SPORT IN PERSPECTIVE

John T. Partington
Terry Orlick
John H. Salmela

Special thanks for the financial assistance provided by

Province of Ontario
Ministry of Tourism and Recreataion
Wintario

Government of Canada
Fitness and Amateur Sport
Sport Canada

Published by Sport in Perspective Inc., and
The Coaching Association of Canada,
August, 1982.

For additional copies write to
Coaching Association of Canada
333 River Road
Ottawa, Ontario
Canada
K1L 8B9

Typeset by Computext, Ottawa (613) 820-8750

Printed by National Sport and Recreation Center

Cover design and overall layout by Vic Mackenzie

ISBN 0-9691170-0-0

PREFACE

Four years ago we responded to the call for a Canadian bid to host the fifth quadrennial meeting of the International Society for Sport Psychology (ISSP). We felt that the combined wisdom and energies of committed scholars and practitioners from across the globe would help stimulate and catalyze positive trends in sport.

In Canada the previous decade had witnessed an impressive number of positive events and developments such as the building of the National Sport and Recreation Center, the founding of the Coaching Association of Canada, the development of the National Coaching Certification Program, widely publicized government reports denouncing violence in sport, First National Conferences on the "Child in Sport and Physical Activity", and on "Women in Sport", the '76 Summer Olympic Games, and the equally impressive Handicapped Olympics, the highly visible and effective PARTICIPACTION program to encourage healthy lifestyles, the National Fitness Survey, and the unplanned, joyful, grass roots running revolution; the list could go on and on.

Within this period the *Canadian Society for Psychomotor Learning and Sport Psychology* strengthened its foundation and more and more Sport Psychologists across Canada began to design research projects and provide consultation services aimed directly at finding ways to improve sport performance and satisfaction.

After making the successful World congress bid in August, 1978, the Canadian delegation received the following instruction from Miroslav Vanek, President of ISSP:

> "Not only should this congress help further the international progress of Sport Psychology, but it should also provide a legacy for Canadian sport."

Almost four years later, the most concrete part of the legacy from this congress is now in your hands.

While four years may seem like a long time to produce an edited international source of information on Sport Psychology, to us the period passed quickly. Over the initial unhurried creative period the basic questions of where we wanted to go and how we were going to get there, preoccupied us. It was our experience that in the past there were a number of dimensions that had not worked in similar ventures. Congresses were too impersonal, too condensed, too theoretical, too boring, quite simply, too inhuman.

Eventually we formulated the congress philosophy, "Sport in Perspective", with the guiding formula to personalize, popularize, and professionalize Sport Psychology. We wanted to ensure three outcomes: First, that the congress would view sport in the wider context of life as it is experienced in the many cultures throughout the world; second, that the congress would identify ways in which sport, and other aspects of our lives, may be out of perspective, and try to redirect these trends through constructive recommendations; and third, that the congress might strengthen our discipline in order that we might carry out our mandate more effectively, thereby improving sport through research, education, and consultation.

This far-reaching dream needed a solid reality base to ensure wide support, extensive funding and tight administration. To this end, in 1980 we founded *Sport in Perspective Inc.* with the following terms of reference: "to improve the quality of life through games and sport for people of all ages. The group is committed to positive change through program development, innovative teaching, and applied research utilizing advanced social science procedures tempered by grass roots wisdom and experience".

Support for our proposal to improve the sport experience through a blend of science and practice came from a number of prestigeous sources who threw their weight behind the concepts *before* the Congress took place:

> "This international manifestation's objectives comply completely with those laid out in the International Charter of Physical Education and Sport". Amadou-Mahtar M'Bow, Director General of UNESCO.

> "There is a definition of happiness that comes down to us from the times of antiquity and which I find particularly appropriate in the context of this Congress. The ancient Greeks, themselves a high-spirited people full of physical vigor, defined happiness as 'The exercise of vital powers along lines of excellence in a life affording them scope'". Pierre Elliott Trudeau, Prime Minister of Canada.

The six days of the Congress gave the first clues that something different was afloat and that it was successful.

In addition to major speakers and reactors from around the world, delegates from all countries were assigned to small work groups who interacted on the theme of that day.

The afternoon session took place in what was called the "Paper Market Place". These sessions replaced the short verbal communications that were so difficult to endure at other Congresses. Instead, the presenters installed their written or audio-visual material in a booth which allowed considerable interaction amongst delegates and contributors. A lively atmosphere was crerated by a special architectural design of the market place, music of different countries and fruit juice or bar service. Computerized opinion surveys were undertaken to tap the collective wisdom of the milling participants on a number of sport issues. Also, to provide children's perspectives on how to improve sport, 800 pieces of children's art on this theme were displayed, which we had obtained from a national survey prior to the congress.

On the weekend, special coaching related sessions related to youth sport, long-term preparation, on-site preparation and retirement were attended en masse by Canadian elite coaches. The final day of the Congress was devoted to practical workshop sessions on mental preparation, concentration, therapy, relaxation and the like. This served as part of the legacy for the improvement of sport.

The physical and social structures that were designed in order to correct what were previously judged to be faults in conference engineering resulted in some positive and unsolicited endorsements from influential participants:

"I congratulate the organizing committee for having forseen such a great amount of time for free discussion. It is during these very moments when new knowledge has the best chance of being produced, integrated, exchanged and diffused for the service of all humanity". Fernand Landry, ICSPE Vice-President for North America.

"The Canadian organizers, our colleagues and hosts, demonstrated quite an untraditional and creative approach. A temperate, realistic approach and ingenious fantasy penetrated all parts of the Congress". Miroslav Vanek, ISSP President.

The material that you have before you is the product of reviews, editing, and in some cases, thinning out of the over 250 contributions to the Congress, by the Theme Editors: Cal Botterill, Terry Orlick, John Partington, John Salmela, Len Wankel, and Nancy Wood. These individuals organized the contents in an effort to provide a coherent package that would be useful to both the researcher and the practitioner. The series editors then integrated the sections to form three volumes that seemed most thematically appropriate: Sport in Perspective, New Paths to Sport Learning, and Mental Training: for coaches and athletes.*

Our contribution is small in light of the challenges which face us. Much more international collaboration of this kind is needed to extend the boundaries of our science, and to maximize the potential of the sport experience in our lives. In the next 20 years our practical knowledge in the field of applied sport psychology is expected to grow in leaps and bounds. By the 10th World ISSP Sport Psychology Congress in 2001, this field should have blossomed for the practitioner. We are hopeful that the readers of this book will not only gain from this growth but also contribute to it.

J.T.P.
J.H.S.
T.O.
Ottawa, Canada
August, 1982.

SPORT IN PERSPECTIVE

An international team of Athletes, Coaches, Sport Psychologists, Administrators, and Journalists challenge current de-humanizing practices in both sport and society. Concrete recommendations for immediate changes in sport are given in the context of proposals for fundamental reorientations of our lives.

NEW PATHS OF SPORT LEARNING

The skill acquisition field has taken fresh directions that depart from traditional approaches. New discoveries in perception, decision-making, and action are revealed within sport contexts. Now a master plan is available for understanding the pertinent dimensions of sport performance and learning.

MENTAL TRAINING: FOR COACHES AND ATHLETES

From countries east and west the best collection of international Sport Psychology material ever amassed for athletes, coaches, and Sport Psychologists. Chapters include the Psychology of Self-Direction, Youth Sports, Training, Psychological Preparation for Competition, and Retirement from high level sport.

---

[1]All available through Coaching Association of Canada, 333 River Road, Vanier, Ontario, Canada, K1L 8B9

Acknowledgements

This book was made possible by those who contributed to the ISSP Fifth World Sport Psychology Congress — delegates, donors, endorsers, school children through the sport art event, speakers[1], supporters, and as part of the congress/publication team-advisors, chairpeople, consultants, contacts, drivers, friends and lovers, fund-raisers, technicians, thinkers, translators, workers and writers. Our sincere thanks to all of you.

The Right Honourable Pierre Elliott Trudeau
Prime Minister of Canada — our Honorary President
Adidas
All About Us
Canada's Capital Visitors and Convention Bureau
Canadian Society for Psycho-motor Learning and Sport Psychology
Carleton University
Carling O'Keefe
Coaching Association of Canada
Fitness and Amateur Sport Branch — Sport Canada and Fitness Canada
George Gross — Toronto Sun
International Society of Sport Psychology
Mathieu, Williams Associates, Sport and Culture Division
Meyer's Chev Olds
Ministry of External Affairs, Federal Government
Ministry of Culture and Recreation — Province of Ontario
National Sport and Recreation Centre
Nepean Sportplex
PARTICIPaction
Secretariat d'Etat — Government of Canada
Skyline Hotel — Ottawa
University of Montreal
University of Ottawa
UNESCO
Wintario

Canada Packers Ltd.
Charline Bass
R.D. Christie
A. Cirko
Dome Petroleum Ltd.
Gulf Canada Ltd.
Merck, Sharp and Dolme Canada Ltd.
National Drug Ltd.
Quebecair
Standard Brands
Peter Van Toorn
The Snowgoose
Tsow-Pollard Partnership Architects

Mohamed Allawy
Ferruccio Antonelli

Christine Blais
Joe Blimkie

Cal Botterill
Geoff Brown
Carolyn Buick

Lise Colton

Sharon Dean
Dorothy Dickie

Stirling Dorrance
Joanne Dowsley

Andrew Fodor
Cathi Foley

Roger Gauthier
Lise Gauvin
Hugh Glyn
Liz Gordon
Geoff Gowan
Luc Gravelle

Erwin Hahn
Madeleine Hallé
Wayne Halliwell
Dorothy Harris
Mike Harris
Abby Hoffman

Berdanette Irvine

Jerry Jones

Fouad Kamal
John Kane
Nikolaj Khudadov
Jane Knight

Susan Laberge

Fern Landry
Sylvie Lavoie
Jack Leavitt
Lou Lefaive
Carol-Anne Letheren
America Lopez

Ron Marteniuk
Osmeil Martinez
Iwao Matsuda
Vic Mackenzie
Gregg McKelvey

Steve Newman
Betty Nickerson

Tom O'Hara
Sally Olsen
Gertruda Olszewska
Bill Orban
Terry Orlick

Carol Parsons
Gail Partington
John Partington
Gilles Paquette

Al Rae
Guy Regnier

Hermann Reider
Daniel Rousseau
Tom Ryan

Mike Sachs
John Salmela
Sheila Salmela
Brigitte Schellenberger
Phil Sharp
Lynn Sinclair
Bob Singer
Dan Smith

John Thorsen
Seymour Trieger

Miroslav Vanek

Len Wankel
Penny Werthner
Joan Westran
Annette Wildgoose
Nancy Wood
Rita Wyczynski

[1]Addresses of principal authors may be found in the Appendix.

FOREWORD

John T. Partington

This book is based on Proceedings of the *Fifth World Sport Psychology Congress,* held in Ottawa, Canada, August, 1981. The major papers, prepared reactions, panel discussions, short papers, and delegate survey results were selected on the basis of their relevance and implications for helping us to understand and deal with current problems in sport.

The result is a powerful message from an international team of Athletes, Coaches, Sport Psychologists, Physical Educators, Sport Administrators, and Journalists. They challenge current dehumanizing practices in both sport and in other dimensions of society. Their concrete recommendations for immediate change in sport are given in the context of broader proposals for fundamental reorientations of values, priorities, and policies which govern our lives. The book comprises three modules, each of which is introduced by a detailed *Foreword* and *Table of Contents.*

Module I. Hidden Curricula in Sport and Society. This section has three parts: The first includes a critical evaluation of Canada's sport system as well as international and Olympic systems; the second focuses on the role played in the athlete's life by parents, school, coaches, community, spectators, referees, media, business, and government; finally, the third part discusses the actual and potential roles played in Sport by the discipline of Sport Psychology.

Module II. The Meaning of Sport Throughout Life. The personal meanings of sport to individuals, as well as socio-economic-political implications are discussed from North American, European, and Eastern European perspectives. A major section on the psychological significance of physical activity in general is also included.

Module III. Cooperation in Sport and Life. This section provides fitting closure to the book by directly confronting the value issues associated with many of the problems reviewed in the first two sections. Writers from diverse cultural sources describe how cooperation, as a play style in sport and everyday living, can nurture individuals, teams, and societies toward greater harmony and fulfillment.

MODULE I

Hidden Curricula in Sport and Society

MODULE I

HIDDEN CURRICULA IN SPORT AND SOCIETY

FOREWORD

John T. Partington, Canada

This section is based on Proceedings from the "Sport in Context" theme, and related presentations, from the *Fifth World Sport Psychology Congress*. The module is organized into three parts. The first includes perspectives of athletes, coaches, and sport administrators whose daily lives are directly affected by the attitudes and values which comprise the cultural context of sport. Contributions in the other two parts were made by specialists in Sport Psychology, Physical Education, and Journalism from Canada, France, Japan, the Netherlands, Scotland, Switzerland, the United States, and West Germany. They provide a plethora of concrete recommendations for improving sport at all levels.

Part I begins with a critical yet constructive review of Canada's sport system. In her first official message as Director of Sport Canada, Abby Hoffman uses examples of her frustrations with bureaucratic bungling and red tape encountered during her athletic career to identify how Canada's sport system must become more athlete-centered. Points in her paper are reinforced by a lengthy discussion by an invited panel; members included the Director of Fitness Canada, a national level coach, a provincial coaching coordinator, two well-informed journalists, and two Sport Psychologists. This discussion brings into clear focus the awesome bureaucratic network, with resultant jurisdictional wrangling, which often destroys the sport experience for many participants. Carol Anne Letheren, Sport Consultant, then reacts with some "hard-nosed" recommendations for problems of growth in Canada's sport system. She holds that management positions at all levels be staffed by people who can at least match the expertise and committment of the athletes they serve. Finally, my own reaction provides concrete ways of humanizing the sport system, not only in Canada, but also in relation to policies concerning the Olympic Games.

Next, Toller Cranston, renowned figure skater and artist, and Jack Donahue, Head Coach of Canada's National Men's Basketball Team, both focus on the impact of values and priorities emphasized by the International Sport Establishment. Toller rejects the emphasis on technical merit over self expression, and encourages us to search for, and express our unique talents. Jack is appalled by the emphasis on winning at all costs and reports how opportunities for fun and excellence are being frustrated by dishonesty in international competition.

Finally, Kathrine Switzer, first woman to run the Boston Marathon, and recent parent of the Women's Marathon event to be included in the 1984 Olympic Games, shares many of her personal experiences as victim of prejudice and discrimination in a male-dominated sport. Against this background she describes how she has combined the most constructive forces in business, the media and sport to provide promising new sport opportunities for women throughout the world. The running program for women, which she developed with the support of the Avon Corporation, is strengthening a new identity and confidence in girls and women throughout the world — a trend which will benefit all of us. Excerpts from a panel discussion of this paper are reported.

Part II begins with a prologue in which I view problems in the sport context as resulting from the "institutionalization" of playfulness. Ways of preserving the playful attitude are suggested.

The first major paper is by Leo Hendry, Senior Lecturer in Education, University of Aberdeen. He shows how our development can be affected by a "hidden curriculum," the unplanned, unrecognized values about sport and life taught outside the traditional school curriculum by parents, peers, the community, media, and even within school by some physical education teachers. He endorses a humanistic model for physical education, and a curriculum which values the "flow" of personal satisfaction in sport.

Three prepared reactions to Hendry's paper follow. First, Raymond Thomas, editor of the Vigot series on sport, seriously questions the role of Sport Directors in France, and examines effects on mass sport participation of the growing program which serves elite competitors. Next, Guido Schilling, President of the European federation of Sport Psychology (FEPSAC) draws our attention to the many varieties of sport, and particularly notes that the role of sport in general varies across different societies in terms of the political and economic system of each nation. I provide the third reaction in which Hendry's concept of "hidden curriculum" is transposed and applied to children's own largely implicit values and expectations in sport. I argue that their civilized curriculum could do much to reduce the alarming incidence of athletic injuries in youth sports.

Stephen Bindman, a student at the School of Journalism, Carleton University, Canada, next examines media effects of sports portrayal on sports participation habits, on societal tendencies toward violence, and on the values we attach to sports participation. He recommends that the media establish a commission to study its own role in sport, and that the media organize, and provide wide-scale coverage of a conference on the role of the media in sport.

The fourth major paper, by David Beaver, a physical education specialist from the United States, notes the reluctance of the Sport Establishment, including Sport Psychology, to work toward the realization of the positive potentials in sport for enhancing the lives of disabled people. The prepared reaction of John McKay, a Canadian physical education specialist emphasizes the need to help disabled people develop athletic skills. In this regard, he notes that if disabled athletes were given training, they might provide the best combination of coaching skills for disabled people. Finally, he draws attention to the positive "fall out" in equipment design, such as more mobile wheel chairs, which could result from a more active program of sport for the disabled.

Y. Matsuda from the *Leisure Development Center* in Japan provided the final paper in this part of the volume. Noting the geometric population growth curve, he suggests that all of us have to shift our expectations in life away from material wealth to a more experiential criterion of satisfaction — from product to process. He combines this point about life goals, with another he makes about the escalating context of leisure time, to support his proposal for us to begin to develop an interest and capacity for "quality sports." Quality sports are those we do just for fun. He says that we are in the dawning age of "secondary culture," a time when the pursuits and interests of average people will become valued in their own right.

This section concludes with fourteen short papers selected to represent the thinking and findings of Sport Psychologists on a number of problems in the macro system which affects sport. Targets include parents, coaches, spectators, aggression and violence, referees, Olympic regulations, and physical education curricula and training.

Finally, Part III focuses on the discipline and practice of Sport Psychology, and how it forms part of the overall context of sport. The context provided by Sport Psychology is really that which is done on a day-to-day basis by Sport Psychologists in 42 countries: What we choose to include and emphasize in our curricula; how we train students; what we elect to study in our research; how we conduct and report this research; who we choose to consult with and/or counsel; what interventions, tools, tests and therapeutic techniques we utilize; what fees we charge; and what other roles we play in relation to athletes, coaches, parents, educators, sport administrators, related Sport Sciences, the media, business, and so on.

The contents of this book, and the other two based on the congress Proceedings, disclose much about the context which Sport Psychology can and does provide for sport. But throughout these hundreds of pages one sees reflected the challenge, and often the explicit invitation from coaches and even senior sport administrators for Sport Psychology to play a more active role in working to solve the many context problems which affect sport participation.

The first paper in this section is by Miroslav Vanek, President of the *International Society for Sport Psychology* (ISSP). His brief review of the development of Sport Psychology includes a timely warning against "Wonder Psychologists" who promise more than can be accomplished.

Reinforcing this warning Bob Nideffer of the United States discusses the ethical practice of Applied Sport Psychology. Bob sensitizes us to the personal and professional consequences of malpractice. He illustrates how Sport Psychology can contribute to problems of athletes by raising false hopes for success, by generating feelings of failure, and by developing over-dependency. The paper argues that such negative effects might be avoided, and positive outcomes maximized if our discipline were to become more organized. Nideffer advocates the establishment of standards for practice, wide public education about Sport Psychology services, as well as taking serious steps toward professional certification.

Concluding this focus on professional practice are two related papers which I reconstructed from notes and transcripts of workshops given by Tom Tutko, a leading U.S. professional Sport Psychologist, and Guido Schilling, Swiss President of the European Federation of Sport Psychology (FEPSAC). Each emphasizes an athlete-centered model for our professional interventions. In addition, Schilling challenges Sport Psychologists to play a more important role in the training of teachers, community leaders, social workers, journalists, and so on, who influence the sport experiences of the masses — recreational participants, the elderly, disadvantaged people in ghettos, drug addicts, prisoners, etc.

The next paper by Wayne Halliwell, former President of the *Canadian Society for Psychomotor Learning and Sport Psychology*, switches our attention from professional practice toward the discipline of Sport Psychology as reflected in published research. He describes a set of procedures for assessing what I choose to call the "net gain" from published research on any topic. Applying these procedures to all the published literature will show how much, or how little, the scholarly discipline of Sport Psychology has contributed to the context of Sport, and to an understanding of this context.

The final series of papers describe the role of Sport Psychology in the lives of the millions of people in three non-industrialized nations — Malaysia, the People's Republic of China and India. These papers provide important insights into the future role of Sport Psychology as a force in the Third World. The paper on Sport Psychology in China shows how much can be accomplished when a discipline receives a strong mandate and full support from the Establishment. The three papers serve as an addendum to the recent review of the status of Sport Psychology in 31 countries, reported by John Salmela in, *The World Sport Psychology Sourcebook*. Montreal: Mouvement Publications, 1981.

PART I   THE SPORT SYSTEM

SURVIVAL IN THE CANADIAN SPORT SYSTEM

Abby Hoffman
Canada

In keeping with the theme of the Congress — "sport in perspective " — the purpose of this presentation is to identify some aspects of the Canadian sport system which have a particular significant (and often adverse) effect on the athlete-participant. In general, it will be argued that while the Canadian system has dramatically improved the range of opportunities for athletes (in terms of facilities, coaching, competition, training camps, etc.) and thus the prospect of achieving excellence in an absolute sense, there has been insufficient consideration of the "human" dimension of high performance sport.

The paper is presented by someone who does not profess knowledge of sport psychology in any academic or professional sense. However, the critique of the system should be carefully considered by sport psychologists who, hopefully, will find some fertile ground for investigation, which would not only help athletes but also make the discipline of sport psychology more relevant.

The description of the system will often depend on my personal experiences. In many instances it is unlikely that such events could occur in Canada today. I'm going to relate my experiences because I think they identify some of the things I'm talking about; about how the system has an impact on sport performance. One of the things that has led me to this sort of approach to the topic is my current role as Director of Sport Canada, and the type of administrative role I've had in the last couple of years in Provincial sport. As sport becomes more sophisticated, and the complexity of the delivery system becomes layers upon layers of bureaucracy, I find very often that I can sit in my office for an entire day, or an entire week, or sometimes an entire month, without really feeling that I've done anything that has a positive impact on the athletes in whose interest I'm operating. That's a matter of concern to me, and I think it should be a matter of concern to all of us who work in sport. I think it's important that we anticipate the results and the impact on the athlete of everything we do in sport. While that's a simple statement, I think often it's a process we don't go through.

The experience that stayed with me the longest during my career, and I suppose what threw up a red flag with the sport system from the day I first became involved in sport, was when I tried to play hockey, my first attempt at competitive sport. As some of you know, because the story has been recounted many times, I tried to play on a boys team. I was told, after my true gender was discovered half way through a season, that girls were not allowed to play on a boys team. The point I'm raising concerns who makes the rules in sport, and how do unreasonable rules get made in sport. As far as I could tell, I was very well qualified to play on this team. So when I grew up I wanted to be a sports administrator who could make the rules for sport.

My next experience that told me something about the system and the arbitrary rules under which we operate was when I started track and field and decided I wanted to be a distance runner. I was told that because of my age and my sex I wasn't allowed to run more than one mile. Given that at the time I was running about 30 miles a week with no apparent ill affects, it concerned me again that someone, somewhere had the right to arbitrarily decide that 14 year old females shouldn't run more than one mile.

On a slightly more serious level, at the time when I first entered into the high performance picture, I competed in my first trials selection competition in July of 1962 for the Commonwealth Games. The Games were being held in November of 1962. I knew nothing about "periodization." I'd never heard of "micro-cycles," and I'd never heard of "macro-cycles," but I knew that to have a selection trials in July for a competition that was taking place in November didn't make any sense. But when I asked about why the selection competition was in July, I was told that it took 5 months to stage the team, to order the uniforms, to file the entry forms, to make the travel arrangements, etc. Well that was almost 19 years ago. Sad to say, I think that one of the key determinants in establishing the dates for selection trials for international events in this country is the time it takes to order the uniforms, to stage the team, to make the travel arrangements, etc. Clearly the impact on performance, of having athletes peak six months before a major competition, is self-evident to people who know anything about sport.

A couple of years after that in 1964 I had the good fortune of being selected for the Olympic Games. I went to Japan along with the rest of the Canadian team with a great flurry of publicity, basically around the medals the Canadian athletes were going to win at the Games. I was perhaps too assiduous a reader of Athletic Weekly, Track and Field News, etc., but I knew bloody well that I was not going to win a medal at the up-and-coming Games. I think it shows the kind of mindless adulation that sometimes our athletes are accorded in this country, and the kind of pressure that is put on them through the media. Because, while it was delightful on my departure to be predicted as a potential medal winner, my return to Canada was not as pleasant when my classmates at school, who were already sufficiently envious that I had gotten the time off school, wanted to know why I hadn't won the medals that had been predicted for me.

A few years after that in 1968 the Olympic Games were held in Mexico City. One of the bizarre aspects of my career that I remember, was the non-preparation of the Canadian team made by Canada to train at altitudes and to prepare to compete in Mexico City. Reading those same magazines that I mentioned a few minutes ago, I remember reading that France was building a high altitude centre, that the British team had made some arrangements with the French government to train in that centre, that the Russians were building camps at high altitudes, and so on. In other words, the people with whom I was expected to compete were going to all kinds of preparation in order to adapt to the high altitude conditions of Mexico City. Fortunately, at the eleventh hour so to speak, Canadian athletes were indeed provided with what turned out to be a satisfactory altitude training experience in the southern United States. But I think it was typical of the Canadian system, and not atypical today either, that the insecurity and the indefiniteness of our plans was something that caused considerable consternation for athletes throughout the preparation period.

In 1972 the Olympic experience provided another opportunity to see how the system has an impact that is often adverse, not only for our athletes, who are not as well prepared as they ought to be for international competitions, but also for our coaches as well. It was interesting for me because this was the first occasion that I was given almost carte blanche to prepare for the Olympic Games. In fact it was quite a marvellous set up. I was contacted in late 1971, and told that funds were available for me to do whatever training programme I wished for the 10 months leading up to the Olympic Games. I took full advantage of that and trained in the United States and Norway, and arrived in Munich before the Olympics, after a quick trip back to Canada so that I could compete in the selection trials that were 7½ weeks prior to the Games — no doubt a scientifically determined date. I considered myself at that time to be self coached, and to use my coach in an advisory capacity. But one of my strongest recollections was my coach coming to the warm-up field in Munich. I always liked to have him come and warm up with me because after all, hadn't he been seen on the warm-up track with me? Anyway as we jogged around to because after all hadn't he been seen on the warm-up track with me. Anyway as we jogged around to warm up he had his hand in his sweat pant pocket and was rattling change. Now women's slacks don't come with pockets so we don't have change in our front pocket, but I think we all know that if you see a male standing rattling change in his front pocket that he is a little nervous. But I had never seen anyone doing it while he's jogging. You know I was

going out to run the Olympic final. But I think he was about as nervous as I was. Probably coaches of our Olympic Teams on many occasions are as inexperienced as our athletes in coping with the rigours of high level international competition. However, the clanging coins was not the end of it. Those of you who have seen Olympic competition know that athletes are allowed to go out on to the track and do some last minute preparations for about the 15 minutes prior to the event being called to the start line. Well with 10 minutes left to go, the referee told us to take off our sweats and line up on the start line for the start. The reason was that the 50 Km walk, which had been started some hours previously in the stadium, was going much more rapidly than had been anticipated and the lead runners were approaching the stadium. Thus, there was some urgency to get this bloody women's 800 metre final on the track, off, and finished, so that the incoming 50 Km walk would not interfere with us. I was offended with this travesty. After all, I had known that at 6:20 on the afternoon of Sept 2nd, 1972 the women's 800 M Olympic final was going to be run. I had read about it 3 years earlier. So for me it was a travesty that anyone would have the nerve to move up that race by 10 minutes, and least of all in Germany, where I had expected that if the race was going to be at 6:20 it would not be one minute sooner and not one minute later. Well what I didn't understand, and should have understood was that once the referee turns the starting commands over to the starter, that's it, there's no discussion about when the race is going to start. If the starter insists that the racers are going to be called to their marks in 30 seconds, that's when the race is going to start. Even with the amount of experience I had had at that time, I was not aware of the rules governing the start of races, and chose to get into an argument with the starter about whether the race was going to start then or in 10 minutes as scheduled. I finally woke up to the fact, when I realized that I wasn't concerned that I needed the additional 10 minutes to prepare, after all I had been preparing for four years, I was just appalled that they were changing the time. But it was a real indication of a lack of understanding, by a supposedly experienced athlete, of the rules governing international competition.

Over the next few years some other things started to happen. The period before 1976, the quadrenniel before the Olympic Games in Canada, was the first time in Canadian sport that we really began to prepare properly for international competition. The motivation was clearly the Olympic Games in Canada. Regular athlete assistance grants were available albeit at a small level. One of the things that athletes had to do was to fill in yearly training charts. I wonder if any of you ever wondered: Who read those charts? Where did they go? Who looked at them? Did you ever hear anything back about them? We actually figured out that four coloured pencils was actually the ultimate, seven was suspicious, and two showed a lack of interest. I say that facetiously but seriously. The only time that athletes ever received their training charts back, and didn't get their money, was when it was decreed that there was insufficient detail on the training chart that was submitted. At the same time there were special grants made available, depending on the basis of A, B or C carded status, for special training and competition rerquirements. At this time I really was self coached, with ultimately disastrous results. One of the things I really needed was a split-hand stopwatch that would not go off time when I ran with it. That item was fairly expensive. I guess these days they are down to $19.95, but they were over $200.00 in those days. So I submitted in my special needs request for $275.00 to buy a stop watch. I was told that I could not get a stop watch. I could go to certain training camps, and I could go to certain competitions, and I could buy extra food and nutritional supplements, but I could not buy a stopwatch. That concerns me to this day. Who decides what an athlete needs, and how bureaucratized is that process? Anyway, I eventually got the stopwatch and carried on training to 1976.

I'll just cite two instances from the Olympic Games that gave athletes, myself included, cause for concern. Five minutes before the first Track and Field event in the Olympic Games competition, an athlete, who was a member of a relay team which had a genuine prospect of winning a medal in the Olympics, was thrown out of the Olympic village and off the Canadian team for an alleged and rather serious, if true, disciplinary infraction. The effect on the rest of the team was absolutely disastrous. This was five minutes before the first event started. Two of his fellow athletes were in that event. Many other members of the team were slated to compete that day. I make this comment, not to defend, and I don't wish to go into that disgression in any detail, but the point is, there was no system in place, no mechanics to deal with the infraction in a way so that the individual athlete could be dealt with appropriately, and the effect on the other athletes could be minimized. In fact, the Canadian contribution to the track and field competition was to have a scene on the warm-up track five minutes before the first event, because the officials concerned came to the warm-up track and physically grabbed this individual and advised him that he was no longer a member of the Canadian team. I trust that we have better ways of dealing with these things today.

The other thing that concerned many Canadian athletes living in the village, particularly in my own sport, was that we seemed to be the only team who had residency in the village for any length of time. The DDR was in Sudbury, the American team was in Plattsburgh, various other national teams seemed to be all over the place, and the only ones who were putting up with the noise, and the pressure, and the aggravation of living in the village, seemed to be the Canadian team. It gave me cause for concern that in our country, the special treatment seemed to be accorded to athletes from other countries.

I am sure that any athlete who has competed in this country, not only at the national level but at any level, could probably offer a littany of comparable examples. But I think that they are instances of things that have been done without adequate

foresight, and without adequate thought about the ultimate affect on athletes.

These personal experiences lead me to target the following problems in the Canadian Sport System.

(1) *From an athlete's standpoint the sport system is a confusing maelstrom over which the individual athlete has little or no control.* Just as the school teacher and the student are caught in a web of pressures constructed by principals, inspectors, superintendents, curriculum consultants, local Board officials, Ministry of Education officials, parents, trustees, the media, special interest groups (each one more moral than the next), and legislators, athletes are caught up in a similar network of conflicting and countervailing forces. And many of these influences are simply confusing to athletes.

From the outset of involvement in competitive sport, an individual must deal with the consequences of actions by a coach, a manager, the team or club sponsor, the club or league administration, the rule-making authority of the regional, provincial, national (and even the international governing body), his/her own parents, other athletes' parents, the media etc. As the athlete progresses through the ranks, added to the scene are provincial and national coaches, the staff of national and provincial sport governing bodies, selection committees, technical experts who administer physiological and psychological tests (individuals who, perhaps on the basis of an hour or even less contact with the athlete have then been given the authority to select — or not select — an athlete for further training and competitive opportunities), sport medicine practitioners, the rules of the international federations, codes of conduct, government officials wanting both to contribute and to buy a piece of the action. In some, the influences are myriad and they have the capacity collectively to be enabling, motivating, inspiring and challenging — and, at the same time to be oppressive, enervating, incapacitating, frustrating, and potentially destructive.

I can see several attributes of the system that we really need to think about in terms of their impact: One is that the system is highly insecure. I think we often forget that athletes live, if not from day to day, then from month to month, and certainly from year to year, highly dependent on such things as selection for the national team, selection for assistance, often under situations where the rules and the guidelines and the criteria are very, very vague. They also operate in a system that has a distinct lack of control. Coaches in most sports have a very clear idea that they ought to be responsible for the athletes training programme on an exlusive basis. But in most sports the athletes to a very high percentage feel that they, in conjunction with the coach, should be involved in establishing the yearly training programme. I wonder to what extent we have ever thought about who indeed, and what sort of collective enterprise it should really be, in terms of control over such things as the training plan. A third factor affecting athletes within the system is that many, many decisions are made, over which they have no involvement, and into which they have no input.

I think it is fair to point out that in the Canadian context, the whole environment in which high performance athletes in amateur sport operate is a rather hostile one. Without generalizing too much about the Canadian cultural environment with respect to sport, I think a few points can be made. One is that we are not a country that puts a particularly high premium on excellence per se. We certainly are a country that has very little understanding about what excellence in sport is about. Team Canada, which could theoretically refer to any Canadian sport team, we all know, refers to the Canadian entry in Olympic Hockey competition or the Canada Cup of Hockey. Our reference point in sport is still professional sport, and the Canadian population generally doesn't have much understanding of why an athlete would be involved in sport, particularly with the little monetary reward that is available. We certainly have an inferiority complex when it comes to sport, and we have relatively little understanding of what's involved in the level of international competition. I will never forget getting off the plane coming back from the Olympics in 1968 when I was 7th in the 800 M final at those Games. I just happened to run into a friend at the airport who knew that the team was returning from Mexico on that day, and she asked me how I had done. I was quite ecstatic actually, and I said "Well I was 7th." She said "Gee that's too bad." Well enough said on that subject.

(2) *If we are serious about helping athletes realize a positive experience in sport, we must ensure that they understand the system and that all actions are taken only after very careful assessment of the full range of effects on athletes.* By *full* range we mean both the intended and unintended consequences. Athletes are subjected to more rules, more guidelines, more restrictions than anyone in our society with the possible exception of members of the miltary. Even a simple entry form to a recreational road race usually contains several pages of instructions. For the high performance athlete the verbal and written directives from coaches, administrators, competition organizers and from government is considerable. Not only is the stream of well-intended (and over-plentiful) guidance often difficult to comprehend (if not in conflict with other information available to the athlete), but it is subject to frequent change. The rules governing residency and league eligibility for 9 year old hockey players in this country are so arcane that even the highest level of the judiciary has difficulty rendering an interpretation. Is it any wonder that athletes often find the system alienating and the experience oppressive.

When events occur over which athletes and others involved in sport have no control, it is important that we understand the impact on the motivation of athletes. The most outstanding example is that of the Olympic boycott of 1980. How many sport psychologists or indeed any of us involved in sport has any clear understanding of the lasting effects of the boycott — not just on this generation of athletes but on the generations to come?

There's been some information put together through a survey conducted by Pat Reid (Sport Canada Consultant) and a few others, conducted on athletes who were influenced, because they were likely team members last year. Some of his findings are pretty interesting. They demonstrated to me that we've erred in advising athletes, and not working with them to help them understand some of the realities of sport, and that sticking our head in the sand is not a very realistic way of coping with those issues. Even now, it's just as if our approach to the Olympic boycott, and the effect it has had on a whole generation and succeeding generation of Olympic athletes, is that we're basically trying to forget it, ignore it, and pretend it didn't really happen. Let me cite one item from the statistics that have been collected that suggests to me that there is some fertile ground here for sport psychologists to do some work very specifically on this item. One of the things that athletes who were affected by the Olympic boycott were asked six months after the boycott, was to identify the level of concern, the level of intensity, the impact on motivation at various times leading up to the boycott, and 6 months after. One of the most interesting findings was that there was just as much rage, and certainly as much bitterness and frustration, and certainly a greater negative impact on motivation to train 6 months after the games, as there was in the period between the announcement of the boycott by Canada, and the time of the Games themselves. I think that should be a concern to us, given that, because of the boycott, a very, very large number of those athletes have chosen to carry on with competition, and to carry on at high level training. But what they are saying is that even though they are carrying on, they are doing so with lesser motivation than they would have under previous circumstances. One of the other findings from this survey, is that many athletes have identified that they no longer regard the Olympic Games as the ultimate objective of their athletic career. In fact one athlete made a rather remarkable comment, "I have abandonned the one-dimensional life necessary to make the Olympic Team. Now I just want to throw, I just want to throw as far as possible." In many respects this individual probably has a healthier attitude towards sport than what he had previously. But the question remains what are we doing, those of us who work in sport, what are sport psychologists doing, to work with athletes to assess the impact of last year's events, so that we can achieve some salutory benefits over the next few years? How well have we prepared athletes (and ourselves) to deal with the political realities of sport? Do we simply choose to ignore the issues because they are seemingly beyond our ken and thus we parrot a mindless idealism of the separation of sport and politics? There is a certain amount of gamesmanship (if not outright attempts at cheating) in international sport, and we should prepare athletes to deal with it.

(3) *The recent decade in Canadian sport has created a new level of performance demands on athletes. The system (while increasing the oppor-*

tunities for high level training, better coaching, more competition and the application of sport science) has become callous, cynical and inhumane. A concern about the lack of fitness among Canadians and our poor performances as a nation in international sport led to the promulgation of the Fitness and Amateur Sport Act in 1961. The next decade saw a gradual but significant growth in government involvement in sport and the promotion of fitness. But it was the fact of the 1976 Summer Olympics in Montreal that gave a major impetus to the development of high performance sport in Canada. National objectives for sport achievement were set for the first time and a new sophistication was acquired. When Canadian athletes did not perform quite as well as had been expected in Montreal (even though they improved dramatically to 10th place overall), key Canadian sport leaders announced that Canadian athletes suffered from a "choke" syndrome, and those athletes who did not live up to expectations were publicly maligned.

Prior to the Olympics, the Canadian system failed to take into consideration the material needs of athletes, and only when athletes mounted a major media campaign and threatened to withdraw their services (i.e. boycott the Olympic competition) was adequate financial assistance made available. But even then, athletes were required to move thousands of miles across country to national team training centres where their non-athletic needs (jobs, education etc.) were (if considered at all) inadequately met. At the and of the Olympics, the grants to athletes ceased, and there was a year-long hiatus before support resumed.

Government became increasingly demanding of sport performance. Instead of talking about creating the conditions in which athletes with excellence potential can reach world standard, we talk about medal production. Athletes are often dots on performance charts — barely individuals. When the criteria for selection for international teams is established the term "tourists" is used to refer to those who fail to reach the minimum standard. When criteria are developed with the intent of setting more stringent standards for acceptance into assistance programs, a magazine produced specifically for nationally carded athletes carried the headline "Sport Canada cuts deadwood." What kind of system refers to dedicated individuals who have spent years of their life and thousands of dollars in the pursuit of excellence as DEADWOOD? The point is that government (and in turn the public) have come to expect a great deal from Canadian athletes and the question must be raised whether our expectations in sport can be reached with the resources made available by the very people who have created the expectations.

We should question as well whose objectives are being met in sport. So pervasive was the influence of one Minister of Sport, that at the end of the Commonwealth Games (in which Canada placed first as a nation), the individual who was feted and carried around the stadium at the end of the Games was not a successful athlete or a revered coach, but

the politician. The involvement of the state in sport is not only inevitable but necessary and highly desirable — government should show leadership in the nurturing of excellence, but not by exploiting the achievements of athletes or by demanding a higher level of performance than that for which it is prepared to pay.

An athlete who participates in Canada's high performance sport system must undertake a "contract" of questionable legal status, be subjected to selection criteria incapable of passing minimum legal standards of fairness, and subject him or herself to disciplinary codes which often embody not even basic aspects of due process. Athletes are certainly human beings and at the international level mainly of adult age — and they should be treated as such.

(4) *The Canadian sport system pays insufficient attention to the non-athletic life of Canadian sportsmen/women.* Canadians frequently accuse their more successful East European counterparts of being full-time athletes dedicating their lives from early ages exclusively to sport training. In fact, many East European countries are more aware than are we of the need to deal with athletes as complete human beings. For most Canadian athletes there is constant conflict between sport, education and career — set in an environment which does not put a very high premium on excellence for its own sake (the metier of the Olympic athlete). The drop-out rate in Canadian sport is one major contributor to an over-all Canadian sport record below our real potential. If we want our athletes to excel, then we must ensure that the motivation is a system which provides for integration of the athlete's total life. The Seneca Gymnastic School in North York is an example of a public education authority which seeks to integrate educational and athletic needs of athletes, by contrast with our general system which compartmentalizes athletes and deals only with their sport requirements. I think the Seneca School initiative is a good sign of things to come, but we need a great many more like these.

My conclusion is that we must do more than build additional facilities, hire more coaches, send more athletes to higher level competitions and provide more opportunities for sport scientists to work with athletes.

We must also retain the perspective of the athlete and understand that the system must be athlete-centred. We must assist athletes to cope with "the system" and we must insist that all sport programs be evaluated not just for their technical merit, but also for the impact (in the broadest sense) that they will have on athletes. Our expectations for achievement in sport as a nation must be brought in line with the opportunities available to achieve excellence even if it means that more modest goals must be set. While it is reasonable for business and industry, and government, to speak of "cost efficiency" and the goal of maximum production for minimum cost, we must remember in sport that we are dealing with human beings for whom the vocabulary of microeconomics and the price system is neither appropriate nor likely to yield much prospect of success.

DISCUSSION

Joe Hauser, Director, Fitness Canada

As director of Fitness Canada I'm just here to encourage Canadians to be more active. But I do find in my job, that I have more of an influence on the sport system than I used to realize. I am reacting to your speach and I'm reacting to something you haven't said. I guessed that you would concentrate on the high performance athlete and not on the athlete that I know. I myself am an athlete. This spring I ran in the National Capital Marathon. I think that is a feat worthy of an athlete. My daughter who is nine years old is a gymnast, a super, natural athlete. She has competed in one single competition. But she's an athlete. But we are not the athletes to whom you, Abby, have directed your comments tonight. And in my view, we are not the athletes to whom many of the people in the sport system — the coaches, the administrators etc. direct their attention. And so that's what I'd like to do tonight.

I think the issue of survival for athletes such as my daughter and myself is very real. The question is "will my daughter survive to continue to participate in gymnastics?" "Will she drop out?" "Will she, when she has children, encourage them to participate in competitive gymnastics?" "Will I survive?" "Will I continue to participate with my age group in marathons and other fun runs?" So I think the issue in athletic survival is — will the athlete survive to continue to participate throughout life. And I think Abby, you touched on this tonight when you talked about athletes connecting their non-sport life with their sport life. But I think that it is unfortunate that the sport system concentrates on the elite and I think it is also unfortunate that the system in sport concentrates on its dollars. And you've indicated tonight that you do plan to make some changes.

I'd like to suggest that the pursuit of excellence at *any* cost is not in the best national interest. I think that that thinking pervades the thinking in all competitive sport right down to minor league hockey. I think that that is not in the best interest of our children and those who would like to compete to have fun. And I wonder whether we in Fitness and Amateur Sport are putting enough energy into ensuring that the sport system allows people to survive while participating, and participating throughout their lives. I wonder whether we offer alternatives and whether we are developing those alternatives. I have observed changes — we do have, in our rules, provisions whereby kids who are participating in competitive sport as athletes have to participate, and the coaches have to ensure that. But the concentration is still on winning and that does concern me, because I came through that system and I still concentrate on winning. But let me tell you when you participate in the Marathon with 4000 others you soon lose the urge to win because you know you just won't. You made a number of very interesting comments, and you'd like to look forward to the development of a sport system in which excellence can flourish and I think that is terribly important, and I think that quote could become a by-word of how you develop the system.

I think that change can come from within. You suggested that the athletes themselves should find out about the system so they can change it. I also think that those athletes who are participating for fun don't understand the system. They never will. I think the elite athletes have to. But for the great majority of athletes who are participating, I think the change has to come from the top.

In Canada, Sport Canada has the role of supporting national and international competitions, and it leaves what it calls, "sport development at the local and regional level," to the provinces. But I do believe Sport Canada has a leadership role in changing the system — in helping change the values within the sport system — far more that it realizes. And I think, Abby, that this is one of your responsibilities as the Director of Sport Canada over the years. As I mentioned earlier, I've begun to realize that Fitness Canada can help change the sport system in a way I didn't realize. We do give dollars to national sport governing bodies, and dollars are very powerful motivators for change. We are beginning to tie some conditions to the dollars we give to sport governing bodies, to encourage them to use the money to get people to participate, but participate in throughout life. While I am working alongside those in Sport Canada, I sometimes feel that I'm a subversive by doing this; that I'm distoring the system. But I do feel that in the work we are doing in Fitness Canada, we are actually helping the athlete survive.

Betty Baxter, Head Coach, Canada's National Women's Volleyball Team

I guess when Abby talks about some of the horror shows that have happened in her career and Joe talks about survival in the system, I can relate at a very gut level to both of these statements. I just returned, two days ago, from 41 days behind the Iron Curtain, and the theme, "survival in the system," has a very special meaning to me these days. I'm sad to say that maybe my time in this past journey had made me lose my sense of humour, but the more Abby talked, the sadder I became, because many of those kinds of instances are still happening. There's definitely been some improvement in caring for our athletes, but there has also been improvement in our coaches and athletes in how to beat the system, and get a little more pat on the back, or a little more profile for what's not always the best in the long run for the athlete. When Abby talks about the difficulties as an athlete — yes they are still happening, but perhaps they can be reduced if we can plan with more foresight for the next Olympiad, or with more than just our immediate athletes in mind. Perhaps we should look at some of our juvenile and junior athletes who are now being pushed for excellence at the age of 11, 12, 13 and dropping out at 19. Perhaps we should look at survival after 10 or 20 years in the sport. I wonder how many of you and how many of us as coaches question how long we'll survive in the system.

I think we should all work together a little bit on the kinds of things which Abby mentioned. For example in this past experience I've had with my own athletes in Europe this summer I found that a little education about the system gives tremendous response. If an athlete can understand some of the difficulties in travel arrangements, or the difficulties in getting funding, or the difficulties in making a long term plan, instead of cursing those administrators up there making all those horrible mistakes and making life miserable for us hard workers down here, they actually come through as very stable, patient and mature human beings. So I don't think we can ever underestimate giving those people we serve a little more knowledge about what kinds of things we're trying to do and what kinds of difficulties we're having doing it.

Abby's paper touched briefly on some problems with officiating. I think in Canada we're very timid to talk about problems we have with officials being perhaps slightly coloured more towards one team than another. If we can educate our coaches and our athletes, and our officials and our administrators to understand what happens in the international sport arena — to the fact that an official will give you perhaps 2 or 3 or 4 discredits at a time when it is very crucial to win or lose. When we hear about that kind of information we all blush and turn away, and say the bad countries do it, but not here in good old Canada. Recently at the FISU Games in Roumania we had many discussions about difficulties with officiating. We agreed that in 1983 when we hold the FISU Games in Edmonton if we ever cheated, the media would kill us. I think that's very true. We're a fine, upright kind of people here in Canada. But I think we need to sell our athletes on the fact that Canadian officials know who they are, and that we need to help them as much as we can both as administrators right down to referees who are judges. But in other countries we may not get the break, the home team is generally a very strong team to be on. So I think we need to be a little bit more aware or realistic about what's happening out there, and I don't think we need to be too optimistic about our work here making a tremendous amount of change out there. There's going to have to be a lot of work in setting up our sport system to make even one place, or even ½ a place, or even better performance.

Abby touched on the knowledge of the people who are involved in sport. Recently I was in Czechoslovakia for 10 days. They have a sport newspaper with colour photos of sport that is available on the street. Our bus driver, to the humour of all of us, would stop as soon as we got out of our little hotel, he would stop within the first two blocks, jump out of the bus and run to two or three different newsstands, and the sport newspaper was always sold out. On the one or two days when he could find it he was so proud when he could show all the color photos of the soccer games, boxing, as well as our exhibition matches. That kind of interest from the public in many countries in Europe is also very important in terms of their own athletes performance. Another example, that I've just come back from living with, concerns how many other countries look after their athletes, or have a system for detraining, or job counselling, or job placement. In Bulgaria about one week ago, our interpreter was in fact the promotions and public relations director for the club she used to fence with. She now fences recreationally and doesn't coach. In the same club, virtually every administrator or coach, right down to the groundskeeper and the nurse, etc., 90% of the people who work in the operation of the club have been former athletes at one time, and with that club. I think that we can take a few lessons from that kind of a system. Naturally, we have to be a little bit cautious, because what seems to be successful, whether it's in the Orient, or in eastern Europe, or in western Europe, or in Russia, or wherever, may not be the most successful for our athletes.

The point that Joe brought up about survival is something that we have to work in very closely with the education of people who aren't in sport, as well as bringing our athletes back into sport as a part of their everyday life. We shouldn't build a little box around them while they are elite athletes. That may be a difficult thing to do, but I like to think that the people at this Congress and the people involved in the sport scene in Canada will all be working toward that. I know as a coach, although I have lost my sense of humour for a while, I hope I will be able to come back and have some sort of influence on that in the future.

Doug Fisher, Journalist and former Parliamentarian

I have very little quarrel with what Abby had in her paper. I think both the descriptions and the analysis are very sound. I can't really speak very much about the point of view of the athlete because most of my relationships since I got involved in working as a lobbyist for amateur sport has been with the administrators and with policies, and with questions of funding.

Her first point is that from an athlete's standpoint the sport system is a confusing maelstrom over which the individual athlete has little or no control. I don't know the truth of that from the point of view of training or coaching or development, but there is no question about it, our sport system so far as it is concerned with administration, regulation, control and funding, is exceptionally complex. In fact, it's a mirror of our political system. Our political system has to be complex, not just because of our history, but because of the sheer scope and scale of this country, and the various levels of jurisdiction.

It was intriguing to me, I was in parliament and voted and spoke for the Sports and Fitness Act in 1961, but the truth was, nothing happened for 8 or 9 years with that first initiative. Things didn't begin to go until 1968 or 1969 when, as a result of the enthusiasm from one or two politicians, and a commitment from the government to create some organization, all of a sudden we began to create such things as the sport centre, and the whole idea of funding and administration.

One of the consequences of the way we operate in Canada, is that as soon as the federal government takes initiative, then the provincial governments take the same initiatives within their area of jurisdictions. So right away we get that nemisis that you get so often in Canada, whenever anything develops an interest group. You almost find that even if it stops at a local point. I could give you a classic example from the history of sport. In 1867 George Beers got the first Lacrosse group going in Montreal. Within six months he'd formed a National Lacrosse Association, had a meeting in Kingston, which is the half way point, and things began to roll. Within a year, the people in Ontario weren't very happy and they wanted a provincial association. This is the way we operate.

Now I'm talking about systems and layers, and Mr. Hauser

made a reference to the national and international direction of the federal programme. This is one of the imprinted consequences of our political system, and it is one of the reasons of the complexities in sport. You see Abby has to concentrate now in her role on excellence because, quite frankly, the whole question of recreational sport, sport for fun, isn't really her business. It may be her business as an individual. She can do a certain number of things. But it really isn't her role or function. That's the kind of system that we have in Canada. One of the consequences of the last 10 years that concerns me the most is that we have put into place an administrative apparatus. Most of the people in the administrative apparatus are from the sport world. They are not really from the business world, the commercial world, or the journalistic world — a few of them are but not very many. And I think in fairness, because of funding at the federal and provincial level, what we now have at least at a worthy minimum is the housing and the support of which you might call basic administration. Now I quite agree that many of these administrations are not working. I know that there has often developed a gulf between these people who are working full time, and who have to go to bureaucracies, and have to report and have to account and justify their requirements. I know there has developed almost a gulf and impatience with the people who are out there with the athletes and the parents. That to me is one of the things I think we need to spend a lot more time on to clear up; that is the responsibility of this administrative set up, which is necessarily complex because of Canada, with the reminder that by creating a bureaucracy it doesn't do anymore than give you an administration. We've got the same problem in pure politics. The separation that has developed between the pure bureaucrats and the politician. You probably know on the political scene one of the most difficult problems we have today is that the politicians in a way are increasingly divorced at the common level of the elected member from the expertise and the knowledge that exists in the bureaucracy proper. So more and more we are drifting into a situation where the elected members are really not responsible in a real sense for what goes on. Now I suggest to you that that is one of the things that has happened in the last 10 years in sport. And that is one of the problems about the complexity and about the information and understanding that is going on there. It's almost as if when people become bureaucrats, whether it is sport, or medicine, they begin to inch away from the roots of what is being done. And the one point I wanted to reinforce in connection with this first point is that if there is a confusing maelstrom over which the individual athlete has little or no control, I think you start first with the sport structures themselves and the sports administrators to begin to remedy that. Secondly, with the political administration such as Sport Canada, Sport Ontario, or the Ministry of Culture and Recreation, to get them to appraise that what they are doing in their bureaucracy, is in a sense almost giving arthritis to the bureaucracy in sport that is out there.

I want to discuss now Abby's next point which concerned making sure the athletes understand the system and that all actions are taken only after very careful assessment of the full range of the effects on athletes. Concerning this I see weaknesses in our standard education system and the University system. I sometimes think that there has been an almost absolute divorce between reason and purpose in terms of sport and officialdom, which you might call the manager or controllers and directors of Universities and Colleges. It's not just a problem that relates to the governmental bureaucracies.

The third point that she made concerned the new level of performance demands on athletes, increasing the opportunities for high level training, better coaching, but also that the system has become callous, cynical and inhumane. I feel that something began to sour five to six years ago. I think a lot of it relates to the deficits that governments were running up. So we began to get a cynicism towards government and its spending that began to be applied to the spending that went into athletes. So we are not as starry eyed and optimistic, as a whole community, as we were just a decade ago, and everybody is talking about "the bottom line," and how we are going to get the government deficit down. This is what makes the bureaucrats within the government look all the time for performance. An obvious way to prove that you are doing something is with medal counts and point standings and victory. This is beginning to build and it has created a general atmosphere, and it certainly tends to premeate the sports journalism in this country. Now how do you meet that? I don't know how you do until we get more prominent athletes to speak up in a lot more forthright way, more directly in a critical way about our sports journalism and about this attitude. In some ways, as a result of the change in our whole Canadian approach to lifestyle and achievement, we've gone sour; and in some ways, athletes, because of the prominence and attention they get, are bearing more of this cynicism than anything else.

The system itself, that is, this administration and bureaucracy we are talking about that we've built up also tends to reflect it. What scared me more than anything when I was doing the sport enquiry for the province of Ontario last year, is when I got talking to what I thought to be some of the more able sport administrators. They all had this bloody ghost sitting on their shoulders that they had to get better results. They had to show more. When you begin to get that as a priority, then you are in a pretty desperate situation for the good health of the whole thing. I think you have got to get that kind of thing out in the open much more, and it's difficult because the administrator, whether he's within a sport or within the government, doesn't particularly care to be open because immediately people begin to ask questions. Again, that begins to put the pressure on him. So the system tends to seal itself. I suppose what I'm really saying is that we have to drag more of these things out into the open, and athletes have to be candid. Athletes, ex-athletes, and coaches have to lose some of their fear about the bureaucratic apparatus which funds them and provides them with so much that they have come to expect in the last ten years.

Another point I must make because Abby is here, and I made it in my report in Onatrio, that the whole tradition in our system of government is that the bureaucrat or the official is anonymous, and that the Minister, the elected person, is the person responsible, and who speaks. One of the problems this creates in sport is that most of the dealings at a senior level that coaches and administrators have in sport governing bodies can't be done on a day to day basis with the Minister or politician. They deal with the bureaucrats, and it is extremely difficult to deal with a person who, by the very nature of the parliamentary system has to be largely anonymous. This is because you can never get anything out in the open. I remember when Roger Jackson was head of Sports Canada or acting head of Sport Canada and Abby took a run at him in the Globe and Mail, I remember Jackson saying to me, "I don't mind the criticism, but what does it do to me within the system." Because immediately the Assistant Deputy Minister and the Deputy Minister say "What the hell are you up to? Here you are, a federal civil servant, on the top item in the sport pages of the Globe in a critical way. That's not it." Now one of the things Sport has to begin to insist upon is that because of the very nature and contentiousness of sport, and the fact so many sports are in competition, is that they have got to get a lot of this stuff out into the open. And if their main dealings are with bureaucrats like Pete Lesaux or a Bob Secord, then Pete and Bob are public figures. So is Abby Hoffman as head of Sport Canada. In other words, I'm really saying that we need to think in this particular field that we are dealing with not the normal routine, traditional kind of operation in Canadian bureaucracy, but establishing some new approach. I welcome the fact that Abby showed the courage here, which I knew she had, to bring some of these things out in the open.

The last reaction I wanted to make in connection with this paper of Abby's concerns her point that the Canadian sport system doesn't pay enough attention to the non-athletic life of Canadian sportsmen and women. That's true, but I don't know where you'd turn to begin to get a better appreciation. We could begin to demand that the people who are responsible for sport begin to provide much more of a public profile in print, or some other terms, of what the situation is, what happens to athletes, and what plans there are to help athletes adjust both after they are through, but also in connection with the kind of relationships they have when they are coming up through the system. It's an enormously large topic. The Canadian sport system pays insufficient attention to the non-athletic life of Canadian sportsmen and women. Absolutely true — but my God, there is so much more before we get into that one. Someone should be working on that one, and maybe in some sports they are. I know in hockey there is a little bit being done. I'm particularly interested in the transition from some of the sports that engage younger athletes, particularly swimming and gymnastics. That is something that is easily studied. It should capture grants; it should even intrigue and interest the volunteers and the parents that are involved.

So all in all I just want to say that Abby has touched on a number of things that open up the system. I think it is just a dandy piece of work, and that it will inspire some of you to carry on with it. You may not be as vulnerable as her, and perhaps you can be even more irreverent.

Len Wankel, Canada's first Doctoral graduate in Sport Psychology

It bothers me to hear that Joe Hauser feels somewhat subversive in getting involved in sport for the ongoing participation throughout life. I would like to plead that Abby and Joe get together and work out some way so that the average participant doesn't get lost in jurisdiction debate between Sport Canada and Fitness Canada. Do you have any ideas of how you might take some action to make sure that this doesn't happen, so that there isn't just the concentration on medals on the one hand, and on pure fitness on the other. I say this because I feel that emphasizing sport is the way to motivate the average Canadian to get into physical fitness. I don't think we can do it just on the basis of health.

Abby Hoffman

There are some jurisdictional issues with respect to who is responsible for excellence and who is responsible for participation. I would agree that there is a federal and a national role for sport participation, and currently through Fitness Canada. Joe will talk about that in a second. National sport governing bodies can play at least a coordinating role in what might be generally termed the recreational sport competition. I think that that is a legitimate role nationally. However, 'he delivery of those programmes rests with the provincial government, and the provincial sport governing bodies. But I think there is one point which is particularly difficult at this point in time, and Doug Fisher touched on it from a couple of angles; it is the push for production, and there is no doubt about it that some rather simplistic indicators are demanded of us right now in Sport Canada to justify the dollars we have now, and to justify any future financial allocations we wish to get. Regrettably, those will be justified almost entirely in terms of our international success record. This may mean that it is perhaps more difficult than it should be for us to meet some of the objectives you have identified, in terms of the competitive recreational participant. But I still feel there is a lot that needs to be done at the national level and can be done through Sport Canada and Fitness Canada.

Joe Hauser

With respect to jurisdictional issues in sport and fitness, I think that they are resolved between the federal government and the provincial offices. There are no major difficulties in that area. Because the provinces have the primary role in participation does not mean that the federal government has to step out of the field, and I think the same goes for sport. Although Abby's main concern is national and international competition, I think with respect to sport development and participation in sport, she and her organization, and the Minister, can show leadership in this country, important leadership. With respect to surviving, as an administrator at the federal level, you have to produce indicators of performance. It's much easier for Abby to produce medals as indicators of performance than it is for me. But I think one of the most important indicators of performance is information about participation of Canadians in sport. The extent to which kids get involved in sport; the extent to which they drop out; the reasons why they drop out. The same thing goes for adults. Which sports do they get involved in? Which sports would they like to get involved in if they had the available facilities, infrastructure, coaches and so on? What sports do they get involved in and then drop out because of difficulties with leadership at the local level? That information is what I need to give me indicators of performance which allow me to argue for the funds necessary to do the job. Last year we initiated the national fitness survey, and the data collection is now complete. We should have the findings by next year. I think it will be very useful and fundamental data in determining where we go with respect to encouraging participation in sport.

Ken Daley, Provincial Coach Coordinator

The jurisdictional problem that I see coming up is a geographical or regional one. In order to develop any athlete at a high level, he must be trained some place; in Canada this means in one of our provinces or territories. In order to make a successful athlete it has to happen at local level, even though he is working at an international level. How are you people going to bridge that gap between taking this elite desire and bringing it to the local level? It is at the local level where real change has to take place. The giving of dollars, when an athlete reaches a certain level, is one thing. But how do we take them through the system? We've used the word "system", but to me system is orderly. At the present time I don't see very much order within the system. It's much too haphazard.

Abby Hoffman

I certainly agree that it is not very helpful to provide assistance to athletes on sort of an award basis, because they've managed by their own bootstraps to pull themselves up to the level of performance necessary to be within the jurisdiction of the federal government. I don't think is very helpful, and it certainly isn't very comprehensive. I think some, if not most of the provinces in this country, have recognized the importance of sharing responsibility for excellence in sport. They have introduced their own athlete assistance programme that deals with athletes up to, but not included in, the national team (carded) programme. I think we made one attempt at defining those various responsibilities among various jurisdictions for excellence with Game Plan, '76. This was a combined attempt among the provincial governments, the federal government, and the Canadian Olympic Association (C.O.A.) to combine forces in pursuit of excellence. Unfortunately it broke down because the two levels of government didn't feel they were getting a fair visibility or profile for their respective contributions, and equally the C.O.A felt that their contribution was somehow or other being lost in all this morass. I think it's important though that the various levels of jurisdiction have to work together. Because, as you say, an athlete works in a local gym, or track or pool. We can't ignore that virtually all the training facilities for high performance sport in this country belong to either Universities, which are funded at the provincial level, or to municipalities whose tax base is the local assessed mill rate in that particular community. So I think there are tremendous problems. But I think it is worth pointing again to the Seneca-North York project. This involved two levels of government, a Community College, borough Board of Education, other Boards of Education, but the program had an elite focus. A training centre for track and field has been established at York university. This also involved three levels of government, the sport governing body, and the University. I think those are difficult arrangements in this country, and Doug Fisher was correct to point this out, but they are inevitable arrangements that have to be worked out. No single level of jurisdiciton can claim monopoly or exclusive responsible for excellence, or for that matter, neither is there an exclusive responsibility for general participation. There is certainly a "lead" responsibility, but that is something different.

Doug Fisher

I think the main problem today is between the provincial government, the municipal bodies, and the educational system. We are not badly fixed in Ontario for facilities, and most of them are in the municipality, and owned by the municipalities, either by the Boards of Education or others. However, we need to reach municipal recreation, and link it with Boards of Education. We also have to get some fair standards of what are provincial responsibilities in terms of funding. I think we all know that the athlete doesn't really give a damn, and he shouldn't have to give a damn, about whether he is operating at one of the three or four levels of government. He does his training. He deals with his coaches. Most of his competitions can be attached to a locale, at least in its early stages. We have some marvellous model communities in Ontario, but we have a lot that are not up to standard.

One of the things I didn't mention that has happened in the last 10 years, is we have had a rise in provincial pride and provincial bureaucracies. The majority of them — particularly Quebec, Ontario, B.C. and Alberta — are not going to sit still and wait for federal leadership or the old kind of carrot and stick that used to be there. That's why it seems to me, in jurisdictional terms, the breakthroughs of the next 10 years are going to come through the provinces, between them, their municipal leadership, their educational leadership and the local community.

I'm pessimistic, in the short run, about the educational systems and their roles. I'm not about the municipalities, because there are enough municipalities in Ontario and the West with good plans, good community spirit, pride and desire to develop. I come from Thunder Bay and I had tears in my eyes at the opening of the Canada Games, because I couldn't believe that this community could put 1500 girls out onto a field, dancing, and dancing well. It was magnificent that they could do this, and that the girls were there, and that there were people to teach them, and the music and everything could be fitted in. The other thing I couldn't believe, and it was even more responsible for bringing tears to my eyes, was that the community enjoyed it, appreciated it, and rose to a feeling of pride. There is a lot out there at the community level.

Cal Botterill, Sport Psychologist

I get excited about the shift in goal concentration. To have an athlete concentrating on how far he can throw, rather than on an Olympic medal, may in fact be the key to the future. I was listening to the gentleman from Sweden this afternoon during a work session commenting on two of the world's most outstanding athletes, Stenmark and Bjorg. He explained that their tremendous success comes from concentrating on a model of ideal performance, and on improving that, each time out. This is why they show tremendous consistency and such a wide margin of victory in events where other athletes are distracted by conditions which the competitive environment presents.

Another point concerning goals in sport can be made from what we know about intrinsic and extrinsic motivation. You can't visit the Soviet Union without developing all kinds of emotions and strong feelings in all kinds of ways. In societies like the USSR, there is tremendous potential for the utilization of extrinsic rewards. This is because the effectiveness of pay-offs to motivate people is determined by how valuable they are relative to other things. In North America, athletes make millions of dollars, but relative to what the average citizen has, that is not as motivating as what you can get from success in sport in the Soviet system. This is very important for us to remember. In order to compete with the kind of intensity that people like the Soviets are able to generate in their athletes we in the Western world have to really love what we are doing. Our athletes will never undergo the kind of training necessary and the kind of rigours involved unless they totally enjoy and love the activity they are pursuing. Our job in the sport system is to create conditions for this to happen.

Joe Blimkie, Coaching Association of Canada

I'm wondering is it the bureaucracy we have, is that why things are getting tied up in the Canadian sport system, or is it the people behind bureaucracies making the decisions that are actually clogging up the system?

Doug Fisher

What we had for about 8-10 years was a tremendous surge of facility building, and institutional creation, The Coaching Association and the Sport Information Resource Centre. Now we have the system. I'm suggesting to you that the system has become stalled, bureaucratized, routinized, marking time.

Some fresh air needs to be blown in to it. We need to be more critical of it. We need to be more candid with it. We have reached the stage where we need more people, not only Abby Hoffman, who have bona fides credentials in sport, to really begin to put issues out in the open, lay them on the line, not only to ask questions, but to go after the answers.

Maybe I can just make one comment on whether it's the system or the people in it. I think that large scale systems end up doing some bizarre things. Let me give one example. Sport Canada says to the National Sport Governing Bodies, that if they wished to be eligible to receive some sort of money, which is in turn for athletes, they would have to undertake some sort of contract with their sport associations. As a result of this policy, the NSGB's developed and established various lists of athletes' commitments. One sport association adopted the following regulation as part of their contract with their athletes: "Athletes who do not abide by team rules, including the unwritten rules of the past, will be liable to penalty." Now are athletes supposed to be historians? There's nothing wrong with the person in that sport who wrote the rule. There's nothing wrong with the association. There's nothing wrong with Sport Canada. The request that there be contracts between athletes and the association is probably not a bad thing. But once you have all those remote, alien forces, that are ultimately an establishment of 6-7 layers, between the athlete and the cheque, things like this invariably occur. My plea here tonight is for the injection of some sort of reasonableness into the system.

George Young, Sport Journalist

I have two points I'd like to bring up. First I question what has happened in Roumania at the FISU Games, where politics played probably the largest role it ever has in international competition — flagrant violations. I'm wondering what that does to the survival of the Canadian athletes who are time after time placed in duress like that in international competition. I think a lot of athletes are saying, "Hey, do we really need that?" And I know some sports in the western hemisphere are saying, "Maybe we should put our money and our emphasis on competition in the western world and when the eastern block countries are ready to play the game again maybe we shall go back into truly world competition." The second thing I'd like to talk about is the media. Perhaps those responsible for sport should hold a seminar for the Canadian sport media, because I think not only do athletes not understand the system, but neither does the media.

As an aside, I don't think the only devils are in eastern Europe — if I were to speak personally I can recall, and without going into the details, that the times I was cheated in sport, those occasions were within the boundaries of this country, I regret to say, rather than abroad. Certainly there are some difficulties undoubtably in international sport.

In conclusion I want to restate a point that Cal made. He referred to the kind of incentives that athletes have in this country. I think it is fair to say that Olympic Athletes are not involved in high performance sport for the material or monetary awards. One of the questions asked in Pat Reid's questionnaire on the Olympic Boycott, was to put a price tag on what they thought their sacrifice had been over the past quadrennial, as they prepared for what eventually became a non-Olympic opportunity. The dollar figures listed were generally in the tens of thousands. Athletes had taken several years off school or work in order to prepare. I think it is because the rewards in this country are not material, that I am more concerned that the sport system be humane in the way in which it deals with people. The only reason for Canadian athletes to aspire to international excellence is because they achieve some personal satisfaction. It's a dilemma, because at one and the same time we want to be reasonably hard nosed, we want to make good judgements, we want to spend money in places where it is going to get results; but at the same time, we know that the only thing that will retain athletes in our system is for the system to be more humane than it is in other societies, where the material rewards play a much higher role.

Carol Anne Letheren, Sport Consultant

Thank you Abby. The message from this discussion is that systems, however you want to define them, what they are or who they are, and no matter what we want to do with them, have to become more responsive; they have to be more open; they have to allow for more creativity. By so doing they will avoid some of the self-serving that is going on within sport and the administration of sport in this country, and become more serving and giving to the people whom they are really affecting.

Reaction 1. Outcomes of Growth:
"Hard-Nosed" Solutions

Carol Anne Letheren (Canada)

Amateur sport in Canada has grown rapidly. From less than $1 million of federal government money 20 years ago, it now spends approximately $35 plus million of federal government money. Over the last decade, this financial growth encouraged the institution of organizations such as the National Sport and Recreation Centre and the Coaching Association of Canada, a layer of "professional" full-time administrators and an amount of money for program development not available before. Opportunities were/are available for individuals in sport to contribute to the building of the sport structures and to personally grow and develop. Performance in world competitive environments was/is significant. From 21st in 1972, we literally leapt to 10th in 1976. Canadian sport and its progress was the "talk of the town".

Growth is critical to progress and is powerful. It impacts on all aspects of any organization. The sport insitutions in this country were no exception and today it is valid to ask: Have we or are we not moving away from an athlete, participant-centered, environment? Abby begs this question in her address and it has relevance.

Prior to 1976, money and energy both were thrust behind the

athlete's preparation and technical development. While late in starting, almost everyone acknowledges the success of this impetus and certainly the results in 1976 bore this out. The question to be addressed is: WHAT WAS THE OUTCOME OF THIS IN THE LONGER TERM?

Five years later, 1981, and looking back: i) Some sport governing bodies lacked the necessary management controls and practices to keep up with the fast pace of spending and program needs. Following the 1976 Games, many of these organizations found themselves in financial difficulty and on the verge of bankruptcy. What had occurred was investment spending by both government and sport alike to get to a position of recognition on a world wide scale. ii) Instead of acknowledging this investment in program and evaluating with pleasure the results, we, in sport, ran scared and headed for the "weeds". Tight controls were "slapped" in place by government; sport governing bodies became extremely administratively oriented and in some cases, this was to the detriment of ongoing program development.

Some of the subsequent results have been unfortunate: The investment up front in programming lost momentum as the heavy emphasis on administration took over. Administration became an end unto itself — in fact in many instances it has become another program unit. The business of being in business became in some cases, the sole focus of the organization. This overemphasis and impulsive move brought with it "not-so-qualified" "sport" administrators who then passed judgement on what is good for an athlete and the program. Further, they became intent on direct involvement personally including travel, meetings, rewards for their efforts and contribution. (An article in one of the Toronto newspapers prior to the '80 Olympics captured the essence of individual involvement by indicating that in no other social or work institution in this country can an individual rise so fast to a position of influence, power, and stature without any significant qualifications as they can in amateur sport.) Layered decision making was prevalent. Administrative overload and layered decision making result in: Significant time delays, collective decisions (very little individuality), and adherence to strict, administrative, often irrelevant procedures and eventually bureaucratization.

The conflict the above creates is particularly apparent in high performance sport which requires: Flexibility, attention to the *individual* needs and requirements of athletes/participants, and increased sophistication and research which in turn demands more professional "technical" expertise.

Following 1976, we should have been in a plateau phase, reassessing and preparing for a new thrust forward. Instead, we regressed a little to accomodate this "fear-ridden" administrative push.

Administration is and should be a process and in fact, a facilitating process for pre-determined programs. It should not be, in a program service organization, determining and dictating program direction, focus and content. Decisions taken that relate to budget priorities, policies of the organization, staffing, fund raising etc. should all relate to and reflect the needs of the athlete and the participant. To ensure that the process and focus are correct, those serving on the Boards of Directors of sport governing bodies in this country should be the best people we can find in the business — the business of *sport*. Admittedly, to be skillful as Board members and sensitive to business life are important member attributes; equally important is a *sensitivity and commitment* to amateur sport.

In sport we assume too much. We assume that top professionals, business personnel and educators alike automatically will transfer all their skills to amateur sport. We should prepare them — we should introduce them to our organizations: which have limited numbers of full-time people managing them; which have multitudes more who both *make* and *implement* decisions but on a voluntary basis; and organizations in which the volunteer actually *directs* the work of the full-time professional.

To keep the administrative process in perspective and to professionalize it we will have to introduce training/educational techniques that climatize contributors to the unique administrative and program features of sport.

The adiministration of amateur sport, in particular high performance sport, operates in two environments: national and international. While domestic, national concerns are critical, it must be noted that high performance sport is international sport. The "performances" are Canadian but the ultimate performance takes place in international environments.

An understanding of how international sport works is important for preparing top athletes and in assisting/protecting them in order that they can perform to their maximum. To ignore the administrative idiosyncracies of the international arena is naive. If knowledgeable, prepared administrators, both volunteer and professional, full-time are required to effectively handle national affairs, then it is logical to assume that equal attention should be given to those who represent Canada, sport and our athletes in the international boardrooms.

Canadian sport governing bodies often send the President of the organization to all international functions. Little or no thought seems to be given to whether or not he/she is the best qualified, most sensitive or most knowledgeable individual to perform the task that has to be performed. All too often, these trips are treated as rewards, prestigious jaunts or travel excursions.

The international competitive arena is "tough". It is full of talented, well-prepared athletes all vying for the top position.

Further, and unfortunately equally important, the international boardrooms are full of well-prepared politicians/representatives, all vying for the top position for their country's athlete(s). Canadians do not to seem to realize the impact that the international administrative mechanisms have on the eventual sporting results. While true in all sports, obviously, the subjective, judgemental sports are more adversely affected.

By way of example, in 1976, I was elected to a seven person international committee at the technical level in the sport of gymnastics for women. This was the first time a Canadian had been elected to an authority body in a European based sport. For 4 years, I attended meetings along with six colleagues who were from DDR, Roumania, Sweden, Holland, Czechoslovakia and the U.S.A. Together we debated the rules, regulations, compulsory exercises — all the important criteria by which an athlete is measured in terms of success and performance. In those meetings, I was able to represent my sport governing body's viewpoint but never my country's. Yet those representing DDR, Roumania and Czechoslovakia, were always alert to not only their sport's position but also that of their country. Often the weight of the political importance of the decision outdid the technical/sport significance. It was so obvious that we are prepared differently to perform such roles. They understood the impact of a single rule change in gymnastics on their other sport negotiations and government to government relations. The closest I felt I came to such harmony and understanding as a Canadian sport official was before and during the Pan American Games in 1979 when all forces (government, C.O.A., Sport Governing Body) cooperated and shared resources and strengths. The strength in manpower and negotiation terms that this set up at that event encouraged and, in fact, directly impacted on results. While we may not agree with the mix of politics and sport, and I don't, I still declare that we have to acknowledge its existence and l;earn to control its influence if we are to protect our athletes. We can only do this by being involved and involved with qualified expertise.

The horror stories about officiating, boardroom discussions, timetables for events, competitive draws, amateur versus professional, drug abuse, to name but a few, circle the globe and premeate the locker rooms of sport. They are true. They cannot be "fought", "altered" from outside with comments like "how awful of *them*" — we, if we compete, are part of the "them" and must do everything in our power to alter and control such happenings to the eventual benefit of our athletes.

Because we have used international travel in sport as a reward or an opportunity for someone to feel important, jealousy and personality disputes have often directed our "sense of justice" in decision-making. Again, a personal example: As a member of the seven person committee described above, I was viewed "world-wide" as one of the authorities in international gymnastics. In 1980, we, Canada, hosted the World Cup — a F.I.G. (Federation International de Gymnastique) event. The Canadian organizing committee found it difficult to include me in their planning meetings, discussions, and even social gatherings. This was particularly evident when members of the international organization were in Canada to inspect the progress. In order, I suspect, that my presence would not detract from others who needed the recognition, I had to tell my boss — the President of the Women's International Technical Committee, that due to a family illness and commitment, I could not attend the dinner organized in honour of her. In truth, I was told specifically by the Canadian Organizing Committee that I was not invited. What is critical is not whether I personally was invited to a dinner or not but whether we, in Canada, are supportive of elected positions once we put them forward and whether we want them to be viewed externally with respect and authority so that they can be exploited and have the potential impact on our athletes. We must realize that that type of behavior simply weakens our sport position internationally — it reflects on Canada, on sport and directly impacts on our athletes.

And so, Abby, "surviving in the system" is complex — I agree. It requires, in fact demands, that we become "hard-nosed" in our approach to the administration of high performance sport at home and abroad. We are dealing with a "career-segment" of people's lives — in some cases 10-15 years worth of dedicated participation. We are spending the Canadian public's money to be involved. We should maximize the return on both time and dollar invested.

16

It is inappropriate and indeed unacceptable to select officials, athletes, representatives to travel abroad because "they haven't been to that country before" or "they really want to see their friends or parents". Those are nice "percs" if they *happen* to occur along with the criteria that are job-oriented and results-oriented. There is no room for ego, petty jealousies or individual and personal needs to be number one.

It is equally inappropriate and unacceptable to elect officials to our Boards because they have been around a long time or didn't get in as President so let's put them in as Vice-President. There is no longer room for this potential "incompetency" — we have to match the expertise and professionalism of the Podborski's, Schlegel's, Brill's, with equal professionalism and expertise in all management positions, administrative and technical, in all organizations in amateur sport.

If we are interested in the athlete as a human being and the eventual "after-life" when sport careers are terminated, then the climate that surrounds and assists an athlete during their career should be: harmonious, co-operative, highly professional, operating on researched facts, contemporary, committed, knowledgeable, accountable both administratively and technically to pre-determined standards. All of these qualities are necessary in all sport, but they are accentuated in importance in high performance sport. Too much time and money is required in this program area for success. To let it be poorly or inappropriately administered is counter productive and detrimental directly to the people involved — in particular to the athletes today and when they retire.

High performance sport could be titled "a medium size business". Whether you agree wich such terminology or not, one still has to ask: "Would you run a medium-sized business with volunteers *directing* the affairs?" The answer is an obvious "No."

It is time to rationalize the respective roles of our volunteer and full-time leaders and workers by: type of expertise required, commitment required, roles, responsibilities, accountabilities, and relationships between the volunteer and full-time.

The volunteer *was* amateur sport. They had to plan and to do everything. Then we employed full-time people and the era of a small business with a permanent office emerged. Now we have a medium-size business by sport and quite a "huge" industry when all sports are considered. We have not made the transition for either the full-time or volunteer. Both continue to be important contributors but perhaps the "how" needs review.

The time is now.

Reaction 2. Humanizing the Sport System: An Olympic Proposal

John T. Partington (Canada)

The Director of Sport Canada, Abby Hoffman, has called for a humanization of Canada's sport administrative systems. This paper offers a few suggestions toward that end. The dilemma is that our administrative systems are created by human beings, to help other human beings, but unfortunately, systems don't always function like healthy human beings.

What does it mean to be human? The recipes of most psychological authorities on this question include equal portions of three ingredients — play, work, and love. The lives of healthy human beings mirror the importance of fun, achievement, and care for self and others. My suggestion for improving sport administration systems derive from this recipe for being human.

Playful attitude: Antedote against "The Trapped Administrator"

One way in which our administrative systems fall short of being human is that they lose the playful attitude. Playful human beings remain curious, flexible, and experimental toward the world. This attitude is the source of artistic expression and scientific creativity. Games and sport are created out of the playful attitude, along with social and administrative systems and even cultural diversity.

Sadly, the administrative systems we create from our playful attitude lose the openness and flexibility which characerize the playful nature of healthy individuals. Compared to their conduct in other settings, when most people enter roles within administrative systems they often begin to behave in a more conservative manner. Eventually, the entire system becomes slow to adjust to changing realities. Such systems seem to take on a life, and set of purposes of their own. They become top-heavy, self-fulfilling-perpetuating monoliths. This is especially the case when those in charge feel trapped by their commitment to certain priorities or mandates of the System.

There are ways to avoid this dilemma. The entire system can remain playfully open and flexible if those at the top can retain the playful attitude as a daily antedote against becoming trapped. I strongly advocate that our top administrators try to adopt the kind of participatory experimental approach we see practiced by the natural leaders among children in free play situations. These leaders listen to what the other players suggest, sometimes they combine these suggestions into new alternatives, and then they suggest playing this new way for awhile. If the game doesn't go well, such leaders listen to the players' complaints and then suggest modifications such as switching players from team to team, or modifying the rules before resuming play. If children can be that civilized, why can't we?

To avoid developing the dogmatic, authoritarian syndrome of the trapped administrator, our top administrators should establish goals and priorities for their systems through close consultation with the clients who are directly served by the system — athletes, coaches, etc. Programs and procedures developed to achieve these goals should be set up as if they are hypotheses in an experiment. Moreover, criteria for assessing achievement of goals should be established in consultation with clients, and data about program effectiveness should come directly from the clients served. In this way, the top administrator doesn't have to cover-up, or get defensive if things aren't going as planned. Within this model the facts are always friendly, because the actions proposed, and the results of actions, come from the clients themselves. Negative results simply mean that priorities have to be adjusted, or that programs need to be modified to achieve those goals. A playful attitude, and a democratic stance are necessary pre-requisites to avoid the role of the trapped administrator. I strongly recommend this orientation to ensure that administrative systems will function like healthy human beings.

Work Orientation: Antedote Against "Burn-out"

Healthy humans enjoy the challenge and satisfaction of doing a good job. However, employment in large administrative systems can destroy the joy of work. This is another way in which bureaucracies can become less than human in their functioning.

The work environments of many administrative systems transform their human employees into system-serving robots who blindly follow rules, and who seem no longer to be interested in providing service to clients for whom the system was originally conceived.

A useful perspective on this dilemma is given in the psychological literature on "burn-out." This literature reports that people working in large centers like hospitals, which are supposed to provide direct help to others, often experience stress from trying to cope with the mismatch between the scope of service demanded from them, and their power and resources to deal with problems directly and completely. When this chronic stress becomes unbearable, people in such settings try to detach themselves personally from their role as provider of services. When this happens they are said to be "burned-out". There are a number of ways of withdrawing: taking long breaks; having short office hours; writing formal memos rather than having personal meetings; rationalizing decisions by arbitrary reference to system rules; referring to the people in need of service with stereotyped, often derogatory labels, such as, "the trouble-makers"; and even by becoming apathetic and just doing nothing for long periods of time.

There are a number of ways to ensure that the work and service of an administrative system doesn't suffer from staff burn out. First, we should recognize that, certain kinds of people are more likely to burn-out then others. These are the "Workaholics" whose personal lifestyles do not comprise a balance of play, work, and love. One way to avoid burn-out is to select, and employ, healthy balanced human beings.

Other suggestions concern improving the administrative system. For example, systems might be less likely to induce staff burn-out if they were organized on a smaller scale. This might ensure that staff would feel more capable of providing manageable service directly to clients. Some support for this suggestion comes from the findings that people in small communities are more likely to help in emergencies than are people in larger communities.

Another way of avoiding staff burn-out is to ensure that those within the system be given frequent and regular opportunities to change their roles and responsibilities within the system. They might also be encouraged to actually work outside the system from time to time in order that they don't become system bound. Working sabbaticals are excellent ways of maintaining a fresh, open perspective.

Efforts should also be made to ensure free communication among individuals who work in the system. Frequent encounter sessions with staff, supervisors, and top administrators, as well as the provision of suggestion boxes are important for helping people within the system to remain open with each other, to feel like a vital part of the system, sometimes just to "blow off steam", and to give each other emotional support.

Similarly, it is important for those in the system to keep in touch with the needs and interests of people outside the system, especially with those for whom the system was established to serve. Group-think, the tendency for all those decision-makers in a system to begin to think alike and to support each others' arguments, is to be avoided at all costs, if an administrative system is to remain open and flexible. Group-think may be avoided by including, in important discussions, the views of people outside the system. It is therefore adviseable for those in the system to engage in regular dialogue via community open-line radio and television programs, to conduct interview and questionnaire surveys, and to hold public forums in educational, occupational, and recreation settings.

The *Children's Sport Art Event* which we arranged in connection with this Congress is an example of what can be done to keep the sport system well-informed and person-centered. The materials we received from the young children across Canada reflect an impressively civilized perspective. In fact, I would like to propose here, that if we want to guard the future of sport against further decay brought on by adult, professional priorities, then we should endeavour to include more children among our Sport Consultants. I am convinced that children's perspectives will help us to keep sport in perspective.

Love: Guarantee for System Success

Finally, an administrative system must express a caring attitude toward its clients if it is to function humanely, like a healthy human being. Although love is not something which can be turned on like a tap, caring behaviour, like any other behaviour, can be "shaped." The behaviour of people within administrative systems toward their clients can be made more caring by establishing appropriate expectations and contingencies. The System should reward those who are helpful to others. This could be achieved by providing financial incentives, promotions, and perhaps even public recognition to those members of staff who have provided good service to clients. For example, there could be a "public servant of the month" award given on the basis of

reports by clients concerning how they were treated by those within the administrative system.

Last year, I proposed to the International Olympic Committee that such an incentive system become an integral part of procedures for selecting the site of each Olympic Games. I would like to conclude my brief remarks to you, about making sport systems human and person-centered, by repeating that proposal herein.

Olympic Proposal: Everybody Wins

It seems to me that previous Olympic sites have been selected primarily on economic criteria. The main question was whether or not the bidding nations were rich enough to provide adequate facilities, transportation and security. It is not apparent to me that the suitability of possible sites has been assessed in relation to the philosophy of the Olympic ideal.

The Olympic ideal embraces two activities: The Olympic Movement, concerned with mass participation; and the Olympic Games, concerned with the highest forms of excellence in sports. Both activities serve the same philosophy — the cultivation of complete, balanced human beings.

My proposal addresses two problems: First, the widening credibility gap between the founding ideals of Olympic Games and the shocking Olympic realities which we are beginning to witness, ranging from bad sportsmanship to boycotts and bombings; the second problem is the unfair economic discrimination which now prevents economically underendowed and/or underdeveloped nations from hosting the Olympic Games.

The Nobel Peace Prize serves as the model for this Olympic site proposal. Each year a panel selects one, or sometimes two individuals to receive the coveted honor. Using clear criteria they decide who's life, and work, serves as the best example of individual effort to improve human conditions.

I suggest that a similar strategy be followed for assessing the suitability of nations to host the Olympic Games, and that the site selection be entrusted to a universally representative, non-partisan international group — perhaps even selected from among the athletes themselves.

These fair-minded people could identify criteria or activities that evidenced the extent to which each nation in the world is operating according to Olympic ideals. Then they could decide which nation has done most toward improving human life in terms of those criteria.

Sport and fitness criteria which come to mind include greater allocation of play spaces by urban developers, greater allocation of time and resources in school curricula for physical education and outdoor pursuits, and greater efforts to bridge the gap between the physical and financial pre-requisites of current sport programs, and the abilities and interests of certain people for example, the poor, the disabled and the aged.

Moral and social criteria could include improved shelter and nutrition for people, greater opportunities for meaningful work and involvement in society, as well as evidence of attempts towards greater international cooperation.

The proposed site selection process would not have to be influenced by the ability of a nation to pay for the construction of Olympic facilities. Instead, an Olympic site fund would be created. To be eligible for Olympic participation, every nation each year would be required to contribute a fixed percentage of gross national product to that fund. The nation hosting the Olympics could use this fund to pay for construction of necessary facilities.

The honor of being judged as the nation most appropriate to host the Olympics, together with tangible benefits from the site fund, should provide tremendous incentives for nations to compete in a very different manner.

My proposal suggests that the Olympic Movement, which generates international sport competition, culminating every four years in the Olympic Games, could also serve to initiate and sustain continuous international competition to improve the quality of the human condition within all nations. I admit that this proposal is Utopian, but I trust that it may provide a model to enable you to imagine how sport systems, even giant international ones, might be changed to become more person/athlete centered.

Opinions obtained from a survey of Congress delegates show considerable support for the proposal as seen below.

%

45.0 Selection of future Olympic sites should be based primarily on criteria reflecting the Olympic ideal. . . the cultivation of complete balanced human beings. The nation selected would have to show evidence of the best record over the previous four years, of internal and external policies, and practices reflecting the Olympic ideal.

33.3 The Olympic Games should always be held in Athens.

13.0 Olympic sites should be selected according to economic criteria alone; that is, whether or not the bidding nation is rich enough to provide adequate facilities, transportation and security for visiting athletes, coaches, and official delegates.

8.7 The practice of selecting just one centralized site for the Olympic Games should be discontinued.

GOALS BEFORE GOLDS

Toller Cranston (Canada)

The reason I skated was because I loved it. Had I listened to what people said about me, or had I listened to people that really knew the ins and outs of skating politics, I never would have continued. But because it was always such a pleasure for me, a joy for me, I never really found the work to be difficult, and I never really believed that I couldn't make it — that I couldn't ever win the appreciation of the establishment. It was my stupidity that propelled me along in my skating career.

One of the reasons that kept me going was that I had another career all together — something that kept me enlightened, that kept me interested in a whole other field that served as a departure from the skating world. I think that people that spend their whole lives doing only one thing are going to burn themselves out very quickly. This is one point I really want to make — as far as creativity in sports goes — I feel that the only way that one can really improve in their sport is if the brain is also being nurtured and groomed. This can be done in many ways. In North America, most skaters at the age of 13 or 14 leave school and they go out and they skate all day. Those skaters, the ones who do that, rarely achieve a high level of skating. I believe it is because their brains just cannot handle it. You've got to grow both physically and mentally.

Another thing that I think is important in the artistic sports, those being gymnastics, diving, figure skating, is the enlightenment that one derives from studying other things. I know that while I took time out with my painting career and spent a lot of time painting, where I suppose I could have been jogging around the block or skating more hours, I know that what I usurped from studying painting, studying music, studying literature, all of those things, other people's ideas came into me and I felt that this was an inspiration to me. I cannot impress you people enough of how important it was for me. The people that prevent other things from coming into their life are on a dead end street.

For example, let's talk about the Russian gymnasts — I feel that as far as the free mat exercise goes, they are the only ones who have it together. Because there is no doubt in my mind — I'm talking about the females — that those people are dance trained — they are not just dance trained, where you go and take a little dance class — but they are Bolshoi trained. They have an understanding that their movements have a motivation behind them. By doing that, they achieve a certain greatness, where in fact their sport is second to the art. I think when one watches even somebody like a Nadia Comaneci, I say to myself, "it's great, it's wonderful." But really we are watching a machine. I feel it has very little to do with creativity.

One performance I will remember to my dying day was the performance of, I believe the name was Turisheva, a Russian gymnast, who to me was the total and complete athlete, she was the total artist — she transcended sport and brought it to an art, yet few people were able to see it.

Sport today is anti-creativity. In fact, it is kind of silly for me, it's redundant to talk about it. In fact for me, sport today is old fashioned. Creativity today in sport is old fashioned. I think that I was in the era in figure skating when It was at its height, not because of me but because of all the other people who were exploring, who were interested in creating new and different routines, who were interested in music, who were interested in style and the choreography — well all of that has fallen by the wayside. Because the athletes who are winning today, who are on the top — are the ones, who have a triple jump — it has nothing to do with creativity. I suppose the Turisheva, that kind of athlete, if she is going to compete against somebody who does a double black flip on the mat, how do you compete against that? You can't, because people, spectators, judges, coaches, etc., are so programmed to those technical achievements that they are not able to discern how valuable the fully rounded athlete really is. I don't know in particular why the male skaters use music. I think they should set an obstacle course, and see who can do the most triple jumps, and declare them the winner. Because that's really where it's at today.

The athletes I bumped into during the 1972 era were great personalities, they were great individuals. Their personalities transcended their work, even when they were off the ice. They were incredible. Now I don't see that anymore. I see trained animals, people that are programmed; it's anti-creativity, it's anti-individuality. People are no longer looking inside themselves and pulling out something that is unique and different because they are only thinking in terms of the technical aspects, and not falling down, and how many triple jumps they can do. I'm sure this is the trend in sport all over the world. The technique has totally eroded any ability to become an individual, to become an artist. There is no room for that.

There are some skaters in the world today, one in particular, luckily enough, was good enough technically to be seen by the world. He was an actor, an artist and an athlete and it was terrific that he was seen in the World Championships. His name was Igor Vogrin. I sent him a telegram. Told him how great he was. That really is the answer. But those few and far between performers and artists are not a product of the establishment — they are driven by their own personal goals and they have sacrificed medals for being themselves.

If I were to do my career again, I certainly don't think I would do it any differently. What I haven't lost is the joy of performing. What I haven't lost is the ecstasy that one feels when you are performing. I am sure that people like Igor are also in tune with that sort of higher level of performing, where medals are actually not important to them.

When we see the great performances in sport, no matter what sport it is, the greatest moment in sport are the human moments. They ignite a spark of ecstasy that we will carry to the grave. They give us a memory. The technical side, of course it is important, but the greatest moments that one sees are the things that bring a certain light into your life.

I guess sports are the most authentic drama that there is on earth because it's pure, there's no script, it's the most real. The people aren't performing in front of the television screen. For example, in the Montreal Olympics, I remember there was a Canadian girl standing on the edge of the diving board, and just before she was going to dive, somebody clicked a camera in the audience, and she lost her balance. When you do that, when you go back from the dive, you are penalized in some way. But an East German girl went out, put her arm around her and said, I presume, "Come on, you can do it, don't worry." And for me the highest moment in sport was seen because it was an authentic human drama, and of course, the girl went and did it. I don't know who won the diving competition in Montreal. But there is something to learn from this.

I think that one has to actively cultivate the moments of ecstasy that sport is really about. You have to perform your sport as though you are an actor. You have to perform it like a theatre. I would make sure that whatever I wore (if I were a diver, a skier) was absolutely unique and different. I would want to assert my individuality. I'm against being just one of the group. I know that there are teams, but I feel that in a sense the individual is really so important in sport. I feel that we are no longer in touch with that. We are in touch with medals, and the one that wins, and all the others are forgotten. The discipline is a very heady drug for almost any sportsman. I know that with my life, the education, discipline that I got out of skating and training, has only now been channelled into my life as a painter and anything else that I do. I think that any sportsman can come out at the end of the road with

or without a gold medal around his neck, but if they can say, "God, it was the best moment of my life, it was fantastic, it was super," surely that's what sport is about.

And yet I feel that because of the way things are developing, that kind of attitude is almost impossible these days. Sports are becoming dangerous. Sports are becoming so technically expert that how can we enjoy it? How can you go and tell your gymnasts that today we are going to learn a triple salto? How can you really enjoy that, knowing that at any second, you could fall on your neck and break it? In figure skating, with the pairs, I don't know if any of you noticed, there may have been 20 pairs of contestants in the World Championships years before. Now we are lucky if we have 10 — why? Because it is too dangerous. Because it is the ones who do the triple throws, where the girls are thrown from tremendous heights and land on their knees — they don't want to do it anymore. They don't want to do it because they don't want to be hurt. The whole art of sport has been bypassed and the whole techical aspect of sport is the deciding factor.

There is no way you can compete with that kind of performance. I guess it is in the name of "progress." And yet surely that is not the answer. Surely that is not where it is at. Is the greatest skater the one that can do the quadruple? Is that what it is all about? I don't think it is. I think that the golden age of skating was in the 50's when skaters were all-round skaters.

DISHONESTY IN INTERNATIONAL COMPETITION

Jack Donahue, Canada

As a basketball coach I have a great concern for a problem that you Sports Psychologists may be able to help us with. We have to take a number of very selfish people, and we are interested in selfish people, and have them play together as a team in what may be the most complete team game. The athletes, though, and the coaches, must be prepared for certain things when they go into international competition.

I think our players are prepared for the games themselves. They are prepared physically, we have a doctor and a trainer who take care of those needs; however, psychologically there are some things that they must be prepared for. By the way, I've already tried to handle these, or paid attention to these by trying to minimize the importance of all these things. We spend a lot of time with our players, one-to-one and in group meetings, trying to prepare them for what will happen in international competition. But we really need an awful lot of help in this area.

Our players, even our Olympic players, start off by realizing that their first goal is to enjoy themselves. Our program is too long and intense for us to have any other ultimate goal, except first of all, that everyone playing with this group of people can have more fun than by doing anything else during this period of time. The second goal is to play as well as they can play. We set no other goals. Others do. They talk about medals and all that stuff. That's fine. It is important to do well because these are the best athletes that we have. But we just have the two goals of having fun and playing well.

But there are distractions. Here are the things that distract us from playing basketball. First, players have to be prepared to spend a tremendous amount of time away from home — parents, girlfriends, wives, children, friends, school. This is because there is no way that they can prepare for our team in their own locale in the prescribed period of time. Our period of time is thirty days.

Second, they have to be prepared for new, very quick and very close relationships which must develop in a short period of time. Some people are not ready for this. It is not the normal way. You usually have more time to develop friendships. In our case we

have a player from the west coast, put in a room with a stranger, perhaps with a very different background, from somewhere else, and they will have to live together for a period of time. You Sport Psychologists might be able to help us with this problem.

We also have unbelievable physical demands. We practice very, very hard for short periods of time, sometimes two or three times a day. The practices are exactly the time it takes to play a full game, ninety minutes.

Travel incidents happen every single trip. Consider a typical day. We played the night before. We got up at 5 a.m. to catch a train at about six. We rode for about an hour, then someone is informed that this is not the correct train. We got into Milan where there were 20 tracks. There were 16 people in the group and 30 large pieces of baggage — balls and medical equipment. We were told that the train we needed to get on was four tracks away. We ran across the tracks. We were chased by the police because it is wrong to run on the tracks. We got to the train, rode for another hour, and were told that this train is the wrong train. While we are on this train we pulled into a station and ended up next to another train. We were told that it is the one we must take. We threw our baggage in through the open windows, but the players on the inside threw it out because the train was the first one we had been on. Anyway we got it all straightened out. We arrived at our destination at 6:30 p.m. after travelling for 12 hours. We hadn't eaten yet. We got on a bus and travelled for another two hours. We changed on the bus, got off the bus, and played a basketball game. That is international competition. Or, have you sat for 12 hours in London airport while someone is on strike? Or have you been in Tel Aviv, in the aeroplane on the runway for four hours, while no one told you what was going on? All those things are not uncommon to our athletes. These youngsters have come up through a minority system which is a completely different world.

The Olympic villages: In Canada there were 10 people to a room, 30 people to a bathroom, with coaches and players all mixed together. The food: While we were in Romania our players lost from 10 to 16 pounds each in 14 days. The media: Our players are not used to being on T.V. and being quoted. When we beat the U.S. there was a line-up of media people who wanted to talk to us.

Finally, politics are a major part of sport. In Roumania we had a situation in wrestling. It had to do with grouping or matching the athletes. It is usually done by drawing names at random out of a box. No one from Roumania wrestled anyone from the Soviet Union in the first round. That could have been a coincidence. But during the weigh-in for the second round, a Cuban wrestler was seen passing a draw number to a Soviet wrestler before he reached into the draw box. This happened four times along the line. The athletes were cheating. I imagine the coaches were in it too. But most important of all, the people running the wrestling tournament had to be involved, because at the end of the draw you can't have extra numbers left in that bowl. Those numbers must have been taken out for the set up. You know what the solution should be? Put all the numbers back and do it again. But there were no official protests, no sanctions, and no official report written about the incident. That is sick. I don't know how you could work for 4 years, or in the athletes' case, maybe 24 years, to get to the World Student Games and have someone cheat — dead against every rule, emotion, philosophy of sport, and then someone say, "Well, boys will be boys."

Consider another incident in basketball. It illustrates the major problem in international competition — that no one must be embarrassed, and that the last people considered in international competition are the athletes. Because of politics, or bureaucracy, the athletes who have devoted their lives to excellence in sport are being frustrated. In this incident, Roumania was playing Brazil in a basketball game which was part of the Student Games. I saw the game and feel that Brazil should have won by a lot. But Brazil didn't play that well.

The clock, probably worth $20,000, stopped working in the first half. They reverted back to what I was used to in New York City when I was 12 years old. A guy sat on a chair with a clock in his hand and no one else could see the clock. They announced that there was two minutes left to play in the first half. Someone in the crowd from Brazil had a watch with a stopwatch on it. He was sitting right behind me. He set it to time the last period of play. The buzzer rang to end the half which was favourable to Roumania. This guy jumped up to show everyone that there was still 35 seconds left to play. There was yelling and screaming, but the players left the court.

I went to the technical committee, a group of people authorized by the sport to oversee the game. I asked them what the problem was. They spoke very nicely to me, "My dear friend from Canada, you realize that there is always discrepancy between when the official blows his whistle and the time when the whistle is heard, and the clock is stopped. Of course, the Brazilian with the watch may not have anticipated the whistle each time it blew." I asked them what the time lag would probably be for each whistle. They said about ½ second. So I said that the whistle would have had to blow 70 times in the last two minutes to explain the disrepancy. But the whistle only blew three times in the last two minutes. They waved me away, telling me that I didn't understand.

About 14 seconds before the end of the game there was a problem — a player from Brazil took his fingers and poked them in a Roumanian player's eyes. Brazil had been playing badly and was losing by this time. A fight started. Everyone got involved. It went out into a lobby, and into the street. It lasted 35 minutes.

After the fight was stopped, here is what they did. Remember Roumania was ahead by 15 points and there was only 14 seconds to play. Now this reflects the current philosophy of international competition. The players had to play the last 14 seconds of basketball. After this, both teams had to shake hands. Not everyone from Brazil shook hands, but enough did to make it look alright. When they shook hands, everyone clapped, because that is sportsmanship. What they don't know is that they *must* shake hands, because if they didn't shake hands, there would be all kinds of reports, because they were unsportsmanlike. It is against international philosophy, against ethics, not to shake hands.

There was no report filed on that game. The technical committee didn't feel that it was necessary. They said that the fight was just an emotional outburst. I told them that I hoped from now on that they would schedule an extra thirty minutes for riots, because the committee was assuming that what took place in that basketball game was a normal, to be expected, occurrence.

Before each game, I now go to the technical committee and yell and scream at them for 20 minutes because I found that's what works. But I want to tell you that it's sickening. It makes people who are involved in international sports wonder if it's worth all the trouble. I don't see how anyone in authority can allow those things to happen.

Now what do we do to change it? I'm trying to get on all the international committees to yell and scream. But I'm telling you that our athletes will have to be prepared for realities, and those are some of the realities that are going to happen the next time there is an international event unless somebody changes things. Perhaps you Sport Psychologists can help us with this.

CREATING SYSTEMS OF OPPORTUNITY

Kathrine Switzer (U.S.A.)

I am a trained athlete and an expert in the field of sports promotion. Therefore I think the experiences I've had of a personal nature, in the field of sports promotion, and as an athlete might be helpful to you. I'm going to discuss everything from my personal experiences, and let you draw your own conclusions.

When I was a little girl I didn't know the differences between a girl or a boy. My parents contributed greatly to this attitude by raising my brother and me in exactly the same manner. I always thought that if my brother could run faster or throw farther than me, it was only because he was three years older than me. As I got older I realized there were differences between males and females, but still to this day I realize that those differences aren't negative or positive. They are just differences. I grew up with the notion that males and females were as good as each other, and that the capabilities of females are just as good as the capabilities of males, but are different. As Physical Educators and Social Scientists we know those differences. Males are stronger and bigger, and Women are more flexible and have better balance.

I remember my first really super athletic experience. When I was about 12 years old and wanted desperately to be accepted by my classmates, which I guess happens to all of us when we are growing up, and the nearest thing to teen age nervana when I was 12 years old, was to be a high school cheerleader. It was the only thing my parents refused me. They insisted that I could not be a high school cheerleader. My mother said she didn't like me trailing along after the guys. But my father was more to the point. He said that if you are going to take part in something, participate in it, don't spectate. So, fortified with the excuse to my classmates, I went out and did what I wanted to do in the first place. I played Field Hockey. I ran up and down the field, huddled and did team strategies, bashed the hell out of the ball, and got involved in the same manner that I saw young boys getting involved.

I was also then concerned about not making the team. Once again my father came to my rescue and said, "Listen Kid, if you want to be a good Field Hockey player, all you have to do is run a mile a day." Well this mile a day sounded like Kilimanjaro to me, but if my father said you could run a mile a day, it meant one could do it. So I went our there every day of the hot summer and ran a mile a day. Well that first mile took me about 14-15 minutes, and every single day I ran a mile. I did not stop. Somehow I was thinking through a limited frame of reference that I would make the Field Hockey team.

As a young girl running that mile a day taught me. It gave me the basis for the rest of my life. In fact I have grown from it both personally and professionally. I learned how to set a goal, and to plan objectives, and how difficult some things are some days, and how easy it is sometimes to run that mile. I learned for the first time that I was not just a human being on this earth, but was part of this environment. I learned that there was no real differentiation between grass and sun and rain and sweat and me, that we all blended together. It was a fantastic revelation. Maybe even at age 12 it was the first inkling of the running high that we are all talking about now. That was a very special thing for me.

Of course when the Field Hockey season came along I tried out for the team, being a very nervous, skinny, speckled freshman, hoping I would make the team, hoping beyond hope. Well, I not only made the team, but I was the best player on the team. Suddenly I realized it had nothing to do with my skill but it had to do with my condition. I was a well conditioned athlete. I could learn skills on top of conditioning because I never got tired. I could run endlessly. I never got sore. This running to me became a very secret sort of weapon. I figured that if it had to be good for Field Hockey, I could use it for Basketball later, or any sort of sport I might want to get involved in. In fact, it became a training base for me, all the way to the point where I started thinking about entering College.

At the same time I was running this mile and playing sport in school, I became very aware that I was a different sort of person. Society was not ready for me. People would stop and offer me a ride along the road. People would go to my mother and say that something was wrong with her child, out there running in circles. Other girls would snicker and giggle; boys would snicker and giggle. Certainly if I kept this up I was going to get big legs, grow a mustache, turn into a Lesbian, never be able to have babies, certainly never have a boyfriend.

But there was another group of people who accepted me for what I was — that I was a well rounded person, that I did well in school, that I was the High School editor of the newspaper, that I was on the Prom Committee. I was then allowed my athleticism, as this was somehow my one peculiarity that I would eventually outgrow.

I never outgrew it because it was probably the one thing in my life that was truly objective. It was there, it existed. It required absolutely no explanation. Running is a beautiful thing because you get from point A to point B, and you actually do that. There is no judgement involved. There is no second guessing about what you are as a person.

And so people were saying that this athleticism was a peculiarity with me, when it might have been the basis for my whole life. So I didn't talk about it. I just went out and did it more and more. If it feels good do it. I felt a sense of accomplishment, strength, a sense of movement, that I knew I was good, and I thought it transcended explanation, so I didn't talk about it a lot with other people.

When I got into College, I became extremely frustrated with the fact that the other girls involved in sport there, were playing *at* them, and were not doing them for any athletic reason, or for self-accomplishment or self improvement. I suddenly realized they were playing with each other, and it was just another social. I had a very big falling out one day when there was an important Field Hockey game, and I was racing for a goal, and the person behind me missed the ball as I passed it, and I got so frustrated and I yelled, "Just Move, get it." She threw down her stick, walked off the field and said, "Oh Kathrine, it's only a game for heaven's sake." Sure it was only a game, but when you're in it, I presumed everybody should play it as hard as I played it. I suddenly felt so terribly, terribly isolated and went out and continued my running. I ran at the beginning and end of every practice which didn't endear me to any of my coaches because they assumed that if I could run after my practices that I wasn't "putting out" in practices. It was difficult to explain to a coach that these workouts alone weren't demanding enough for me to work out my own aggressions.

Anyway when I was out running I had decided that I had reached, at the age of 19, a turning point in my life, and that sports weren't for me in terms of a team concept, which was really wrong. There was a particular point in time, about in the mid 60's, being a woman in sport in the mid 60's, honest to God, I think you all understand the mid 60's was the dark ages for women in sport, but I thought that maybe team sports were not an alternative for me. I regret that now. I would love to be involved in a super team effort with everybody putting out 100%. I think it would be an incredible experience. But anyway, I realized then that for me perhaps it was going to be an individual sport, and I thought about what sport it would be. Could it be Tennis? Could it be Golf? None of these offered me any challenge, and I suddenly realized that I am going to do what I am doing now, and that is running.

It didn't matter if there were no track and field, or

cross country teams, I would just run and enjoy the experience of running every day. I therefore dropped all my sports and told my coaches that I was just going to run. They all thought I was crazy. I just enjoyed going around the college's lake, or running from town to town, and just adding more and more miles every day. The sense of self accomplishment, and those of you who run, or know of it, understand that when you run around the block or run ten miles, the sense of accomplishment is still the same — you did it all yourself. It's really overwhelming.

I continued doing this until one day the College cross country coach came out and watched my running and said that one of the eleven lettermen had flunked off the team and asked whether I would consider running the mile for the track team next week and even pick up points. I said, "Sure coach — whatever will help the team out." He had sort of asked me in the same manner. If he could keep his pet basset hound in the inside lane for four laps, then the team would get points, and wouldn't I be glad to help out. And I was. I was very glad to help. At any rate, little did I know that my running the mile for the college track team was going to cause the scandal it caused. It was an incredible scandal and people who didn't even know me, either loved me or hated me, and everyone had an opinion about what I was doing. Somehow my running with the men's track team and being on the track for four laps in short-shorts was tatamount to something very anti-social. I couldn't understand why, because running was the most natural thing I've done in my whole life. A beautiful thing. I ignored all those things. Or I was sustained by those who thought it was a terrific thing. By the way my first mile was a 5:69 — so you're getting the idea that I was never any great athlete. But that's also part of the story.

At any rate as I became more involved in this running thing. I met people who were involved in similar activities, as we all do, and at the same time transferred into Syracuse University to study sport journalism because I wanted to be a sport journalist. I have always maintained that if you love something very much there is no reason why you have to live for it as an avocation. That maybe a Utopian viewpoint. I believed that if I loved sport so much, and I believed that sport and intellect were in balance, and that your life worked together, that I could somehow earn a living doing things that kept you involved with the activity. In my case I did not ever want to be a professional athlete, and get paid for performance. I did want to use my mind and I was a good student, and I did love journalism, and I thought that becoming a sports journalist would keep me in the mix of sports writing all my life.

So I went to Syracuse to study journalism and while there began working out with the men's cross country team. This time I really began to understand what distance running was, because these guys were running 7-8 miles a day. I had never heard of anyone who ran 7-8 miles a day and while I was out running with these guys, and always finishing lamely

behind them, there was one little guy who is a track coach there, whose name is Barnie Briggs who had trained with the men's cross country team for 20 years. He had a knee operation this particular year and thought he'd never run again. He saw me running lamely behind the men and came out and said, "Look why don't we run together? I can't run very fast but I can coach you a little." So every day we'd be out running together, and with all this 20 years of cardio-vascular conditioning, he couldn't run very fast, but he could talk while he ran. I couldn't talk at all. Arnie would talk and every day he would tell me, "Gee you're getting a lot better, gee, you can really improve, drop your arms, but stretch out a little bit." And then he'd go off on all these tales as runners often do. Barnie had run 16 Boston Marathons. Anyone in the '60's who had run Marathons was weird. Arnie had to be the weirdest of anyone I had ever known, but he was also my hero. I wound up growing up on tales of all the top runners but I also got sick and tired of hearing about the Boston Marathon.

One night we were out running, and I was really cranky and tired, and I suddenly realized that we had been running about 10 miles a night in sleet and blinding snow. The cross country team had long given up and were training in the field house. And Arnie was out there telling me how great I was and, "gee, I've never known any of the guys to stick with me out here in the sleet and snow," and he started in again on the Boston Marathon — and I said, "Arnie let's quit talking about the damn thing and run it." He didn't miss a beat. He'd just told me how good I was and he now said, "That's impossible, you can't run the Boston Marathon." And I said, "you got to be kidding. Why can't a woman run the Boston Marathon? I'm running 10 miles a night, why can't I run 26?" He said, "I don't know, I think with women it must be something like the law of diminishing returns." I said, "Arnie, that's preposterous, if a man can run 26 miles, a woman can run 26 miles." Now we were arguing, cars were sliding into us, and suddenly Arnie and I came face to face with the fact that we didn't know anything about anything. I'd been running every day. It felt good, I was getting better. I was adding more distance, Arnie was saying, "Gee you're terrific." And then when we looked at the idea of running 26 miles we realized we didn't know anybody who had done it, and we really didn't know if I did do it whether I might get big legs grow a mustache, and become a Lesbian, if I went beyond the 12 mile point, or whatever. Whatever it was, as early as, or as late as, 1966, we were sailing, or, in this case "running on a flat earth." We didn't know at what point we were going to fall off the other side. I again, thank God, for my naivety and my optimism, but I insisted that it could be done. Somebody telling me something can't be done, Arnie especially, is like raising a red flag in my face. And Arnie said, "All right, if you can do it in practice, you show you can run 26 miles, and I'll be the first person to take you to the Boston Marathon." Well, now I was like a kid in the candy shop, because I'm the type of person that does my homework, and would not want to go to Boston anyway unless I could do it. I knew that I was going to be peculiar in Boston among the 5700 men, that I would be noticed and I wanted them to know I was serious, and that all women could do it.

At the same time that this was going on in my athletic life, I adapted very well to my social situation. I tried to tell everyone what I was doing. I lived in a residence cottage in Syracuse, and all these women tolerated my athleticism, but they were curious about what would drive anyone to go out and run 10-12 miles every afternoon in that kind of snowy, sleety weather. I tried to relate to them my sense of accomplishment. I tried to explain that it was the same kind of return as they got from their involvements. One was an artist/photographer, and one a ballerina. They didn't understand, but liked me just the same.

I then began to develop a very bad attitude. It was the same thing I had in team sports, where I felt very smug and very superior. I began to feel that I had some inside knowledge about the balance of life — of intellect and physicality. I didn't feel at all sorry for my roommates, that their concerns about life — being concerned about boys and school — were quite frivolous compared to mine. In retrospect it is clear that I didn't have a smug, superior attitude. It was with this attitude that I was training for the Boston Marathon and feeling quite special about myself. I've changed a lot about that, but that was my attitude then.

I'd like to relate to you the training that took place in connection with the Boston Marathon. Arnie continued running with me 10 miles a day and on Sunday we ran a long run which I always liked because we didn't have to worry about time. We had all day and didn't have to worry about getting back to class or to bed. And we built up to a 12 miler and 16 and then 20. One day we were going to run 26 and I was more "psyched" for that workout than for any of the competitive 35 Marathons I've done since, and probably even more than the first Marathon, even more than the Marathon I ran my best time in. We began at 8:00 a.m. because we thought it might take all day to run this 26 miles. We ran roughly a 10,000 meter route that we kept repeating and adding on the miles. We came round and round and I felt terrific. Towards the end of the day we were coming into our imaginary finish line, which was a country lane coming onto the main road that we were running on. Anyone who takes part in any sport knows that it's usually when you are coming down the road into your driveway that makes it all worth while, because for you, it's coming into Olympic stadium, there are 20,000 people there, and they've got the gold medal hanging up, and they are screaming for you, and it doesn't matter that maybe it's just a paper boy or a milk truck driver, or you're alone on this country lane — you're coming home to Olympic stadium and you have just won a big one. That's what always makes a workout fun for me because it is that mixture of fantasy and reality and physical accomplishment that kind of got me there in the first place. Arnie was telling me, "You're not

going to run 26 miles, I don't believe it." But, for the first time I didn't feel like I was running into Olympic Stadium — I didn't feel like we had done the whole distance, the whole thing. I said that maybe the course was short and suggested that we run a little more to be sure we had run 26 miles. "Don't be ridiculous," he said, "We've run this course every day." He said, "Well, what do you want to do?" I said, "Let's do another 4 mile loop." He felt the course was long if anything. He said, "If you're up to doing it." I said, "sure." He said, "Well, if you can do it, I can do it." So I said, "Let's go." We took off for a 5 mile loop, and we were a mile from home and I began to hear the distant cheers. I was talking to Arnie, but Arnie was suddenly gone. His eyes were rolling and his legs were like rubber. I put my arms in his and said, "Come on, we can do it." We only had a mile to do, but he was all over the place. We finished our mile and I was jumping up and down, so happy because I knew then that I could run the Boston Marathon. I clapped Arnie on the back and said, "damn it, we did it, we did it." Arnie passed out cold. The first thing he said when he came to was, "you can run the Boston Marathon." The next day, little Arnie was like so many men I've met the rest of my life. He was going all over the campus saying, "Women have hidden potential and endurance. Women are much stronger than we ever realized, why, that woman ran me into the ground." Arnie was in heaven. Arnie came by the dorm and gave me an entry form to the Boston Marathon.

This was a big moment of celebration for us. I filled out the form and mailed it off. I filled it out the same way I sign my name which is K.V. Switzer. But in those days before the race you had to go to the school's infirmary and take a physical, they took your heart rate, etc. Arnie warned that I was going to be embarrassed in Lockington Gym at the start of the Marathon because all the men are running around nude.

I have to tell another side story, at the same time, it is a social story. At the same time I was also dating a nationally ranked hammer thrower, a super athlete, national potential, Olympic potential. I always felt like a klutz around him because all I could do was run 10 minutes a mile, mile after mile. About 2 weeks before the Marathon we were sitting in a bar having a beer and I decided I better tell him that I was going to run the Marathon. So I told him that in fact this summer I was going to Boston to run the Marathon. And this was one of those slow laughs that begins with a giggle and goes into an uproar and pretty soon he has fallen off his bar stool and onto the floor and said this is one of the funniest things he had ever heard. I said I was serious. Then he said if you can run the Boston Marathon then I can too and I'm coming too. I said, "Tom, you weigh 235 lbs and you have to train for this kind of thing." He said, "Don't worry, I'll come out and run tomorrow." We went out and ran. I have to hand it to the guy, he ran 13 miles and he thought that was enough — if I could run it, he could do it.

So two nights before Boston, another member of the cross country team, Arnie who is now 55 years old, a woman, and a hammer thrower piled in a car to go to Boston to run the Marathon. It was fortuitous because it was snowing and sleeting the day of the race, and I had put on a heavy sweatsuit and they were really tatty old clothes. Arnie had told me to take old clothes because you warm up in them and then throw them away and may never see them again. I really looked bad. I say it was fortuitous because I had all these heavy clothes on and underneath them you could not tell that I was a woman.

I did not know that it was against the rules for a woman to run the race, I just thought I was going to be the odd man out. I didn't know it was against the rules. I just knew I was going to be noticed. The easier I could start into the race and just get running along the better it was going to be. It was snowing and sleeting and you couldn't tell I was a woman. I wouldn't be here talking to you today, I probably wouldn't have the job I have, we wouldn't have had the recent International Women's Marathon in Ottawa if it had been a sunshiny day that day in Boston and I would have had on shorts and a T'shirt and an official would have come up to me and said, "you're not running the race." I would have been embarrassed and probably not begun.

Anyway the gun went off, and like a band of merry Indians we all went down the street. I'm in heaven. I have gone to Mecca, I've met the wailing wall, I'm doing everything at once. I've trained the whole year in snow and sleet to run the 26 miles, I'm with 600 wonderful people. They were all men. I must admit, the men in my athletic career have been the most wonderful supporters in the world. It's only been society and some officials who have given me a hard time. The men on the cross country team always regarded me, and I them, as runners. I was never female and they male — we were just runners together and we superceded all the sexual stereotypes.

Four miles into the race I had shed my sweatsuit and the race official saw that I was a woman in the race, he became so incensed, he jumped from the truck, ran down the street, tackled me and tried to rip my numbers off and throw me out of the race, screaming at me to get out of the race. I burst into tears. Big Tom came to the rescue and threw a cross body block at the official. I went on to finish the race in 4 hours and 20 minutes, and the official instead went out of the race.

The poor timing of the official again probably put me in a position I'm in right now, because he had the audacity to do that in front of the press truck. The next morning, in fact by the time I had finished the race, on the front pages of the world newspapers was a series of a woman running and being saved by her husky boyfriend.

Society was outraged again in two camps. One camp said it was ridiculous for women to be involved in such activities, and it was ridiculous for women to force themselves into such environments. The other camp said, "She did it. She beat a lot of men in the race. Why can't women be involved in sports?"

For me, it was a very radical experience. I said to myself that no longer is it important for me to feel smug or superior to other women. The reason I'm in this race in the first place is because I've been given encouragement from the beginning to do whatever I wanted to do, and try to do it well, and to have no sense of limitation. And I suddenly began to feel sorry for all other women in the world, who maybe got to be 19 years of age without it ever occurring to them to run in a Boston Marathon. I decided then, that if life had given me that kind of insight, it behooves me to change as much as I can.

I have devoted the rest of my life to creating a system of opportunities for other women in sport. After working for a number of years in an official capacity as Chairman of the AAU, and working in different international governing bodies and structures, I realized that what was going to change the system for women in sports, not just in running but in all sports, was a system of opportunity, and opportunity was going to come from Economics. I felt that if I could create a system of events around the world, starting with North America, that women would literally come out and answer the cry for an opportunity. They would take the incentive and run with it.

People kept telling me as years went by, "You want to run in North America, but the women in Japan don't want to, the women in South America don't want to run. They will get big legs and get mustaches and turn into Lesbians. It's anti social and anti feminine." I answered that they won't if they are given the opportunity. Because opportunity means it's okay. It's like reading something in the newspaper. I can tell you something and you won't believe it, but if I tell you something that gets printed in the newspaper, and you read it in the newspaper, it becomes perfectly acceptable and believable. It's the same thing with opportunity. I can tell a woman it's okay for her to run, but she won't believe me until we create a race for women only, and they come out and watch and they think it's wonderful. It's the same thing with athletic governing bodies, and I've been telling them this, and telling them this. But I realize first of all that they can't put on the event, no matter how much they believe in it, because they don't have the money. So my mind is clicking, over the years I'm realizing it would behoove a major corporation to get behind such an effort to put on these events. To put on something incredibly worthwhile, in the community and in the international environment, and that they are going to get a fantastic return on their investment and visibility.

Timing has always been fortuitous for me. I happened to meet some of the executives of the Avon company. I told them about my idea. I gave them my 50 page proposal. They said, "We may never do anything in sports, but anyone who can write like this we'd like to work with us." Which again is giving me my inch, and I immediately had myself hired on by Avon. Whereupon, the door being open an inch, I kicked it open a mile and convinced them that they should begin a series of athletic events for women, and showed them the kind of return they could get.

Their return was so overwhelming, they became freer and gave me more and more latitude. I created a series of international events, beginning with a pilot series of five little races. Suddenly we began putting on races around the world, putting on events in 12 countries, involving athletes from 32 countries, and created a grass roots system running around the world. This has all culminated in two major Avon international championships, including the one held in Ottawa last week-end.

This international marathon was designed to fill the void in the Olympic Games, because as you know, until last February, there was no event longer than 1500 M for women in the Olympic Games, because of all the stereotypes I've told you about. In many countries people would come to me and say, "I understand what you are saying, and I know intellectually you're right, but I'm not going to let my daughter run, or my wife run." It was a matter of going into these countries and putting on the event and showing officials first hand that it was going to be safe, that it was a wonderful thing, and we put on events.

Let me give you the example of Brazil. They said no women would be interested. First race in Brazil — 580 women; second race in Brazil — 1600 women; two weeks later a race in Chile, first race ever in the country — 2100 women came out and ran 5 Km; same in Japan — 10 Km race, the first one — 780 women. So everyone knew that they were interested.

From these races we gathered statistics, data, medical evidence, and put it into a major status report. I was invited by the International Amateur Athletic Federation to come to Paris and present this report. I presented it, and received and repudiated every argument there ever was about women's ability, particularly in endurance. I pointed out that women may excell in physical capability, particularly in endurance, while men may excell in speed and strength events. I lobbied tirelessly, not just by myself, but with a lot of other women. As you know, as of February, that evidence was voted on overwhelmingly 7 to 1 to include a marathon for women in 1984. To say that that was a high priority in my life was probably an understatement.

But I think probably the highest points of my life have come in a series of events that I'm priveleged to see, watching each woman come across the finish line in her first ever marathon which she never thought she could complete. To see that expression on her face, and to see it manifested around the world on 30 or 40,000 women a year, who never thought before they could do anything. These women were limited only by their experience, and by the myths and preconceptions they had had fostered on them from an early age. To see those broken away repeatedly is a continuing high point for me, and for any women who are involved in sports, and for any who have seen that, and been involved in women's activities.

It is awsome to think at this point in time, that we really are at the tip of the iceberg in terms of not only women's opportunity, but women's sense of limitation, and therefore the human sense of lack of limitation. When all of us have realized, at any point in our lives, that we have no limiting factor, that we in fact can do anything, we forever change our thinking about everything we do in life, and in our children's thinking, and their children's thinking, and things begin breaking down just so fast that it is awsome. To see a mutual understanding between ourselves, maybe through the act of playing together, through a simple act of physical accomplishment together, that transfers into every other aspect of life. Males and females, maybe for the first time may start getting to know each other again, on that level I told you about, that humanistic level, and have a sense of understanding of each other, that is going to make this world a much better, brighter more exciting place than we can, right now, even imagine. I think it is a very exciting threshold.

Discussion

Question: Why focus on running?

Kathrine: Running is universal. Even women in Brazil who can't afford shoes can still run.

Question: The question is one of motivation. How to get started. What was it in your family that caused you to be so strong?

Kathrine: You have to start some place. I can't go into two million families across the world and try to change women. But if you give a particular idea, at a particular point in time, it may be the only way to start. I've seen young women who have never had a sports experience say, "I think I can run 3 Km" — and they do. From then on it changes their whole focus, and their ideas about their capabilities. That's what I mean. At some point you have to take a stand, make a start, and branch out from there.

Comment: I'd like to pursue the point about the family because sometimes these educational programs come and go, but the family continues. I tend to think of the nuclear family as the traditional two parents with two children. But a recent study in Aberdeen Scotland showed that 70% of the teenagers in one inner city school were from single parent, mother-led families. This may have a tremendous impact on sport modelling within the family. If this family trend continues we will need proper education for physical education teachers to help them to provide positive messages about everyday sport and fitness to girls — because they will be the mothers of the future single parent homes. Education of the physical education teachers is the key.

Question: Your participation rates are very high. How did you get the media to participate in promotion?

Kathrine: The media has been the key factor in women's participation in running. It has been so effective recently because women's sport coverage has not been done very thoroughly in the past. I try to get as much worldwide media exposure as possible for the top Avon runners so that other women can use them as role models. When sending a runner abroad we do hometown stories on her development as a runner. We tie this in with the development of the sport. For the major events, we invite the world media to attend. We offer them incredible amounts of background and statistics for their stories. Actually, we bombard them with information on a year round basis. We also set up a complex communication network of Telex & Telecopiers. We have twenty professionals working on the media outlet.

The women's international marathon in London England was the first time in history that downtown London was closed for a sport event. Elite and fitness competitors representing 27 countries in five continents ran together through downtown London. This commanded world-wide media attention. NBC and BBC joined to produce a telecast. We showed the world that it could be done.

Question: With media focus on the élite, aren't you concerned that the cultural message comes across once again about the importance of competitive success rather than mass participation?

Kathrine: No. The media thrust is to encourage women of all ages and abilities to participate. Our approach has been a broad based triangle with élite at the top. But now that the women's marathon has been accepted into the Olympic Games our emphasis now is to create systems of opportunity for health and fitness. With every event, in every center, we give a series of clinics in schools and work places. Kids and participants can come to these clinics and meet athletes, doctors, and physiologists, and talk about their sport at any level. This education is not just for the runner, but for the whole family.

PART II   THE MACRO SYSTEM

PROLOGUE: THE MURDER OF PLAYFULNESS

John T. Partington (Canada)

When I think back to my old football days, my clearest, happiest memories are about the playful times — smearing mud in my teammate's face during rainy practices, singing together in the showers, and carrying coach off the field after a well-played game. If you think seriously about where sport came from in your own lifetime experience, or in our history as a people, you will recognize that sport emerges from play. The experiential context of sporting activities is the playful attitude. When things go wrong in sport it is usually when the participants have lost their playful attitude toward the game.

To illustrate, consider the following historical analysis[1] of how the game of football in the United States became transformed, in less than a century, from an opportunity for play and exercise to something quite different.

The informal football games of the 1860's and early 1870's between groups from the same campus led, little by little, to challenges for games with other institutions. This led to travel expenses, more formalized rules, nonpartisan officials, and uniforms. The increase in interest led to larger groups of spectators. What could be more natural than to pass a hat among these spectators to raise monay for the players' expenses? Defeats led to desire for revenge, and thus to stricter rules of team membership, practice, and training. All of this led gradually to more formalized coaching. This task rested at first with the captain and more experienced players, but, as established intercollegiate rivalries began to grow, an experienced player of previous years, usually the last victorious captain, was asked to return from the outside world to coach intensively during the week before the "big game." As other colleges adopted this pattern and several "big games" a year emerged, the demands on graduates to return to the campus for coaching duty became more than could be fulfilled. The obvious solution, a full-time paid coach, made it essential to have an established team income. "Passing the hat" among the spectators was replaced by sales of tickets at a fixed price. But sold tickets entitled spectators to a seat, which led very quickly to the building of the first modern stadium (1903). In time stadiums were being built with borrowed funds, with the result that their mortgage charges, along with coaches' salaries and other expenses, made it essential that the stadium's seats, no matter how numerous, must be filled, or nearly filled, on the eight or so Saturdays a year it was used.

Gradually the interests of the spectators and the need for football income became dominant over the interests of any undergraduate who liked football or needed exercise. The team had to win, at least most of the time, and the game had to be spectacular to watch. Scouts looked for able players outside and, in one way or another, persuaded them to come to the scout's college to play football. Financial rewards proved, in may cases, to be powerful persuaders. Thus the game shifted from undergraduates who needed exercise to those who had already had too much exercise. At some institutions, where football incomes were earmarked for educational uses such as for building funds, almost all games were played in baseball parks of large cities remote from the campus, with the result that the team could rarely be seen by its own students. Teams that played on the East Coast, the West Coast, and the Gulf Coast on successive weekends spent much of the autumn traveling and might be away from their college halls for weeks.

When the depression cut attendance in the early 1930's, many games were scheduled in the evening to attract working spectators. For the same purpose the rules were manipulated to give more open play, high scores, and superiority to the offensive. By reducing the diameter of the ball, it was made easier to pass and harder to kick, in the belief that spectators preferred passing. Restrictions on passing requiring a minimum distance behind the scrimmage line for the passer or penalizing successive incompleted passes were removed. To keep the ball moving on offense, the referee was instructed to move the ball in fifteen yards from the side lines when it became dead closer than that distance from the sides. At no point in this process did many persons stop to ask themselves, "What is the purpose of football anyway?" But those who look at football's ninety years of development can see quite clearly how an organization which originally rose as an instrument for undergraduate exercise had become something quite different, to the jeopardy of undergraduate exercise. This process, which we call the institutionalization of instruments, is found in almost all social phenomena.

Following the above analysis, questions about improving the context of sport begin to translate into the more fundamental question, how do we prevent the "institutionalization" of play and sport?

In what follows, I will try to define play in terms of what it feels like; I will discuss what play can do for us as individuals, nations and as a species; I will show how we murder play; and finally I'll suggest a few ways for us to resurrect playfulness in our lives and thereby prevent the "institutionalization" of sport.

What Play Feels Like

Insight into feelings during play have been given by Csikszentmihalyi, whose work appears in another module in this book. In one study, he aimed to discover what teenagers do most, what they enjoy most, and how they actually feel when doing liked and disliked activities. To avoid entirely disrupting the teenagers lives a system was developed for notifying each subject with a soundless signal. This was sent at various times of the day and night using a transmitter which covered a 50 mile radius. Teenagers received signals seven times per day for seven days. Every time a signal was felt, the teenager recorded in his diary what he was doing, whether he wanted to be doing anything else, and how he was feeling at the moment. Results showed that teenagers experienced greatest enjoyment, and didn't want to be *anywhere* else, while playing games and sports, and while talking with other teens. In sports they reported feeling strong, active, free, excited, and sociable. When talking with friends they reported feeling happy and friendly. At the opposite extreme, the teens felt least enjoyment when watching T.V. and studying. Strangely, although T.V. watching was the second most frequently occurring activity in their lives, the teens described a "feelingless, mindless" state associated with it. Finally, studying school work, made them feel least free and excited. In sum, this study of adolescents suggests that when they are "doing their own thing", a condition which for me seems not unlike children's play, they feel strong, excited, free, friendly, and happy.

The same investigator's research on adult "flow" and "peak" experiences provides another perspective on what play feels like. I want to cite this work because many play scholars believe that children's play provides the training ground to get us in shape for emotional highs and peak experiences in adult life. Flow experiences have been reported by athletes, artists, surgeons, and people from all walks of life. The experience is usually

---

[1] Carroll Quigley, *The evolution of civilizations.* Indianapolis: Liberty Fund, 1961.

triggered in challenging situations wherein you find yourself operating at the outer bounds of your abilities. These situations provide clear goals, immediate feedback, and help us to focus our attention. In such a context, people report being fused or merged with the activity and surroundings — part, not apart from, the action; time seems to stand still; they feel a tremendous sense of power which makes evereything seem effortless; they feel as if they are outside of themselves, and yet feel more in touch with who they really are, or could be. Above all, in flow, people report feeling very happy.

These are life's really meaningful moments, when we are self actualizing, when we are truly in touch with our human nature. It excites me to know that serious scholars are beginning to believe that children's play may prepare us for these peak experiences, which add so much to life satisfaction. Incidentally, two senior citizens reported to my research assistant that they regularly experience flow. An 80 year old lady said that she flows when engaged in handicrafts like macramé, while an 81 year old gentleman confided that he flows when conversing with close friends and relatives who really understand him.

This lengthy section on what play feels like was intended to illustrate that we are talking about a mode of awareness, an experiential state, which is unlike any other human condition. When playing, that which we do and feel differs from the serious state of ordinary instrumental activity; differs from the frightened state of being threatened; differs from the apathetic state of being totally controlled; differs from the mindless state of habitual living; and differs from the altered states of consciousness induced by chemical agents, allergins, meditation, acute physical and mental effort, and high fever. When talking about the play state, we are talking about a very real potential in human nature. In fact, noted ethologists and anthropologists believe that playfulness may be *the* unique human trait.

What Play Can Do For Us

We turn now to a consideration of what play can do for us — for individuals young and old, for our interpersonal relationships, for our society, and perhaps for our future survival.

It seems just a little strange to be talking about the products of play, when we all know that play is a process, destroyed by serious concern for outcomes. However, rightly or wrongly, we are in an era which stresses accountability. Actually I am delighted to have the opportunity to shout the merits of play. We can only hope that some who read our message are in a position, and are willing, to change the priorities which daily rule out valuable play experiences from the lives of our developing children and youth.

First, in terms of individual development, research using standard measures of creativity and problem solving clearly indicates the cognitive benefits of play. There are several explanations for this. Some feel that the neurophysiological "idling" mechanism associated with play, which temporarily screens further outside information from the player, is thought to aid the child in the consolidation of newly acquired information. Others hold that play experiences provide the psychological security necessary for the kind of suspension of reality important for creative thought, and for subsequent reality testing of new ideas. Still others hold that, within play, children generate an arsenal of cognitive, affective, and behavioural subroutines. These behavioural potentials are thought to prepare us for adaptation to problem situations now, and even for those which have not yet been encountered or even anticipated.

Findings and explanations of this nature suggest that the school curriculum should provide regular and frequent time outs, in order that children might play with the information they have been given in their formal lessons. Such play will help each child consolidate and elaborate the information given by the teacher, in ways far beyond the expectations of those who develop the curriculum.

Play also aids social and moral development. Role playing not only builds self identity, but also strengthens empathy for others — helps us to see things from different perspectives. Inventing and playing games leads to a deeper appreciation of rules, and of the origins of control in our lives. Cooperative game playing also leads to greater readiness to share and help others, even outside play episodes. Finally, participants of team sports, drama groups, and glee clubs can, and often do, increase their capacity for coordinated social action.

Play is also necessary for the maintenance of our moment-to-moment psycho-economy. If we are bored, suffering from too little stimulation, we can generate new information for ourselves by entering the play state. Miraculously, we can re-frame and thereby transform meanings of the old stimuli around us, so that we are no longer bored. On the other hand, if we are overstressed by too much information, we can "tune out" by entering the play state, perhaps in the form of daydreaming, which allows us to control our own self-created world of information. For example, after a long grammar class, during which the child has been swamped by linguistic rules, he can engage in speech play, and make and break his *own* linguistic codes. I really believe that play helps at least some children to survive the awesome pressures and injustices which often occur in school.

My last, and most important point, concerning the role of play at the *individual* level, is that child's play supports and develops the playful attitude. This attitude is crucial for both artists and scientists; moreover, it is crucial for all of us to avoid "psycho-sclerosis" — hardening of beliefs and closing of the doors of perception, and the doors of opportunity for vital living. Even our sex life is implicated, since there is evidence that achievement of orgasm is related to capacity for fantasy.

Finally, I want to add some serious considerations, concerning the role of play in our cultural identity, and in our future survival. Play is significant for our cultural identity because the play that we ourselves engage in, and what we observe around us, tells us, and tells others, what is meaningful and important in life. Much of our play is bounded and influenced by the objects, settings, time schedules, and rules recommended by our society.

To illustrate, consider play objects like toys. If the business establishment in our society provides a steady diet of racing cars, trucks, tanks, and bulldozers recommended by cartoon illustrations, for boys and dads, then daily play with such toys teaches boys something about our society and something about themselves. Specifically, our toy curriculum tells boys that they are different from girls, who play with dolls, and that cars, tanks, and bulldozers are central ingredients in our lives, and perhaps even that driving fast, powerful and destructive vehicles is more important or manly than driving ordinary cars.

What about settings? If play is not allowed in the streets, or near apartment doorways in high rises, as is still the case in some parts of the "modern" industrialized world, then children in such areas are learning something different about play, and about themselves, than are children in "primitive" cultures, where their joyful shouts are welcomed throughout the entire village. In "advanced" cultures, which insist on separate play spaces such as recreation rooms below the underground parking lot, and large far-from-home playing fields, children are taught that play must somehow be apart from the more serious, and more acceptable side of living. In "primitive" villages, children do not have to develop a split human nature.

Similarly, our time scheduling for play also contributes to our cultural identity. If our school boards grant thirty minutes per day for free play at recess, in contrast to five hours for school work; if they allow one or two course options for expressive subjects like physical education, art, and music, in contrast to the more emphasized analytic subjects; if they steal large chunks of leisure time for homework assignments; if some recreation authorities designate 10% of rink or pool time for free activities, in contrast to 90% for serious training and competition; if our society prescribes and sanctions all these temporal policies, then we learn from our opportunities for play, that playfulness is not a valued trait in our culture.

What about rules? Examine the table games available in most toy stores. Their explicit rules are invariably competitive. Moreover, even though the explicit rules of hockey disallow purposeful tripping, our competitive culture has begun to sanction implicit rules which prescribe that, under certain conditions, tripping is a "good penalty". Thus, a "win-at-all-costs" Canadian cultural identity is inescapable when we consider, in this way, the fact that most of our "playing" of games and sports is framed by explicitly competitive rules, which are further supported by implicit rules which advocate that "anything goes" in the interest of winning.

The last play product I want to discuss is the role of play in protecting our future survival. Really what I mean here is that the free play of ideas, especially the ideas of children and youth, is the only guarantee for the survival of potential futures. Let me explain. If the 1984 "Big Brother" suddenly erased all fresh thinking about ourselves and the world, then what would happen next week, and next year, would be determined solely by growth curves of current forces, resources, descision styles, and governing policies. Without significant policy changes, based on creative inferences and projections about alternative futures, we would bleet blindly toward almost certain extinction; pollution, depletion of resources, and/or nuclear "solutions" would guarantee this. Our only hope lies in new conceptions of the future, generated by younger people. Most adults can't understand and adapt to what seems to be escalating and inevitable changes in our world. This is because our understanding is impaired by the ways we were taught to think about things.

Children, on the other hand, seem to have a natural capacity to think about everything in the world in the manner adopted by modern physics. For children there is no separate reality outside themselves, time and space are one. Most of us have had too much practice in logic and reductionistic thought to appreciate the potential in children's views of the world. But their topsy-turvy playful perspectives provide a daily buffet of infinitely varied possibilities for us to consider. It is along these lines that I mean that our future survival, or survival of futures, may depend on children's play. I believe that the likelihood of our future survival will vary directly with the freedom and encouragement we provide for children to play, to create, and to be themselves.

Recipe for the Murder of Play

To this point I have tried to establish that playfulness represents a unique side of our human nature, and that the activity and process of playing has extremely important individual and social consequences, now and for the future. At play, the individual is most fully alive; without play the species may not survive. For these reasons I choose the term "murder" to designate practices which fail to nurture play in our lives.

Our multiple roles give each one of us opportunities to murder, or to nurture play. First, as parents, if we fail to be playful with our infants, and to give them appropriate nutrition, security, freedom, and challenge, their playful attitude will be strangled. This means that we will have murdered the psychological prerequisite for play.

But even with this prerequisite, play of the developing child can be murdered by eliminating any one, or combination of, the following ingredients from the recipe for play. Basically, for someone with the playful attitude to enter the play state, and begin the process of playing, requires the subjective perception of freedom, which usually requires some measure of real freedom. The major aspect of freedom to which I refer is the freedom not to be overly concerned with reality, in the form of consequences, such as rewards and punishments for the end products of play — ideas, drawings, structures, game scores, and so on. Ingredients for such freedom include time for play, space for play, privacy for play, mobility for play, ability for play, together with a responsive environment which provides freedom of information — uncertainty, freedom for risk — challenge, and freedom of choice.

Most of you are painfully aware how the specific policies of parents, educators, recreators, sport administrators, coaches, personnel managers, media producers, and those in municipal, provincial, and federal government can and do murder play opportunities in our daily lives by reducing or eliminating the above ingredients. We are aware of this because each one of us contributes to this genocide of play. But we are all good people. Most people, in most circumstances, want to be good people. So how do we become murderers?

Most of us become murderers of play by unknowingly conforming to any social order, system of thought, culture, ideology, religion, paradigm, bureaucracy, organizational structure, curriculum, or set of rules which is not person-centered. So total is our immersion in systems which value achievement, in the narrow forms of production and profit, over life satisfaction, in the infinite forms of meaningful self expression and discovery, that we accept the yoke of curricula and time schedules as readily as we do the inevitable downward pull of gravity.

Imagine bounding gleefully like the astronaut temporarily freed from earht's gravity! Similarly, imagine living in a society whose policies were shaped more by life-centered than by econocentric criteria. In such a society, little Susan Cummings, the Canadian girl who wanted to be a hockey goalie, wouldn't have had to fight right through to the Supreme Court, finally to be denied the freedom to play hockey with other boys in the neighbourhood.

In a life-centered world, the United Nations *Declaration of the Rights of the Child* would not have been necessary. Think back to 1959 when we all celebrated the assertion, in Article #2 that, "the child shall enjoy special protection, and shall be given opportunities and facilities by law and by other means to enable him to develop physically, mentally, morally, spiritually, and socially in healthy and normal manners and in conditions of freedom and dignity . . .", and recall Article #7, third paragraph, "The child shall have full opportunity for play and recreation . . .".

The system of established power, which quasi-legally entrench against such freedoms, made it necessary, twenty years later in 1979, to declare the International Year of the Child (IYC) to push again for these rights. We now have a new set of recommendations concerning play and recreation from our own Canadian Commission for IYC. These were presented to the Standing Committee on Health Welfare and Social Affairs in the First Session of the Thirty-second Parliament. But I'm pretty pessimistic about these high-level, time and energy consuming deliberations.

Consider the widening gap between recommendation #7.1 in the IYC report, *For Canada's Children,* and the real estate realities we face in urban Canada. Article #7.1 states that, "Governments and local authorities give the same priority to the out-of-school life of children and adolescents as they do to the provision of formal education, or the building of roads and parking places". But a recent *Canada Mortgage and Housing* report on play space allocations in urban centers throughout the world revealed that Canada's guidelines are far behind many other European countries. Furthermore, we all know what generally happens in our own towns; even with these guidelines, developers can and do get away with murder — with the murder of our children's play spaces. Developers, in league with local politicians, cheat our children with cash rather than land settlements, and by "contributing", as play space amenity areas, balconies of high rises. The concrete, steel, and asphalt products of this daily cheating destroy play opportunities, not only for our own children, but even for their children and grandchildren. I could go on and on with examples.

The point which I have been leading up to is that advocates of play and fun-filled sportsmanship must become more than good-hearted guys and gals. Serious play advocates should begin to consider themselves as revolutionaries, as enemies of many parts of the Establishment. I say this because the realization of Canada's IYC recommendations for the child, and the realization of self-fulfilling life styles for all citizens, young and old, will require fundamental changes in our distribution of property and time, as well as fundamental changes in the locus of decision making, toward a more human, person-centered society. The rip-off has got to stop. We have to begin playing a different life game, with new rules, and differently defined goals.

The Resurrection of Playfulness

I'd like to close with some suggestions about how we can avoid the "institutionalization" of play and sport. Playfulness, fun, and satisfaction can be nurtured in our lives. Consider suggestions by the experts — children. Two years ago, in preparation for some workshops on "Children's Perspectives in Recreation Planning", I asked a large number of elementary school children to tell me how they would like to improve a number of aspects of their daily lives. I'll repeat some of their replies for you.

The children made the following interesting recommendations for sports, parks, school, their neighbourhood, home, parents, and other children: Sports — "Kick out people who cheat and fight"; Parks — "Get rid of the punks"; School — "Have more parties"; Neighbourhood — "Keep teenagers from goofing around little kids"; Home — "Have no arguing"; Parents — "Have them not get so mad at you"; and Children — "Have them be nice to each other".

It is clear to me that children are much more concerned about the quality of interpersonal relationships in their lives than they are with material possessions and the temporary status of being a winner. From the child's perspective, it may be safe to assert that they are less in need of lend-a-toy libraries than they are of depots for supplying happy playmates, friendly neighbours, and loving parents.

But none of us can revolutionize human nature overnight. However, there may be some significant adjustments to be made in our day-to-day lives which could support an evolution of playfulness and joy. A host of possible adjustments follow logically from an understanding of the necessary conditions for attaining the state of flow, which we mentioned before. We are most likely to experience flow when there is a fine balance between the opportunities and demands of an activity, on the one hand, and our readiness and abilities to meet those demands. Furthermore, it seems as if satisfaction is maximized when our minds and bodies are stretched beyond what is usually required by daily living.

For every play activity, whether informal game or organized sport, there are many combinations and permutations of conceivable adjustments in rules, equipment and playing areas for ensuring an appropriate balance between challenge and skill. Of course, our freedom to make such adjustments in sport situations is frequently limited by the rigid rule enforcement of league officials. In such cases we have to ask ourselves whether we value playful enjoyment over whatever it is that such officials think they are trying to accomplish.

The most serious limits on our ability to make these simple and obvious adjustments are psychological rather than procedural. Many of us, and many of our children and youth, are "play cripples". That is, we have lost, or perhaps never developed, the playful attitude. For the play cripple, game rules and definitions of winning are absolutes to be followed dogmatically. It's as if the rules are part of some kind of devine revelation or sermon from the mount. Just try to mess with game rules when you are around such play cripples. You will find yourself in serious trouble. The play cripple can't allow himself to make hockey more fun for children by changing the rules — no. That would be spoiling the game; thus, he simply buys them more milkshakes after the game, and perhaps drinks more beer himself.

In the short run, the best way to preserve and nurture the playful attitude, in my view, is to provide as much effective modelling of the attitude as possible. In this regard, I believe that television can become our greatest ally. Expectant mothers, when they become bulky, and mothers with little ones at home, often watch a lot of television. Also, we know that many children and youth spend more time with the television set than they do with parents, peers, and teachers. We also know, from the Canadian La Marsh report on Violence in the media that television provides a very influential curriculum.

Why not use television to model the playful attitude? With carefully selected child and adult models, and an entertaining format, we could reach and teach expectant mothers how to play with their infants; we could show mothers at home how to make inexpensive toys and materials like playdough for their pre-schoolers; we could illustrate how young children in free play change their game rules to have more fun; we could show classroom simulations of students and teachers playing together with ideas from the formal lesson; and we could show coaches in live discussions with their pee-wee players concerning such matters as players' personal goal setting, and how to attribute success and failure after a game. I'm very excited about what can be done to nurture playfulness in our lives both within and outside sport.

THE "HIDDEN CURRICULUM" IN PHYSICAL EDUCATION AND SPORTS

Leo Hendry (Scotland)

1. Introduction

This paper sets out to consider interpretations of the "hidden curriculum" as a conceptual framework for studying the social context of sport, and the ways in which resultant social processes have psychological influences on the individual — his or her attitudes, self-evaluations, interests, and involvement in physical activities. A number of social settings and groupings are particularly emphasized namely, the family; the role of the school; the media; community sport; and competitive sport. The paper concludes by looking critically at the possibilities for sport and sports participants which may be inherent in a re-orientation towards principles of humanistic psychology.

2. What is the "hidden curriculum"?

The "hidden curriculum" has been described as the unplanned and often unrecognised values taught and learned through the process of schooling (e.g. Apple, 1971; Ridwell, 1972; Dreeben, 1968; Henry, 1966; Jackson, 1968; Overly, 1970; Silberman, 1971; Snyder, 1971). Various writers (e.g. Dreeben, 1968; Hargreaves, 1967; Holt, 1964; Illich, 1970; Jackson, 1968) have offered somewhat different versions of the "hidden curriculum", but all of them have indicated that it interpenetrates with, and is communicated alongside, the official curriculum in teacher-pupil interactions, and can be as highly structured and organised, detailed and complex as the formal curriculum.

Henry (1966) has pointed out that communication systems, such as telephones and radios, generate "noise" along with the official, intended communication. In the classroom the teachers' communications to the pupils — usually communications about the official curriculum — also generate noise. This noise is the "hidden curriculum".

"If the spelling, arithmetic, or music lesson were only what it appeared to be, the education of the child would be simpler ... The striking thing about the child is that along with his arithmetic — his 'message about arithmetic' — he learns all the noise in the system also. It is this inability to avoid learning the noise with the subject matter that constitutes one of the greatest hazards for an organism so prone to polyphasic learning as man.

An objective observer cannot tell which is being learned in any lesson, the noise or the formal subject matter. But — and mark this well — it is not primarily the message (let us say the arithmetic or the spelling) that constitutes the most important subject matter to be learned, but the noise! The most significant cultural learnings — primarily the cultural drives — are communicated as noise."

Henry then documented this thesis with a series of brilliant and insightful analyses of events taken from his observations of apparently inconsequential classroom events, such as a game of spelling baseball. Within these events he detects various strands of the "hidden curriculum", particularly the important theme of competition and competitiveness. It becomes clear that to succeed, or even to survive in school, the pupil must learn this complex hidden curriculum.

"School metamorphoses the child, giving it the kind of Self the school can manage, and then proceeds to minister to the Self it has made ... School is indeed a training for later life not because it teaches the three Rs, but because it instils the essential cultural nightmare, fear of failure, envy of success and absurdity."

Thus it has been suggested that the "hidden curriculum" teaches the pupil norms and values necessary for transition to, and integration into, the adult world (e.g. Dreeben, 1968; Haller and Thorsen, 1970) and so an emphasis on socialization — order, control, compliance and conformity — has been persistently reported (e.g. Adams and Biddle, 1970; Jackson, 1968; Leacock, 1969; Rist, 1970). On the other hand, some writers have criticised these implicit qualities as stressing consensus and social orientation not in the best interests of the individual (e.g. Apple 1971; Friedenberg, 1963; Henry, 1963; Silberman, 1970). Further, the "hidden curriculum" has been described as a vehicle for possibly unjustified differential treatment of pupils often on the basis of race, academic ability, social class or sex (e.g. Apple, 1971; Frazier and Sadker, 1973; Hargreaves et al, 1975; Illich, 1970; Rist, 1970; Willis, 1977).

Eggleston (1977) argued that the "hidden curriculum" and the official school curriculum are, in fact, two perspectives of the total curriculum, in that the official curriculum is predominantly a teacher perspective and the "hidden curriculum" is predominantly a pupil perspective. This interpretation of curriculum-interactions between teachers and pupils, inferred from consistencies in class organisation, teacher behaviours and procedures, have been assumed to have a powerful impact on the values, norms and behaviour of pupils. While Eggleston's interpretation of the "hidden curriculum" might well be questioned, I want to utilise this model simply because it stresses the possibility of differing perceptions, expectations and values between teacher and learner. Thus this model of the "hidden curriculum" can be usefully extended beyond the academic curriculum and schooling to include physical education and sports, and utilised

in order to gain insight into a number of important psychological issues within physical education and sport.

3. Interpersonal relationships, sport and the "hidden curriculum"

In one sense at least, consideration of the "hidden curriculum" involves an examination of social relationships between the individual and various others in his social environment — parents, peers, teachers, sports coaches . . .

a) Parents

Firstly, it is necessary to ask what may be the role of parents as social facilitators and as behavioural models with regard to human movement and sports? The importance of the family in establishing children's general life-styles, and attitudes to the educational system is well established. Fraser's (1959) study identified the most important factor determining a child's progress at school as "parental encouragement". Douglas (1964), Wiseman (1964), Mays (1965), Douglas, Ross and Simpson (1968) also investigated the relationship between home and school and found similar results. Klein's (1965) analysis suggested that the causal relationships between socioeconomic variables and attainment might be due to sub-cultural differences in children's levels of aspiration and in their ability to postpone gratification. These dispositions, it was argued, may have their origin in the distinctive child-rearing and socialization practices in different social groups.

The family then is a potent force in motivation, academic success and attitudes to schooling, sex roles, *and* physical abilities development. Movement skills and attitudes acquired in the family may reinforce dispositions towards sports participation and evaluation of specific physical activities. This in turn, can lead to interest and performance in physical activities by the individual. Parental influences on movement behaviour may be related to the extent a child identifies with parents. Even in the early years of life, the evidence suggests the possibility of a "hidden curriculum" in terms of the social relationships which emerge through movement exchanges within the family.

To briefly outline the main thrusts of the argument, non-verbal interactions between mother and infant is an aspect of movement behaviour that has been well documented over the last two decades (e.g. Schaffer, 1975). Stern (1977), for instance, described these interpersonal exchanges as "dances" and "choreographies". Thus the "catching" of movements from parent to child has been demonstrated (e.g. Birdwhistell, 1962). Birdwhistell (1970) has further argued that movement behaviour is just as much:

"Learned behaviour as is language behaviour, we simply have not, heretofore, known enough about it to teach it."

The important point, however, is that within these communicative movement exchanges and interactions exists "noise" — a potent "hidden curriculum". For example, Campbell (1972) wrote:

> "The mothers of more active infants were more demonstrative towards their children and appeared to form a stronger and earlier attachment to the baby."

Further, Schaffer (1977) has commented on the negative effects in family relationships when the movement behaviour of either mother or child displays "rejecting characteristics"; and Bowlby (1965) and Furneaux (1973) have illustrated how the deprivation of a warm intimate communicative relationship between mother and child can result in:

> "an apathetic withdrawal from all emotional entanglements" (Bowlby, 1965)

There is unconscious rejection because the movement qualities in the social encounters produce insufficient interaction and emotional stimulation for either parent or child. In contrast, Stern (1977) stated:

> "The goal of face-to-face play interaction is to have fun, to interest and delight and be with one another."

To demonstrate the possibly divisive effects of different types of movement experiences, Lowen (1977) pointed out that a rejecting mother deprives her child of opportunities to experience the pleasure of its body through physical intimacy with her; while an over-possessive mother denies the child the right to experience its body as a separate entity — she seems to usurp the child for her own personal pleasure and satisfaction. The correct balance of intimacy and freedom seems vital. As a result of being involved in a reciprocal relationship the infant begins to realise that his non-verbal behaviour *communicates;* that he can influence the actions and reactions of others, that others respond to him, positively or negatively. The styles and patterns of expressive bodily movement characteristics between parent and child can create a "hidden curriculum" with either potentially reinforcing or divisive effects in subsequent social relationships. Fathers seem to figure significantly in achievement training, and parental encouragement and attitudes to success in physical tasks has been investigated, for example, by Rosen and D'Andrade (1959).

Without labouring the point further, it seems clear that the influence of the family can range from "hidden curriculum" of bodily exchanges in the process of socialisation to the more specific induction of children into particular sports activities by interested members of the family. On the latter topic, Orlick (1972) has indicated that any "average" child placed in a very positive family sports environment will almost surely be an early participant in sports regardless of other factors. In several cases brothers described as complete opposite in terms of personality, level of activity, size, ability, were either both participants or both non-participants in sports, depending upon their family sports environment. Once a child does become an early sports participant, whether or not he continues, becomes largely dependent upon the positive and negative reinforcements operating in the organized sport environment as well as in the home.

As reflected by Orlick's study the family appeared to be a significant factor influencing early participation in sport. Two major factors within the child's environment appeared to be directly related to his attraction to, or avoidance of, sports participation: (a) the significant sport role models which were available to the child (i.e. parents), and (b) the sport related reinforcement contingencies to which the child was exposed.

Previous sports related research which looked, albeit superficially, at the family influence upon participation has tended to support this perspective. Studies by Rarick and McKee (1949); Skubic, (1965); Behrman (1967) and Malumphy (1968) indicated that parents of participants were (or had been) active themselves and/or encouraged their children to participate.

Parents of children who elected to participate in sport were found to provide both a model of participation and positive reinforcement for sports behaviour (as evidenced by their own participation, their viewing habits, their expectations regarding their child's participation, and their encouragement for their child's participation).

Fear of failure, or the psychological stress of disapproval, appeared to influence certain children to the extent that they were afraid to participate (Orlick, 1972). 80 per cent of the mothers interviewed by him expressed a strong dislike for the winning emphasis, and the competitiveness in children's sports. They indicated that emphasis should be put on fun and enjoyment, along with giving each child an equal opportunity to play. As far as sport is concerned, this cultural transmission is supported in a British investigation by Cruden (1970). He contended that:

> "The value a child places on sport will in large measure be culturally induced."

In his study, Crunden found that the children under investigation did not avail themselves equally of the opportunities which existed for participation in sport, and these differences could be stratified in relation to sex and family background.

b) **School**

A "hidden curriculum" may then exist within families in terms of both movement experiences which encourage social acceptance and affection or rejection, and in terms of experiences related specifically to sports participation. Nevertheless, I want to emphasise the role of the school's "hidden curriculum".

In this process various elements of the school system can combine to differentiate pupils in terms of their attitudes toward teachers, their self images, and their scholastic success. Hargreaves (1972), for instance, has offered a theoretical framework for studying the social processes and school relationships linked to academic attainment. He suggested that the teacher's conception of a pupil's ability, the pupil's own conception of his ability, and whether or not the pupil values the teacher's approval, all have a part to play in bringing about an educational self-fulfilling prophecy. Empirical support for such social processes is available (e.g. Hallworth, 1966; Hargreaves, 1967; Keddie, 1971; Nash, 1973; Rich, 1975; Silberman, 1969). Hurn (1978) has also argued that the teacher's expectations, which are shaped by ascribed characteristics of pupils and by means of stereotyping, are translated into differential treatment of pupils, and these treatments in turn have powerful effects on subsequent student learning. In this connection it may be important to note that school sports participants tend to produce better academic results than non-participants, and have higher educational aspirations (e.g. Schaffer and Armer, 1966; Schaffer and Renberg, 1970; Spreitzer and Pugh, 1973). As Start (1966) has postulated, pupils who play for school sports teams also tend to accept the academic pupil role so that sport becomes another manifestation of school culture. Thus it can be hypothesised that a "hidden curriculum" of sport may exist in schools (cf Jackson, 1968).

Hargreaves (1972) has pointed out that in evaluating pupils in the classroom, the teacher gives approval to those pupils who conform to his expectations. Further, Nash (1973) has written:

"The most important point to understand about this evaluation is that it is not wholly (or even mainly) about academic matters . . . Teachers are concerned about their pupils' liveliness, sociability, and simply how likeable they are."

This may, to some extent, depend on the particular teacher's teaching style (e.g. Bennett, 1976). The labels which teachers may use in "getting to know" their pupils have been outlined by Hargreaves et al (1975): 1) Appearance; 2) Conformity (or its opposite) to discipline role aspects; 3) Conformity (or its opposite) to academic role aspects; 4) Like-ability; and 5) Peer group relations. Similarly, a number of researchers have demonstrated the effect of pupils' physical attractiveness on teachers' expectations and evaluations (e.g. Clifford and Walster, 1973; Dion, 1972; Dusek, 1975; Rich, 1975), even when teachers have been made aware of teaching bias (Foster et al, 1975). It can be argued that confirmity, attractiveness, skill, and even "hidden" sex roles, could be major factors in the teacher's expectancies of pupils' performance especially (but not only) in practical subjects like physical education. Physical education teachers may use certain perceptual impressions of pupils to construct an overall evaluation of their physical ability and personal qualities, which is conveyed to pupils, setting up matching self estimations in these pupils as part of the differential effect of a "hidden curriculum" within school sports. Some supporting evidence for these ideas about the "hidden curriculum" in sports emerged from a study carried out by the author (Hendry, 1978)[1] on over 3,000 fifteen to sixteen year old pupils attending 15 comprehensive schools in an area in Central Scotland, together with their physical education teachers (N = 75). Pupils were classified on the basis of their involvement in extracurricular (i.e. voluntary) school sports as: competitors, recreational participants, or non-participants.

Briefly, the findings showed that physical education teachers' perceptions of pupils revealed differential views of active and non-participant pupils, with teachers having more favourable attitudes towards sports participants. Of the three groups, competitors were seen by teachers to be most enthusiastic, friendly, popular, reliable, and of attractive appearance, as well as being highly skilled physically and highly muscular. (Additionally, women physical education teachers considered competitive schoolgirls to be the most socially poised group of girls and to be more likely than other groups to come from a "good" home background, although no differences were found among the three groups of boys in these characteristics.)

In their turn, pupils who were participants in extra-curricular school sports had more favourable opinions of physical education teachers than non-participants; yet the majority of pupils, regardless of participation category, perceived physical education teachers as even-tempered, friendly and approachable, able to get on well with pupils and to establish good relationships with pupils.

At the same time they were seen by most pupils as competitive individuals, giving differential treatment to pupils by paying more attention to the more highly skilled and by being less interested in pupils who were not especially enthusiastic about school sports.

There were interesting differences in the way teachers were perceived by the three groups of pupils. For instance only competitive boys, in any major way, regarded the physical education teacher as a "counsellor", while recreatives and non-participant girls seemed more acutely concerned with teachers' differential attention and time devoted to high skilled pupils than competitors. Additionally, teachers were perceived as more friendly and approachable, and better able to give pupils confidence firstly by competitors, then by recreatives, then by non-participants.

In the light of such varying perceptions it is perhaps not surprising that pupils' self-evaluations revealed a rather similar pattern, with active pupils having greater self-esteem than non-participants.

[1]Most research on the "hidden curriculum" has used intensive naturalistic observations in a small number of classrooms (e.g. Cowell, 1972; Jackson, 1968; Rist, 1970; Keddie, 1971). Because of this, and the lack of statistical analyses, findings are not easily generalised to other situations (cf Hargreaves, 1967). Additionally, cause and effect can be hard to disentangle, and delayed effects in pupils difficult to trace. One way of avoiding some of these limitations is to examine the cumulative differential effects of the "hidden curriculum" by investigating pupils towards the end of their compulsory schooling and to consider how these possible influences are manifested in the way in which teachers and pupils view each other. This was the approach taken by the author although it is acknowledged in turn that a general examination of differential perceptions obviates value inferences at the level of daily classroom (or sports field) interactions.

FIGURE 1:
MINIMUM VARIANCE CLUSTER ANALYSIS:
DIAGRAMMATIC REPRESENTATION OF ADOLESCENT PUPILS' INVOLVEMENT
IN PHYSICAL ACTIVITIES.

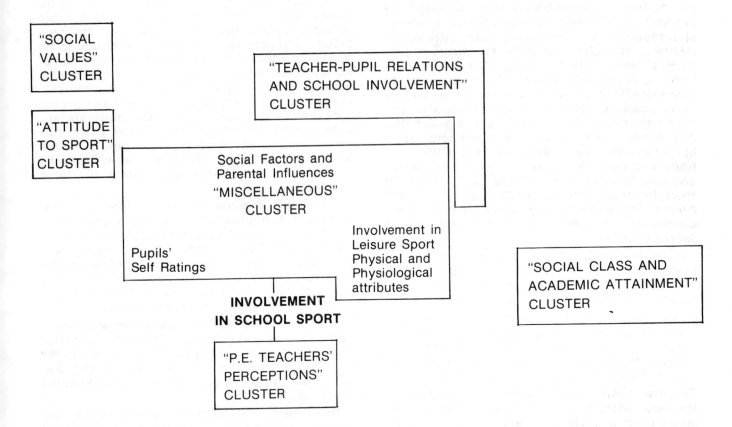

In physical ability, enthusiasm, desire to improve physical skills, and in perceptions of the attention given to them by the physical education teacher, a greater percentage of competitive pupils possessed highly positive views of their own personal qualities, talents and interests than in the other two groups. Nevertheless, it should be noted that around 70 per cent of non-participants, as well as a high percentage of participants, wished to improve their personal physical ability level and to develop their sports skills.

At a more impressionistic level, non-participant pupils reported feelings of neglect and isolation from physical education teachers within the learning procedures adopted in school sports programmes. When questioned, a large number of non-participant pupils indicated feelings of isolation and neglect within the compulsory time-tabled programme. By far the most frequent comments were directed toward physical education teachers' decisions about teaching procedures and choice of activities without any *real* pupil understanding of reasons behind these decisions. Whitfield (1971) has referred to this as "curricular trade secrets", where pupils are excluded from knowledge of what is happening to them in terms of changes in behaviour. When sports groups were formed teachers appeared to give much of their attention to skilful athletes, so that other pupils felt there was a lack of opportunity to be helped in making personal progress. In other words, many felt they were being ignored by teachers and received little coaching as a result. While physical education teachers might well justify their actions in terms of learning strategies, the important point is that from the pupils' perspective, their main concern may be about the social context of learning.

On the face of it, there would seem to be less need within education for a teaching bias or for pupils to seek the teacher's approval in the classroom (cf Silberman, 1969). Physical education teachers are associated with a fairly popular and wide ranging subject — or so it would appear from a report into attitudes and preferences of fifteen year old pupils (e.g. Morton-Williams and Finch, 1968). Sixty-four per cent of boys, and fifty-six per cent of girls thought physical education interesting, which placed it well ahead of Art, Crafts and Music in terms of popularity with pupils. Taking a different view, however, Hendry (1978) has suggested that there may be a much greater affinity between the physical education teacher and muscular, physically skilled, competitive children who reveal similarities to the teacher in both physique and behaviour; and by implication, there may be a neglect of children who do *not* conform to this "desired" social image: a "hidden curriculum" of sport.

As further support for a "hidden curriculum" a cluster analysis was carried out (see Figure 1). A fairly coherent pattern was apparent for both boys and girls:

A clustering of physical education teachers' perceptions, pupils' own estimations in relation to their sporting prowess, together with a number of physical and physiological components can be seen to be most closely associated with school sports participation.

(Within a second circle of constelled variables were items linking "home factors" such as parental encouragement, watching sport on television; "social aspects" like leisure sports involvement, "relational considerations" and "personal factors" like extraversion, attitudes to sport, body esteem, and so on).

In rather the same way as classroom teachers, certain personal characteristics may be used by physical education teachers as the basis for differential treatment of pupils. The differential perceptions of teachers, and the reported differential treatment of pupils can create a "hidden curriculum" of school sports potentially every bit as divisive as one operating within classroom subjects (e.g. Hargreaves, 1967; Willis, 1977).

What is being argued here is that the interactions between the teacher and pupils, either in the classroom or on the games field, may be crucial in conveying "messages" of praise or disapproval, and attention or neglect, which subsequently influence different pupils' attitudes, interests and performance in school activites; and if such self-fulfilling prophecies do arise in educational contexts, then perhaps greater research attention should be given to the mechanics and processes and effects involved in the encounters of teachers and their pupils.

Of course it might be argued that other factors may influence the pupils' involvement or non-involvement in extracurricular sports: out-of-school interests; perceived lack of ability; parental discouragement; part-time jobs and so on. But Hendry (1978) has reported that active sports participants are as frequently engaged in part-time employment as non-participants which suggests that interested pupils are able to arrange employment to fit in with their sports commitments. Further, Hargreaves (1967) and Sugerman (1968) have claimed that it is pupils who are disillusioned with, and alienated from, school that turn to pop oriented leisure interests. Such a division of interests might be seen as additional evidence for a "hidden curriculum" within school sports (e.g. Hendry and Thrope, 1977).

c) Community Sport, the Media and Peers

The patterns established in relation to school sport and its divisive "hidden curriculum" may well repeat themselves in leisure sports within the community. In connection with school, such differentiation was summed up by Reid's (1972) provocative question about the social integration of extracurricular activities when she asked:

"Why don't a higher percentage of (academically) able pupils belong to activities other than the 'prestige' activities? (i.e. sports teams, school choir)."

This suggests a hierarchy of extracurricular leisure activities in terms of "worthwhile" values and pursuits (e.g. Scarlett, 1975), while Murdock and Phelps (1973) have argued that for many pupils school is a "contradictory" setting which can only be redeemed in leisure pursuits of various kinds supported within certain sub-cultural groupings away from school. Linked to this Sugarman (1967) has claimed that it is adolescents who are alienated from school who turn to pop culture for alternative roles to copy and follow. Longland (1969) pointed out that the many hours spent on arts and crafts, and on physical and cultural developments, are not reflected in the activities of young people after school. If this is so then school based leisure education as presently constituted may have little interest or relevance for many pupils in later life.

"The influence of thousands of hours in schools given to arts and crafts and to physical education and cultural development is only partially discernible in post-school leisure interests."

(Simpson, 1973)

In this connection Leigh (1971) has argued that school based activities and sports interests bear little resemblance to the out-of-school leisure pursuits of teenagers. He suggested that the failure in school based pursuits lay in the teaching emphasis and organisational patterns; in other words, its "hidden curriculum".

From the above discussion it is clear that school influences provide important constraints and opportunities for young people's leisure. The educational system provides a potentially valuable structure within which interests may be aroused and cultivated; but mainly for middle class pupils happily involved in school sports and activities. On the other hand, there is a possible stifling of interest development that frequently attends a large number of working class adolescents who are destined to leave school as soon as possible (e.g. Morton-Williams and Finch, 1968; Bone, 1972).

The reasons for the decline in participation in community sports for many adolescents are important to seek and understand. It is clear, for instance, that the solution to *non-participation* in adolescence does not lie simply in giving more time or attention to the physical education in schools or by providing better recreational facilities. There are complex attitudinal and sub-cultural factors to be taken into account, as is clear if we consider why girls in particular tend to lose interest in sport when they reach adolescence (Spry, 1977; Moir, 1977). This may be due (in part) to a continuance of values conveyed by a "hidden curriculum".

Emmett (1977) has reported in a "follow up" study of 2,000 19 year olds that factors of gender, social class, occupation, academic attainment, and peer group allegiances continued to exert an influence on recreational involvement. Further, Emmett concluded that some of the reasons to which post-school sports decline can be attributed are:

1. some participation in school sport is compulsory and competitive, and this affects attitudes to out of school activities;
2. post-school years are courting years;
3. young people at work have more money and greater freedom from parental control in choosing leisure pursuits; and
4. at eighteen years of age they are *legally* entitled to drink in public houses.

It is possible to suggest, therefore, that the differential effects of schooling on particular interests create attitudes and perceptions about leisure sports pursuits which persist into later adolescence. These attitudes may be directed more towards organisation and structure than to the leisure activities themselves. A "hidden curriculum" of leisure sports. A reputation for success in school sports may provide greater incentives for continued involvement in post-school life. A series of post-school studies have shown that despite an association between school sport and leisure sport and between past and current involvement in sport, there was a pronounced tendency to reduce the extent of participation or stop participation in sport as pupils reached leaving age, but this tendency was less marked among the group who were competitors in school (e.g. Hendry and Douglass, 1975; Hendry, 1976).

Additionally, a number of reports have underlined the importance of links between schools and local sports clubs (Sports Council of Wales, 1980); Dunfermline College Report, 1979) though Hendry (1978) has indicated that school competitors were best informed about, and most involved in, community leisure activities.

The Social and Community Research Project (1977) concluded that there was little evidence of new links between school and community in the provision of joint centres, even in relation to sporting activities. This is consistent with their finding that the use of sports centres is very selective. Although the bulk of users are young people it would be impossible to conclude from this that the leisure needs of adolescents are adequately met by community facilities. Nisbet, Hendry, Stewart and Watt (1980) have reported similar findings in one Scottish region.

Because of the costs of commercial leisure, adolescents often make use of facilities provided by community (i.e. youth) services in their various forms. Youth service provision has been criticised on the grounds that it has been "more concerned with amenity than community" (Smith, 1973). On the other hand, Davies (1970) has argued that the desire to do something, or participate in an activity, usually emerges out of a reasonably happy social situation, and that the provision made for young people will be most suitable and attractive where it has the reputation of being a happy place. It can be said that between the ages of 14 and 20 years a very high proportion of young people are attached to youth

service provision for at least some period of time. Equally it is fair to state that many being "disenchanted" are only briefly attached to youth clubs. Why should this be so?

In studying youth and community centres, one of the models which Eggleston (1976) found to be of major relevance was what he called the "socialization model" in which the young are seen to be socialized or made ready for adult society-learning and accepting approved patterns of social behaviour, social structure, skills, knowledge and values. There are other models, but Eggleston noted "the original and still dominant concern with socialization". Clearly, not all young people will be attracted by such traditional conformist institutions, and the activities offered will not fit in with their general leisure styles. The nature and organisational structure of youth provision are at least partly responsible for the disengagement of many adolescents.

Yet even amongst those who attend local authority provision there are differences in motivation and satisfaction derived. It is interesting to ask, therefore, if like-minded adolescents group together around similar activities within community centres, and to consider how they perceive their own group, other users of the centre, the leaders, the facilities themselves, and so on.

A study by Hendry and Simpson (1977) and a replication study by Hendry, Brown and Hutcheon (1981) — on regular users of an urban sports and community centres revealed a differing pattern in terms of leisure pursuits and life-styles. It was clear from these studies that two distinct and separate teenage groups existed with little or no contact between them: one group following sports activites, the other using the facilities as a social amenity, sitting around the community area, chatting, drinking coffee, listening to pop music.

This brings us to the important question: why do the majority of young people in the neighbourhood of the centre choose *not* to attend the sports area? Many of the community area members complained that there were too many rules surrounding the sports area, that sports area leaders were unable to mix well with young people and were unsympathetic. They agreed with the necessity of rules and were not advocating a sports area without rules. Instead, rather than subject themselves to the strict discipline and rules, they preferred not to attend, thus opting out of the organised atmosphere of sports for the relaxed, informal, less restrictive atmosphere of the community area.

An interesting observation noted by the researchers was that younger users of the sports area were less likely to be reprimanded than older members. It would appear that not only do young people come to an age when they more critically perceive rules and regulations, but that these written and unwritten rules are likely to be enforced more strictly by leaders as adolescents progress through the teenage years. It became clear during conversations with community users that their dislike of or disinterest in the sports area was often due to confrontations with sports leaders over enforcement of these unwritten rules.

One further observable feature of the sports area was that groups were already formed creating possible difficulties for such adolescents in "infiltrating" these activities. In other pursuits "star" performers were seen as individual attractions with their own band of "groupies". For serious sports participants one obvious sign of difference was their "uniforms" of tracksuits, specialised clothing and equipment which may create a symbolic barrier between them and other adolescents who might want to follow sports simply for recreation and enjoyment with no great interest in the pursuit of excellence.

Together with an antipathy to organised sports and its trappings, there was also a pull towards the social amenities provided by the community area at a time when many adolescents are exploring the possibilities of relationships with the opposite sex (cf Coleman, 1979). Several young people interviewed admitted that the main reason for attending the centre were: that "it was better than sitting at home", but especially that it provided an opportunity to meet other teenagers of the opposite sex.

The two groups however differed in their views of the centre, and perceived themselves as clearly different from those in the other group. Feelings of group solidarity were quite clear. They were loyal to their own area and its leaders, and revealed a need to belong, to identify and to support their own particular group, seeing it as a mirror image and reinforcement of their own qualities and characteristics.

Further differences in academic attainment, career aspirations, involvement in school based leisure and school sports teams, between sports area and community area users were found.

Nevertheless it was not possible to describe community users as completely non-sport-loving, nor to argue that sports members had no need for more socially oriented activities. Several community area boys played for local soccer teams (but not school teams) and girls went to places such as swimming pools, ice rinks and bowling alleys though not necessarily for serious or competitive involvement. Similarly, sports members indicated that going to cinemas, discos, youth clubs and pubs was common outside their sports involvement in the centre.

With regard to an investigation of a rural centre by Hendry, Brown and Hutcheon (1981) it was found that teenage boys in general attended the centre for the activities offered, whereas girls claimed to attend to meet established friends or to make new ones. The club seemed to have a bias towards activities such as team sports, "pool", darts or table tennis while girls felt that more could be provided for them (a finding which parallels that reported by Hendry and Simpson, 1977). In this there may be some conscious or unconscious subscribing to expected sex roles. The idea that males should be aggressive, dominant and sports-loving is a potent one (e.g. Emmett, 1971; Sharpe, 1977) while Sharpe (1977) argued that girls quickly "tune-in" to things that bring social approval, picking up cues, and responding to pressures from inside and outside school to look "sexy", decorative and alluring. Linked to this, a considerable percentage of "non-attenders" at the senior youth club stated that they preferred commercial provision to the centre — a finding which agrees with Bone's (1972) assertion that girls are the most enthusiastic supporters of commercial leisure provision. Eggleston (1976) also believed that commercial facilities satisfied the older teenagers need to be independent.

It may be that the break with the formal leisure club situation at senior level signifies a greater independence on the part of the adolescent (rather in the same way as certain urban teenagers reached the stage where the rules of the sports area became intolerable to them). Alternatively it could be argued that their allegiance had changed from the establishment to the values and norms dictated by peers. Whatever reason is more acceptable, these findings are closely aligned to Coleman's (1979) ideas that the adolescent's focus of interest changes across the teenage years.

As the adolescent grows older he becomes more critical, questioning and sceptical of adult-oriented organisations, and he wishes to use his peers to reinforce his emergent self-image. The need to feel independent may be a vital reason why the older adolescent moves towards commercial leisure provision. Thus Eggleston (1976) believed that many problems in youth clubs might be solved by allowing a greater measure of "shared responsibility" between leaders and members. Adolescents, because of their different experiences and life-styles have varying perceptions of leisure activities, whether or not certain pursuits are worthwhile, and whether the organisation is truly democratic or authoritarian.

Those who provide structured leisure activities and who organise them may perceive these organisations differently from the clients. Adolescents may perceive these organisations as being more structured and authoritarian then do the organisers:

> "Like the school itself, like the education system as a whole, like the Duke of Edinburgh Award Scheme, like the Scouts, like the Youth Service and like school based leisure, Youth Clubs describe themselves as non-authoritarian."
>
> (Corrigan, 1979)

Further, the very attraction of leisure pursuits seems to be grounded in the peer group. In Hendry's studies (1976, 1978) boys often indicated an interest in mildly aggressive rough and tumble games; or just "hanging about" with a group of friends in their leisure time. Obviously these activities can be less culturally approved for girls, and other pursuits such as dancing, dating, meeting friends for coffee, listening to records, seemed to satisfy their need for social contact. Pop music and discotheques, as Murdock and Phelps (1973) have outlined, are in many ways central elements in adolescent leisure — particularly for girls — from which many subsidiary activities flow. In Hendry's (1978) study most replies given by adolescents showed that the nature of their leisure pursuits included activities which were designed to cater almost exclusively to adolescents, which were undertaken within peer groups; dancing, youth clubs, drinking, dating, going out "on the town", and "hanging around" with friends. Such findings closely match recent major surveys: visiting friends, pop music, pub going, cinema attendance, discotheques and dancing appeared to be popular leisure activities for Scottish teenagers, whereas playing sports or going to youth clubs were not so interesting to them (Scarlett, 1975). Dancing, visiting, drinking in public houses, at home, or at a friend's home, together with some small interest in swimming, sports and games were the pursuits of English adolescents (Fogelman, 1976).

At this stage it is possible to suggest the influence of the "hidden curriculum" of community sport in its values, rules, regulations, dress, adult dominance in structure and organisation . It is attractive to certain adolescents, and like school sports, enables them to absorb values of adult society and to interact socially with caring adults. The same system, however, creates antipathy to *organised* sports in many others — though a desire to participate and enjoy physical activities may remain.

How does this "hidden curriculum" operate with regard to teenage girls?

There is an ever increasing interest in women in relation to sport and leisure, especially since the rise of the feminist movement and the concern with equal opportunities for women (e.g. Talbot, 1979). Yet the decline in sports participation by adolescent girls seems a general and continuing one (e.g. Emmett, 1971; Spry, 1977; Moir, 1977; Hendry, 1978). Moir (1977) made a telling point concerning sport and physical activities in the early stages of secondary education when she wrote:

"Quite a number of girls . . . seem to resent being forced to take part and some feel they should have more choice of physical activities at school."

In considering the wider social context, sport appears to be a fairly popular activity for young people, only surpassed by television and social activities (e.g. Bone, 1972; Fogelman, 1976; McCann-Erickson, 1977). Yet when examining comparisons between boys and girls' interest and participation in leisure sports marked differences have been noted (e.g. Morton-Williams and Finch, 1968; Emmett, 1971; Bone, 1972; Spry, 1977; Hendry, 1978). For instance, both Morton-Williams and Finch (1968) and Spry (1977) demonstrated that girls listed television, dancing, cinema, visiting friends, domestic pursuits, reading, courting and playing records before sport. It would appear that adolescent girls give up sports in high numbers after leaving school — or in the last few years of secondary school — irrespective of whether or not the sport or activity is associated with school (cf Spry, 1977). Emmett (1977) claims that three years after leaving school roughly twice as many boys as

girls belonged to sports clubs; girls tended to enter casually into physical activities which could be undertaken with friends of the opposite sex without necessarily joining sports or activity clubs.

In a study by Hendry and Singer (1981) a fairly high proportion of girls said they would continue with school based sports in their future leisure. On the other hand, certain school sports such as hockey and cross-country running emerged as being particularly unpopular with the majority, while more less competitive individual activities enjoyed high popularity. These pupils greatly appreciated the organizational nature of sports activities afternoons where there was a wide range of available choices, and a stress laid on enjoyment rather than on skills development. An emphasis on individual activities, with wide choice and a loose organisational structure where pupils enjoy themselves seems important to mid-adolescent girls. The popularity of sports in activity afternoons demonstrated that such arrangements may well help to maintain the adolescent girls' interest in sport. This would seem to suggest that in response to a variety of social pressures many adolescent girls relegate "serious" sports to a lower level of priority in favour of social activities:

"The general feeling . . . is not that girls on the whole are not interested in physical activities but that they have conflicting interests which make it difficult for them to participate in physical activities with ease."

(Moir, 1977)

In their leisure, schoolgirls interviewed by Hendry and Singer (1981) stated that they were able to find time for a variety of pursuits — watching television, listening to records, meeting friends — yet the reason most often cited for non-participation in school-based and leisure time sport was "lack of time". Money, independence, and having friends were found to be important to these schoolgirls, especially after fourteen years of age. This concurs with Coleman's (1979) theory, that adolescents have "peaks" of interests occurring at different stages of the teenage years. After this, although perhaps thought by many adolescent girls to be a fairly interesting pursuit, sport is never the focal point of their leisure lives as it can be for some boys. Adolescent girls seem much more concerned with what Moir (1977) called "conflicting" interests and these are mainly social activities involving friends and having an enjoyable time. Even when they attended the local sports centre it was mainly to use the social amenities as a meeting place. The Social and Community Planning Research Project (1977) showed that there was considerable difference between adolescent boys and girls in the interest they showed in playing sport *outside* school. Almost half the girls did not take part in sports in *leisure time* compared to under a quarter of boys. (Hendry's [1975] corresponding percentages for leisure sports involvement were: girls — 53% did not take part in leisure sports; boys — 32% did not take part.)

Physical activity is linked to notions of manliness.

Mating and considerations of physical attractiveness seem important to the adolescent girls' role, thus courtship is a dominant leisure activity for many young people (Barker, 1972). Adolescent heterosexual encounters begin with social events like dancing, going to a pub, cinema-going (Schofield, 1973) rather than competitive sports events. Changes in women's role in society may over time create changes in attitudes, and these in turn may well be reflected in future patterns of leisure activities. Already there are many inroads into previously exclusively "male" sports territories. It can be suggested on the basis of Hendry's (1978), Emmett's (1977) and Social and Community Planning Research Project (1977) findings that while many young people engage in physical activities *in their leisure time* — facilities and organisations are more likely to attract adolescents exhibiting certain characteristics (e.g. middle class, academically able, securely employed etc.), and equally, leave a relatively large number of teenagers untouched and uninfluenced. The attitudes, value systems and lifestyles of these latter teenagers are embedded in a social structure which may create difficulties in responding to sports provision and sports "hidden curriculum", even if they have an interest in sports activities per se. There is little doubt that discotheques and some other forms of commercial leisure provision are popular with some sections of young people, possibly due to the independent adult status such places usually confer on them.

A different variety of "hidden curriculum" may exist when we come to consider the interactions of individuals with the mass media. The importance of watching television as a highly popular home-based leisure activity is well established (Bailyn, 1959; Himmelweit, 1958, 1962; Sillitoe, 1969; Murdock and Phelps, 1973; Scarlett, 1975; Fogelman, 1976; Youth Survey, 1977).

A number of studies have implied that boys and girls differ in their use of television in accordance with stereotypic sex roles (Murdock and Phelps, 1973; B.B.C., 1974; Hendry and Patrick, 1977), and this may be seen as a continuance of the theme that cultural influences and values affect adolescents' interests and behaviour (e.g. Sharpe, 1977).

These differences further determine the amount of sport watched on T.V., and favourite televised sports — soccer and car or motor-cycle racing for boys, swimming and tennis for girls (Kenyon, 1968). Apparently, at present, notions of femininity do not include sportiness, whereas notions of masculinity do.

"The picture of girls' lives which emerged . . . shows them spending more time with their families and more time at home than boys, but when not with their family, more likely than boys to be courting."
(Emmett, 1977)

Yet few researchers have attempted to relate televiewing patterns to other aspects of leisure behaviour. In a study by Hendry and Patrick (1977), high and low frequency adolescent viewers were found to have different attitudes and values to life. For example, as might be expected both logically and empirically, high frequency viewing was associated with a low level of sporting activity (e.g. Coleman, 1961; Sillitoe, 1969; Emmett, 1971) and such adolescents were less committed to school values but considered pop culture as more important (e.g. Murdock and Phelps, 1973).

Maccoby (1954), Bantock (1968) and Murray (1973) have all noted that the media provide "a variety of possible images for conduct" and that they foster "the ability to project oneself into a number of life-styles". Despite such ideas, and despite Bantock's (1968) proposals that a critical understanding of the mass media should be included in the curriculum of young people, there have been very few studies centred on the ways schools utilise the media, or the effects the media may have on adolescents' social and leisure behaviour. Nevertheless Murdock and Phelps (1973) have argued that middle class pupils would be more inclined to have mass media included within the school curriculum in order to experience varying life-styles and leisure patterns vicariously; whereas working class pupils would maintain a work-leisure division because they experience particular leisure styles and use argot at first-hand (e.g. Mungham and Pearson, 1976). Hendry and Thornton (1976) have argued that television programme preferences may be related to particular life-styles. The mass media may also have an influence on the way adolescents match their own self-esteem against social norms (Hendry and Gillies, 1978), and may even affect or induce aggressive behaviour (e.g. Belson, 1978).

In a comparison of the relative influence of prosocial behaviour versus violence in television viewing by Sprafkin and Rubinstein (1979), correlations obtained between viewing habits of children and prosocial behaviour were lower than those obtained between viewing habits and aggressive behaviour. Possible reasons for such findings were, firstly, that television prosocial content basically reiterates what children already know, and prosocial behaviour is often subtly and verbally mediated, whereas aggressive behaviours are blatant and physical. Children learn from simple, direct, active presentations and they may therefore be more likely to learn from violent rather than prosocial portrayals on television. Additionally, content analysis has shown that televised prosocial behaviours are predominantly performed by female and non-white characters and that aggressive behaviours are most often performed by white males who are also the most successful and powerful character types in television dramas (e.g. Donagher et al, 1975; Gerbner et al, 1979). Without further research it is only possible to speculate on the possible implications for televised sport, and the "messages" of aggression or prosocial behaviour which it may convey to a wide audience of young people via the "hidden curriculum".

d) Competitive Sport

These differential emphases of a "hidden

curriculum" of community sport may be paralleled in competitive sports. Cratty (1970) has written:

"... That critical personality qualities including authoritarianism, success and dependency in both coach and participant will influence the manner in which each will accept the decisions of the other."

On the British scene, Hendry (1968) found coaches to be bright, driving, aggressive individuals who were also anxious and insecure. In America, Ogilvie and Tutko (1966) have shown that:

"Top American coaches from a variety of sports were sociable, highly organised, dominant, conscientious, emotionally stable and mature, open and trusting, could freely express aggression, had low interest in the dependency needs of others, and were intelligent but inflexible."

Ogilvie and Tutko went on to argue that these driving, aggressive individuals in seeking success and achievement, "weeded out" poorer athletes ruthlessly and swiftly. Such attributes have led Scott (1970) to suggest that the coach is one of the most authoritarian individuals in American society. "He is an authoritarian among authoritarians!" Other writers have stated that authoritarian coaches destroy the athlete's natural joy of sport (e.g. Cerruty, 1970), and that coaches intimidate athletes with feelings of inadequacy and guilt (e.g. Murdock, 1970) rather than supporting, encouraging and counselling them. Scott (1970) stated:

"... this is little hope for the development of sport programmes where the emphasis will be on athletics for athletes until there is also a concomitant emphasis on education for students within the total education structure."

This quotation presents the view that a "hidden curriculum" of sport and academia exists within the total educational system, emphasizing similar values and qualities, and creating a situation of mutual reinforcement. There is also evidence to suggest that dependent athletes are "created" for the coach's ego satisfaction (e.g. Rushall, 1967; Tattersfield, 1971). Hendry (1968; 1972) has also claimed that top class teenage athletes are centred within a rather limited and restricted sub-culture where there is continual reinforcement of a "hidden curriculum" of commitment, achievement, aggression, authority, conformity and traditional rules.

But, having said this, when stereotypic personality profiles for coaches are presented for examination we must consider how many coaches do not match the stereotype and consider the fact that some coaches may be completely different in character from others.

As Hendry (1972) wrote:

"Stereotypes are a simplification, categorised in terms of the predominant attributes common to a particular group, with less emphasis on individual differences between them. This process produces a tendency to minimize differences between members of a category, but maximizes differences between different categories."

This claim was substantiated by a study which compared top level coaches and physical education teachers (Hendry, 1974). There was close similarity between the two groups in only two factors — namely, dominance and authoritarianism — and a wide range of differences in other personality dimensions. Further, coaches from more individualized sports revealed a greater psychological difference in personality terms from a core of team and combat sports coaches, who shared high similarities of temperament and characteristics. Irrespective of the possible variety of personality types among coaches, however, coaches who do stress commitment, aggression and achievement via a "hidden curriculum" have been criticised for the influence they may have upon athletes:

"... Society has got the whole approach to sport wrong. We breed competitive types in a society which has a need for cooperative types."

(Butt, 1972)

Sport is not a universal panacea. It may have serious detrimental effects on the individual as well as beneficial ones. The former are equally important considerations which should weight heavily with coaches at certain levels of their role performance and should be as important as a consideration of the beneficial effects of participation, or the production of highly competitive individuals or groups who come nearer to the requirement of winning at all costs.

4. **Another "Hidden Curriculum" — The Athlete's Perspective?**

Recently there have been some signs of changing values and a re-orientation of the conditions of learning in sports which takes more account of the athlete's perspective. These are the learning strategies offered, for instance, by "inner game" techniques (e.g. Gallwey, 1977; Dunlop, 1979). There are connections here with Mead's (1934) ideas of "I" and "me", of a reflexive, evaluative "self" and an action "self". With "inner game" strategies the attempt is to effect performance, enjoyment and the process of self-learning for the athlete simultaneously. The techniques involved include: focussed but relaxed concentration; experiencing awareness and "feeling", rather than absorbing technical information and coach's evaluation; receiving positive feedback for problem solving and being given "playful" key points with no overload of information. Some examples may serve to provide a flavour of how the learning process is "given over" to the athlete: one Gallwey standby in tennis is to ask a student, "Tell me, on a scale of one to five, exactly how much tightness you feel in your elbow as you make contact with the ball." Often, the student will be able to correct errors simply by being aware of the situation. Another is "bounce-hit", in which he has beginners say "bounce" every time a ball bounces, and "hit" whenever it hits their own or their opponent's racket. Yet another idea is to get the learner to experience the boundaries of play by encouraging him to deliberately "hit the ball out of court". A further example of these strategies (from Gold) is the name of "film star".

"Imagine you're an actor in a movie and you're playing the role of a famous golfer. In this scene, you will be hitting balls, but the camera will be shooting closeups — only your head and shoulders will appear in the footage. The director will be looking for the same facial expressions of supreme confidence and lack of self-doubt shown by the pro. It's also important to realize that results don't matter — whether the balls are hit straight or not is of no consequence — the ball flight pictures will be shot separately. Now, step into the shoes of your chosen star. You are he for the period of the drill."

(Gallwey, 1977)

Clearly, in these situations where fun and self-learning is highly valued, the role of the coach changes. The coach becomes a mentor and guide, switching emphasis to the athlete, hinting and questioning, being non-critical and, in the best sense, non-involved. There is a stress on individual techniques, where experiences, not outcomes are important and where there are no rights and wrongs or technical advice given. The coach becomes a creative instructor, the athlete responds by being trusting and giving relaxed concentration to the sporting task.

Without exploring the "inner game" (or this particular "hidden curriculum" further) I want to stress two points:

1. The potential for experience, pleasure and self-discovery for the athlete;
2. The creative, humane functions available to the coach.

In this approach there is a switch in ideology towards principles of humanistic psychology (e.g. Rogers, 1967; Maslow, 1970). Humanistic teaching has been described as the self-actualization of the individual. Much of that which has developed in educational practice based on this philosophy has hinged on Maslow's concept of self-actualization. Ideas such as "self-identity", "self-acceptance", "self-hood", "unique potential", "students' concerns", and those characterizing affective learning (interests, appreciations, emotions, motives) are emphasized in this approach. Although the variety of goals of humanistic education are not easily unravelled, Alschuler (1975) suggested that most courses in humanistic education have the common goals of development of a person's imagination by using one's fantasy, development of better communication skills by using nonverbal exercises, exploration of the individual's emotional responses to the world, and emphasis of the importance of living fully and intensely here and now. Some of the many techniques and strategies developed under the sobriquet of humanistic education include free-learning or open classrooms, creativity training, sensitivity training, encounter groups, role playing, psychodrama, aikido, yoga, zen, body awareness, strength training, simulation games, movement exploration and movement-oriented tasks, and many other experiences designed to develop self-awareness. Most humanistic conceptions of physical education focus on human movement experiences as a way to facilitate the development of self-actualization and to experience the full range of human feelings.

Importantly, the spirit of joyful play and humane teachers who are caring sensitive and empathic seem crucial to these ideas (cf the authoritarian coach; Hendry, 1973). To be a humanistic teacher, from most vantage points, may be to strive to be humane and to recognize humane qualities in others. To be humane is to be capable of being agonized; to have feelings, to have a benevolent attitude toward others — caring, sensitive, empathic — as opposed to seeing one's more urgent problems in terms of the deficiencies and shortcomings of others.

5. **Concluding Remarks: Emergent Issues for Sports Psychology**

In re-assembling the two perspectives of our "hidden curriculum" of sport — the coach's and athlete's perspectives — a number of questions need to be discussed:

a) **What should be the role of the sports teacher or sports coach?**

The ideology of humanistic leadership gives emphasis to an empathetic identification with others, an openness to experience, acceptance of a wide and rich perceptual field for information from which to draw, and a commitment to enhancement of a positive self concept of those with whom the leader comes in contact. In this approach, leadership is perceived as one of freeing people to be more open to their experiences. In contrast, the traditional coaching model, presents emphasis on a relatively rigid structure, imposition of conformity through requirements, direction and control exercised through a formal hierarchy of authority — with the coach as the all-powerful authority figure — and a fixed system of rights, duties, and procedures. No matter how much emphasis is placed on such other qualities as coaching techniques, equipment, facilities, the humanity of the coach is the vital ingredient if athletes are to learn self-identity, self-responsibility, self-direction.

Athletes cannot be expected to develop wise choices in relation to their own sports involvement and success if all choices are made for them (e.g. Laughlin, 1974).

. . . When you get to college and professional levels, the coaches still treat you as an adolescent. They know damn well that you were never given a chance to become responsible or self-disciplined."

(Scott, 1971)

Maslow (1965) noted that the great leader is one who has the right combination of humility and flexibility while at the same time possesses a strength of character to stand alone when an important principle is involved. A critical factor with regard to the legitimate use of authority by the coach is scope:

"Determination of the precise limits of authority in the end must depend upon the good judgment of the sensitive coach, although athletes can hardly be faulted for increasingly resisting the authority of the unnecessarily intruding and controlling coach and for demanding that he stay within his justifiable limits in controlling their lives."

(Schafer, 1971)

b) What is the correct balance between self-expression and self-discipline in sports?

To be human is in itself a continual act of self-assertion. However, at what point and how deeply does one have a concern for other individuals? Further, does the coach or teacher who believes that it is as important to feel as to think need to be apprehensive about what happens emotionally to the young person who is expected to obey adult authority? Is the coach or teacher less than human if he believes that authority is a part of living? Moreover, how should what is to be taught and the variability of the athletes-gradations of interest, purpose, and talents — be taken into account? There are many implications here for sports teaching, learning and participating. I would like, however, in concluding to emphasize the ethos — the social context — of sports.

c)[1] How should the social context of sports learning and sports playing be structured? Is the spirit of play in sport repressed by the competitive spirit?

While humanism gives preference to cooperation over competition, it does not reject competition in a sport context. Competition, within limits of sport, is accepted for its own pleasure. But, except when carried out as fun in itself, there is a belief that intensive competition has the danger of generating conditional self-worth, role-specific relationships, excellence based on competitive merit, and the subjection of self to external control (Schafer, 1971). Perhaps the important issue is one of choice: perhaps no child should be "forced" to compete, though competition should be available for those who enjoy its challenge, seek excellence, admire competence. But as Ingham and Loy (1973) said:

"Sport needs no other justification than that it provides a setting for sociability and fun."

From this perspective, enjoyment of the process of *what* is being attempted as well as dwelling upon *outcomes* is important. Czikszentmihalyi (1975) investigating the inner experiences concerned with joy and pleasure in play games and life styles described a common form of experience enjoyed by the instrinsically motivated. He called this experience *flow* which incorporated feelings of exhilaration, of creative accomplishment and of heightened functioning. He wrote:

"They concentrate their attention on a limited stimulus field, forget personal problems, lose their sense of time and of themselves, feel competent

and in control, and have a sense of harmony and union with their surroundings. To the extent that these elements of experience are present, a person enjoys what he or she is doing and ceases to worry about whether the activity will be productive or whether it will be rewarded."

Perhaps this is the "hidden curriculum" we should aspire to in all our sporting endeavours.

REFERENCES

ADAMS, R. and BIDDLE, B.J. (1980) *Realities of teaching.* York: Holt, Rinehart and Winston.

ALSCHULER, A.S. (1975) Humanistic education. In *"Humanistic Education Sourcebook"*, READ, D.A. and SIMON, S.B. (Eds.) Englewood Cliffs, N.J.: Prentice-Hall.

APPLE, M. (1979) The hidden curriculum and the nature of conflict. *Interchange* 2, 27-43.

BAILYIN, L. (1959) Mass media and children: A study of exposure habits and cognitive effects. *Psychol. Monogr.* 73, 1-48.

BANTOCK, G.H. (1968) *Culture, industrialisation and education.* London: Routledge.

BARKER, D. (1972) Young people and their homes: Spoiling and "keeping close" in a South Wales town. *Sociological Review* 20, 4.

BEWHRMAN, R.M. (1967) Personality differences between swimmers and non-swimmers. *Research Quarterly* 38, 163-171.

BELSON, W.A. (1978) *Television violence and the adolescent boy.* London: Saxon House.

BENNETT, N. (1976) *Teaching styles and pupil progress.* London: Open Books.

BIDWELL, C. (1972) Schooling and socialization for moral commitment. *Interchange* 3, 1-27.

BIRDWHISTELL, R.L. (1962) *An introduction to kinesics.* Louisville: University Press.

BIRDWHISTELL, R.L. (1970) *Kinesics and context.* England: Penguin.

BONE, M. (1972) *The Youth Service and similar provision for young people.* London: HMSO.

BOWLBY, J. (1965) *Child care and the growth of love,* 2nd Ed. England: Penguin.

BRITISH BROADCASTING COMPANY GENERAL ADVISORY COUNCIL (1974) *Children as viewers and listeners.* London: BBC.

BUTT, D.S. (1972) Psychological motivation in sport. *"Issues in Physical Education"*. McGlynn, G.H. (Ed.) San Francisco: University Press.

CAMPBELL, D. (1972) Activity and attachment in early life, *Proceedings of the British Psychological Society, London Conference.*

CERRUTY, P. (1970) Cited in MURDOCK, S. The dissident varsity. *The Nation,* 305-308, 16th March 1970.

CLIFFORD, M.M. and WALSTER, E. (1973) The effect of physical attractiveness on teacher expectations. *Sociol. Educ.* 46, 248-258.

COLEMAN, J.C. (1979) *The school years.* London.

COLEMAN, J.S. (1961) *The adolescent society.* Glencoe: Free Press.

CORRIGAN, P. (1979) *Schooling the smash street kids.* London: Macmillan.

COWELL, R.N. (1972) The hidden curriculum: A theoretical framework and a pilot study. Doctoral dissertation, Harvard University.

---

[1] Another important question to be answered (which is beyond the scope of the prresent paper) is: Can "inner game" techniques and humanistic approaches to sport be evaluated by accepted psychological evidence? What research strategies should be employed in an attempt to verify these basically experiential sports processes?

CRATTY, B.J. (1970) Coaching decisions and research in sports psychology. *Quest* 13, 46-53.

CZIKSZENTMIHALYI, M. (1975) *Beyond boredom and anxiety.* San Francisco: Jossey-Bass.

DAVIES, R.D.S. (1970) Youth service as a part of further education. In BULMAN, I., CRAFT, M. and MILSON, F. (Eds.) *Youth service and inter-professional studies.* London: Pergamon Press.

DION, K. (1972) Physical attractiveness and evaluation of children's transgressions. *J. Personality Soc. Psychol.* 24, 207-213.

DONAGHER, P.C., POULOS, R.W., LIEBERT, R.M. and DAVIDSON, E.S. (1975) Race, sex and social example: An analysis of character portrayals on inter-racial television entertainment. *Psychol. Reports* 37, 1023-1034.

DOUGLAS, J.W.B. (1964) *The home and the school.* London: MacGibbon and Kee.

DOUGLAS, J.W.B., ROSS, J.M. and SOMPSON, H.R. (1968) *All our future.* London: Peter Davies.

DREEBEN, R. (1968) *On what is learned in schools.* Reading, Mass.: Addison-Wesley.

DUNFERMLINE COLLEGE OF PHYSICAL EDUCATION REPORT (1979) *Education outdoors.* Dunfermline College of Physical Education Research Report on the Outdoor Education Programme in Lothian Region Secondary Schools 1978/79.

DUNLOP, S. (1979) *Golfing bodymind.* London: Inner Game Ltd.

DUSEK, J.B. (1975) Do teachers bias children's learning? *Review of Educational Research* 45, 661-684.

EGGLESTON, J. (1976) *Adolescence and community.* London: Arnold.

EGGLESTON, J. (1977) *The sociology of the school curriculum.* London: Routledge and Kegan Paul.

EMMETT, I. (1971) *Youth and leisure in an urban sprawl.* Manchester University Press.

EMMETT, I.(1977) Unpublished draft report to the Sports Council on decline in sports participation after leaving school. London: Sports Council.

FOGELMAN, K. (1976) *Britain's sixteen year olds.* London: Nat. Child. Bur.

FOSTER, G.G., YSSELDYKE, J.E. and REESE, J.H. (1975) I wouldn't have seen it if I hadn't believed it. *Exceptional Children* (April) 469-473.

FRASER, E. (1959) *Home environment and the school.* London: University Press.

FRAZIER, N. and SADKER, M. (1973) *Sexism in school and society.* New York: Harper and Row.

FRIEDENBERG, E.Z. (1963) *Coming of age in America.* New York: Random House.

FURNEAUX, B. (1973) *The special child,* 2nd Ed. England: Penguin.

GALLWEY, T. (1977) *The inner game of tennis.* London: Inner Game Ltd.

GERBNER, G., CROSS, L., SIGNORELLI, N., MORGAN, M. and JACKSON-BEECK, M. (1979) The demontration of power: Violence profile No. 10. *J. Communication* 29, 177-196.

GRUNDEN, C. (1970) Sport and social class: A study of 13 and 15 year old children. *Bull. Phys. Educ.* 7, 6.

HALLER, E.J. and THROSEN, S.J. (1970) The political socialization of children and the structure of the elementary school. *Interchange* 1, 45-55.

HALLWORTH, H.J. (1966) Perceptions of children's personalities by experienced teachers. *Educ. Res.* 19, 3-12.

HARGREAVES, D.H. (1967) Social relations in a secondary school. London: Routledge and Kegan Paul.

HARGREAVES, D.H. (1972) *Interpersonal relations and education.* London: Routledge and Kegan Paul.

HARGREAVES, D.H., HESTER, S.K. and MELLOR, F.J. (1975) *Deviance in classrooms.* London: Routledge and Kegan Paul.

HENDRY, L.B. (1968) The assessment of personality in the coach-swimmer relationship and a preliminary examination of the father-figure stereotype. *Res. Quart.* 39, 3, 543-552.

HENDRY, L.B. (1972) The coaching stereotype. In *"Readings in Sports Psychology",* WHITING, H.T.A. (Ed.). London: Kimpton.

HENDRY, L.B. (1973) The physical educationist stereotype. In *"Personality and Performance in Physical Education and Sport",* WHITING, H.T.A., HARDMAN, K., HENDRY, L.B. and JONES, M.G., 123-148. London: Kimpton.

HENDRY, L.B. (1974) Coaches and physical education teachers: A comparison of the personality dimensions underlying their social orientation. *Internat. J. Sports Psychol.* 5, 1, 41-53.

HENDRY, L.B. (1975) School, sport, leisure: A study of personal, social and educational factors. Report to the Scottish Education Department, Edinburgh.

HENDRY, L.B. (1976) Early school leavers, sport and leisure. *Scottish Educational Studies* 8, 1, 48-51.

HENDRY, L.B. (1978) *School, sport, leisure: Three dimensions of adolescence.* London: Lepus.

HENDRY, L.B., BROWN, L. and HUTCHEON, G. (1981) Adolescents in community centres: Some urban and rural comparisons. *Scott. Jour. Phys. Educ.* (Forthcoming).

HENDRY, L.B. and DOUGLASS, L. (1975) University students: Attainment and sport. *British Journal of Educational Psychology* 45, 299-306.

HENDRY, L.B. and GILLIES, P. (1978) Body type, body esteem, school and leisure: A study of overweight, average and underweight adolescents. *Journal of Youth and Adolescence* 7, 2, 181-194.

HENDRY, L.B. and PATRICK, H. (1977) Adolescents and television. *Journal of Youth and Adolescence* 7, 2, 321-334.

HENDRY, L.B. and SIMPSON, D.O. (1977) One centre: Two sub-cultures. *Scott. Educ. Studies* 9, 2, 112-121.

HENDRY, L.B. and SINGER, F.E. (1981) Sport and the adolescent girl: A case study of one comprehensive school. *Scott. Jour. Phys. Educ.* (Forthcoming).

HENDRY, L.B. and THORNTON, D. (1976) Games theory, television and leisure in adolescent study. *Brit. Jour. of Soc. Psych.* 15, 369-76.

HENDRY, L.B. and THORPE, E. (1977) Pupils' choice, extracurricular activities: A critique of hierarchial authority? *Inter. Rev. Sport Sociol.* 12, 4, 39-50.

HENRY, J. (1966) *Jules Henry on education.* New York: Random House.

HIMMELWEIT, H.T. (1962) *Television revisited.* New Society, 15-17, 1st November, 1962.

HIMMELWEIT, H.T., OPPENHEIM, A.N. and VINCE, P. (1958) *Television and the child.* Oxford: University Press.

HOLT, J. (1964) *My children fail.* London: Pitman.

HURN, C.J. (1978) *The limits and possibilities of schooling.* London: Allyn and Bacon.

ILLICH, I. (1970) *Deschooling society.* New York: Harper and Row.

INGHAM, A.G. and LOY, J.W. Jr. (1973) The social system of sport: A humanistic perspective. *Quest.* 19, 3-23.

JACKSON, P.W. (1968) *Life in classrooms.* New York: Holt, Rinehart and Winston.

KEDDIE, N. (1971) Classroom knowledge. In YOUNG, M.F.D. (Ed.) *Knowledge and control.* London: Collier-Macmillan.

KENYON, G.S. (1968) Values held for physical activity by selected urban secondary school students in Canada, Australia, England and the United States. United States Office of Education, Contract S-376, University of Wisconsin.

KLEIN, J. (1965) *Samples from English cultures.* London: Routledge and Kegan Paul.

LAUGHIN, N.T. (1974) Existentialism, education and sport. In *"Issues in Physical Education and Sport",* McGLYNN, G.H. (Ed.) Palo Alto, California: National Press Books, 169-180.

LEACOCK, E.B. (1969) *Teaching and learning in city schools.* New York: Basic Books.

LEIGH, J. (1971) *Young people and leisure.* London: Routledge and Kegan Paul.

LONGLAND, J. (1969) In SIMPSON, J. (Ed.) Education for leisure. *Trends,* No. 7. London: Department of Education and Science.

LOWEN, A. (1977) *The language of the body.* New York: The MacMillan Co.

McCANN-ERICKSON (1977) *You don't know me: A survey of youth in Britain.* London: McCann-Erickson Advert. Ltd.

MACCOBY, E.E. (1954) Why do children watch television? *Public Opinion Quarterly* 18, 239-244.

MALUMPHY, T.M. (1968) Personality of women athletes in intercollegiate competition. *Res. Quart.* 39, 610-620.

MASLOW, A.N. (1965) *Eupsychian management.* Homewood: Ill. Dorsey Press.

MASLOW, A.H. (1970) Peak experiences in education and art. *The Humanist,* 29-31 (Sept.-Oct.)

MAYS, J.B. (1965) *Education and the urban child.* Liverpool: University Press.

MEAD, G.H. (1934) *Mind, self and society.* Chicago: University Press.

MOIR, E. (1977) *Female participation in physical activities — A Scottish Study.* Edinburgh: Dunfermline College of P.E.

MORTION-WILLIAMS, R. and FINCH, S. (1968) *Enquiry 1: Young school leavers.* London: HMSO.

MUNGHAM, G. and PEARSON, G. (1976) *Working class youth culture.* London: Routledge and Kegan Paul.

MURDOCK, G. and PHELPS, G. (1973) *Mass media and the secondary school.* London: MacMillan.

MURDOCK, S. (1970) The dissident 'varsity. *The Nation,* 305-308, 16th March, 1980.

MURRAY, J.P. (1973) Research coordinator, surgeon general's advisory committee on television and social behaviour. Quoted in LIEBERT, R.M., NEAL, J.M. and DAVIDSON, E.S. *The early window.*

NASH, R. (1973) *Classrooms observed.* London: Routledge and Kegan Paul.

NISBET, J.D., HENDRY, L.B., STEWART, C. and WATT, J. (1980) *Towards community education: An evaluation of community schools.* Aberdeen University Press.

OGILVIE, B. and TUTKO, T. (1966) *Problem athletes and how to handle them.* London: Pelham.

ORLICK, T.D. (1972) A socio-psychological analysis of early sports participation. Ph.D. Thesis: University of Alberta.

OVERLY, N. (Ed.) (1970) *The unstudied curriculum: Its impact on children.* Washington, D.C.: Association for Supervision and Curriculum Development.

RARICK, G.L. and McKEE, R. (1949) A study of twenty third-grade children exhibiting extreme levels of achievement on tests of motor proficiency. *Res. Quart.* 20, 183-195.

REID, M. (1972) Comprehensive integration outside the classroom. *Educational Research* 14, 2, 128-34.

RICH, J. (1975) Effects of children's physical effectiveness on teacher's evaluations. *J. Educ. Psychol.* 67, 5, 599-609.

RIST, R.G. (1970) Student social class and teacher expectations: The self-fulfilling prophesy in ghetto education. *Harward Educational Review* 40, 411-51.

ROGERS, C. (1967) *On becoming a person.* A therapist's view of psychotherapy. London: Constable.

ROSEN, B.C. and D'ANDRADE, R. (1959) The psychosocial origins of achievement motivation. *Sociometry,* 22, 185-218.

RUSHALL, B.S. (1967) Preliminary personality work with swimmers. *Brit. Sw. Coach. Assoc. Bull.* 44, 7-27.

SCARLETT, C.L. (1975) *Euroscot: The new European generation.* Edinburgh: Scott. Stand. Confer. of Volunt. Youth Organs.

SCHAFER, W.E. (1971) Sport, socialisation and the school: Towards maturity or enculturation? Proceedings of the Third International Symposium on the Sociology of Sport. Waterloo, Ontario, Canada. August.

SCHAFER, W.E. and ARMER, J.M. (1966) Participation in high school athletics and academic achievement. Proceedings of the International Sports Congress, Madrid.

SCHAFER, W. and RENBERG, R. (1970) Athletic participation, college expectations, and college encouragement. *Pacific Sociol. Rev.* 13, 182-186.

SCHAFFER, H.R. (1975) *Studies in mother-infant interaction.* London: Academic Press.

SCHOFFIELD, M. (1973) *The sexual behaviour of young adults.* London: Allen Lane.

SCOTT, J. (1970) Athletics for athletes. In "The Dissident 'Varsity". MURDOCK, S. *"The Nation",* 305-308, 16th March, 1970.

SCOTT, J. (1971) *The athletic revolution.* New York: Free Press.

SHARPE, S. (1977) *Just like a girl: How girls learn to be women.* Harmondsworth, Penguin.

SILBERMAN, C.E. (1970) *Crisis in the classroom.* New York: Vintage Books.

SILBERMAN, M.L. (1969) Behavioural expression of teachers' attitudes towards elementary school students. *J. Educ. Psychol.* 60, 402-407.

SILLITOE, K. (1969) *Planning for leusire.* London: HMSO.

SIMPSON, J. (1973) Education for leisure. In SMITH, M.A., PARKER, S. and SMITH, C.D. (Eds.) *Leisure and society in Britain.* London: Allen Lane.

SKUBIC, E. (1965) Studies of little league and middle league baseball. *Res. Quart.* 27, 97-110.

SMITH, C.S. (1973) Adolescence. In SMITH, M.A., PARKER, S. and SMITH, C.S. (Eds.) *Leisure and Society in Britain.* London: Allen Lane.

SNYDER, B.R. (1971) *The hidden curriculum.* New York: Knopf.

SOCIAL AND COMMUNITY PLANNING RESEARCH PROJECT (1977) *Joint provision, the school leaver, and the community.* London: Sports Council.

SPORTS COUNCIL FOR WALES (1980) Report of the Working Party of School Sports, Welsh Council for School Sports.

SPRAFKIN, J.N. and RUBINSTEIN, E.A. (1979) Children's television viewing habits and prosocial behaviour: A field correlational study. *J. Broadcasting* 23, 265-276.

SPREITZER, E. and PUGH, M. (1973) Interscholastic athletics and educational expectations. *Sociol. Educ.* 46, 171-182.

SPRY, R. (1977) Leisure and the school leaver in Stoke-on-Trent. In FOX, W.M. (Ed.) *Leisure and the quality of life.* London: HMSO.

START, K.B. (1966) Substitutuon of games performance for academic achievement as a means of achieving status among secondary school children. *Brit. J. Sociol.* 17, 3, 300-305.

STERN, D. (1977) *The first relationship: Infant and mother.* London: Fontana Open Books.

SUGARMAN, B. (1967) The social system of the school. British Sociological Association Annual Conference.

SUGARMAN, B. (1968) The social system of the school. *Brit. Sociol. Assoc.* Annual Conference.

TALBOT, M. (1979) *Women and leisure.* London: SSRC Sport Council.

TATTERSFIELD, R.C. (1971) Competitive sport and personality development. Ph.D. thesis. University of Durham.

WHITFIELD, R.C. (1971) *Disciplines of the curriculum.* London: McGraw-Hill.

WILLIS, P. (1977) *Learning to labour.* Farnborough: Saxon House.

WISEMAN, S. (1964) *Education and environnemt.* Manchester: University Press.

Reaction #1   Raymond Thomas (France)

The research conducted by Hendry in Scotland shows us that the interest of the pupils in certain sports is determined by numerous factors, but in particular by the attitude of Physical Education instructors, by the kind of perception they have of the pupils, and by the fact that the children feel that they are treated differently according to their abilities. These points should be underscored. It is known indeed that the image a teacher has of a pupil plays an important part in the success of the latter. Since the work of R.A. Rosenthal in the United States drew attention to it, this phenomenon is well known. In the research he conducted in a school, he has established that when a teacher is led to believe that a pupil is going to make important progress during the following weeks, that pupil does indeed make progress. This work of Rosenthal is part of a more general area of research devoted to the fulfillment of these prophecies.

However, something which has not been examined as much is the importance of the general attitudes of physical education instructors. This factor must carefully be examined, for according to public opinion the lack of sports practice after a pupil leaves school or college is due often to the small amount of time spent on physical education in school. In fact, it is the teaching method which is also a deciding factor. At any rate, this is the conclusion that can be drawn from the works of Simson and Leigh, mentioned by Hendry. This view, as expressed in the speaker's paper, should be developed further, for we have noticed that in France and, I believe, in many countries there is a decline of sports practice and competition in the adolescent years. In order to explain this phenomenon, the French coaches first proposed a physiological reason. In their opinion, the root of the problem was a wrong system of training devised for the young people before the years of adolescence. The coaches felt that they had been mistaken in emphasizing resistance work, instead of endurance work.

To simplify all this, let us say that resistance is the capacity to sustain an intense effort as long as possible, and endurance is the ability to make an effort of average intensity as long as possible. According to the coaches, resistance work resulted in a cardiac development different from that produced by endurance work. The thickness of the heart muscle was increased, but not the volume of the cavities. This, in the long run, produced bad sports results; and because the young people were not having good results, they gave up sports. However, the theory that cardiac development differs according to the type of training has not had scientific confirmation, and the coaches have had to find other explanations for the decrease in the number of pupils taking up sports at the time of adolescence. They now blame social factors and try to explain in this way the bad results obtained by the elite athletes.

It now appears that adolescence represents a period when there is a change of values and discovery of other goals. It is especially true that the cultural pressure that is brought to bear upon the adolescents increases with age. As the adolescent grows up, exams become increasingly difficult. No civilization has imposed on this age group such a load of school work. Parents, teachers, all the members of society are always telling these young people that their future depends on their school results. Accordingly, the adolescent puts school success at the top of his list of values. Of course, when questions are put to the parents about this matter — and surveys provide proof of this — most of them always declare that young people should practice more sports, that the school schedule should include more hours of physical education. But when these same parents are asked to rank the school subjects in order of importance, they place mathematics and French at the top of the list and physical education last. It is this last message which is communicated to the adolescent as he is growing up. This is something to be included in the "hidden curriculum" file.

It must also be pointed out that society as it is today requires constant adaptation on the part of the adolescent, but at the same time does not provide models for this because society progresses so rapidly. The adolescent therefore discovers for himself new types of relationships and must constantly make adjustments.

All these constraints bring about a psychological crisis and an abandonment of the practice of sports for many adolescents. Often the facilities of modern life are blamed for this withdrawal from sports. However, I don't think at all that this is the reason, for adolescents are capable of being deeply interested in great causes. It must be pointed out though, that they have a tendency to reject authoritarianism. Now, in certain sport clubs this authoritarian climate exists and they are repelled by it. We are living at a time when authority is being questioned.

It is therefore appropriate to re-examine the function and behaviour of the sports director whose motives are not sufficiently known. In France, Georges Magnane, in a work dealing with sports sociology, has called the directors "gerontocrats", that is, "authoriatrian old men." Indeed, is it not true that some directors are persons who have economic power, in particular those dealing in big business, but also do not have any power over men, and therefore seek to control and influence others by investing in sports? We do not have in hand sufficient studies on the psychology of the French sports director to answer this question. Anyway, it can be said objectively from observation that those who have attempted to conduct studies on social psychology in the sports world have often encountered more or less obvious refusal to co-operate or obstacles raised by responsible persons. We suggest that the directors are responsible for this situation, for unconsiously they do not want their motives to be brought to the light of day.

After having taken up again certain ideas developed by Hendry, I shall now raise an objection which seems important to me. His paper does not take into account a fundamental aspect of modern sport, which is that of the diversification of the levels of participation and of the evaluation of their relationships in industrialized countries. The scope which he suggests is one sport. From now on it is necessary to distinguish between different types of participation. For example we must distinguish between the champion, who devotes 5 to 6 hours of training per

47

day under the supervision of an expert in his particular discipline, following a rigorous, very precise plan, based on the most recent scientific information, and using very sophisticated techniques on the one hand, and on the other we consider the person who runs a few hours every weekend to maintain his physical condition; or the person who plays a tennis match with a friend occasionally. There is a wide gap between the competitive athlete and the recreational participant, yet these entirely heterogeneous activities are all called sports.

In my opinion it is proper to distinguish between at least three kinds of sports participation: the high level of sports, the mass sports and the recreational sports. A high level sport is one that is practiced by champions, by those who participate in Olympic Games or in major international competitions. It is a sport for the élite. The federations have given it a precise definition. They are obliged to do it, for particular credits and advantages are granted to those who make up their membership. In certain disciplines which provide a measurement, such as track and field or swimming for example, the performances of the athletes are a means of marking the boundary of a high level sport; in other sports where a simple hierarchical system is maintained, in group sports for instance, it is the "standing" in the classification which determines whether or not a person belongs to the élite.

Mass sports are practiced by those who are holders of certificates from clubs. They are members of federations and try to climb up the hierarchical ladder by passing, for example, from the departmental to the regional level. Mass sports are distinguishable from elite sports, not only from the standpoint of level, but also from that of the recruiting, which is done differently and thus makes the two kinds of sport entirely heterogeneous, as we shall see further on.

Recreational sports bring together those who carry out physical activities for the purpose of keeping fit and relaxing the body and mind. These physical activities may eventually become competitive. However, the kind of motivation here is only secondary.

The relationships between these three types of sports participation have changed and, as a result, the sports scene may be transformed completely.

During a first period which ended around the Second World War, mass sports and high level sports were linked by a sort of cohesive relationship which might be represented graphically as a pyramid. A large base, made up of people who took up mass sports, was producing an elite at the top. Alongside this system there existed recreational sport, but hardly developed.

Under the pressure of the competition between countries, which have made use of sports to assert the superiority of their social system, the results of the elite have improved. Little by little high level sports have become an independent aspect of mass sports. Indeed, countries anxious to increase their prestige have first of all tried to improve the training methods and then to place athletes in particular life conditions, in order to enable them to carry out very sustained training. Next, the responsible officers thought of a way of raising further the level of the élite and, for that purpose, they developed a system for the discovery of talented young people. They tried to find among the very young children those who were most likely to become champions. At first, this system worked very well within the federations; and then it was the entire population who became interested. From then on, an independent body of mass sports was created. The prospective athletes discovered among the population were placed in special situations, where they found a structure which allowed them to pursue their studies by following a special time table, flexible enough to give them the possibility of carrying out a sustained and consistent training program.

But, from now on, the subjects who enter the domain of mass sports, that is, in the usual federal structure, cannot claim to have the same results as those who are in special structures, because on the one hand, they have less ability as a rule. Indeed, they were not selected during the talent-scouting operation; and, on the other hand, they do not enjoy the same advantages. Consequently, those who take up mass sports gradually withdraw from a competition which they know beforehand they have lost. And so, they turn back to recreational sports.

This model I am presenting must logically lead to a collapse of mass sports. This phenomenon is especially true for sports where measurements or evaluations of performance can be made, such as track and field or swimming, for example. It is true that in these disciplines, the young sportsman has a very specific idea of the distance which separates him from the best. He has also a clear idea of the distance which exists between himself and the young athlete of the same age who has been placed in a special structure. He sees the gap widening and, consequently, his motivation for taking up a particular sport diminishes.

In France, the development of the athletes of the federations confirms the hypothesis I am putting forward. For example, the number of certified athletes of the French Track and Field and Swimming Federation, is not increasing and has even diminished. These sports which have an obvious ascetic aspect, but include no play activities at all, cannot easily be reconverted into recreations.

I think therefore that this evolution of relationships between types of participation plays an important role in the selection of individuals and that specific surveys must be conducted rapidly, in order to appraise better the psycho-sociological forces that come into play. Unfortunately, the government authorities do not seem to have become aware of this necessity. When an analysis is being made of the progress of the athletes of the federations, it is fitting to take into account the composition of the certified athletes and not to limit oneself to the consideration of gross figures. Thus, for the last few years, the number of athletes of the French Track and Field Federation has remained stationary, but the ratio between the number of members of the male sex and that of the female sex has varied. The percentage of female athletes has increased. This means that the number of certified athletes of the male sex has diminished, and is a confirmation of the hypothesis we have put forward concerning the pernicious influence of the new structures of high level sports on mass sports. But other phenomena are added to the one we have just described, and this makes it necessary to make a thorough study of the evolution of sport participation as a whole.

Reaction #2   Guido Schilling (Switzerland)

The task of evaluating the policies of sport and the rights of athletes is quite a delicate one in that sport policies usually are established in accordance with the political and economic systems of the country in which people engage in a given sport. There are many differences between the East and the West, but also between the North and the South. I will therefore give a personal answer to the question of how sports psychology or sport psychologists can help solve present and future problems.

1. "Sport" does not always mean "Sport"

Sport today has many facets and is always full of contradictions. Everyone understands the term according to what he or she has experienced in the past or is still experiencing now in connection with sports. For some people, they may bring back good or bad memories of physical education classes in high school, and today when they hear the word they perhaps think of the next volleyball game in a regional league they have to play or of a tennis match against an opponent, or again of the national league games that they will enjoy watching on television or at the stadium next weekend.

The term "sport" is a difficult one to define today. Sport does not always mean just that. The smooth transition from recreational to competitive and elite sport is no longer valid. Recreational and elite sports have developed independently and established their own rules. Active recreational and elite athletes as a group stand by themselves, as compared to non athletes or passive sports consumers.

In elite sports, also called high performance sports, it is the delivery that counts. Everything is centered around the establishment of records. Financial sacrifices are great and the amount of time devoted to training varies according to the discipline. In professional elite sports, athletes can work more "professionally" than amateur athletes. Finally, professional elite sports attract the mass media.

In recreational sports, on the other hand, performance is still a factor but a more relative and personal one. What counts foremost is satisfaction. Recreational sports may lead some athletes to participate in elite sports and others who are lazy to abandon sports altogether. Among recreational sports may be included Competitive Sports with league championships, individual tournaments, team tournaments, and competitions in every discipline, as well as sports for Fitness which are usually physical activities involving no organization, definite schedule or competition.

Finally among the non-sport people we find some who are spectators, some who lack interest in sport, or are lazy, and some who reject sport for ideological reasons.

What about school sports?

School sports, are at the root of Hendry's paper. The role of school sports varies according to the development of sport in different social systems. Its importance depends on the objective of school sports, on the place held by the school in the given society, and on the importance of sport in the school system.

Phrases such as "Chinese athletic schools", "physical education students in France" and "Sports scholarships in the United States", for example, show what close ties exist between the educational system and elite sports in these countries.

Needless to say that school sports are not always so closely related to elite sports. They can also mean recreational sport, competitive sport or, unfortunately, no sport.

Tentative Definition of Sport

- Sports involve physical activity
- Sports are based on the innate desire to move and to compete with one's self, others, or the forces of nature
- Sports preserve and develop physical, social and psychological fitness (according to the Swiss Sport Association).

The fundamental elements of sport are movement, play and performance. The importance given to each of these is not the same in recreational, competitive or high performance sports. If one or other of these fundamental elements is lacking, the sport no longer corresponds to the definition of sport as we see it: For example, is there physical activity in motorized sports; Is the knock-out truly a conscious affirmation of the boxer's responsibility; and finally, is "high performance" a part of sport if it is attained through "doping" at the expense of health?

2. **The Context of Sport**

The family, school, neighbourhood, and models presented by the mass media, play an important role in the decision whether or not to angage in sports. A child will obviously become a skier if he lives in a ski area. And how many mothers who always dreamed of excelling in skating make of their daughters figure skating stars? The son of a pool lifeguard also has very good chances of becoming an excellent swimmer.

The Evéquoz brothers, who for a long time were part of the Swiss fencing team, agreed that it was normal for them to practise the same sport as their father, a Maître d'armes. Their father does not want to hear about manipulation or intervention on his part and justly so: "My children took to fencing quite naturally," says he.

The Family and Sport

The family as a way of life and a structure of interpersonal relationships in our society has undergone many changes in the last few years. Other institutions have assumed responsibilities which were once the family's, such as education, the production of food, the care of the sick and the elderly. The family has also become smaller and less stable.

Children always need a family, responsible persons to whom they can turn or on whom they can depend in order to live. Spitz (1960) examined 91 children in an orphanage. All of them had been separated from their mothers after the age of three months. The orphanage provided them with everything they needed physically: food, drugs, and health and medical care. But since only one sister had to take care of up to twelve children, the infants received very little affection, approximately one tenth of what they would normally have received in the usual mother and child relationship. After three months of separation, alarming symptoms slowly began to appear. The children almost always stayed on their backs, completely passive in their cradles. Their motor development was slowed to the point that they could not even turn over onto their stomachs in their cradles. The first year, the mortality rate neared 30% as compared to 1% in nurseries where babies were under the care of the mothers. At the age of four, five of the 21 children still at the orphanage could not walk, twelve could not feed themselves with a spoon, twenty could not dress themselves, six could not talk, five knew only two words and eight knew only three to five words.

The family of today is still a type of laboratory where we learn to live in society. This applies particularly to sports. The participants at a symposium in 1979 stated clearly that most students are motivated to practise sports firstly by their family and only secondly by their school or friends. Family sports are more common today than in the past. Families hike together, spend ski holidays together. This is certainly due to the fact that people now have more free time and freedom to spend their money. The woman's role is also more open today: housework and children are no longer her exclusive field. In the same way, sports are no longer the man's exclusive territory.

The State and Sport

In most countries, physical education has been included in the curriculum in public schools. The State wants the young to be fit, but students do not practice sports to preserve their health. Physical education is rather an alternative to the other type of teaching. (see: Sport and Youth, unpublished paper, 1979) School sports and physical education are part of a child's education and, as such, are state responsibilities.

Hendry (1981) has shown that the three following categories can be found in school sports:

- *high performance athletes — competitive athletes*
  These students are spoiled by the physical educators, who consider them to be polite, attractive and enthusiastic. In turn, these students like their teachers, and relationships between them are good. (Hendry 1981)

- *non athletes*
  It takes very little to turn a non athletic student into a non athlete. He feels inferior in the eyes of the physical educator and soon finds himself excluded. These students abandon sports often as early as during their school years and at the latest when they finish school

- *recreational athletes and fitness athletes*
  These athletes stay active in school sports only if they are very interested in physical activity and if they practice recreational sports for example with their families or friends.

It is therefore clear that the State and the school, in general, do not succeed in encouraging young people to practice sports during their entire life.

In some countries, school sports are a testing ground to select elite athletes. In such cases, school sports become high level sports in themselves. Special attention is paid to these talented students, who are developed (or literally "trained"), especially in sports where the champions are still children, such as artistic gymnastics, figure skating and swimming.

Some governments continue to assume the responsibility of developing elite athletes even longer and make them train and win as students or soldiers working for the glory of their country. Is it the State's responsibility thus to encourage elite athletes? Why not? Does it not equally encourage artists and scientists?

Free Sport Organizations

Toward the end of the last century, independent athletes began to form clubs. Associations were necessary if those interested were to compete in such meets as football championships, gymnastic competitions or rowing regattas. It was also the time when the first Modern Olympic Games were held. International federations are still today establishing competition rules.

The rapid development of elite sports after the Second World War led the international and also some national sport federations to deal only with competition sports and therefore elite sports.

Members of a club who performed well were held in higher regard than the others. All that counted in such teams was performance. At some other time, an attempt was made to eliminate recreational athletes and fitness buffs by including them among the category of non athletes. Many clubs and federations had difficulty understanding that only a minority of their members wanted to become high performance athletes. But what were the alternatives? What could be offered to athletes who were not interested in competition as such, but wished to practice sports?

Several administrators became aware of these difficulties in the sixties. International and national federations initiated campaigns for recreational sport. "Sports for all", with gymnastics for the elderly, jogging, family sports and citizen races attracted thousands of participants. Government departments have also taken over the responsibility of recreational sport and fitness. Occasionally, difficulties arise with regard to jurisdiction. Who is responsible for what? Must clubs and federations promote elite sports in particular? Is the State responsible for school and recreational sports? A third party which has recently discovered the potential athlete in man, namely the leisure industry, is becoming extremely interested in sports. The responsibilities are becoming all the more difficult to divide.

This competition for input to sport is, however, a great advantage. The opportunities to practice sports must be as varied as possible, so that anyone may be able to participate. Neither the government, the federations nor the leisure industry must hold the monopoly on sports.

Sport and the mass media

The triumph of elite sports was supported by the mass media, particularly by television. Few events hold the interest of as many viewers as sports. One was perhaps the royal wedding of Prince Charles and Lady Diana. Still today, there is an increase in television set sales just before Olympic Games or World Soccer Championships get under way. Direct transmissions ensure tremendous returns in terms of money and viewer interest.

The number of armchair athletes continues to grow. This fact, however, is regrettable:

1. One who sits passively to watch sports on television cannot practice sports himself during that time.

2. It is by actively engaging in sport that one can experience competition with one's self, an opponent or the forces of nature. Although television allows the viewer to feel emotions, it still provides only second-hand experiences.

3. The image of the perfect elite athlete shown often and sometimes even in slow motion is fascinating. It satisfies expectations of success that cannot be met in the viewer's daily existence, to the point that the viewer stops seeking personal success in sports because it seems out of his reach.

BIBLIOGRAPHY

Illich, I., Entschulung der Gesellschaft, München 1972. "Deschooling Society"

Mander, J., Schafft das Fernsehen ab, eine Streitschrift gegen das Leben aus zweiter Hand, Reibek bei Hamburg 1979, "Four Arguments for the Elimination of Television"

Silberman, Ch.E., Die Krise der Erziehung, Weinheim und Basel 1973, "Crisis in the Classroom"

Spitz, R., in Psychologie du développement, Trainer-Information-Entraîneur, no. 8, Macolin 1980, p. 13.

Sport! Sport? (1979)

a) film from the Ecole fédérale de gymnastique et de sport (F. 70.19)

b) special issue: der Berufsschüler, 58/1 1979

c) Maggligen/Macolin, Symposium: ETS/EFGS Schulklassen im Gespräch — Sport and the Young — Lo sporto nel mondo dei giovani, unpublished paper.

Reaction #3   John T. Partington (Canada)

I'd like to borrow Leo Hendry's "hidden curriculum" concept and use it to refer to a hidden curriculum which most interests me — our children's own values and expectations regarding sport. I want to use this translated version of the term to develop a better understanding of how we can make sports safer for children and youth.

It is my opinion that a growing number of children's sport injuries are *not* accidental. We can understand what happens to children, physically and emotionally, while participating in sports by considering two sets of forces, or curricula. On the one hand, there is an explicit sport curriculum which expresses adult's attitudes, expectations and policies; and on the other hand, there is the hidden curriculum of children's own personal needs and interests related to sport.

Children's safe, playful sport spirit, in my view, is being crucified by certain elements in the explicit adult sport curriculum for children. Resurrection of the safe, playful spirit requires that we do everything in our power to nurture children's natural, but increasingly hidden curriculum.

I refer to the children's sport curriculum as "hidden," because I don't see much evidence of it in organized league play, which claims so much of our sport facilities, budgets, and leadership resources; nor do I see any reference to it in the Sport section of our local newspaper; and finally, because I fail to note any reference to it in the Federal White Paper on Sport.

I have tried to learn about the hidden curriculum of children's interests and needs related to sport by watching and talking to my own children, and by interviewing and conducting questionnaire surveys of children and youth. My first study focused on 31 girls who had dropped out of a competitive swimming club. Their recommendations to improve the program included the need for more enjoyment in swimming, the need to start a program for non-competitors, and to recognize the achievements of the lower "C" level swimmers.

Last year my friend, Terry Orlick, attended a youth conference in Saskatchewan. I suggested that he try to ask the young delegates what aspects of sport make them "flow." Flow refers to the peak experience of being fused with the action; being part, not apart from what's going on. Their replies suggest that friendly, playful elements are crucial to their sport curriculum, and that an over-emphasis on serious competition and bad sportsmanship is to be avoided. Seventy percent said that sport makes them happy when — "You are with all your friends playing something, everyone is out for a good time"; "It is just fun without pressures";

"You feel comfortable with your surroundings"; "The better help the lesser ones"; "It's a clean fair game." Also, a considerable number stressed the joy of effort, as reflected in remarks like: Sport makes me happy when, "people stretch and really push themselves to do the impossible"; ". . . myself and my team has done the best of its ability, and you can laugh even if you lose." On the other hand, over one third of the group reported that sport makes them anxious when, ". . . You go out there to kill and win, and then everybody gets on each other's back"; ". . . people are pushed to gain something, and if they don't accomplish it, they are looked on as a failure." Incidentally, the issue of winning/losing per se had little significance for this group of young people.

These very recent findings simply confirm the mounting evidence reported by researchers across Canada from boys and girls, and children and youth, that playing sports just for fun is the guiding principle in their own hidden sport curriculum.

If children were free to play sports according to their own curriculum, I propose that injuries would decrease, and participation would increase. Certainly there would be accidents, but I feel that such accidents would be an inevitable, and even acceptable, consequence of the child's quest in sports for greater self-expression, and for a more fun-filled, zestful life.

But many Canadian children, especially those in the urban centres, are not free to play naturally. They are bound by an explicit sport curriculum imposed on them by adults; by an alarming number of parents, teachers, coaches, sport administrators, journalists, and some of the power elite in business, media and politics.

Some elements of this curriculum are good, even as life-supporting as the children's own natural curriculum. Consider, for example, the Physical and Health Education curriculum recommended to local School Boards by the Ontario Ministry of Education; it includes such goals as the following:

1. To expose students to a variety of enjoyable activities and experiences related to physical and health education;

2. to develop in students a habit of, and love for, daily vigorous activity by providing opportunities for them to experience a total fitness feeling that can be maintained throughout their lives;

3. to help individuals develop a sound understanding of their total development, and enable them to attain positive self-images;

4. to provide opportunities for students to solve problems and make personal decisions related to their intellectual, social, physical and emotional development;

5. to allow students to experience social relations that will encourage desirable attitudes and behaviour, especially in regard to sport, leadership roles, respect for rules, and cooperation with others;

6. to help students improve their physical and motor fitness through activities designed to develop stamina, strength, endurance, flexibility, balance, speed, agility, coordination, and power.

This all sounds very positive, until one recognizes that all of these fine-sounding goals must be realized in two class periods or less per week, and that there is often a wide discrepancy between this curriculum, and how it is operated; for example, many teacher-coaches still send in plays to their quarterbacks in the interest of winning, rather than allow student-athletes to learn from their mistakes, and grow through both victory and defeat.

A new chapter in the explicit sport curriculum has recently been provided by the Coaching Association of Canada. It includes their developmentally oriented accreditation program for those who plan to coach children. This program reflects the following principles from their *Bill of Rights for Young Athletes*:

1. Right of the opportunity to participate in sports regardless of ability level

2. Right to participate at a level that is commensurate with each child's developmental level

3. Right to have qualified adult leadership

4. Right to participate in safe and healthy environments

5. Right of each child to share in the leadership and decision making of their sport participation

6. Right to play as a child and not as an adult

7. Right to proper preparation for participation in sport

8. Right to an equal opportunity to strive for success

9. Right to be treated with dignity by all involved

10. Right to have fun through sport.

Again, I have to say that this all sounds fine, but . . . but what about the newly educated humanistic coach who gets ousted by a few red-neck parents because they want their sons to play tough hockey to attract the professional talent scouts . . . and what about the top-scoring midget superstar whose dad tells him always to smash his first shot at the goalie's head?

Just talk to the silent and suffering majority of concerned hockey or baseball moms and dads; they could write encyclopedias of examples to illustrate how a sick sport ideology has penetrated and poisons the daily context of their children's lives in sport.

Somehow, at some point in our history, the positive need for achievement and excellence in life and in sport has changed to an irrational hunger for personal control and for the exercise of unlimited power; somehow, competition, which served at one time to yield the excitement of an uncertain outcome, and the joyous, momentary release at the end of the match, has also changed. Sport competition now serves as the arena for judging whether or not our children are "cut from the right cloth" to make it in the competitive world. Results of competitive sport in general are like stock market reports; they provide simple daily criteria for helping to judge whether our city, province, nation, or political/economic system is superior to others. From this we can "borrow" a temporary ration of feelings of power and purpose for which many of us hunger. However, the interest on this "loan" is escalating in terms of higher sport injuries, and mounting dropouts from children's sport.

The "good penalty" to prevent a goal from being scored, and "dusting the batter" to prevent him from hitting with confidence are common-place sport strategies, practiced by many youthful players in the service of winning at all costs. Sport injuries sustained from these practices are not accidents, they represent felonious assaults.

Children and youth who decide to drop out from sport rather than be murdered are not "lazy chickens," as I heard one adult coach remark; in my opinion, they are sensible citizens whose natural needs for friendship and fun are not being met by the sport context provided by adults.

The problem of child safety in sports, as I have defined it, will not yield to a simple prescription. But one thing is certain to me, that most of our previous attempts to help have been misguided. Take, for example, the usual technological solutions: If children are sustaining facial injuries, we must invent a better face mask; if they are getting more concussions, we need better headgear; if collarbones are the problem, then let's make better shoulder pads. These quasi-solutions are costly and miss the point. They assume that something is wrong with the children's bodies. But there is nothing wrong with children's bodies as long as they play according to their hearts. I'm afraid that our technology is just not ingenious enough to keep up with accelerating violence in sports. And even if it was, no amount of hardware can protect our children against the psychological injuries which they are more and more exposed to in sport — whithering blows to their self-esteem if they are cut, and overwhelming levels of competitive stress if they are not.

I think that the most promising direction to pursue involves recognizing children's innate wisdom in relation to play, and supporting their hidden curriculum. If children haven't been completely socialized into the competitive ethic, they can play for hours without adult supervision, without referees, and without external rewards. Children in their natural play state are very civilized.

However, there are millions of children and youth whose natural capacities and attitudes for play have been warped by our explicit adult sport curriculum. These play cripples need our assistance. Somehow we have to help them forget about our false goals of winning at all costs, and to define for themselves their own personal goals in sport. Somehow we have to help them to regain control over their lives in sport. I feel that improved sport commentary, as well as special pro-social modelling programs on television would help a great deal.

But we mustn't lose sight of those directly responsible for the existing context of children's sport. It will be impossible to change youthful sport participants without recognizing the needs of their parents, teachers and coaches. These are all good people who want the best for their children. How can we redirect children's sport without making these adults feel guilty and ashamed about what they have been doing? How can we avoid public confrontations and painful denouncements of the high priests of the sick sport ideology? We all know that violence begets violence. The challenge is to identify gentle, peaceful solutions for the violence in children's sport.

THE ROLE OF THE MEDIA IN SPORT

Stephen Bindman (Canada)

A symbiotic relationship exists between the mass media and sports that is beneficial to both social segments. (1) While the relationship may not be equal in nature, both the media and sport serve their own interests by protecting and promoting each other. (2)

No element of twentieth century life has played a more significant role in promoting sports interest than TV. (3)

Sports and the media have lived together now for a considerable period of time. Each now needs the other. (4)

These quotes are representative of a vast area of research, both by sociologists and mass media analysts. When studying sports, it is no longer possible to exclude the media from the discussion, for it is indirectly through the media that most people have the most contact with the world of sport.[5] Likewise, when examining the media, sports must be an important consideration. Every newspaper, no matter its size or market, usually contains some sort of sports section whether it is a full section in an urban broadsheet or a few local scores in a small weekly. In terms of consistent space each and every edition, few newspaper sections get as much as the sports section. On television, up to 30 percent of all programming may involve sports.[6] Television networks spend many millions of dollars each year in transmitting sports programs.

The literature abounds with studies on the mass media and its effect on the organized sports world. Such analyses look at various rule changes and shifts in scheduling designed to accomodate television, or how extensive media coverage and press "playups" have led to higher player salaries and increased professionalization among athletes. There has also been a good deal of work done on how sports has changed the media.

But while our knowledge of how sports has influenced the media, and the media sports, is fairly detailed, little effort has been devoted towards investigating how mass media portrayal of sports has affected us — the viewer. There is a third party in this sports-media relationship, namely the people who tune into sports on TV or purchase the papers in which sports is reported. We have seen how it affects the sports and media establishments themselves, but little is known about the recipients of this media influx. Does this portrayal cause us to get out and do it ourselves? Does it make us more violent when we participate in sports? Does it makes us want to win at all costs?

This paper will attempt to survey some of the literature in an attempt to fill in these gaps. It takes a "we-orientation." While a lot of questions are posed, unfortunately the state of the research in this area is such that firm and conclusive answers will be limited and few in number. In light of this however, it is hoped that from a few current examples, this essay can point out new directions in which the research path should lead in the next few years in this crucial area.

This paper is, however, not an attempt to evaluate the pros and cons of media sports coverage — whether it is done well or not. There has already been a good deal of work done in this area. Many have concluded that because of their relationship with players and team owners, many reporters are nothing but a propaganda arm of the sports establishment[7], and that many of the true facts and real stories are not reported.* These areas too are beyond the parameters of this essay. It is concerned with the person orientation.

Most of the analysis will be on the medium of television for it is the one which reaches the most people, and not unrelatedly, it is the medium which has been the subject of most of the small amount of research that has been done. As well, it is on TV that the most distortion of reality occurs.

The media effects of sports portrayal will be examined under three general categories:

— its effects on our sports participation habits,
— its effects on our violent and aggressive tendencies and
— its effect on the values we attach to sports participation.

NOT THE REAL THING

It is important to distinguish content effect from media effect. An attempt must be made to isolate those effects specifically caused by the actual media portrayal of a sport event, from those that are caused by the event itself. For example, a TV network may

---

* Harry Edwards is typical of this school of thought: "Significant social injustices in athletic arenas are slanted to minimize embarrassment to the sports establishment . . . facts are ignored or misstated . . . Consequently, the sports world in America has been portrayed as a citadel of racial harmony and purity and this distorted image has been fostered by sports reporters."[8]

broadcast a hockey game in which there are an abundance of fights. Those fights may influence the viewer's behavior patterns, but it is how that TV network's portrayal of those fights influences the audience that is of concern here. The fact that this distinction is more often that not, blurred and hard to distinguish, goes far in explaining the lack of research in this area.

It is clear however, that sports spectators in front of their televisions do not necessarily see an unbiased, true and reliable representation of the game that fans in the arena or stadium see.[9] What one sees on TV may be vastly different from what one would see in person at the event being covered. The TV transmission is not just a restatement of the game being played:

> The TV coverage of a live unscripted event imposes its own structures and unity and provides its own ideological viewpoints . . . points of reference and emphases which are unique to the medium event. (10)

TV watchers are exposed to a "media event," the production of a team of professional gatekeepers and embellishers.[11] There is a director who edits the game by choosing from between several closeups, long shots, replays and cutaways. CBS had 15 different cameras stationed in every part of the stadium at last year's Super Bowl alone. Someone has to choose between all those alternative views of the action and it certainly isn't the viewer who turns the lever (unless of course he/she changes channels):

> Through the electronic eye we have become accustomed to specific segments of athletic performances being isolated, blown up, slowed down, repeated and otherwise detached from the overall sports configuration. (12)

Brien Williams[13] analyzed the third quarter coverage of six different NFL football telecasts in 1975 on each of the three major American networks. Among his conclusions were that there were vast similarities between the networks' coverage. All three tended to present the action of the game "in terms of individual performances rather than team efforts."[14] 29 per cent of all the shots recorded were individual closeups. Aside from this focus on individuals, Williams also found that the media

> — disregards the stadium event (those activities that take place off the playing field) except for infrequent shots of the crowd, cheerleaders, mascots or banners and signs. However for a live spectator at a sports event, the stadium event is more likely to be in focus than the game. Most spectators know more about what the people in front of them are doing, than what the leftfielder is doing.

> — coverage is kaliedoscopic and visually dynamic (someone or something is always moving).

> — focuses attention on the ball and ball carriers to the exclusion of other players and the overall geometry of the game.

> — creates its own time frame. The coverage begins right at the opening kickoff, is a cutaway to a studio during halftime and stoppages in play and ends right after the game. The person watching at the game experiences a different perception of time.

While exposure to media sports is a focussed event, live sports spectating is a diffuse experience.[15] TV does not allow the spectator the freedom to choose the segment of action he wishes to follow. In the stadium there are many different things a spectator can focus on: the flag, the girl in the next row, the quarterback, the coach . . . On TV those decisions are made by someone in a control booth outside the stadium.

In addition, TV viewing is itself a different experience. Watching TV transmissions serves a different function than watching sports events on the spot. It doesn't provide the fan with the high degree of social interaction with other fans and with the nature of the game experience.[16] You lose the whole atmosphere of contact with other people, in front of the TV or at least you interact with a different set of people:

> Watching at home, you lie in your sofa with your beer and your wife next to you and the children on the other side. But if you go to the game, this has another function. You go and you leave your wife, perhaps that's what you like, and you have some friends there. Afterwards you buy a beer. This is pretty different. (17)

Orrin E. Dunlop Jr., a writer for the *New York Times,* lamented in the early days of televised sports:

> The fan does not see the half of what is going on to make baseball the pleasure it has become in 100 years. The televiewer lacks freedom; seeing baseball by TV is too confining, for the novelty would not hold up for more than an hour if it were not for the commentator . . . what would oldtimers think of such a turn of affairs — baseball from a sofa. TV is too safe. There is no ducking the foul ball. (18)

A more recent interpretation emphasizes the point and extends it to other sports:

> TV networks with their zeppelins and zoom lenses, their dreamlike instant replays of colour and violence have changed football watching from a remote college pastime to something very much like voyeurism. No matter how fine his TV reception, no beer and armchair quarterback can hope to see the true game. For all the paraphernalia, the tube rarely shows an overview.[19]

Sapolsky and Zillmann[20] found that the enjoyment of sports on TV is not affected by the social conditions of watching. They showed the United States — Yugoslavia 1976 Olympic basketball final to their subjects under different social conditions (alone, with one other viewer, in a small group and in a large group.) They found, to their surprise, that the social conditions under which the game was watched did not exert an influence on the enjoyment of U.S. baskets. They had expected the enjoyment of U.S. scores, and hence the disappointment with Yugoslavian successes, to increase with group size.[21] Studies have found that this indeed does occur when viewing an event live amongst a partisan crowd. It is harder to cheer for one team if the rest of the stadium is cheering for the home team.

On TV there is no crowd magic or a sense of being out of doors to capture and hold the viewer's attention. There is nothing there but a small, dark screen. That is why a sport, to succeed on TV must be dramatic and must have the qualities "of good theatre"[22] in order to maintain the interest of the viewer. As Chandler[23] points out, not all sports have an equal capacity for this "good theatre." He says football, with its lateral action, patterned series of crises, controlled violence, problem solving, excitement, flamboyance, fast pace and visual power[24] makes it, whereas British soccer does not.

This may influence a TV network's decisions about its choice of sports covered.

And finally, there is the distorting effect on TV Dunlop alluded to, the commentator or announcer. The commentator can serve two functions. He can explain complicated or ambiguous situations and compensate for the imperfections of the visual modality of the medim.[25] It is not in this function that the negative effects usually result. But if the action sags so that the TV viewer's interest declines, the commentator will often try and keep this enthusiasm alive by embellishing the drama of the event to make it more palatable.[26] In this effort to generate excitement, the event is dramatized, suspense is created and tension is sustained where often there is none. It makes the viewer "feel they have participated in an important and fiercely contested event, the fate of which was determined in the climatic closing second of play."[27] With his endless supply of statistics, the commentator may also propagate false standards of achievement. The need to generate excitement often narrows the vision and draws attention to incidents (such as bench-clearing brawls) simply because they are dramatic:

> The rise of the sportscaster as a TV personality, therefore the real star, followed logically from the role these "play by play" and "color" people performed in translating games into mass entertainment. They are now the celebrities, selected primarily for their appearance as much as their knowledge of the game; selected as much for their reputation to event "mix it up" on the screen, to argue with players and managers, and in short to actively participate in the contest they are presenting. Howard Cosell is the best example. They have become the new players. (28)

Therefore what the TV viewer sees is not necessarily what he gets. Despite this, audience figures for sports events on TV are staggering and viewers seem to be happy:

> The new techniques of sports broadcasting seem to enhance the sports experience for the fan rather than diminish it. Although it removes him from the true context of sport, the American spectator seems more than happy to accept the televised sports experience. TV has trained Americans to focus on particular bits of action and ignore, or perhaps never come into meaningful contact with, a live sports experience. Perhaps this explains why many disgruntled fans leave a live game complaining that they could have seen it better on TV.[29]

PARTICIPATION

One area of investigation has been the effect of sports programming on people's engagement in sports. Investigators have sought to determine whether watching sports on TV (or reading about them in newspapers) is a reason for them to take up some sort of sports activity, either as a participant, coach or supporter. Is there a relationship between the use of the mass media on the one hand, and active sports practice on the other hand?

The conventional wisdom in this area is that those who watch don't participate, and those who watch on TV don't go to the stadium to watch in person.[30]

This however seems to be an oversimplification, as is most Reader's Digest wisdom. The literature has identified several possible effects resulting from watching sports on TV.

There may take place a DISPLACEMENT effect, where in order to find time to view sports on TV, a choice must be made to sacrifice some other leisure time activity. According to this view[31] sports activities may be the first to go. There may not be time to watch sports on TV and actually participate, so a choice is made to forego the latter in favor of the former.

Because of the propensity of sports available on TV, a SATURATION EFFECT may take place, whereby all the sports on the tube may tie us down to the passive recipient role, restraining us from active sports interests.[32] We all may become "armchair quarterbacks", with TV socializing us into the role of immobile spectators at home. A regular TV sports viewer may say to himself, "Why should I bother straining myself doing sports when I can get a steady diet of it on TV right in the comfort of my own home?" This view of course overlooks the many benefits to be gained from sports participation, but this could be because the media is guilty of emphasizing the wrong values.

Some analysts have identified a DISASSOCIATION EFFECT. Because the majority of TV sports coverage emphasizes elite sports, top world class athletes competing in beautiful facilities with the best of equipment, it may give some viewers the impression that sports should, and can, only be practiced by a special group of top trained athletes.[33] This may lead to paralyzing inactivity.

> Some individuals might be discouraged by seeing performances of such exceptional standards that they remain inaccessible for the majority of participants. (34)

"I can never do that as well, so why should I bother?" might say the viewer. How many times are we warned by TV commentators not to attempt such feats as we are watching without the proper training or expertise?

Watching such elite competitions such as the Winter Olympics may also create frustrations in viewers, if in certain activities there are no public facilities for people to follow up what they have seen on TV, by taking part in the sports they have watched.[35] "Where am I ever going to get equipment like that or find a field that size?" may be the typical reaction. It is only recently that we have seen an upsurge in the availability of physical recreation facilities so that there are fewer sports that are beyond the limits of most people. But what about watching sports like bobsledding, where there is only a single facility in all of North America to learn, practice and train? If the emphasis of TV sports were more on mass participation sports, it is less likely that either of these two DISASSOCIATION EFFECTS would occur.

But TV sports may not be all that bad. They may have a STIMULATORY EFFECT, whereby watching others do on TV stimulates new interests and activities. "I've never seen that before. It looks like fun. I think I'll try it myself" may be the reaction of some viewers. By stressing the values of top athletes and international competitive sports, TV may motivate us to do it ourselves. It may encourage rather than curtail our active participation and interest in personal physical activity.[36] This has been the aim of campaigns such as Participaction:

> Live TV is the best window shop any sport can have . . . in these days of wide choices in leisure, major sports need TV to keep people interested so that today's viewer becomes tomorrow's spectator or participant.[37]

Finally some writers have suggested a TRANSFER EFFECT where viewers, both young and old, identify themselves with a particular sports hero and try and emulate and copy their achievements. The media portrayal of the stars of sport may do a lot to encourage viewers to take on and participate in sports:

> It is true that the image of champions attracts the young to the practice of sports. (38)

"I want to be like Wayne Gretsky. He says all it takes is practice, so that's what I'll do." A challenging example set by the media and the positive and pleasant emotional rewards that may result, may therefore trigger active personal interest. It may make people take an interest in sports with the hope of sometime equalling the achievements of the sports hero who is the object of their identification.[39] Nor must this phenomenon be limited to youngsters. Many an adult is equally affected.

While there are certainly enough theoretical explanations, there are not very many firm answers. There appears to be evidence to support each of the various effects, which may suggest that there is no hard and fast rule. The effect may depend on the individual viewer. One person may be affected in one or more of the suggested ways. Because media watching is often a very individualistic process (we all do it differently and at varying times), people may, and likely do, react in different ways.

The difficulty of isolating exposure to the media as the sole factor in a subject's level of sports activity may also contribute to the lack of consensus among researchers.

One survey lends support to both the stimulatory and transfer hypotheses. It found that the interest in gymnastic clubs skyrocketed after the world watched Olga Korbut's brilliant performances at the 1972 Olympics.[40] A similar upsurge in the popularity of tennis was recorded in Sweden when Bjorn Borg began to be successful in international tennis competitions. The Wolfenden Report in Great Britain[41] concluded that "watching, as often as not, encourages those who can, to try it for themselves."

Puali Vuolle attempted to measure the effect of TV coverage of the Olympic Games on the sports behavior of the general public of Finland.[42] He measured the sports interest and level of physical activities of a group of subjects three months before, and three months after, the Olympic Games of 1976. He also measured how actively the subjects had followed the media's coverage, and whether the success of the Finnish athletes in the Games had ful-

filled the subjects' expectations. This latter measurement was to ensure that the viewers did not turn off the sports because of a disappointment in the performance of their national representatives.

Vuolle was surprised to find that although his subjects had all followed the games closely, and the success of the athletes had fulfilled or exceeded their expectations, there was no increase in interest.[43] In fact, he found that both active (actual participation) and passive (following sports in the media) interests in sports actually diminished in the second period of investigation (three months after the Games). Vuolle could not isolate the media as the cause of this decrease in activity, but he concluded that it did not have a stimulatory effect. He said the change in climate between the two test periods may have been important in explaining the decrease in active participation (people tend to be more active and interested in sports in the summer and spring.) Nonetheless, the dissociation effect may have been at work, though Vuolle was not able to prove this.

Host, a Norwegian researcher,[44] claims to have disproven the displacement effect. He found that people try and organize their time in order to also have time to do some exercises, even if they are going to sit in front of the TV.[45] He found that it is usually not sports that are sacrificed in order to make way for sports viewing on TV (assuming the viewer does participate in some sort of activity related to sports regardless of his TV watching behavior) but rather other passive leisure pursuits (movies, reading etc.):

> TV sports are not a serious rival for those who regularly engage in sports, but are for those who only on occasion engage in sports. TV would be a rival for those who are inactive. TV could eventually be a retain for putting aside time to devote to active participation. (46)

Host bases his conclusion on the fact that on a Sunday when those surveyed said they viewed four hours of sports on TV, 39 percent also said they engaged in some form of exercise. Several Sundays later when there was no sports on TV, 37 percent still participated. Based on this study, one can picture the beer commercial where the group of guys get together on a Sunday morning for some softball, and then spend the afternoon at home in front of the television, watching football and drinking beer.

Another Norwegian, Kari Fasting, has undertaken an extensive study of the viewing audience of sports programs on Norwegian TV. In *Sports and TV — A Description of Sports Programs on Television As Seen In Relation to Personal Engagement in Sports and Social and Geographic Conditions*[47] he breaks the audience down into categories of sex, occupation, and location. He concluded that those who are generally classified as "passive" watch less sports on TV than those who were "active." Those surveyed with the most personal activity were the ones who watched sports on TV the most. Fasting concludes that

> . . . a high degree of engagement in sports (personally active, member of sports clubs or participant in sports competitions) is characteristic of those who watch almost all sports on TV.

This is true of children and adults . . . there is so far no reason to assume that sports programs on TV have any passivity causing effect with regard to the viewer's own physical activities. (48)

He also found that people watch more often on TV the sport which they themselves practice actively.[49] Fasting also investigated the TV watching habits of the sports viewer — whether they watch sports on TV just because the TV happened to be on (secondary watching) or because out of a genuine interest they actually turned the set on (primary watching). He concluded that the percentage of those who turn on the TV out of particular interest in watching increases systematically with increasing degrees of activity.[50]

Despite Fasting's firm conclusions, he has failed to establish the stimulatory effect, that is, a cause-effect relationship between viewing and participating. He has not identified whether it was this TV watching that actually encouraged these "active" people to take up some form of activity, or discouraged the "passive" group from so doing. While he feels viewing does not cause passivity, he has not established that it actually causes activity. Thus while his work may go far towards disproving the saturation or disassociation effects, it is not as successful in verifying the stimulatory effect. Nonetheless, his results are encouraging.

Van Loon[51] has found that education level is more significant than mass media exposure as a predictor of sports practice.

Perhaps an empirical study might be designed to help clarify matters. One might take two groups of subjects. A control group would be selected that has had no prior access or exposure to the media portrayal of sports, while the experimental group would be given regular, monitored exposure to media events. Then some sort of long term comparison of their engagement in sporting activities could be undertaken to assess the impact of the media. What makes this task difficult though, in our increasingly TV-oriented environment, is finding a representative group of subjects who have had no access, they may, a priori, not be representative of the public at large. We could go up to the North where media access is more limited, but then certain cultural differences might come into play. Perhaps we could compare a group of non-TV exposed Inuit to a group of media-exposed Inuit.

While there is no general agreement on this question, there seems to be at least a tacit accord that sports programs on TV do keep some people away from live sports events and do cause somewhat of a reduction in live attendance at stadia. This has led to much bitterness on the part of some:

The transmission of important sporting events often leads to the emptying of sporting grounds. (52) Television is doing great harm to the game which once ruled the everyday life of so many people in so many British towns not long ago . . . Clubs outside the First Division are desperate for support — as long as TV continues to saturate the public with the cream of the game — we'll be left waiting . . . (53)

For most professional sports owners, it is a matter of weighing losses in attendance against the tremendous revenues brought in by the sale of television broadcasting righfs.

Most of those surveyed by Fasting who said they did not attend sporting activities in person, attributed the availability of the events on TV as the main reason for staying away.[54] But again the cause-effect relationship is not clear; if there had been no access to TV, would those surveyed have still attended in person? It is very easy to say; it is another thing to actually do. His results also do not indicate whether these people had previously attended games in person, but had deserted the practice with the advent of extensive TV coverage.[55]

Later in his research, Fasting gave his subjects the choice of attending a game in person, or viewing it on TV. While most said they would prefer to attend, almost 40 percent said they would prefer the mediated version, indicating that the media do steal at least some spectators. The degree to which those questioned would rather attend in person, was found to increase with their degree of involvement in sport.[56] The more involved sportsperson prefers to watch in person.

Fasting would by no means claim that the media coverage was the sole reason for the decision not to attend. A host of other factors have been identified: economic conditions, management, performance of both home and visiting teams, publicity and promotion, employment, kinds of games and scheduling, general population, weather, ticket prices, individual attraction and competition of other sports.[57] But the competition from TV is one that must be considered. This in part explains the NFL rule that a game will not be televised in the city or surrounding area in which it is played, unless it is sold out a specified number of hours before game time. This is a recognition that TV does steal some fans away, and that if there were no televised option to choose from, more fans might decide to take in the game in person.

Availability of TV alternatives will be more of a factor if reinforced by other conditions. For example in pouring rain, a loyal fan might stick it out if he/she knew the game was not being televised. But if it were available in the warmth and dryness of a living room, they might think twice about braving the elements. Minor league sports suffer most from TV because most fans would prefer to watch the best on TV than attend a lower calibre exhibition in person. The same is true of boxing:

In the early 1950's, boxing matches were so common on TV that most fans stopped attending local fights. As former middleweight champion Gene Fullmer put it:
    Television made fans but it also killed boxing. The small clubs couldn't exist anymore and colleges dropped the sport.
Even the fight center of the world, Madison Square Garden suffered greatly . . . The reason for the disparity between increasing numbers of supporters for local clubs are tied to the logic of television. (58)

The competition from TV may not be as fierce now:

What is clear however is that the public are more difficult to satisfy than previously. They have a very keen sense for elite sport. But no true sports enthusiast would trade their presence at a sports event for a TV screen if they sense good sport. (59)

56

EFFECT OF TV VIOLENCE ON PERSONAL AGGRESSIVE BEHAVIOUR

While professional sports team owners may be concerned with the effect of TV on the attendance at their events, and while the influence of TV on people's sporting habits are an issue of major consequence to recreational authorities, work is also underway on another, perhaps more vital area — the possible effects of continued exposure to aggressiveness in TV sports on our individual behavior. Researchers are trying to establish whether there is a connection between the pro and anti-social models that sports on TV present, and the high level of aggressiveness and violence that now seems to be dominating North American sports.

This research is not taking place in isolation; the look at the effects of TV sports violence is part of an overall effort to assess the impact of all TV violence in general. This has been the subject of many Canadian and American federal, provincial and state commissions, most of whom have started with the premise that TV violence does have harmful effects.[60] Though there are many theories on this relationship, there have been two in particular which have dominated the appraisal of TV violence in general, and hence TV sports as well:

1) LEARNED THEORY — aggressiveness and violence begets aggressiveness and violence. (61) This theory holds that TV violence provokes the imitation of violent behavior. This was used as a defence in a murder trial in Florida. The lawyer maintained that the defendent could not control his behaviour as the result of the subliminal effect of watching aggression and violence on TV. (62) While the capacity to aggress is inherited, the ability to do so is learned and must be brought out. "You have to learn violence somewhere . . . and TV is where."

2) CATHARTIC THEORY — viewing of aggressiveness and violence on TV reduces the need to be aggressive and violent. TV violence acts as an agent of relief, a way of channelling innate aggressiveness and destructiveness into socially acceptable channels (63) (TV channels). This theory holds that people take out their hostilities and frustrations watching others beat themselves silly, instead of actually doing it themselves.

As in the case of participation, there is again no consensus among scholars.

Michael Smith of York University[64] makes a strong case that one of the social determinants for youth hockey violence is the mass media portrayal of the professional game. He admits it certainly is not the sole factor, but says it is one of the important ones. Sportscasters seem to highlight and comment approvingly on the more sensational aspects of the game (because of the need of the TV medium to be dramatic and visually dynamic) — dirty tactics and fighting — and not on the sportsmanlike behavior.[65]

One need only pick up any daily newspaper or watch a TV newscast or telecast for evidence of Smith's point. In the papers there is often a big picture of a fight along with an attention-grabbing headline ("Fight mars . . . " "Record number of penalties handed out . . . ") There may be articles overtly or covertly glorifying tough guys or reminiscences about famous brawls of the past. Smith excerpts the following from a magazine article about Gordie Howe on the occasion of his fiftieth birthday:

It's not as if he plays some Caspar Milquetoast game, shying from the corners, relying on speed and finesse. He is of the generation that disdains the now accepted protection of helmets and he was never one to skate from a fight. After he was nearly killed from a check into the boards by Ted Kennedy of Toronto Maple Leafs — a skull operation saved his life — he returned as one who knows it's better to give than to receive, that retribution is best administered quickly and decisively. With Lou Fontinato of New York Rangers he participated in what many regard as the greatest hockey fight in the history of the NHL. Fontinato was the terror of the league then, intimidating everyone, pulverizing even the mighty Rocket Richard, but Howe destroyed him in that fight. He broke his nose, splattered Fontinato's blood over his face and jersey and Fontinato was never as terrifying again. (66)

If this is the treatment a player like Howe receives, one can just imagine what some of the real badboys get.

TV is no different. On an actual broadcast, there are always slow motion replays of key punches. The announcer's voice is always several octaves higher as he describes a fight. TV highlights of a previous night's games will almost always include footage of an "exciting" fight in between clips of the various scoring plays. The spotlight is usually focussed on fouls, fights, combat, brutality and even lawsuits, but rarely on competence. While the TV newscaster may shake his head in disgust when showing these fights, and may say some sort of punitive action should be taken, just by showing these fights again he is giving them unneeded exposure. While the media may not overtly condone such violence, the simple act of constantly exposing it and highlighting it helps to glorify it, and convey the idea that fighting and the like are acceptable, even desirable forms of behavior.[67]

Some suggest that to suppress this violence and not report would be just as improper as the current overplaying of it.[68] Why? What were to happen if everytime a fight broke out, the TV cameras shifted elsewhere, to a studio shot or commercial for example? What if newspapers would not report on fights and TV newscasters did not highlight them? Surely without this tacit approval from the media, violence in the game would decrease. While the media has not created these problems, their simple act of reporting, and sometimes over-reporting of fights, serves to enhance and condone it and keep it "alive in the national consciousness."[69] Many analysts claim the role of the media in society is merely to act as a mirror of society.[70] It can be argued that in this case, this mirror magnifies and distorts.

Comisky, Bryant and Zillman[71] provide an even more frightening example of the role of the media in condoning or legitimizing violence. They conclude that no one person in sports is more able to produce this distortion than the announcer. In their study "Commentary as a Substitute for Action," they examined two segments of videotape from an actual broadcast of an NHL game — one that contained very rough play and another with normal, not as rough play. They then showed the segments to a group of subjects, both with the commentator's audio commentary, and without it.

In analyzing the commentary on the play, the researchers found that in the normal hockey (video showing no roughness) the commentator convinces us that we're witnessing rough and tough hockey at its best, when in fact the visuals showed little roughness. However, when the play was visually rough, the announcer said little and let the video carry the action. Thus roughness in action and commentary were negatively related.[72] As a result, the viewer may see fierce, rough competition and aggressiveness when it doesn't really exists because of the sportcaster's play-by-play embellishment. We seem to get caught up in the way the sportcaster interprets the game and we apparently allow ourselves to be influenced by this suggestion of violence.[73] We see more violence than there actually is:

> Commentary can substantially alter the viewer's perception of the play in a sports event . . . perception of play as being rough is largely a function of the commentary . . . the commentary is more important to us than the visually present action of the game. (74)

Our dependence on commentary is epitomized by those fans who bring a pocket radio to the baseball park to get the play-by-play account of the game they are viewing right before their eyes. The poor audience reaction to an experiment by NBC earlier this year of a telecast of a football game without an announcer, again emphasizes the results of Comisky's study. People were lost without the commentator to point them in the right direction of the game.

People watching the NBC game simply didn't enjoy it as much without the little voice talking to them. Comisky and his associates got the same results in their study. They found that not only does dramatic commentary affect the perception of play, but it apparently is also a factor in the enjoyment of the game as well.[75] They found that differences in the rating of entertainment value (how much the viewers said they enjoyed the action) was related to the degree the play was perceived to be rough, and even violent. Since ultimately that is determined by the commentator and not the visual action, they found that the announcer controls the enjoyment of the game. If he calls the game a yawner, so will most of the viewers. Monkey see, monkey do:

> The enjoyment of televised sports events closely corresponds to the perception of roughness, enthusiasm and even violence in play. Since the perception of all these aspects is strongly influenced by broadcast commentary, it appears that to a high degree, the sportscaster is a critical contributor to the spectator's appreciation of televised sports. (76)

Not surprisingly, the segment that was perceived to be the most entertaining was that featuring normal play with commentary presenting it as rough. This emphasizes Smith's point of reference of the media as an agent of legitimation for sports violence.

Newspapers may also act in the same way with a hidden bias towards violence. In 1959, Tannenbaum and Noah [77] studied what they termed "sportugese," the use of verbs in newspaper sports stories. They studied the use of verbs in reporting on high school basketball games in Illinois and Missouri and found

84 different verbs were used ("The sports writer releases a barrage of exact words . . . "[78]). Predominant among them were those with violent connotations, such as "annihilated," "whipped," "crushed" and "defeated." Teams with names like Indians and Braves scalped their opponents; Eagles and Hawks soared to victory; Lions and Tigers clawed out victories; Rough Riders roped up their opponents and Stampeders galloped off. These terms help create a mental set of images for the reader that are vividly violent. Although this study was done in 1959 and was limited to high school basketball in Illinois and Missouri, one only has to pick up the *Citizen* or *Globe and Mail* . . . or unfortunately *The Charlatan* for similar examples.

Despite the implications of these studies, none of them really measures the direct impact of this glorification or enhancement of sports violence on our behavior. SIR/CAR (University of Windsor Sports Institute for Research/Change Agent Research) attempted to do that in a study for the Ontario Royal Commission on Violence in the Communications Industry (Lamarsh Commission).

They studied[79] a group of 259 lacrosse, hockey and baseball players ranging in age from 7 to 17 (thus including sports with allowable body contact and non-contact sports as well), their aggressiveness and sport behavior and their use of the media in watching sports. They used the following criteria to determine pro- and anti-social behavior models:

1) cooperation or lack of cooperation towards team members and opponents,
2) verbal aggression towards team members, opponents, coaches, referees or umpires,
3) acts of direct physical violence,
4) team cohesion displayed by encouragement and reassurance for performance,
5) team alienation displayed by disapproval and condemnation of performance,
6) sportsmanlike or unsportsmanlike behavior,
7) attitudes of players being friendly or hostile,
8) positive or negative reinforcement by coaches,
9) crowd reactions as supportive or non-supportive.[80]

They studied the players either at the beginning of their respective seasons or in leagues focussing on instruction as opposed to competition because it was felt that aggression and violence increased as the season progressed towards the playoffs and tournaments.[81] In assessing the normal TV viewing habits of these youngsters, they found that the hockey players generally watched more aggressive sports on TV than did the baseball players (hockey being a rougher sport generally than baseball, the link may be there). Generally though, "of the sports shows shown regularly on television, those classified as aggressive athletic activities are viewed most consistently."[82]

They also did research in an experimental setting, where they observed the subjects, then exposed them to pro- or anti-social models and then reobserved them. They also used a control group with similar observation periods, but neutral or no TV treatment. They concluded that exposure to anti-social programming had less effect on the subjects' behavior than did exposure to pro-social patterns. They said individual factors were probably what determined the reaction to viewing both anti- and pro-social media:

> Exposure to anti-social media does not necessarily lead to increased levels of aggressive behaviour among children and youth participants in organized sports. Neither the experimentally provided anti-social media inputs nor the aggressiveness of programs watched by the children at home show any strong and consistent relationships with aggressive behavior on the playing field. In general, a rather strong relationship did appear between exposure to pro-social media models and high levels of pro-social behavior. Symbolic aggression (non-verbal and verbal) also tended to be higher among those groups whose viewing was relatively pro-social. (83)

In other words, they found that it wasn't that the bad was so bad; just that the good was good. In light of these findings, the SIR/CAR study recommended action in this direction to emphasize pro-social coverage:

> — increased coverage of events which emphasize playing for fun and recreation (school and amateur sports) rather than the "winning at all costs" ethic. They suggested sports such as tennis and golf where, aside from Ilie Nastase, pro-social behavior is common and part of the customs of the game. Win or lose, players shake hands at the end of a match.
>
> — increased coverage of events which convey the distinction in goals, methods and means between amateur and professional sports.
>
> — increased pro-social input in events where the sport itself does not usually provide such pro-social models. For example, they suggested showing more NFL players helping crippled children and charitable organizations during commercial breaks of a football game where the players usually are hitting each other. (84)

The authors of the study identified several limitations with the study. It focussed only on group behavior, those youngsters who played on teams in organized leagues. This in itself may pose some biases. No control group of youngsters who did not participate in organized sports was included to see how they would react to media input of both types. As well, the study only focussed on short term effects of media input; the real effect may in fact come in the long term. As well, the study found very different patterns in the behavior of the baseball players as a group and the lacrosse and hockey enthusiasts. At times they were "diametrically opposed"[85] to each other. They suggested that the characteristics involved in choosing to participate in one sport over another may influence reactions to media input.

The SIR/CAR study also investigated adults' views on the effect of TV sports on their children.[86] They found that most were sceptical that aggressiveness in sports on TV led to increased aggressiveness in amateur sports. When asked "Does athletic aggression on TV affect you or your family?" 50 percent responded "not at all or little," 20 percent said "somewhat" and only 16 percent said "a great deal."[87] Women, Quebeckers and older people were generally the most concerned. Younger people were the most sceptical of any connection.

While the direct effects of TV sports violence may not be clear, there is agreement that the conditions for learning violent and rough techniques in sports (especially hockey) are ideal on TV. What better place to learn the dirty tactics of the game than from the media? It is as if TV hockey presents a showcase on how to play rough. While intermission features may teach youngsters how to shoot or pass, the actual game itself teaches them how to check or elbow. In a sample of 604 Toronto minor and junior professional players,[88] 56 percent said they had learned how to hit another player illegally by watching pro hockey on TV. Among the things the educational medium of TV served to teach:

> I learned spearing and butt-ending.
> Sneaky elbows, little choppy slashes Bobby Clarke style.
> I've seen it and use it: when you check a guy elbow him.
> If you get in a corner you can hook or spear him without getting caught.
> Butt-end, spearing, slashing, high sticking, elbows in the head. (89)

The violence one sees in TV sports is real-life violence. It is really two people hitting each other. There are no stuntmen, like in movies. The punches and checks are for real:

> Boxing, football, hockey, car racing and demolition derbies are only exceeded in real-world violence by the news reports of homocides, hijackings or modern "limited wars." (90)

Because of this reality, there has been the fear expressed by some[91] that continued exposure may desensitize viewers to other violence in the real world. Such analysts try and explain cases such as passerbys in New York doing nothing to help mugging victims, on the continued exposure to media violence. The SIR/CAR study found no evidence to support this hypothesis:

> Regarding the issue of desensitization to violence as a result of observation of anti-social media, our results do not provide conclusive answers. The indication is . . . exposure to anti-social media tends to sensitize rather than desensitize viewers. Those players exposed to anti-social inputs had a slight tendency to see more aggression than did those who had been exposed to pro-social inputs. The trends observed were not statistically reliable. It should be noted that these findings do not necessarily indicate that the same sensitization would be present in the observations of an actual aggressive act.[92]

OTHER EFFECTS
CREATION OF MEDIA PERSONALITIES

In their search for vivid material, certain performers may be brought on by the media unwisely. Coverage of that athlete may be premature and out of proportion to that player's ability or potential.[93] Exposure may become more important than performance. The failure to live up to the heightened expectations of the media may lead to disillusionment and suffering, both for the player and those around him.

This syndrome brings to mind the case of Wayne Gretsky, the 20-year-old millionaire superstar for the Edmonton Oilers. There is no doubt in anyone's mind that he is an unbelievable hockey player. But when hockey announcers call him "The Great Gretsky" everytime he touches the puck (or "the incredible one," "Mr. Hockey"[94]) one has to wonder what will happen to the youngster if he ever loses his touch and becomes just another player. Will he be able to live up to the expectations the media has created for him? Will he be able to meet the superlatives the media has designed for him? One has to wonder what will happen to players like Gretsky then; how they themselves feel about themselves and the treatment they receive from the media.

Today Magazine recently featured a young hockey player which it labelled the "Next Wayne Gretsky." It told of the antagonism other parents felt towards him and his parents, and how when he met his idol in person, Gretsky told him "to get yourself an agent." Again one has to wonder what will happen to this boy if he never does pan out, if he loses his ability and never reaches professional hockey stardom. What if he later decides he would rather study law than play pro hockey? Will he be allowed this choice, given all the media buildup of his hockey ability? The premature media hype he has received now could ruin him psychologically for life. He may have a heightened conception of himself and failure to live up to it could spell trouble.

SOCIALIZATION OF POLITICAL VALUES

Prisula [95] found that heavy viewing of televised sports was the best predictor of conservative values among high school students. The more the students watched TV sports, the more they were found to possess values defined as "conservative": beliefs in authoritarianism strict regulation of activity, emphasis on property, male domination and ethnocentricity.[96] The viewers learn these values by a process of affective, implicit socialization. The process is not direct. But TV sports coverage implicity imparts certain realities about law and order, fairness and the rule of law (the referee is always right).

> The values which are most often stressed by coaches, players and sportcasters, most of whom were once athletes themselves, epitomize the business values of competition, personal success and corporate obedience to the managerial hierarchy. In general, coaches stress the importance of end-states and of the characteristically masculine values of aggressiveness, dominance and assertion . . . They are apt to believe that their own philosophies and strategies are responsible for the success of their teams, and there is thus conveyed a spirit of rugged individualism. There is little room in this schema for also-rans, liberals or females. (97)

As observers of televised sports, viewers are constantly exposed to these values. TV sports therefore act as an agent of socialization of these political values.

THE HIDDEN CURRICULUM IN TV SPORTS

Mass media coverage of sports also conveys particular social values about the purpose and nature of participation in sports. The media creates a mental model on which viewers may judge their own sports participation. This has been labelled the "competitive achieving ethic."

In the media we are constantly exposed to a series of catch phrases which are repeated ad infinitum:

> I will demand a commitment to excellence and to victory, and that is what life is all about — Vince Lombardi
> Winning isn't everything, it's the only thing — Lombardi
> To play this game you must have fire in you, and there is nothing that stokes fire like hate — Lombardi
> Every time you win, you're reborn; when you lose, you die a little — George Allen
> The winner is the only individual who is truly alive — Allen
> In this country, when you finish second, no one knows your name — Frank McGuire
> Defeat is worse than death because you have to live with defeat — Bill Musselman
> Nice guys finish last — Leo Durocher[98]

The media makes out most sports as zero-sum games[99] — there is always a winner or a loser. Winning, or OUTCOME, always seems to be emphasized as the major goal, rather than participation or PROCESS. Participation by itself is made to seem as insufficient as an end.[100] From reading the sports pages or watching Wide World of Sports, it seems participation can only be motivated by extrinsic rewards, in most cases the defeat of one's opponents. They usually overlook, or at least de-emphasize, style and process or the values of competition. Rarely does the media attach importance to the aesthetics of sport, except for diving and figure skating. Even in these sports, there is an undue emphasis on scores and standings:

> Without the awareness of the intrinsic psychological and social implications of a sport to its participants, sports writing has little value. Within the words of many newspapers is a harsh, combative and brutal representation of sport in which the true strength is ironically passed by. (101)

As viewers, we are exposed to these values, whether we recognize them or not. Goldstein and Bredemeier[102] say it therefore effects the values we attach to participation in our own sporting endeavours. The effects of participation, say the researchers, would be socially different if the process of play were seen as paramount:

> Emphasizing extrinsic motivations for participation leads to the derogation of opponents and undermines subsequent personal satisfactions which might otherwise accompany sports participation. Intrinsic personal motivation and satisfaction to engage in sports is diminished . . . there is an inherent notion that losers are in some fundamental sense inferior to winners and that opponents should be regarded as foes . . . the assumption that sport is a mirror of society in which only the most physically fit survive. (103)

Because we watch sports on TV, Goldstein and Bredemeier say we too attach inherent meaning to victory and see participation itself insufficient as an end. It is not psychologically rewarding and should not be taken for its own sake but as a means to some other objective. They say this has also led to a professionalization and formalization of amateur sports.

> Whereas fifteen years ago, pre-high school youngsters could play hockey, soccer or football only in pickup games, today there are dozens of junior leagues replete with uniforms, sponsors, coaches and all the trappings of their more senior counterparts, including the emphasis on outcome rather than process. It seems fair to say that sports in which youngsters participate are modelled on professional leagues, made familiar by television exposure. (104)

They say the effects of televised sports are therefore "dysfunctional."

But there really is a lot more to sports than simply winning or breaking records. Further, there must surely be sports enthusiasts who do not pursue sports necessarily to see a team win, but are interested in the skills of the game and their execution. Certainly the media must be denying these interests.[105]

Without necessarily defending it, it is easy to see why the media does place the emphasis on outcome and not on process. Many broadcasters (although fewer print reporters) are themselves former athletes who were brought up in this system of winning at all costs. Furthermore, by the nature of sports reporting, they come into contact with this "winning or else" environment on a daily basis — in the locker room after the game, on the field, even at the dinner table or in the bars. They must be responsive to the desires and needs of the sports industry. They themselves are part of this jock mentality and it seems only natural that they pass it on. It is natural, but not correct.

As well, reporting scores is simply easier for the sports writer or broadcaster. It is much simpler to emphasize the most objective aspect of the competition, the outcome and score, than it is to subjectively evaluate a performance . . . as good or bad. As well, focussing on wins and losses makes it easy to arrive at quick conclusions for success and failure after the fact.[106] "They lost because of poor pitching" is easier to conclude than "it was a good performance because . . . "

ELITE SPORTS

The range of sports covered by the media is limited to certain "elite spectacle" sports. In Canada we get a steady diet of hockey, football and baseball. Unless there is a special event, a big tournament or great scandal, other sports rarely get covered to the same extent. A content analysis done last year on the Ottawa *Citizen* and the now-defunct *Journal* found that in the given week of analysis, items dealing with professional sports made up 50 percent of all sports stories.[107]

This is not a problem unique to Canadian, or even North American media. Britons complain that all they are given is soccer and cricket (and only top-level Division I soccer at that). A study of Norwegian TV found that 95 percent of all sports programs featured competitive sports.[108] Thus while the individual sports may vary, the general pattern across the globe does not. There is rarely extensive coverage of events featuring non-competitive, cooperative behavior, where the emphasis is equally on fun.[109] The 1975 PreOlympic Seminar on "The Role of Television in Promoting the Practice of Sport" concluded that:

> Comparatively little time on TV is devoted to sport for all and to educational sport programs. Such programs as there are, are frequently broadcast at inconvenient times for the viewers concerned and at low audience hours. (110)

There are several exercise classes which currently air on TV at the ungodly hours of 6:00 a.m.

M. Marie Hart[111] in a study of the content of sports magazines, found that often sports fads take precedence in content for short periods of time.

There can be several explanations, but few justifications, for these biases. They may be explained by the fact, as discussed earlier, that not all sports are suited to the medium of television:

> Although leisure sport is becoming more and more important in our society, it has great disadvantages on TV — lack of topicality, lack of popular personalities, lack of the fascination inherent in the unusual, and above all, lack of excitement . . . lack of sensational suspense and identification with well known sports personalities. (112)

A BBC report on sports on television[113] emphasizes this point:

> BBC TV sets out to cover all sports which are *televisable* and has even had a shot at one time or another at covering a number of sports such as rifle shooting which are recognized as presenting formidable difficulties in television terms. (114)

There may be economic reasons as well. Because of limited resources, television is forced to report on, and examine, only exceptional events. This is obvious in all fields — news, art, politics and sport. Therefore we learn only of exceptional events, the deeds of the elite, champions who break records. There may be yet another dollars and cents reason:

> Noncompetitive games, or competitive games where the emphasis is equally on end-states and processes are relatively ignored by the Western mass media, despite the growing movement towards process orientation in American physical education . . . An emphasis on intrinsic satisfactions associated with participation in sport might be economically detrimental to the networks, for people might then conclude that they would enjoy themselves more by playing tennis than by watching Connors and Borg playing tennis on TV. (115)

There are plenty of journalistic adages which insists that public demand is what must ultimately govern the content and style of the media. People like to identify themselves with the elite.[116] Media moguls will claim, as they do in other areas of programming, that they are merely giving viewers what they want. They point to audience ratings for top sports programs. There are studies, such as a Polish one[117] which confirmed that Polish viewers prefer the passive consumption of record seeking sport. Those surveyed preferred it, and showed minimal interest in "programmes whose function was to popularize physical culture rather than transmit a sports event."[118] In Greece the programs which have the highest audience figures show the best in top performance sport.[119]

This however is countered by the "which came first, the chicken or the egg" argument. How can you know, it is asked, what the viewers and readers want if all they are given is competitive sport? They have no alternative but to like it. Perhaps they flock to such programs because that is all they are offered in terms of viable alternatives. The debate drags on. As in so many areas, there are no right answers . . . yet.

CONCLUSION

The tone of this paper should not be interpreted as all bad — that the media portrayal of sports only implies negative consequences. As we have seen, TV sports may actually be an impetus, rather than a hindrance, to active sports participation on the part of viewers. The media have also brought sport to the attention of many who have themselves never participated in such activities. They may help to keep sports on the forefront of people's minds as a topic of constant interest. After a big hockey game, almost everyone riding the bus to work next morning has one thing on his/her mind. "Did you see that game on TV last night? Did you read that article about. . ." This may be healthy both for sports in particular, and society in general. The media may act as a social facilitator. In international competitions , the media in its coverage of sporting events may promote international understanding[120] and foster goodwill between nations. It has been through media coverage of USSR-Canada hockey series that Canadians have come to learn more about life in the Soviet Union. As well, the media may help stimulate interest in sports which had previously not attracted widespread support. There has been a noticeable upsurge, for example, in the popularity of soccer in Quebec since the arrival of the North American Soccer League franchise, the "Montreal Manic."

But what does clearly emerge from this survey of the literature, are some serious doubts about the hidden effects of sports in the media. There emerge serious questions about the hidden curriculum in TV sports, the excessive violence and the concentration on a few select sports. These questions and doubts are so serious because the media has such an all-pervasive effect on us.

The fact that these effects are probably not the result of deliberate policy by those who control the media is no relief. Just because there is no conscious intent to deceive the public does not make matters any better. Rather it may make matters worse, because these effects are hidden and cannot be seen. Perhaps if they were more overt, and we realized they were there, we could control them with greater ease.

Nor should the fact that no direct causal link has been found to implicate the media, lessen our concerns. Mass media analysts no longer view the media acting like a "hypodermic needle" or "bullet" in which it has a message to deliver which is directly injected into the viewer's head with no intermediary stages. The media do not work in isolation, but rather hand in hand with a large number of other societal factors. The media cannot be divorced from the rest of life. The values and value systems in a society will almost certainly be reflected in the media. Therefore attempts to isolate a direct media-behavior cause-effect relationship will likely continue to prove fruitless unless attention is also paid to these other influences in the equation. A more complicated model must be developed that includes other elements besides the media and the viewer.

What has also emerged is evidence of a dearth of knowledge in this area:

> There is a dearth of scientific analysis about the fundamental relationship between sport and mass media. It is therefore urgent that research be undertaken in this field, using, e.g., the methods of the psycho-social sciences and of the science of communications. (121)

> However, while the socially significant area of sports/athletics pervades the life of a vast majority of children on the Canadian/American scene, we do not know the effect of televised sports/athletics upon youth since . . . this deplorable lack of empirically based data . . . Recommend study/research commissioned and conducted by the television industry as well as government commissions on the Canadian-American scene to show the high level of concern regarding the actual and potential effects of TV upon North American children/youth . . . It is the opinion of the principal investigators and those of us involved in SIR/CAR research studies in the areas of children/youth sports that a concerned and beleaguered media would welcome some suggestions and readily join in a partnership to achieve this goal. (122)

One can only echo this plea, together with a hope that it take place soon. Because our dependence on the media continues to grow, our children are more and more growing up on a lifestyle weaned on TV, and TV watching is now our greatest leisure-time pursuit (it has passed active sports participation), we should take heed from a recent TV commercial: "The Time Is Now, Before It's Too Late." The time has come to reckon with these concerns. It will be in the interest, in the long run, of all the parties concerned — certainly the viewers, sports organizations, scientists and even the media themselves — to take a fast hard look at the question of sports and the media and attempt to answer at least some of these questions and allay some of these fears.

Perhaps a conference or commission could be organized with all the parties involved. Perhaps the media could be persuaded to commit itself to give the conference good media exposure. This would allow the public at large to know what was taking place. It could itself begin to question certain media practices. All too often, conferences are held behind closed doors and the results shared by a select few. But this is a problem that directly affects every one of us TV addicts, sport enthusiasts and "arm chair quarterbacks."

ENDNOTES

[1]*The Role of TV In Promoting The Practice of Sports*, Pre-Olympic Seminar, Greece, October 1975, Proceedings p. 145.

[2]Eldon Snyder and Elmer Spreitzer, *Social Aspects of Sports*, New Jersey, 1978, p. 122.

[3]Terrence Monnington et al, *British Sports in The Seveties: An Assessment of Some Factors Affecting Sports and Physical Recreation in Great Britain*, Warwick, 1975, p. 17.

[4]BBC General Advisory Council, *Coverage of Sport on BBC TV*, London, 1974, p. 5.

[5]G.H. Sage, ed. *Sports and American Society — Selected Readings*, Mass., 1974, p. 27.

[6]David L. Altheide and Robert P. Snow, "Sports vs. The Mass Media," unpublished paper presented to the American Sociological Association 72nd Annual Meeting, Chicago, 1977, p. 5.

[7]Harry Edwards, *Revolt of the Black Athlete*, New York, 1970, p. 167.

[8]Ibid.

[9]Paul Comisky et al, "Commentary As A Substitute For Action," *Journal of Communications*. 27(3), 1977, p. 150.

[10]Brien Williams, "The Structure of Televised Football," *Journal of Communications,* 27(3) 1977, p. 133.

[11]Ibid.

[12]Snyder and Spreitzer, p. 127.

[13]Williams op. cit. pp. 133-139.

[14]Ibid. p. 134.

[15]Susan Birrell and John W. Loy, "Media Sport: Hot and Cool," *International Review of Sport Sociology,* 1(14) 1979, p. 12.

[16]Ibid.

[17]Role of TV, p. 116.

[18]Ibid.

[19]Ibid.

[20]B.S. Sapolsky and D. Zillman, "Enjoyment of a Televised Sport Contest Under Different Social Conditions of Viewing," *Perceptual and Motor Skills,* 46(1) 1978, p. 29.

[21]Ibid.

[22]J.H. Chandler, "American Pro Football in Britain," *Journal of Popular Culture,* 12(1) 1978, p. 149.

[23]Ibid.

[24]Ibid.

[25]Role of TV, p. 112.

[26]Comisky, p. 150.

[27]Ibid.

[28]Altheide, p. 14.

[29]Birrell, p. 13.

[30]R.H. Prisula, "Televised Sports and Political Values," *Journal of Communications,* 29(1) 1979, p. 96.

[31]British Sports, p. 19.

[32]Pauoli Vuolle, "Influence of Mass Media on People's Sports Behavior in Finland," *7th International Seminar on Sports and Leisure.* Warsaw, 1977, p. 54.

[33]British Sports, p. 19.

[34]Role of TV, p. 171.

[35]Ibid.

[36]British Sports, p. 16.

[37]Ibid.

[38]Role of TV, p. 168.

[39]Vuolle, p. 53.

[40]Role of TV, p. 155.

[41]quoted in British Sports, p. 29.

[42]Vuolle, p. 50.

[43]Ibid.

[44]quoted in Kari Fasting, "Women, Sport and TV," paper presented to the First International Conference on Women in Sports, London, 1979, p. 12.

[45]Ibid.

[46]Role of TV, p. 117.

[47]Kari Fasting, *A Description of Sports on Television As Seen In Relation To Personal Engagement In Sports and Social and Geographic Conditions,* Oslo, 1977.

[48]Ibid.

[49]Ibid.

[50]Ibid.

[51]Lamon Famaey and F. Van Loon, "Mass Media and Sports Practice," *International Review of Sports Sociology,* 4(13) 1978, p. 37.

[52]Hans Gmelin, quoted in Role of TV, p. 82.

[53]British Sports, p. 34.

[54]Fasting, p. 20.

[55]Ibid.

[56]Ibid.

[57]Role of TV, p. 115.

[58]Altheide, p. 8.

[59]Rolf Rusta quoted in Fasting, p. 59.

[60]Dick Moriarty, "Violence/Aggression in Sports/Athletics on TV," *New Zealand Journal of Health, Physical Education and Recreation,* 2(2) 1978, p. 45.

[61]Dick Moriarty, "SIR/CAR Studies of TV and Youth Sports," *International Journal of Sports Psychology,* 10(2) 1979, p. 122.

[62]Violence/Aggression, p. 42.

[63]Ibid.

[64]Michael Smith, "Social Determinanats of Violence in Hockey — A Review," *Canadian Journal of Applied Sports Sciences,* 4(1) 1975, pp. 72-86.

[65]British Sports, p. 27.

[66]Ibid. p. 77.

[67]Ibid.

[68]BBC, p. 6.

[69]*Hooliganism in British Football,* ch. 6.

[70]Ibid.

[71]Comisky, op. cit.

[72]Ibid. p. 151.

[73]Ibid.

[74]Ibid.

[75]Ibid. p. 153.

[76]Ibid.

[77]quoted in Hilmi Ibrahim, *Sport and Society: An Introduction to Sociology of Sport,* California, 1975.

[78]Ibid.

[79]SIR/CAR, p. 124.

[80]Ibid. p. 123.

[81]Ibid. p. 124.

[82]Ibid. p. 125.

[83]Ibid.

[84]Ibid.

[85]Ibid. p. 123.

[86]Dick Moriarty and L. Leduc, "Skeptical Public Favors Self-Regulation of Aggressiveness in Televised Sports," *CAHPER Journal,* 45(1) Sept./Oct. 1978, p. 38.

[87]Ibid.

[88]Smith, p. 77.

[89]Ibid.

[90]Violence/Aggression, p. 46.

[91]Ibid.

[92]SIR/CAR, p. 126.

[93]BBC, p. 7.

[94]*Hockey Night in Canada,* Edmonton Oilers vs. New York Islanders, Fri. April 24, 1981.

[95]Prisula, p. 97.

[96]Ibid.

[97]Jeffrey H. Goldstein and Brenda Bredemeier, "Socialization — Some Basic Issues," *Journal of Communications,* 27(3) 1977, p. 154.

[98]Ibid. p. 158.

[99]Ibid. p. 155.

[100]Ibid.

[101]Harry Edwards, *Sociology of Sport,* Illinois, 1973.

[102]Goldstein, p. 156.

[103]Ibid.

[104]Ibid. p. 156.

[105]D.S. Butt, *Psychology of Sport: The Behavior, Motivation, Personality and Performance of Athletes,* New York, 1976.

[106]Goldstein, p. 159.

[107]Stephen Bindman, "The Ottawa Citizen and Journal Sports-Reading Audience: Who They Are, What They Want, What They get and Why," unpublished paper, Carleton University, 1980, p. 32.

[108]Fasting op. cit.

[109]Role of TV, p. 123.

[110]Ibid. p. 171.

[112]Ibid. p. 115.

[113]BBC, op. cit.

[114]Ibid. p. 5.

[115]Goldstein, p. 155.

[116]Role of TV, p. 29.

[117]Witold Rekawski, "Popularization of Mass Physical Culture by Television Sports Programmes," *7th International Seminar on Sports and Leisure*, Warsaw, 1977.

[118]Ibid.

[119]Role of TV, p. 123.

[120]Peter McIntosh, "Mass Media: Friends or Foes in Sports," *Quest*. June, 1974, p. 43.

[121]SIR/CAR, p. 122, 129.

BIBLIOGRAPHY

Altheide, David L. and Robert P. Snow, "Sports vs. The Mass Media," unpublished paper presented to the American Sociological association 72nd Annual Meeting, Chicago, 1977.

BBC General Advisory Council. *Coverage of Sport on BBC TV*, London: BBC, Dec. 1974.

Bindman, Stephen. "The Ottawa Citizen and Journal Sports-Reading Audience: Who They Are, What They Want, What They Get and Why," unpublished paper, Carleton University, Ottawa, 1980.

Birrell, Susan and John W. Loy. "Media Sport: Hot and Cool," *International Review of Sport Sociology*, 1(14) 1979.

Butt, D.S. *Psychology of Sport: The Behavior, Motivation, Personality and Performance of Athletes*, New York: Van Nostrand Reinhold, 1976.

Chandler, J.H. "American Pro Football in Britain,"*Journal of Popular Culture*, 12(1), 1978.

Comisky, Paul et al. "Commentary As A Substitute For Action," *Journal of Communications*. 27(3), 1977.

Edwards, Harry and V. Rackages. "Dynamics of Violence in American Sports: Some Promising Structural and Social Considerations," *Journal of Sports and Social Issues*, 1(2) Summer/Fall, 1977.

Edwards, Harry. *Revolt of the Black Athlete*. New York: Free Press, 1970.

_____ *Sociology of Sport*, Holmwood, Illinois: Dorsey Press, 1973.

Famaey, Lamon and F. Van Loon. "Mass Media and Sports Practice," *International Review of Sports Sociology*, 4(13), 1978.

Fasting, Kari. *A Description of Sports Programs on Television As Seen In Relation To Personal Engagement in Sports and Social and Geographic Conditions*, Oslo: Norwegian Confederation of Sports, 1977.

_____ *Sport and TV — Research on the Interrelationship*, Oslo: Norwegian Confederation of Sports, 1978.

_____ "Women, Sport and TV," paper presented to the First International Conference on Women in Sports, London, 1979.

Goldstein, Jeffrey H. and Brenda Bredmeier. "Socialization — Some Basic Issues," *Journal of Communications*, 27(3), 1977.

Hendry, L.B. and D.J. Thornton. "Games Theory, Television and Leisure — Adolescent Study," *British Journal of Social and Clinical Psychology*, 15, Nov. 1976.

Hooliganism in British Football.

Ibrahim, Hilml. *Sport and Society: An Introduction to Sociology of Sport*, California: Hwong Publishing Co. Inc. 1975.

Milshteyn, U.A. and S.V. Molchanov. "The Shaping of Public Opinion Regarding Sport By The Mass Media As A Factor Promoting International Understanding," *International Review of Sports Sociology*, 11(3) 1976.

McIntosh, Peter. "Mass Media: Friends or Foes in Sports," *Quest*, June, 1974.

Monnington, Terrence et al. *British Sports In The Seventies: An Assessment of Some Factors Affecting Sports and Physical Recreation in Great Britain*, Warwick: University of Warwick, 1975.

Moriarty, Dick. "SIR/CAR Studies of TV and Youth Sports," *International Journal of Sports Psychology*, 10(2) 1979.

_____ and L. Leduc. "Skeptical Public Favors Self-Regulation of Aggressiveness in Televised Sports," *CAHPER Journal*, 45(1) Sept./Oct. 1978.

_____ "Violence/Aggression in Sports/Athletics on TV," *New Zealand Journal of Health, Physical Education and Recreation*, 2(2) 1978.

Prisula, R.H. "Televised Sports and Political Values," *Journal of Communications*, 29(1) 1979.

Real, M.R. "Super Bowl: Mythic Spectacle," in Yiannakis A. et al. *Sports Sociology: Contemporary Themes*, Dubuque: Kendall-Hunt, 1976.

Rekawski, Witold. "Popularization of Mass Physical Culture by Television Sports Programmes," *7th International Seminar on Sports and Leisure*, Warsaw, 1977.

Sage, G.H. (ed). *Sports and American Society — Selected Readings*, Reading, Mass.: Addison-Wesley, 1974.

Sapolsky, B.S. and D. Zillman. "Enjoyment of a Televised Sport Contest Under Different Social Conditions of Viewing," *Perceptual and Motor Skills*, 46(1), 1978.

Smith, Michael. "Social Determinants of Violence in Hockey — A Review," *Canadian Journal of Applied Sports Sciences*, 4(1) 1975.

Smith, G.J. "Use of the Mass Media for Sports Information as a Function of Age, Sex and Socioeconomic Status," in *Proceedings — International Congress on Physical Activity Sciences*, Quebec City, 1976.

Snyder, Eldon and Elmer Spreitzer. *Social Aspects of Sports*, New Jersey, 1978.

The Role of TV in Promoting the Practice of Sports, Pre-Olympic Seminar, Greece, October 1975.

Whitson, D. "Authority, Legitimation and the Distribution of Knowledge," *Journal of Psycho-Social Aspects*, 3 April 1977.

Williams, Brien. "The Structure of Televised Football," *Journal of Communications*, 27(3) 1977.

Vuolle, Pauoli. "Influence of Mass Media on People's Sports Behavior in Finland," *7th International Seminar on Sports and Leisure*, Warsaw, 1977.

SPORT FOR THE DISABLED

David Beaver (Canada)

In the constant struggle to prove or gain superiority, one over the other, East-West have raced to conquer outer space, harness nuclear energy, increase food production and a myriad of other aspects affecting the totality of life. The application of psychology to sport is no exception, as attested to by a recently published article of Dr. William P. Morgan appearing in *Psychology Today*. The author explains the Russians' ambitious program in sport psychology, noting that coaches can utilize test results for both selecting and training top athletes to become better prepared mentally for future competitions. Naturally, with such a secret weapon as "sport psychology" in the hands of such an athletic rival as Russia, Western coaches will demand more from their own sports psychologists so as not to fall behind their Soviet counterparts. Thus, a continued growth in sport psychology is assured.

But where, in light of all the relatively recent interest in sport psychology does the disabled community fit in? Practically nowhere! A very few studies directed at psychological parameters have been done on spinally paralyzed wheelchair athletes and one or two on extraordinary blind distance runners. Even here the surface has barely been scratched. The population is relatively small and the conclusions are not really generalizable to the vast population of the disabled; and, certainly there is a dearth of research from sports psychologists as it might pertain to the disabled.

In the United States alone, according to recent census figures, there exists a disabled subpopulation that numbers between 31 and 37 million persons. This number will rise dramatically as medical knowledge increases and life expectancies are raised well above the 67-72 years of age currently averaged by men and women within the general population. It has only been since World War II, especially since the Korean War, that medical science has increasingly become aware of the handicapped and has generally developed a greater humanistic appreciation for the disabled and the quality of life available to them.

Naturally, the Kennedy Family's personal and political interest with those who are mentally handicapped has contributed to an increased public awareness in this sector. Long before it became fashionable to jump upon the special education band wagon, Dr. Charles Buell of the United States, was championing the need to develop sound physical education practices for the blind and visually impaired. Likewise, a vast number of those traumatized by accident or disease, resulting in amputeeism and/or spinal paralysis may be thankful for the life work of Sir Ludwig Guttmann and the research conducted at the famous National Spinal Injuries Center housed in the Stoke-Mandeville Hospital at Aylesbury, England.

The Attitude of Society in General Towards the Disabled

It is an undeniable fact that for centuries the prevailing attitude of society towards the disabled was basically negative, one of neglect, even treating those that were handicapped as outcasts of society. The fathers of disabled Greek or Roman children were instructed to take their child's life or to abandon it to the fates of the elements so as not to have the child become a drain upon the group and lessen its chances of survival. Even today one of the largest nations of the world refuses to admit that it has any disabled people.

Up to and even following the Second World War, with its millions of disabled people, many handicapped persons were hidden by their relatives, shut inside and kept from the eyes of the community in a conscious effort to avoid bringing shame or discredit to the family. This was especially true in those cases where the disability was misunderstood. Fortunately, time and attitudes change. Yet only recently has public opinion altered significantly to recognize the advantage to the community as well as to the disabled individual of utilizing the residual talents of such people and in fitting them into the mainstream of the community, both economically and socially.

The introduction of modern concepts of rehabilitation has been responsible for much of the attitudinal change within the medical profession. State and governmental legislation has focused societal attention upon heretofore discriminatory practices inflicted upon the disabled, thus enabling greater access to facilities, employment, recreational and sporting activities by all disabled persons. However, there is still room for improvement. We must enlighten society as a whole to the point of view that the disabled person does not want sympathy or pity, but empathy.

I am reminded here of the often repeated words of advice that I give every semester to my students, "Make every effort to see the individual at first, foremost and always a HUMAN BEING, then note the individual's particular handicapping condition!" Until one is able to accomplish this feat, psychologically all the individual sees is the disability and in turn any potential relationship between the two is doomed. To empathize is to project one's own being, one's own personality into that of another; in this case, that of the disabled, thus acquiring a truer understanding and/or a fuller comprehension of what the problem or the individual's life is all about.

The Attitude of the Disabled Towards Society

At the outset, I must point out that there is a marked psychological difference for individuals who are born with or acquire very early in life, their handicaps, than for those who have received an injury or disease which results in a severe disability, such as blindness, deafness, the loss of limbs and/or partial or complete paralysis of the nervous system. Obviously, the later such trauma occurs in one's life, the greater is the initial psychological adjustment that correspondingly must be made.

Affliction upsets to a greater or lesser degree the precision, the efficiency and most assuredly, the appearance of normal motor patterns of the body. Abnormal patterns are characterized by paralysis, weakness, disjointedness, stiffness, change in speech and coordination. Psychologically, the sudden realization and/or awareness of the changed body self image causes greater internal tension and helps to create a withdrawal function in the individual from his/her surrounding world. In turn, this makes social contact with one's able-bodied counterparts more difficult, sometimes even impossible.

There is an old socio-psychological axiom that is applicable here; "What you think of me I will think of me, and what I think of me I will believe." If the individual is regarded as out of the ordinary by society and is continually confronted with embarrassment, the disabled person's attitude may deteriorate to the point of inferiority characterized by shyness, anxiety, a loss of self-confidence and dignity which ultimately might be expressed as self pity, in anti-social behavior, even self-imposed withdrawal.

The Significance of Sport for the Disabled

In 1976 I was priviledged to be a coach with the first national team of blind athletes to compete for the United States during the Olympiad for the Physically Disabled in Toronto, Canada. This event has left an indelible imprint on my total being. I believe that there is no better way to proceed in this section than to recap a situation that was later to be immortalized in the Olympic Book. It deals with a conversation that was overheard at the opening ceremonies between two young men in athletic dress and standing very close to the passing procession of athletes. With tears in his eyes, one young man turned to the other saying:

> You know, this is what the Olympics is all about. Look at those athletes' faces! They are so happy to be here and to be able to march and compete in front of a cheering crowd that really loves them. I do not feel it was quite like this in Montreal, or Munich for that matter. They are clapping for each other and smiling and singing to each other. I wish I had half the dedication and spirit that each and every one of these athletes must have in order to train and compete at such a high level. Just think what they'd be capable of doing if they were physically normal. It's beautiful just watching these people loving life the way they are right now. It would sure be nice if some other people could follow their example. You know, I'm going to go and try and get a few autographs . . .

The person speaking had just finished representing Canada at the Olympic Games in Montreal and the person he was addressing who nodded agreement was in Munich to represent his country in the 1972 Olympics. Unknowingly, these two had paid a tribute to all disabled athletes. Later, all of us connected with the Toronto Olympiad were to realize for ourselves that we were seeing fully actualized human beings in all their magnificent glory.

I am reminded also of a U.S. Chaplain's words:

> The first thing I thought about when I stepped on that mine in Viet Nam was, and this was before I even hit the ground, how in the world am I gonna be able to play golf? I found a way to play golf and ski. I don't know of anything that's been more enlightening, joyful and uplifting to me than sports. There's only one place to go, and that's up.

The Chaplain lost his leg in Viet Nam.

In March 1972, eleven amputees, all Viet Nam veterans from Walter Reed General Hospital participated in a skiing rehabilitation program at Steamboat Springs, Colorado. According to the army surgeon's report following the experience, the surgeon related:

> Physically, every one of the eleven patients demonstrated definitive, objective improvement in strength, range of motion and/or decreased pain . . . all within 2½ days of this training. These individual improvements were apparent to my own observation and were substantiated by others in the group, as well. Every patient, regardless of disability, showed definite physical improvement and demonstrated commendable proficiency and progress in the early techniques of downhill skiing, traversing and turning, regardless of prior pre and/or post amputation ski experience. Mentally, there was a singular and very obvious change noted in every individual . . . changes in general deportment, carriage and general attitude. Specifically, the initial outward signs of minor dependency and psychological defense could be seen in all of these men in varying degrees, some significantly obvious and disconcerting. The various signs of dependent regression secondary to such severe traumatization and lengthy hospitalization were manifest, initially, by poor carriage, adolescent behaviorism, unfounded boisterousness, defensive solitude and selfishness, the high pitched whining voice of the spoiled child, a lack of humor, fixations on disability, inability to perform at true physical capability and dependency on medication. It must be emphasized that these men manifested varying degrees of the above psychological traits, some to a minimal degree, others to greater, none beyond the limits of proper deportment or social acceptance but all definitely involved. This does not mean any failure of previous rehabilitative efforts but rather some residual but significant problems. By the end of the 2½ days of training, every one of the above psychological traits was observed to have completely resolved or abated by a significant margin. Every individual looked upon the training as an extremely important personal experience. Every individual began to show a much more evident "can do" attitude with an outward renewed sense of independence and confidence. The whining reverted to the deeper voice of a young man, self-interest turned to interest in others, brashness and boisterous behavior melted to sincere and adult dialogue. Every man voiced a deep expression of gratitude for the experience and each witnessed meeting a challenge of great importance of a very personal nature.

It is not difficult to understand from all I have said why sport is of even greater significance for the well-being of the disabled than it is for the able-bodied. Broadly speaking, the aims of sport embody the same principles for the disabled that they do for the able-bodied. Additionally, however, sport is of immense therapeutic value and can play an integral role in the physical, psychological and social rehabilitation of the disabled.

In a society where physical fitness, athletic prowess and good appearance are continually promoted, sport and physical recreation give the disabled person a chance to compete, be appropriately acknowledged and admired. Being able to participate in a sporting activity at an equal proficiency level with one's peer group counterpart and/or at an equal or nearly equal proficiency level with one's able-bodied counterparts provides the disabled person with a key element to his/her overall psyche and well-being. This ability to compete, first from within one's self, then amongst one's peers and later perhaps with the able-bodied athlete, goes a long way in compensating for a disabling condition. Thus, the aims of sport for the disabled can be generalized from three significant standpoints: Sport as a Curative Force; Sport as a Recreational and Psychological Force; and, Sport as a means of Social Re-integration.

Sport as a Curative Force

As a part of the "team" approach for the remediation of the body or an afflicted part of the body, sport represents a natural form of remedial exercise and is complimentary to the efforts of the physical therapist and/or those of the occupational therapist. It is invaluable to the successful restoration of the disabled person's physical fitness, especially those aspects relating to one's muscular strength, muscular endurance, flexibility, balance, cardio-vascular efficiency, kinesthetic coordination, etc.

Certainly the most formidable obstacle to the newly disabled is the ever present aura of physical fatigue, a predominant symptom in the early recovery program. By increasing the physical fitness and efficiency of the body, fatigue looms less and less an obstacle to the disabled.

Sport as a Recreational and Psychological Force

While never to be thought of as a panacea for all problems connected with a disability, sport has a deeper meaning than merely being a form of physiotherapy. Exercises, even when set to music, become old very fast. The great advantage of sport over formal exercise lies in its recreational values. To be re-created, rejuvenated is the goal of recreation. Thus, an additional motivator for the disabled person, sport rekindles the inate passion for playful activity while providing a substantial release for tension through experiencing sheer joy and pleasure of life.

There is little doubt in my mind that much of the benefit of sport as a rehabilitative tool would be lost if the individual did not perceive pleasure from the total experience at this stage. Thus, participation as opposed to competition is the key; it is of paramount importance.

Obviously then, sport as a means of recreation becomes an important factor in promoting or re-establishing the psychological equilibrium which enables the disabled individual to gradually come to terms with his/her physical defect. Remember our earlier axiom, "What you think of me I will think of me and what I think of me I will believe!" Thus, the aims of sport through its recreational approach are to instill in the disabled an active and forceful mind, self-confidence, self-dignity, self-discipline, a competitive spirit, team mindeness. In short, to contribute to all those psychological attributes essential to a well rounded personality, an improved life style and good mental health. Therefore, the oft repeated slogan, "Mens sana in copore sano, a sound mind in a sound body" holds just as much importance for the disabled as it originally signified for the able-bodied.

Sport as a Means of Social Re-integration

Finally, the aim of sport with the disabled is to help to restore the individual's contact with the real world. In this context sport is utilized as a facilitator to accelerate individual social re-integration amongst the able-bodied.

Involvement on a regular basis with an occupational therapy department and eventually in sheltered workshops or similar settings are generally recognized as viable steps in the total treatment of those individuals with physical disabilities. In addition to increasing efficient motor-patterns within the real world of a working experience, such involvements counteract boredom and help to restore an active mind, a sense of self-worth, of self-confidence and dignity. Obviously, the aims of sport for the disabled are indeed identical with those sought through occupational therapy and gainful employment. However, they greatly magnify them.

Remember, until the trauma point occured in the individual's life, a "normal" life style was an accepted fact. However, following the trauma point the effect of the trauma was felt psychologically. Involvement in a carefully selected sports program can be of tremendous help towards insuring proper recovery and the avoidance of depression.

Naturally, initial *participation* must be chosen wisely so as to allow for small *successes,* which will compound to make larger successes. Success felt deep within one's self prompts an *interaction* with others. First, as a form of narrative sharing, then in physical demonstration and eventually in competition. Once the latter has occured a *tenacity* to improve sets in as the individual becomes motivated to excell. The physiological benefits are immediate. Psychologically, realization of the thrills and fulfillment available through the medium of sport comes slowly, until, as for all athletes, the individual achieves a proficiency within a particular sport. Gradually, he/she realizes the intrinsic values of participation.

On the other hand, without increased impetus of the sports experience, the individual could just as easily have followed the route of *fear, dependency,* becoming *isolated* from others, and subsequently withdrawing from the environmental setting. Finally, this avenue would lead to mental *depression* and a self-concept of *failure*. Such an individual falls victim to a willed self-helplessness, which once ingrained becomes extremely hard to reverse.

Naturally, one would expect those of the medical profession to be strong advocates of sport as a viable tool for the rehabilitation and the successful social re-integration of their patients. However, this seemingly is not the case at the moment. During the 1980 Olympic Games for the Disabled, staged in Arnhem, Holland, a poll was taken among the athletes from 18 countries. The result showed that only 8 percent had been urged by a doctor to take up sports. In 54 percent of the cases the impetus had been derived from friends, spouses or relatives. Seventy five (75) percent averred that sport had improved their social contact with non-handicapped people, while 92 percent claimed to take full part in a normal social life. Additionally, 74 percent held jobs and 18 percent were students. Thus, it would seem, in summary, whenever a doctor or other interested party urges a handicapped person to take up sports as an integral part of his/her life, not only has the individual promoted the health of the disabled person, but also helped his/her integration into society.

In closing, I am reminded of a recent conversation with the executive director for the National Association of Sports for Cerebral Palsy in the United States, who stated:

> In summary, sports is a challenge to the individual. Our philosophy is for athletes to earn; one must train and struggle. Through struggle and training one grows. This growth is immeasurable and of course, is reflected differently through each athlete. For some individuals, who have adjusted to their disability, sport is sport. For the majority of our athletes, sport is more than sport, it is a positive therapeutic activity that leads to the overall growth of the individual.

Can there be any doubt? Sport is obviously a means by which the disabled person enhances the quality of his/her everyday lifestyle; I think not!

Reaction — John McKay (Canada)

David's interest appears to be in the general field of sports psychology and how it relates to the disabled. My interest is in a fairly specific area — in the development of skill with the disabled and how we can enable disabled performance to become skillful.

Skill sets the boundary on how much sport can help people with disabilities. From David's presentation I am left with the impression that all one has to do is make sport available for people with disabilities and almost everything would be fine. I guess that is the one thing I don't completely agree with in David's presentation. I think that's not even half way. Simply making facilities available and allowing individuals with disabilities to participate is not enough.

I think that government sports for the disabled can have value only if the individuals are given the opportunity to achieve some degree of skill. I've identified skill performance as the ability to achieve on a regular basis some self determined goals in an effective and efficient manner. If the individual cannot set his or her own goals as to the amount of performance of the sporting activity he might be involved with, I don't think that he has skill; or, if he cannot achieve these goals then he hasn't attained the skill; and if he cannot attain these goals on a regular basis or consistently, I don't believe that he has attained skills in that sporting activity.

What are some of the things that we can do to allow disabled people to achieve skill? Disabled people are no different than non-disabled performers in the acquisition of skill; for example, you have to practice, and you have to have the opportunity to recognize and make corrections in the areas of performance. In Halifax, my home town, I frequently ride back and forth to the University on a bus. The bus goes by numerous outdoor playgrounds, basketball courts and volleyball courts. I've lived In Halifax for six years and I've seen one disabled athlete shooting baskets once in that whole six year period. I've ridden on this bus perhaps 500 times.

It's very difficult for disabled athletes to utilize certain facilities. They're not easily accessible to these individuals. Allowances should be made for these individuals to practice when they can, when they have an opportunity of shooting baskets or swimming or doing whatever activity they want to. One hour a week in a rink to play hockey is pretty much a standard time, and if you happened to be busy at that time, you don't get an opportunity to play hockey.

The second point that I would like to mention is that we have to allow disabled performers to recognize and to make corrections in their areas, again to become more skillful performers. In the case of unsighted athletes, it is impossible for these individuals to recognize the errors visually. We have to build into their sport activities some means of providing an artificial form of feedback, here in an auditory sense. Or, we have to have coaches who can act as eyes for the individuals who are performing, providing information back to them in the form of knowledge of results about the outcome: What happened to the object that they threw or the object which they kicked?

My experience as a coach with the Montreal disabled athletes was quite rewarding, but I quite quickly reached a stage when I just could not come up with any suggestions about what they could do with their wheelchairs to make them more effective basketball players. This has suggested to me that perhaps disabled performers themselves may become the best coaches. These individuals, in the future, will be experienced wheelchair athletes themselves. They are the individuals who have experienced the sporting activity. They are the individuals who can relate directly with the athletes themselves.

There are a couple of last points that I would like to make. I think that there is perhaps a major difference in the method of performance of disabled athletes who have achieved a disability later in life, compared to individuals who have sustained it quite early in life. It has been suggested that there is a tremendous traumatic effect for those whose disability occurs later in life. But from an athletic standpoint, there appears to be some advantage for the disabled athlete if the disability occurs later. In Halifax, there was an unsighted runner who set a world record in running for the unsighted. He has recently taken up skiing, an activity he was involved with up until about the age of 10. He was on Canada's Blind Ski Team. He believes that it wouldn't have been possible for him to develop the necessary skill had he not had this previous experience as a sighted performer. Such gifted athletes could be utilized more to teach and coach those who have been disabled since birth.

One of the advantages of sport for the disabled is that it can force individuals to deal with more than one thing at once. I've done some work with individuals who are attempting to learn to control devices such as arms that have electric motors in them. These individuals are very accurate in their movements as long as they are looking at the device that they are controlling. I have suggested to some of these individuals that they should consider taking up a sport which will allow them to control their device while they are concentrating on something else. What they have to do now is to stop whatever they are doing, and look at this device they have to control. Sport, I think, is an ideal activity to incorporate into these individuals' lifestyles. I think that the carry-over value of using their special devices while playing sports would be tremendous from an information processing standpoint. Sport allows individuals to interact with the environment in a much more complex manner than normal existence requires. This is good preparation for emergency situations such as getting caught going across a street and the light changes on you and the driver can't see over the hood and starts to go forward. Individuals with a sporting background might be in a better position to process the information and make the correct changes and maybe to get out of the way.

My final point is that sport for the disabled creates stronger needs and expectations in disabled athletes for better supportive equipment, such as faster, more mobile wheelchairs. Thus the "fall out" from sport programs could be better designed devices to aid disabled people in their daily lives outside of sport.

Editors' note: Sports Psychologists fully endorse David Beaver's committment to sport for the disabled, as shown by results below, obtained from a survey of congress delegates.

Fitness, physical recreation, and sport has much to offer the disabled person. There is a great need to —

	% agree
• develop strategies to remove the many psychosocial barriers to participation presently encountered by the disabled population	82.1
• assess the effectiveness of present approaches and design new strategies	83.9
• examine the motivational factors that affect their participation and performance in these activities	87.5

SPORT AND LEISURE IN 2001

Y. Matsuda (Japan)

1. Change in the structure of life time in Japan

It is said that the life time of Japanese will soon be 75 years, 650,000 hours, for men and 80 years, 700,000 hours for women. If we apply to it the Western vacationing system and five day working week etc., we find that the time given to work will be less than 10% of our life time and that to free time increase to over 30%. In a society so amply supplied with free time, the way we spend it becomes very important.

Yet, in spite of this change in the composition of life time in Japan, society is very slow to adapt to this new situation. The education system in particular is still aimed at preparing one for the working hours of a hundred years ago, giving first priority to "reading, writing and arithmetic", with but little care for music, art and sports. However, it is quite plain that the abilities to read, write, and do arithmetic only, are quite inadequate to fill 30% of our lives. Here, music, art and sports should take the lead. This is not to say that the work oriented subjects have lost their significance. On the contrary, they are just as important as ever to support and enrich our economy. But the point is, in the coming age, we need the skill to both work *and* play, or else we shall find ourselves out of work, and also out of leisure.

Looking closer into the 30% free time of Japanese, 22% is spent dozing in front of the TV, 5% in mental leisure activities such as reading, and only 5% in sports activities. Obviously there is a great deal too much napping with the TV. If we add to this the 35% of our life time given to sleep, we would be spending more than half our life sleeping. The Japanese whose free time is employed in such a way may indeed be called semi-"out of leisure"-ers.

In days gone by, the Greek philosopher Aristotle said in his *Nicomachean Ethics,* "we busy ourselves that we may have leisure". Its modern interpretation would be, "we work that we may have leisure", "we work that we may build and enjoy cultured life". But somehow from a certain period, work itself became the object in life, and the moral changed to "we live that we may work". However, in a recent survey on human values carried out by the Leisure Development Centre in 13 countries including U.S.A., West Germany, France, and England, it was found that the Japanese and West Germans among the developed industrial countries still wanted many material things and therefore wished for a high income. The French wanted mental rather than material wealth, and the English and Americans were following suit.

Perhaps we ought not to be unnecessarily anxious about the future, but by the year 2,000 the world population is estimated to increase from the present 4,000 million to 6,000 million, and by 2030 to 10,000 million. If these people were all to aim at and realize a materialistic life, there would be a serious shortage of supplies. As such, we seem to have arrived at an age when we must change our values from a life in quest of materialistic riches to one of mental and cultural affluence. It is indeed very difficult to determine what would be the material standard of living necessary to enable us to enjoy a cultural life, but I believe that at least we in Japan have come to a point when such things must be given serious consideration.

In a country like Japan where the productivity is high, the way to slacken economic growth is to cut down working hours. The resultant increase in free time will be consequently given to leisure activities such as sports, art, learning, travelling, gardening, various do-it-yourself's etc. Public organizations such as the state should be active in providing the facilities necessary to meet the growing demand in this field, while private organizations should be fully aware of the influence leisure services have on the public, and be mindful of their respective responsibilities.

I previously quoted from Aristotle that the Greek word *schole* means leisure, or that which is done during leisure time, a school. Psychiatrist Dr. K. Doi interprets leisure as "ease", i.e. "we work that we may have ease". However, if our desires become boundless into wanting everything and anything, and we work with the sole view of satisfying this wish, we shall be called not only work addicted but, like the nicotinic and the dipsomaniac, one with an uncontrollable craving for "ownership". I am glad that an "ease" period has been included recently in the school curriculum, and can only hope it will be considered in relation to leisure.

2. Sports as a Leisure

What is leisure? This is a very difficult question but here, I would like to make a few observations with reference to Abraham Maslow's "Theory of Human Motivation". Maslow maintained that human motivation evolved from basic needs to cultural needs and divided this hierarchy into 5 levels:

1. Physiological Needs.
   The most basic biological need to stave hunger, thirst and cold.

2. Safety Needs.
   Needs for law and order, limits, stability, protection, regular occupation, freedom from anxiety and chaos.

3. Belongingness and Love Needs.
   The need to love and be loved; the need for friendship, for a place in his group.

4. Esteem Needs.
   The need for self-esteem and recognition from others. The former to be satisfied through exertion, achievement and development of one's abilities etc., the latter through dignity, fame, praise, status etc.

5. Need for Self-actualization.
   After the 4 prior needs have been satisfied comes the need to express oneself, to become actualized in what one is potentially.

According to Maslow's hierarchy, the needs become harder to realize as we go down the list, but the last need for self-actualization is the most important with reference to leisure, as the need itself is the object and goal. Of course there are opportunities for joy, gratification and self-actualization in the prior levels too, but there one's actions are not in themselves the object but a means for other ends. To fulfill the needs for self-actualization, i.e. in the leisure level, one must have the prior needs 1-4 satisfied, and be free from their worries.

Let us look at this in connection with the development of the economic and social systems. In primeval society, running, throwing and jumping were all connected with the work of hunting game. It was not enough to be able to throw a spear a long way; it had to hit its prey bull's-eye. We may say that the greater part of a day's life time was spent to meet the first physiological needs. However, in the agricultural; society, the ways to satisfy the physiological needs have been secured, and the time formerly spent in gratifying this need may be given to meet the second safety needs and third belongingness needs. Here running, throwing, and jumping come to form part of festive and ceremonial activities. In the industrial society the time spent for the first 3 needs are further reduced. Running, throwing and jumping become commercial entertainment to form part of mass leisure, and they are used as a means of acquiring status, fame and wealth. Leisure thus becomes big business. And in the fifth, need for self-actualization stage, cultural activities are released from the economic and industrial systems, for here it becomes more and more difficult to harmonize the various needs of the individual with the standardized systems. However this last stage has yet to be realized, and is but an optimistic conjecture. I know it is not easy for such a society to come true, but I sincerely hope it will.

Thus, when we correlate the evolution in the socio-economic system with the life time given to the human needs, we can see quite clearly the human activities, for example, of running, jumping and throwing released from work, from feudalism, and from commercialism, to become a sports activity in itself the object and the goal. What counts is the human side of sports, the enjoyment of the quality of sports.

Similar observations may be made not only with regard to sports but also to music, art, gardening, survival art, craft, travelling, reading etc. The free time in our life which will soon increase to 30% will be allotted not only to sports but to all kinds of leisure activities. Thus sports, or art or music, as a leisure is but one aspect of this varied world.

5. Quality Sports and The Age of Secondary Culture

In days gone by, Takeo Kuwabara, professor emeritus of Kyoto University, greatly provoked the haiku poets by observing that "Haiku is a secondary art. Such (i.e. writing haiku) is a suitable pastime for the aged and the bedridden to kill time. But can such a diversion be considered an art worthy of the devotion, heart and soul, of the modern man? Is it not a misuse of the language? If one must use the word 'art', I would call modern haiku a 'secondary art', to be set apart from the other arts." I.e. haiku is not an art, and if so, one of lower rank with the prefix "secondary" attached to it. However, the interesting part of it is that the great haiku poet Kyoshi Takahama just let it pass with the observation, "Whatever the criticism, everybody's enjoying it, so what if it is secondary art? It's fine with me!"

No doubt what he meant was that if an art is given social recognition, then so much the better, but why should such a gauge be dragged into what one is doing for one's private enjoyment? Indeed, the current trend is to call first class art, first class culture, that which is given national recognition, acknowledged by the mass media, and which fetches the highest price in the market. We seem to be unsatisfied unless culture itself is evaluated according to its utility and reputation. To those who are motivated by personal preferences and enjoyment, such a tendency appears quite absurd.

This phenomenon of secondary art however, can be seen not only in the world of haiku poetry but also in that of sports, learning, crafts, music, fine arts, literature, etc. We might even borrow Prof. Kuwabara's words and say that it is the dawn of "the Age of Secondary Culture".

It is as yet only at its germination stage, both from the number of people taking part as well as from its standing as a custom. But if we foster the seedlings we Japanese may still be able to transform ourselves from being leisure-poor to leisure-rich. More and more students are joining sports activity groups of their own rather than entering the established college clubs; more and more coterie magazines are going round; more and more amateur musical bands are formed; all of which foretell the coming of a new age. Young people are not carried away by social ratings but are each seeking enjoyment after his own values.

Let us take a closer look at this, for example with regards to sports. If someone came and broke the world record for the 100 metre dash, he deserves praise regardless of race or nationality because it is a great accomplishment on behalf of mankind. Similarly, if a physically handicapped person who took 30 seconds to run the same 100 metres managed one day to cover it in 25 seconds, he also is worthy of praise. To the runner himself the joy is a joy proper, whether it is a world record or a 25 seconds, and it would be futile to debate which is the more meritorious.

Last year in the general Physical Education class, I came across "N" who suffered from severe infantile paralysis. When he first came to university "N" was unable to stand on his own. Fortunately there was Kato, studying for his M.A. on sports physiology, who assisted him to class and in every other possible way. After a month or two, "N" was able to stand and to walk 4 or 5 metres, and after another few months, he could receive a soccer ball and head it back. We rejoiced together that here was the pleasure of moving the body, the joy of a good sweat, in other words the root of sports.

The point I wish to make is that the quality of sports, or as I think we may call it, the pleasure and joy of Quality Sports is to be found not in its social values but in the human values of each individual player, same as in the case of haiku poetry dubbed secondary art.

Leisure in the self-actualization stage is often called a state of mind, a state of meditation, a state of highest mental freedom. Thus quality sports is a state of physical and at the same time of mental satisfaction, to be enjoyed not only by sports champions, but equally by everybody. Encouragement of people's sports, citizen sports, national sports etc. should be in the shape of furthering quality sports, and not in that of looking for potential sports champions.

PARENTS AND COACHES:
NOTES FROM TUTKO'S "SPORT PSYCHING" WORKSHOP

This brief report is based on notes from Tom Tutko's "Sport Psyching" Workshop. Although his main thrust was on how to introduce Sport Psychology to athletes and coaches (See Part IV), I felt that his aside remarks and tangents about parents and coaches should be preserved.

Parents

Little recognition is given to the possible negative impact of some parents in Youth Sport. Parenting in general is very demanding, and often provides very little positive feedback. Since sport provides a public forum, some parents see their child's sport performance as an indirect reflection of their child-rearing practices, and thus, of their own self-worth. Because of their daily self-denials, and sacrifices as parents, and their need for feedback, they over-identify with their child's sport successes and failures. Hence, when their child trips, some parents see the whole family image tumbling down. This kind of parent often becomes a problem spectator at practices and games. He screams at the referees and coaches, and often imposes terrible pressures on his children through unrealistic demands and destructive criticism.

These problems can be avoided by opening communication among league officials, coaches, players, and parents. For example, some leagues have tried to help parents improve their "sport parenting" by organizing a family day picnic prior to the beginning of the seasons. This event makes it possible for all the players in the league and their parents to meet together in a happy, non-pressured atmosphere. League officials and coaches can dialogue with players and parents about their personal expectations for the coming season, and about overall objectives of the sport program. Sometimes respected well-known athletes are invited to the picnic to reinforce what the league is trying to do. During the day each coach can meet parents face-to-face, discuss the program and the individual child, and invite parents to keep in touch about their child's development during the season. The aim has been to try to enlist the support of parents toward furthering the positive general developmental goals of the sport program.

This open approach will usually work with most problem parents. However, there are a few who don't seem to benefit from any kind of appeal. Some youth sport programs have found it necessary, as a last resort, to ban such parents from practices and games.

Coaches

The coach is a very important model in the context of sport for children and youth. This is because the coach shares the fate of the players, when the team loses, the coach is a loser; when the team wins, the coach is a winner. Psychologically, this is a different experience of success and failure than usually occurs between students and teachers in school. The players know that their coach is really "part of the action." Hence, how a coach defines winning and losing, and how he or she responds personally to winning and losing, can have a profound effect on the players. It should be noted in passing that since most participants, young and old, are now seeking self-satisfaction through sport, coaches should redefine winning. The traditional concern for being "#1" should be changed to a concern for how well the players and the team are working toward their potential.

Two overlapping, but distinct coaching orientations are required to satisfy the different developmental needs of children and youth in sport. According to Erikson, children 6 to 12 years are in the stage of industry; they are active and curious. Sport represents to them exciting physical activity doing what others are doing. At this stage players are more interested in the process of sport, the fun and excitement, rather than the products, such as scores, wins and losses, public recognition, and so on. Children at this stage need a positively oriented coach who will ensure that their needs are satisfied, for fun, excitement, and shared activity.

Youth 12 to 18 years, on the other hand, especially those 12 to 14, are in the stage of ego-identity. They are striving to discover who they are, and what life can mean. They are ready for a different kind of sport program. They want to challenge themselves and are looking for performance feedback from the activity, from other players, and from the coach. Their need for adult feedback sometimes becomes obscured behind what appears to be rebelliousness, because their quest for identity and meaning demands that they continually question and challenge everything and everybody around them. The coaching orientation required for youth should combine the positive attitudes of the children's coach, with the following:

(a) a keen sensitivity and respect for individual differences; (b) good judgment for setting challenging yet realistic goals; (c) a thorough knowledge of the sport in order to provide constructive performance feedback; and (d) maturity enough to accept rebelliousness but still maintain firm limits.

EFFECTS OF EXTRINSIC REINFORCEMENTS ON INTRINSIC MOTIVATION IN SPORTS: IMPLICATION FOR COACHES

Robert J. Vallerand (Canada)

This paper presents a personal stand on the use of extrinsic reinforcements in sports based on the literature on intrinsic motivation as well as this author's own research. Sport and physical activity represents activities which are generally engaged in for their own sake. Since intrinsically motivated behaviors are generally defined as those behaviors which are engaged in for their own sake in the absence of external contingencies, it follows that sport and physical activities represent a class of intrinsically motivated behaviors in their own right. As physical educators, we believe that sport can produce several beneficial effects on an individual's quality of life. It is believed that it falls upon the role of the sport psychologist to study the intrinsic motivation of sport participants in order to uncover ways to increase one's enjoyment derived from participation in the activity and consequently help individuals to persist in sports and related areas.

An aspect of intrinsic motivation which has been under much scrutiny recently is the effects material rewards may have upon one's intrinsic motivation. Generally the results of the literature indicate that rewards which are expected, salient, and contingent on participation decrease intrinsic motivation. This effect happens because individuals receiving reward for participation come to perceive the reason for their participation as being the reward and not the activity itself. When no more rewards are available, individuals may leave the activity since the reason for their participation is no longer present. This undermining of intrinsic motivation through the reception of rewards has been termed the overjustification effect.

On the other hand, rewards which are given contingent on high performance levels (e.g. champion scorer) have been found to increase recipients's intrinsic motivation. This latter finding has led sport psychologists to recommend that rewards in sport should be offered contingent on high performance levels. However, Vallerand, Gauvin and Halliwell (1980) have shown that rewards presented contingent on high performance levels provide information of incompetence to all other participants who fail to win the reward, resulting in a decrease of intrinsic motivation relative to those winning the reward. Thus performance-contingent rewards may produce two types of effect on participants intrinsic motivation. It may increase the intrinsic motivation of recepient's rewards as well as decrease the intrinsic motivation of those failing to win such rewards. Since trophy recipients only represent a minority of participants in sport, the use of such rewards may do more harm than "good". It is thus seen that both participation and performance-contingent rewards may have detrimental effects on one's intrinsic motivation. This is the reason why it is suggested that they should not be used anymore in sports.

Another type of reinforcement which is used extensively in sport, and thus which deserves our attention, is verbal feedback of performance. Verbal feedback affects intrinsic motivation through the effect it has on feelings and perceptions of competence. When performance feedback is positive, there should be an increrase in feelings and perceptions of competence leading to an increase of intrinsic motivation. On the other hand, when performance feedback is negative, there should be a decrease in feelings and perceptions of competence leading to a decrease of intrinsic motivation (Deci & Ryan, 1980). Recent studies in the realm of sport and physical activity have provided evidence for this proposition. Vallerand, Reid, and Marisi (1980) showed that positive verbal feedback presented at a fixed ratio (FR:4) increases, while negative verbal feedback presented at the same ratio decreases perceptions of competence as well as the intrinsic motivation of college male subjects toward an intrinsically motivating motor task (stabilometer).

Further, positive verbal feedback may also be presented at a very high rate and still increase intrinsic motivation. In effect, Vallerand and Halliwell (1981) demonstrated that positive verbal feedback presented at different ratio schedules from every fourth trial, to every trial, increase the intrinsic motivation and feelings of competence of male adolescent hockey players toward a hockey-related task. Finally, taking into consideration the finding that positive verbal feedback does not influence the intrinsic motivation of males and females differently (Vallerand & Halliwell, 1980), it appears that its use should be encouraged with both male and female athletes, at the expense of negative verbal feedback and material rewards.

Based on this author's own research as well as the literature on intrinsic motivation, the following implications are proposed:

- The use of material rewards be they participation or performance-contingent should be abandonned.
- Positive verbal feedback should be used by coaches in their interaction with both male and female athletes.
- The use of negative verbal feedback should be kept at a minimum since it decreases one's sense of competence and intrinsic motivation.
- Finally, verbal feedback should be provided more often contingent on effort and not merely contingent on attainment or performance. This type of feedback may be especially important after a loss where the coach can encourage his/her players to look forward to the next game by working harder in practice.

REFERENCES

Deci, E.L. & Ryan, R.M. The empirical exploration of intrinsic motivational processes. In L. Berkowitz (Ed.), *Advances in Experimental Social Psychology*, Vol. 13. New York:

Academic Press, 1980.

Vallerand, R.J., Gauvin, L.I., & Halliwell, W.R. *When you're not good enough: The effect of failing to win a performance-contingent reward on intrinsic motivation.* Paper submitted for publication, 1980.

Vallerand, R.J. & Halliwell, W.R. *Comparative effect of positive verbal feedback on males and females' intrinsic motivation.* Unpublished manuscript, Université de Montréal, 1980.

Vallerand, R.J. & Halliwell, W.R. *Toward an inverted-U relationship between positive verbal feedback and intrinsic motivation.* Paper submitted for publication, 1981.

Vallerand, R.J., Reid, G., & Marisi, D.Q. Effects de reinforcements verbaux et matériels sur la motivation intrinsèque face à une tâche motrice. In C.H. Nadeau et al. (Eds.), *Psychology of motor behaviour and sport — 1979.* Champaign, IL.: Human Kinetics, 1980.

SPECTATORS PROFILES AT SPORTING EVENTS

Hans J. Stollenwerk (West Germany)

Every week hundreds of thousands of spectators go to stadiums and halls to watch sport performances. Speaking of the Federal Republic of Germany, this is mainly valid for football, as one knows, although other kinds of sports equally attract a lot of spectators, such as ice-hockey and tennis.

A considerable discrepancy is, however, to be observed between the lively interest in sports, its social significance and its respective scientific valuation. This is especially valid for the sport spectator.

In order to fill this gap a little, I developed a questionnaire, which I distributed to spectators at football matches, ice-hockey and tennis matches. The obtained figures cover an experience period of four years. These inquiries were made on the basis of comparable studies in the domain of music.

The inquiries about football and ice-hockey were always made at the level of the German top league, the so called "Bundesliga" and those made about tennis at two Grand-Prix-tournaments in Cologne. About 2,500 persons were questioned.

The small amount of previous research concerning the spectator has focussed on juvenile spectators who stick out of the crowd, because of their hooliganism, their extreme outfit with symbols of their team and because of their regular attendance in the stadiums.

This minority is often falsely considered to be *the fans*. Research does not give any consideration to the majority of the association football spectators amongst which can be found a large number of fans in the real sense of the meaning.

But, as shown in my research, only an insignificant minority is made up by fanatic spectators, whilst the majority is emotionally bound to a favourite football or ice-hockey team, that applies even to the older visitors.

On the other hand, the typical behaviour of the fan characterized by collected symbols of his team like stickers, flags, scarves and autographes — diminishes with age. The fan's degree of depression after a defeat of his favourite, correspond to his identification with his team. The older the spectator is the less he becomes emotionally involved.

Both in football and in ice-hockey 90 per cent of the spectators on an average sympathize from the beginning with one team. We see that the neutral spectator is part of an insignificant minority. But, this minority rarely remains neutral during the game.

One half to three quarters of the association football and ice-hockey spectators respectively is normally prepared to demonstrate its affection by applaus and vivid encouragement.

On the other hand, about one half of the association ice-hockey spectators and about two thirds of the association football spectator believe that whistling and booing are appropriate means to disconcert most of the players.

This in mind, one third of the ice-hockey and the football spectators try to disconcert the players of the rival team by such manifestations of disapproval with a view to reduce their efficiency. Speaking of ice-hockey, the goal-keeper is the preferred target for such whistling and booing.

Inspite of being aware of the negative effects of these manifestations of disapproval one of three football spectators occasionally hoots at athletes of his own team.

Spectators, who come quite often with high and even exaggerated expectations to the stadiums, are very quickly annoyed at failures of the athletes.

Players of the "Bundesliga" football team 1. FC Köln describe the effects of such reactions as follows: "Most of us are hampered, because the spectators already start whistling at the first bad shot." — "We are in great fear of our own public and don't believe in ourselves." — "If two or three failures occur and people start whistling, one is somehow hampered and one fears to make a mistake and then quickly shoots the ball to another player, as one has no longer the courage to take any risk."

A decisive difference can be observed here as against the specifications of the association tennis spectators. The investigation of the association tennis spectators was made on the occasion of Grand-Prix-Cups, where national aspects were of secondary importance, because the German players as potential sympathy bearers were quite early withdrawn from competition.

Before the matches started, only one third of the questioned spectators had chosen one player or a double as their personal favourites. In the course of the match another third sides with the one or the other. But 90 per cent of the tennis spectators are ready to reward a good performance by applaus and encouragement and thus support the respective player. The inner compassion of the spectator must be acquired by the player by offering a good performance. One of the reasons why the association tennis spectators are less reready to tie down its sympathy right from the start might be seen in the fact, that most of them are active tennis players themselves. Top performances for them range at a higher level than the orientation of persons toward teams.

The Hungarian player Balazs Taroczy, who often managed to win the sympathy of his public because of his appearance and his playing style, says: "It is a considerable handicap for me, when I have to play in the morning, when only a few spectators are present. I need the large "side-scene" and the full support of the public to show my best."

Though the spectator permanently tries to influence the sport event and the athlete, until now little importance was given to him in the domain of research and in sports psychology practice. We need to do more in this area.

AGGRESSION AMONG SPECTATORS AT SOCCER MATCHES

Hans van der Burg (The Netherlands)

Almost weekly, acts of violence are perpetrated by soccer supporters on and around Dutch soccer fields. These acts of violence may be directed at players, referees, or spectators. Outside the stadiums also there are often acts of violence carried out in the form of damage to buses and trains. Why do sportgoers behave in such an aggressive way? Unfortunately we know all too little about this. In spite of the overwhelming interest in soccer which exists in the world today there is still very little scientific attention devoted to public behavior at soccer matches.

There are two ideas that are still popular which deal with the effect on spectators of seeing soccer matches. In the first place is the supposition, developed by Vinnai (1970), that the sport of soccer is a sop to the public provided by the present political and economic system. That is, *those people who experience dissatisfaction with the social system, diverted from direct resistance to the system by the events at soccer matches.* One comes across the above theory in various forms. It is essential that such people make themselves angry now and then during the match. After the match is over the incentive for aggression is removed. They will be less inclined to behave aggressively in circumstances which have no connection with the sporting event.

On the other hand, it is argued that observation of certain behavior, e.g. aggression, and the positive effect that such behavior has for aggressors can equally lead to the development or the strengthening of aggressive habits whenever people are violent themselves (e.g. Bandura, 1978). Also it is possible that certain players see the use of violence and similar behavior as a positive value. Violence then becomes acceptable behavior in the stadium.

These theories have reference to the effect of violent behavior seen from (violent) sports contests, but offer little insight into the question of which situational factors increase the chances of the development of violent behavior by spectators.

In this paper we occupy ourselves with that question. We attempt to provide an explanation for violent behavior at soccer matches.

We will distinguish between two different groups of factors. In the first place are the factors which have to do with the match itself, or are directly connected with it, such as exciting or unexciting play, winning or losing, and expectations about the end result. In the second place are the circumstances which apply for the spectator when he sees the match, such as the number of other spectators and the presence of supporters of the opposing team. These situational factors will be put successively under discussion with the help of a treatment of relevant literature and my own research on this subject. The research data were obtained by means of analysis of newspaper articles and an experiment. Before we go further into the meaning of the above situational factors we give first a description of the ways in which both research projects were carried out.

Analysis of newspaper reports

Use is made of incidents that were reported in newspaper articles about soccer matches in Dutch professional soccer. The analysis is carried out on newspaper articles which were written in detail about sporting events. The newspapers analysed were De Telegraaf (The Telegraph), Het Parool (The Password), and De Volkskrant (The People's Paper). The style of reporting was not a subject for study. These newspapers are used because of their information value which is relevant to the object of the study. The research period was spread over 8 seasons from 1971-1979. Of the matches during which incidents cropped up a number of particulars were noted and later assessed. Every disturbance reported in the newspaper that was caused by spectators was regarded as an incident and also noted and assessed. Thus, disturbances that were caused by players remained outside our consideration, except when these disturbances involved spectators. Also verbal aggression in the form of provocative chanting and slanging matches was not included in the research. Subject of the research was divergent violent behavior directed against the referee, players or supporters, destruction of property, and the throwing of objects inside and outside the stadium by spectators at soccer matches.

The following aspects of the match served as the independent variables: The result of the match, the score at the moment that the incident took place; the point in time when the incident occurred; which side the aggressors supported; and, finally, the target of aggression.

The experiment

In the experiment we got 112 pupils at LTS (Lower Technical School) level from Amsterdam to see a summary of an English soccer match between the first division teams Queens Park Rangers and Stoke City. The video-tape summary of the match lasted for about 25 minutes and in the last minute Queens Park Rangers scored a goal to win 3-2. A week before the experiment took place a question list was filled in by the potential subjects of the experiment to assess interest in soccer and by means of a series of aggression questions to check beforehand whether or not their aggression level was approximately equal in order to validate the various conditions of the experiment. At the end of the summary of the above match the subjects of the experiment were given a question list in which they were asked their opinion about various aspects of the match. In the experiment 3 experimental conditions were introduced: Group size (6 or 16 persons); Composition (homogenous or heterogenous in terms of team favoured); Winning or Losing.

Conclusion

On the strength of our newspaper analysis and our experimental research, we discovered that situational factors foster anger and aggression among spectators at soccer matches. It has to do with two groups of factors. From the factors which concern the match itself the following are of direct significance: slight strength-difference between the teams, and having your team lose, especially if you expected the team to win are factors related to aggressive incidents. We could not decide with complete certainty whether the number of spectators is of significance or not. Further research will have to show if, in fact, a large number of spectators has a disinhibiting influence or that such an effect is not real and must therefore be ascribed to an illusion on the part of the perceiver of crowd behavior. The presence of supporters of the opposing team seems to be of influence on the degree of anger among spectators. Our research results suggest that this influence is restricted to spectators in close proximity to one another. It is necessary to realize that these last research findings are the result of an experiment from which the results cannot be easily translated in terms of the situation in the stadium. This does not mean that such a restriction in any way invalidates the significance of our rersearch findings. No other research method in my opinion gives such a clear insight into the influence of certain situational factors. We have to realize that supporters who are hostile to one another very often express this hostility in the context of the group and that groups which behave in this way can often influence one another in the way of provocative chanting, showing of denigrating notices, slogans and so forth. Research carried out in the stadium situation would be of great additional significance to these research results.

References

Bandura, A.: "Aggression, a Social Learning Analysis". Prentice-Hall, 1973.

Blumer, H.: "Symbolic Interactionism: Perspective and Method". Prentice-Hall, 1969.

Deutsch, M.: "The effects of Cooperation and Competition Upon Group Processes". In: D. Cartwright and A. Zander (eds) "Group Dynamics". Evanston, 1953.

Goldstein, J.H. and Arms, R.L.: "Effects of Observing Athletic Contests". In: Sociometry 34, 1971.

Schulz, J., Weber, R.: "Bedingungen agressiver Handlungen von zfussballzuschauern". In: Sportwissenschaft Jhrg. 9-3, 1979.

Sherif, M.: "Intergroup Relations and Leadership". New York, 1962.

Turner, R. and Killian, L. (eds): "Collective Behavior". Prentice-Hall, 1973.

Vinnai, G.: "Fussballsport als Ideologie". Frankfurt, 1970.

Zimbardo, P.G.: "The Human Choice; Individuation Reason and Order versus Deindividuation, Impulse and Chaos". In: Arnold, W.J. and Levine, D. (eds) "Nebraska Symposium on Motivation", Vol. 17. Lincoln, 1969.

VIOLENCE DANS LE SPORT

Bernard Morelle (France)

Dans les milieux sportifs comme dans le public, les explosions de violence sont dénoncées comme le témoignage de malaises nouveaux difficiles à cerner. De nombreuses interprétations sont données qui ont chacune leur valeur. Dans le domaine sportif qui est celui d'un affrontement constitué en spectacle où l'aggressivité est privilégiée, cette montée de la violence est particulièrement sensible dès lors que les procédures habituelles (arbitrage, sanctions, . . .) ne suffisent plus à la contenir. Peut-être faudrait-il alors examiner ce qui se passe ailleurs que sur le stade et en particulier dans l'environnement sportif?

Revenons d'abord sur les notions de violence et d'aggressivité: Le terme de violence est descriptif. Il rend compte du sentiment subjectif d'un sujet ou d'un groupe au niveau des conventions sociales: la violence d'un match de boxe serait inconcevable sur un terrain de basket. La violence verbale dépend des conventions de lieu, du moment, des interlocuteurs.

S'il est vrai qu'une certaine frustration suscite l'aggressivité, son accroissement engendre l'inhibition et croyant évacuer le mal on n'arrache que son symptôme. Il paraît donc essentiel de tenir compte des manifestations de violence: c'est qu'il se passe quelque chose qui est d'autant plus importante que le signal a été dramatisé publiquement. Que les responsables sportifs en soient convaincus peut dèjà constituer une étape importante vers une évolution. Si en plus, l'effort en vue d'une amélioration pouvait passer par une étude sérieuse en vue d'une meilleure organisation plutôt que de se contenter de sanctions souvent superficielles, une autre étape essentielle serait franchie.

AGGRESSION CONTROLS IN SPORT

Larry M. Leith (Canada)

Man has more than a detached, scholarly interest in aggression. His difficulty in living harmoniously with nature and with his fellow men now threatens all forms of life, and his own future may depend on his ability to understand and control aggressive behaviour (Johnson, 1972:1).

Man indeed does have more than a "detached, scholarly interest in aggression". All too often, however, we have been content to explain aggressive behavior in terms of philosophical theories or hypothetical inner constructs. While this approach has aided our basic understanding of aggressive behaviour, and served a heuristic function at best, it has done little to provide workable solutions towards curbing goal aggression in the sporting environment. Our complacency in this regard has done little in bettering our sporting environments.

Concept Definition

For the purposes of this paper, athletic aggression will refer to those acts performed in an attempt to injure another participant, either physically, verbally, or symbolically. These acts are performed outside the rules, as ends in themselves. Goal aggression is not to be confused with instrumental aggression, which is performed as a means towards an end, and not as an end itself.

Purposes of the Paper

1. To point out the futility in philosophical or nonmeasurable approaches to aggression control;
2. To delineate the major contingencies of reinforcement for aggressive behavior operative within the sporting environment;

3. To provide some practical implications and suggest guidelines for aggression control in sport.

Types of Reinforcers Operative Within The Sporting Environment

Rushall and Siedentop (1972:50) have defined the term reinforcer as "a stimulus which occurs as an event after the performance of an operant and causes a change in the probability of that operant occuring again". The following types of reinforcers control almost all aggression behavior in the sporting milieu:

Social Reinforcers

Perhaps the most common source of positive reinforcement for the athlete is social in origin. Examples of social reinforcers would include praise, affection, social approval, encouragement, attention, and adult proximity. The reinforcement strength of these secondary reinforcers would depend upon each individual's different reinforcement history. According to McCandless (1961), the part of society which administers the reinforcing function varies between age groups. The social world of very young children consists essentially of parents, siblings, close friends and relatives. As the child grows older, more people comprise their social world. They begin to react to other adults, hero figures, and peers. Eventually, the peer group becomes the major reinforcing agent in the young adult's life. A major implication of these findings is that the coach must select social reinforcers based upon each athlete's level of social development.

In regard to social reinforcers, Rushall and Siedentop (1972:54) have made a cogent observation. They have suggested that "inappropriate (bad) behaviors are often maintained by social reactions that are reinforcing. The reactions to these behaviors often have a stronger reinforcing function than negative consequences that may also be associated with them. In many cases, if there were no reaction to inappropriate behaviors, they would occur less often". The implication here is that reinforcement should be forthcoming from constructive rather than aggressive behaviors.

Intrinsic Information Reinforcers

Intrinsic information feedback refers to bodily sensations arising through Kinesthetic feedback. The "feel" of a thrown punch, a body-check, or tackle would be examples of this type of reinforcer. While intrinsic performance information is difficult for the coach to manipulate, it could be suggested that alternative kinesthetic sensations be stressed. An example in this regard would be the "feel" of a perfectly executed skill.

Internal Reinforcers

There are two main types of this secondary reinforcer: vicarious and self-control.

Vicarious reinforcement refers to a change in an athlete's behavior as a result of watching another player's behavior and the concomitant reinforcement following the act. For example, if an athlete witnesses another participant's aggressive exchange, and that individual is socially rewarded by the coach, team-mates, and fans, then the viewer would "learn" that rewards will accrue from aggressive behavior. He would then be more likely to act aggressively in a similar situation. It has been suggested that the more popular the model, the greater the likelihood that the behavior will be copied. The tremendous impact of professional aggressive role models on children is obvious. Similarly, the elimination of any form of goal aggression in the practice situation would decrease the social learning of aggressive behavior which could later be manifested in the game situation.

Self-control reinforcement refers to internalized stimuli of behavior. For example, an athlete might say to himself "if I get in a fight with an opposing player, my team-mates will be impressed", or "if I don't fight, the fans will think I'm a coward". In either case, attribution of outcome is responsible for the aggressive behavior. In other words, the athlete perceives that the positive reinforcements resulting from fighting will outweigh the negative reinforcement of receiving a penalty. This is a learned phenomenon resulting from the individual's past learning history.

Material Reinforcers

There is a vast potential for utilizing material reinforcers in the sporting environment. This type of secondary reinforcer involves such tangible rewards as prizes, money, badges, awards, candy, and tokens. One thing to keep in mind when applying material reinforcers is that the reinforcing strength will vary with the type of reinforcer and the individual. In other words, what might be highly reinforcing to one individual might be completely ineffective to another.

Material reinforcers provide major implications for the coach. Their utilization in the form of prizes, badges, tokens, etc. for skilled, non-aggressive behavior provides tangible potential for decreasing goal aggression in the sporting environment. The exact methods are limited only by the coach's degree of ingenuity.

Proposal and Practical Implications

1. First and foremost, the coach, parent, and sports governing officials must honestly ask themselves if they indeed *want* to curb the incidence of goal aggression in their respective sports. If the answer is yes in more than "lip-service", then operant psychology can provide the means.

2. More effort must be made in the area of public education. To date, this is an area that has been largely overlooked. It is important that aggression research be made available to the parent and weekend coach, since these individuals are in the best position to start curbing aggressive behavior. Newpapers, popular home journals, coaching clinics, and presentations to community groups are popular avenues to employ.

3. Closely related to the preceding point, it is imperative that coaches be made aware of the reinforcers that are operative within the sporting environment. Since these reinforcers are ultimately shaping their athletes' behavior, it might prove beneficial to start training coaches in behavior observation techniques. Establishing baselines of aggressive behavior is a prerequisite to exerting any measurable form of control.

4. In view of the information provided regarding social reinforcers, a major implication is that coaches must consider the athlete's stage of social development in determining significant reinforcers. This will be a major feature in aggressive behavior control.

5. We have to avoid bestowing social recognition on negative behaviors such as aggression. A major implication here is to socially make less of the aggression issue, and more of alternative more positive behaviors.

6. Coaches and parents can help internalize substitute values that could then be modelled by the athlete. For example, by making an issue of skill level, effort, conditioning, etc., attribution theory would predict an increase in these types of behavior. Conversely, by ignoring goal aggression, we would expect a decrease in this type of behavior.

7. If it becomes necessary to take concrete steps to eliminate goal aggression, aversive control would be a recommended technique. Rather than utilizing punishment, this approach merely makes the anticipated negative consequences outweigh the anticipated positive consequences. Hence the athlete chooses an alternative to goal aggression. Operant Psychology provides the ammunition for this technique.

8. Finally, it should be concluded that a more pragmatic form of aggression research is needed to supplement our theoretical knowledge. It was the intent of this paper to suggest operant psychology as a tool for providing observable and measurable dimensions to aggression research.

REFERENCES

Johnson, R., *Aggression in Man and Animals*. Philadelphia: Saunders Co., 1972.

Lefebvre, L., Leith, L., and Bredemeier, B., "Modes for Aggression Assessment and Control — A Sportpsychological Examination" *International Journal of Sport Psychology*, 1980, 11, 11-21.

Leith, L., "The Psychological Assessment of Aggression in Sport — A Critique of Existing Measurement Technique". Paper presented at the International Symposium on Psychological Assessment in Sport, Wingate, Israel, 1977.

Rushall, B., and Siedentop, D., *The Development and Control of Behavior in Sport and Physical Education*, Philadelphia: Lea & Febiger, 1972.

Skinner, B.F., *Science and Human Behavior*, New York: Macmillan, 1953.

Skinner, B.F., *The Technology of Teaching*, New York: Appleton-Century-Crofts, 1969.

VIOLENCE IN SPORT

Thomas Wilke (USA)

For several years now, the overwhelming empirical evidence in support of a social learning analysis of aggression (e.g. Lehrman, 1953; Kuo, 1960; Montagu, 1968; Berkowitz, 1969; Bandura, 1973) has induced most scientists and physical educators to accept the view that, like any other behavior, aggression is a learned habit which has been reinforced and can be extinguished according to the laws of conditioning. Accordingly, social scientists interested in eliminating violence, hostility, and aggression have focused upon changing the environmental stimuli and eliminating the social conditions which lead to the learning of such responses. It seems, in fact, that a premature complacency has set in, as if the whole question of the nature of human aggression has been resolved. The notion of cathartic discharge of pent-up aggressive energy has become unfashionable in spite of the fact that an irritating question remains: Why do many of us recognize within ourselves a fascination with physical violence and sometimes experience a sense of release rather than a strengthening of a tendency when we exhibit it? Such questions force us to re-examine the catharsis idea, and somehow achieve a large enough perspective on the nature of human aggression to see that both the social learning and the catharsis views are valid.

The institution of American sport offers such a perspective. Sport is a microcosm of life itself, a crystallization of the human drama. The totality of a participant's psyche (i.e. emotions, motives, learning capacity, memory, developmental history, psychopathological tendencies, etc.) inevitably gains expression through his or her demeanor and performance. In athletics, the entire spectrum of types of aggression is seen, ranging from the most benign and ritualized to the cruel and malicious. Sports can enable us to discover the psychological functions served by aggression and violence, and how and why cathartic release occurs in some situations while reinforcement of the aggressive response occurs in others.

Scott (1970) argues that we should keep aggressive sports because they teach a number of useful values, such as how to control one's aggression. Adopting a social learning perspective, he convincingly shows that we could change the rules and the values surrounding sport and thereby program or condition athletes to exhibit only certain forms of aggression. This position is widely recognized as a very sensible and humane one. However, the assumption that this would facilitate the evolution of happier human beings and a more peaceful society is questionable, for Scott's view evades the deeper issue of the nature of the unspent energy supressed by "passive inhibition." That is, there is no evidence whatsoever that the "malignant" forms of aggression (Fromm, 1973) can be reduced by behavior modification. On the other hand, we must not embrace any of the simple catharsis theories which from Freud (1923) to Lorenz (1966, 1973) have been problematic in their blindness to the obvious fact of the extreme flexibility of the human information processing system and the consequent complexity of his motives. However, this paper will attempt to show there is a sense in which a sort of catharsis does occur.

Fromm (1973) makes an important distinction between "instincts" serving physical survival of a species, which dictate almost all animal aggression, and the "higher" existential needs of man. Aggression, admittedly, sometimes occurs in man purely in the service of physical survival. However, the means by which aggression promotes survival in the higher social species is not the killing of conspecifics. Both Eibl-Eibesfeldt (1961) and Bernstein and Gordon (1974) have demonstrated that innate aggression consists in a sequence of fixed action patterns whereby two animals can communicate, as harmlessly as possible, which roles each should adopt for the good of the social unit. Eibl-Eibesfeldt states: "Fights between individuals of the same species almost never end in death and rarely result in serious injury to either combatant. Such fights . . . more nearly resemble a tournament than a mortal struggle" (1961, p. 112). Fighting exists to minimize harm and solidify social bonds, not to eliminate competitors. Also, there is evidence that the axiom "Only the strong survive" may be false, even in the wild. Snow (1958) reports the case of a male blackbird which was extremely aggressive, defended a large territory, and attracted a healthy

female, but was so aggressive toward his mate that he inhibited her nest building behavior and thus jeopardized his own ability to reproduce. Excessive aggressiveness does not make sense in nature, and it is an error to assume that physical survival is at the root of man's hostilities.

In our culture, we are strongly encouraged to develop large egos, more so than in some other countries such as India and China. It is only people whose childhood conditioning led them to believe that they needed a bigger ego than everyone else in order to survive and be happy who become possessed by this violent tendency. In reality, life flows more smoothly in a person for whom the ego does not have to be constantly defending itself, for the little frustrations that constantly torment a person with a big ego are not even noticed. This ego, then, is conditioned, or learned, and must be deconditioned to achieve psychological health. Jung also realized that the ego is too limiting, and that to become a fully self-actualized (i.e. individuated) human being, one has to slay the ego.

In a sport like American Football, if a defensive back tackles an opposing player with unnecessary viciousness, he is diverting the destructive energy from himself to the other player, for that player constitutes a threat to his ego, in the sense of causing him physical pain, loss of financial security, public embarrassment, loss of status, etc. The result of this projection is that the athlete salvages his ego, but loses the opportunity to discover a truth about himself which would ultimately make his life much happier. That is, there is something in his unconscious which he hates, and which has been eating away at him. If he could see his anger as a projection of his self-destructiveness, and could begin to notice the situations in which it comes up, he could eliminate it from his psyche, which would produce a healthier personality which would then attract other healthier personalities. On the other hand, if he does not recognize the message behind his anger and aggression, no catharsis will occur, and he will simply reinforce the ego and its defenses, and his discomfort can only increase. The next time a similar situation arises, the intensity of his self-destructiveness is greater, and therefore his projection of it in the form of violence is less controllable.

If you merely find "outlets" for your aggression, you not only delay the discovery of its true cause, but you intensify the problem by strengthening the ego defenses (in Freudian terms). It is true, that if an athlete has reached such a pathological stage with his violence that in a given situation, he cannot but act it out, it would be better to project it where it can do the least damage, but he should immediately thereafter be encouraged to look into himself to discover what is happening to him before the same situation recurs. It is only when the physical discharge of aggression is coupled with the insight of what it is the athlete is attacking in himself that true catharsis takes place.

A player may be pre-occupied with remorse at having injured a teammate or opponent. Guilt consists of recurring self-punishing thoughts which are an effort by the mind to put aside the cause of the violent act. Remind him of what the purpose of sports participation is — to learn from your mistakes and achieve excellence. Explain to him that the best way to deal with guilt is not to deny it or pretend the harm was of little consequence or well-deserved, but to go into the guilt and get some relief by understanding it.

But there may be a better way to deal with aggression which does not even require that it be acted out in any form at a physical level. This technique, called active imagination, was developed by Jung. Simply stated, to perform it, the athlete would have to trace back his violent tendency as far back into his past as he can, and then revivify a specific event, complete with all the emotions and feelings that accompanied it. For most males, the event would be either being physically punished by a father figure, or being humiliated by a male peer.

An athlete can derive a great deal of insight about himself, his teammates, and his opponents by looking deeply into the violence in his sport, and can also in the process satisfy some of his highest existential needs as a human being. Malicious violence can always be inhibited by a conscious decision not to harm. This decision not to harm can be facilitated by helping a person see that underneath all the games he plays with people is a valuable human being.

REFERENCES

Bandura, A. *Aggression: A social learning analysis.* Englewood Cliffs, N.J.: Prentice Hall, 1973.

Berkowitz, L. Simple views of aggression: An essay review. *American Scientist*, 1969, (57), 372-383.

Bernstein, I.S. & Gordon, T.P. The function of aggression in primate societies. *American Scientist*, 1974, (62), 304-311.

Eibl-Eibesfeldt, I. The fighting behavior of animals. *Scientific American*, 1961, (205), December, 112-122.

Freud, S. "The ego and the id." In J. Strachey (Ed.) *Standard edition of the complete psychological works of Sigmund Freud.* London: Hogarth Press, 1923.

Fromm, E. *The anatomy of human destructiveness.* New York: Holt, Rinehart, & Winston, 1973.

Gillespie, W.H. Aggression and instinct theory. *International Journal of Psychoanalysis*, 1971 (52), 155-160.

Jung, C.G. *Collected Works*, G. Adler et al. (Eds). Princeton U. Press, 1970.

Kuo, Z.Y. Studies on the basic factors in animal fighting: VII. Interspecies coexistence in mammals. *Journal of Genetic Psychology*, 1960, (97), 211-225.

Lehrman, D.S. Problems raised by instinct theory: A critique of Konrad Lorenz's theory of instinctive behavior. *Quarterly Review of Biology*, 1953, (28), 337-364.

Lorenz, K. *On aggression.* New York: Harcourt-Brace-Jovanovich, 1966.

Lorenz, K. *Civilized man's eight deadly sins.* New York: Harcourt-Brace-Jovanovich, 1973.

Maslow, A.H. *Toward a Psychology of Being* (2nd Ed.) Princeton, N.J., Van Nostrand, 1968.

Scott, J.P. "Sport and aggression." In Kenyon, G.S. (Ed). *Contemporary psychology of sport.* Chicago: Athletic Institute, 1970.

Snow, D.W. *A study of blackbirds.* London: Allan & Unwin, 1958.

Wilke, T. Reconsideration of Human Aggression and Violence: A Fresh Perspective on Some Old Theories. Unpublished, 1981.

REFEREE PROBLEMS IN FOOTBALL

Leif Isberg (Sweden)

Decisions in sport are often made on subjective grounds. Most branches of sport have some form of rules governing the behaviour of the participants and the assessment of the result. One difficult problem consists in the interpretation and application of these rules. Disputes often arise concerning the interpretation of these rules in team games. One reason may be that body contact is permitted to some extent. This creates complicated situations, so that it is more difficult for the referee to determine the actual course of events. Football is Sweden's major team sport, and developments in the game have made the referee's role far harder than before.

The problem of football, seen from the referee's viewpoint, includes four components:

The *process* is composed of the decisions made by the referee.

The *result* consists of the reactions which the decisions provoke in the group concerned.

Frame factors in this context are factors in the football environment which can be manipulated by the organization, but in the present process curtail the freedom of actions of players and officials.

Other environmental factors which may delimit action are, for example, weather conditions, but since these are beyond the organization's control they are of minor interest in this context.

Aims of the investigation

1. With the help of an analysis of the job of the football referee, to survey his duties and the demands made by referees and various contact groups on the performance of the job.

2. To examine the qualifications of the referee to carry out these duties in accordance with the demands.

3. With the help of the results which emerge, to suggest measures to facilitate the referee's situation.

Method

1. *The referee's duties and demands*

The analysis was made with the help of the Critical incident technique, direct observation and interviews.

The subjects are

- referees in division I and II (population)
- players and leaders from teams in division I and II (random selection)
- teaching staff (population)
- journalists

2. *The referee's training*

Interview, questionnaire and analysis of a first division referee course. In addition a testfilm (video) about the interpretation of different situations was used. The analysis was carried out according to a model in which intended and observed factors were compared. The subject matter of the observed course was then compared with the duties and related demands which emerged in the investigation.

Results

The most important demands made on the performance of the referee's job were

- to cope with specific patterns of behaviour and demands in the referee's situation (courage, consistency)
- to make certain decisions together with the linesman
- to punish correctly by means of warning and sending off.

During the match, controversial decisions, i.e., those in which the observers considered that the referees made a wrong decision, or where the referee did not blow his whistle although he should have done so, are chiefly concerned with penalty kicks and warning situations. The controversial decisions evidently increase with distance from the incident. The disputed situations observed here were followed up with interviews. The incidents were later classified according to the same principles as were used by critical incident technique. The comparison show 87% agreement and the validity is underlined.

From the questionnaire one can see that the positive side of the referee's job is the companionship, while the negative consists of irresponsible criticism by mass media and management. They became referees first and foremost because of their interest in football. But a desire for achievement also plays a large part.

The proposals to improve the referee's situation concern the frame factors.

A Proposals concerning external Qualifications

1. *Criticism from outsiders*

The referees regard irresponsible criticism from mass media and management as a higly negative element. The Football Association can counteract this by

- arranging courses (information meetings) for journalists
- putting in a "rule column" in our major daily newspapers
- having the loudspeaker to describe a specific rule before every match
- having the loudspeaker to mediate decisions to the spectators
- arranging a discussion after the match, where the parts discuss the decisions made

Implications:

- Information has been given to the journalists
- The match programs often contains a rule column
- The discussion of the decisions is now and then arranged

B Proposals concerning Rules and Regulations

1. *Division of labour*

The results show

- that the referee has difficulties in perceiving the linesman in time
- that the majority of the referees prefer a one referee system with two linesmen who have wider powers

Implications:

Today one can see that the linesmen are more active during the match. (They often signal for penalty kicks in their areas).

The problem to see the linesman in time is still there.

2. *Rule changes*

The proposed change in order to reduce the referee's risk of making wrong decisions, was that the indirect free kick would be replaced by a direct free kick.

Implications:

This proposal has not been applied.

C Proposals concerning individual qualifications

1. Physical training

Information should be provided on modern training methods which are also put into practice. Possibly an endurance test lasting at least 25 minutes will be introduced.

Implications:

An endurance test has been introduced.

2. *Other individual characeristics*

The referees display serious defects with regard to courage and consistency. They desire training in psychology and hope thereby to learn both how people react in different situations and how they can remedy their defects by mental training.

Implications:

A compendium has been given to the referees where they can read about coaches' and players' reaction in different situations and how to remedy their own defects by using mental training.

3. *The referee's function in general*

The referee should receive increased information on the sports movement in general. They should be given an understanding of the situation of management and coaches in order to fix their own role into the whole.

Implications:

The courses for referees and coaches are now partly held together. Everybody is very satisfied with this arrangement and they understand each other much better.

4. *Follow-up*

A thorough follow-up of the referee's achievement is essential. The opportunities for communication between instructors and referees are open to improvement. The referee's committee should acquire both a personal opinion and a substantial pictorial material about the situations which are to be discussed.

Implications:

The opportunities for communication has been improved and a better pictorial material is used.

5. *Planning of the instruction*

If the instruction is to yield a satisfactory result in terms of the referee's competence, then it is necessary to analyse their qualifications and the aims, content, and method of instruction.

a *Qualifications*

The authorities must be cognizant of the referee's motives in attending the course and their experience as players and as referees.

b *Aims*

The chief aim must be that the referees learn facts which are relevant to the performance of their duties. Furthermore, it is advisable to discover each referee's personal goal, since these affect the participants' involvement in the course.

The final aims should be defined in concrete terms.

c *Method*

Consideration should be given to the usual phases when the course is planned. E.g., the activity phase must satisfy the participants' need for action.

Implications:

The instruction is better, planned, but one still misses the referee's personal goal.

Before I started my work I looked for references related to the subject. But I found hardly any from 1970-1978, so this work must be seen as one of the first on this particular focus.

REFERENCES

Flanagan, J.C., 1954: The critical incident technique. *Psychological Bulletin*, 51, 327-358.

Heisterkampf, G., 1975: *Die Psychodynamik von Kampfspielen. Am Beispiel der Beziehung zwishen Schiedstrichtern und Zushauern.* Stuttgart: Karl Hoffman Verlag.

Thorndike, R.L. (Ed.) 1971: *Educational measurement* (2nd ed) Washington: American council on education.

SOURCES OF INFLUENCE IN SPORT SUCCESS

Thomas J. Sheeran and Jerry Freuschlag (USA)

This study was designed to examine factors contributing to the success of high level athletes in order to facilitate understanding of developmental variables associated with quality performance.

During the summer of 1980, a sample of 3,443 athletes were surveyed. This sample represented 64% of the total population in attendance at the Empire State Games in New York. Male and female competitors from twenty five sports in open and scholastic divisions comprised the subject pool and represented the best athletes from among 80,000 preliminary competitors.

A demographic profile of the "typical" athlete engaging in the Empire Games competition shows an academically successful, white, 19 year old from an upper middle class family. This athlete resides in a large suburban or small city environment. The athlete's parents are well educated and well-off financially. This profile agrees with previous research (Pavia, 1976, 1974; Jaques, 1975) which indicates that high level athletic competitors generally come from middle and upper classes of society. One notable exception was in the combative sports of wrestling, boxing and judo.

The sources of influence and motivation of athletes have considerable, but undetermined impact on sport success. In theory, of the several influences on athletic achievement, parental nurturance has been recognized as having subtantial bearing on the athlete's development. Additionally, the contribution of coaches on sport achievement has not been systematically examined. Research was undertaken to determine the nature and extent of the contributions of these several factors on sport success.

Among the motives examined relative to participation in high level competition, the principal reason given was the opportunity to compete at a high level. Other reasons for involvement were the association with other athletes, Olympic aspirations, free warmups, and exposure to college recruiters. The opportunity to compete at a high level was a consistent view across all events involved in the games with the exception of synchronized swimmers who expressed association with other athletes as the primary reason for their involvement.

An understanding of developmental factors associated with high level athletes requires the examination of sources of influence on their sport success. Analysis of the collected data was performed by sport and sex. An athlete's mother was found more influential to females than to males. This was especially true among female gymnasts, swimmers and synchronized swimmers. Parental influence was also evident when the father's role is considered. Females, once again, attributed more of their success to the parent than did their male counterparts. Surprisingly, the impact of coaches on athletes was relatively small, ranking below that of the parents, other family members and peers. Of the three coaching groups examined, high school coaches had the most impact on the athlete's development, youth coaches were found to be second in importance while the college coach ranked least effective in providing impact on the development of sport success. These findings are consistent with research by Jaques and Pavia, (1975) and Orlick (1974) which conclude that a direct relationship exists between athletic achievement and parental attitude.

Interactive effects of ethnicity and their sources of influence on athletic success were also analyzed. Recognizing that subcultural values, opportunities, and relationships shape different behaviors, this research indicated that the influence of the athlete's mother is similar among Whites, Blacks, and Latins. The father was seen as less influential on athletic success by Blacks than by either Whites or Latins. There was no ethnic difference with respect to peer or family influence exclusive of parents. All three coaching groups: you''-, high school, and college, were viewed as more influential by blacks than by other ethnic groups.

Examination of family background revealed significant demographic patterns. A majority of competitors come from families where one or more parent possess a college diploma. Only a small percentage of the sample (7%) come from families where neither parent had finished high school.

In analyzing family composition, several observations are of interest. The typical competitor comes from a family of two to three children, however, a substantial number (23%) are "only" children. Surprisingly, first born children account for 27% of the sample which would indicate an extraordinary small percentage (4%) of participants who were from families with more than one child and were first born.

The breakdown of siblings by sex did not produce unusual findings. It did, however, lay to rest a common misconception that high level female athletes come from families which are predominantly male.

An additional finding of interest is the amount of participation in other sport activities. The majority of respondents reported that the sport they were competing in was the only activity they participated in on a regular basis. Fully 80% of the sample reported that they participated in no more than two athletic activities. This finding confirms the "athletic pipeline" theory which suggests that the most effective means of achieving a high degree of skill in one activity is to focus exclusively on that sport.

Identification of the developmental processes which propel young athletes toward national prominence is an important function of the sport psychologist. Oftentimes, research efforts are directed only to those who have attained the highest levels of athletic achievement. Unfortunately, such research results in biased retrospective judgements.

Comprehending why athletes compete and understanding who has the greatest impact on their psychological development as athletes will make it possible to both modify and enrich programs to take advantage of the roles that parents and coaches play during the athlete's formative years.

Results of this investigation permit the following recommendations:

1. Athletic administrators must encourage parental involvement in programs to insure development of the athlete's potential.

2. Ethnic differences must be recognized with regard to motivation for participation and efforts must be undertaken to introduce these motivational factors into the athlete's program.

3. Parental influence on athletic success is significantly greater for females than for males, suggesting that increased parental involvement is warranted when the athlete is female.

4. The influence of school coaches on the development of high level athletes bears testimony to the belief that people trained to work with children will have a more positive and lasting effect on their athletic achievement. This pronounced supportive effect is particularly true among Blacks and females. Efforts must be made to provide increased opportunities for athletes to receive coaching during the school years.

5. In order for athletes to pursue sport at high level, it is necessary to come from a background which is middle class or above. The middle class nature of sport is confirmed by factors including family composition, educational level of parents and income level. Programs must be developed which eliminate this restriction.

6. The development of interest and ability in a single activity appears relatively early in an athlete's career. A byproduct of this development is the exclusion of almost all other athletic activities. Although this appears to be a sound process for developing high level athletes, it does not seem educationally sound for developing a wide range of motor skills or providing an enriched developmental environment.

REFERENCES

Balazs, E.K. *A Psycho-Social Study of Outstanding Female Athletes.* Unpublished doctoral dissertation, Boston University, 1974.

Collins, L.J. Social Class and the Olympic Athlete. *British Journal of Physical Education.* 1972, 3, 25-27.

Cramer, P.M. *Active Participation in Sports and Family Cohesion in the various Social Strata.* Unpublished doctoral dissertation. University of Southern California, 1974.

Freischlag, J. *The 1980 Empire State Games: Background and Training of Participating Athletes.* Unpiblished study, 1980.

Jaques, T.D. and Pavia, G.R. *An Investigation into the Educational Socioeconomic and Parental Background of Successful Australian Male Cricketeers.* Paper presented at the Conference of Sport, Society and Personality. La Trobe, Australia, May, 1975.

Loy, J.W. Social Origins and Occupational Mobility Patterns of a Selected Sample of American Athletes. *International Review of Sport Sociology,* 1972, 7, 5-23.

Orlick, R.D. Family Sports Environment and Early Sports Participation. *Proceedings of the Fourth Canadian Symposium, Psycho-Motor Learning and Sports Psychology.* Department of Health, Canada, 1974.

Pavia, G.R. An Investigation into the Sociological Background of Successful South Australian Footballers. *Australian Journal of Physical Education.* 1974, 63, 9-15.

Pavia, G.R. *An Investigation into the Socioeconomic Background, Academic Attainment and Occupational Mobility of Syracuse University Letterwinners.* Unpublished doctoral dissertation, Syracuse University, 1976.

Sheeran, T.J. and Freischlag, J. *Selected Characteristics of 1979 Empire State Games Athletes.* Paper presented at the 1980 state conference of the New York State Association for Health, Physical Education, Recreation and Dance, 1980.

OLYMPIC ATHLETES: AMATEUR OR PROFESSIONAL?

David A. Rose (USA)

In both American intercollegiate athletics and in international competition in the Olympic Games, there has been extensive conroversy about the nature of participants; i.e., whether they are amateur or professional. As these terms are presently understood, an amateur is one who plays for the fun of the experience, a professional is someone who plays for money. The controversy over the nature of the activities has grown because in both American college athletics and the Olympic Games, neither definition seems applicable (in spite of official retention of the "amateur" label). A major problem has been the provision of financial support so that athletes may continue their training. This matter is disputed in American college athletics under the notion of the athletic scholarship and in the Olympic Games under the notion of the broken-time payment.

In a recent investigation, I resolved this controversy by pointing out a theoretical deficiency in American (and implicitly international) sport sociology. This resolution is based on the insights that (1) there are three methodological orientations to research in American sociology of sport and (2) the issue regarding participation has been contained heretofore within an inadequate orientation, namely, one which defines concepts according to the motive of the participant. To overcome the inadequacy, I argued it is necessary to define the concepts of amateur and professional sport in a sociological way — by emphasizing the context in which participation takes place. By so doing, it is possible to resolve the long-standing controversy.

More specifically, it is appropriate to define "semiprofessional sport" as sport undertaken to represent the quality of the sponsoring organization. Using this definition, it can be shown that both American intercollegiate athletics and the Olympic Games are semi-professional sport — *at the least.* In the former case, individuals are expected to be student-athletes; in the latter case, citizen-athletes. In both cases, relative priority is to be given to the former role; e.g., citizens first and athletes second. What must be understood, however, is that if the semi-professional sports competition is grounded in an important political economic competition, organizations are tempted to shortcut the representative relationship — in order to increase their chances of being "well-represented." In this situation, the organizations shift the relative priority of the roles by exchanging their financial support for the athlete's labor in the programs they control. In so doing, the competition is converted to a peculiar form of professional sport. It is a peculiar form because while some forms of reimbursement are acceptable, not all forms are acceptable. Those which are not acceptable break the representative relationship between outcomes on the field and the quality of the organization. In college athletics, for example, this break occurs if a school hires individuals who cannot succeed as students. In the Olympic Games, this break arises if an individual's occupation and income are dependent upon his athletic performances. In other words, the issue of broken-time payments should be understood not as an issue of amateur or professional athletes but as an issue of acceptable or unacceptable professional sports programs.

Thus, as these matters relate to the Olympics, it must be recognized (a) the Olympic Games are prominent today precisely because of the political economic competition represented by the sports competition; (b) the controversy over acceptable versus unacceptable professional sport will not go away until political economic antagonisms which feed them have been resolved; and (c) attempts to resolve this controversy in a way consistent with the Olympic ideal of promoting peace through sport must be grounded in efforts to critically examine the structural contexts in which Olympic athletes are produced by their respective countries.

In this latter regard, one must be further aware that there are different definitions of "athlete's rights." These definitions align more or less with the methodological orientations alluded to above. (1) Under the normative right (conservative) orientation, the phrase embodies an individual's "right to choose" to participate. (2) Under the normative center's (politically uncommitted) approach, the phrase means an athlete's right to participate to the highest level of skill to which (s)he is capable. Both capitalist and socialist versions of this meritocratic principle exist: the best participate and all participate, respectively. (3) The normative left (progressive) approach uses the phrase to mean the rights of the people to determine who gets to participate; i.e., what structures are to be erected in which individual choices will be made.

BIBLIOGRAPHY

Killanin, Michael and John Rodda (eds.) (1976). *The Olympic Games.* New York: Macmillan.

Rose, David (1980). "Physical culture. A critique of the American sociological study of sport." Unpublished Ph.D. dissertation, University of Massachusetts, Amherst.

Segave, Jeffrey and Donald Chu (eds.) (1981). *Olympism. A Cross-Disciplinary Analysis of the Olympic Movement.* Champaign, Illinois: Human Kinetics Publishers.

Zornow, Gerald (1977). *Report of the President's Commission on Olympic Sports, 1975—77.* Washington, D.C.: U.S. Government Printing Office.

COACTION AND SPECTATOR EFFECTS IN THE CLASSROOM: IMPLICATIONS FOR PHYSICAL EDUCATION TEACHERS

Mary Jo Weaver MacCracken (USA)

Studies have demonstrated that social facilitation or the influence of the presence of others on performance is a real force, but its strength needs harnessing in an endeavour to lead the educational process to new paths of excellence. Educators should recognize the hidden implications of the environment and become aware of the social enhancing or detrimental effects on performance when an individual acts in the presence of others compared to alone.

Because of the dire lack of field studies on social facilitation regarding young boys and girls, and to extend the testing of simple and complex motor skills, this study was undertaken examining the effects, if any, of acting "alone", together (coaction), and before spectators with evaluative potential upon the performance of 4-, 6-, and 8-year-old children. Psychomotor achievement of boys and girls with high or low developmental dynamic balance skill levels was compared on simple and on complex balance tasks with the use of a paradigm common in classroom organization. Individuals were tested, performing "alone", together in groups of two, and alone before five spectators.

In a major overview of recent social facilitation research, Geen and Gange (1977) concluded that Zajonc's (1965) drive theory was the most parsimonious explanation to date on social facilitation, but Cottrell's (1968, 1972) modification appeared justified. Zajonc's hypothesis suggested that with subjects who are still in the learning stage the dominant responses are principally incorrect, and the audience or coaction conditions facilitate the incorrect responses and thus impair performance. But during performance of well learned tasks, since correct responses generally dominate, they are facilitated, and thus, performance is enhanced.

Later investigators of coaction and spectator settings verified this principle but added that the responses were not necessarily unidirectional. Cottrell explicated that in the coaction setting with the unskilled, through rivalry and the opportunity to take cues from coactors, dominant incorrect responses may be decreased. Hence, performance is enhanced and not impaired as in the spectator paradigm, where evaluation apprehension directs performance. With skilled subjects in the coaction setting, according to Cottrell, performance may improve, due mainly to the degree of the individual's competitiveness and the motivation to take cues. In the spectator setting, aware of evaluation and reinforced by past experience regarding success, skilled subjects may perform better than when "alone".

Overall, the findings in the present study appeared to corroborate Zajonc's hypothesis and indicated that motor performance is, indeed, affected by both coaction and spectator paradigms. But in addition, the results tended to support Cottrell's refinement of Zajonc's drive theory. No significant effect appeared contradictory to what was termed Cottrell's learned drive theory.

The intensity of the effect in the spectator situation was evidenced especially with the high skilled 8-year-olds on complex tasks. In contrast, the 4's demonstrated no significant performance change in the spectator condition over the "alone". Two reasons for the enhanced performance of the 8's may be suggested: evaluation apprehension (learned) and/or maturation (innate). While nobody can deny the genetic effect of maturation, facilitation effects might be due to anticipation of evaluation; they might even be in addition to, and summate with, those due to mere presence (Wankel, 1980).

Motivation has been credited as a prime component of evaluation potential. When observed in this field situation, older children especially the high skilled, appeared to be more highly motivated than the younger. The 8's seemed more competitive, more able to take cues and to perceive their peer group as a source of evaluation. In the field situation the youngest children often appeared not to apprehend that their peers were evaluating them. Their lesser facilitation may have been somewhat due to task novelty, new environment, strange evaluators, distraction, and/or fatigue.

The dichotomous nature of performance according to skill level was a principal finding in this study. In the spectator setting high skilled 6-year-olds evidenced improvement of performance over the "alone" state, while their low skilled peers demonstrated impairment on simple tasks. These opposing findings with the same aged children of opposite skill levels demonstrated bidirectionality of performance according to skill.

Between the situations, coaction tended to be more constant than the spectator condition and was modified to a lesser degree by the interaction of the setting with sex, age, and skill over the "alone" state. The crucial variable in both settings was skill level. The implication for the educator is to acknowledge the importance of adapting the right situation in accordance with the pupil's needs. Pinpointing skill level is the key to choosing the helpful situation.

The improved performance apparent in the coaction paradigm of this study may have been due to competition and/or the opportunity for modeling. Cottrell had emphasized that without these components in the coaction setting, the effect of the presence of others would be eliminated.

In addition to skill level, age appeared to affect performance profoundly. Evidence also demonstrated that environmental influences relative to dynamic balance may be similar for all children regardless of sex.

Based upon the findings of this study, the following implications about social facilitation effects might become a part of the professional's expertise relating to children.

1. Educators should be cognizant of the organizational influence of the classroom regarding performance. Teachers should use that knowledge to facilitate performance and to promote a successful learning experience for all children.

2. Cottrell's learned drive theory may be used to improve techniques for teaching motor skills to children.

3. Environmental conditions should be controlled *before* children perform in coaction and/or spectator situations.

4. The coaction setting may facilitate performance of the unskilled. The spectator setting may aid performance of well learned tasks and impair performance of complex or poorly learned tasks.

5. Coaction settings should be included for children who need the challenge of competition or the opportunity for modeling to improve performance.

6. Coaction learning centers may be based on skill level, pairing those of like skill. When paired alike, competition should aid performance.

7 The spectator setting should be used only when skills are simple or well learned. The evaluation potential of the peer audience should facilitate the skilled child's performance. Youngsters might take turns acting and observing.

8. Tasks of dynamic balance should not be too long nor repetitious for young children. Motor tasks should arouse the youngster's interest and should be appropriate to age and skill level.

9. All children, regardless of sex, should be given equal opportunity to perform dynamic balance tasks in the various settings.

10. The teacher's major problem in determining the best environment for any one phase of learning/performance is to determine the relative position of the students on the skill level continuum in order to adapt the most suitable paradigm to needs. A "common sense" assessment of skill level to determine which responses are dominant is imperative.

11. The curriculum plan ought to be analyzed and revised to offer teachers more options in preparing lesson plans to apply valuable knowledge about the force of the environment.

12. Teacher education programs need redesigning to help professionals diagnose and assess what is imperative at different stages of learning/performance in order to provide a prime setting

for the optimal development of each child.

REFERENCES

Cottrell, N.B. Social facilitation. In C.G. McClintock (Ed.), *Experimental social psychology*. New York: Holt, Rinehart & Winston, 1972.

Geen, R.S., & Gange, J.G. Drive theory of social facilitation: Twelve years of theory and research. *Psychological Bulletin*, 1977, *84*, 1267—1288.

Hunt, P.J., & Hillery, J.M. Social facilitation in a coaction setting: An examination of the effects over learning trials. *Journal of Experimental Social Psychology*, 1973, *9*, 563—571.

McCullagh, P.D., & Landers, D.M. A comparison of the audience and coaction paradigms. In D.M. Landers, D.V. Harris, & R.W. Christina (Eds.), *Psychology of motor behavior and sport* (vol. 2). Champaign, Illinois: Human Kinetics, 1975.

Wankel, L.M. Social facilitation of motor performance: Perspective and prospective. In C.H. Nadeau, W.R. Halliwell, K.M. Newell, & G.C. Roberts (Eds.), *Psychology of motor behavior and sport 1979*. Champaign, Illinois: Human Kinetics Publishers, 1980.

LA DANSE POUR LES PERSONNES DU TROISIEME AGE

N.A. Gomez, F. Péronnet, D. Massicotte et M. Gagnon (Canada)

Quel type de programmes d'activités physiques sont susceptibles de répondre aux besoins des adultes du troisième âge? Quels sont les avantages particuliers, pour cette population, des programmes d'activités physiques à caractère expressif? Dans le but de formuler des réponses à ces questions, deux programmes d'activités physiques: conditionnement physique classique et danse, furent comparés quant à leurs effets physiologiques, psycho-moteurs, socio-affectifs, et quant à la participation et la satisfaction des participants. Un résumé des principaux résultats de cette étude (Gomez et al., 1981) sont présentés et discutés ici, ainsi que leurs implications pour l'organisation des activités physiques destinées aux populations du troisième âge.

Méthode

Sujets. Les participants à cette recherche ont répondu à une annonce faite dans les journaux et la radio et affichée dans des centres des loisirs qui offrent déjà des programmes d'activité physique pour cette population. Des 38 personnes qui ont commencé, le programme 26 ont complété l'étude: examen médical, pré-test, post-test, entraînement du 1er décembre jusqu'au début d'avril à raison de trois rencontres d'une heure et demie par semaine (congés et suppressions imprévues exclues). Dans le groupe de danse (DAN) il y avait 3 hommes et 10 femmes; leur âge moyen était de X = 66. 47 ans, O = 6.41. Dans le groupe de conditionnement physique (CP) il y avait 4 hommes et 9 femmes, leur âge moyen était de X = 62.15 ans, O = 4.81.

Protocole. Le programme de CP classique comprenait des activités de réchauffement, de la marche ou de la course et des exercices de force, de flexibilité et de relaxation. L'intensité des exercices était contrôlée individuellement.

Le cours de danse comprenait trois formes de danse: danse folklorique, sociale et claquette (une classe chacune par semaine). La structure des cours était celle d'un cours de danse régulier avec les phases de réchauffement, d'apprentissage des éléments nouveaux et de répétition des séquences chorégraphiques. Il y avait une alternance dans l'intensité des exercices. La durée de pratique de différentes séquences de mouvements fut augmentée graduellement pendant les 16 semaines.

Les pré- et post-tests, administrés une semaine avant le début et à la fin de la période d'entraînement respectivement, mesuraient des aspects: (1) de la condition physique (capacité de travail aérobie, force, flexibilité), (2) des aptitudes rythmiques, (3) de la cordination, (4) du bien-être psychologique tel que défini par le questionnaire d'Everett Shostrom (1963), le Personality Orientation Inventory (P.O.I.), (5) de la satisfaction avec l'activité. Les descriptions détaillées de ces instruments sont reportées ailleurs (Gomez, et al., 1981).

Résultats et discussion

Un premier résultat important de cette étude est le fait que, malgré la durée et la fréquence de l'entraînement, il n'y a pas eu d'amélioration significative dans la condition physique, telle que mesurée par la capacité aérobie, la force ou la flexibilité, pour aucun de deux groupes. Des résultats semblables ont été obtenus par Gauthier et Poulin (1980) lesquels ont également comparé les effets de deux activités physiques (yoga et conditionnement classique) chez des sujets du troisième âge.

Plusieurs facteurs peuvent expliquer ces résultats. D'abord, les sujets qui ont choisi de participer à cette étude étaient déjà relativement actifs physiquement. Deuxièmement, il semble plus difficile d'obtenir des effets d'entraînement significatifs chez des personnes âgées (Pollock et coll., 1976).

Cependant, il est à nôter qu'il y a des améliorations significatives dûes à l'entraînement pour les autres aspects mesurés: aptitudes rythmiques, coordination motrice, actualisation de soi (P.O.I.). Des effets d'apprentissage sont particulièrement évidents surtout pour le groupe DAN (e.g. aptitudes rythmiques) dont les scores au pré-test sont un peu plus bas que ceux du groupe C.P.

Un autre fait important qui ressort de cette étude est que les participants de chacun des groupes semblent appartenir à des populations relativement différentes. Le groupe de C.P. était un peu plus jeune que le groupe de DAN et légèrement plus habile dans certaines preuves de coordination motrice, tant dans le pré-test que les post-tests. Les profils dans les 14 échelles d'actualization de soi du P.O.I. sont aussi relativement différentes pour les deux groupes.

Les différences des deux groupes sont aussi très évidents dans le taux de participation aux cours et le degré de satisfaction exprimé avec l'activité choisie. Le groupe C.P. a maintenu un taux moyen d'assistance de 64% sur 45 cours, par rapport à 74% sur 49 cours pour le groupe DAN. Ce dernier taux est très élevé, si l'on considère que les cours se donnaient pendant l'hiver et à raison de trois fois par semaine. Les réponses aux questionnaires sur la satisfaction avec l'activité, ainsi que les commentaires des participants indiquent les raisons principales pour lesquelles les cours de danse ont mieux soutenu la motivation des participants. Les questions sur lesquelles le groupe DAN a exprimé un plus haut degré de satisfaction concernaient des aspects tels: 1) la possibilité d'échanger avec d'autres, 2) la présence de défis stimulants, 3) la possibilité d'augmenter leur expressivité, 4) la certitude face à la possibilité d'une amélioration personnelle, 5) la contribution de l'activité à leur aisance de mouvement, 6) l'effort mental requis, 7) le degré de satisfaction ressenti après chaque cours, 8) l'assurance d'avoir fait une bonne performance pendant les cours, 9) l'importance de l'estime du groupe, 10) le fait d'avoir un professeur compréhensif, 11) le fait de trouver une bonne communication dans le groupe, 12) le fait de trouver une atmosphère amicale, 13) le fait de trouver le groupe enthousiaste, 14) le fait qu'il n'y ait pas des mésentente entre les membres du groupe, 15) le fait que le groupe ne soit pas autoritaire.

Selon les résultats de cette étude, c'est l'encadrement de l'activité danse qui a contribué en grande partie à maintenir un haut niveau de participation et de satisfaction (Gomez, 1980). D'abord, la variété de cours (social, claquette, folklore) permettait de répondre à des goûts et des attentes diverses. Deuxièmement, la méthode d'enseignement employée assurait: l'intégration des personnes ayant des niveaux de compétence différentes, des progressions dans les exercices axés sur des habiletés de base très simples, l'entre-aide et l'échange entre tous les participants, la rétroaction individuelle et de groupe (e.g., dire au professeur ce qu'ils avaient trouvé particulièrement difficile après chaque cours), l'opportunité de participer et d'organiser des activités à l'extérieur des cours qui mettait en relief l'importance de leurs acquisitions (e.g., démonstration de leurs chorégraphies aux personnes de l'extérieur).

Références

Gauthier, P. et Poulin, N. Etude comparative des effets physiologiques et psychologiques de deux programmes d'activité physique pour les personnes âgées. Rapport soumis au M.L.C.P. Gouvernement du Québec, 1980.

Gomez, N.A. La danse pour les personnes du troisième âge. *Le Desport*, No. 17, juillet 1980.

Gomez, N.A., Péronnet, F., Massicotte, D. et Gagnon, M. Etude des effets sur la condition physique, les qualités psychomotrices, les dimensionssocio-affectives, les habitudes de vie, ainsi que la satisfaction des participants à des programmes de conditionnement physique et de danse chez des personnes du troisième âge. Rapport final soumis au M.L.C.P., Gouvernement du Québec, 1981.

Pollock, M.L., Dawson, G.A., Miller, H.S., Jr. Ward, A., Cooper, D., Headley, W., Linnerud, A.C. and M.M. Noemir. Physiological response of men 49 to 65 years of age to endurance training. *Journal of the American Geriatrics Society*, 24: 97-104, 1976.

Shostrom, E.L. An inventory for the measurement of self-actualization. *Educational and Psychological Measurement*, 1964, 24, 2, p. 210.

ACHIEVEMENT MOTIVATION TRAINING OF FUTURE PHYSICAL EDUCATION TEACHERS

Hosek, V., Man, F., (Czechoslovakia)

Application of the theory of achievement motivation in social practice showed that predominance of success oriented motivation is more useful than motivation oriented towards avoiding a failure in an activity. Motivation variables form in children during the period if 6-10 years of their age; the achievement set of a teacher — especially a PT teacher — has a great effect on children in this period. A teacher who has undergone a motivational training can be expected to form achievement sets in children more successfully. This is the reason why in our psychological-pedagogical experiment we decided to verify the following hypothesis: it is possible under the conditions of a pedagogical faculty curricula to organize — in a form of seminar, motivational training that would increase achievement motivation and, subsequently, also social activity.

Method

The experiment included four comparable homogenous study groups (N = 80). Two groups were used as experimental ones, two as control ones. 37 students went through motivational training. The training program consisted of 12 training units (each lasting 90 minutes), carried out in one week interval. Theoretically the program was based on the concept of active social learning (Linhart, Perlaki, 1975), including the explication of the theory, achievement thoughts planning, causal attribution and interpretation training, adequate role playing, motivational games using sports elements.

Before the experiment started, achievement motivation was tested projectively with the use of McClelland's (1953) and Heckhausen's (1963) methods. The same measurements were carried out repeatedly in all groups immediately after the termination of the training, half a year and one year after the termination of the training. School achievements were evaluated in the same intervals by means of average study results. Social activity was evaluated by means of both objective data, and a standard interview.

Results

Statistical treatment of the results (ANOVA, analysis of variance) showed a significant increase of achievement motivation after the termination of motivational training in experimental groups. The changes were especially conspicuous, when comparing experimental groups with control ones; they showed in persons' behaviour as well as in factual significance of observed differences. A significant decrease of achievement motivation was observed in the experimental group after the termination of the training, however, one year after the termination of the training this variable exceeded original values at 5% level of significance.

A significant increase of the fear of failure due to the motivational training was found but there were no differences in this variable between experimental and control groups one year after the termination of the training course. The increase of the fear of failure is connected with the use of Mc Clelland's concept which works diffusively in this area. It can be also assumed that motivational training has a different effect on individual members of a group whose motivational structure was not differentiated in advance. More precise results could probably be achieved by modifying the training program with regard to the motivation structure of the subjects who would be included in training groups with a differentiated program according to the results of the initial diagnosis of motivation.

Social activity in the experimental group increased significantly compared to the control group. On top of that, differential scores showed that students who "profited more" from the motivational training course were subsequently more active in social sphere.

There was no significant change in absolute values of study results in the experimental group. Study results decreased significantly in the control group in the same period. This was due to the fact that all the groups sat for a series of rather difficult exams during the period of investigation. The results can be interpreted as a relative increase of study achievements of the experimental group students who — in contradistinction to the controls — maintained the average of their study results in more difficult conditions.

Practical implications

1. Designed and experimentally tested program of forming achievement motivation in future teachers can be fully utilized within their professional training.

2. Individual elements of the program of achievement motivation training based on the concept of active social learning can be used in the psychological training of sportsmen as factors of re-education.

3. At present a program of achievement motivation training of top sportsmen is being designed and tested. This program includes those elements that proved competent in the program of achievement motivation training of future teachers and that are directly connected with the performance in sport (such as performance planning, regulation of aspiration level on the basis of success and failure in the sequence model activities, risky decision making, selection of the level of difficulty of one's own future activity program, choice of suitable partners for group activities based on social sensitivity, regulation of will strain).

Conclusion

In terms of the initial hypothesis we consider a motivational training of future physical education teachers a meaningful means of the forming of a teacher's personality and thus also a determinant of later development of sports motivation in pupils.

REFERENCES

1. Alschuler, A., Tabor, D., Mc Intyre, J.: Teaching achievement motivation. Middletown, Conn. Education Ventures, Inc. 1970.

2. Hechhausen, H.: Hoffnung un Furcht in der Leistungsmotivation. Meisenheim, Hain 1963.

3. Hosek, V., Man, F.: Aktivni sociálni uceni jako teeoreticky základ vycviku sociálne psychologickych dovednosti trenéru. "Cs. psychologie" XXI, 5, 1977: 488-497.

4. Hosek, V., Man, F., Vondrysova, M.: Achievement motivation training college. In: Materialy svetového psychologického kongresu v Lipsku 1980.

5. Linhart, J., Perlaki, J.: Model aktivniho socialniho uceni. "Cs. psychologie" XIX, 3, 1975: 235-248.

6. Mc Clelland, D.C. et al.: The Achievement Motive. New York, Appleton-Century-Crofts 1953.

7. Norakidze, V.G.: Tipy charaktera i fiksirovannaya ustanovka. Mecniereba 1966.

8. Vorwerg, M.: Adaptives Training der Leistungsmotivation. Zeitschrift für Psychologie 185, 1977, 2: 230-236.

9. Weiner, B.: Human Motivation. New York, Holt, Reinhart and Winston 1980.

Etude longitudinale de la personnalité et des motivations des éducateurs physiques en formation.

Catherine Garnier (Canada)

La publicité faite aux faits sportifs fournit des arguments contradictoires aux éducateurs qui, ou bien rejettent le sport à cause de ses déviations, ou bien n'en retiennent que les vertus éducatives. Quelque soit la position que l'on prenne, il est indéniable que le sport est devenu un fait social puissant (Zeigler, 1977). Rechercher ses bienfaits devrait retenir l'attention des éducateurs dont la mission est de transmettre la culture aux jeunes générations.

Pour véhiculer les valeurs positives du sport dans les différents milieux où ces éducateurs agissent: école, loisir, entraînement, ils devront donc soit être convaincus de ces valeurs avant de s'engager dans leur formation, soit les découvrir au cours de cette formation. Par sa nature synthétique le sport conduit à un développement harmonieux de la personne. La corporéité retrouvée dans une pensée occidentale autrefois culpabilisée, s'ouvre vers un point de vue humaniste du sport, l'individu considéré dans sa totalité. Par le sport, coopération et compétition se marient (Zeigler, 1977) pour le meilleur du développement de l'intelligence sociale de l'enfant. Bouet (1968) insiste sur ces aspects de l'activité sportive qui apparaissent aussi dans les 6 dimensions qu'énuméraient Barrel et Holt (1980) dans leur étude sur les attitudes des étudiants vis à vis de l'éducation physique.

L'ensemble des rôles ou fonctions accordés à l'activité sportive peut s'exprimer en parte à travers deux valeurs essentielles: — la première selon laquelle le sport contribuerait à l'épanouissement de la personne, — alors que la seconde, centrée sur les inter-relations sociales inhérentes aux sports, favoriserait pour chacun son intégration dans les groupes en développant des attitudes saines vis à vis de la coopération et de la compétition. Ces fonctions ne peuvent être ignorées par les auteurs soucieux d'un processus éducatif complet, et parmi ceux-ci, Zeigler (1977) suggère que le sport, aspect intégral de la culture, soit un objet d'étude dans les universités, en même temps qu'une partie importante de la formation des maîtres.

Il incombe donc à ces futurs maîtres de propager et de développer les idéaux reliés à la pratique de l'activité sportive. C'est pourquoi l'étude longitudinale présente a porté sur les motivations et le personnalité des étudiants de 1er cycle à l'Université du Québec à Montréal dans un programme de formation des maîtres en éducation physique et sportive de 1977 (64 étudiants) à 1980 (retest de 35 étudiants). Un des buts de cette investigation était de vérifier du statut du sport chez les étudiants avec les exigences de la mission imparties aux éducateurs, ainsi que les effets de la formation reçue par les étudiants par rapport à ces valeurs.

Ces deux dimensions furent étudiées au moyen d'un questionnaire de recherche. De plus, un questionnaire de personnalité à validation factorielle a permis d'identifier les traits distincts de cette population. Celle-ci se différencie quelque peu d'une population normale, en étant significativement plus imaginative,

plus intelligente et audacieuse que cette dernière (.008 — p — .035). Les résultats tendent à montrer qu'elle est particulièrement concernée par l'épanouissement de la personne et par la fonction de formation des diverses catégories de population. Toutefois, bien que globalement les motivations n'aient pas changé après trois ans d'études, il semble que le programme accentue l'intérêt du groupe dans la personne "biologique", que l'aspect social retienne moins l'attention, et que les jugements sur la compétition et son rôle soient plus partagés.

L'influence de cette appréhension biologique de la motricité dans les programmes a été analysée dans une étude antérieure (Garnier, 1977) qui rejetait le point de vue réductioniste et limité de l'enseignement au profit d'une vision plus englobante de l'homme dans le sport ou l'activité physique. A l'opposé d'une formation en miettes (Parlebas, 1967) par sommation cumulative, ce serait une formation par quête exploratrice vers "les concepts fondamentaux" et les "principes interdisciplinaires" selon l'approche des systèmes (Bertallanfy, 1968) qui devrait être préconisée.

Pour être menés à bien, ces projets seraient expérienciels et insérés dans le temps et l'espace de différents milieux, de telle sorte que le développement de la personne et l'appropriation des connaissances soient assurés. C'est l'authenticité du vécu qui permettrait d'atteindre les mécanismes sous-jacents aux phénomènes globaux et non partiels. De plus, cette implication sollicitant la prise de responsabilité, l'autonomie, la continuité dans l'action et l'intérêt soutenu serait garant d'une formation complète.

Les 4 principes suivant seraient donc à la base de la formation des étudiants:

• l'activité est étudiée dans le contexte social dont elle est forcément issue afin que la reflexion porte essentiellement sur son rôle dans la vie de l'homme.

• la formation de l'éducateur ne peut se réduire à l'acquisition de connaissances; elle doit aussi établir les conséquences individuelles de la mission de chacun, et une éthique car "science sans conscience" ne peut mener qu'à une impasse.

• la formation s'inscrit dans l'histoire de l'individu et doit lui permettre d'acquérir l'habileté de se développer et de s'intégrer à l'évolution culturelle dont il fait parti.

Une démarche logique est nécessaire pour répondre à ce dernier principe, c'est-à-dire que les mécanismes fondamentaux sont extraits d'une situation concrète, alors que les principes d'intervention sont établis à partir de ces mécanismes.

Cette conception aurait pour conséquence une prise de conscience de la part de l'éducateur quant à son rôle dans la société qu'il traduirait par le genre de vie qu'il adopterait et tenterait de développer autour de lui en accord avec les valeurs véhiculées. Quant à sa formation, dorénavant inscrite dans un processus permanent et non ponctuel elle serait axée sur l'expérience, la pratique des connaissances, une éthique adaptée aux mouvements culturels.

Enfin, l'ensemble de cette étude suggère les recommandations suivantes: tout d'abord au niveau de l'élaboration et l'évaluation des programmes:

● en établissant les finalités de ceux-ci relatives aux valeurs à développer ou à acquérir par rapport au sport.

● en concevant des programmes où savoir, savoir-être et savoirfaire ne sont pas juxtaposés mais conçus dans un système d'intégration justifié par les finalités.

● en évaluant systématiquement les modifications apportées par le programme chez les étudiants afin de débusquer les échecs concernant le développement des valeurs attachées au sport.

Ensuite. au niveau des contenus:

● en recherchant une implication de l'étudiant par des stages de pratiques sportives et des stages d'intervention dans différents milieux où l'activité sportive est implantée ou à être implantée.

● en organisant un développement individualisé à travers des projets de longue durée où le style et le rythme de l'apprentissage de l'étudiant seront respectés,

où le passage du pratique au théorique et retour au pratique seront assurés

où le systeme des valeurs attribuées au sport sera considéré d'un point de vue éthique, en général et professionnellement.

● en développant la compétence des éducateurs par des stages universitaires de réflexion périodiques, pour que le processus entamé lors de leur formation se continue à travers des échanges organisés et favorisant l'adoption de chacun au milieu culturel changeant.

Références

Barrel, G.V. & Holt, D. Attitude changes of specialist students of physical education towards physical activity during teacher training courses (1980), Sous presse.

Bouet, M. *Signification du sport.* Paris: Edition Universitaires, 1968.

Cattell, R.B., Eber, H.V. *Manuel d'application du test 16PF de R.B. Cattell.* Paris: Les éditions du centre de psychologie appliquée, 1972.

Garnier, C. L'E.P.S. au Canada Programmes de formation *Revue E.P.S.* 1978, *154,* 63-65.

Parlebas, P. L'éducation physique en miettes. *Revue E.P.S.,* 1976, 85-88.

Von Bertalanffy, L. *Théorie générale des systèmes,* Paris: Dunod, 1973.

Zeigler, E.F. *Physical education and sport philosophy,* Englewood Cliffs: Prentice Hall, 1977.

PART III THE ROLE OF SPORT PSYCHOLOGY

SPORT PSYCHOLOGY COMING OF AGE

Miroslav Vanek (Czechoslovakia)

The psychology of sport became an institutionalized discipline in the twenties of this century. Since that time the number of scientific articles and monographies, as well as textbooks is growing. Departments of psychology are established at universities and institutes of training of physical education teachers and coaches. National societies for sport psychology are founded, conferences, symposia and seminars are arranged, and within the range of sports sciences the psychology of sport is included in the interdisciplinary international congresses. The need for a greater international contact and cooperation opened the way to the foundation of ISSP in the sixties in the First International Congress of Sport Psychology in Rome (1965). The congresses that followed were arranged in Washington (1968), Madrid (1973), Prague (1977) and at last in Ottawa 1981.

Is it possible to say then that the psychology of sport has grown up to adulthood? Undoubtedly - we are more numerous, we have specific journals, national, continental and international societies, the sport psychology subjects are not only larger, but also structured and differentiated, system and sub-system approaches are employed, and the problems of complexity, multidimensionality and multidisciplinary investigations arise, as well as questions of professional ethic, since sport psychology becomes a profession in many countries.

Regarded from all those points of view the psychology of sport is certainly a grown-up and distinctive scientific branch.

However at present the focus is not only on research undertakings and professional and institutional promotion of psychological questions of sport activities. More and more attention is now paid to effective use of the psychology of sport in social practice.

Effective application of psychological findings cannot of course be regarded only as reinforcement of instructions or as an interpretation of scientific language. The psychic phenomena of individuals and groups are so complex and situationally determined that they form a dynamic and variagated mosaic of sociopsychophysiological events. Individual cases may be generalized only approximately; and also all directions, patents and techniques of auto- and hetero-regulation are of the same approximate character.

In the previous period we had to face an underestimation of the psychology of sport; nowadays the situation has changed and we feel that sometimes a real danger of overestimation of sport psychology is threatening. It is an overestimation on the part of the psychologists themselves and it may become one of the greatest problems of a further progress in sport psychology. The extreme marketing of "wonder-psychologists" who promise attainment of unrealistic achievements to athletes, coaches, administrators and sport associations discriminate the psychology of sport in the eyes of both experts and public. But perhaps it belongs to the development of any scientific discipline - miraculous instructions and pills, as well as impostors exist in every branch of man's activities.

This concerns, of course, not the greatest part of our colleagues who preserve the principles of fair psychological work. It should be accepted only as a sigh of a man who for many years - including several Olympic Games - was working in the demanding sphere of superior sport, and who frequently was astonished to hear opinions of the following calibre: it is not necessary to require a hard, strenuous sport training - when hypno-suggestive instructions and tape-recorder casette bring the same result.

The psychology of sport is justified for its humanistic positive aims in motor therapy both in sport and adjoining social spheres, since physical culture represents a high value for every society.

ETHICAL PRACTICE OF APPLIED SPORT PSYCHOLOGY

Robert M. Nideffer (USA)

Until recently, the primary focus in sport psychology had been in the areas of research and education. Although our Eastern European colleagues have been traveling with athletic teams for some time, and have been providing a variety of psychological services, the same has not been true in North America or much of the rest of the world.

Since the middle of the 1970's we have seen a rather dramatic shift in interests, with more and more professionals becoming interested in the applied aspects of sport psychology. This growing interest has tended to follow just behind the increase in interest being shown by athletes, coaches, and various governmental organizations.

Discussions with applied colleagues throughout the U.S., Canada, and Australia indicate that they are experiencing increases in requests for information from psychologists and counselors who have declared themselves specialists in the area of sport psychology, from athletes and coaches who want to know what psychology has to offer (or who want to dictate what they want psychology to provide), from researchers who want to do post doctoral training in the applied areas of sport psychology.

The Canadian government through Sport Canada has come to the Canadian Society for the Psychology of Sport and Physical Activity to find out what sport psychologists can contribute to the total development of the athlete. Sport Canada has provided funds for committees so that information about the resources and services available can be identified. Sport Canada has been concerned about quality control and needs help in determining just what it is that sport psychology has to offer to Canada.

Unfortunately, as interest in the area of sport psychology develops, so does the opportunity for professional jealousies and unethical practice. At the present time there are legal constraints in North America that will prevent the majority of individuals who currently identify themselves as sport psychologists from representing themselves in that way to the public. The title psychologist is licensed and to use it an individual must meet the educational and experiential requirements for licensure, as well, pass a licensing examination (an examination and set of experiences that has little if any relevance to the area of sport psychology). Various members of CSPLSP and NASPSPA have been informed by members of the American and Canadian Psychological Associations that these organizations are looking for violations of the licensing laws in order to enforce legal constraints.

This year marks the first time in history that a school of psychology will attempt to enter doctoral level students into a sport psychology specialty with an applied focus (there are many masters and doctoral level programs with a research or motor learning, motor development focus). The quality of the program, the quality of the faculty and the quality of the students has yet to be evaluated. It will be at least four years before we graduate anyone with a focused educational experience in the area of sport psychology.

In the meantime, there are those of us who are (and want to continue) providing services, there are agencies and sport governing bodies who want help now. What can we do to protect ourselves and the public. Can we, or do we need to, work toward some balance between excessively repressive legislation on the one hand, and unconstrained permissiveness (let the buyer beware) on the other? It is my contention that professional organizations like NASPSPA, CSPLSP, ISSP, and perhaps to a lesser degree FEPSAC, should take an organized position and work rapidly towards the development of ethical guidelines for sport psychologists. I would further contend that it is these organizations, and not organizations like the various psychological associations (which lack the applied experience), that should define the roles that sport psychologists fill. It is only with an operational definition of roles that we can determine the legitimacy and quality of service that is provided. It is only with the definition of roles that we can determine whether or not a relevant body of knowledge exists which is related to an individual's ability to provide service.

The idea that national and international associations should take upon themselves the role of defining sport psychology and of developing an explicit set of ethical standards is threatening to some of the membership. Who will be included, and who will be excluded? How much will it cost in time and money? Do we have the knowledge base and expertise to take such a step? Do we want to assume the responsibility that will be associated with making such judgements? Should we be involved in application at all?

Intellectually, I believe that we can provide rational, well thought out answers for most of the questions I just raised. Emotionally, it is a different issue, one that is affected by our personal values and ideologies. I would suggest that even though we may have strong negative emotional reactions towards moving in the direction of certification, the development of ethical standards, and role definition in the area of sport psychology, many of us have no choice if we wish to survive. Let me continue by discussing some of the questions I have raised.

Perhaps the first (and most central issue) to be discussed when we think of the need for role definition and/or ethical standards has to do with whether or not some type of protection is required, either for the profession, or more importantly, for the consumer. As a professional you may need to be protected in two ways. First, your right to practice may be interfered with by others. This is what any type of licensure results in whether it is controlled by the government, various states and/or psychological associations, or by sports governing bodies. Most of us are currently discriminated against in this way in that we cannot legally call ourselves sport psychologists.

Many individuals attempt to get around licensure laws by adopting new names or titles. We have "personal advisors", "spiritual readers", "counselors", "astrologers" etc. All individuals who are providing "psychological services" for fees. Momentary reflection on these titles and the services that are often provided is sufficient to make most of us realize that quality of service is not controlled when people go their own way. The individual's reputation, no matter how effective they are, is hardly enhanced by some uncontrolled or poorly defined title. If a name change is necessary for those of us who are not psychologists, then it should be a name that the various sport psychology associations agree on, one that has defined roles, a set of ethical standards, and professional expertise behind it.

A second problem that the professional faces is the damage that the practice of others, who call themselves by the same name, yet perform in an incompetent or unethical way, can create. Should you doubt that you are affected by the reputation of others, simply ask yourself how various colleagues react to individuals who have degrees from different institutions. Psychologists feel discriminated against by the medical profession because they are Ph.D.'s and not M.D.'s. Unfortunately, the public still does not know what a psychologist is, let alone what a sport psychologist is. By title you may be mistaken for a psychiatrist, a spiritual advisor, a person who studies extra-sensory perception, a magician, or a color coordinator. Individuals looking for publicity and newspapers looking for excitement are getting together more and more frequently to talk about the role of psychology in sport. Unfortunately, often the most colorful people to the papers are those with the least expertise, the loosest ethical standards, and the most "far out" ideas.

It would be nice to believe that an "informed consumer" would be able to make judgements about who can help, what service might be useful, etc. Certainly one of the services that associations like ISSP can provide is to educate the consumer. Presumably if the public were educated there wouldn't be any need for the profession to establish standards for itself. I believe that it is fair to say that this position is extremely idealistic. In fact, it has been the experience of associations like the American Medical Association, various psychological associations, and every police department around the world, that educational programs fall on a great many deaf ears. There are many good reasons for this.

First, everyone has something that they would like to educate us about. We can't possibly listen to them all, so we pick and choose on the basis of what we feel is important or relevant. If I'm not an alcoholic or a drug addict, if I'm not a sinner, if I don't perceive a need for a sport psychologist, why should I listen? Then too, we are skeptical because we have learned a great many people are out for themselves. It is because we don't know who to believe that we go to associations, brand names, or familiar people for their recommendations. A third reason that it is difficult to educate the public is especially apparent in sports.

Most coaches and athletes don't want to take the time to become psychologists. Most coaches and athletes don't want to be educated. What coaches and athletes want are straight answers to specific questions. "Can you increase my player's confidence or not?" For the most part, individuals don't care what you use, they want results. It is this intensity, drive, and lack of knowledge, that either makes them susceptible to quacks and false promises, or causes them to avoid sport psychology altogether.

Alright, so there are people making promises they can't keep, are they hurting anyone? Does the person who promises a service and doesn't know what they are doing in the area of sport psychology create serious enough problems that we need to think of certification? It has been my experience that they can and do!

Can a diving coach hurt (physically, emotionally, and in terms of ultimate development) a diver that he/she gets to attempt a dive off of a ten meter tower before the diver is ready? Of course they can. Then can't the sport psychologist make the same type of mistake by promising individuals that techniques like hypnosis will give them greater control than they had before?

If the sport psychologist's input (whether if comes from interviews, behavioral observations, psychological and physiological tests, and/or past history) is used in the selection and screening of athletes, do you suppose the decisions made could have a critical impact on the athlete's life. On what basis should such decisions be made?

How should a sport psychologist react to the examples of child abuse that occur quite frequently in sport, especially in sports like gymnastics and skating? If the sport psychologist fails to recognize that the athlete who is lethargic is clinically depressed, and instead sees them as lazy, does that create problems? If a sport psychologist had told management that J.R. Richards (the pitcher) was simply a problem ball player where do you suppose that sport psychologist would be practicing today?

To have an impact, to be able to get the athlete to take the steps required for ultimate development, the sport psychologist, like the coach, must establish a very strong relationship. Most often, the changes an athlete makes to perform more effectively and control arousal level result from increased confidence in either themselves and/or in the coach or sport psychologist. It is the confidence that a given technique or procedure will be effective, and that the professional knows what they are talking about, that allows the athlete to take needed risks.

The sport psychologist is effective through development of respect and trust of the athlete. Along with this trust and confidence goes a certain amount of emotional involvement and at times dependency. It is this special relationship and trust which makes the athlete potentially vulnerable to abuse or to the mistakes of ignorance. To do away with the emotional involvement would be to destroy much of the effectiveness of the sport psychologist. Can't we teach professionals to use their influence ethically?

Certification programs and ethical standards do not guarantee that the most competent people will always be certified. These programs do not guarantee that mistakes won't be made. Such programs do insure that those certified have been sensitized to certain critical issues. Such programs let the public know that the professional has had certain relevant experiences and training. Finally, these programs do increase the accountability of members. The argument should not be that explicit ethics or standards result in perfect performance. Rather the argument should be that the average level of performance is higher when certain requirements are met and in addition, performance variability is reduced.

Some people might argue that sport psychologists are not clinical psychologists or psychiatrists. They are working with normal, healthy people in an educational environment so why do they need to adopt ethical standards like those of other service providers. I believe that there are several reasons for this.

First, although we are working with healthy individuals, we are often working under extremely stressful conditions. The average individual does not butt heads with someone who is 300 pounds. The average individual does not attempt a triple axel, or a reverse two and one-half. The average individual does not play a set of tennis for $22,000, or have the expectancies of an entire country placed on them during the Olympics.

Second, in youth sports we may initially be dealing with healthy children and find ourselves having to contend with unhealthy parents. Often, sport psychologists find themselves in the middle, having to make a decision to respond to the needs of the individual, or the parent, team, or country, etc. An explicit set of ethical principles helps the individual make that decision and lets the consumer know what to expect.

I have tried to make the point that sport psychology has achieved enough status, and notoriety that it is time to develop a more formal structure. I hope that the 1980's will see the emergence of sport psychology as a respected and recognized discipline. It is my belief that if this is to occur we must make our positions known. It is time for organizations like ISSP, NASPSPA, CSPLSP and FEPSAC to take a stronger political, administrative, and educational role.

It is my fear that if we don't lobby for ourselves, we will find others deciding our future. In North America it will not be long before psychological associations take the title "sport psychologist" as their own. It will not be long before they make an organized effort to be seen as the experts. Currently, sports governing bodies and governmental agencies are waiting to see if we will get our house in order. Their patience cannot continue for long. Soon, they will either respond to the person with the best pitch or lose confidence and respect in the area.

The ISSP has already recommended that its membership consider a modification of the Ethical Standards established by the American Psychological Association. Both CSPLSP and NASPSPA will soon do the same. The adoption of these standards by the membership in addition to establishing some working guidelines, will provide nonprofessionals and outsiders with some evidence that we do have a professional identity, and that we are concerned about quality in the provision of service.

I believe we need to move much beyond this first step however. I think we must begin to define the roles that sport psychologists can be expected to fill. Such a definition will allow the public to determine the personal relevance of what we have to offer. A definition of roles will allow the profession to determine the skills and experiences that should lead to quality service. This role definition can help reduce the anxiety of other professionals. Many clinical psychologists would relax if they knew that sport psychologists didn't consider themselves clinical psychologists specializing in athletes.

We need a body of respected professionals who will make a concerted attempt to educate the public. We need to establish organizations, the place to come with questions about the psychology of sport and it's practice.

I don't believe that we should attempt to license or legislate sport psychology. I do believe we should establish our own standards, standards that are based on the services provided. I believe we should be flexible in determining the ways in which individuals can meet those recommended standards. A Ph.D. degree from a certain institution is not the answer. Certainly not the only one.

I do believe that we should move in the direction of certification. Unless, we do that, I don't feel we will have any real impact on the policy or practice of various sports governing bodies. We should establish standards and we should certify individuals as having met those standards. This does not say that the individual is an ethical or qualified or competent service provider. It does say that they have been exposed to relevant theory and experience.

The final question or point I would like to address has to do with "the state of the art." In suggesting that sport psychology has reached the point where we need to establish a code of ethics, to define roles, and to certify individuals, am I being delusional? These suggestions are based on the premise that we have enough content to offer to potential consumers. Do we have a "science" of sport psychology? Do we have a "religion" of sport psychology? In either case, are there identifiable techniques and/or processes that are reliable and valid. Can we demonstrate that the systematic application of certain procedures (e.g., relaxation training or biofeedback), and/or ways of communicating (e.g., confronting, supporting) do affect performance in any lawful way. Are we sophisticated enough to be able to use information about situational, interpersonal, and perceptual factors to facilitate performance. Is there a body of knowledge we can teach others?

Obviously I feel that we have reached that point in the development of both theory and technique. We do have an identifiable body of knowledge. There are laws and principles associated with behavior modification that affect outcome in systematic ways. In a similar way, research in the area of cognitive behavior modification is resulting in the demonstration of systematic changes as a function of various types of interventions.

In the area of psychological assessment we can

enhance our ability to predict and control behavior. Tests can serve a useful purpose. At the same time, we know that test results can be abused, particularly if the user does not know his/her own limitations, or those of the tests. We can identify a set of skills (including knowledge about statistics, reliability, and validity) that an individual using tests should have. In the areas of stress management we can identify methodological issues and concerns associated with the use of techniques like biofeedback and progressive relaxation. Sensitivity to individual differences in confidence and self-esteem can allow us to better balance confrontation and support in our work with athletes.

MODELS FOR PRACTICE I:
NOTES FROM GUIDO SCHILLINGS WORKSHOP

John T. Partington (Canada)

Sport Psychologists must not work exclusively with élite athletes. They should take a more important role in the training of Sport Directors and instructors, and even journalists and teachers, inside as well as outside sport. Training about sport is hopelessly lacking in the preparation of many types of community leaders and social workers, as well as for those working in most reintegration projects with drug addicts, prisoners, elderly people, groups in ghettos, etc. It is lacking because Sport Psychology has generally stayed within the parameters of élite sport.

Sport Psychologists who do work actively with élite competitors should not aim solely at increasing skills for athletic performance. They must try their best to introduce concepts of Humanistic Psychology to sport. They could, for example, teach the methods of interaction applied by Ruth Cohn (see Bidder von K. Psychologische Beratung im Sport — Themenzentrierte Interaktion als Beitrag, Diplomarbeit, Zürich, 1980). Moreover, they should especially try to help children and young athletes who are competing at the élite level.

The model represented in Figure 1 is suggested to guide the practice of Sport Psychologists who work with élite competitors. The model illustrates the following principles: The athlete is shown at the top of the triangle to assert that he/she alone is most important in the sport enterprise. It also illustrates the stark reality that there comes a time, just before the starting signal, after all the lengthy preparation is over, when the athlete alone becomes totally responsible for achievement in the event. It is not the theory of coaching, the Sport System, or the Political-Economic Ideology which wins or loses — it is the athlete. That is why the athlete should be more in control of his sport experience.

Coaches and Specialist Assistants are shown at the base of the triangle to make the point that their most active role with the athlete should be in the earlier stages of preparation. Ideally, as the time for actual competition approaches, the athlete should assume more autonomy.

The solid double-headed arrow between athlete and coach emphasizes the desirability of close rapport and continuous collaboration between athlete and coach. Similarly, the solid double-headed arrow between coach and the team of Specialist Assistants underlines the mutual, shared responsibility of all these individuals to work closely together in the service of the athlete. The Sport Psychologist is listed first among the specialists only to emphasize that he should be involved early in the preparation period and play his most active role in long-term planning.

The dotted two-way arrow represents three points. First, the athlete should be free to consult with the Sport Psychologist, or other specialist, without permission from the coach. The dotted line indicates, however, that this would not be the most desirable arrangement because over-dependency of the athlete on others should be avoided. This is the paradox of our practice — to build trust without dependency. Finally, the fact that this dotted two-way arrow points both ways shows that Sport Psychologists should be free to approach athletes directly, when research requires, to ask for their involvement in crucial research issues. The opportunity for direct links with the athlete is especially important for ensuring confidentiality.

Although there was no opportunity to assess support for this model among congress delegates, results shown below of a survey item given the congress indicate the considerable degree of commitment felt by Sport Psychologists in general toward athletes.

Question: To whom should the Sport Psychologist be most accountable?

Answer:		%
	The athlete	50.0
	The coach/teacher	14.3
	The parent	5.4
	The client ("owner" who pays)	3.6
	All of the above	23.2
	None of the above/no opinion	3.5

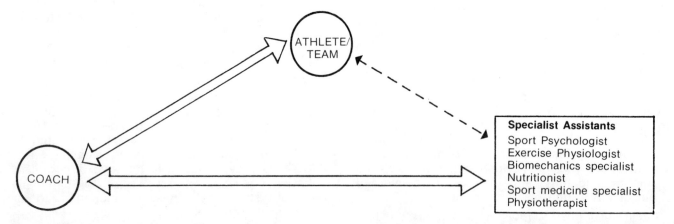

Figure 1. An Athlete-Centered Model to Illustrate the Ideal Role of the Sport Psychologist Working with Elite Competitors.

MODELS FOR PRACTICE II:
NOTES FROM TOM TUTKO'S "SPORT PSYCHING" WORKSHOP

John T. Partington (Canada)

Initial Contact

The athlete should be the one to decide whether psychological services are needed; but regardless who makes the contact, everyone in the system should know what you are going to do.

Ideally, the Sport Psychologist (SP) should be consulted long before competition begins, but unfortunately he/she tends to be called in when the athlete or team is already in trouble. This can have unwanted consequences. First, it can lead to a "negative Hawthorne Effect." If an athlete appears to have a problem and a SP ("shrink") is called in, it may confirm and strengthen the athlete's belief that he has a problem, thus generating or compounding a real problem. Also, when psychological problems are solved, the SP may look good; but if the athlete was already in the process of gradually working and developing through the problem, the SP's intervention may deny the athlete the confidence building which might have resulted from his recognition that he had solved his own problem.

Role

The SP should be an educator who works behind the scenes, rather than a practitioner, like an M.D., doing things down on the bench. Before you can help, you have to learn what is going on. The best teacher for this is systematic and continuous observation. Also, to encourage everyone to communicate openly about what is going on, an open-door, totally confidential policy should be established from the outset. The aim is to get everyone connected with the team to trust you. Without trust no one will tell you anything, and nothing you try will work.

The team is like a family and the coach is the father. The SP should help the coach become better at performing the psychological part of his role. This means that he helps the coach to recognize and deal with individual differences among his players. It also means that he might even teach the coach how to administer, score, interpret, and utilize psychological tests for athletes. With most standardized objective tests this can be done in a day or two, but it is better for the coach to work on this with the SP for a few months.

Overcoming Resistance

The SP has to be prepared to deal with problems when he tries to initiate a program of psychological assistance for athletes: Coaches and other specialists may feel that their territory is being invaded; athletes, on the other hand, may not want to change their own ways of coping.

Role disputes can be avoided if the SP explains very clearly to everyone what he can and cannot do, how he would like to function, and how he intends to avoid infringing on someone else's special area of responsibility. To ensure that everyone understands and feels part of the psychological program, it is recommended that everyone (coaches and general managers in professional sports, and physical education teachers and principals in school sports) should undergo whatever the SP has planned for the athletes in the system. The key is to establish and maintain open communication.

The SP should also inform coaches and athletes about how other athletes and teams have benefitted from learning psychological skills. This will help to build rapport by overcoming some of the doubts and suspicions. Every sport has at least one or two successful athletes who are well-known for their use of psychological strategies.

Before starting the psychological program the SP should learn in detail about the athlete's present ways of preparing and coping. Most high level performers develop an implicit, complex set of beliefs about what they have to do in order to succeed. Their training rituals and superstitious beliefs and behaviours have been associated with previous success. They are bound to be resistant to change, even during a slump, due to partial reinforcement. When the SP helped the athlete to recognize that he may have alrerady been using naive psychology, the SP can then begin to explain the program and techniques which he thinks will help the most.

The best way to get started is to invite the athlete to participate on a trial basis for a couple of weeks. If his initial voluntary compliance is reinforced by constructive feedback, the athlete will usually commit himself fully to the program.

The Sport Psychology Program

The SP should be prepared to offer more than a collection of tests and techniques. He should develop a well designed, fully organized, total package of services. Tom Tutko's "Sport Psyching" program has three components — testing, feedback, and psychological training.

Since athletes are generally action-oriented, the testing should not overtax their patience, nor their abstract reasoning skills. Tutko uses the *Athlete Motivation Inventory* (AMI) to test for motivational and emotional strengths and weaknesses.

The manner in which test results are to be used should be discussed with the athletes before testing is done. Several feedback models are possible. In one the SP gives each athlete a confidential, individual interpretation of the profile of test results, with recommendations about how to try to improve certain characteristics. This feedback is spelled out in clear behavioural terms. However, some athletes prefer not to know their test results. In this case, the SP can give feedback to the coach, with the athlete's permission of course. In the case of teams, the ideal model is to have all players, and coaches fully aware of everyone else's test results, and targets for change. All test profiles can be displayed in a quiet corner of the locker room. This encourages players to help each other with the psychological aspects of their training (e.g., relaxation, imagery, mental rehearsal, etc.), just as they traditionally do to improve physical skills.

Tutko's "Sport Psyching" is a six week program of 20 minute per day sessions aimed at teaching relaxation, imagery, and mental rehearsal skills. This program provides the techniques and confidence necessary for the athlete to work further on those areas of weakness revealed in the test profile. His examples of the program in action illustrate close collaboration among the athlete, coach, and SP. Finally, Tutko stresses that there are no magical cures — psychological skills must be practiced by the athlete like all of the other learned components of excellence.

INTEGRATING AND INTERPRETING RESEARCH FINDINGS: A CHALLENGE TO SPORT PSYCHOLOGISTS

Wayne L. Halliwell and Lise Gauvin (Canada)

"Our problem is to find knowledge in the information" — G. Glass. "Where is the knowledge we have lost in information?" — T.S. Eliot. "Knowledge exists in minds, not in books. Before what has been found can be used by practitioners, someone must organize it, integrate it, extract the message." — K. Boulding.

1. Why is it important for sport psychologists to integrate, interpret and disseminate research findings?

• During the past decade researchers in the field of sport psychology have produced an impressive amount of data on a variety of topics related to the psychological aspects of sport participation and performance. However, reviews of the literature in areas such as "personality and sport" have typically led to the conclusion that empirical findings are equivocal and inconclusive. As a result both researchers and practitioners have obtained very little useful knowledge from the information contained in research findings.

It is contended that the failure to extract knowledge from information may be due to a lack of sophistication in the methods presently being used to integrate research findings in the field of sport psychology. Thus, it is suggested that sport psychologists should follow the lead of educational psychologists who are developing new methods for synthesizing the results of completed research studies. In this regard, Gene Glass (1976), an innovative pioneer in the area of synthetizing research outcomes, calls for *the need to think differently than we do about reviewing and integrating research*" (p. 6). He suggests that "the best minds are needed to integrate the staggering number of individual studies. This endeavor deserves higher priority now than adding a new experiment or survey to the pile" (p. 4).

Both in education and in sport, practitioners are searching for more effective ways of dealing with students and athletes. Hopefully, in the 1980s sport psychologists will recognize the integration of research findings as a worthy, scholarly undertaking which will produce a body of useful knowledge.

2. What methods are available for integrating and synthesizing research findings?

• There are essentially three methods for integrating research findings

    (i)   The narrative literature review

    (ii) The vote-counting method or box score method

    (iii) The techniques of meta-analysis

3. What are the advantages and limitations of using the narrative literature review?

• As its name suggests the narrative literature review consists of a literary report of the content and conclusions of existing research papers. This traditional method of research integration is the most commonly employed by researchers. If well-conceptualized and well-written, it has the advantage of providing a meaningful synthesis of a wide body of research which can be tailored to readers of all levels of expertise. However, social and educational psychologists such as Cooper (1978), Glass (1976, 1977), Light and Smith (1971), and Pillemer and Light (1980) as well as Rosenthal (1978) have recently remarked that the narrative literature review is deficient in certain ways. These scholars point out that this type of review can be highly subjective, as well as lacking in objective scientific standards as it is a product of the reviewer's own judgment. As a result of this subjectivity, the reviewer tends to draw "impressionistic" conclusions concerning the state of the art of the body of research being integrated. In this regard, Morgan (1980) criticizes existing narrative reviews of the sport personology literature as being characterized by ". . . a tendency to include certain types of research in these reviews and exclude other types of research. . ." (p. 53). It is this tendency of researchers to be "selectively inclusive" which reflects the type of subjectivity to which the use of the narrative literature review is particularly susceptible.

4. What does the vote-counting method consist of?

• In this second type of research integration the results of all studies pertaining to one particular hypothesis or question are gathered together and categorized as either showing a positive significant relationship, a negative significant relationship or no significant relationship. The number of studies falling into each category is tallied and the category containing the largest frequency count is then viewed as the one reflecting the true relationship between the independent and dependent variables under scrutiny (Glass, 1977; Light and Smith, 1971; Pillemer and Light, 1980). In the field of sport psychology, Martens' (1971) categorization of the results of studies dealing with the arousal-performance relationship provides a good example of how the vote-counting method has been used to synthesize research findings.

5. Is the vote-counting method superior to the narrative literature review?

• The vote-counting method is certainly more systematic than the narrative literature review as it employs a criterion in order to classify and thereby derive meaning from a group of studies. In this respect, it is superior to the narrative literature review. However, a recent discussion by Hedges and Olkin (1980) revealed that the vote-counting method of research integration has very low power. That is, the labelling of the results of a group of studies as being positive significant, negative significant or non-significant may not enable the reviewer to detect the presence of effects of the magnitude usually encountered in the social and educational psychology literature. Consequently, erroneous conclusions may be drawn from the results of this type of research integration. Moreover, Glass (1977) has argued that by simply classifying studies into three categories a large amount of descriptive information is disregarded and hence potentially insightful notions are overlooked. In sum, the vote-counting method is more systematic and objective than the narrative literature review, but it nevertheless has certain important deficiencies which render it inappropriate for some types of research integration.

6. What is meta-analysis?

• Meta-analysis constitutes a third level of research whereby the reviewer is able to integrate a large body of research findings in order to establish the state of the art in a certain field of study. More specifically, Glass (1876) has called for the recognition of three levels of research. The first level of research, also called primary analysis, is a procedure by which the researcher collects data from the subjects of a sample, and analyzes these data by means of statistical procedures in an effort to answer the question underlying the research. Primary analysis is the type of research most frequently employed by researchers in sport psychology and in the social sciences in general.

The second level of research termed secondary analysis, requires that the researcher gather together the data obtained from the subjects in a primary analysis, and subsequently these data are reanalyzed by means of different statistical procedures. Such a procedure allows the researcher to answer new questions or to provide a more elaborate answer to the original research question. It differs from primary analysis in that the data under scrutiny are not collected from subjects as they are already available from other studies.

Finally, a third level of research has been delineated by Glass)1976), and labelled meta-analysis. This level of research can be distinguished from the two previously outlined levels of research in that the unit of analysis is no longer data collected from subjects in a sample but rather data retrieved within a study. That is, in meta-analysis the researcher retrieves information pertaining to treatment, subject and design characteristics of a group of studies, and this information enables the investigator to examine the covariation of these characteristics with the results of these studies. This in turn permits the researcher to integrate findings relative to one particular research topic.

In sum, to echo Glass' (1976) definition, it can be stated that meta-analysis is: ". . . the statistical analysis of a large collection of analysis results from individual studies for the purpose of integrating the findings" (p. 3).

7. What are the advantages of the use of meta-analysis?

• Meta-analysis as a method for research integration has mainly three advantages over its counterparts. First, by way of coding, indexing and retrieving study characteristics and results, reviewers can avoid falling into the pit-falls of incorrectly combining results of studies. As was outlined previously, inadequate combining of studies can result from the subjectivity inherent in the narrative literature review or from the oversimplification and loss of information which may occur in using the vote-counting method. Meta-analysis therefore provides a useful and practical alternative to the more traditional methods of research integration.

Second, the use of meta-analytic techniques provides reviewers with new perspectives on the information available. That is, by including a wide array of descriptive information from the various studies being integrated, and by organizing, synthesizing and presenting this information by means of graphs, summary statistics and other statistical tools, reviewers can acquire valuable insight into the relationship between variation in outcomes and study characteristics. Glass (1976, 1977) contends that due to its ability to furnish additional insights into the research findings meta-analysis is more appropriate than traditional methods for research integration.

Finally, the coding, indexing and retrieval procedures involved in conducting meta-analysis allow the reviewer to establish a practical bibliography of the topic being reviewed. This advantage is by no means to be disregarded, because establishing such a methodological tool represents a considerable economy in time as well as energy spent searching for and locating various research articles. To recapitulate, meta-analysis constitutes a most efficient and powerful means whereby data synthesis may be accomplished.

8. What are the limitations of the use of meta-analysis?

• Users of meta-analysis risk encountering three main problems. The first problem pertains to the fact that meta-analysts possess only a limited amount of information on the studies being integrated, namely, that which is available in the articles or research papers. If the authors of the various investigations failed to include certain essential details concerning the treatment and design characteristics, or the result of their studies, then the integrator's effort would produce a weakened meta-analysis. However, this risk can be minimized by the use of very strict coding procedures, as well as precise defining of studies to be included in the meta-analysis. Moreover, if the integrator suspects that some indispensable information is missing s/he can contact the researchers concerned and obtain the missing data. The second caution to be reckoned with when conducting meta-analytic data synthesis relates to the need for appropriate human resources. The use of meta-analysis involves formulating guidelines for inclusion of different studies, making decisions about how to code various information, retrieving the values of various summary statistics and computing measures of experimental effect and the like. Hence, if the integrators are somewhat naive with respect to the body of literature being integrated or basic statistical principles, then incorrect data could be included in the meta-analysis, thereby weakening the resultant overall integrative analysis. However, integrators can lessen this problem in one of two ways. On the one hand, the studies to be integrated can be coded by two integrators and the resulting coding can be compared and discussed until agreement is reached as to the best way to solve any coding discrepancies. On the other hand, formulation of very strict, precise and elaborate coding procedures might just as well fulfill this purpose.

Lastly, because of the prefix *Meta* in the word meta-analysis, one might be lead to believe that meta-analysis is a useful tool for solving conceptual dilemmas. This in fact is not the case. The task of dealing with conceptual problems and determining the meaning of results of a meta-analysis are still clearly under the researcher's jurisdiction. What meta-analysis can do, however, is provide the researcher with otherwise unavailable insight into the relationships between study characteristics and study outcomes, and hence ultimately aid the researcher in debating conceptual issues.

9. What techniques and strategies are available to users of meta-analysis?

• There are a number of techniques and strategies of meta-analysis which can be used to integrate findings. Selection of the most appropriate strategy will be determined by the purpose of the integration. To this end, the pioneering efforts of Glass, Rosenthal and Pillemer and Light, are particularly noteworthy. Space does not permit a detailed elaboration of the intricacies of all these strategies and techniques, however one description should suffice to illustrate the logic with which meta-analysis is accomplished. One meta-analytic technique that integrators can use to synthesize findings requires that all the studies pertaining to the effects of one treatment on one dependent variable be gathered together and coded as to their design, treatment measurement and sample characteristics. Then an "effect size" measure which is a standardized quantified measure of the magnitude of experimental effect is computed. The coded information relative to the design, measurement, treatment and sample characteristics are viewed as

the independent variables, whereas the quantified effect size measure is seen as the dependent variable. Subsequently, these data can be submitted to analysis of variance or other types of univariate parametric tests in order to identify if different effect sizes are attributable to differences in treatment, design, measurement or sample particularities. This strategy provides the reviewer with a wide body of quantified information which can facilitate his/her interpretation of the meaning of the body of literature being integrated.

In sum, it can be seen that there are a variety of strategies and techniques potentially useful to integrators. Selection of a strategy depends on the purpose of the integration as well as the characteristics of the body of literature being reviewed. The reviewer must exercise both creativity and critical thinking to decide which strategy is most appropriate to his/her ends.

10. What is an example of an effective use of meta-analysis?

• Robert Rosenthal, author of "Pygmalion in the Classroom", used meta-analytic techniques to summarize the results of 345 studies of interpersonal expectancy effects. Results of his integrative efforts (Rosenthal & Rubin, 1978) led to the clear conclusion that in academic settings teachers' expectancies do indeed have a strong influence on students' academic performance. Thus, teachers were provided with the important message that expectancies do have effects and this knowledge should be useful to them in their interactions with students.

11. How can meta-analysis be useful to sport psychologists?

• Meta-analysis can be used by sport psychologists to integrate the results of a large number of studies dealing with a given topic such as personality and sport. By conducting a systematic, objective integration of research outcomes, meta-analysis can provide a means of formulating new research questions and drawing useful implications for practitioners.

Since sport psychologists studying a research problem frequently adopt an electric approach by gathering information from a number of branches of psychology, meta-analytic techniques can provide an effective means of uncovering the knowlege available in these fields of study. Thus, meta-analysis offers sport psychologists a tool which can be used to systematically and objectively synthesize this information. Instead of arriving at equivocal, ambiguous conclusions, as is so often the case with narrative reviews, integrators using meta-analytic techniques will be able to provide fellow researchers and practitioners alike with meaningful conclusions based on an unbiased, objective method of reviewing the extant literature.

12. What are some areas of research that could advantageously be synthesized by means of meta-analytic techniques?

• Potential areas of application of meta-analytic

techniques is sport psychology would include those topics for which there exists a substantial data base. Since sport psychology research dealing with personality, anxiety, and more recently, attributions, has generated a large number of studies, these topics would appear to be areas in which meta-analysis could be used to summarize research findings.

REFERENCES

Cooper, H.M. Statistically combining independent studies: A meta-analysis of sex differences in conformity research. *Journal of Personality & Social Psychology*, 1979, *37*(1), 131—146.

Glass, G.V. Primary, secondary, and meta-analysis of research. *Educational Researcher*, 1976, *5*, 3-8.

Glass, G.V. Integrating findings: The meta-analysis of research. In L.S. Shulman (Ed.), *Review of Research in Education*, (vol. 5), 1977.

Hedges, L.V., & Olkin, I. Vote-counting methods in research synthesis. *Psychological Bulletin*, 1980, *88*(2), 359—369

Light, R.J., & Smith, P.V. Accumulating evidence: Procedures for resolving contradictions among different research studies. *Harvard Educational Review*, 1971, *41*, 429—471.

Martens, R. Anxiety and motor behavior. *Journal of Motor Behavior*, 1971, *3*, 151—179.

Morgan, W.P. The trait psychology controversy. *Research Quarterly*, 1980, *51*(1), 50—76.

Pillemer, D.B. & Light, R.J. Synthesizing outcomes: How to use research evidence from many studies. *Harvard Education Review*, 1980, *50*, 176—195.

Rosenthal, R. Combining results of independent studies. *Psychological Bulletin*, 1978, *85*, 185—193.

Rosenthal, R. & Rubin, D.B. Interpersonal expectancy effects. The first 345 studies. *The Behavioral and Brain Sciences*, 1978, *3*, 377—415.

DEVELOPING SPORT PSYCHOLOGY AROUND THE WORLD: A MALAYSIAN PERSPECTIVE

Leonard A. De Vries (Malaysia)

Malaysia (population approximately 12 million) became an independent nation state on the 31st of August 1957, and since then, has been striving to achieve the following goals. First, national integration into a Malaysian nation of the three major races, namely, indigenous Malay, comprising approximately 50% of the population, the Chinese, and Indians. Second, national development, a process to transform a traditionally agricultural society into an industrialized and technological society, with a more even distribution of wealth among the people. Third, political stability, so that plans for both national integration and development can be implemented.

Social science as an area of study and research has had a slow start when comparisons are made with the humanities and pure sciences. In the latter's case, the government has provided for greater resources because of the more immediate contributions to economic development, while for the humanities, primarily because of the influence of the British academic tradition in Malaysia. Perhaps political elites have been suspicious and fearful of the social sciences, with its analytical and critical study of man in society, which could present a threat to their positions and instability in the new nation. Psychology as a discipline is a case in point. Out of five universities, one has a division of psychology, while at the others, psychology is studied as a minor area in other faculties, and this was acccomplished only in the early 1970's.

Physical education and sport is in no better position, having a much more recent development. In 1979 the first bachelor's degree was offered at a university in Kuala Lumpur, while at the others it is studied as a subject for the preparation of science and humanities teachers. Besides this, the 22 teachers colleges preparing teachers under a two and three year programme offer physical education for general and specialist teachers. In terms of sport participation, the problem can be quite simply stated as one of recognizing the societal need for mass participation in sport on the one hand, and on the other, striving to compete internationally.

These brief introductory background remarks are necessary for understanding the discussion which follows.

Sport psychology is an extremely new area, with only very superficial understanding and use of its body of knowledge. If the subject is to be introduced to any appreciable extent, considerations should be given to these three basic areas.

Knowledge and Research - One of the reasons generally expressed for the late start of physical education and sport as an area of study and research, is the lack of understanding of political and government leaders of the contributions of sport to national life. The brunt of criticism has been directed to physical educators for failing to convince leaders by precise and persuasive arguments of its role. Scarce budgetary resources for large scale development of physical education and sport ultimately depend on them. What limited resources available are generally channelled towards the preparation for international competition for what Anthony (1979) calls symbolic nationalism. A rationale needs to be given for mass sports, which should include research data derived from the study of the connection between sport, national development and integration; two important concerns of Malaysian society. In other words, it should be the contention that sport might be a unique medium which could help prepare persons, communities and nations for the personal and social revolutions which face them. Knowledge and research, particularly relating to sport psychology has important contributions to make in this connection. Within this perspective, a sampling of research possibilities are highlighted below.

(1) A theory with relevance for developing countries and sport psychology is that expounded by Hagen (1973) who proposes how traditional society becomes one in which continuing technical progress is occuring. His theory suggests that there are two requirements needed for this change, namely (1) a fairly widespread creativity, problem solving ability and a tendency to use it in a country, and (2) attitudes toward manual technical labour and the physical world, such that creative energies are channelled into innovation in the technology of production. The theory does not suggest that these are the only factors, but they should be considered important among others. Galbraith (1964) also

sees this as crucial, for although the developing countries have the good fortune of learning from the experiences of the developed countries, adaptation, he suggests, is as demanding in its own way as innovation. A criticism which is generally directed towards our university students is that although they have acquired knowledge in their respective disciplines, the flexibility of mind to use and apply knowledge to the unique problems and situations is lacking. What contributions then could sport make to creativity and problem solving abilities?

Morris (1967) believes that gymnastics, games and sport as well as music, singing, dancing, writing, speech, etc., are complex, specialized forms of exploration and experiment. The function of this exploratory behaviour is to provide man with subtle and complex awareness of the world around us and our own capacities. What we acquire is developed in a generalized way and can be applied anywhere at any time.

Sports and games as a medium for developing creative and problem solving ability are exciting research possibilities in Malaysia. From my personal observation, the home and school, two important socializing institutions, are plagued with authoritarian practices, the very antithesis for creative ability to develop. In both the homes of the working and middle class, the child's freedom to move and explore are restricted, for more practical and safety reasons and less because of the influence of traditional practices. The middle class, although familiar with new theories and practices of child development, still tends to be over-protective. The working class family, unable to provide constant care and attention because of difficulties earning a living, is forced to confine the child to restrictive areas. In schools, the influence and importance of national examinations, quality of teacher preparation, over-crowded classrooms and traditional attitudes are some of the causes for authoritarian teaching methods.

(2) Malaysia, like most other developing countries, is experiencing the rapid migration of rural youth to urban areas, in search of jobs and life styles which cannot be supported in rural areas. The change from a more indigenous traditional culture to the modern, industrialized, consumer oriented environment requires new knowledge, skill and attitudes. At our universities we have observed feelings of inferiority, poor self-concept and other inhibiting qualities generally associated with our first year students from rural areas. A period of orientation is necessary, and the sports group might serve this purpose by taking the place of the extended family. The focus could be to provide support and understanding as well as the other qualities needed for inserting the individual into the modern technological life. The sports group might also facilitate the development of a more healthy self-concept, for the successful sportsman could learn that in sport at least, a poor economic background, a low social status and other discriminatory factors can be overcome by hardwork and talent. These sports groups, in particular soccer, at both formal and informal settings are popular with rural youth and found in all cities. They could be the focus for study and research.

(3) Spectator sport is on the rise in Malaysia. In terms of our cultural modes of expression (see Maheu, 1970) sport has the largest following. It does not take a required level of literacy to appreciate the beauty of movement and physical skill. Sport provides for many people, perhaps, their only chance to experience and often create beauty and in so doing utilize the artistic resources of people. If sport is to contribute to development, which should not be confined, primarily to economic development for "man does not live by bread alone", the connections between sport and the development of the artistic resources of people could be studied and researched.

(4) Malaysian society has often been called an experiment in multi-racial living, because of cultural, linguistic, religious and economic diversity. The government naturally is pre-occupied with national integration, by trying to break down barriers which have traditionally kept the communities apart. Research into the role of sport and integration to determine the extent to which such qualities as tolerance, understanding, and a general change of perception towards each other, would be a valuable contribution.

(5) Malaysia, I would like to suggest, has not made enough efforts to introduce and expand indigenous sports and games, including the martial arts, into the school curriculum and adult life. We are told that cultural activities are necessary for the healthy self-concept of people. This is related to national self-reliance, advocated by third world leaders (see Nyerere, 1973). In Malaysia, where societal or group goals are emphasized in order to facilitate national development, the indigenous activities, in particular the martial arts, take an added importance. The philosophy underlying the various forms of Malay and Chinese martial arts has been on the relationship of the person to the activity and persons with the activity, and not its contributions to something else. The major emphasis is on experience and experiencing; the goal being to master oneself and not to master the world and others. These activities which give primary importance to the development of self, instead of societal goals determined by the state, should be studied.

(6) Research should also be made and intensified into the preparation for a new type of physical education specialist, conscious of his role as a development agent.

The above is a sampling of research possibilities having relevance to sport psychology, for the justification of increasing resources for the development of sport and physical education. The perspective taken is one of relating sport to national development and integration. Presently, as indicated, most of the resources are given to the preparation of our national teams for international competition. However, knowledge and research facilitating performance at this level of competition should not be neglected, especially the psychological preparation of sportsmen. And finally, cross-cultural studies in motor learning offer significant contributions to the teaching of physical education and sport in Malaysian schools.

Professional Preparation — The development of sport psychology, through knowledge and research relevant to the needs of Malaysia, is dependent on an increasing number of qualified specialists in the area. Unfortunately, institutions preparing physical education teachers and specialist have not begun to understand fully the scope of sport psychology and its contributions to education and national life. At the 22 teachers colleges the physical education programme considers sport psychology very superficially in the various courses on teaching sports. Methodology here is based primarily on conventional wisdom and practice and not on theories, concepts and data from motor learning. Sport psychology needs to be improved and emphasized. This also applies to university physical education. The University Pertanian which offers a bachelors degree in physical education has given more consideration to the physiological aspects of exercise and sport. There is scope for much more concentration in sport psychology. At the other universities opportunities are limited, since physical education is only studied as an introductory course for science and humanities teachers. However, university psychology departments or divisions could include sport psychology as an area of study and research.

Relations with Developed Countries — This analysis of the status of sport psychology in Malaysia has indicated the potential contributions of sport psychology to national life and the unability to fulfill this role because of constraints associated with knowledge, research, specialist, national leadership and financial resources. Clearly, the developed countries with their abundant resources and longer tradition of university physical education and sport has much to offer.

In terms of professional preparation, a more liberal policy in admissions and scholarships for developing countries would be a great help. Perhaps a well planned exchange programme of teachers, coaches, administrators and scholars from both countries could be established for the mutual benefit of countries.

In terms of sport psychology literature, there is a tremendous shortage. Some structure could be set up, preferrably in North America, whose function would be to disseminate information about sport psychology, including titles of publications, journals and seminars. The various international professional organizations in physical education and sport should establish closer cooperation and a deeper understanding of the needs of developing countries.

And in terms of research, Malaysia, as indicated in this paper, and for that matter other developing countries, offer exciting research possibilities for the mutual benefit of both countries.

REFERENCES

1. Hagen, Everett, E. "How economic growth begins: A theory of social change", in Masannat, George S. (ed)., *The Dynamics of Modernization and Social Change: A Reader.* California: Goodyear Publishing Company Inc., 1973).

2. Adams, Don and Bjork, Robert. *Education in Developing Areas.* (New York: David McKay Company Inc., 1975).

3. Hanson, John W. and Breinbeck, Cole S. (ed). *Education and the Development of Nations.* (New York: Holt, Reinhart and Winston, 1966).

4. Anthony, Don. "The Analysis of Sport and Physical Education in Developing Countries". In Howell R. et al., *Methodology in Comparative Physical Education and Sport.* Champaign, Illinois Stipes, 1979).

5. Myerere, J., *Arusha Dectaration,* Tanzanian Government, 1973).

6. Morris, *The Naked Ape* (Cape, 1967).

7. Galbraith, *Economic Development* (Harvard University Press, 1964).

8. Maheu, R. "Education and Man's Development". *Unesco Chronicle,* Vol. 1., 16/4 (April, 1970).

SPORT PSYCHOLOGY IN CHINA

Ma-Qi-Wei (The People's Republic of China)

Since the founding of the People's Republic of China, 12 institutes of physical education and 116 departments of physical education in normal universities and colleges have been established, and the courses on general psychology were offered. At the end of the 1950s, the contents of the courses began to combine with the practice of physical training and athletic competitions. At the same time, psychological research works in connection with the practice of sports activities have developed. Books and materials concerning this aspect from other countries have also been translated into Chinese.

But the development of sports psychology in China suffered great damage during the period of the "cultural revolution". Courses of sports psychology were entirely cancelled from the teaching programs of the institutes because it was condemned as idealistic by the "gang of four". With the overthrow of the "gang of four" in 1976, the spring of science was here again in our great land and the reputation of sports psychology has been rehabilitated. Since then sports psychology has rapidly developed.

I. The Establishing of the Society of Sports Psychology

During the second annual meeting of the China Society of Psychology in Paoting at the end of the year 1978, with the proposal of seven comrades and the approval by the Board of Directors of the China Society of Psychology, the preparatory group of the Special Committee of Physical Culture and Sports Psychology was set up. Through a series of work of the preparatory group, by working out plans and strengthening the ties between the teachers of psychology and the institutes of physical education, the Special Committee of Physical Culture and Sports Psychology was formally established at the third annual meeting of China Society of Psychology in Tienjin, Nov. 1979. This is the first organization of sports psychology that has been established since the founding of new China.

During the time when China Society of Sports Science was setting up, the Society of Sports Psychology was also established which is affiliated to the former. The members and the leading bodies of the Special Committee of Physical Culture and Sports Psychology and the Society of Sports Psychology are identical. They are subjected to the leadership of both China Society of Psychology and China Society of Sports Science.

Eleven comrades are elected as committee members, five of them as members of the standing committee, who take care of the routine matters.

II. The Development of Research Works

The research work on sports psychology now in China is still in its initial stage. Before the setting up of the Society, physical educators and psychologists in many cities had already done some research works. But there was no unified direction or schedule. The themes that had been studied were scattered rather in a wide range. After the setting up of the preparatory group in 1978, a new and dynamic atmosphere appeared in the research work. Not only psychologists, but also physical educators, especially coaches, took part in the research work. At the academic discussion of the Special Committee of Physical Culture and Sports Psychology in 1979 many papers were read, such as "On reinforcements the athletes in competition", "The starting reaction of the basketball players and the selection of athletes", "The study on the temperament of the young table-tennis players", etc. Some of the articles of other countries were also introduced at the meeting, they are: The classification of personalities; the personality testing methods; the function of the application of the relaxing reaction in sport training; the recovering after competitions and the eliminating of psychological abnormalities; the general aspects of sports psychology in other countries, etc.

After the full discussion by the committee members, the meeting pointed out that the direction of research work must be clear and definite, it should be put on the problems associated with psychological training and psychological selection of athletes. At the same time, it was made clear that psychologists should do their research work in cooperation with physical educators and coaches. Then a schedule of research work from 1980-1982 was drawn up in accordance with these principles.

The common effort of psychologists, physical educators and coaches reaped splendid fruits. At the conference of

China Society of Sports Science in November 1980, in the special field of sports psychology, 42.81% of the papers were written on the subject of psychological training; 14.28% of the papers dealt with the problems of the selection of athletes, and the others were concerned with the analysis of psychological reaction in the teaching of physical education courses, etc.

Now let me give a brief sketch about some of the research works that have been done recently.

1. "The Study of Psychological Training for Archers" by teachers from Hobei Normal University and Beijing Institute of Physical Education.

Testing subjects: 103 national and provincial athletes on archery.

Testing methods: 1) Relaxation training (including muscular relax, concentration training, verbal adjusting, respiratory regulation, etc.)

2) Heart rate adjusting training through feedback processes.

3) Covert practice or mental rehearsal practice.

4) Mood control training.

During the testing processes, the heart-rate, rate of respiration, superficial body temperature and EEG (electroencephalogram) had been recorded.

The results of the test:

1) During the processes of relaxation training, the heart-rate, superficial body temperature and the rate of respiration can be adjusted, and the psychological diathetic conditions can be improved.

2) Under the heart-rate feedback control training during the shooting practice, the increase of shooting scores had been resulted.

3) With the application of the mood control training, the alpha wave reflected in EEG showed the improvement of the psychological stability.

This study showed the possible positive effectiveness of the psychological training to athletes.

2) "Psychological Analysis of the Stability on Balance Beam" by a coach-researcher from Sichuan Research Institute.

Through the investigation of 154 gymnasts during the 1980 National Competition. The results of investigation showed:

1) Among the 154 gymnasts, 20.77% were good in stability, 52.57% were fair and 26.66% were poor.

2) An average of .62 point lost because of the unstableness. There are many factors that influence the stability. According to the results of the investigation, they are mainly: the period of years of training, number of times of participating in competitions, percentage of failures before competition, body condition and psychological status.

3) Among the reasons of dropping off from the beam, 59.5% were on account of psychological factors.

During the period of the competition, the ability of eliminating the interferences and the type of nervous system of the gymnasts had also been investigated and it was found that there were 39.52% among them low on the ability of eliminating both the external and internal interferences (such as, interferences from the apparatus, the spectators, the accompanied music, the failure of a teammate, etc.), and 44.2% were of the highly excitable type with low perceptiveness or over sensitiveness which affected stability.

We have just started to work on the psychological training and the psychological selection of athletes. There are some studies in the field of special characteristics of personality, temperament and type of the nervous system, with the purpose of trying to find out the criteria for psychological selection of athletes.

3. A teacher from Shantung Teacher's College made a study on the type of temperament in correlation with the different kinds of sports. 450 athletes from different kinds of sports have been tested and it was found that athletes from different kinds of sports showed distinctly different tendencies in types of temperament. And it was also found that the differences of ages, sexes, period of years of training gave certain influences to the types of temperament.

4. A teacher from Shanghai Institute of Physical Education studied the special characteristics of personality of the sportsman in fencing. During this study, a special method of testing, the CH Comprehensive Personality Test was satisfactorily designed. It is composed of three different methods of testing: (1) basic psychological method — questionnaire, (2) social investigation for comparative retification, and (3) supplementary psychological tests.

From the study the major characteristics of the personality of the fencers that influence the consistency of the achievements in competitions were found to be independence, decisiveness, intelligence (thoughtfulness), and self-confidence.

5. A graduate student in my Institute (Beijing Institute of Physical Education) made a study on "Whether the Type of Nervous System Can Be Used as One of the Psychological Criteria in Selection of Volleyball Players".

Testing Subjects: 214 volleyball players from 22 A class volleyball teams and the national teams (97 male and 117 female)

Testing methods: 1) Anfemov testing table

2) Reaction Time

3) Social investigation

The results of the test:

1) Volleyball players have their special characteristics on the type of nervous system.

2) The volleyball players of different roles — spiker, co-spiker and setter — with different types of nervous system: 64.5% of spikers were of the vivid type, 61.5% of men co-spikers were of the vivid type and 68.8% women co-spikers were of a steady type, etc.

3) The testing results from this study showed: there is the possibility that the type of nervous system may not be changed by years of training.

6. A teacher from Jiangsu Teacher's College made a study on "The Testing Method of the Type of Nervous System".

After a thorough study a project of testing form 803 was designed. It consists of only simple symbols, with no alphabets and no numbers so as to eliminate the possible influences of educational level. The form thus designed had been put into test with 26,852 subjects, including students from kindergarten, primary schools, high schools, colleges, universities and athletes. On the basis of the test results, the project had been remoulded into testing form 808. The 808 form had been put into test with 10,000 subjects and the testing results were very satisfactory. The test has shown that there is a "leap" of the development of the cerebral function at the age of 6-7. It illustrated that this age period may be considered as the suitable or important period for the selection of athletes.

Due to the fact that our research work is only in its initial stage, the experimental methods with the instruments that we are using in our research works are absolutely necessary to be improved. At present, the vast numbers of psychologists and physical educators are working very hard according to the program of 1980-1982. There will be another seminar of sports psychology at the fourth annual meeting of China Society of Psychology in December this year. The stresses of the seminar will still be put on the psychological training and the selection of athletes.

III. Teaching and the Popularization of Sports Psychology

In order to develop the research work, there is an urgent need of the popularization of the knowledge about sports psychology. We have translated articles and books on sports psychology from the United States, Soviet Union, Japan and other countries. They have enriched our knowledge about the research work on sports psychology of other countries. We have also planned to compile popular science books on sports psychology. These books will be published within two or three years. On the other hand, in order to raise the standard of teaching in the institutes and colleges of physical education, we have decided to offer intensive courses on sports psychology. We have the intention to invite specialists to give lectures. Scholars from other countries to give lectures in China are welcome. We hope to establish further academic relations with other countries, to strengthen academic exchanges so as to promote the development of sports psychology, to enhance our mutual understanding and friendships.

SPORT PSYCHOLOGY IN INDIA

Gurbakhsh Singh Sandhu (India)

The growing area of the psychological science through its branches, educational psychology and social psychology, started exerting its influence on physical education and sports. The origin and development of sports psychology was conditioned by the out-growth of the social sciences on the one hand and the academic expansion of physical education with an increased emphasis on performance on the other. In 1961, the opening of the National Institute of Sports at Patiala facilitated the environment for the synthesis of the theoretical knowledge related to coaching and performance. There appeared a discernible role of the psychological aspect of training which at that time was at a rudimentary stage.

The sixties also witnessed the academic development of physical education when the master degree courses were started in some of the major institutions. Subsequently, the facilities for Ph.D. were made available at some places.

These developments in physical education and its allied social sciences led to awakening for the development of sports psychology which actually started developing as a separate branch of knowledge from the early seventies and has recorded a respectable level of growth during the past decade.

The establishment of the Indian Association of Sports Medicine stimulated the interest of some of the clinical experts and acknowledged the role of psychological training in the total fitness of the athletes. Recently, the Indian Association of Sports Psychology has been formed which is yet to make its contribution in this area.

Today, sports psychology is a part of the master's curriculum in physical education in some of the institutions. It is also taught at the master's level in the National Institute of Sports, Patiala. To strengthen research, the laboratories have been established at the N.I.S. and at the Lakshmi Bai National College of Physical Education, Gwalior.

Research in this area is being facilitated by collaboration of the departments of Psychology, Education and Sociology at various universities. The main problems being investigated are:

1. Role of Yogic asanas on rehabilitation of the psycho-physiological processes of the athletes.
2. Study of Socio-psychological impediments in sports participation.
3. Arousal and performance.
4. Attention and performance.
5. Pre-competition preparation of the athletes.

The SNIPES journal is the main source of publication for the sports psychologist in India. Also, the I.A.S.M. facilitates such publication through its annual proceedings.

Today, we have the following types of sports psychologists.

1. Those engaged in the study and practice of yoga.
2. Those engaged in teaching and research at the colleges and departments of physical education in various universities.
3. The coach as a psychologist and psycho-therapist.
4. The psychiatrist as a clinical psychologist.

MODULE II

MEANING IN SPORT THROUGHOUT LIFE — FOREWORD
Leonard M. Wankel (Canada)

Victor Frankl (1963: 1978) has clearly identified "The quest for meaning" as a central issue facing modern man. He notes that as hunger and other physical needs are increasingly taken care of, at least for the industrial world, a "poverty of riches" results. A malaise termed the "existential vacuum" results, wherein feelings of meaninglessness, boredom and emptiness prevail. In Frankl's words . . . "Affluent society has given vast segments of population the means, but people cannot see an end, a meaning to live for. In addition, we are living in a leisure society; ever more people have ever more time to spend, but nothing meaningful on which to spend it" (1978: 95).

Frankl suggests that sport can help to fill this void by providing "artificial challenges" which stimulate the individual to more fully develop his/her potentialities. Such challenges for optimal development take on significance both for the individual, a meaningful challenge to improve one's own performance and abilities, and for the society at large, the adaptive social value of the further development of human potentiality.

Although aspects of Frankl's analysis are certainly subject to question, this recognition for the importance of sport to modern society by a world renowned authority on human adjustment and meaning draws needed attention to this topic. Despite the apparent prominence of sport in the modern world as amply documented by sport participation figures and by expenditures on sporting goods and **services**, the whole question of meaning in sport has received little systematic study. Sport psychologists in the main have adopted a narrow scope with research activities being focussed primarily upon the learning and performance of physical skills. Relatively little attention has been given to such larger but more difficult questions as: why do people engage in sport? what are the psychological consequences of sport involvement? how can desirable consequences be maximized and undesirable outcomes minimized? how can more people be provided with positive lifelong sport experiences?

Consistent with the holistic approach of the "Sport in Perspective" conference, the "Meaning in Sport" theme was designed to address these important albeit more difficult issues. While not minimizing the importance of performance (it follows from a holistic perspective that outcomes, meaning, enjoyment, etc. are related to performance), this theme encouraged authors to look beyond performance to consider how more people could enjoy and benefit from positive sport experiences. The initial promotional materials sent to prospective conference participants outlined the meaning theme as follows:

"This theme explores the personal significance of sport, the joy of sport, the beauty of sport, the 'flow' and the inner meaning of the sport experience. Sessions on this theme are designed to identify ways in which more people might experience sport as a way of lifting the quality of everyday life."

Four individuals representing different perspectives were invited to present papers on this theme. George Sheehan, (U.S.A.) a physician, avid runner, and popular spokesman and author on the philosophical dimensions of running was invited to present his views on how sport might be made a more personally meaningful experience. Paul Kunath (G.D.R.), a former competitive athlete, current director of the German Academy of Sport Culture in Leipzig, and author of over 150 articles or books was asked to present an East European perspective of how meaningful sport throughout life can be facilitated. Mihaly Csikszentmihalyi, (U.S.A.), Chairman of the Department of Human Development, University of Chicago, whose research on the "flow experience" is central to a discussion of intrinsic interest in sport was invited to share his views on the implications of his research for promoting greater involvement. Finally, Juhani Kirjonen, (Finland), a behavioural science researcher in the health field, was invited to serve as a discussant for the three initial presentations. Due to communication difficulties created largely by a national mail strike Dr. Kirjonen did not receive copies of the papers until arriving at the conference. Consequently his paper also became an independent contribution rather than reaction to the other papers.

Edited versions of the four invited papers are printed in these proceedings along with a number of submitted papers from the Congress. In addition, papers from a special symposium pertaining to the "Therapeutic Effects of Exercise and Sport" are included under the "Meaning in Sport Throughout Life" theme. Although these papers focus more on non-competitive activity engaged in largely because of health benefits, they are relevant to the meaning theme as they address the question of what are the psychological benefits of activity and how can more participants be motivated to participate and experience these outcomes:

In an earlier paper on "The Meaning of Athletic Performance", Sir Roger Bannister opened with the following remarks:

"The problem is this. How is it possible to describe the meaning of what we enjoy, whether it be Mozart, Cezanne, or sport? One would need to be a sociologist and philosopher as well as a doctor to do justice to this subject" (1964:   ).

The contributors to this theme indeed represent all of these mentioned disciplines in addition to the cenral discipline, psychology. Hence, a truly multi-disciplinary perspective of "Meaning in Sport Throughout Life" is presented through the assembled papers.

In the first paper, George Sheehan writing in his own inimitable style laced generously with quotations from past masters and references to personal experiences, presents a philosophically oriented perspective of how widespread involvement in physical activity throughout the lifespan might be facilitated. He presents the case that to be a fully functioning human being, physical activity is essential. Further, he says, there are essential differences between the sub-categories of physical activity — exercise, play, and sports. He observes that each refers to a distinctive type of activity which has a distinctive and essential role for human fulfillment. Sheehan argues that only by appreciating these distinctive and complementary roles will significant progress be made in motivating mass involvement in healthy physical activity.

Sheehan's paper is followed by a submitted paper, "Dimensions of Meaning" by Peter Arnold (Scotland), which provides a further philosophical examination of essential differences of sport and play. Arnold elucidates how sport is different than play but at the same time emphasizes the importance of the spirit of playfulness to sport. "Without it (play) sport would not be all that it can be. Unless the spirit of play is present in sport from time to time much that is done in its name would lack lustre and be empty of exuberance and joy."

Arnold points out that a logical analysis of the characteristics of sport (e.g., competition, established rules, emphasis on physical prowess, etc.) does not explain why people participate in sport. He emphasizes that opportunities for self-expression and self-realization through the process of being involved in sport may be more important thatn the instrumental reason of winning, gaining recognition, etc. In developing this thesis Arnold discusses how sport involvement can relate to moral, aesthetic, and psychological dimensions of human development. His concluding statement has particular relevance to the meaning theme as he cautions against an overemphasis upon the instrumental use of sport for accomplishing extrinsic goals. "In conclusion it can be said that if sport is to be a source of intrinsic value and provide opportunities for the discovery of authentic being it must, like play, be left to pursue its own ends and not be used as a means to further other ends whether social, political or economic, that are extrinsic to its nature."

Kirjonen, in the third paper, "The Meaning of Sport — Health Care or Modern Rituals", addresses sport involvement from the perspective of its potential as a form of preventive health. He presents information pertaining to the involvement of Finnish adults in "leisure time physical activity." Following a Sociological perspective, descriptive statistics on amount of involvement and relationship of involvement to occupational status, age, and sex are presented. Kirjonen then presents more psychologically oriented data pertaining to motives for involvement in sport and physical activity and notes that non-health related motives (e.g., recreation, relaxation, love of nature) may be more important for involvement than health and fitness motives. Consistent with other research (cf Wankel, 1980, 1981) Kirjonen notes that people generally hold positive attitudes toward the health aspects of physical activity regardless of whether or not they are personally active.

In his paper Kunath presents a socialistic perspective in which the meaning of sport to the individual is framed within the broader perspective of the individual's relation to the larger society. Kunath argues that the value of sport and physical culture must be viewed in terms of its social value as well as in its contribution to an individual's personality development. The social learning opportunities offered through sport are seen as an important means of developing personal characteristics desirable for social living. Within this ideological framework, Kunath describes the growth of sport involvement within the German Democratic Republic. Reference is made to factors related to sport participation at different age levels and to the different organizational structures (e.g., schools, camps, sport unions) important to the delivery of sport opportunities.

Csikszentmihalyi, in his paper, addresses the topic of sport outcomes. He points out that the outcomes of sport, either for the individual or for society generally, are not intrinsically good or bad but rather there is potential for either. Csikszentmihalyi suggests that the role of sport psychology in this area is to delineate the conditions under which the outcomes of sport will be beneficial and contrarily those conditions under which they will be negative. He proposes a theoretical model for guiding such an investigation of sport outcomes. The model incorporates four main types of consequences of sport involvement — personal enjoyment, personal growth, social harmony, and social change (growth). It is suggested that optimal activity would be one that privdes for all four outcomes. Research is reported pertaining to personal enjoyment outcomes associated with various activities. The practical significance of such research is pointed out in that if it is possible to identify the situational and leadership characteristics associated with positive experiences it would then be possible to prescribe or at least recommend, certain conditions.

Morgan's paper, "Psychological Benefits of Physical Activity", is a good illustration of Csikszentmihalyi's recommendation that a key role of sport psychology is to delineate the conditions under which sport or physical activity will have beneficial outcomes. In a scholarly review of the research pertaining to the effects of non-competitive physical activity on young adult populations, Morgan questions the common interpretation that physical activity "causes" numerous desirable psychological outcomes (e.g., reduced anxiety and depression; desirable personality changes). He notes that methodological shortcomings in much of the research precludes such a casual interpretation. Although involvement in various forms of acute and chronic physical activity has been shown to be related to different positive psychological states it is not clear whether it is the physical activity itself, the social aspects of the program, or some other facet which accounts for the relationship. Morgan suggests that biomechanical and neurophysiological research will be required to uncover any direct casual relationship between exercise and affect.

In the final major paper in this section Dishman addresses the topic of adherence to health-related exercise. He thus delimits his discussion to that type of physical activity which has a clear Instrumental focus and which thus is distinct from most sport programs. In fact, Dishman indicates that exercise compliance of this type basically parallels general medical compliance. Dishman briefly reviews the research pertaining to exercise involvement while focussing primarily upon his own research in developing a psychobiologic prediction model for exercise adherence. He advocates this as one possibility for moving from the general group based descriptive research, which has been the norm, toward a more clinically effective individualized approach. Dishman notes the importance of developing self-motivated behaviour for facilitating long-term involvement outside of the formal program setting. This topic has been addressed in considerable detail in previous papers by this author (Wankel, 1980, 1981).

A number of subsidiary papers or abstracts are included which complement and extend issues raised in the previously mentioned papers. Bergen, in a paper giving specific attention to female runners, addresses both the psychological effects of running and guidelines for implementing a running program designed to have positive psychological outcomes. Moxley also discussed considerations for implementing an exercise program in order to facilitate positive psychological outcomes. Tiainen, Lintunen, and Vainikka report a study of how a school exercise program (pause gymnastics) effected performance on tests of various mental processes. Uson and Larrosa as well as Dallaire, report studies examining the effects of a physical activity program upon the psychological adjustment of an elderly population. McConnell reports how running has been incorporated into both a therapy program and an educational program in clinical psychology. The reader is cautioned to critically review the results of these various studies, reporting psychologocal effects of physical activity, as Morgan's observations concerning inappropriate causal interpretation of results when methodological difficulties prevent adequate experimental controls are applicable to several of the presented reports.

In a general discussion paper, Sachs departs from the previous emphasis on the positive psychological effects of exercise to identify a potential problem. He discusses the concept "negative addiction to running" and suggests some general guidelines for therapy programs for negatively addicted runners. Ostrow and Spiker, in their paper, discuss one important factor which tends to prevent lifelong sport involvement. They indicate that the reduction in sport and physical activity participation with age may be due in considerable measure to age stereotypes (Ageisim) of what is appropriate. A number of suggestions are presented as to how such discriminatory labelling practices might be alleviated.

The next three papers deal with psychological factors influencing involvement in physical activity. Silvennoinen reports information on age related changes in intrinsic and normative motivational factors in Finnish school children. Bonaiuto and Bonaiuto present information from five Italian cities concerning how developmental and situational factors influence interests in sport and physical activity. Salman reports a study investigating the attitudes and actual physical activity behaviour of a group of female students at a Canadian university. Finally both Bregiroux and Rioux present perspective from France on personal meaning, choice and expression in movement and sport.

Following the presentation of the papers some brief concluding remarks on the "Meaning of Sport Throughout Life" are given.

TABLE OF CONTENTS

RUNNING AND BEING
George Sheehan (USA)

Emerson, at the age of sixty-one, wrote in his journal, "I look inside and I don't see wrinkles or a tired heart, I see an unspent youth." I am going to urge you to spend that youth again and suggest to you things that may not have occurred to you.

The first is that there is no verb for sport. And because there is no verb, we have been in all kinds of difficulty in our thinking about sport and play and physical education. When you read in the books about sport you keep seeing the verb "playing" "playing" "playing". Now there is an essential difference between play and sport. Unless we understand that, we will not be good teachers, we will not be good coaches, we will not be good athletes. We will not lead the full life.

There are three things involved as I can see it. There is exercise, which is labour; there is play, which is a craft; and there is sport which is a profession.

We are all athletes or should be. Some of us are in training and some of us aren't. Let's put it that way. What we have to understand is the essential differences of these three things and see what we have to do to integrate them. Among other things, we are, all of us, one - animals, two - children, three - artists, four - heros or saints. And it is in those functions that exercise, play and sport enter. You cannot have the good life without being an athlete. Our education system has failed to see this.

In Santayana's novel *The Last Puritan*, his protagonist, Oliver Alden, learned to scull when he was a youngster and when he got to Harvard he would go out on the Charles and scull. He loved those afternoons. You read of this in Oliver Wendell Holmes also. The great feeling you have sculling. Those meditative moments, the contemplative moments. And we've got to go back again to think about those words we're using - "contemplative". That syllable in the middle, "temple" means holy ground.

When he was sculling on the Charles he made it holy ground because he was thinking of the eternal verities, you see. Well, he happened to be observed by the captain of the Harvard crew who said to him, "Why don't you come out for the crew? And he said, No, he was having fun on the Charles. He had no intention of going out for the crew and going through all that sweat and toil and agony and pain and suffering. He said, "I'm having fun" and the captain of the Harvard crew said, "We're not here to have fun. We're here to beat Yale."

But we are here to do both. We are here to have fun and we are here to beat Yale. That's the thing. These two diametrically opposite things have to be attained. When we start talking about Vince Lombardi and put him down, we do not understand Vince Lombardi. Vince Lombardi was "the perfect Vince Lombardi". He was a perfect competitor. If we think that football is all aggression and violence,

witness those athletes after the games. It is the spectators that have aggression and violence, it is not the players. The players are shaking hands and throwing their arms around each other. These athletes who would resort to anything ten seconds before the whistle is blown know when it is over.

Games are necessary. The race is necessary. When I race - when someone comes to my house and they say "Where's George?" and they say "He is out for a run", that is one thing. If they say "He is at a race" that is another and you know it is different.

Peter Berger has just written a book called *The Heretical Imperative*. It is about religion but what he is saying is that we have to accept both traditional religion and secular humanism and the way we do it is to use our experience. When we are in that no man's land between science and religion, we have to resort to the individual experience. And the individual experience says there is a difference between exercise and play and sport. And that difference is essential. You see sport is the experience. Play is the aesthetic expression of that experience. That is what everyone will tell you. You read the Thinkers....Nietzsche said "Every creative act came about in play." Every thinker you read you will find they were in motion and on their feet walking when they created. They were playing. They were using their bodies.

It shows that we are mixed up when we say playing football. People are not playing football. We say playing tennis. They are not playing tennis. It is true there are some people who want to play tennis with the net down, that is playing tennis. There are some people who don't want to keep score in basketball, that is playing basketball. But that is not basketball, and that is not tennis and that is not sport because we need competition. We need it for reasons as Montague said, in his earlier address, it brings out the best in us by bringing out the best in others.

I remember that Bob Giegenback, the track coach at Yale, had an argument with Paul Weiss, the philosopher, because he said that competition is necessary. It would be unfair to Harvard, he said to field a team that didn't want to do its best. This is the great Emersonian idea, you see. Emerson never told us what to do. He just said we had to do it. Get off your duff, he said. Be your best. To do less than your best is not to be worthy of you or this day, which is an everstanding miracle, or the people you do these things with. That is what sport is. Play is the coming back and then from inside yourself comes the artistic effort or the solution.

Every philosopher you read will say that man is an animal. We are animals. Do not forget it. Therefore, we need exercise, we need motion, we cannot sit still, we are not cats that wear napkins and sit at a table. That's the trouble, we have been domesticated; not only civilized, we have been domesticated. Spencer, back in the 1800's, said if you wish to be a success in this life, you must first be a good animal. Where do we hear that in school? Where do we hear as they said in Greece, seven years for the teacher and seven years for the trainer. Where do we hear what was done in the Renaissance, one-third gymnastics?

But hear Spencer further. He said that exercise should not be gratuitous. Observe children at play, he said. That's what we want. We are animals. "The body is the source of all energy and initiative," said Plato.

That's where you start, but what else are we? We're social animals, we're problem solving animals, we're technological animals, we're theological animals. I believe what Ernest Becker said. We're here to be heros, he said and then kept raising the ante. He wanted us to be cosmic heros. But if we are here to be heros, you are not a hero in play. You are only a hero in sport. We are born to be a success, but the only time we believe it, is when we see an athlete. The only truly successful man is the athlete. Everything else we do is problematical...Are those the best words in the best possible order? Is that the solution? Is that the most loving thing to do? Who knows? The most successful man is the athlete, the most successful woman is the athlete.

What is play? It is simply problem solving. As a child it is problem solving, as a man, a woman, it is problem solving. Any number of runners you know and I know go out and take their problems on the road. And there they solve them. They turn on this billion cell computer and release the bedlam of signs and sounds and touches that we have had from day one of our lives. We can only make them available to us in play. Szentgyorgi, when he was up at Wood's Hole, said, if he had a problem he would put it in his head and go fishing.

If I have a problem I put it in my head and go running. That is where the aesthetic achievement comes. That is where I write my column, that is where painters paint pictures. Out there is a virginal canvas ready for those thoughts. And where do you get the thoughts to use - from sport.

I remember a story about Robert Frost when he was posing for Joe Brown at Princeton for a bust. A student came up from the college paper and interviewed him and said "...how often do you write poems?" Mr. Frost said "not too often". And the student said, "Well, I write one every day," and Frost said, "That will improve your penmanship". If you want to write a poem you have to have an experience, if you want an experience you have to test yourself, you have to challenge yourself and that is what the race is.

The race is so many things, you see. The race is drama, it's a drama where you act out the ancient Grecian emotions. The race is also competition. Competition, what is that word? "Petere", the Latin, to seek excellence but "com" is "with", not "against". Competition is to seek excellence with other people. We know that.

And the race is also a contest as Paul Weiss says. It is a struggle. It is a place of self discovery. The Latin meaning again for contest is to testify with. The other runners are witnesses of what you do and those witnesses come up and congratulate you, even if you are 2,578th. And you accept those congratulations.

They are witnesses and because they are witnesses, what is the corollary of that? I am under oath, I have taken my word of honour in that race. How many times I ask you have you taken your word of honour for anything in the past year? Two years? Ten years? When have you put yourself on the dock and tested yourself? Only in sport. It's true, we should bring that out and use it in every other area of our endeavour but it is in sport where we put ourself on the line, you see. That is the place we have to be heros.

James said, we need the moral equivalent of war. Where is it? It is, of course, in sport. The virtues of sport are the martial virtues, courage, dedication, endurance, discipline, and all those things. I had a basketball coach tell me once that there are days when you can't put the ball in the basket, no way, no matter how hard you try. But there is no excuse for not playing defence. You see, that is sport. Sport is defence. Offense is art. You know - you just get lucky. Things were going in for Bill Bradley that day against Wichita. He scored 56 points. He was throwing them in over his head, blind, everything. There was no way he was going to miss, but that's art. That's like a vision. The mystics have them. They don't tell anybody because they know it is going to be taken away from them. You don't boast about art, that is play. That is something that is given to you. But defence you earn, by God. That's you. That's you on the line and that's what sport is. I think we have to understand that each one of these elements is necessary.

In sport, you become a member of a crowd. Not only a crowd, but a good crowd, and you can tell the race is typical of that. What do crowds feel. They feel invincible. You stand on the line with four thousand, you feel invincible. Forget about that 26.2 mile course. It is nothing. It is a piece of cake. And then there is contagion and the gun goes off and there's 26 miles and people are running like they're anchoring a mile relay, you see. And you get the feeling, yes, I can hold this pace. And finally because you're in this crowd, because you are a member of it, they take you in. You are part of these little suffering platoons that make this journey from Hopkinton to Prudential Centre.

When you read Huizinga's *Homo Ludens* - the great book on play, what is Huizinga speaking about? He is not talking about play, he is talking about sport. Witness the characteristics that Huizinga says about play.

The occasion, he says, is sacred or festive. Play doesn't have to be sacred or festive. I went out today and played. There was no sacred or festive occasion about it. I ran down the Ottawa canal. I played for an hour with my brain and my body.

The occasion must be sacred or festive. I think specifically of a race I have run. The fourth of July, Pepsi Challenge, Ten Kilometre Race over the George Washington Bridge into Manhattan. Can anything be more sacred or festive that that event? Did that ever happen to you that you congregated on a plaza on the George Washington Bridge and ran over that span with not a vehicle on it to Manhattan and up past the Cloisters and down into Baker Field, the athletic facility for Columbia University. Ten kilometres of suffering with three thousand other people. And, said Huizinga the mood is one of enthusiasm and rapture. "Enthusiasm", the greatest word the Greeks ever gave us, said Pasteur, because "Thus" is God, Theos. Enthusiasm and rapture, the same root as rape. Seized, of course, we were. There wasn't one of us there who knew more than our own name. I mean this event was it. This was the world we were in, we were seized with this reality. And then Huizinga said, it is played out with feelings of tension and exultation. Of course. It is the one thing we do that we don't know the outcome and the outcome depends on us. There is tension in sport because there is something at risk. And then finally this exultation because I am fulfilling myself. In Maslow's words I am self-actualizing myself. I am pure runner. I am pushing to my limits and I am having people drag that out of me and so when I come out I come down into Baker Field and I look at that digital clock and that's the enemy, not the person beside me. There was the time...38:38, my best time of the year.

The single most distinguishing attribute of sport is that closure, or result, a completion. I remember James Galway, the flutist, was once asked "How good are you?" "I don't know," he said, "there's no world's record in the flute." Well, I want to tell you I have a world's record. I have a personal record. And when I go under that clock I know what I've done. I know what I have gone through and I know what I have done and that's what sport is. There is a result to it, there's a completion.

You know C.S. Lewis said one time, the reason we love this world is because it is so like the world we left. The reason we love sport is because it is even more like the world we left. I was in this race in New York, I remember a ten mile race in Central Park. It was a very tough course, "rolling hills" is the way they usually describe these things. That means rolling agony, you see. And it was ten miles of rolling agony including the 110th street hill which is pure agony, 110th street hill never stops, it just keeps winding, and winding, and winding. And so we finished and I had done a very good time and was up where I hadn't been for awhile and I had beaten people I had not beaten for a long time. And after the race we go across the street to the Church of Heavenly Rest, you know. And Huizinga said that, at the completion there is mirth and relaxation.

Sacred and festive, enthusiasm and rapture, tension and exultation, mirth and relaxation, what have you given up for this. What have you given up

for that? What do you do with your time that's worth that, that you don't do it every Sunday? So I went over and we were sitting around and having bagels and coffee and we tell each other how wonderful we are. Not in words, you know, not in so many words, but with our eyes and gestures and that kind of bearing everybody has. And I was sitting there on the floor with George Hirsch, a friend who is another runner, and I turned to him and said, "George, right now I could pull the sword out of that stone". That's what it is, it is that return to innocence, that return to being the child, that return to being a saint. You are now animal, artist, hero, saint. And that is available to everyone.

What did Emerson say about the common man? "What Plato thought, he can think; what the saint felt, he can feel; what happened to any man, he can understand". That's what we should understand, our experience does count. We have a vision that no one else has, "The world exists for the education of each man", said Emerson. Again and again, we see that experience is it. William James spoke for the individual, he was the philosopher of becoming. He believed that life was made in doing and creating and suffering, and so does the athlete. So do each one of us, and he said that anyone who avoids those things knows he has not been initiated. He feels he is lacking in something. Victor Frankl feels the same. Suffering is something we would like to avoid but once having gone through it we are delighted that we had it. Pain is a big subject. It has sent psychiatrists to other psychiatrists. It has confused everyone and very few people have written of it in a way that we can understand.

I call to your attention today one book that I have found so marvellous in this respect. It is by Yuki Mishima. It is called "Sun and Steel". Mishima, as you know was a Novel candidate for Japan and committed suicide at the age of 46. This was written the year of his suicide and in this he described his rebirth from an intellectual to an athlete. And because he uses words the way Reggie Jackson hits baseballs, he is able to put something into words that very few athletes can do. And in this he describes what occurred to him. He said, "My body does not speak Japanese". Our body does not speak our native tongue. Our body speaks another language. It teaches us things we cannot learn in any other way. What have you exchanged for that? Books? Have you exchanged books for experience? Have you exchanged an old age for a childhood that's not yet spent? Are you subjecting your students to sport without having play? Do you understand the need for all things?

I'd like to close now with something I have written. In essence it was this. Running is being. Racing is becoming. Running is the creative act. Racing is the experience. When I race I am going to the ultimate limits and I am experiencing something I cannot do otherwise. I cannot get it out of books. When I run, on the other hand, I am filled with peace and confidence and serenity and all those things that James spoke about. And sometimes I think to myself, what is the point of racing? And a lot of people say, why race? But it is essential. When I run I do one thing. When I race I do another. It is that dialectic that goes on that makes it so necessary that we have both. We need the experience. We need the drama. We need these things that come out of what Huizinga said. The enthusiasm and exultation. But we also need this peace and confidence and serenity and this getting into the head. You see, in the race you are completely occupied with space and time, every moment seems like a minute, pain increases with every step and every second on the clock. But in play time disappears. You enter into what Maslow calls, those little heavens that are available to us. You escape into some area where time stops.

We have failed to understand that both of these things are part of what we call play and sport. And the chief reason, as I see it, is the need of a verb to indicate the sporting action rather than the playing action and to stop saying playing football, playing tennis, playing baseball. Otherwise we are going to forget about this essential difference between play and sport.

Right now we are having a fitness revolution, but if we get so scientific that we destroy the play, or if we remove the race by saying that competition is bad, we will fail our students and our athletes.

Believe in your own experience and the experience of those people that you have control over, or influence over. The idea now has to be to provide the experience. What was the Renaissance? What is any Renaissance? It is the raising of someone's consciousness to the ability to do something and then providing the opportunity. That's why we have this Renaissance in fitness. Their consciousness is being raised and the opportunity is there. Now the physiology of fitness you could put on the head of a pin. But nobody is attending to the psychology of fitness. We are having a massive dropout problem, we are having a massive success rate too. And the reasons seem to escape us. The reasons are purely this, that there are three things--in the beginning there was exercise and there was play and there was sport and we need all three.

DIMENSIONS OF BEING IN SPORT

Peter J. Arnold (Scotland)

Dimensions of being in sport or dimensions of being that can arise in sport are conceptual as well as existential. I shall begin therefore by looking at the concept of sport and then go on to suggest why I think certain aspects of being, whilst not confined to sport, find a natural location in the variety of activities that are called sport.

The concept of sport is greater than that which is held in common by its different instances. It defies simple definition and embraces many activities not all of which are characterized by the same features. Some sports are marked by their dependence on machines, others upon balls, others still upon forms of equipment without which it would be impossible to proceed. Sport is a collective term and today embraces a large number of disparate activities. It includes motor-racing, water polo and weight-lifting, no less than "field games" such as rugby, cricket and hockey or "field pastimes" such as hunting, shooting and fishing. So far as sporting activities can be identified at all they seem to be associated in varying degrees with such factors as whole-bodied exertion, competition, the employment of skill, uncertainty of outcome and some element of danger. Most sports too, are rule-bound, ritualistic and institutionalized. They are in a word miniature "forms of life" that put a premium on physical prowess and frequently also on speed, strength and stamina. Although some sports are like others in a number of respects - tennis, squash, and

racquets, for example - they each have their own distinctive ways of proceeding; their own strategies and tactics. If any one phrase can usefully be applied to the diverse and yet related series of activities that go by the name of sport it is probably that of "family resemblances".

If sport is held together at all by something "common" it surely lies in the notion of sportsmanship. For many, sprtsmanship is an inbuilt element of the concept of sport. Keating has even written of it as being a moral category and associates it with such virtues as courage, courtesy and magnanimity. Whilst it may be a mistake to regard sportsmanship or the qualities and dispositions that make it up as "special" or "peculiar" to sport in some way, it may well be true that such qualities and dispositions find a more ready home in sport that leads to their acceptance and expression. The point here is that if virtues are to be "moral" virtues they must be universalisable and generally applicable and therefore not be tied nor restricted to one type or group of activities no matter how well associated such virtues have come to be with these activities. What seems true is that at least for some participants to engage in sport entails *being* a sport or behaving in a sportmanlike way. It invokes the injunction to act in a particular manner. This means more than paying a deferential lip service to the legal code of "fair play". It involves the living out of a moral dynamic based upon the principles of equality and justice that becomes a constituent and characteristic part of the action. What the ethics of sportsmanship invokes is that the participant should not merely do his duty by following the rules that identify and regulate *that* activity as being the one it is, but go beyond what is required in any formal or "self contained" way by acting in accord with moral principles that exemplify a regard and concern for the other. Clearly not all sporting encounters are so conducted. Sometimes the very opposite is true; that the cheat and the spoilsport prevail. When this occurs one dimension of the nature of sport gets damaged and "bad faith" ensues. "Good" sport, by contrast, is not destructive of mutual respect and goodwill: rather, it is enhanced. Features that constitute the moral life — impartiality, benevolence and liberty — are lived out in a climate of friendship and comraderie. In the pursuit of context and effort the true sportsman is thankful to his opponent for the giving of his best in a climate of shared understanding and brotherhood.

If participation in sport can lead to an enrichment of the moral life, so too it can provide distinctive ways of entering the aesthetic life. Whilst it seems clear that all sporting activities are capable of yielding aesthetic experience it is perhaps true to say that some sports because they are inherently aesthetic in their make-up are more predisposed to do so. Whereas it is perfectly possible, for example, to put the shot without reference to aesthetic criteria it would not be possible to do so in an activity like ski-jumping for here the *manner* or how something is done is as important as *what* is done. In the shot put, providing the rules are kept, it is the distance that counts, whereas in ski-jumping, line and form are no less important than the distance achieved.

Whilst it is important to recognise that "aesthetic sports" like figure skating are partially characterised and evaluated by reference to aesthetic criteria it should not be thought that other sports which are not, are thereby rendered aesthetically barren. On the contrary as I have suggested elsewhere[1] in such facets of sport as the skillful, the dramatic and the phenomenon of "the good contest", the aesthetic response is likely to be evoked. In the mastered skill, for instance, not only can the informed spectator be afforded delight, but the bodily-aware performer pleasure. The hammer thrower is no less able to feel the rhythmical sequence of his controlled gyrations than the onlooker is able to admire the fluency, poise and balance of their execution. It is by attending to the familiar gestalt of his kinaesthetic flow patterns that the athlete, as the agent of his actions, can and does derive aesthetic gratification. For the athlete a mastered skill can become a kind of aesthetic manoeuvre — something akin to a well-known melody. It can not only be functionally employed to meet a particular task in the context of sporting action but, when attended to kinaesthetically, enjoyed for its own sake. It is both an aspect of self and a source of pleasure.

Too much emphasis upon analysing the features by which a sport can be identified can lead to a neglect of its psychological elements. Originally

110

sport meant to find amusement, diversion, fun or pleasure, particularly in games and play but with the coming of professionalism and commercialism it became a more serious business.* The nature of sport, however, cannot be adequately grasped if attention is confined to an examination of the observable features of its separate instances. The raison d'être of a sport lies not in its outward characteristics and procedures so much as in the needs, craving and satisfactions of those who participate in it. Although those who engage in competitive sport agree to abide by the rules and try to win, it should not be thought that these "definitional features" are in any way equivalent to or commensurate with the reasons and motivations, if they are known at all, as to why people take part. The logical characteristics of a sport in other words do not necessarily offer an explanation of why people want to participate in it. The fact that a person tries to win, for example, when playing a game in no way suggests that to win is his purpose, least of all his chief purpose, in playing it. For many the attempt to win is but a procedural feature of competing.

Some people take part in sport not in order to win per se but because in taking part they find value and satisfaction in its processes and outcomes. This can take the form of such dimensions as social experience, excitement, catharsis or health and fitness or a combination of them. The point then is that although the attempt to win is a necessary procedural feature for engaging in sport this by no means is the same as saying that winning is the reason why people participate in it.

One dimension of being that sport can help satisfy is the quest for authentic existence. Such is the pervasive and alienating power of the mass media and the anonymous "they" that the soul of man cries out for a sense of individuality and freedom. To live inauthentically is to de-personalise one's existence by giving way to amorphous collective. To live authentically on the other hand enables the existent as agent to take possession of himself and live in accordance with his choices and decisions. Sport is authentic to the extent that it provides a meaningful forum in and through which the person can both find and make himself. Whereas the reflective life is concerned with theory and ideas and proceeds from thought to thought, the practical life of which sport is a paradigmatic case, proceeds from intention to action. To intentionally act in the world is to make our mark on the world. It is concerned with doing and being involved *in* the world not simply formulating thoughts *about* the world in propositional terms. It is because thoughts without action achieve nothing that praxis is more fundamental to being in the world than theory. In sport man re-affirms his presence in the world by doing and becoming. In sport one competes as much to self-actualize and to find out who one is as to seek recognition or glory.

Related to the question of sport as action is the notion of bodily being. Here the concern is not with

---

* See Huizinga, J. Homo Ludens   Paladin, 1970) Chapt.12

regarding the body as an object to be looked at or an instrument to be used in order to accomplish and achieve but as an indissoluble part of self that can be "let be"* in terms of the experience it offers. To put the matter another way the sportsman learns to dwell in his body and attend to its animate nature. In such events as the discus throw the athlete performs a particular action and is able to test and experience his vital powers. He becomes acquainted with the demands, rhythms, pains and excitements of his physicality. The skilled athlete then, like the skilled dancer, is not only able to perform and give an informed account of what he is doing, but experience and feel his body as an inherent part of his presence in the world. Being-in-the-body is not meant to convey any sense of possession or dualism as in the phrase my-body-and-me or "I have a body", but rather in the composite but unitary sense of I-em-embodied or "I am a bodily being". The person engaged in sport, by attending to what he experiences as well as to what he does, becomes more fruitfully aware of his own incarnate consciousness. In the lived-body event of the throw, the jump or the run, the athlete becomes more firmly established in his own bodily being. More than this, in such "peak" moments of the perfect chip at golf or the perfect triple somersault dive, the performer can enter a transcendent state whereby he temporarily becomes "golfer" or "diver".

Although sport is not play it is doubtful if "modern" sport would have come into existence let alone survived unless something of the spirit of play were encapsulated by it. Whereas play is immediate in its attractiveness and takes what it can from the passing moment, sport reflects more an attitude of disciplined application; whereas play is essentially an expression of disinterested absorption, sport is committed more to the fulfilment of its own rule-governed ends. Certainly when fun and spontaneity cease to be a part of sport it can become a dull and serious business. This is why it is the amateur rather than the professional who is the guardian of sport, for it is the amateur, the lover of what he does that keeps the nature of sport alive. The amateur participates because he takes pleasure in doing so, not because he sees it as a means of earning a livelihood. It is because of this that the Olympic ideal, abused and corrupted as it has been, is still worth preserving.

Despite the fact that play is not sport it is doubtful if the notion of "good" sport can be grasped without reference to it. Somehow in the attitude to life that is characteristic of play there is an important message for sport. As has been shown it is possible to identify the conceptual features of sport without reference to play. Yet without its spirit it remains for the participant deficient. Play then is a vital but gratuitous element in sport. Without it sport would not be all that it can be. Unless the spirit of play is present in sport from time to time much that is done in its name would lack lustre and be empty of exuberance and joy.

The illusiveness and value of play in relation to sport lies in its paradoxical nature: it is at one and the same time both "serious" and "non-serious". It is serious in that it appears to "step aside" from the realities of life and thereby to some extent becomes escapist, yet in the very act of doing so becomes serious again but this time at a more profound level. There are two points to be made about this second sense of seriousness. The first relates to the belief that play is a necessary ingredient for the living of the good life and stems from both Aristotle and Acquinas, who thought that in the interests of the good and balanced life man should be neither over earnest or idiotically buffoonish. Eutrapelia was the name given to this reconciling playful element in the good life. The second point about play in relation to sport (when it is not taken too seriously) is that it seeks nothing but its own satisfaction, its own pleasure. When this occurs refreshment is the outcome. The play element in sport then is important for it helps sport to remain a harmonising and restorative pursuit and prevent it being turned into a dehumanising, dedicated, routinised and zestless occupation.

In conclusion it can be said that if sport is to be a source of intrinsic value and provide opportunities for the discovery of authentic being it must, like play, be left to pursue its own ends and not be used as a means to further other ends, whether social, political or economic, that are extrinsic to its nature.

REFERENCES

1. Keating, J.W. "Sportsmanship as a moral category" in Ellen W. Gerber and William J. Morgan (eds.) *Sport and the Body,* Lea and Febiger, 1979, pp. 264-271.
2. Arnold, P.J. "Meaning in movement, sport and physical education" Heinemann, 1979, pp. 143-161.

---

*For Heidegger "letting be" is a form of freedom. See his "On the essence of Truth" in "Existence and Being" edited by W. Brock. Pegenery 1968, pp. 305-307.

THE MEANING OF SPORT — HEALTH CARE OR MODERN RITUALS?

Juhani Kirjonen (Finland)

1. Background

One of the traditional ways of evaluating the meaning of sport involves a tendency to polarize the way of thinking: motives for competition are seen in contrast to motives for health improvement, the interests of youth are differentiated from those of adults, also the effects of team sports and those of individual sports are even regarded as opposite etc. It is not clearly understood that modern sport really touches only a part of the people, and furthermore only in a certain cultural environment. Involvement is, however, manifold and changes slowly without any sharp phases during the life history of an individual and with developments in the society. My general thesis is that in order to obtain the most accurate and complete idea of the personal meaning of sport, physical exercise and sport interests should be seen as a varying stage in the life style of a person. Research which is directed towards questions concerning the way of life or life style, has to consider at the same time phenomena at the individual as well as the collective level. In contrast to the traditional positivistic approach, this kind of research is oriented to some extent historically and anthropologically. Modern social psychology might offer good examples. I therefore think that the most successful scientific approach — also the empirical one — to the phenomena of sport and physical culture, is interdisciplinary by nature and aimed at gaining a thorough, overall understanding of the structure of the individual way of life.

It would be time-consuming in this instance to try to present the theoretical background of the meaning of sport using old classical models: priorities of the agent of all cultural and societal development, which were ideas put forward by Weber and economical relations by Marx. Instead it might be sufficient to ascertain that a prerequisite for the rise and growth of sport, as well as other sub-areas of our culture, has been a highly-advanced, modern society (Kiviaho 1974, Wohl 1964). The necessary preconditions for the rise and development of sport as an institution were some kind of *urbanized structure of society* and a system of *division of labour*. The distribution of the work force resulted in a class of people whose main responsibility was to train physical and military skills in readiness for war. At the same time, the social division of labour also provided opportunities for other groups in society to participate in some way or another in various competitions and performances. Such mass performances have been an essential part of militaristic ideology from the very beginning of our societies' history. Regardless of the economical and political system of the society, some of the motives and also functions of sport are parallel to this ideological background.

Socialization institutions, which are partly or totally maintained by society, such as the educational system, have incorporated sport as an essential component of their formal program for a long time. On the other hand the system of health care is only gradually starting to utilize physical exercise methods and other applications of corrective sport. In any case these activities have a relatively short history as a part of officially accepted medical treatment in most countries.

2. Some concepts

I have the tendency to understand phenomena related to sport and physical culture as being determined primarily by the development of the society, without forgetting the role of the individual. This role is especially meaningful in the development of motives for action, which has an organic link with concrete preconditions of action. Such preconditions may vary from physical and material facilities to appropriate instruction and even as far as the availability of a team or companion. However, the extent to which the objectives of the activity and the changes in these objectives are defined by a person itself are also essential. I am using here an expression "the level of individual autonomy". Thus by adapting both these dimensions together, we first can have three categories of the social functions of sport and physical exercise, and secondly a kind of sliding scale of individual autonomy in the definition of the objectives and the nature of the activity (Table 1).

Table 1 Categories of the social function of sports and physical exercise. Examples of the activity types according to the level of individual autonomy in determining objectives for the activity

Social function	Activity types		
	High ———————— Low		
	Level of autonomy		
1. Ambition and gaining social and material benefits	Various games	Amateur sports	Championship and international sports
2. Advancement of socialization	Forms of plays and dances	Physical education	Military exercises
3. Reproduction of work force	Outdoor activities	Conditioning exercises	Physiotherapy

Using this frame we can obtain several combinations of activities with different social functions and levels of autonomy and then identify certain typical forms of physical activities. Some examples of these activities can be seen in the table. I am mainly concerned in this presentation with the activities in the first and second column and other similar activities. This is due to the fact that I am regarding "sport" as a population-related term, which has a multidimensional and epidemiological nature in this context. It comprises a vast variety of physical activities ranging from the playing of children to conditioning exercises and competing sports for adults. One common characteristic of these activities is a personal and purposeful participation in physical performances, which are not immediately related to work activities. The interpretation of the concept follows the same usage of the term, which our research team has adopted with a synonym "leisure-time physical activity" (Telama 1977), the third column in Table 1 being excluded.

In the following chapters my aim is at first to review certain selected empirical findings, by means of which I will attempt to link "leisure-time physical activity" (LTPA) to certain phenomena at the collective and demographic level. Secondly I will discuss and question certain conventional explanations of the interest in LTPA. And thirdly I will make some suggestions for theoretical models, which could be used to make advances in studying the personal meaning of LTPA as an essential part of the individual life style.

3. Interest in sport among the adult population in Finnish industrialized cities

In this chapter a short description of the situation in Finland in the 1970's will be given by presenting some empirical survey results concerning general interest and active participation in organized and unorganized sport. The point is that even very rough figures depicting interest distributions by principal demographic factors presuppose certain specifications of the topic, when we are talking about the meaning of sport.

3.1 Interest in organized sport

Results from a survey concerning employees of an engineering factory in an industrialized city in Central Finland, showed that most people had some contact with organized sport in one way or another. The average proportions were 86% for men and 59% for women (Table 2).

Table 2. Interest and participation in organized sport among urban adult Finnish men and women. Examples from a survey (METELI, 1975).

	Men %	Women %
1. Interested via mass media:		
total proportion	86	59
via newspapers	78	35
via television	46	52
2. Members of sport clubs		
total	21	9
mainly as competitors	11	3
mainly as officials etc.	11	2
(sample size)	(886)	(288)

However most of those showing an interest were only passive "consumer" enthusiasts and spectators, who read the sport news (78% of men) or watch TV (52% of women).

Furthermore, our results showed that active participation was clearly infrequent since only 21% of men and 9% of women were members of a sport club and 11% of men and only 3% of women were active competitors, "producers". Thus the "producer/consumer"-ratio was about 1:8 among men and about 1:17 among women (METELI 1975). Naturally the ratio would be dramatically decreased, if rural areas and rather low participation frequences were to be included in the study.

3.2 Interest in unorganized sport

Spontaneous, unorganised sport and leisure-time physical activity encompass various forms of conditioning exercises and outdoor activities. The general finding in earlier studies has been that far more than 50% of Finns regularly participate in spontaneous leisure-time recreation. Selected results from our studies are presented in Table 3. The most popular activity for both sexes is outdoor activity, strictly speaking walking, and about 85% of the sample selected it as the preferred LTPA using tne alternative "at least once a week". The proportion of those stating "at least twice a week" was about twenty percent lower in both sexes. Two thirds of the sample are thus regularly active, this level corresponding very well to previous results concerning the Finnish adult population in urban areas.

Table 3. The amount of participants in the preferred sport or outdoor activity during summertime among urban adult Finnish men and women. Examples from a survey, (METELI 1975).

	Men %	Women %
1. Outdoor activities and sport		
at least once a week	84	85
at least twice a week	61	67
2. Intensive sport or conditioning exercises		
at least once a week	36	21
at least twice a week	17	7
(sample size)	(886)	(268)

If we define the criterion for LTPA very narrowly, let us say by using its physiological effectiveness for fitness (for example estimating the average energy consumption in each kind of activities mentioned and the taking into account only the most intensive), then the proportions of active people of both sexes are considerably lower than above. We found that about one out of six men and one out of fourteen women are actively interested in this kind of intensive sport and physical exercise (see Table 3, 2nd paragraph). It is also interesting to see that less than a half of the "LTPA-intensive" people are regular sport competitors.

3.3 Distribution of sport interests

The same population was used as the target group when we carried out one year later a health examination combined with questionnaires, in which the same or respective items concerning LTPA were used as previously.

We constructed a general index of strenuous physical activities, which included LTPA-activities as well as some of the heaviest home chores. The index was a combination of all those activities engaged in during a period of one year in which the estimated energy consumption was more than 500 Kcal/h. This index score correlated highly positively with the score for intensive sport and physical exercise, which we used formerly (see Table 3). We were attempting, among other things, to compare the shape of the distributions of various activity variables. The results showed that the distribution of most of these variables was very skewed. For example, in the distribution of strenuous activities 42% of men and 60% of women had a zero-score (Figure 1).

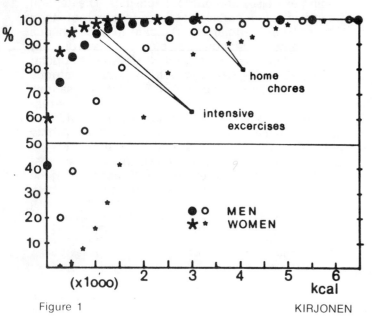

Figure 1   KIRJONEN

Cumulative percentages of the distribution of physical activity: estimated energy consumption per year, 1) for (METELI 1975)

A less skewed variable was the score for home chores, which approaches a normal curve in case of women. One rather logical conclusion is that really effective physical activity, especially sport or conditioning exercise, does not have a very dramatic role in the life of most people. A significant exception from the general tendency is the activity spent on home chores, in which the scores are most evenly, almost normally distributed. However, the inequality between sexes is also clearly seen in these results.

In addition, some interesting differences between age groups are demonstrable. It is generally known that the time budget of girls and boys changes abruptly during puberty and interest in sport then becomes markedly less. The same decreasing tendency is also seen in our results for young male workers. The level of interest remains nearly unchanged until the age of fifty,

114

whereupon there is a conspicious decrease in interest (Figure 2).

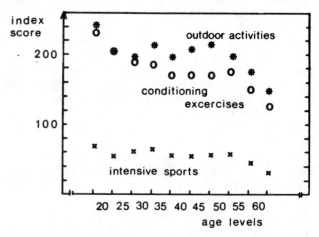

Figure 2   KIRJONEN

Total amount of sport and physical acyivity by age (average index scores in five-year intervals) among men.

Qualitative differences between age groups are not very marked: active participation in competitive sport seems to persist as an interest for a minor group of men. Outdoor activities (walking), on the other hand, are very popular in all age groups and reach their peak at the age of about fourty. I would like to point out here, that we are looking at cross-sectional results, so that it is not really correct to speak about "changes" by age.

The supplementing factor in analyses of quantitative variations in LTPA is the type of work in which people are engaged in. We have used categories of occupational status in representing this dimension. General trends in LTPA differences can clearly be seen when they are put in cross-tabulation form, in which proportions of those people who are not at all interested in sports are classified by occupational status categories and by age groups (Table 4).

Table 4. Proportions of those adults, who *are not actively* interested in sport of any kind or intensive exercise. (Examples from a survey, METELI 1975).

	Younger than 30 years	30-49 years	Older than 49 years
MEN			
Managers	11	36	57
Other clerical & technical staff	31	38	53
Skilled workers	43	40	65
Semi-and unskilled workers	37	61	70
Together	31	41	60
(Number)	(351)	(365)	(162)
WOMEN			
Clerical etc. staff	46	48	55
Workers	74	73	74
Together	55	64	69
(Number)	(88)	(131)	(49)

Our results are in good agreement with some eralier findings (for example Grusin 1970, Hogseth et al. 1973, Lüschen 1963, Takenoshita 1967). According to these results, the amount of sport and leisure-time physical activity is positively correlated with occupational status measures, which, on the other hand, correlated negatively with passive interest, like spectatorship (METELI 1975). It was also shown by detailed analyses that the strenuousness of a person's job correlated negatively with all kind of LTPA-measures. These negative correlations were highest among women, when the loading due to home chores was also taken into consideration (compare Figure 1).

3.4 Typical portrait of the physically inactive and the physically active person

Summarizing our results as regards the reverse side of the portrait, it can be said that the person non-active in sport is most likely to be a member of the following groups:

1. Woman, especially married (or divorced) with children
2. Man of middle age or most probably older
3. Worker, especially less educated, regardless of age group

When some detailed results of regression analyses are also included, the portrait of the physically active adult person is as follows:

- the person is a man, he is rather young, well educated, is living in a well-furnished apartment, and has received positive influences as regards interest in sport from his parental home;
- if the person is a woman, she has good earnings, is most likely in a white collar occupation, has received positive influences as regards an interest in sport from her parental home, and is not over-weight.

3.5 The background to interest in sport and its interpretation

We are now in a situation in which we have sufficient knowledge to answer the question — which are the most prominent explanative factors regarding interest in LTPA among a normal, adult population. I have constructed a theoretical framework for this purpose in which explanative factors are located on two levels called determinants and moderators (Table 5). The point I am trying to make is that moderators are likely to be extremely important when analyses of the individual meaning of sport are made.

Some additional comments are relevant here. It should first be emphasized that definitions of those interest characteristics which are concentrated on the investigation are of primary importance. It is a totally different thing to analyse the intensity of interest than the frequency or total amount in a time unit. Clearing-up the persistency of interest by using only the cross-sectional approach, to say nothing of changes in interest motives along life history, is particularly problematic. Another comment concerns the selection of the scientific point of view. Traditionally, characteristics of certain interests are

Table 5. A theoretical framework for analysing the effects of determinants and moderators on active interest characteristics in sport and physical exercise.

Determinants	Moderators	Characteristics of active interest
AGE		
	PSYCHO-PHYSICAL EFFECTIVENESS	intensity,
SEX		amount,
	FAMILY STRUCTURE AND DISTRIBUTION OF TASKS	
OCCUPATION		persistency
	NATURE OF JOB AND WORK LOAD	and quality
STANDARD OF LIVING		
	MATERIAL AND SOCIAL CONDITIONS (I.E. HOUSING)	

frequently studied separately and by using representative samples. Such facts are valuable. However, we also need more intensive approaches, which consider various aspects of the general background (determinants and moderators) and in which the same individuals are followed up over a period lasting for several years in order to study qualitative changes in their life history. I am well aware of existing problems, of which economical ones are not the least significant, but new ideas are really needed.

4. About restrictions and motives in physical exercise

In the preceding chapter, some tentative answers to the question — which are the most common factors restricting physical exercises — were put forward. As we have seen, ageing, living habits related to educational background, interests other than sporting ones competing for the time available are examples of such factors. We also asked the respondents to specify how meaningful the effects of certain restrictive factors were. The results showed that the most important were fatigue due to work, lack of time and other interests among men, and lack of time, home chores and fatigue due to work among women. The proportion of those respondents who mentioned these factors was more than double the proportions for other alternatives (METELI 1975).

Motives in LTPA were also asked by submitting a list of statements, which included items from such areas as health, competition and social relations (see Kenyon 1968). Our results showed that the most commonly accepted motives among this sample were: promotion of health, acquiring refreshment and maintaining working ability. More than 50% of the respondents were positive as regards these motives. On the other hand, competitive performance and efforts, as well as a need for social contacts, were only 20 percent or less. It should be mentioned that only one out of four respondents regarded physical exercises as being indispensable for health. Thus there is a rather big gap between the expressed positive motivational opinion and actual manifested activity. This would be interpreted to mean that responses to this kind of general statements mainly reflect the normative and conventional attitudes towards all-round positive effects of sports and physical exercise without revealing any kind of personal motives. The information obtained by means of structured questionnaires would appear to require supplementary data obtained using other methods.

Some other results have recently been published which indicate that the methodological problem really exists. In a study, carried out in the same city as our previous investigations, the respondents were again adults, but in this case employees of a number of municipal offices (Telama et al. 1981). An unstructured interview was partly used as the principal method and the interview was based on a questionnaire completed in advance. The interviews were made only with respondents who were actively interested in LTPA. According to the results the most commonly preferred motives were recreation, relaxation and a love of nature. These were clearly more frequent than health and fitness among both sexes (Table 6). Motives which included a recreational tone were especially dominant among female respondents. General motives for health and for prevention of illnesses were rather infrequent (10% or less of the respondents).

Table 6. Most frequently selected separate motives for interest in sport and physical exercises. Results from interviews with urban, adult men and women (Telama et al. 1981).

	Women	Men	All
Refreshment, recreation	61	41	51
Outdoor activity, fresh air	59	38	48
Conditioning, generally	32	38	35
Nature, landscape	41	25	33
Calming oneself, relaxation	30	23	27
Physical, effectiveness	27	18	23
Generally interest in ph. a.	21	23	22
Joy, fun, pleasure	29	12	21
...			
Mental health, mood	18	17	17
...			
Prevent illnesses	14	10	12
...			
Health generally	10	10	10
(Sample size)			(336)

By using specified and diverging categories of motives it was possible to obtain a more clearcut and manifold picture of the structure of motives. It seems that without reservations and further definitions, application of such positively loaded terms as "health", "fitness", "preventation" in a questionnaire is extremely risky. This finding, even though not a very new one, might be significant when we are talking about changes in the personal meaning of the sport throughout the life history. The term "health" is especially problematic, because precise

changes in it, for instance an increase, are very difficult to define even subjectively. We need further facts concerning more complex methods for mapping the structure and variations of motives. Emotionally loaded, "soft" categories like joy, relaxation, inspiration etc. then might also be emphasized more than in traditional studies. In addition to this, it should be kept in mind that empirical findings as regards causal relationships between physical exercise activity and the improvement of health status do not justify the drawing of positive conclusions only.

5. Understanding the personal meaning of LTPA

Findings which I have demonstrated in the preceeding chapters have not notably augmented our knowledge about the generality of sport interests, nor about the motives of exercise or about its restrictions. Instead, I hope that I have been able to indicate that:

1. the meaning of sport in the normal population necessarily varies at least according to age, sex, occupation, and educational background; this is why the primary preconditions set by these factors have to be taken into consideration in studies which deal with the personal meaning of sport,

2. certain changing circumstances during the life history, such as physical fitness, the family structure, the distribution of tasks between the family members, characteristics of the job and the level of housing all obviously act as moderators between active interests and the preconditions (determinants mentioned before). Thus they most likely either promote or impede active interests and thus indirectly lead to alterations in the meaning of sport during the life span.

3. the classical means of motivation in sport and other physical exercise which emphasize health effects, are evidently too one-sided and partly also ineffectual, because they do not correspond with the actual structure of real personal motives; more emotionally loaded, affective motives might be of more importance than they have seen to be before.

4. characteristics of interest in LTPA vary in several dimensions: besides intensity there are variations in its total amount, quality persistency and naturally also in its individual objectives; The LTPA-area is a very versatile field encompassing many phenomena, in which many-sided approaches are most relevant, and which is an exceedingly suitable target for cross-disciplinary research strategies.

6. Concluding suggestions

There are two remarkable points clearly more evident than others which arise during discussion concerning empirical research in question of the psychological meaning of sport. First of all we need more information about the individual and combined effects of social and material conditions on an active interest in sport, and how these effects change during the different stages of the person's life history. Secondly we also need to know more about the various types of motives, and their role in stimulating active sport and physical exercise in various groups of people, whose backgrounds differ. In this respect affectively-loaded motives (for example joy, relaxation, refreshment) might prove to be important. According to an eminent Soviet psychologist Oznadze (1969), psychic processes have two principal levels: "the plane of sets" and "the plane of objectivization". The first mentioned level includes, for example, emotions, perceptions and memory functions, and the latter comprises, for example, cognitive processes and will. Everyday activities are primarily dependent on processes pertaining to the first level. Roughly speaking, such activities are principally directed by the motives, which are closely related to "the plane of sets", in which "the outside world consists of unending and unceasing change" (op.sit., 118). Cognitive processes and related motives direct the behaviour of a person in situations in which there are problems to solve, in which a person's attention is directed profoundly at the world of reality, is "objectivated". It is also possible that this theory, which is not so well-known, might prove valuable in studies of the psychological meaning of sport.

One alternative or supplementing theoretical frame can also be used, the frame of the formation of the individual way of life. In this sense the process of socialization is of primary importance. The role of sport interests could be considered to be determined by certain social rules on the one hand, but on the other hand it is also seen as an agent for change, which has a specific meaning in each stage of an individual life span in the formation of the way of life. By adapting the scheme of successive factors, which are mediating social deprivation (Berthoud, 1976), a varying meaning of sports in a socialization process and in the formation of a way of life could be studied (Figure 3). In the meantime we have an excellent opportunity to enjoy all the effects of sports, be they either health-promoting or ritualistic by nature.

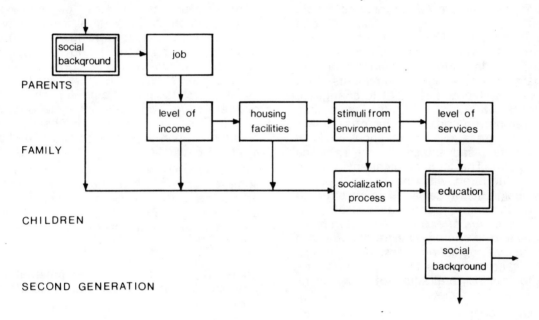

Figure 3   KIRJONEN

A model for analysis of various types of socialization "agents" and their functions in forming the individual way of life.

REFERENCES

Berthoud, R.: The disadvantages of inequality. A PEP report. MacDonald and Jane's, London 1976.

Grusin, B.: Die Nutzung der freien Zeit in der UdSSR. in: Die Freie Zeit als Problem (Autorenkollektiv Grusin, B. et al.) Berlin Verlag, Berlin, 1970.

Hogseth, K., Mork, I.V., Railo, W.: Fysisk aktivitet of idrettsintresse i den norske befolkning. Norges Idrettshogskole, Oslo, 1973.

Kenyon, G.: A conceptual model for characterizing physical activity. Res. Quart. 39:96-105, 1968.

Kiviaho, P.: Sport oroanaization and the structure of society. Studies in Sport, Physical Education and Health, No. 4. University of Jyväskylä, Jyväskylä, 1974.

Lüschen, G.: Soziale Schichtung und Soziale Mobilität bei Jungen Sportlern. Kölner Zeitschrift für Soziologie und Sozialpsychologie 15, 1, 74-93, 1963.

Mantz, G.: Zur Auffassung von der Lebensweise und dem Lebensniveau in der sozialistichen Volkswirtschafts-plannung de DDR; in Koskiaho, B., Tanninen, T., Steaufenbiel, F. und Brand, K. (Eds.): Lebensweise und Lebensniveau, Wohnen und Wohnumwelt, pp. 12-22, Tampere, 1979.

METELI: Kolmen metallitehtaan henkilöstöjen liikuntakäittäytyminen (Leisure time sport and psychical activity of employees in three plants of the machine industry, in Finnish). Liikunnan ja Kansanterveyden julkaisuja 11, Jyväskylä, 1975.

Takenoshita, K.: The social structure of the sport population in Japan. Int. Rev. Sport Sociology 2:5-18, 1967.

Telama, R.: The relationship between leisure time physical activity, physical fitness and mental health among employees of machine industry in Finland. Proc. 4th World Congress of the Int. Soc. of Sports Psychology, Prague, 1977.

Telama, R., Vuolle, P. & Laakso, L.: Terveys ja kunto aikuis-väestön liikunta-motiiveina. (Health and fitness as mo-

tives for physical exercise among adults, in Finnish) Liikunta ja tiede 18, 1, 33-40, 1981.

Uznadze, D.N.: The psychologyof set. New York (Original Russian text was published in 1961, in Tiflis) 1969.

Wohl, A.: Die gesellschaftliche-historischen Grundlagen des bürgerlichen Sports. Wiss. Zeitschrift DHfK 6, 7, 5-93, 1964.

PERSONAL MEANING IN SPORT — GDR PERSPECTIVES

Paul Kunath (GDR)

Sport gains an ever greater importance for the development of social life and for every individual within modern societies. This is true for the developed industrial countries as well as for the developing countries. The individual must be increasingly better prepared to meet the requirements for a happy and healthy life and to react to changes in his/her personal way of life. At the same time, however, obtaining the consequences of scientific-technological progress and urbanization would be desired without the disadvantages for one's physical and mental health. The technological environment having vastly interfered with the private spheres places only insignificant demands upon strength, endurance or flexibility. *Sport has, therefore, to prepare the individual better for a life under changing conditions and to compensate for the effects of the scientific-technological progress on his physical and mental functions.* It, thus, fulfils an increasingly larger task for the self-realization of man and his happiness in a given society.

I think that it cannot be left, therefore, to the choice of the individual to take part in sports or to reject them. A society that is responsible to the human being and its self-materialization should do everything to guarantee everybody's physical-athletic engagement. To achieve this, adequate material-technical conditions have to be provided and as well, capable officials, instructors, sport teachers, sport physicians, and sport journalists have to be trained to support that process.

We consider this World Congress also to be a forum for an exchange of various experiences which have been collected in different states or societies. The World Federation of Sport Psychologists (ISSP) thereby supports the efforts of UNESCO, including those of CIEPS and modern Olympic movements to intensify and to promote the world-wide process of an ever stronger utilization of sport or athletic activities, respectively, for an individual self-materialization.

There have been efforts by states and institutions in many countries, for rather long periods and with varying effects, to come to a healthy way of life, to organize working, learning and living conditions in a health-promoting manner and to support a large-scale propaganda campaign corresponding to these aims to interest people in sport. I see the reasons for varying efforts and effects for and by sport, in different states with different social orders, particularly in the close inter-relations between sport and economical pre-suppositions and conditions of life in certain societies.

I would, therefore, like to present in my paper some *experiences and findings* that we have been able to collect in the *German Democratic Republic* concerning the growing importance of sport, for the development of our citizens, but especially of our youth.

Social Conditions and Developmental Factors of Physical Culture and Sport in the GDR

Physical education and physical-athletic activities start in the *family* during early childhood. During the last 30 years a *generation of parents* has grown in the GDR that has an extremely positive attitude towards physical culture and sport. 56% of these parents encourage their children to take part in sport activities several times per week. Another 22% expect their children to participate (cf. 1, p.32). Parents, grandparents and relatives spend ever more money to buy toys and sport equipment. Sports goods, athletic toys, and clothing are produced in increasing amounts. At the present time, the demand is higher for some sports goods than the supply. Such processes are intensively screened within the state planning process and steps are taken into consideration in accordance with the economic total development.

State-owned crèches and Kindergardens. More than 80% of young or pre-school age children enjoy Kindergardens — which give high preference to daily physical-athletic activities, in addition to health education and hygiene. The educators' and parents' work is increasingly better supported by appropriate literature for the guidance of sport and playing activities of their children. Newspapers and magazines publish a lot of articles to inform parents and educators about the values of sport and physical culture for the development of personalities and about the possibilities for mass involvement in sport and physical activity. During the last few years the mass media has also started to give more examples of the physical-athletical activities appropriate for physically or mentally handicapped children. The state has taken a large number of measures to increase the participation of physically handicapped children in physical activity.

Physical education and athletic activities are promoted on a wider scale during the *compulsory school years* (7 to 18 years of age). There are two to four sport lessons in the classes that are compulsory. Sport teachers (more than 15,000) have had a four-year university or college training. About 72% of all the school children take part in extra-curricular sports within their school sport clubs or in the children's groups of the sport organisation's unions (DTSB). Schools and sport organisations are currently attempting to encourage the last third of children and adolescents to participate in an organized athletic activity. We, the sport psychologists, support these efforts of schools and sport organisations to include, if possible, all the children and adolescents in *organised, regular athletic activity*. We hold the opinion, and our studies have confirmed this fact rather convincingly, that a regular and organized athletic activity possesses the highest value for the development of personalities. Children and adolescents that are taking part in sports on an organized level differ in several personality traits from those who participate in some individual sports or who do not take part at all. We found such differences particularly in their *attitudes towards life* and *to other people*, in *value orientations*, in *a large variety of interest*, more *enthusiastic social activities* and *increased active behaviours*. We found for example a five times higher frequency in participating in hobby-circles, theatre performances, scientific projects, advanced studies and social engagements for those who were actively taking part in sports as compared to those who were athletically passive (cf. 4, p.43). According to our research findings there is an increase in athletic activities with children and adolescents during their *leisure-time* or *weekends* in the *local areas* or *territorial centres*. *Holiday camps during school holidays*, are being organized in beautiful landscapes throughout our country with an adequate athletic and touristic program (Tab.1: Number of children participating in holiday camps).

A large-scale *competitive system* has been established for the athletic engagement of children and adolescents, on local and central levels. Schools and sport organizations are closely cooperating with the youth organization. The *Spartakiad-system* has been shown to be a particularly effective program for the development of athletic performance efforts of children and adolescents in our country. Best

Children and adolescents of school age (1-10 class) in total	= 2.300,000
out of it: participants in central and factory camps (3 weeks)	= 800,000
• in local camps (3 weeks)	= 750,000
• camps for specialists (for instance to learn swim)	= 100,000
Assistance (Camp- and groupleaders; kitchen-, health- and sport-staff, physicians, life savers etc) in total	= 250,000

Table 1: Participation in holiday camps in summer 1981

performers are found in summer and winter sports, starting with intramural competitions, in towns and countries in district competitions and on a national level every two years. This system is especially useful to give *athletically-minded children and adolescents that are talented* the chance to develop their athletic talents and to compete in sport events with their age groups. (Tab. 2: Participation in Spartakiad-competitions).

Participation	Year	children	adolesc's	in total
in district Spartakiad-competitions	1965	202,000	119,000	321,000
	1970	353,000	191,000	544,000
	1975	561,000	285,000	846,000
	1980	622,000	318,000	940,000
	1981	641,000	329,000	970,000
in central Spartakiad competitions	in summer sports			11,000
	in winter sports			1,200

Table 2: Participation in Spartakiad-competitions 1965-81

Families are participating in athletic activities in an increasing number. Parents and their children go for trips to *recreational resorts* run by state or factories and situated near to their local areas. They use the various facilities offered there to keep fit. *Family competitions* of many different kinds enjoy ever greater popularity. *Holiday services of the Trade Unions* have reached a high level. Professional sport teachers or physiotherapists are employees of all the holiday resorts or centres to guide physical-athletical activities during vacations. During the school holidays (July/August) families with school-aged children are given preference to recreate themselves in Trade Union holiday inns. In summer, bathing or swimming facilities are used at the seaside, in lakes, open-air swimming pools, rivers or channels, according to our climatic conditions. In winter (about 3 months) skiing is a favourite weekend or holiday activity, especially in the uplands. (Tab. 3: Some statistics from the Trade Unions' Holiday Services).

Holiday places (c. 14 days) in total	= 4.400,000
out of it: places in factory vacation hostels	= 2,600,000
places with professionals with children in school age during summer and winter holidays	= c.50%

Table 3: Some figures on the Free German Trade Union's (F.D.G.B.) holiday services

The GDR sport organisation, the Deutscher Turn- und Sportbund (German Gymnastics and Sports Union) is the initiator and organizer of all the sport throughout our country. About every 5th citizen is a member of this sport organisation. It continuously enlarges its *exercising, training and competitive program*. In accordance with the economic capacities of the state, facilities are established for a growing number of people to take part in sports. The sport organisation promotes a vast athletic and touristic life beyond the competitive system in various sports.

Sport is connected in quite versatile manners *with the intellectual-cultural needs of the people.* Many cultural events, festivals in local areas or companies have programs that include athletic activities of the people living or working there or their children and youth groups.

The sport organisation trains ever more and competent *officials, instructors, coaches, judges and referees* and other groups of *assistants* to run sports events to meet the increasing demands of our citizens to take part in sports. An adequate number of *sport physicians* and *First Aid assistents* has been trained in cooperation with the state health service for the support of the exercise, training and competitive program. About every 8th member of the sport organisation is an official, every 14th an instructor or coach, and every 30th a judge or referee (6, p.76).

The efforts of the sport organisation to develop ever broader and more varied physical culture and sport throughout our country are strongly supported by the *united sport program* conducted by the sport organisation, the Trade Unions and the youth organisation. There are 200,000 sport organizers in Trade Union groups only, and another 36,000 sport officials in the Free German Youth's groups to organize their sports programs on a voluntary basis (Tab. 4: The DTSB of the GDR in figures).

Physical culture and sport become an ever stronger *component of our citizens' way of life.* Changing positions of man in the social production and towards the distribution of material, cultural, intellectual, and social values produced, also bring about new relations or needs, respectively, of our

Members of German Gymnastics and Sports Union D.T.S.B.) od GDR 1981 in total		= c.3.200,000
out of it: Children (still to 14 years)	=	693,000
1978 adolescents (15-18 years)	=	499,000
Trainer and instructors (1981)		209,000
Judges and referees (1981)		127,000
Officials (1981)		400,000
Sport utilities in total (1981)		35,000

Table 4: Some statistics of German Gymnastics and Sports Union (D.T.S.B.) of GDR

people for physical culture and sport. This process concerns all the social classes and strata, all levels of ages, and both the sexes. The majority of the GDR population are right now actively and regularly engaged in some kind of sport. The male percentage is here somewhat higher than that of the female part of our population.

It is interesting in that connection that the *positive attitude of men and women to athletic activities* has almost equally been expressed. "The participation in athletic activities is also with women highly dependent on the activity-profile of the personality. Women in leading positions or who are socially active are more frequently engaged in sports than women who do not go for social activities. This is also supported by the fact that women in professions take part in sports at a far higher percentage than house-wives do (37%, compared to 15%)." (1, P.33).

As we know from sociological studies, there is a highly significant connection between peoples sports activities and their education and their professional qualifications. From 1965 to 1977 for instance, the number of people engaged in sports, who left the school after the 8th grade decreased from 36% to 31%. Participation of the graduates of the 10th grade went up, from 52% to 61%, and for graduates of the 12th grade up to 67%.

Referring to professional qualification the statistical connection is still stronger. Whereas only 15% of unskilled workers are engaged in physical activities, there are 44% of skilled workers and 68% of college or university graduates.

Physical culture and sport contribute — under our social conditions — to a *reasonable, dynamic, joyful, and health-promoting life, i.e. to an increasing fitness and proficiency.* We have to carefully investigate the *causes* of why about 30% of the children and adolescents do not use sport actively for their development and to more effectively bring the values of sport for the development of their personalities into effect.

Physical culture and sport become, under our social conditions, an ever more important component of our way of life. Our empirical results clearly show that the conscious interest in and the utilization of physical culture and sport to consolidate their health, to promote their zest of life and to increase their proficiency, is coming increasingly into play as a particularly significant trait within the behaviour of our people. Therefore *knowledge* about the importance, the *values*, and *effects* of physical culture and sport becomes a decisive criterion when the recruiting of human beings for an active regular athletic activity is at stake. *Information and propaganda by mass media and their quality are thus becoming especially important.* A type of mass media that is orientated upon sensations, single happenings or peculiarities in competitive sports are not only not-accepted in our country but are not available at all. All the state and social institutions and organisations are presenting, in a versatile and interesting manner, a sport-like way of life as being the standard. People are encouraged to follow this line.

Sport science supports this process with its findings and results. As sport psychological investigations have shown, there are quite rich reserves for a broad development of sport in our country. Prof. Dr. Erbach, State Secretary for Physical Culture and Sport stated: "We should try to ever better inspire joy for movements in children's and youth ages, in an active physical and athletic engagement, to consolidate the knowledge on the importance of a good physical condition for health and fitness, and to make visible the personality-forming value of regular sport activities possibly to every young boy or girl. The all-social responsibility lies in the fact to guarantee the required physical training and education throughout the whole process of forming personalities in children and adolescent ages, i.e. twice weekly sport lessons, and two to three times exercises or training sessions per week." (3, p.35).

The Socialist Type of Personality

The contribution of physical culture and sport for the development of a personality can only be understood and implemented as a *unit of social development and individual self-materialization.* (8, p.124). As athletic activities are always implemented within a social relation, the sporting human being is tackling social effects in form of ideals, aims and many different conditions during his athletic activities. Thereby the *social inter-relations of sport become also important for the "social quality" of his personality.* Under such conditions physical culture and sport contribute to the formation and consolidation of the *type of a socialist personality.* We see this value as follows:

- Athletic activities at first widen the motor activities of man. They promote the strengthening of his health and the increase of physical fitness. Zest of life and optimism are consolidated. New

education level \ year	n	graduates of 8th class	graduates of 10th class	graduates of 12th class
1965	3486	36	52	
1977	2246	31	61	67

Table 5: **Participation in sport activities, corresponding to education level; comparison 1965-1977 in %**

aspects of human getting-together in connection with physical efforts and successes and failures in sport competitions enlarge social ways of experience.

- Athletic exercises, training and competitions have a special importance for the development of personalities. They are characterized strongly by activity and conscious cooperation or co-construction of social relations. The athlete establishes relations to the aims and objectives of sport, to his coach, and to his team-mates, to the sport fans, spectators, and to his opponent. All these self-established relations have a large influence upon the formation of abilities of social conduct and corresponding behaviour.

- Physical culture and sport have varying effects on those who are actively engaged in sports and others who are connected to sports only in a more passive manner. Their intellectual, moral and esthetical abilities, opinions and behaviours are differently intensive, called and formed. Athletic activities in organized sport groups or individuals jogging during leisure-times have very different importance for the development of the respective personality. Athletic competitions play another role for the active athlete than for the spectator. Both are more or less intensively connected with the attitudes or results achieved during the athletic activity concerned, e.g. a football play or a gymnastic event. Experiences of success or failure are immediately incited in the athletes. The spectators are stimulated to agreement, or to refusal, to joy or disappointment. They may even keep their reserve from the behaviour watched or results achieved.

- Finally, physical culture and sport help to cement individual particularities of the individual, especially of the athletically active and talented young boy or girl. They thereby enable these people who possess specific biological gifts and individual interests in sports to develop them ever better — in coincidence with the social possibilities — and to meet these needs. (12)

The social conditioning and inter-relation, respectively, of physical culture and sport with their social background in a given society do not — under

121

Professional qualification	unskilled workers	skilled workers	graduates of trade schools	graduates of colleges and universities
engaged in sports	15	44	58	68

Table 6: Participation in sport activities; difference of professional qualifications, 1977, in %

socialist conditions — lead to a restricted or unilateral development of personalities, but to their universal and all-round development based upon their biological pre-suppositions and in accordance with their individual history while consciously applying the social possibilities available. (9)

Winding-up we may state that *a human being taking part in sport does not behave indifferently toward the conditions of social life, but consciously cooperates in organising social relations in sport, too.* The athlete induces social efficiency within the framework of his sport system. He expresses his attitudes, standards, and traits during his athletic activity.

We educate our athletes in a way that *they do not only arrange themselves into given social conditions in their teams, groups, clubs, associations or into society at all, but cooperate ever more consciously and independently.* They help thereby to develop their society and serve their own self-materialization.

REFERENCES

1. Bierstedt, H.: Die Einbeziehung der sportlichen Betätigung in die Lebensweise der Familien. Theorie und Praxis der Körperkultur 30 (1981) 1, S. 32-34.

2. Bujewa, L.P.: Sozialstruktur der Gesellschaft und soziale Tätigkeit der Persönlichkeit. In: Über die sozialistische Persönlichkeit. Berlin: Deutscher Verlag der Wissenschaften 1978, S. 26 f.

3. Erbach, G.: Körperkultur und Sport in der sozialistischen Lebensweise. Theorie und Praxis der Körperkultur 28 (1979) Beiheft 2, S. 30-38.

4. Friedrich, W.: Stellung von Körperkultur un Sport in der sozialistischen Lebensweise der Jugend. Theorie und Praxis der Körperkultur 28 (1979) Beiheft 2, S. 39-44

5. Harmel, M./Piech, St. und U. Wille: Die Startakiade ruft. Theorie und Praxis der Körperkultur 30 (1981) 6, S. 407

6. Herrmann, H.G.: Gesellschaftliche Bedingungen und Entwicklungsfaktoren für Körperkultur und Sport in der DDR. Theorie und Praxis der Körperkultur 28 (1979) Beiheft 1, S. 26-28

7. Judin, E.G.: Die Tätigkeit als erklärendes Prinzip und als Gegenstand wissenschaftlicher Untersuchung. Sowjetwissenschaft (Gesellschaftswissenschaftliche Beiträge) 33 (1977) 3

8. Kossakowski, A.: Psychologische Aspekte der allseitig entwickelten Persönlichkeit. Pädagogik 31 (1976) 2

9. Kunath, P.: Sport und Entwicklung sozialistischer Persönlichkeiten. Theorie und Praxis der Körperkultur 26 (1977) Beiheft "Körperkultur und Sport in der entwickelten sozialistischen Gesellschaft der DDR" — Gesellschaftswissen — schaftliche Beiträge, Kapitel, 7, S. 177-205.

10. Kunath, P.: Psychologische Grundlagen der Persönlichkeitsentwicklung in der sportlichen Tätigkeit. Theorie und Praxis der Körperkultur 28 (1979) Beiheft 1, S. 26-28

11. Kunath, P.: Der Beitrag von Körperkultur und Sport zur Herausbildung des sozialistischen Typs der Persönlichkeit. Theorie und Praxis der Körperkultur 30 (1981) 6, S. 419 ff.

12. Schwidtmann, H. und H. Kogel: Zum Verhältnis von Persönlichkeitsentwicklung und leistungssportlicher Tätigkeit. Wissenschaftliche Zeitschrift der DHfK 17 (1976) 1, S. 19-36

13. Vorwerg, M.: Explikation weiterer Grundprobleme der persönlichkeitspsychologischen Forschung. Berichte aus der Sektion Psychologie der Karl-Marx-Universität, Lepzig 1978, Heft 13

14. Vorwerg, M.: Grundlegende Probleme der persönlichkeitspsychologischen Forschung. In: Zur psychologischen Persönlichkeitsforschung. Berlin: Deutscher Verlag der Wissenschaften 1978, Heft 1

THE VALUE OF SPORTS
Mihaly Csikszentmihalyi (USA)

The critical approach to sports

Most sport psychologists can afford to be uncritical; that is, they can ignore the question of value in their investigations. As long as they study the physiology of motor performance, or the social psychology of teamwork, or the motivation of elite athletes, they need not be concerned with goals and values. They can do this because sport psychology by and large operates within the value system of society at large, which takes for granted the importance of "records", of squeezing ever higher performances out of the human body. No researcher needs to justify why he wants to know how to maximize the physical energy output of the organism. In the symbolic universe in which we live, that goal has a self-evident value.

But when sports are viewed as psycho-social processes in a historical context, a truly scientific psychology cannot take goals and values for granted any longer. The psychologist must eventually confront the question: what good is sports, and to whom?

When such a question is asked, the answers are often contradictory. On the one hand, some critics have condemned sports for breeding violence, exploitation, and a constricting conformity to authoritarian social systems (e.g. Hammer, 1970; Geiringer, 1972, Mann, 1979; Hoch, 1972; Leonard, 1975). On the other hand, scholars have praised sports for contributing to personal health, a sense of community, self-actualization and transcendence of cultural limitations (e.g. Michener, 1976; Novak, 1976; Ravizza, 1977; Kleiber, 1978; Anderson and Stone, 1980).

This discrepancy does not mean that the critics of sports are right and the supporters wrong. Nor does it mean the opposite is true. It just means that some writers prefer to abstract the positive elements out of the complex reality of sport, whereas others abstract out only the equally real negative elements. It is time we stop acting as if it were possible to say: "Sport is good" or "Sport is bad" in the abstract. Fire in itself is neither good nor bad - it is good when used for cooking, and bad when it burns someone's house down. The same is true of atomic energy, and everything else, including sports. Whether a thing is to be valued or not depends on how it is used; on its consequences within a context of goals.

A scientific approach to the value of sport requires us to specify the conditions under which it might be considered beneficial, and the conditions under which it is likely to be harmful. In real life, every historical example of sporting activity has some beneficial as well as some harmful consequences. The task of the sport psychologist is to be able to tell the two apart, and then to maximize the positive elements while reducing the negative ones.

A model for evaluating sports

To take a critical atitude one must use a theoretical model. The model must be able to define what the potential positive and negative consequences of sports are. It is an indispensible tool without which one simply cannot perform a critical evaluation.

There are several theoretical models to choose from. Some are more explicit than others, some are more clearly developed than others. Currently one finds Marxist, Freudian, structural-functional, sociobiological, humanistic theories being used as critical perspectives from which to evaluate sports, and there are many others as well. The one I shall present here I have been working on for a number of years (Csikszentmihalyi, 1975; 1979; 1981). It is certainly not unique in any of its elements, because it is based on previous theories as well as my own research. A theory need not be right, and certainly it can never be complete. As long as it helps to order old knowledge in more satisfying ways, or if it stimulates the acquisition of new facts, a theory has served its purpose. With this brief introduction, let me present a model - which is not in itself theoretical, but is based on theory - that might facilitate the evaluation of sports activities.

The model is based on the premise that there are four main types of consequences one should take into account when evaluating a sport activity. These are represented schematically in Figure 1. Two dimensions concern the individual: personal enjoyment and growth; two concern the community: social harmony and growth.

According to this model an "ideal" sport activity will be enjoyable to the athlete, will allow him or her to grow as a person, it will contribute to social solidarity, and at the same time it will promote organic social change. In Figure 1, this ideal type is represented by the central space labelled 1.2.3.4.

A sport activity or event that does not match this definition falls short of its potential, and to the extent that it lacks one or more of the four dimensions, it might actually be harmful. For instance, let us consider a purely enjoyable physical activity ("1." in Figure 1). If this activity neither fosters personal growth, nor social harmony or change, it might be considered an inefficient investment of psychic energy even though it provides a pleasant feeling of well-being. The space marked with a "2." in the figure represents a different kind of limitation. Here the person is learning something new, is acquiring new skills, but is not enjoying the activity and neither is he contributing to the community. An activity that fits the space marked "3." would be one which the athlete neither enjoys nor is learning anything new from. Although his acts fill a need for society as presently constituted, they do not help its evolution. A common example would be the professional athlete who is bored by his sport and performs it routinely for purely extrinsic reasons. As it is probably clear by now, sports that could be classified as "1.", "2.", "3.", or "4." in Figure 1 are more harmful than beneficial, because they fail to develop the potentials of the activity, and thus end up wasting scarce physical and psychic resources.

Presumably most sports activities fit best the smaller spaces in Figure I. Some are enjoyable and socially synergistic (1.3), but do not lead to either personal or social growth. Others might lead to personal learning and social solidarity, but provide little enjoyment or social change (2.3). Whether such sports are to be considered beneficial or harmful depends on what alternatives are available. If this is the best one can do at the moment, they might serve a useful purpose. But there is no question that compared to an optimal activity, which combines all four dimensions of sports, the other combinations are limiting and therefore wasteful.

The question to ask this or any other theoretical model is, how can it be used? How do we measure the amount of enjoyment, growth, or social harmony that a given concrete sport activity provides? Are these dimensions really quantifiable? If these questions cannot be answered with precision, then the model might still be useful heuristically, but it cannot claim scientific status.

I will use the rest of this presentation to describe a method of investigation and a set of findings which attempt to measure the quality of experience people report when doing various things, including sports. This method makes it possible to compare rather precisely the amount of enjoyment one derives from one type of sport against another, or from sports in general versus other activities like working, eating, or watching television.

Thus the method to be described is a way to operationalize the first dimension shown in Figure 1. The remaining three might be more difficult to measure, but there is no reason to believe that they cannot be quantified also. After all, if the quality of experience can be reliably measured, despite its inherent subjectivity, the other dimensions ought to yield eventually to systematic inquiry.

The Experience Sampling Method

To develop a comparative science of subjective states, we have been experimenting at The University of Chicago with a procedure we have called The Experience Sampling Method, or ESM for short. This consists in giving persons an electronic pager, or "beeper", similar to the kind doctors wear in hospitals, and a booklet containing identical response sheets. Eight times a day, at moments chosen at random, a radio transmitter sends a signal to the pagers, which start making a beeping sound; when this happens, the respondents fill out a page of the booklet. Each page contains about 30 items of information, ranging from where the respondent is at the moment, to his or her feelings on several dimensions. (see Fig. 2)

In this way, over a week's period, we get between 40 and 50 reports from each person, which permit us to compare the quality of experience in a great variety of situations that naturally occur in everyday life. At this point we collected thousands of records from several hundred persons. The advantages of the ESM are that it gives a quantified measure of subjective states in real time; thus it is more relevant than most laboratory experiments, more precise than interviews, and provides much more concrete data than questionnaires do. In our work, however, we always combine interviews and questionnaires with the ESM to obtain the most complete information possible about our respondents.

Figure 3 shows a week in the life of a fairly typical high school boy, as reconstructed from the ESM records and the subsequent interviews. The line that zig-zags down the figure shows changes in the average mood of this boy; it is the sum of his ratings on eight variables like "happy", "cheerful", or "strong". The "0" point in the graph indicates neutral moods, while the negative numbers represent times when the respondent felt sad, irritable, weak, and so on. One can see how quickly the moods of this boy oscillate from positive to negative extremes. Like most of his colleagues, this boy felt worse when in class, going to church with his parents, or when alone. His best moods tend to occur when he is with this friends, and when he is involved in sports - in this case, informal games of basketball and softball. It is with this kind of data that we might begin to describe the quality of experience that sports provide.

Sport in the lives of adolescents

To show how sport compares to other activities in terms of the quality of experience, I will present some data from 75 normal adolescents from the Chicago area, approximately half of whom are male, half are lower class, and composed of equal numbers of 14, 15, 16, and 17 year olds.

Of course sports are more important for teenagers than for adults, so the patterns to be shown will be more extreme than they would be for grownups. Still, it is surprising how similar the experience of sports is across age; thus the data for adolescents represent quite accurately the pattern of older respondents as well.

When we compared teenagers' reports in 15 major kinds of activities on the variable "Activation", we could immediately see that they report being most active (which is the sum of the responses on the variables "active", "strong", and "alert") when they are involved in sports. At such times, their average activation level is almost a standard deviation above the mean. The lowest activation is reported when they are resting, this time they report being almost one standard deviation below the mean. It is to be noted that there were 111 responses involving sport activities. This means that, on the average, these adolescents spent about 4 percent of their waking time playing sports or about 4 hours during the week. By comparison they watched TV almost twice as often. In the lives of these teenagers, sports take about as much time as work, reading, personal care, transportation, and resting.

It is not too surprising that people rate themselves most active when engaged in sports. Although *activation* is an important component of the quality of experience, it is certainly not the only one. Two other crucial aspects are *affect* (how happy, cheerful, sociable a person feels) and *motivation* (how much a person wishes to do what he or she is doing). In our studies these three dimensions of experience, which are quite independent of each other, have emerged as the best measures of the quality of subjective experience.

How do sports compare to 14 other major activities on these three dimensions (i.e. classwork, studying, work, eating, personal care, transportation, chores, rest, socializing, television, music, hobbies, reading, idling)? Sport is highest on activation. It is also an activity quite high on positive affect; teenagers are more happy only when they socialize with each other, when they eat, and when they travel in a car. If we turn to the third dimension, we see that adolescents are strongly motivated to do sports; only when resting, listening to music, doing hobbies, and eating do they wish more to be doing what they are doing.

Considering all three dimensions of experience, sport appears to be over-all the most positive. Hobbies are also enjoyable, but the quality of affect when doing hobbies is much more neutral. Eating and socializing are also very positive, but the activation dimension is much lower than in sports. Thus one can say without qualification that in the lives of these teenagers sport provides the most positive experiences.

The Evaluation of different sport activities

The results confirm that sport *in general* is a very positive experience for adolescents. But at the beginning of this paper I stressed that it makes little sense to speak of sports in general; one must instead evaluate each concrete sport activity separately to see whether or not it is beneficial. Unfortunately we have not yet collected enough data to be able to make the necessary comparisons between different types of sports.

But one comparison was possible to make: that between sport activities supervised by adults, and those that were unsupervised. Teenagers rated both types of sport as much more positive than the rest of everyday experience. But there were also some large differences between supervised and unsupervised sports. When adults were in charge, teenagers reported higher levels of challenge, of concentration, and control; they also rated themselves much more active. When no adults were present the adolescents reported more positive affect, and rated themselves as more "open" and "free"; they also reported having significantly higher levels of skills. Despite these differences, they reported almost exactly the same levels of high motivation in both activities. Thus adult supervised sports and free peer play have different consequences for the quality of experience. The former might contribute more to growth, by forcing the teenagers to concentrate and develop control; the latter seems to be a more enjoyable, relaxing experience.

The same sport, when organized or played out in different contexts, provides radically different experiences to the athletes and the spectators. Thus it makes no sense to say that "soccer is good for youth", or that "swimming builds character". It all depends on the social system in which the sport is embedded.

If the psychology of sports is to be a useful discipline, it will have to learn to deal scientifically with questions of value. It will have to be able to discriminate between a sport that athletes enjoy, that builds up their personal resources, that helps

the community in the present and in the future, and perhaps the very same sport that played under different conditions inhibits joy, growth, and social solidarity.

At present, the psychology of sports operates largely at a pre-scientific level. The conclusions we reach, either pro-sport or anti-sport, tend to be based on unexamined values. Most of us do not even question what the consequences of swimming faster or jumping higher might be for the athlete who is being trained; what counts is breaking the record, come what may. This attitude, while understandable, is no longer a responsible one. It resembles the so-called "objective" approach of the physical scientists before the discovery of atomic energy. A generation later we can no longer ignore the fact that true objectivity must reckon with the long-term consequences of the phenomena we study. A science of sport must be objective, precise, and elegant; but it must also assess its findings within a framework of explicit human values.

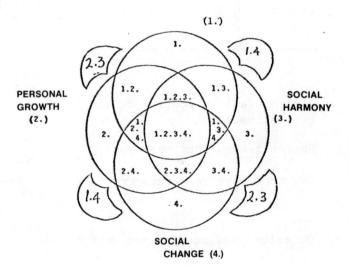

Figure 1. A model for evaluating sport activities. A given sport might produce any combination of the four main consequences.

REFERENCES

Anderson, D., & Stone, G. Sport: A search for community. Paper presented to the annual congress of the North American Society for the Sociology of Sport, Denver, Colorado, 1980.

Csikszentmihalyi, M. *Beyond boredom and anxiety.* San Francisco: Jossey-Bass, 1975 (a).

Csikszentmihalyi, M. The value of leisure: Towards a systematic analysis of leisure activities. *Research papers on leisure and cultural development,* #2. Waterloo, Ontario: Otium Publications, 1979.

Csikszentmihalyi, M. Leisure and socialization. *Social Forces, 1981 (in press).*

Figure 2
Sample Experience Sampling Method Sheet

Date: _H-20_   Time Beeped: _9:00_ (am)/pm   Time Filled Out: _9:00_

As you were beeped...

What were you thinking about? _PROJECT I AM WORKING ON_

Where were you? _AT WORK, IN OFFICE_

What was the MAIN thing you were doing? _COFFEE BREAK_

Why were you doing this particular activity?
( ) I had to do it
(X) I wanted to do it
( ) I had nothing else to do

What other things were you doing? _DRINKING COFFEE, SMOKING_

	not at all	some what	quite	very
Did you feel in control of the situation?				⊙
How self-conscious were you?	⊙			
How much were you concentrating?		⊙		

Describe your mood as you were beeped:

	very	quite	some	neither	some	quite	very	
alert	0	⊙	.	-	.	o	0	drowsy
happy	0	o	⊙	-	.	o	0	sad
irritable	0	o	⊙	-	.	o	0	cheerful
strong	0	⊙	.	-	.	o	0	weak
angry	0	o	.	-	⊙	o	0	friendly
active	0	⊙	.	-	.	o	0	passive
lonely	0	o	.	-	⊙	o	0	sociable
creative	⊙	o	.	-	.	o	0	dull
free	0	o	.	-	⊙	o	0	constrained
excited	0	o	⊙	-	.	o	0	bored

126

COMPOSITE MOOD

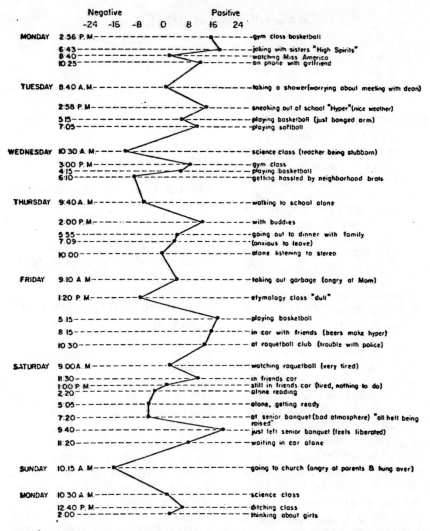

Fig. 4. Explanations for the ups and downs of one person's week. The figure shows the moods reported by a young man during one week in his life, with the explanations he gave for these moods.

(From: Larson, Csikszentmihalyi and Groef, 1980)

Geiringer, E., *Sport as a threat to physical and mental health.* Bulletin of Physical Education, 1972, 9 (3), 19—27.

Hammer, W.M. Anxiety and sports performance. In G.S. Kenyon (Ed), *Contemporary Psychology of Sport,* Chicago: Athletic Institute, 1970.

Hoch, P. *Rip off the big game.* Garden City, N.Y.: Doubleday, 1972.

Kleiber, D. Play and sport in a psychology of aesthetics. Paper presented at the American Psychological Association Convention, Toronto, September, 1978(a).

Larson, R., Csikszentmihalyi, M., & Graef, R. Mood variability and the psychosocial adjustment of adolescents. *Journal of Youth and Adolescence,* 1980.

Leonard, G. *The Ultimate Athlete.* New York: Viking Press, 1975.

Mann, L. Sports crowds viewed from the perspective of collective behavior. In J. Goldstein (Ed) *Sports, games and play.,* N.Y.: Wiley, 1979.

Michener, J. *Sports in America.* Greenwich, Connecticut: Random House, 1976.

Ravizza, K. Peak experiences in sport. *Journal Humanistic Psychology.,* 1977, 17(4), 35-40.

PSYCHOLOGICAL BENEFITS OF PHYSICAL ACTIVITY

William P. Morgan (USA)

INTRODUCTION

The purpose of the present paper shall be to review the existing literature dealing with the psychological benefits of physical activity. Special attention will be paid to the potential role of exercise in prevention and restoration of psychopathologic states where possible. Prior to beginning the general discussion of this topic it would appear necessary to delimit the review. First of all, personality is usually taken to mean the sum or totality of an individual's psychological states and traits. The distinction between state and trait psychology with special reference to exercise and sport has been reviewed extensively in several recent papers (36, 37, 38, 40, 40), and, therefore, this matter will not be discussed in the present paper. The actual review, however, will deal primarily with affective measures such as anxiety and depression and, to a far lesser degree, with psychological traits--the primary reason for this decision being that traits are regarded as relatively enduring features of one's personality structure and, as such, not readily amenable to change.

It will also be necessary to delimit the topic of exercise since it is possible to include various activities under the exercise rubric. Physical activities performed at various metabolic costs (e.g., light, moderate or heavy) such as (i) walking, cycling, swimming, and running, (ii) competitive or non-competitive recreational activities (e.g., bowling, golf or tennis), and (iii) highly competitive team or individual sports (e.g., football, baseball, or track and field athletics) can all be subsumed under the rubric of exercise. These exercises can also be approached from the standpoint of age which brings into consideration such seemingly diverse activities as "little league" or "age group" baseball, football, soccer and swimming, as well as "master's competition" in various sports. The psychological consequences of sport have been reviewed in several recent papers (20, 32, 36, 38, 39, 40) and, therefore, this topic will not be addressed in the present paper.

The existing research involving the psychological consequences of physical activity *per se* has utilized either young or middle-aged adults as subjects. Indeed, research involving the psychological benefits of exercise on the elderly is almost totally nonexistent. The present review, therefore, will deal primarily with the influence of non-competitive physical activity on selected psychological states of young and middle-aged adults. Occasional reference will be made to psychological traits and sport *per se* where necessary, but these particular topics have intentionally not been addressed in detail since they have been recently covered in other reviews.

Much of the research conducted in this area of inquiry has been characterized by statistical and design inelegancies. First of all, much of the work has been cross-sectional rather than longitudinal, and this has eliminated causal attribution. Second, most of the available investigations did not even employ control groups, much less placebo groups (35), and these are simply imperative in order to quantify Hawthorne effects (i.e., any treatment versus no treatment).

METHODOLOGICAL CONSIDERATIONS

Prior to proceeding directly to a review of the literature dealing with the psychological beneficence of physical activity it would appear appropriate to first comment on selected methodological considerations which must be considered in evaluating the available literature. The intent of this brief section is to highlight some of the more fundamental or basic considerations.

It is imperative that control groups be employed in research dealing with the psychologic effects of exercise. While this may seem rather obvious, most of the studies to be reviewed in the following sections have not relied upon such a "design strategy." Also, use of a control group in such experimentation should be viewed as a *necessary,* not a *sufficient* design consideration. It is equally important, indeed, it is imperative, that a placebo group or sham strategy be routinely employed. Numerous behavioral artifacts are permitted to profoundly influence one's interpretations of results otherwise.

The types of behavioral artifacts referred to are: demand characeristics, compliance, "pact of ignorance," response distortion, halo effect, Hawthorne Effect, and so on (35, 43). There are various ways in which these behavioral artifacts can be minimized or evaluated such as use of: appropriate experimental designs, sampling procedures, and statistical models; single, double, and/or total blinds; placebo or sham conditions; debriefing; cross-over and counter-balancing procedures; "hold-out" control where necessary; and so on (35).

The importance of adopting such design strategies is readily reinforced in our contemporary literature. For example, it has been demonstrated by Michaels *et al.* (23) that transcendental meditation (TM) is *associated* with a decrement in circulating plasma catecholamines which are known to be related to anxiety. Hence, it would be easy to jump to the conclusion that TM *causes* anxiety or catecholamines to decrease. However, their control group experienced a comparable decrement in catecholamine levels. This, of course, raises the classic question of causality, and forces one to conclude that while TM may reduce plasma epinephrine and norepinephrine, it is no more effective in doing so than simple rest in a quiet room.

The result of Michaels et al. (23) have recently been supported by investigators employing substantially different procedures. de Vries et al. (10), for example, reported that a simple rest break was just as effective as biofeedback in reducing tension. Tension was measured electromyographically by de Vries et al. (10). In a somewhat related experiment, Bahrke and Morgan (1) found that a control group of subjects who rested quietly in a sound-filtered room experienced a decrement in state anxiety which was comparable to decreases observed following acute physical activity or "non-cultic" meditation. State anxiety was measured with a standardized self-report inventory (STAI) in this study.

These investigations demonstrate that transcendental meditation (23), biofeedback (10), exercise (1), and "non-cultic" meditation (1) are all capable of reducing anxiety. It is also noteworthy that this finding applies to anxiety whether it is defined biochemically (23), neurophysiologically (10), or in a traditional psychometric sense (1). More importantly, however, is the serendipitous observation that a quiet rest is just as effective as more sophisticated procedures.

It has been reported by Kavanagh et al. (21) that post-myocardial infarction patients who participated in a physical activity program experienced significant physiological gains, but these gains did not surpass those of a sedentary group who practiced a form of autohypnosis. In other words, a presumed placebo treatment was just as effective as exercise. The placebo effect, however, can be just as effective as potent pharmacologic agents or even surgery in the reduction of pain (35).

The report by Chien (6) should be regarded as required reading for any investigator contemplating psychological research with older individuals. Chien (6) assigned forty patients who lived on a geriatric ward to one of four groups. One group was administered the drug thioridazine, a popular psychotropic drug treatment in geriatric settings, and the remaining three groups received a beverage in a specially designed "pub" situated in the hospital. These groups received either beer, fruit punch, or fruit punch with thioridazine in the pub setting five days per week for a nine-week period. Social interaction (sociotherapy) was encouraged in the pub setting, and each session lasted for one hour. The greatest psychological improvement resulted from "beer sociotherapy," and while both drug groups improved, their improvement was not as great as the group receiving beer. In other words, "beer sociotherapy" was found to be superior to an already established drug therapy. The "punch-in-the-pub," or placebo, group received the smallest amount of change.

Chien's (6) work might be considered by those exercise scientists who, for reasons not yet specified, imply that physical activity is inherently capable of achieving results not possible by more "traditional" procedures. If one is willing to accept the results presented earlier (3, 54, 58) suggesting improved psychological states in older individuals as a consequence of chronic exercise, a reasonable question would seem to be, "Would these gains equal or exceed those of a sedentary group receiving 'beer sociotherapy' in place of exercise?"

The purpose of the present section has been to identify some of the basic considerations which must be made in evaluating research designed to study the psychological effects of exercise. The importance of these considerations will become apparent in the next section. While the present discussion has been limited to behavioral artifacts of a self-report nature, it should also be emphasized that test subjects can also comply at a biological level as well. For example, resting and exercise heart rate, blood pressure, oxygen comsumption, skin temperature, muscle tension levels, catecholamine levels, and even amine metabolites in the cerebro-spinal fluid (1, 10, 21, 23, 42, 53) can be modified by most compliant individuals. In other words, physiologic, as well as psychologic parameters are subject to artifactual responsivity.

BENEFICENCE OF PHYSICAL ACTIVITY

The psychological benefits of involvement in physical activity have been studied primarily from the standpoint of long term or chronic effects. These investigations have typically ranged from six weeks to several months, but shorter as well as longer time periods have occasionally been employed. While the immediate or acute physiological effects of exercise have been studied extensively, there has been very little attention paid to the psychological effects of acute physical activity. It may well be that acute or transitory psychological effects occur in the absence of chronic effects. Daily exercise, for example, may have the primary effect of reducing tension states or anxiety in an episodic manner with the result being that chronic changes are not observed. If this, in fact, were the case, then the chief psychologic benefit of exercise would reside in its preventive powers. The present review will consider research which has utilized both acute and chronic paradigms.

As mentioned earlier there have been quite a few investigations involving comparisons of athletes and non-athletes, but this particular research will not be addressed in the present paper since most of these studies have been cross-sectional in nature. It is noteworthy, however, that athletes have consistently been found to possess more favorable psychological profiles than non-athletes from the standpoint of mental health (20, 36, 38, 40, 43, 46, 47). The issue of causality has seldom, however, been studied in this earlier research. In other words, do athletes and non-athletes differ from the outset, or does involvement in sport produce psychological change? This question has been addressed in earlier papers, but it remains unanswered (36, 40).

Acute Effects

There has been very little research involving the psychological effect of acute physical activity, and the limited existing research has been concerned with anxiety. The prevalence of anxiety states in both the general and psychiatric populations (1, 37, 42, 51, 52) suggests that the effect of exercise on anxiety warrants attention. Also, it has been proposed by Pitts and McClure (51) and Pitts (52) that acute physical activity will produce anxiety symptoms and anxiety attacks in persons suffering from anxiety neurosis, as well as normal individuals under certain circumstances. The fallacy of the Pitts-McClure hypothesis, however, has been challenged in several subsequent publications (8, 9, 10, 13, 15, 37, 38, 48, 59, 55).

One of the first investigators to examine the effect of physical activity was Byrd (4) who reported that bowling produced a reduction in tension as measured by a self-report inventory. This peculiar investigation was characterized by numerous design flaws, and even if bowling did "cause" the reduction in anxiety it was probably due to the *diversional* impact of the activity, not exercise *per se*.

In a series of well-controlled investigations by de Vries and his associates (8, 9) it has been demonstrated that both acute and chronic physical activity of vigorous nature produces a reduction in tension as measured electromyographically. Furthermore, in one of these studies (9) exercise was found to be superior to a commonly employed tranquilizer (meprobamate) in reducing anxiety (i.e., resting EMG). It is well known, of course, that other seemingly diverse "inactive" therapies involving techniques such as progressive relaxation, biofeedback, meditation, and hypnosis are also capable of reducing anxiety, and this is true whether anxiety is measured electromyographically or psychometrically.

One of the most frequently prescribed exercise therapies employed by physicians has been walking (5). Morgan *et al.* (34) tested the effect of walking one mile at 3.5 mph on the state anxiety of young adult males and females. The subjects were randomly assigned to exercise groups which walked on level grade or 5 percent grade, and their responses were compared with those of a control group consisting of subjects who simply rested quietly in the supine position. The control, 0 percent grade, and 5 percent grade walks resulted in heart rates of 73, 126, and 144 bpm, respectively, for the women, and 69, 111, and 125 for the men. This particular experiment did not demonstrate an exercise effect on anxiety. One possible explanation would be that exercise might need to be more vigorous in order to demonstrate an effect. A second possibility would be that the anxiety scale employed in this investigation, the IPAT 8-Parallel-Anxiety Battery, was not sensitive to changes since it appears to be more of a trait than a state measure. On the other hand, shifts in anxiety consistently have been demonstrated with this instrument under a variety of circumstances (31, 32, 38).

Sime's (57) recent research indicating that light exercise does not modify state anxiety corroborates the earlier work of Morgan *et al.* (34) reported above. It is also noteworthy that Sime (57) employed a more universally accepted measure of state anxiety, the STAI. These reports (34, 57) seem to suggest that exercise of a light nature does not alter state anxiety.

A series of investigations dealing with exercise performed at 70 percent to 80 percent VO_2 max have now been completed, and these investigations reveal that state anxiety is consistently decreased following such exercise (37, 40, 45). In other words, it appears that exercise must be of a fairly high intensity in order to provoke decrements in anxiety. It should be emphasized, however, that meditation, both "cultic" (23) and "non-cultic" (1), "time out" therapy (1) and simple rest breaks (10) are also capable of reducing circulating catecholamines, electromyographic activity, oxygen consumption, heart rate, and self-report measures of anxiety. These findings have special relevance from an applied standpoint since certain therapies, for a variety of reasons, are often contraindicated in the case of specific individuals.

Partial support for the research described above (37, 40, 45) has recently been presented by Wood (59) who administered the state anxiety scale (STAI) to college males and females before and following a 12-minute run test. The males (n = 62) experienced a significant reduction in state anxiety, whereas the females (n = 44) did not. These results were in disagreement with those of Morgan (37) who reported a significant decrement in state anxiety for both adult males and females following vigorous physical activity. It also appears that Wood's (59) study may have suffered from behavioral and/or statistical artifacts since a subsidiary analysis described in his paper reveals that high and low anxious males and females regressed toward the mean following the exercise treatment.

Exercise has been successfully employed by Orwin (50) to treat agoraphobia, as well as a specific phobia. It appears that the anxiety response is inhibited as a result of the exercise induced autonomic arousal "competing" with the anxiety reaction. Driscoll (11) has compared the efficacy of systematic desensitization and exercise plus "pleasant fantasies" in their ability to reduce anxiety. The two procedures were found to be comparable. While exercise or fantasy alone produced a decrement in anxiety as well, the decrease was not as great as that produced with exercise and fantasy combined.

None of the investigations reviewed to this point attempted to evaluate the time course of anxiety changes observed following acute physical activity. A recent attempt to clarify this issue has yielded some interesting results. Seemann (55) evaluated the state anxiety of middle-aged men and women before and following aerobic jogging for approximately 45 minutes. Both groups experienced a significant decrement in state anxiety following acute physical activity, which is in agreement with the earlier research described above (37, 40, 45). Seemann (55) also evaluated the state anxiety of these subjects across the following 24-hour period, and it was observed that anxiety gradually returned to the base-line levels within 4 to 6 hours in both groups. In other words, the tension reduction associated with this vigorous exercise was found to last for about 4 to 6 hours on the average. This finding suggests that one of the major benefits of regular exercise may reside in its ability to reduce anxiety on a daily basis and, hence, *prevent* the development of chronic anxiety.

Chronic Effects

There is a great deal of evidence available concerning the physiological effect of chronic physical activity, but there is very little evidence on the psychological consequences (40, 41, 42). It is widely reported by investigators who work in this field that individuals report an increased sense of well-being following the adoption of an exercise program (28, 33, 42). The "feeling better" sensation which accompanies regular physical activity is so obvious that it is one of the few universally accepted benefits of exercise. Indeed, individuals who themselves do not exercise will even readily admit that exercise ". . . is good for you!"

Despite the absence of a substantial experimental literature supporting the value of physical activity in the prevention and restoration of psychopathologic states, there are a number of indirect and theoretical bases for suggesting that chronic exercise possesses psychologic beneficence. First of all, if one accepts the totality of mind and body, it is not difficult to accept that psychic or somatic health, or disease, are likely to influence one another. To the extent that exercise improves physical health, and there is considerable evidence to suggest that it does (7, 8, 14, 21, 49, 61), a concurrent improvement in, or maintenance of, mental health should follow. The unity of mind and body is such, of course, that it is only one's vantage point that permits a distinction between the two.

In addition to the theoretical basis for the belief that chronic exercise possesses psychologic beneficence, there is a substantial amount of correlational evidence in this area (18, 19, 28, 40, 56, 60, 61). While such evidence cannot be offered as causal support, the relationship is consonant with theoretical expectations.

While former athletes and non-athletes appear to be more alike from the standpoint of general health and longevity (24), it is of interest that athletes consistently have been found to possess more desirable mental health profiles that non-athletes (20, 36, 38, 40). These reported differences, while consistent and statistically significant, have not been of a remarkable magnitude. Also, it is of further interest that former athletes have been found to

possess more favorable *attitudes* toward physical activity and greater *estimates* of physical ability than non-athletes, but their *actual* levels of physical activity and aerobic power have been reported to be comparable (40, 44).

Psychiatric patients have consistently been found to score low on standard measures of physical fitness (25, 27, 28, 29, 33, 39), but there is not a consensus on the issue of whether or not degree of psychopathology is related to physical fitness (25, 27, 28, 29). On the other hand, it has been demonstrated that level of physical fitness at the time of admission to a psychiatric facility is inversely related to length of hospitalization (30); that is, the higher the muscular endurance and strength at the outset, the shorter the duration of stay.

There is also evidence that hyperponesis or heightened muscle tension levels increases as a function of psychopathology (26). In other words, hyperponetic states are more common in anxious, neurotic, or depressed patients than in normal individuals or even patients not suffering from these particular problems. Since there is considerable evidence suggesting that either acute or chronic exercise decreases resting muscle tension levels (8, 9), it is reasonable to *predict* that exercise would improve behavioral states such as anxiety and depression.

In addition to the theoretical, correlative, and epidemiologic reports summarized above, there have also been a number of experimental investigations conducted over the past ten years which address the issue of whether or not chronic exercise would produce improvements in psychologic states. These investigations will now be summarized and critiqued.

One of the first experiments was conducted at the University of Missouri, and it involved the influence of various physical activity programs on the level of depression in adult males (33). While approximately 85 percent of the individuals who exercised reported an improved *sense of well-being*, none of the groups differed significantly from the control group on depression as measured by Zung's Self-Rating Depression Scale. It was found, however, that a significant (P > .01) reduction in depression occurred for those individuals (n = 11) who were clinically depressed (SDS = 50 >) from the outset.

The finding that psychological changes did not occur in those individuals who scored within the normal range on the SDS should not be surprising. This observation was in agreement with an earlier report by Naughton et al. (49) who found that daily exercise for a period of one hour did not alter the MMPI profiles of their subjects following six months of exercise.

In a more recent report by Kavanagh et al. (22) the MMPI was administered to patients between 16 and 18 months following myocardial infarction, and those with severe depression were studied for 2 to 4 years. These patients, who took part in a regular running program, experienced a significant improvement in depression as measured by the

MMPI scale. The improvement in depression was not accompanied by alterations in other MMPI scores. Therefore, it is quite possible that the decrement in depression represented chance alone, or it may have reflected the course of recovery *per se* rather than an exercise induced effect. As with most research in this area, however, adequate controls were not employed.

The psychological effect of participating in a jogging program was evaluated in college students by Folkins *et al.* (12). The psychological measures were performed at the beginning and conclusion of a semester-long course, and comparisons were made with a control group of subjects enrolled in archery or golf courses. Significant improvements in anxiety and depression accompanied gains in physical fitness for women in the jogging program, but changes were not observed for the men. The changes for the women may have represented statistical regression since they scored significantly higher than the controls from the very outset on the various psychological measures. At any rate, there is no evidence presented to suggest that exercise *caused* the improvement in psychological state.

In a similar investigation Sharp and Reilley (56) administered the MMPI to 65 male students before and after an aerobics conditioning class that met twice a week for 45 minutes per session. The length of the course was not specified, and it is not clear whether or not an actual psychological training effect resulted. However, correlative data were presented relative to change scores, and the authors stated that,

> ". . . changes in aerobic physical fitness are related to score changes on selected scales of the MMPI for college males who participated in an aerobic exercise program (P. 430)."

The statistical analysis employed in this study (i.e., 160 bivariate r's) makes it very difficult to interpret the psychologic effect of the aerobics program. However, the present investigation, like most others in this area, did not employ a control or placebo group and, therefore, the issue of causality cannot even be entertained.

A frequently cited investigation in this field is the paper by Ismail and Trachtman (16) who reported that middle-aged men who embarked on a regular exercise program experienced an alteration in their personality as measured by the 16 PF. However, it would be hazardous to suggest that exercise *caused* the change in personality since neither a control nor placebo group was employed for comparison purposes. Also, Ismail and Trachtman (16) made no attempt to evaluate response distortion in their study. Deceptive subjects can not only fake behavioral self-report measures such as the 16 PF with ease (43), but it has also been shown that simulation can actually result in biological alterations as mentioned earlier.

The Cattell 16 PF test was administered by Ismail and Young (17) to 56 middle-aged subjects before and following a 4-month physical fitness program. These authors feel that their results ". . . tend to suggest that the physical fitness program helps in stabilizing the factors affecting personality (P. 56)." Employing the phrase "tend to suggest" is certainly appropriate since there were no controls with which to draw comparisons. It might be argued, of course, that these subjects served as their own controls. While such an argument is acceptable for certain experimental designs, it does not appear to be appropriate in the present case. The same criticism can be leveled at subsequent papers by Ismail and Young (18), Young and Ismail (60), and Ismail and Young (19). These investigations, in the author's opinion, have been characterized by biologic, psychometric, and statistical rigor of what appears to be the highest order. Furthermore, these writers themselves do not argue vigorously that exercise causes personality to change but, rather, they suggest that factor structures change following chronic exercise. Nevertheless, the implication has been that exercise causes personality to change, and that has not been possible to convincingly demonstrate with the design employed in the afore-mentioned studies (16, 17, 18, 19, 60).

Anxiety and depression has been reported by Folkins (13) to decrease significantly in a group of adult males who exercised three days per week for twelve weeks. These individuals had previously been judged high-risk from a coronary risk factor perspective, and they were matched by age, occupation, and risk factors with a group of non-exercise controls. The control group did not change on any of the psychological variables measured. Also, it is noteworthy that the exercise group only changed on two of the five measures. Alterations in self-confidence, adjustment, and body image did not occur. These findings suggest that chronic exercise was *associated* with a reduction in anxiety and depression, but there is no way of evaluating whether or not the exercise program *caused* the change. Use of a placebo group, in addition to the control group, would have been preferred.

It has been reported by Buccola and Stone (3) that a group of men ranging in age from 60-79 years experienced a change on two of the factors of the 16 PF Inventory following a walk-jog program. Exercise was performed three days per week for fourteen weeks. A group of subjects in the same study participated in a cycling program, and while they experienced physiological changes similar to those of the walk-jog group, they did not experience psychological changes. Therefore, exercise *per se* must not have been responsible for the changes observed in the walk-jog group. In view of the fact that only two of the multiple comparisons were significant, these changes may have been due to chance alone. Also, since appropriate control groups were not employed it is difficult to evaluate the meaningfulness of these observations. In other words, both groups might have improved significantly on a number of variables, but there would be no way of determining whether this was due to the (i) exercise programs,. (ii) "special attention effect" (35), or (iii) interaction of both of these forces.

A recent investigation has been described by Griest *et al.* (14) in which a unique experimental design was employed. Thirteen men and 15 women patients who sought treatment for neurotic or reactive depression were randomly assigned to running therapy, time-limited psychotherapy, or time-unlimited psychotherapy. The findings revealed that running was just as effective as psychotherapy in the treatment of moderate depression. In other words, rather than comparing the effect of exercise with a control group (i.e., "any treatment" vs. "no treatment" paradigm) or no group at all, an attempt was made to quantify exercise effects within the context of more traditional therapies. Running was found to be just as effective as psychotherapy in the treatment of young men and women with *moderate* depression in the study.

SUMMARY

In the present paper an attempt has been made to summarize the existing literature dealing with the influence of exercise on personality. Theoretical, correlational, epidemiologic, and experimental evidence have been presented. While most of this literature suggests that exercise, both acute and chronic, is *associated* with an improved psychological state, there has been no attempt to identify the *mechanism* underlying such improvement. The tacit assumption in most of the experimental research has been that exercise was responsible for, or *caused,* the observed changes. Such an assumption, however, must be regarded as questionable in light of the fact that quasi-experimental designs have been the rule. If, in fact, this research had been conducted with acceptable designs, it would remain rather difficult to address the *why* of the matter. The challenge for future investigators in this area will be to adopt rigorous research designs, and it is suggested that answers to the question of "why exercise improves affect" will be found at a biochemical and neuropsychological level.

REFERENCES

1. Bahrke, M.S. and Morgan, W.P.: Anxiety reduction following exercise and meditation *Cog. Therapy Res., 2,* 323, 1978.
2. Brown, R.S., Ramirez, D.E., and Taub, J.M.: The prescription of exercise for depression. *Physician Sportsmed., 6,* 35, 1978.
3. Buccola, V.A. and Stone, W.J.: Effects of jogging and cycling programs on psychological and personality variables in aged men. *Res. Quart., 46,* 134, 1975.
4. Byrd, O.E.: Viewpoints of bowlers in respect to the relief of tension. *Phys. Educ., 21,* 119, 1964.
5. Byrd, O.E.: The relief of tension by exercise: A survey of medical viewpoints and practices. *J. Sch. Hea., 42,* 238, 1963.
6. Chien, C.P. Psychiatric treatments for geriatric patients: "Pub" or drug? *Amer. J. Psychiat., 127,* 1070, 1971.
7. Clarke, H.H. (Ed.): Exercise and aging. *Phy. Fit. Res. Dig., 7,* 1, 1977.
8. deVries, H.A.: Immediate and long term effects of exercise upon resting muscle action potential. *J. Sports ,ed., 8,* 1, 1968.
9. deVries, H.A. and Adams, G.M.: Electromyographic comparison of single doses of exercise and meprobamate as to effects on muscular relaxation. *Amer. J. Phys. Med., 51,* 130, 1972.
10. deVries, H.A., Burke, R.K., Hopper, R.T., and Sloan, J.H.: Efficacy of EMG biofeedback in relaxation training. *Amer. J. Phy. Med., 56,* 75, 1977.
11. Driscoll, R.: Anxiety reduction using physical exertion and positive images. *Psychol. Record., 26,* 87, 1976.
12. Folkins, C.H., Lynch, S., and Gardner, M.M.: Psychological fitness as a function of physical fitness. *Arch. Phy. Med. Rehabil., 53,* 503, 1972.
13. Folkins, C.H.: Effects of physical training on mood. *J. Clin. Psychol., 32,* 385, 1976.
14. Greist, J.H., Klein, M.H., Eischens, R.R., Faris, J., Gurman, A.S., and Morgan, W.P.: Running as treatment for depression. *Comp. Psychiat., 20,* 41, 1979.
15. Grosz, H.J. and Farmer, B.B.: Blood lactate in the development of anxiety symptoms. *Arch. Gen. Psychiat., 21,* 611, 1969.
16. Ismail, A.H. and TRachtman, L.E.: Jogging the imagination. *Psychol. Today, 6,* 78, 1973.
17. Ismail, A.H. and Young, R.J.: The effect of chronic exercise on the personality of middle-aged men by univariate and multivariate approaches. *J. Human. Ergol., 2,* 47, 1973.
18. Ismail, A.H. and Young, R.J.: Influence of physical fitness on second- and third-order personality factors using orthogonal and oblique rotations. *J. Clin. Psychol., 32,* 268, 1976.
19. Ismail, A.H. and Young, R.J.: Effect of chronic exercise on the multivariate relationship between selected biochemical and personality variables. *Multivariate Behav. Res., 12,* 49, 1977.
20. Johnson, R.W. and Morgan, W.P.: Personality characeristics of college athletes. (In preparation).
21. Kavanagh, T., Shephard, R.J., Pandit, B., and Doney, H.: Exercise and hypnotherapy in the rehabilitation of the coronary patient. *Arch. Phy. Med. Rehabil., 51,* 578, 1970.
22. Kavanagh, T., Shephard, R.J., and Tuck, J.A.: Depression after myocardial infarction. *Can. Med. Assoc. J., 113,* 23, 1975.
23. Michaels, R.R., Huber, M.J., and McCann, D.S.: Evaluation of transcendental meditation as a method of reducing stress. *Science, 192,* 1242, 1976.
24. Montoye, H.J.: Health and longevity of former athletes. *Science and Medicine of Exercise and Sports.* W.R. Johnson and E.R. Buskirk (Eds.), New York, Harper and Row, 1974.
25. Morgan, W.P.: Selected physiological and psychomotor correlates of depression in psychiatric patients. *Res. Quart., 39,* 1037, 1968.
26. Morgan, W.P.: Hyperponetic states and psychopathology: A review. *Amer. Corr. Ther. J., 22,* 165, 1968.
27. Morgan, W.P.: A pilot investigation of physical working capacity in depressed and nondepressed psychiatric males. *Res. Quart., 40,* 859, 1969.
28. Morgan, W.P.: Physical fitness and emotional health: A review. *Amer. Corr. Ther. J., 23,* 124, 1969.
29. Morgan, W.P.: Physical working capacity in depressed and nondepressed psychiatric females. *Amer. Corr. Ther. J., 24,* 14, 1970.
30. Morgan, W.P.: Physical fitness correlates of psychiatric hospitalization. *Contemporary Psychology of Sport.* G.S. Kenyon (Ed.), Chicago, Athletic Institute, 1970.

31. Morgan, W.P.: Psychological effect of weight reduction in the college wrestler. *Med. Sci. Sports, 2,* 24, 1970.

32. Morgan, W.P.: Pre-match anxiety in a group of college wrestlers. *Int. J. Sport Psy., 1,* 7, 1970.

33. Morgan, W.P., Roberts, J.A., Brand, F.R., and Feinerman, A.D.: Psychological effect of chronic physical activity. *Med. Sci. Sports. 2,* 213, 1971.

34. Morgan, W.P., Roberts, J.A., and Feinerman, A.D.: Psychologic effect of acute physical activity. *Arch. Phys. Med. Rehabil., 52,* 442, 1971.

35. Morgan, W.P.: Basic considerations. *Ergogenic Aids and Muscular Performance.* W.P. Morgan (Ed.). New York, Academic Press, 1972.

36. Morgan, W.P.: Sport psychology. *Psychomotor Domain: Movement Behavior.* R.N. Singer (Ed.), Philadelphia, Lea and Febiger, 1972.

37. Morgan, W.P.: Influence of acute physical activity on state anxiety. *Proc. College Phy. Educ. Assoc.,* Pittsburgh, 1973.

38. Morgan, W.P. and Hammer, W.M.: Influence of competitive wrestling upon state anxiety. *Med. Sci. Sports, 6,* 58, 1974.

39. Morgan, W.P.: Exercise and mental disorders. *Sports Medicine,* A. J. Ryan and F. L. Allman, Jr. (Eds.), New York, Academic Press, 1974.

40. Morgan, W.P.: Psychological consequences of vigorous physical activity and sport. In *The Academy Papers,* M. G. Scott (Ed.), Iowa City, Amer. Acad. Phy. Educ., 1976.

41. Morgan, W.P.: Influence of chronic physical activity on selected psychological states and traits of police officers. Technical Report. International Association of Chiefs of Police, Inc., 1976.

42. Morgan, W.P. and Pollock, M.L.: Physical activity and cardiovascular health: Psychological aspects. In *Physical Activity and Human Well-being,* F. Landry and W.A.R. Orban (Eds.), Miami, Symposia Specialists, Inc., 1978.

43. Morgan, W.P.: Sport personology: The credulous-skeptical argument in perspective. *Proc. 3rd Symp. Integ. Devel.* A. H. Ismail (Ed.), Indianapolis, Indiana State Board of Health, 1977.

44. Morgan, W.P.: Involvement in vigorous physical activity with special reference to adherence. *Proc. College Phy. Educ. Assoc.,* Orlando, 1977.

45. Morgan, W.P.: Horstman, D.H., Cymerman, A., and Stokes, J.: Use of exercise as a relaxation technique. *Prim Cardiol.* (In Press).

46. Morgan, W.P. and Pollock, M.L.: Psychologic characterization of the elite distance runner. *Annals N.Y. Acad. Sci.,* P. Milvy (Ed.), *301,* 382, 1977.

47. Morgan, W.P. and Johnson, R.W.: Psychological characterization of national level oarsmen differing in level of ability. *Int. J. Sport Psychol., 9,* 119, 1978.

48. Morgan, W.P.: Anxiety reduction following acute physical activity. *Psychiat. Ann., 9,* 34, 1979.

49. Naughton, J.; Bruhn, J.G. and Lategola, M.T.: Effects of physical training on physiologic and behavioral characteristics of cardiac patients. *Arch. Phy. Med., 49,* 131, 1968.

50. Orwin, A.: Treatment of a situational phobia — a case for running. *Brit. J. Psychiat., 125,* 95, 1974.

51. Pitts, F.N. Jr. and McClure, J.N. Jr.: Lactate metabolism in anxiety neurosis. *New Eng. J. Med., 277,* 1329, 1967.

52. Pitts, F.N., Jr.: Biochemical factors in anxiety neurosis. *Behav. Sci., 16,* 82, 1971.

53. Post, R.M. and Goodwin, F.K.: Simulated behavior states: An approach to specificity in psychobiological research. *Biol. Psychiat., 7,* 237, 1973.

54. Powell, R.R.: Psychological effects of exercise therapy upon institutionalized geriatric mental patients. *J. Gerontol., 29,* 157, 1974.

55. Seemann, J.C.: Changes in state anxiety following vigorous exercise. M. S. Thesis, University of Arizona, 1978.

56. Sharp, M.W. and Reilley, R.R.: The relationship of aerobic physical fitness to selected personality traits. *J. Clin. Psychol., 31,* 428, 1975.

57. Sime, W.E.: A comparison of exercise and meditation in reducing physiological response to stress. *Med. Sci. Sports, 9,* 55, 1977.

58. Stamford, B.A.; Hambacher, W., and Fallica, A.: Effects of daily physical exercise on the psychiatric state of institutionalized geriatric mental patients. *Res. Quart., 45,* 34, 1974.

59. Wood, D.T.: The relationship between state anxiety and acute physical activity. *Amer. Corr. Ther. J., 31,* 67, 1977.

60. Young, R.J. and Ismail, A.H.: Personality differences of adult men before and after a physical fitness program. *Res. Quart., 47,* 513, 1976.

61. Young, R.J. and Ismail, A.H.: Relationships between anthropometric, physiological, biochemical and personality variables before and after a four month conditioning program for middle-aged men. *J. Sports Med., 16,* 267, 1976.

PSYCHOBIOLOGIC PREDICTORS OF EXERCISE BEHAVIOR

Rod K. Dishman (USA)

A renewed interest in the health benefits of vigorous physical activity characterizes contemporary literature in both popular and scientific sectors. Considerable clinical and experimental evidence indicates that individuals involved in a controlled program of regular exercise typically "feel better" (Morgan, 1977b), and this feeling better syndrome appears to have both biometric and psychometric correlates. That is, exercise behavior is known to covary with reduced risk for coronary heart disease (Falls, Baylor, and Dishman, 1980) and with symptom reduction in mental disorders such as tension, anxiety, and non-psychotic depression (Folkins and Sime, 1981). Although continued study of comparative dosage/mode effects and explanatory mechanisms is necessary to reduce prescription errors when exercise is used as an alternative or adjunctive intervention, (Bahrke & Morgan, 1979; Greist, Klein, Eischens and Faris, 1979) it appears there is general consensus that the descriptive association between exercise and health is strong enough to predict *feelings of wellness* for both the typical individual and for certain patient groups as well. Thus, the critical question facing health and exercise psychologists may now focus less on possible benefits of exercise behavior and more on insuring that those individuals who might benefit, or who want to benefit, from exercise do in fact exercise. That is, the effectiveness of exercise and sport-related activity in promoting the life quality of its participants becomes a subordinate consideration if people don't remain actively involved. The focus of the present paper is on this latter issue of exercise adherence.

There are at least two primary dimensions to habitual exercise behavior, and these relate to involvement and adherence. Although Morgan (1977a) has suggested that initial involvement may represent the crucial behavioral variable, the typical clinical observation that 50% of the individuals who become involved in an exercise program discontinue participation within the first six months (Dishman, Ickes & Morgan, 1980) suggests that adherence or behavioral compliance with an exercise regimen represents an equally important issue. Moreover, in the United States, exercise is currently being actively marketed to the consumer public in a proverbial "Madison Avenue" manner, and there seems to be a continued acceleration of involvement (NJA, 1981). Yet, dropout rates in clinical exercise settings still range from 30-70% of those initially involved (Dishman, Note 1). These observations tend to support the fact that involvement may be more sensitive to an intervention than is adherence, and this proposal is at least intuitively consistent with the well known and widely experienced "New Year's Resolution" phenomenon. Adherence to an exercise training program is also a prime consideration in competitive athletics since sport performance cannot consistently exceed biological conditioning, and the following material will also have some ancillary relevance for motivation in athletic training.

The issue of behavioral commitment or perseverence in therapeutic exercise appears, in many respects, quite analogous to the problem of persistence in other health-related intervention settings, such as weight reduction or smoking and drug withdrawal, which require adherence to a behavioral regimen. In fact, a rather provocative behavioral similarity seems to exist between adherence to exercise programs and compliance with medical prescriptions in general (Baekeland and Lundwall, 1975; Dishman, Ickes, and Morgan, 1980; Haynes, Taylor, and Sackett, 1979). In each case, dropout or recidivism rates are extensive and describe a negatively accelerating function of time. And, despite a considerable amount of heterogeneity among treatment settings, there seems to be a rather homogenous pattern of behavior across intervention programs. A representative dropout pattern in exercise programs is characterized by a rapid decrease in participants during the initial 3-6 months of involvement, a plateau effect up to 12-15 months and a subsequent gradual and steady decline thereafter. Moreover, this pattern suggests that the chances for "staying with" an exercise program in a long term sense may be substantially enhanced if an individual can remain involved during the first 3-6 months (Dishman, 1981b). A principal issue thus appears to relate to insuring adherence or compliance during this critical initial period.

Despite the fundamental significance of understanding exercise adherence, it has received little systematic research attention. The work of Oldridge (1977, 1978, 1979) is notable, however, and his paradigm has principally focused on demographic discriminators between compliers and non-compliers in cardiac rehabilitation programs. Also, Wankel and his associates (Thompson & Wankel, 1980; Wankel, 1981; Wankel & Thompson, 1977; Wankel & Graham, Note 3) have examined the clinical significance of cognitive-behavioral intervention strategies in a series of exercise studies. Orlick (1974) has examined the dropout phenomenon in youth sport. The characteristic approach to the study of exercise adherence/compliance has, however, been restricted to descriptive information with limited relevance for practical application. Even recent clinical attempts at facilitating adherence through cognitive-behavioral and contingency modification strategies (Epstein, Thompson, and Wing, 1981; Krumboltz and Thoresen, 1976; Stalonas, Johnson, Iwata, and Riordan, 1979) have described group differences, but as yet, have neither explained nor predicted exercise behavior in the individual case. This limited practical applicability in adherence research has resulted principally from limitations of method and analysis inherent in the paradigms employed. The material which follows in this paper will provide a background for the discussion of a series of studies conducted by the present author which was designed as a first step toward the prediction of exercise behavior in clinical settings. The ultimate goal of this line of research is to complement the implementation of behavioral prescriptions which may facilitate exercise adherence. The work to be discussed has been presented in more specific terms in a series of previously published papers (Dishman, Ickes, and Morgan, 1980; Dishman and Gettman, 1980; Dishman, 1981a, 1981b, Note 1; Dishman and Ickes, 1981).

As previously noted, there are several apparent parallels between medical compliance in general and adherence to therapeutic exercise programs, and these include factors related to the time course of involvement (Haynes, Taylor and Sackett, 1979), spouse influences (Andrew & Parker, 1979; Haynes et al 1979; Heinzelmann & Bagley, 1970), accessibility of the setting (Haynes, et al 1979; Sanne, 1973; Teraslinna, Partanen & Koskela, et al, 1969), and participant characteristics such as health-related disability, self-motivation and program expectations and perceptions (Danielson & Wanzel, 1977; Dishman, 1981a, 1981b; Dishman, Ickes & Morgan, 1980; Haynes et al. 1979; Sanne, 1973). On the other hand, it seems that exercise as a mode of treatment may have a relatively unique potential for enhancing adherence which is not typically inherent in other medical interventions. Namely, a multidimensionality which permits a variety of alternative treatments within the same therapeutic modality and which may thus better permit a matching of patient to treatment (Haynes et al, 1979). This possibility has not been tested, but it is consistent with the finding that exercise behavior is promoted even when participants only perceive a choice in activity mode (Thompson & Wankel, 1981). Simply stated, it may be easier and more effective to fit the program to the participant than to try and fit the participant to the program.

From this practical standpoint of adherence facilitation, initial diagnosis of the dropout-prone participant would appear to offer a distinct clinical advantage. Such a prediction would permit careful monitoring of the likely dropout, subsequent attention to specific individual program needs, and would facilitate the non-random implementation of a variety of intervention strategies designed to enhance adherence. Since medical screening conducted prior to activity prescription in the treatment and "prevention" of coronary heart disease (CHD) routinely measures client characteristics related to health and functional capacity, one approach to adherence prediction might consider biological differences between eventual adherers and dropouts which exist at the outset of involvement. In addition to the pragmatic advantage of employing standard screening information, there are also theoretical reasons to expect a biological connection with exercise adherence. For example, biological differences in the ability to tolerate or adapt to the stress of exercise may influence behavioral decisions (Ingjer and Dahl, 1979). In addition, knowledge of low functional capacity or high risk for CHD might promote adherence in an effort to reduce or retard symptoms of the disease process.

Study 1

To examine these possibilities, a retrospective study was conducted in 1978 at the University of Wisconsin (Dishman, 1981a). Diagnostic profiles for a five year period were analyzed for 362 adult male participants in the Biodynamics Exercise program to determine the relationship of voluntary length of stay in the clinical setting with both biological fitness and clinically diagnosed CHD status. Stepwise multiple discriminant analysis indicated

that body fat, weight, and metabolic capacity discriminated among patients according to their adherence pattern. Specifically, individuals who elected to stay with the program for more than 12 months were leaner, lighter, and less fit at the outset than were those who dropped out within the first month of treatment. Metabolic capacity and body weight were also inversely related to coronary disease symptoms and this added further indirect support for the influence of health status on adherence behavior. Moreover, in a more direct test, adherence and CHD classification variables were positively associated; indicating that patients diagnosed as disease-free tended to be short term adherers (i.e. dropped out within the first month) while patients with clinically established CHD status enhanced the prediction of adherence by 13% above chance. On the basis of these findings, the derived discriminant function equation was used to provide a statistical prediction of eventual adherence behavior for a holdout sample of 181 patients from the initial clinical population. That is, an attempt was made to use the initial screening information in a practical clinical application to predict eventual exercise behavior for individual patients. In an overall sense, the obtained assignment rate was accurate in only 25% of the 181 cases. Assignment accuracy was relatively high, however, for adherence classification in groups which had initially accounted for most of the inter-patient variance in the biologic screening variables. That is, 44% of those patients who dropped out within the first month and 54% of those who stayed for at least 12 months were correctly diagnosed from initial information on body fat, weight, and metabolic capacity. These prediction rates represented gains of approximately 30% above a chance prediction in each case.

Although the findings from the first study suggested that standardly assessed exercise screening information might enhance the prediction of adherence behavior in a statistically meaningful way, the clinical significance of the observed differences was less clear. Considering the apparent clinical limitations of the biological prediction model, a series of prospective studies was conducted to consider several conceptually relevant psychological influences and to determine if the initial biological findings could be replicated in another sample. A review of literature (Dishman, Note 1) dealing with medical compliance, exercise science, and health psychology indicated that, besides factors relating to health status, participant motivation and program attitudes and expectations might best discriminate between adherers and dropouts. Aside from theoretical reasons, there was also an intuitive base for viewing psychological characteristics since "psycho-social" influences are common clinical observations by exercise specialists. Moreover, an abundant literature supports the efficacy of multivariate inquiry and it was reasoned that a psychobiologic model might permit an enhanced accuracy in prediction. Thus, it was anticipated that participants who were symptomatic for coronary disease or who manifested a biological profile indicating low physical working capacity might tend to adhere in order to reduce coronary risk or to increase functional fitness. Furthermore, individuals who viewed exercise as a health promoting activity and who felt they were responsible for their health status were expected to adhere as were individuals who were attracted to physical activity, perceived a personal ability to exercise, and possessed a trait for self-motivation or perseverance.

Study 2

An initial study was designed to develop and refine a psychometric scale for the assessment of a behavioral trait for self-motivation, and this involved the testing of 401 young adult males and females. The decision to examine individual differences in self-motivation was based on several factors. First, the importance of patient motivation has been perhaps the most frequently cited behavioral influence in the medical compliance literature (Baekeland and Lundwall, 1975, Haynes et al. 1979), yet at the time of this research there were apparently no available measures with demonstrated psychometric properties of validity and reliability (Holt, 1967). Second, the similarity in behavior patterns across rather diverse treatment settings suggested individual differences in motivation, and this was consistent with the intuitive notion that some people are simply better able to stay with a behavioral commitment than are others.

Results of a psychometric pretesting yielded an objective 40 item self-report scale which was logically valid (i.e., possessed a univocal factor structure and was valid by appearance), internally reliable (a = .91), and stable across time (r = .86 - .92). Detailed descriptions of self-motivation's psychometric properties may be found in papers by Dishman, Ickes, & Morgan (1980) and Dishman and Ickes, (1981).

Study 3

A subsequent study was designed as a test of self-motivation's construct or behavioral validity and involved 64 undergraduate women involved in voluntary (i.e. "walk-on") 8-month athletic training program for crew (i.e. team rowing) at the University of Wisconsin (Dishman, Ickes, and Morgan, 1980). This training setting was quite demanding in terms of time and effort commitment due to the endurance nature of crew. Also, it offered limited extrinsic reinforcements for continued involvement since no scholarships were awarded, no competitive cuts were made, and since actual intercollegiate competition was not scheduled during the training period. In addition, the training program was quite protracted and extending from early September throughout the harsh Wisconsin winter to early spring. An a priori decision was made to compare dropouts with non-dropouts at three naturally occuring breakpoints during the crew training program. The test conducted at the first breakpoint compared the scores of nondropouts with those of early dropouts who withdrew from the program during the first ten days. The second comparison was made after the first eight weeks. This was the point at which the weather turned cold and the training moved to the boathouse and became more strenuous. The final breakpoint occurred in the 32nd week of training, after the participants had spent the winter months confined to training in the boathouse. At each point, continued adherence required increasing commitment and self-motivation due to increasing intensity of the physical stress of the actual conditioning, increasingly adverse weather conditions, and decreasing attractiveness of the behavioral setting as the activity progressed from autumn on a scenic lake to the uninviting confines of a boathouse during harsh winter weather. This setting provided an excellent opportunity to observe the relationship between self-motivation and behavior patterns in a naturalistic and voluntary adherence setting.

Self-motivation scores for eventual dropouts (N= 42) were significantly lower (p < .05) than those of the adherers (N=22) at each point during the crew training period. In contrast, no differences were observed at any time for other psychological characteristics which were conceptually related to training motivation. These included ego-strength and approval motive and, in fact, the self-motivation differences remained even when the common variance with the other psychometric variables was removed. Moreover, self-motivation was the best predictor of training adherence in a stepwise regression analysis (R=.33), while the other psychological factors did not enhance the significance of the predictive equation. Furthermore, when all crew participants were divided into dichotomous groups on the basis of a median split of self-motivation scores, only 41% (13 of 32) of low self-motivated athletes adhered for the entire training program while 78% (25 of 32) of athletes with high self-motivation stayed with the program for all 32 weeks.

Study 4

A fourth study involved 66 adult males who were involved in preventive medicine and adult fitness exercise programs (Dishman and Gettman, 1980). Each program consisted of medically prescribed and supervised activity conducted 3 days per week for 20 weeks in accordance with guidelines established by the American College of Sports Medicine (1976). Three testing sites were used and these included 1) the Biodynamics Clinical Exercise Program at the University of Wisconsin-Madison, 2) the Adult fitness and Cardiac Rehabilitation Program at the University of Wisconsin-LaCrosse, and 3) the Institute for Aerobics Research — Dallas, Texas. Since the subjects at these sites were statistically similar in terms of their psychological profiles and their actual exercise behavior, they were combined for analysis purposes. This procedure provided a more desirable subject-to-variable ratio and enhanced the robustness of the multivariate test statistics employed. Assessment was made of self-motivation, health locus of control (HLC; Wallston et al., 1976), and certain attitudes toward physical activity, including attraction to physical activity, self-perceptions of exercise ability (ATTR; Sonstroem, 1978) and perceptions of exercise as having instrumental value for health and fitness (Kenyon, 1968). In addition, body fat, weight, metabolic-capacity, and CHD states were also assessed so that adherence might be characterized within a psychobiologic prediction model.

At the end of the 20-week study period, data for eventual dropouts (N=23) and adherers (N=43) were compared by a number of statistical techniques. Results of MANOVA revealed a significant ($p > .01$) overall difference between dropouts and adherers on the biological and psychological variables. Subsequent application of stepwise multiple discriminant analysis as a post hoc test indicated that only percent body fat, self-motivation, and body weight made a significant ($p > .05$) contribution to this group separation. Furthermore, when used in a prediction equation, these variables permitted accurate classification of individual participants into actual adherence or dropout groups for approximately 80% of all cases. This represented a predicition which was 40% better than chance for dropouts and 16% above a chance prediction for adherers. Group means for the discriminating variables revealed that adherers possessed lower values for both percent fat and body weight but had higher self-motivation scores than dropouts.

Stepwise multiple regression analysis yielded similar results, revealing that percent body fat, self-motivation, and body weight entered the regression equation consecutively and were the only variables which significantly ($p - .05$) enhanced the prediction of adherence. Nearly 50% of the variance in adherence behavior could be accounted for by the derived regression equation (R=.67, $p > .01$).

Summary

Replication of body weight and percent body fat's ability to discriminate adherers and dropouts adds considerable support for the influence of body composition on exercise adherence. And, when combined with self-motivation scores in a psychobiological prediction model, these variables appear to be of considerable clinical importance in the initial identification of likely dropouts. The correlation between exercise adherence and self-motivation is noteworthy not only for its magnitude (r=.44, $p > .05$) and the fact that it was a considerably better predictor than any of the remaining psychometric variables, but also because it provides strong empirical support for what previously has been largely only a hypothetical link between motivation and adherence to therapeutic exercise.

There was no difference between adherers and dropouts in metabolic capacity ($p > .05$) in study 4, and asymptomatic participants actually adhered longer ($p < .01$) than did individuals with established

coronary disease. This discrepancy with findings from the initial retrospective study suggests that behavioral influences mediated by cardiovascular fitness or health status are likely to be specific to exercise mode and setting and to the participant population. On the other hand, the relationship between body composition and adherence seems to be more generalizable. These possibilities are each consistent with previous clinical studies related to the adherence question (Dishman, Note 1).

Self-Motivation and Athletic Training

The self-motivation construct appears to also have some relevance for the study of athletic training in *certain* sports. This is not only supported by the consistency of its predictive efficacy in several diverse exercise settings, its generalized scale format, and its intuitive relationship with motivation for endurance training, but also by the endurance nature and sport relevance of both studies 3 and 4 discussed earlier. That is, team rowing involves strenuous muscular conditioning which is similar in many respects to that demanded for many other endurance sports. In addition the Aerobics Institute sample included in study 4 was involved in a weight training program which is readily applicable to supplemental conditioning in a variety of athletic settings, (Dishman and Gettman, 1980; Gettman, Strathman, and Culter, 1981). Moreover, the appropriateness of applying the self-motivation measure to selected sport settings is consistent with a recent exploratory study of training motivation in cross-country runners (Dishman, Note 2). In this investigation, both interscholastic and intercollegiate athletes who trained more extensively in terms of both duration and intensity were characterized by high self-motivation scores, and this relationship was independent of fitness or running ability. While the external validity of self-motivation for sport application remains to be tested, these initial findings are notable considering the practical significance of training motivation for sport and the lack of systematic inquiry in this area.

Facilitation Models

Despite available evidence which has described and, in some instances predicted, exercise adherers and dropouts, very little information is available to support the effectiveness of specific intervention strategies for adherence facilitation (Falls, Baylor, & Dishman, 1980, p. 198). This is directly related to the lack of understanding of the adherence process. Essentially, all that can be said with reasonable assurity is that the likelihood of adherence appears to be enhanced in group settings (Mann, Garrett, Farhi, Murray & Billings, 1969; Massie & Shephard, 1971) which are conveniently accessible (Sanne, 1973; Teraslinna, Partanen & Koskela, et al., 1969). And, in some instances, the accessibility issue may be more significant than possible social reinforcements from an exercise group (Wilhelmson, Sanne & Elmfeldt, et al., 1975). The chances of adherence are also facilitated if a married participant's spouse is supportive of involvement (Andrew & Parker, 1979; Haynes et al., 1979; Heinzelmann & Bagley, 1970) and if the intensity of the exercise is not stressful to the point of injury (Pollock, Gettman % Milesis, et al., 1977). Attainment of training objectives may also influence adherence (Danielson & Wanzel, 1977), and in this regard biological considerations related to excessive weight and body fat or disease-related disability (Dishman, 1981a; Dishman, 1981b; Dishman, Ickes and Morgan, 1980) may have clinical significance in terms of prescribing an exercise dosage which may optimize adherence either through maximizing goal attainment, setting more realistic goals, or preventing discomfort or possible injury (Falls, Baylor & Dishman, 1980). This points to the logical importance of personalized exercise prescription based on behavioral "tailoring" (Haynes et al., 1979; Thompson & Wankel, 1981) and not just an optimal psychological threshold. Subsequently, one approach to adherence facilitation might be situation-oriented in attempts to manage exercise behavior indirectly by first changing critical aspects of the exercise setting (Thompson and Wankel, in press). An alternative approach might be participant-oriented in which exercise behavior is changed directly by using certain contingency-based behavior management techniques such as lotteries and contractual agreements (Epstein, et al., 1981; Krumboltz and Thoreson, 1976; Stalonas, Johnson & Christ, 1978; Wysocki, Hall, Iwata, & Riordan, 1979). Moreover, a cognitive-behavioral intervention in which individuals rationally evaluate anticipated gains (i.e. benefits) and losses (i.e. costs) of exercise behvaior has been consistently effective in promoting exercise (Hoyt & Janis, 1975; Wankel & Thompson, 1977; Wankel, 1981); particularly in individuals who, on the basis of self-motivation scores, are most sensitive to an intervention (Wankel & Graham, Note 3). These are areas which remain to be actively researched, however.

The self-motivation research just discussed and the psychobiologic prediction model introduced suggest that manipulation of the exercise setting may, however, be unnecessary or ineffective for certain individuals. And, it would seem that the ultimate goal in terms of promoting long term adherence would be the development of self-motivated or self-reinforcing behavior which will be perpetuated outside the treatment setting. This is highlighted by the common practice of specified terms of involvement in many clinical settings in which clients are restricted in the time, (e.g. months) they may spend with the formal program. The self-motivation scale discussed may provide a method of evaluating the degree to which exercise behavior may be expected to be perpetuated once clinical ties are severed. Moreover, in both a heuristic and a pragmatic sense, the initial diagnosis of adherence-prone and dropout-prone exercisers at the outset of program involvement might not only facilitate adherence rates in a clinically significant manner, but may also complement controlled interventions designed to enhance the behavicral appropriateness of exercise prescriptions by identifying individuals most sensitive to an intervention attempt. The use of self-motivation scores within the psychobiologic prediction model introduced may represent one effective approach in this regard.

Reference Notes

1. Dishman, R.K. Staying with exercise: Adherence to habitual physical activity. In Sachs, M. & Buffone, G. *The psychology of Therapeutic Exercise,* in press.
2. Dishman, R.K. Motivation for athletic training. Manuscript in preparation, 1981.
3. Wankel, L. & Graham, J. The effects of a decision balance-sheet intervention upon exercise adherence of high and low self-motivatied females. Manuscript submitted for publication, 1981.

REFERENCES

American College of Sports Medicine. *Guidelines for Graded Exercise Testing and Exercise Prescription.* Philadelphia, PA: Lea & Febiger, 1976.

Andrew, G.M. & Parker, J.O.: Factors related to dropout of post myocardial infarction patients from exercise programs. *Medicine and Science in Sports and Exercise,* 1979, *11,* 376-378.

Baekeland, F. & Lundwall, L.: Dropping out of treatment: A critical review. *Psychological Bulletin,* 1975, *82,* 738-783.

Barhke, M. & Morgan, W.P.: Anxiety reduction following exercise and meditation. *Cognitive Therapy and Research,* 1978, *2,* 323-333.

Danielson, R.R. & Wanzel, R.S.: Exercise objectives of fitness program dropouts. In Landers, D.M. & Christina, R.W. (Eds.) *Psychology of Motor Behavior and Sport.* Champaign, IL: Human Kinetics Publishers, 1977, pp. 310-320.

Dishman, R.K.: Biological influences on exercise adherence. *Research Quarterly for Exercise and Sport,* 1981a, *52,* 190-200.

Dishman, R.K.: Prediction of adherence to habitual physical activity. In Montoye, H.J. & Nagle, F.J. (Eds.) *Exercise in Health and Disease.* Springfield, IL: Charles C. Thomas, 1981b.

Dishman, R.K. & Gettman, L.R.: Psychobiologic influences on exercise adherence, *Journal of Sport Psychology,* 1980,*2,* 295-310.

Dishman, R.K. & Ickes, W.: Self-motivation and adherence to therapeutic exercise, *Journal of Behavioral Medicine,* in press.

Dishman, R.K., Ickes, W.J., & Morgan, W.P.: Self-motivation and adherence to habitual physical activity. *Journal of Applied Social Psychology,* 1980, *10,* 115-131.

Epstein, L.H., Thompson, J.K. & Wing, R.R.: The effects of contract and lottery procedures on attendance and fitness in aerobics exercise. *Behavior Modification,* in press.

Falls, H., Baylor, A., & Dishman, R.K.: *Essentials of Fitness.* Philadelphia: Saunders, 1980.

Folkins, C.H., & Sime, W.E.: Physical fitness training and mental health. *American Psychologist,* 1981, *36,* 373-389.

Greist, J.H., Klein, M.J., Eischens, R.R., & Faris: Antidepressant running, *Psychiatric Annals,* 1979, *9,* 23-29.

Gettman, C.R., Culter, L., & Strathman, T.: Physiologic changes after 20 weeks of isotonic vs isokinetic circuit training. *Journal of Sports Medicine and Physical Fitness,* 1980,*20,* 265-274.

Haynes, R.B., Taylor, D.W., & Sackett, D.L. *Compliance in Health Care.* Baltimore: Johns Hopkins University Press, 1979.

Heinzelmann, F. & Bagley, R.W.: Response to physical activity programs and their effects on health behavior. *Public Health Report*, 1980, *85*, 905-911.

Holt, W.E.: The concept of motivation for treatment. American Journal of *Psychiatry*, 1967, *123*, 1388-1394.

Hoyt, M.F., & Janis, I.L.: Increasing adherence to a stressful decision via a motivational balance-sheet procedure: A field experiment. *Journal of Personality and Social Psychology*, 1975, *31*, 833-839.

Ingjer, F., & Dahl, H.A.: Dropouts from an endurance training program, *Scandinavian Journal of Sports Science*, 1979, *1*, 20-22.

Kenyon, G.S.: Six scales for assessing attitude toward physical activity. *Research Quarterly*, 1968b, *39*, 566-574.

Krumboltz, J.D., & Thoresen, C.E. (Eds) *Counseling Methods*. New York: Holt, Rinehart & Winston, 1976.

Mann, G.V., Garrett, H.L., Farhi, A., Murray, H., & Billings, F.T.: Exercise to prevent coronary heart disease. *American Journal of Medicine*, 1976, *46*, 12-21.

Massie, J.F., & Shephard, R.J.: Physiological and psychological effects of training — a comparison of individual and gymnasium programs, with a characterization of the exercise "drop-out." *Medicine and Science in Sports*, 1971, *3*, 110-117.

Morgan, W.P.: Involvement in vigorous physical activity with special reference to adherence. *Proceedings, College Physical Education Conference*, 1977a, Orlando, Florida.

Morgan, W.P.: Psychological consequences of vigorous physical activity and sport. In Scott, M.G. (Ed.) *The Academy Papers*, 1977b, Iowa City: American Academy of Physical Education.

National Jogging Association, Statistical Report, 1981.

Oldridge, N.B.: What to look for in an exercise class leader. *The Physician and Sportsmedicine*, 1977, *5*, 85-88.

Oldridge, N.B., Wicks, J.R., & Hanley, et al.: Noncompliance in an exercise rehabilitation program for men who have suffered a myocardial infarction. *Canadian Medical Association Journal*, 1978, *118*, 361-364.

Orlick, T.D.: The athletic drop-out: A high price to pay for inefficiency. *Journal of the Canadian Association for Health, Physical Education and Recreation*, 1974, *40*.

Pollock, M.O., Gettman, L.R., Milesis, C.A., et al.: Effects of frequency and duration of training on attrition and incidence of injury. *Medicine and Science in Sports*, 1977, *9*, 21-36.

Sanne, H.M.: Exercise tolerance and physical training of non-selected patients after myocardial infarction. *Acta Medica Scandinavica Supplement*, 1973, *551*, 1-124.

Sonstroem, R.J.: Physical estimation and attraction scales: Rationale and research. *Medicine and Science in Sports*, 1978, *10*, 97-102.

Stalonas, P.M., Jr., Johnson, W.G., & Christ, M.: Behavior modification for obesity: The evaluation of exercise, contingency management, and program adherence. *Journal of Consulting and Clinical Psychology*, 1978, *46*, 463-469.

Teraslinna, P., Partanen, T., Koskela, A., et al.: Characteristics affecting willingness of executives to participate in an activity program aimed at coronary heart disease prevention. *Journal of Sports Medicine and Physical Fitness*, 1969, *9*, 224-229.

Thompson, C.E., & Wankel, L.M.: The effects of perceived activity choice upon frequency of exercise behavior. *Journal of Applied Social Psychology*, in press.

Wallston, B.S., Wallston, K.S., Kaplan, G.D., & Maides, S.A.: Development and validation of the health locus of control (HLC) scale. *Journal of Consulting Clinical Psychology*, 1976, *44*, 580-585.

Wankel, L.M.: Involvement in vigorous physical activity: Considerations for enhancing self-motivation. *Proceedings, National Fitness Motivation Workshop*, Geneva Park, Ontario, 1981.

Wankel, L.M., & Thompson, C.: Motivating people to be physically active: Self-persuasion vs. balanced decision-making. *Journal of Applied Social Psychology*, 1977, *7*, 332-340.

Wilhelmsen, L., Sanne, H., Elmfeldt, D., et al.: A controlled trial of physical training after myocardial infarction. *Preview of Medicine*, 1975, *4*, 491-508.

Wysocki, T., Hall, G., Iwata, B., & Riordan, M.: Behavioral management of exercise: Contracting for aerobic points. *Journal of Applied Behavior Analysis*, 1979, *12*, 55-64.

PSYCHOLOGICAL EFFECTS OF RUNNING: IMPLICATIONS FOR PERSONAL SIGNIFICANCE AND SELF-DIRECTION

Bonnie G. Berger (USA)

Running as a form of therapy is increasingly being viewed by psychologists, psychiatrists, and sport psychologists as an effective strategy for helping clients to decrease their elevated levels of anxiety and depression (Berger, Note 1; Morgan, 1979; Sachs & Buffone, Note 8; Dienstbier, Note 5; Rueter & Harris, Note 7; Greist, Klein, Eischens, Faris, Gurman, & Morgan, 1979). Running also can enhance one's self-concept, body image, and self-understanding (Berger & Mackenzie, 1980; Berger, Note 2; Joesing & Clance, 1979; Snyder & Kivlin, 1975). Despite substantial experimental evidence that supports the psychological ramifications of physical activity, this information is not readily available to physical educators. This information is of particular value to physical educators who view physical education as being much more than the teaching of sport skills. It is the thesis of this paper that physical education should prepare an individual to use different types of physical activity for a variety of

personal purposes such as stress reduction, enhancement of cardiovascular health, and improvement of physical appearance. In other words, the physically educated person should be able to knowledgably weave regular and appropriate physical activity into her/his lifestyle. If this objective of physical education is accepted, then information about the value of running in decreasing a person's anxiety and depression and in enhancing self-esteem and self-understanding is of vital importance to teachers and directors of physical activity and ultimately to the general population.

The purpose of this paper is threefold. First, information about women runners will be presented to emphasize the potential differences in psychological responses of women compared with men to running as a result of gender differences in child rearing, enculturation, and role models in the United States. Despite the great strides towards equal rights, the social milieu of women runners in the United States differs from that of men. Sport generally is a male dominated activity which reflects such male values as strength, strategy, and winning. Thus, women who venture into the bastion of male sport report different personal reactions, problems, and benefits than do men.

Physiologically, female and male exercise novices respond similarly. Psychologically, however, they are approaching the activity from two very different positions. Many women who have not participated in sport have accepted and followed the traditional feminine gender role. Extensive sport experience is not expected of women. In contrast, male novice exercisers have rejected their traditional gender role. Thus, it seems logical to examine the psychological responses of novice female and male runners separately.

The second purpose of the paper is to examine the value of running in decreasing anxiety and depression and in enhancing self-concept and self-understanding. These psychological effects of running have direct implications for a major theme of this conference: personal significance in sport.

Finally, the third purpose is to discuss the practical parameters of running programs that are most conductive to affecting the various psychological effects.

Self-Concept, Self-Esteem, and Androgyny

In addition to reducing the negative psychological states of anxiety and depression, running has been found to enhance psychological well-being by positively influencing self-concept and self-esteem (Kraft, 1978; Leonardson, 1977; Martinez, Cheffers, & Zaichkowsky, 1978; Sharp & Reilly, 1975). Self-concept, a collection of tentative hypotheses about one's self, is primarily learned from other people's responses to the individual and does not refer to the person herself, but to what the woman sees when she stands away from herself. Since the self-concept is a primary determinant of behavior (Diggens & Huber, 1976), its enhancement by running is an important ingredient in psychological well-being.

Observed differences in self-concept between women and men indicate that women describe their actual and ideal selves as more tender, submissive, and socially competent than do men (Bledsoe, 1973; Maccoby & Jacklin, 1974; Stoner & Kaiser, 1978). However, high self-esteem which is indicated by little discrepancy between a person's ideal and actual selves is significantly and positively related to a man's masculinity score but not to a women's femininity score (Sappenfield & Harris, 1975). As noted by Sappenfield and Harris (1975), masculinity, which denotes assertiveness, competency, and self-reliance, is a desirable characteristic for women as well as for men. It seems likely that physical activity enhances a woman's image of her body (Joesting & Clance, 1979; Snyder & Kivlin, 1975) and her feelings of competency (Roberts, Duda, & Kleiber, Note 6) which in turn are related to her self-concept (Mahoney, 1978).

Of particular importance when examining the influence of running on women's self-concepts is the possibility that running might create gender role conflict for particularly "feminine" women (Corbin & Nix, 1979; Wark & Wittig, 1979). In spite of the variability of experimental methodology, the inclusion of athletes participating in a variety of sports, the use of different scales to measure self-concept, and the changing role models of women, there is an emerging body of evidence that supports the possibility of a positive relationship between a woman's self-concept and participation in certain types of physical activity (Berger, Note 2). As concluded by Snyder et al. (1976), the expected negative associations between female sports participants and self-concept often are not observed. Supporting the positive effect of running on women's self-concepts, Jorgenson and Jorgenson (1979) found no significant differences between female and male runners' perceptions of self and that an incredibly high proportion (92%) of the runners perceived increased emotional well-being as a result of their running. Further

evidence of enhanced self-concept was that 74% of those who lived in a family environment perceived an increase in their families' appreciation of their physical appearance.

Closely aligned with self-esteem is the concept of androgyny, the possession of both male and female psychological characteristics. Androgyny enables an individual to respond appropriately and competently without being restricted by stereotyped ideas about gender appropriate behavior (Bem, 1974, 1979; Locksley & Colten, 1979; Pedhauzur & Tetenbaum, 1979). The importance of androgyny for a woman's psychological health is emphasized by the observation that it is impossible to be a psychologically healthy adult woman and at the same time a psychologically healthy human being who is defined by male psychological traits (Kaschak, 1976). By emphasizing traditionally masculine personality characteristics such as vigor and physical competency, running may enable women to become psychologically more androgynous (Harris & Jennings, 1977) and thus more competent in responding appropriately in a variety of situations (Bem, 1974, 1979; Spence & Helmreich, 1979). Rather than either androgyny or masculinity denoting negative characteristics for women, they have been found to be related to desirable behaviors and to enhanced self-esteem (Flaherty & Dusik, 1980; Harris & Jennings, 1977).

Self-Understanding

Running also provides a woman with an outstanding opportunity to increase her conscious awareness of feelings, values, and the underlying psychodynamics (Berger, 1979; Berger & Mackenzie, 1980; Besson, 1978). Not only is the woman runner free to explore her stream of consciousness as she runs, she also can begin to question whether she really wishes to run further, faster, and even why she chooses to run (Berger, 1979; Berger & Mackenzie, 1980; Besson, 1978; Schofield & Abbuhl, 1975). As concluded by Berger and Mackenzie (1980), from their case study of a woman jogger, running involves experiencing a wide spectrum of emotions ranging from agony to ecstasy; running is conductive to introspection as well as to thinking in general; running satisfies inner psychodynamic needs; and awareness of private phenomenological experiences associated with running can be useful for gaining self-understanding.

RUNNING GUIDELINES FOR PSYCHOLOGICAL HEALTH

The following guidelines can be followed both by physical educators and by informed members of the general population who wish to consider running as a strategy to reduce on-going levels of anxiety and depression and/or to enhance their self-concepts, self-esteem, and self-understanding. It is quite likely that these psychological effects of running, in addition to the physiological benefits and the ease of participation, may explain the large influx in running and the personal significance of the activity. Further elucidation of the psychological effects of running, dissemination of this knowledge to educators and to the general population, and positive personal experiences in physical education classes are important components in encouraging people to adhere to active lifestyles. Crucial to a person becoming self-directing in her/his lifetime running experience is the following information about running prescription.

Frequent and strenuous exercise is most effective.

Moderately strenuous exercise, in contrast to mild or exhaustive exercise, seems to be most conductive to mood changes (Brown, et al., 1978; Buffone, 1981; Morgan, 1979). In a study of depression, softball players who participated in intermittent rather than in continuous physical activity were similar to a control group who did not exercise and showed no change in depression (Brown et al., 1978). Tennis players showed a small yet significant reduction in depression. Runners who jogged 5 days a week in contrast to those who ran 3 days and those who participated in the other sports reported the greatest changes in depression.

Running Prescription

Since a "moderate" running program varies from person to person and even differs within the same person, exercise prescription must be highly individualized according to the exercise components of frequency, duration, and intensity. Individualized running programs also increase running adherence by minimizing the likelihood of injury and boredom and by maximizing the psychological effects of running.

Frequency. An exercise frequency of 3 times per week provides a training effect that noticably increases the psychological ease of running, serves as an intrinsic reward as the person observes her increasing ability to run, and results in significantly less injury than the 5 day a week programs (Pollock, Gettman, Milesis, Bah, Durstine & Johnson, 1977). Limiting a running program to 3 days a week presents less of a time problem to the participant and reduces the possibility of monotony.

Duration. Running duration can be expressed in terms of time, distance, or calories burned. The total time of exertion, however, is suggested for use because it is easily measured, is often employed in experimental studies of running and allows for easy comparison to the literature. The suggested continuous running duration of 20 to 30 minutes is based on a wide variety of considerations:

1) the reported improvements in cardiovascular health (Hartung & Squires, 1980; Kirby, 1980; Squires, 1980),

2. reduced risk of heart disease (Paffenbarger, Wing & Hyde, 1979),

3) the impressively low injury rate evidenced by running this length of time (less than ½ the percentage of injuries that occur in 45 minute programs) (Pollock et al., 1977), and

4) the practical consideration of an amount of time that can be garnered from a busy day (Berger, Note 3).

From a psychological vantage point, running for 40 to 60 minutes probably results in more positive emotional states and in more frequent occurrences of altered states of consciousness or "runner's highs" than do shorter running periods (Carmack & Martens, 1979; Glasser, 1976; Kostrubala, 1976). However, because of the dramatic increase in injuries (Pollock et al., 1977), runs longer than 30 minutes are not recommended for most people.

Intensity. The moderate levels of running intensity suggested for the recreational runner are characterized by sustained heavy breathing and are performed between 70% and 85% of a person's maximal heart rate (220 beats/minute minus age in years). When running intensity is above the aerobic threshold, running does not produce improvement in aerobic fitness and cannot be performed for the recommended 20 to 30 minutes. Exercise below this intensity may not produce the desirable psychological effects.

CONCLUSION

The psychological effects of running offer new insight into the personal significance of sport. Some people may run to reduce their on-going levels of anxiety and depression. Others may include running in their lifestyle because it enhances their self-concepts, self-esteem, androgyny (if they're women), and self-understanding. The following poem by La Ferne Price (1970) captures some of the personal meaning in running.

Sport holds a mirror to a woman's life
all that she can know
of joy
or sadness
finds its counterpart in sport
she learns not only how she moves
but how she feels
and thinks
and struggles

how she is tormented
triumphs
and then finds peace
as she absorbs the
mood
drama
and emotion
which are the essence of her sport
so she discovers
all the inward stresses
that move her being

Because the sentiments in the poem can be universally meaningful to men as well as to women, it is particularly important that a running program be individually tailored as to frequency, duration, and intensity. It is hoped that as the general public becomes aware of the psychological ramifications of running and of other sport activities and the psychological bases for regulating their programs, they will become self-directing in their lifetime sport experiences.

Reference Notes

1. Berger, B.G. Running away from anxiety and depression: Special considerations for the female client. In M. Sachs & G. Buffone (Eds.), *The psychology of exercise and running; Research and application.* Book in preparation, 1981.

2. Berger, B.G. Running toward psychological well-being: Special considerations for the female client. In M. Sachs & G. Buffone (Eds.), *The psychology of exercise and running: Research and application.* Book in preparation, 1981.

3. Berger, B.G. Running strategies for women. In M. Sachs & G.G. Buffone (Eds.), *The psychology of exercise and running: Research and application.* Book in preparation, 1981.

4. Berger, B.G. *Effects of swimming and yoga on mood during a five month interval.* Manuscript submitted for publication, 1981.

5. Dienstbier, R.A. *Exercise, catecholamines, and personality.* Paper presented at the Third Annual Psychology of Running Seminar, Cornell University Medical College. New York, October 24, 1980. (Available from R. Dienstbier, Psychology Department, University of Nebraska).

6. Roberts, G., Duda, J., & Klieber, D. *Children in sport: Dimensions of motivation and competence in male and female participants.* Paper presented at the annual meeting of the North American Society for the Psychology of Sport and Physical Activity, Boulder, May 1980. (Available from D.D. Kleiber, Department of Physical Education, University of Illinois, Champaign, Illinois).

7. Rueter, M.A., & Harris, D.V. *The effects of running on individuals who are clinically depressed.* Paper presented at the American Psychological Association Convention, Montreal, 1980. (Available from M. Rueter, Department of Physical Education, University of Northern Iowa).

8. Sachs, M. & Buffone, G. *The psychology of exercise and running: Research and application.* Book in preparation, 1981.

9. Wilson, V.E., Berger, B.G., & Bird, E. *Effects of running and an exercise class on anxiety.* Manuscript submitted for publication, 1981.

REFERENCES

Akiskal, H.S., & McKinney, W.T. Overview of recent research in depression. *Archives of General Psychiatry,* 1975, *32,* 285—305

Bahrke, M.S., & Morgan, W.P. Anxiety reduction following exercise and meditation. *Cognitive Therapy and Research,* 1978, *2,* 323—334.

Berger, B.G. The meaning of regular jogging: A phenomenological approach. In R. Cox (Ed.), *American Alliance for Health, Physical Education, and Recreation research consortium papers* (Vol. 2, Book 2). Washington, D.C.: American Alliance for Health, Physical Education, and Recreation, 1979.

Berger, B.G., & Mackenzie, M.M. A case study of a woman jogger: A psychodynamic analysis. *Journal of sport behavior*, 1980, 3,3—L6.

Bem, S.L. The measurement of psychological androgyny. *Journal of Consulting and Clinical Psychology*, 1974,42, 155—162.

Bem, S.L. Theory and measurement of androgyny: A reply to the Pedhauzer-Tetenbaum and Locksley-Colten critiques. *Journal of Personality and Social Psychology*, 1979, 37, 1047—1054.

Besson, G. *The complete woman runner*. Mountain View, California: World Publications, Inc., 1978.

Biaggio, M.K., & Nielsen, E.C. Anxiety correlates of sex-role identity. *Journal of Clinical Psychology*, 1976, 32, 619—623.

Bledsoe, J.C. Sex differences in self-concept: Fact or artifact? *Psychological Reports*, 1973, 32, 1252—1254.

Blue, F.R. Aerobic running as treatment for moderate depression. *Perceptual and Motor Skills*, 1979, 48, 228.

Brown, R.S., Ramirez, D.E., & Taub, J.M. The prescription of exercise for depression. *The Physician and Sports Medicine*, 1978, 6,(12), 34—37; 40—41; 44—45.

Buffone, G.W. *Psychological changes associated with cognitive-behavioral therapy and an aerobic running program in the treatment of depression*. Unpublished doctoral dissertation, Florida State University, 1980.

Carmack, M.A., & Martens, R. Measuring commitment to running: A survey of runners' attitudes and mental states. *Journal of Sport Psychology*, 1979, 1, 15—42.

Chesler, P. *Women and madness*. New York: Avon Books, 1973.

Corbin, C.B., & Nix, C. Sex-typing of physical activities and success predictions of children before and after cross-sex competition. *Journal of Sport Psychology*, 1979, 1, 43—52.

deVries, H.A., & Adams, G.M. Electromyographic comparison of single doses of exercise and meprobamate as to effect on muscular relaxation. *American Journal of Physical Medicine*, 1972, 51, 130—141.

Dienstbier, R.A. Running and personality change. *Today's Jogger*, 1978, 2, 30—33, 48—49.

Dienstbier, R.A., Crabbe, J., Johnson, G.O., Thorland, W., Jorgensen, J.A., & Sadar, M.M. Running and changes in stress tolerance, mood, and temperament indicators: A bridge to exercise and personality change. In M. Sacks & M. Sachs (Eds.), *The psychology of running*. Champaign, Illinois: Human Kinetics Publishers, 1981.

Diggens, D., & Huber, J. Self: How are you affected by the way you see yourself? In D. Diggens & J. Huber, *The human personality*. Boston: Little Brown & Company, 1976.

Flaherty, J.F., & Dusik, J.B. An investigation of the relationship between psychological androgyny and components of self-concept. *Journal of Personality and Social Psychology*, 1980, 38, 984—992.

Folkins, C.H., & Sime, W.E. Physical fitness training and mental health. *American Psychologist*, 1981, 36(4), 373—389.

Glasser, W. *Positive addiction*. New York: Harper & Row, 1976.

Greist, J.H., Klein, M.H., Eischens, R.R., Faris, J., Gurman, A.S., & Morgan, W.P. Running as treatment for depression. *Comprehensive Psychiatry*, 1979, 20, 41—54.

Grove, W.R., & Tudor, J.F. Adult sex roles and mental illness. In J. Huber (Ed.), *Changing women in a changing society*. Chicago: The University of Chicago Press, 1973.

Harris, D.V., & Jennings, S.E. Self-perceptions of female distance runners. In P. Milvy (Ed.), *The marathon: Physiological, medical, epidemiological, and psychological studies. `Annals of the New York Academy of Sciences, 301*. New York: New York Academy of Sciences, 1977.

Hartung, G.H., & Squires, W.G. Exercise and HDL cholesterol in middle-aged men. *The Physician and Sportsmedicine*, 1980, 8, 74—79.

Joesting, J., & Clance, P.R. Comparison of runners and non-runners on the body-cathexis and self-cathexis scales. *Perceptual and Motor Skills*, 1979, 48, 1046.

Jorgenson, C.B., & Jorgenson, D.E. Effect of running on perception of self and others. *Perceptual and Motor Skills*, 1979, 48, 242.

Justice, B., & McBee, G.W. Sex differences in psychological distress and social functioning. *Psychological Reports*, 1979, 43, 659—662.

Kaschak, E. Sociotherapy: An ecological model for therapy with women. *Psychotherapy: Theory, Research, and Practice*, 1976, 13, 61—63.

Kavanagh, T., Shephard, R.J., Tuck, J.A., & Qureshi, S. Depression following myocardial infarction: The effect of distance running. In P. Milvy (Ed.), *The marathon: Physiological, medical, epidemiological, and psychological studies. Annals of the New York Academy of Sciences, 301*. New York: New York Academy of Sciences, 1977.

Kirby, M.S. Secondary risk factors related to coronary heart disease. In R.H. Cox & J.K. Nelson (Eds.), *American Alliance for Health, Physical Education, and Dance Research Consortium papers: Exercise physiology: Exercise and heart disease and analysis of body composition*. Washington, D.C.: American Alliance for Health, Physical Education, Recreation, and Dance, 1980.

Klerman, G.L. The age of melancholy. *Psychology Today*, April 1979, pp. 36—42; 88.

Kostrubala, T. *The joy of running*. New York: Pocket Books, 1976.

Kraft, R.E. Can the movement specialist really influence self-concept? *The Physical Educator*, 1978, 35, 20—21.

Leonardson, G.R. Relationship between self-concept and perceived physical fitness. *Perceptual and Motor Skills*, 1977, 44, 62.

Liliefors, J. *The running mind*. Mountain View, California: World Publications, Inc., 1978.

Locksley, A., & Colten, M.E. Psychological androgyny: A case of mistaken identity? *Journal of Personality and Social Psychology*, 1979, 37, 1010—1031.

Maccoby, E.E., & Jacklin, C.N. *The psychology of sex differences*. Stanford: Stanford University Press, 1974.

Mahoney, E.R. Subjective physical attractiveness and self-other orientations. *Psychological Reports*, 1978, 43, 277—278.

Martinez, T.J., Cheffers, J.T., & Zaichkowsky, L.D. Physical activity, motor development, and self-concept: Race and age differences. *Perceptual and Motor Skills*, 1978, 46, 147—154.

Morgan, W.P., & Pollock, M.L. Psychologic characterization of the elite distance runner. In P. Milvy (Ed.), *The marathon: Physiological, medical, epidemiological, and psychological studies, Annals of the New York Academy of Sciences, 301*, New York: New York Academy of Sciences, 1977.

Morgan, W.P. Anxiety reduction following acute physical

activity. *Psychiatric Annals*, 1979, *9*, 141—147.

Morgan, W.P., Roberts, J.A., Brand, F.R., & Feinerman, A.D. Psychological effect of chronic physical activity. *Medicine and Science in Sports*, 1970, *2*, 213—217.

Morgan, W.P., Pollock, M.L. Physical activity and cardiovascular health: Psychological aspects. In F. Landry & W.A. Orban (Eds.), *Physical activity and human wellbeing*. Miami, Florida: Symposia Specialists, 1978.

Noble, B.J. Cardiac rehabilitation: Psychological implications. In *American Alliance of Health, Physical Education, and Recreation symposia proceedings*. Washington, D.C.: American Alliance of Health, Physical Education, and Recreation, 1976.

Paffenbarger, R.S., Wing, A.L., Hyde, R.T. Physical activity as an index of heart attack risk in college alumni. *American Journal of Epidemiology*, 1979, *108*, 161—175.

Pedhauzur, E.J., & Tetenbaum, T.J. Bem sex role inventory: A theoretical and methodological critique. *Journal of Personality and Social Psychology*, 1979, *37*, 996—1016.

Pollock, M.L., Gettman, L.R., Milesis, C.A., Bah, M.D., Durstine, L., & Johnson, R.B. Effects of frequency and duration in training on attribution and incidence of injury. *Medicine and Science in Sports*, 1977, *9*(1), 31—36.

Price, L.F.E. *The wonder of motion: A sense of life for woman*. Grand Forks, North Dakota: University of North Dakota Press, 1970.

Sappenfield, B.R., & Harris, C.L. Self-reported masculinity-feminity as related to self-esteem. *Psychological Reports*, 1975, *37*, 669—670.

Scarf, M. The more sorrowful sex. *Psychology Today*, April 1979, pp.45—52, 89—90.

Scofield, L.J., & Abbuhl, S. The stimulation of insight and self-awareness through body-movement exercise. *Journal of Clinical Psychology*, 1975, *31*, 745—746.

Sharp, M.W. & Reilly, R.R.: The relationship of aerobic physical fitness to selective personality traits. *Journal of Clinical Psychology*, 1975, *31*, 428-430.

Snyder, E.E., & Kivlin, J.E.: Women athletes and aspects of psychological well-being and body image. *Research Quarterly*, 1975, *56*, 191-199.

Spence, J.T., & Helmreich, R.L.: The many faces of androgyny: A reply to Locksley & Colten. *Journal of Personality and Social Psychology*, 1979, *37*, 1032-1046.

Squires, W.G.: Exercise, diet, and blood lipids in coronary heart disease. In R.H. Cox & J.K. Nelson (Eds.), *AAPHER research consortium symposium papers: Exercise physiology: Exercise and heart disease and analysis of body composition*. Washington, D.C.: American Alliance for Health, Physical Education, Recreation, and Dance, 1980.

Stoner, S., & Kaiser, L. Sex differences in self-concepts of adolescents. *Psychological Reports*, 1978, *43*, 305-306.

Tharp, G.D., & Schlegelmilch, R.P.: Personality characteristics of trained versus nontrained individuals. *Medicine and Science in Sports*, 1977, *9*, 55.

Wark, K.A., & Wittig, A.F.: Sex role and sport competition anxiety. *Journal of Sport Psychology*, 1978, *1*, 248-250.

Wilson, V.E., Morley, N.C., & Bird, E.I.: Mood profiles of marathon runners, joggers, and non-exercisers. *Perceptual and Motor Skills*, 1980, *50*, 117-118.

EFFECTS OF EXERCISE ON SELECTED PSYCHOPHYSOLOGICAL VARIABLES IN ADULT MEN

A.H. Ismail and A.M. El-Naggar (USA)

In a series of experiments on normal subjects, de Vries and Adams (1972) found that properly designed exercise protocols reduced muscle action potential activity of both acute and chronic types. When comparing the effect of a bout of moderate exercise with pharmacologic treatment for anxiety tension states in middle-aged and older subjects, it was found that exercise had a significantly greater effect upon resting musculature than meprobemate; a commonly used tranquilizer (de Vries and Adams, 1972).

This study attempted to examine the *nature* and *degree* of relations among selected psychophysiological (physiological, biochemical, emotional and intellectual) variables before and after a long-term exercise program.

Thirty-five men averaging 42 years of age participated in a four-month physical fitness program; while a comparable group of 13 men matched for age and health status acted as a control group. The control group was advised to maintain their routine, sedentary life style. The physical fitness program consisted of three 90-minute sessions each week for a four-month duration. At each session subjects took part in stretching before jogging for warm-up followed by calisthenics, progressive jogging and self-selected recreational activities. The intensity of exercise was individualized for each participant according to his ability.

Psychological and physiological testing on both exercise and control groups was conducted during the week preceding the onset of the fitness program and again during a one-week period following the conclusion of the program.

Within the limitations of this study it can be concluded that 1.) physiological and psychological performance are highly related in adults, and; 2.) participation in a long-term exercise program does not only affect physiological functioning in a positive manner, but also psychological performance.

It is hoped that the findings obtained in this study will motivate young and adult alike to engage in habitual exercise not as a "preventive medicine" but as a "natural medicine".

REFERENCES

1. deVries, H.A. and G.M. Adams, "Electromyographic Comparison of Single Doses of Exercise and Meprobamate as to Effects on Muscular Relaxation". *American Journal of Physical Medicine*, 51: 130—141, 1972.

2. Ismail, A.H. and L.E. Trachtman, "Jogging the Imagination", *Psychology Today*, 6: 78—81, 1973.

3. Ismail, A.H. and R.J. Young, "Effect of Chronic Exercise on the Multivariate Relationships between Selected Biochemical and Personality Variables", *Journal of Multivariate Behavioral Research*, 12: 49—67, 1977.

4. Ismail, A.H. and R.J. Young, "Influence of Physical Fitness on Second and Third Order Personality Factors using Orthogonal and Oblique Rotations", *Journal of Clinical Psychology*, 32: 268—272, 1976.

5. Elsayed, M., A.H. Ismail and R.J. Young, "Intellectual Differences of Adult Men Related to Age and Physical Fitness before and after an Exercise Program", *Journal of Gerontology*, 35: 383—387, 1980.

6. Powell, R.R. and R.H. Pohnforf, "Comparison of Adult Exercisers and Non-exercisers on Fluid Intelligence and Selected Physiological Variables", *Research Quarterly*, 42: 70—77, 1971.

---

*An extended version of this paper can be obtained from the authors.

AEROBIC EXERCISE AS A TREATMENT FOR NON-PSYCHOTIC DEPRESSION

Sue Moxley (Canada)

The physiological benefits of ongoing aerobic activity have been known for some time. If this exercise is to be used as a psychological intervention, it would be useful to show that these improvements are also associated with improvements in "psychological fitness". Studies using ongoing physical activity programs have shown increased physical fitness to be related to improved self-concept (Collingwood and Willett, 1971), decreased depression (Folkins, Lynch and Gardiner, 1972) and decreased anxiety and muscle tension (Bahrke, 1979). As well, Solomon & Bumpus (1978) have suggested that running gives the person a feeling of being in control over functions such as heart rate, breathing and muscles, and thus gives the person a sense of mastery.

Although aerobic exercise has great potential for relieving depression, few researchers have tested its actual value for depressed patients. Case studies (Blue, 1979; Lion, 1978) suggest that even mild aerobic activity (walking, jogging) is effective in reducing depression. Griest, Eischens, Klein and Faris, (1978), in a controlled experiment with moderately depressed patients, have shown running to be as effective as psychotherapy in decreasing depression on a short-term basis, and to have more long-lasting effects.

To enjoy the beneficial effects of running, depressed patients must become successful runners. Because of the depressed state, these people will have more difficulty than usual initiating a fitness program. They will be more likely to drop out as well. Therefore program design is critical in early stages. Four factors have been identified by various researchers to increase adherence to running programs.

1. Regularity — Stretch/walk/jog/run five days/week, because regularity leads to addiction which can become a positive factor in exercise maintenance. Beginners should schedule regular times to run as an important part of treatment.

2. Gradual approach to capacity — While all fitness literature says "start out gradually", it is often not clear to beginners what "gradual" means. Eischens, Kane, Wilcox and Griest (1979) have put out detailed guidelines for depressed patients to ensure they have "stimulating but manageable stress and conscious avoidance of distress". In brief, the program progresses from 30 min. of stretching and walking, through walking and jogging to stretching and running for 30 min. or more. It is helpful if patients can begin exercising with someone trained to monitor signs of stress, and who can give feedback to patients to enable them to learn to monitor their own feelings.

3. Realistic short term goals: Patients should know why they are running. They should have concrete goals such as walking for 30 min., or running for 15 breath cycles. Some authors have cautioned against competitive aspects of trying to cover so much distance in a certain time, and suggested instead leaving distance open but specifying a minimum time for being active. Thinking while Running; Griest and his colleagues have stressed attention to and concentration upon environment, running form, and both bodily and mental feedback. Especially early in the program patients should concentrate on bodily feedback to idfentify when to decrease or increase activity.

In summary, a program of activity may be designed to induce a depressed patient to become a successful runner and reduce/eliminate depression. However, caution must be exercised in recommending running. As Folkins and Sime (1981) concluded from their review, the research is very limited and much more is needed. As Griest and Eischens (1980) have pointed out there is no evidence that running is suitable for psychotic patients. As well, there is the suggestion from the literature that there may be large individual differences in reaction to running as a treatment. However, there is so much potential for such a low-cost treatment, that further clinical research is definitely needed.

REFERENCES

Bahrke, M.S.: Exercise, meditation and anxiety reduction. *American Corrective Therapy Journal*, 1979, 33(2), 41-44.

Blue, O.E.: Aerobic running as treatment for depression. *Perceptual and Motor Skills*, 1979, 48, 228.

Byrd, O.E.: A survey of beliefs and practices on the relief of tension by moderate exercise. *Journal of School Health*, 1963, 33, 426-427.

Collingwood, T.R.: The effects of physical training upon self-concept and body attitude. *Journal of Clinical Psychology*, 1971, 27, 411-412.

Eischens, R.R., Kane, P.M., Wilcox, J.M. and Griest, J.H.: A new precise guide to running. *Behavioral Medicine*, 1979, June, 14-17.

Folkins, C.H. and Sime, W.E.: Physical fitness training and mental health. *American Psychologist*, 1981, 36(4), 373-389.

Folkins, C.H., Lynch, S. and Gardiner, M.M.: Psychological fitness as a function of physical fitness. *Archives of Physical Medicine and Rehabilitation*, 1972, 503-508.

Griest, J.H., Klein, M.H., Eischens, R.R., and Faris, J.W.: Antidepressant running. *Behavioral Medicine*, 1978, June, 19-24.

Lion, L.S.: Psychological effects of jogging: a preliminary study. *Perceptual and Motor Skills*, 1978, 47, 1215-1218.

Morgan, W.P. and Robert, J.: Psychological effect of chronic-physical activity. *Journal of Medicine and Science in Sport*, 1979, 2, 213-218.

Morgan, W.P.: Anxiety reduction following acute physical activity. *Psychiatric Annals*, 1979, 9(3), 141-417.

Solomon, E.G. and Bumpus, A.K.: The running meditation response: An adjunct to psychotherapy. *American Journal of Psychotherapy*, 1978, 32(4), 583-592.

EFFECTS OF PAUSE GYMNASTICS ON PSYCHIC ALERTNESS

J. Tiainer, T. Lintunen and M. Vainikka (Finland)

Pause gymnastics has been carried out in the elementary schools of Finland to a certain extent as early as in the 1920's. At that time it was thought that even if there was lack of place for physical activities, active breaks for recreation must be arranged for pupils by means of "desk gymnastics". Thus it happened, until need for pause gymnastics and consequently also its fullfillment decreased. Obviously so, because places for physical activities improved and physical activities at school got more hours.

Nowadays it has been suggested again that pause gymnastics should be tried out in school as well, since hours that can be used for physical education have again decreased in the recent upheavals of the school. In addition the space of work at school has become increasingly strained. Poor posture may appear in pupils and they may have symptoms of pain, fatigue and strain like headache, irritability and unwillingness to go at school.

Reasons mentioned above and the fact that among adults it has been found that pause gymnastics hastens the reversal of the heart rate and blood pressure, increases the flexibility of the shoulder girdle (Wojciezak et al., 1967) and productivity, (Prokop, 1972) and that after pause gymnastics the ability to work remains high, (Nifontova, 1962) have been incitements to study the effects of pause gymnastics at school.

PROBLEMS

The purpose of this research was to study:

1. Whether the programme of a half year pause gymnastics affects pupil's capacity for psychic performances?
2. Are the effects of pause gymnastics on pupils' psychic alertness different when the pupils often have leisure time physical activities compared with when they seldom have leisure time physical activities?
3. Whether the programme of pause gymnastics affects pupils' subjectively assessed mental well-being?

RESEARCH METHODS

1. Research design and subjects

This study was carried out in normal school conditions at one urban school and at one rural school. The study was begun in August 1979 and the exercise breaks were carried out once every school day during hald of the school year. The research design was a two-group, pre-post experimental design. At both schools there are two experimental classes (which both have exercise breaks and obligatory physical education) and two control classes (which only have obligatory physical education). About half of the 250 pupils are 13-

year-old boys (29 in the e. class and 21 in the c. class) and girls (e. 29, c. 36). The rest are 16-year-old boys (e. 32, c. 30) and girls (e. 36, c. 42).

2. Treatment

Three kinds of programmes were designed for pause gymnastics periods: flexibility and mobility programmes and muscle power programmes. They were carried out on successive days in the above mentioned order. Daily pause gymnastics periods were organized on each school day beginning mostly at 13:05 and lasting five minutes. The times spent on pause gymnastics programmes were planned by a research team and were carried out by both physical education teachers, p.e. students and pupils.

3. Variables and measurements

The subjects' psychic alertness consists of cognitive performances and subjectively assessed mental well-being. On the basis of earlier studies the following tests were included in the study: short term numeral memory, visual reproduction, verbal memory (repetition of a story), ability to concentrate and perceptual speed (copying test) from the Wechslers test battery. Test of thinking fluency was from Pitkänen and Tiainen and accuracy and attention span test (D_2) from Brickenkamp (Tiaine et al. 1980).

Subjectively assessed mental well-being was measured by asking the pupil to evaluate the frequency of their psychosomatic symptoms like headache, pain in the back and shoulders, tension, fatigue during two past weeks by means of four point scale (Tiainen et al. 1980). In addition pupils were asked about their state of health, evaluations as to how their physical fitness suffices for school work, how long they are able to attentively follow teaching, and about their alertness.

Leisure time physical activities were asked by questionnaire. The pupils of the experiment classes were divided into two groups on the basis of how oftern they had leisure time physical activities at least half an hour at a time. Those who had activities two times or more often in a week made up the group that often had physical activities. Those who seldom had physical activities had them once a week or more rarely.

TABLE I. Tests of cognitive performances. Comparison between the experimental and the control groups by means of one-way analysis of covarience.

TEST	13-year-old boys	13-year-old girls	16-year-old boys	16-year-old girls
MEMORY:				
numeral memory	— 1)	—	—	—
visual memory figure 1.	—	—	—	—
visual memory figure 2.	—	—	—	—
visual memory figure 3 a.	—	—	—	p < .01 (C > E)[2]
visual memory figure 3 b.	—	—	—	—
visual memory total	—	—	—	p < .01 (C > E)
verbal memory	—	—	—	—
PERFORMANCES OF MENTAL ROUTINES:				
copying test (ability to concentrate and perceptual speed) the first half	—	—	p < .05 (E > C)[3]	p < .01 (E > C)
copying test: the second half	—	—	—	p < .01 (E > C)
copying test: total	—	—	—	p < .01 (E > C)
accuracy and attention/D_2: % of the mistakes	p < .05 (C > E)	—	—	—
THINKING				
thinking fluency: the first itme	—	—	—	—
thinking fluency: the second item	—	—	—	—
thinking fluency: total	—	—	—	—

1) — = no significant differences between the experimental and the control group
2) C > E = the control group performed better than the experimental group
3) E > C = the experimental group performed better than the control group

146

4. Methods of analysis

One-way analysis of covariance was used to find out the effects of pause gymnastics. ANCOVA makes it possible to compare the post-test results of the experimental and control groups by holding constant differences observed in the pre-test between the groups. The amount of subjects decreased because of sick absences with a few cases but was still sufficient.

RESULTS

The results concerning the test of *cognitive performances* indicated that pause gymnastics had a positive effect on the ability to concentrate and perceptual speed (copying test) of the 16-year-old girls and boys ($p < .05$ - $p < .01$). When we subtract from the results the effect of learning between the first and the last measurements, the alerting effect of pause gymnastics varies between 8-12%.

Pause gymnastics did not affect memory performances. A contradictory finding was that in visual reproduction 16-year-old girls of the control group improved their performance more than the experimental group ($p < .01$). Further 13-year-old boys of the control groups performed better in the accuracy and attention-span test than the experimental group ($p < .05$ see table 1.).

The results — excluding one exception — indicated that pause gymnastics has more improving effects on performances of those who seldom have leisure time physical activities than on pupils who often have those interests. In all the comparison groups those who seldom have physical activities improved more in visual reproduction ($p < .05$ - $p < .01$). Similarly with the 16-year old boys' ability to concentrate and perceptual speed. The only exception is in the 13-year-old girls' divergent productive thinking in the first and last part of the test. Those who often have physical activities improved here more (table 2).

TABLE 2. The effects of pause gymnastics on pupils who often have leisure time physical activities and on those who seldom have them. The results of one-way analysis of covariance.

TEST	13-year-old boys	13-year-old girls	16-year-old boys	16-year-old girls
MEMORY				
numeral memory	—[1]	—	—	—
visual memory figure 1.	—	—	—	—
visual memory figure 2.	—	—	—	—
visual memory figure 3 a.	—	—	—	—
visual memory figure 3 b.	$p < .01$ (S > 0)	$p < .01$ (S > 0)	$p < .01$ (S > 0)[2]	—
visual memory total	—	$p < .05$ (S > 0)	—	$p < .05$ (S > 0)
verbal memory	—	—	—	$p < .05$ (S > 0)
PERFORMANCES OF MENTAL ROUTINES				
copying test (ability to concentrate and perceptual speed): the first half	—	—	—	—
copying test: the second half	—	—	$p < .05$ (S > 0)	—
copying test total	—	—	$p < .05$ (S > 0)	—
accuracy and attention/D_2: % of the mistakes	—	—	—	—
THINKING				
thinking fluency: the first item	—	$p < .05$ (0 > S)[3]	—	
thinking fluency: the second item	—	$p < .01$ (0 ≷ S)	—	—
thinking fluency: total	—	—	—	—

[1] — = no significant differences

[2] S > 0 = pupils who seldom have leisure time physical activities have improved their performances more than those who often have those interests

[3] 0 > S = pupils who often have leisure time physical activities have improved their performance more than those who seldom have those interests

The effects of pause gymnastics on pupils' subjectively assessed mental well-being concentrated on boys. In the experimental group, 13-year-old boys' feelings of pain in the back, the neck and shoulders decreased ($p < .01$). They also assessed their state of health as better than boys in the control group ($p < .01$). Sleeplessness decreased in the experimental group of 16-year-old boys ($p < .05$) and they also were able to follow teaching more attentively ($p < .01$ see table 3).

DISCUSSION

One of the most important results the finding of the pilot study was confirmed, (Vainikka et al. 1979) namely, that pause gymnastics has positive effects on performances of mental routines demanding ability to concentrate, accuracy and perceptual speed. In the pilot study this result was found in 12-year-old, and in this study in 16-year-old, girls and boys. On the basis of the results of this and the pilot study it can be concluded with considerable certainty that pause gymnastics helps pupils to concentrate on tasks demanding accuracy and perceptual speed.

Pause gymnastics did not have long term increasing effects on the capacity of memory and thinking. However in the pilot study improving effects were also found in thinking fluency measurements that were done immediately after pause gymnastics.

Another chief result can be considered the significantly more positive effect of pause gymnastics on pupils who seldom have leisure time physical activities compared with those who often have them. The result appeared in all the comparison groups, especially in visual reproduction. In 16-year-old boys the same feature was also found in copying test and in 16-year-old girls in repetition of a story.

It is remarkable that here the effect was also seen in the performances of visual memory while in the comparisons of the experimental and control groups it did not appear. This result indicates that pause gymnastics may promote pupils' physical abilities which enables better perception and also for pupils with low level of performances, offer them experiences of succeeding. Pause gymnastics may have greater use as an alerter of the inactive persons' congnitive

TABLE 3. The effects of pause gymnastics on the subjectively assessed mental well-being. Comparison between the experimental and control groups by means of one-way analysis of covarience

VARIABLE	13-year-old boys	13-year-old girls	16-year-old boys	16-year-old girls
headache	—[1]		—	—
sleeplessness	—	—	p < .05 (E >)[2]	—
stomachache	—	—	—	—
distress	—	—	—	—
pains in the back	p < .01 (E > C)—		—	—
tension	—	—	—	—
fatigue	—	—	—	—
poor appetite	—	—	—	—
Sweating of the hands		—	—	—
pains in the shoulder girdle	p < .01 (E > C)	—	—	—
oppression	—	—	—	—
stiffening of the limbs	—	—	—	—
indisposition	—	—	—	—
nervousness	—	—	—	—
the sum index of psychosomatic symptomps	—	—	—	—
• the state of health	p < .01 (E·> C)	—	—	—
• evaluations how pupils' physical fitness suffices for school work	—	—	—	—
• state of mind when living school	—	—	—	—
• how long pupils are able to follow attentively teaching	—	—	p < .01 (E > C)	—
• evaluation of alertness	p < .05 (C > E)	p < .05 (C > E)[3]	—	—

[1] — = no significant differences between the experimental and the control group
[2] E > C = the experimental group performed better than the control group
[3] C > E = the control group performed better than the experimental group.

performances.

It was noticed as the third chief result that pause gymnastics' effects on subjectively assessed mental well-being concentrated primarily on boys.

Pause gymnastics, through relaxation and addition of flexibility, had a curing effect on the pains in the back and shoulder girdle of the 13-year-old boys. These were almost the only symptoms that boys had more often than girls.

In 16-year-old boys the positive effects of pause gymnastics concentrate on psychic functions such as how long pupils are able to attentively follow teaching, and on sleeplessness. This result implicates better resistance to stress through heightened physical condition.

IMPLICATIONS

If the members of school are interested in activities like this pause gymnastics may be recommended as a means to increase alertness during school hours.

• pause gymnastics as a regularly recurring daily activity because it facilitates pupils' concentration on school tasks
• the alerting effects of pause gymnastics are higher on the pupils who seldom have leisure time physical activities than on those who often have them
• pause gymnastics may prevent and correct strain symptoms on shoulder girdle like feelings of pains in the back, the neck and shoulders
• pupils, especially poor ones, get practice and learn new skills

Practical guides:

• It should be mainly used as relaxing exercises to achieve an optimal level of alertness in schoolwork
• concerning practical guides music (tapes, records, accompaniment) stimulates
• the instructor of pause gymnastics may be the teacher of physical education, other teachers and older pupils.

Pause gymnastics during school years may promote positive attitudes and develop abilities to perform conditioning exercises in free time and pause gymnastics later. Pause gymnastics could be carried out more than is now done, not only at school but also at work because it decreases stress at work and increases productivity.

REFERENCES

NIFONTOVA, L. (1962) Investigation of the effectiveness of industrial exercise for people in mental work. Index and abstracts of foreign physical education literature, 9, 75.

PROKOP, L. (1972) Ausgleichsport und produktivität. Leibesubungen — Leibeserziehung, 4, 74-77.

TIAINEN, J., VAINIKKA, M. & LINTUNEN, T. (1980) Effects of pause gymnastics held daily during one term on pupils' psychic alertness and physical fitness. Paper presented at the ICSPE Congress of Sport in Modern Society, 10. — 16.7.1980 in Tbilisi.

VAINIKKA, M., TIAINEN, J. & VEISTOLA, J. (1979) Physical performance and alertness at school of schoolchildren. (English abstract) Stadion (16) 3:86.

WOJCIECZAK, I., LAMERS, H. & POBUDKOWSKI, A. (1967) Physiological and psychological researches upon active rest in factories. HPESR Abstracts vol. 10, No. 4 — 241, 612:796.

PHYSICAL ACTIVITIES IN RETIREMENT AGE

Pepa Pueyo Uson and
Vincente Rubio Larrosa (Spain)

INTRODUCTION

During the last few years we have been witnessing the creation in developed countries of communities the average age of which is progressively older due, on the one hand, to an ever increasing life expectancy thanks to an improved diet and to the development of medical investigation and, on the other, to an ever decreasing number of births, it being possible to find nations where the birth rate is the same as or even lower than that applying to deaths.

In addition, at the present day retirement age is reached earlier than in other periods in history, all this in a society which is becoming increasingly more competitive and in which the profitability of the individual is more highly considered; a society which is subject to constant change and which, as far as individual persons are concerned, demands a great capacity for accomodation and adaptation.

Because of all this, and in agreement with my teacher (Prof. A. Sava Diaz), the elderly person finds himself up against problems and a situation which act upon his psychical makeup in a negative fashion, plunging him into psycho-pathological situations of an especially reactive nature and with a depressive-anxiety content. Problems such as loneliness, the nearness of death, sickness, general decline, retirement, insufficient economic means, the increasingly progressive dehumanization of the structures and of the rhythm of life in the cities, the breaking up of his previous family circle, the widowed state, all these are none other than some of the many problems which beset retirement age with such terrible dramatism. The sudden inactivity brought about by retirement after many years of his life devoted to work having a negative effect on the elderly person, make him feel uneasy with respect to the large amount of spare time he has at his disposal.

In the field of Sports Medicine much has been done in the way of work and studies carried out in an attempt to improve the pathological situation of the elderly; the prevention of cardiopathies, obesity, respiratory problems, amelioration of arthritis and arthrosis, etc., but there are few studies which have been carried out with the idea of improving the situation of the elderly from the psychosocial and psychosomatic point of view, that is to say, the improvement of their mental health.

MATERIAL AND METHODS

In view of the foregoing considerations, we planned the carrying out of a study — which would show whether physical and sports activities could be made use of as therapeutic techniques which would ameliorate the psychosomatic problems — and which would improve the social adaptation of the elderly and, as well, their life expectancy.

For this purpose, we formed a group of 30 persons, 19 women and 11 men, between the ages of 60 and 80, attending two weekly sessions devoted to physical and sports activities during a period of nine consecutive months. The sessions, which lasted one hour, were supervised by a specialized teacher.

The sessions were divided into a preliminary part devoted to warming-up exercises and, following on this, psychomotivity activities were carried out for the improvement of coordination, the improvement of reflexes, laterality, time and space orientation, etc. After this, there followed a series of corrective gymnastic exercises for improving the gait, treatment of cyphosis and spinal column problems and as well, the strengthening of the abdominal wall and exercises of elasticity and, finally, a run taken at a slow pace lasting 10 minutes.

At the start of the experiment, all those attending were medically examined for eliminating a possible organic pathology which might contraindicate the participation of these persons in the sessions.

Once the medical examination had been passed, they were given a folder with a series of questionnaires which they themselves had to administer. The folder contained:

1. An original questionnaire which we had drawn up for this study.
2. Zung's Scale referring to the depression index.
3. Langner's Psychical Health Scale, greatly used in epidemiological studies.
4. Bell's adult adaptation questionnaire.
5. A follow-up card where they had to indicate the occasions on which they visited the doctor and the diagnosis given them by the same.
6. A questionnaire regarding the motivations which led these persons to enrol for this course of physical education.

In addition, at the beginning of the experiment a test was carried out for the appraisal of the psychomotor state of the participants. This test, drawn up by us, was prepared with an adaptation of some items of Ozeretsky's motor tests.

Running parallel to the first, another group was formed of persons in the same age bracket and in identical proportions as far as sex was concerned. This group was formed by visiting clubs for elderly and retired persons and which are institutions where people of advanced years may go to spend their leisure time. These institutions are both private and state run bodies.

This group was formed as a control group, for comparing the results obtained with the first one in regard to the normal population; as in the case of the first group, they were given another folder with the aformentioned tests and questionnaires, and though they were not given No. 6, — the questionnaire concerning the motivations — which led these persons to enrol for these courses of Physical Education, and nor were they made the object of the psychomotor appraisal, as the control group did — nor take part in the sessions of Physical Education.

When the period of nine months, the time during which our experiment had lasted, had come to an end, we re-distributed the questionnaires and tests, both to the group which had regularly attended the two weekly sessions of physical and sports activities and, as well, to the control group which had not carried out any type of programmed physical and sports activities.

None of the persons belonging to either of the two groups which we studied had indulged in organized sport or had taken part in official competitions throughout the whole of his or her life span.

RESULTS

We here below list the results obtained in each one of the tests and questionnaires administered to both groups; in order to make it easier to understand the data, we shall call the group consisting of those persons who had attended the course of physical and sports activities Group A and the group consisting of the persons who had not attended the course of physical and sports activities Group B.

Analysing questionnaire No. 1, drawn up by us especially for this study, we obtained the following significant data:

149

Social class: Group A —Middle   Group B -Lower middle
Widowed state: Group A — 15 women, 3 men/Group B —
  10 women and 6 men
Living alone: Group A — 19   Group B — 10
How many years is it thought they will live: (life expectancy) (average years)
  Group A — 8.5 years   Group B — 8.3 years
Average age: Group A — 70.8 years   Group B — 71.6 years
Educational levels: G.A. Primary education: 16
                         Secondary education: 10
                         Higher education: 4

                    G.B. Primary education: 19
                         Secondary education: 9
                         Higher education: 2

Emigrants: Group A: 8
           Group B: 17
With psychiatric treatment: Group A: 12
                            Group B: 5

After the nine months, life expectancy was an average of 10.1 years for Group A and 7.9 years for Group B.

Zung's questionnaire referring to the depression index; at the start of the experiment, the indexes are high for both groups, indicative of clear depressive traits, logical at this age, the highest indexes coinciding with those persons living alone; after the follow-up period Group A improved its indexes in 70% of its individuals whilst Group B got worse in 40%, a fact which gives an idea of the rapid deterioration of these persons.

With regard to questionnaire No. 3, Langner's psychical health scale, after the follow-up period of nine months, 60% of the individuals in Group A have an improved index; an interesting piece of information is that those who most improve are the widowers and those who live alone. In Group B, 25% are worse and the most affected are also the widowers and those living alone.

The appraisal of questionnaire No. 4, Bell's adult adaptation test, which consists of 160 questions and which, after correction, indicate the adaptation of the individual to his or her family circle, to his or her health, social, emotional and professional adaptation, and total or global, dividing the same in Excellent, Good, Normal, Unstatisfactory and Bad; as is logical, in this study we shall ignore the items referring to professional adaptation as they were unable to be the object of appraisal due to all the individuals concerned being retired persons; drawing up a summerized table, the results are, at the beginning of the experiment: (   ), the arrows indicating if it is low or high:

	Group A	Group B
Family adaptation	Normal ↓	Unsatisfactory ↑
Health "	Unsatisfactory ↑	Unsatisfactory ↓
Social "	Normal ↓	Unsatisfactory ↑
Emotional "	Bad ↑	Unsatisfactory ↓
Total or Global "	Unsatisfactory ↑	Unsatisfactory ↓

On finishing the study the results are:

	Group A	Group B
Family adaptation	Normal ↓	Unsatisfactory ↑
Health "	Normal ↓	Bad ↑
Social "	Normal ↑	Unsatisfactory ↓
Emotional "	Unsatisfactory ↑	Unsatisfactory ↓
Total or Global "	Normal ↓	Unsatisfactory ↓

With reference to the follow-up card (5) the results:

At the start of the experiment:
  a. visits to the doctor during the previous 9 months (average)

     Group A: 6.5
     Group B: 5.3

  b. diagnoses on the occasion of these visits of a psychosomatic or neurotic character:

Group A: 63%
Group B: 57%

Results at the end of the experiment:
  a. Group A: 3.7
     Group B: 5.5
  b. Group A: 47%
     Group B: 59.3%

With reference to questionnaire (6) regarding the motivations for enrolling for this Course of Physical Education. The results coincide completely with the investigation cited by Dr. R. Guillet in his Manual of Sports Medicine, the summary of which is:

- in the majority of cases, (23, amongst all the women) they came because of an aesthetic preoccupation with the question of overweight.
- maintenance of their physical condition, enabling them to grow old better.
- nostalgia for an active youth now past, not an indication of still existing physical possibilities.
- search for a lost equilibrium through physical education.

In addition to the above, in our results there appears a reply which is almost generalized; those asked indicate that they engage in physical education as a positive means of making use of the many hours of leisure which they have due to their enforced inactivity.

Once the experiment was over, it was highly significant that of the 23 who were worried about their weight, only 4 maintained this attitude whilst the remainder came to understand that physical and sports activities had functions which were more important than an aesthetic improvement, such as, for example, the improvement in their health, in their resistance, in their aggressiveness.

Those who, at the beginning, had yearned for their lost youth, learned to accept their own limitations, logical at their age, and they took an interest in their recent activity without making comparisons with past periods in their lives.

The appraisal of the psychomotor test gave us some highly significant results, such as that 26 of the 30 persons taking part had improved their psychomotor characteristics.

CONCLUSIONS

The conclusions arrived at after the carrying out of the comparative study are of great significance, so much so that one is able to affirm that physical and sports activities for persons of advanced years are vital for improving the mental health of such persons and, what seems to us even more important, for drastically reducing the pathological alterations of a psychosomatic type brought on by the problem of retirement age, and all this justifies the necessity of generously increasing those activities and organizations aimed at favouring the promotion of physical and sports activities for these persons.

Physical activities serve as a clear self-assertion of the individual, all the more so when society has already decided to do without him or her.

Neurotic and depressive traits are found to be much improved.

Those persons living alone improve because they have an opportunity to communicate with other members of the group.

The disappearance of psychosomatic pathology and of the fewer visits to the doctor are highly significant.

The carrying out of physical and sports activities delays and even arrests the normal social-type aging process.

The ability to do exercises considered by them as being impossible makes them feel younger, increasing their life expectancy.

Moderate competitions enables them to self-assert their personality.

Physical activities reconcile the individual with his own body, and, to a great extent, enable him or her to avoid acquiring complexes relating to obesity and bodily aspect.

REFERENCES

Antonelli, F. Psicologia dello sport, F.M.S.I. Roma 1966

Chauchard, P. La fatiga — Oikos Tau, Barcelona.

Ey, H. Bernard, P. Tratado de Psiquiatria, Toray Masson, Barcelona.

Layman, E. Psychological effects of physical activities. Exercise and sport sciences reviews, 1974.

Guillet, R. Medicina del Deporte, Toray Masson, Bareclona 1978

Millon, Th. Psicopatalogia Moderna, Salvat. Barcelona 1976

O.M.S. Capacidad optima de rendimiento fisico en adulto, informe tecnoco de l O.M.S. No.436, Ginebra 1969

Rubio V. Marco, N. Aznar, P. Estudio psicosocial de la tercera edad.

Rubio Larrosa, V. Tercera y deporte, Jornadas de Higiene Mental 1981

Rubio Larrosa, V. La unidad de actividades fisicas en el hospital psiquiatrico. I Congreso Nacional de Psiquiatria Social, Madris 1981.

Seva Diaz, A. Psiquiatria Clinica, Espaxs, Barcelona 1979.

REAPPRENDRE A ETRE A TRAVERS SON CORPS AU TROISIEME AGE

Hélène Dallaire (Canada)

L'idéologie d'efficacité, de productivité et de profit pèse parfois lourd sur des groupes d'une société industrialisée. Par exemple, les personnes âgées devenues improductives ou du moins considérées comme telles, se sentent exclues d'une telle société. "La société matérialiste de la croissance, du profit, a condamné la vieillesse parce qu'elle était inutile, parce qu'elle ne produisait plus". (Vellas, 1974:8) Lochet (1972) souligne le fait d'une immense importance dont nous n'avons pas fini de mesurer les conséquences: "En deux siècles, la durée moyenne de la vie humaine a plus que doublé. D'autre part, l'abaissement progressif de l'âge obligatoire de la retraite, impose, à des personnes encore bien portantes tant au plan physiologique qu'intellectuel, un nombre grandissant d'années de vie d'exclusion. "Le drame et la contradiction de ce temps que nous vivons est précisément que l'on donne de plus en plus d'années de vie à une multitude de gens, mais que personne ne sait plus leur dire comment les remplir". (Lochet, 1972: 35) Ainsi, le troisième âge pose à la société technique des questions auxquelles elle ne sait pas répondre. En même temps qu'elle lui assure parfois des conditions de vie meilleures, la société contemporaine tend par ses orientations les plus profondes à dévaloriser la vieillesse.

La société n'est pas seule responsable de cette exclusion. Les personnes âgées d'elles-mêmes, de par l'angoisse qu'elles éprouvent face à l'usure de la santé, à une situation financière insuffisante et un sentiment de rejet développent parfois un caractère difficile. Selon le mot de Vellas, (1974) elles "s'entourent d'une sorte de carapace, s'efforcent de ne pas être sensibles à tout ce qui les entoure, s'habituent à une dureté qui devient naturelle et qui est sans doute favorisée par un lourd passé de souffrance".

Si par son matérialisme notre société tend à enlever toute raison de vivre aux personnes du troisième âge, par l'éducation elle a le devoir de favoriser l'épanouissement humain de ces personnes. Selon Le Boulch, (1961) l'éducation doit permettre à l'homme de se situer et d'agir dans le monde en transformation par une meilleure connaissance et acceptation de soi, un meilleur ajustement de la conduite, une véritable autonomie et l'accès à la responsabilité dans le cadre de la vie sociale. Comprise dans ces termes, l'éducation est de tous les âges. D'une part, l'individu évoluant dans une société de plus en plus automatisée se sent de plus en plus dépersonnalisé, d'autre part le même individu ne voulant pas succomber au joug des pressions constantes de son environnement doit réagir en essayant de préserver son identité constamment menacée. Cette double prise de conscience place la personne devant la question du comment remédier à cette situation.

Lors du 7ième Congrès International des Universités du troisième âge en août 1980, Gilbert Leclerc s'exprimait ainsi: "Réapprendre à être voilà quel pourrait être l'objectif primordial de l'éducation de la personne âgée". Il poursuivait:

> Mais il existe un apprentissage ou mieux un désapprentissage préalable à faire: se départir des fausses images de la vieillesse, des stéréotypes sociaux, des attitudes négatives qui empêchent souvent la personne âgée d'atteindre un fonctionnement optimal.

C'est précisément dans cet esprit que nous concevons l'activité physique comme une force d'intervention auprès du troisième âge. L'activité physique ayant toujours été conçue pour les jeunes et réservée à eux, il nous semble particulièrement opportun à un moment dans notre société où nous parlons de participation et de démocratisation de se conscientiser à l'importance de son *corps* car ce dernier constitue un instrument de communication, un moyen de relation. Travailler avec son corps, c'est engager dans l'action sa propre personnalité, à travers le geste, l'attitude, la mimique, le contact, toute cette communication infraverbale qui parle le langage direct d'une relation authentique. Toutefois l'évidence scientifique nous démontre qu'avec l'âge le processus de détérioration physiologique s'amorce. Afin de retarder les effets de ce déclin biologique nous provilégions la théorie de l'activité (physique) invitant le retraité à trouver des substituts aux rôles perdus par de nouvelles activités afin de minimiser les effets négatifs de la retraite ou de l'abandon du foyer par les enfants. La vieillesse

> n'est plus considérée comme le temps de l'immobilité..., mais elle représente le temps privilégié...le temps du perpétuel loisir... Désormais la retraite est le temps de la vitalité et de la participation (Guillemard, 1974, p.72).

Voyons, à partir de quelques résultats de recherche, pourquoi nous la provolégions: Des remarques faites par Allport (1961), Snyder et Kivlin (1974) ainsi que Jourard et Secord (1955) révèlent que toute expérience humaine se réfère à l'expérience corporelle et que notre corps interagit constamment avec l'environnement.

L'être humain, jeune ou vieux, contitue une entité multidimensionnelle (L'Ecuyer, 1975). L'image corporelle est partie intégrante de la personnalité et agit comme un cadre de référence influençant les modes de perception d'un individu, de même que son comportement (Fisher & Cleveland, 1960). Hunt (1964) suggère que l'image corporelle est l'instrument par lequel les individus entrent en contact avec les autres et le monde extérieur en général. Schilder la définit ainsi: "The picture of our own body which we form in our mind, that is to say the way in which the body appears to ourselves". Selon Jourard (1963), l'individu évalue son corps selon la connaissance qu'il en a et exprime de la satisfaction ou de l'insatisfaction à son égard. Toutes ses perceptions, ses croyances et ses attentes vis-à-vis la structure, les fonctions et l'apparence de son corps dépendent de son image corporelle. Kreitler et Kreitler (1967) soucieux de l'influence du vieillissement sur l'image corporelle disent que les personnes de plus de cinquante ans et physiquement inactives perçoivent leur corps plus gros et plus lourd qu'il ne l'est en réalité.

> They therefore experience their bodily activities as increasingly strenuous, thus establishing a faulty feedback between movement and body image and with it a vicious circle through which a progressive restriction of physical exercise leads to a corresponding alteration of their body image.

Ainsi, si l'image corporelle est une composante fondamentale de la personnalité et l'âge entraîne possiblement sa distorsion, il nous apparaît dès lors d'être physiquement actif tout au long de la vie. C'est ici que se situe l'importance de l'activité physique pour les personnes âgées car en plus d'agir positivement sur l'image corporelle (Harris, 1972, Dayries et Grimm, 1970), elle procure selon Kreitler et Kreitler (1967) une profonde satisfaction émotionnelle et recrée chez le participant un sentiment de sécurité tout en permettant de ne pas intérioriser des tendances agressives.

Cowgill et Baulch (1964) mettant l'accent sur le double phénomène d'une longévité plus grande associée à la retraite qui se prendra à un âge plus jeune, suggère le fait que nous faisons face à une nouvelle classe, celle du leisure class. Ainsi,si les gen âgés ne veulent pas se sentir seuls, ils devront s'impliquer dans des activités de loisir organisées de façon à éviter des moments de dépression profonde dans leur temps libre.

Sherman (1974) confirme ces résultats de Cowgill et Baulch quant à l'utilisation du temps de loisir par les personnes âgées: chez des personnes âgées vivant en institution on retrouve une relation positive entre le degré d'activité de l'individu et sa façon de concevoir la vie en général.

Corbin (1977) indique que les personnes âgées qui sont actives ont tendance à se sentir mieux et ont recours à des soins médicaux moins fréquemment que ceux qui vivent de façon sédentaire et isolée. De plus, (1977) faisant allusion aux difficultés psychologiques auxquelles sont exposées les personnes âgées, telle la perte d'une personne chère, la perte de prestige et d'influence, la diminution de statut accompagnée habituellement d'une diminution de salaire, Corbin (1977) suggère qu'à cause de toutes ces raisons les personnes âgées devraient rester actives afin de maintenir un équilibre.

De Carlo (1974) démontre, après avoir étudié 60 sujets dont la moyenne d'âge était de 85.5 ans et qui furent suivis pendant 20 ans, qu'il y a une relation significative entre la participation à des activités récréatives et le processus du vieillissement.

Sydney et Shephard (1976) ayant fait une étude avec cent vingt-quatre personnes âgées impliquées dans un programme de conditionnement physique de quatorze semaines ont découvert des améliorations et arrivent aux conclusions suivantes:

> 83% of subjects reported improvements in well-being, but there was a decrease on Manifest Anxiety (Taylor Scale) and a greater regard

for physical activity as the relief of tension. Persons who trained frequently and intensively showed improvements for body image and for five of Kenyon's attitude scales.

Une étude de Springer (1973) avec les personnes âgées démontre qu'il y a chez cette clientèle un besoin de discuter de leurs problèmes avec les autres; ils veulent être entendus et sont prêts à s'impliquer et à s'engager.

Même s'il existe peu de recherches quant à l'effet de l'activité physique sur le concept de soi des personnes âgées, celles qui existent prennent une signification particulière pour les gens intéressés à aider des personnes âgées. Gayle Thompson (1972) dit que les personnes appelées à travailler avec les gens du troisième âge devraient s'efforcer de porter une grande attention au phénomène loisir chez cette clientèle. Elle est d'avis qu'en stimulant l'engagement social des personnes âgées, il y a possibilité d'améliorer leurs perceptions quant à leur santé et par conséquent leur moral.

Face à cette position adoptée par Thompson, et au fait qu'il existe peu d'études sur l'influence de l'activité physique sur la personne âgée, le présent auteur a fait l'investigation systématique de l'influence d'un programme de conditionnement physique sur la perception de soi de personnes âgées. Les principales conclusions qui ressortent de cette étude se résument ainsi:

L'activité en général rehausse le moral de l'individu et fait en sorte que l'individu se sent plus efficace plus productif et moins seul. Alors que l'étude quantitative des résultats nous révèle une dimunuation dans le taux de verbalisation dans les structures soi personnel, soi adaptif et soi social lors du post-test, l'étude qualitative nous révèle que la qualité des énoncés dans ces trois structures est plus positive lors du post-test, c'est-à-dire qu'il y a après le programme, une augmentation du pourcentage d'énoncés positifs et une diminution de pourcentage d'énoncés négatifs. Il semble donc d'une part que le programme ait accentué et amélioré la perception de soi au niveau de la structure soi matériel; d'autre part, qu'il ait diminué mais quand même amélioré la perception de soi au niveau des structures soi personnel, soi adaptif et soi social.

Une deuxième recherche de Dallaire (1980) menée avec le même groupe de sujets 21 mois après la fin du programme avait pour objectif de vérifier si les changements opérés au niveau de la perception de soi du groupe à l'étude avaient été des changements durables. Après une analyse des protocoles d'entrevue, l'auteur arrive à la constatation suivante: Les changements opérés ont été peu durables car:

a) Quantitativement, le taux de verbalisation des sujets est sensiblement le même dans les structures soi personnel, soi adaptif et soi social, à l'exception de la structure soi matériel où il est plus élevé que lors du pré-test administré deux ans auparavant, c'est à dire avant le début du programme de conditionnement physique.

b) Qualitativement, les sujets se décrivent plus négativement dans les structures soi matériel, soi personnel, soi adaptif et soi social deux ans après l'expérience du programme.

Dallaire est portée à croire en effet que d'une part le programme a eu une influence très positive sur la perception de soi du groupe à l'étude, et d'autre part, à justifier l'importance d'assurer une continuité au niveau de ces programmes pour les personnes âgées. Enfin ces résultats obtenus dans ces deux études tendent à corroborer les résultats de recherches cités auparavant. A cet effet, l'activité physique au troisième âge peut constituer une novelle forme d'intervention voulant que l'individu réapprenne à être à travers son corps. Par conséquent, nous croyons que l'activité physique peut sensibiliser les personnes âgées à l'importance de leur condition physique et permettre qu'elles se décrivent plus en fonction de leurs ressources (ma condition physique, mes goûts, mes aspirations) qu'en fonction des autres (soi possessif). Se décrire en fonction des autres indique à notre avis, la dépendance et le manque d'autonomie. De plus, nous avons la conviction que l'activité physique peut permettre à la personne âgée de prendre conscience de l'importance de conserver un bon état de santé et de constater que l'activité physique peut constituer une stratégie d'adaptation permettant de contrecarrer les effets provoqués par l'amorce d'un processus de détérioration au plan physiologique, entraînant par conséquent possiblement une détérioration psychologique.

Ainsi, si l'un des objectifs de l'éducation prmanente en 1980 est de réapprendre à être, il nous apparaît devoir faire face à des propositions et des méthodologies nouvelles. Nous devons de plus, penser dès maintenant à de nouvelles formules d'intervention en faveur des personnages âgées. A la lumière de ces quelques résultats de recherche l'activité physique par le biais de l'image corporelle constitue dès lors le tremplin de départ pour un réapprentissage à être à travers son corps.

Bibliographie

Corbin, D., *Brighter Vistas for Senior Citizens: Salient Thoughts*, dans *J.O.H.P.E.R.*, octobre 1977.

Cowgill et Baulch, *The Use of Leisure Time by Older People*, dans *The Gerontologist*, 1964, vol. 2(1), p. 47-50.

Dayries, J.L. et R.L. Grimm, *Oersinality Traits of Women Athletes as Measured by the Edwards Personal Preference Schedule*, dans *Perceptual and Motor Skills*, 1970, vol. 30, p. 229-230.

De Carlo, Thomas J., *Recreation Participation Patterns and Successful Aging*, dans *Journal of Gerontology*, 1974, vol. 29, no. 4, p. 416-422.

Fisher, S. et S.E. Cleveland, *Body Image and Personality*, Princeton, Van Nostrand Co. Inc., 1958, 567 p.

Guttmann, David, *Leisure Time Activity Interest of Jewish Aged*, dans *The Gerontologist*, 1973, vol. 12, no. 3, p. 219-223.

_____, *A Somato-Psychic Rationale for Physical Activity Involvement*, Chicago, W.B. Saunders Co., 1972.

Hunt, V., *Movement Behavior: A Model for Action*, *Quest*, Monograph II, 1964, p. 69-91.

Ismail, A.H. et L.E. Trachtman, *Jogging the Imagination*, dans *Psychology Today*, février 1971, p. 18.

Jourard, S.M. et P.F. Secord, *Body Cathexis and Personality*, dans *British Journal of Psychology*, 1955, vol. 46, no. 2, p. 130-138.

Kreitler, H. et S.H. Kreitler, *Movement and Aging: A Psychological Approach*, dans *Medicine and Sport*, vol. 4: Psychical Activity and Aging, p. 302-306.

Le Boulch, Jean, *L'Education par le Mouvement*, Paris, Editions Sociales Françaises, 1961.

Leclerc, Gilbert, "La Personne Agée Face à l'Education Permanente", 7ième Congrès International des Universités du Troisième Age, Sherbrooke, 1980, p. 4.

L'Ecuyer, René, *La Genèse du Concept de Soi, Théroie et Recherches*, Sherbrooke, Collection Psycho-Péda, Editions Namaan, 1975, 344 p.

L'Ecuyer, René, *Le Concept de Soi*, Paris, Presses Universitaires de France, 1978, 211 p.

Lochet, L., *Principaux Exposés, Congrès de Poissy*, C.T.I.C., Paris, 1972, 64 p.

Schilder, P., *The Image and Appearance of the Human Body*, New York, International Univcersities Press, 353 p.

Secord, P.F. et S.M. Jourard, *The Appraisal of Body Cathexis: Body Cathexis and the Self*, dans *Journal of Consulting Psychology*, 1953, vol. 17, no. 5, p. 343-347.

Secord, P.F., *Objectification of Word Association Procedures of the Use of Homonyms: A Measure of Body Cathexis*, dans *Journal of Personality*, 1953, vol. 21, no. 4, p. 479-495.

Sherman, Susan, R., *Leisure Activities in Retirement Housing*, dans *Journal of Gerontology*, 1974, vol. 29, no. 3, p. 325-335.

Snyder, Eldon E. et Joseph E. Kivlin, *A Study of Women Athletes and Aspects of the Feminine Role, Psychological Well-Being and Body Image*, dans *The British Society of Sports Psychology Annual Conference*, 8th Proceedings, England, septembre 1974, p. 118-137.

Springer, D.G., *A Study of the Relationship Between the Self-Concept and the Adjustment of Aging of a Selected Urban Population*, dans *Dissertation Abstracts*, 1973, vol. 33B-5, p. 1865B-2419B.

Sydney, K.H. et Roy J. Shephard, *Attitudes Towards Health and Physical Activity in the Elderly: Effects of a Physical Training Program*, dans *Medicine and Science in Sport*, 1976, vol. 8, no. 4, p. 246-252.

Thompson, G.B., *Adjustment in Retirement: A Causal Interpretation of Factors Influencing the Morale of Retired Men*, dans *Dissertation Abstracts*, 1972, vol. 33A-1, p. 402.

Vellas, Pierre, *Les Chances du Troisième Age*, Paris, Stock, 1974, 216 p.

Wray, Stephen D., *The Social Factors Associated with the Happiness and Mental Health of People in the Middle Years and Early Old Age*, dans *Dissertation Abstracts*, 1975, vol. 36A-3, p. 1848A.

EDUCATION AND THERAPEUTIC APPLICATIONS OF RUNNING

H. Keith McConnell (USA)

This article presents a description of how the experience of running has been incorporated as an integral part of both an educational program in clinical psychology and a therapy program for personal growth. In an educational context the course "Running As An Adjunct to Group Therapy" is for students pursuing a Master's degree in psychology in one of the applied areas of counselling or mental health practice.

In a typical class, I meet with the students (8-12 in number) about 9 times for 2½ hours plus a couple of extended sessions. With rare exceptions, we run together during each meeting, usually during the first part of class. A run, which might involve a short drive first, could be anywhere from 20 minutes to an hour or more and would periodically include some facilitating guidelines or exercises by myself as instructor, e.g., run alone in silence, run in couples with one person leading, vary strides, focus on breathing, run with certain images. Initially I observe the students' running styles and encourage them to increase their own self-awareness without much direction just as I allow the process of the group to unfold with members taking an active part in their own personal growth. Subsequently I provide input and suggest ways they can experiment with their running. After our run, we function as a group and explore the experience with focus on material stimulated by the run be it personal, interpersonal, or group level in nature.

The inclusion of running in certain group courses consistently generates personal issues and group themes directly relevant to the kind of education and training that we are trying to provide. Students report experiencing and learning about a spectrum of issues such as self-confidence, body/mind relations, competition, trust, inclusion/exclusion, and cohesiveness. In comparison to other groups I have conducted, these issues come up faster and with more emotional charge when running is a central and shared vehicle to the group's development. The group interaction and structured awareness exercises assist the students in the process of making connections between the running experience and other parts of their lives, e.g., the resistances experienced in relation to running frequently are found to parallel other similar life patterns of avoidance, and significant personal changes are reported to occur.

When taught as a university course, the preceeding activities are supplemented with readings, class discussion, and student assignments. It is via the assignments that I have become aware of some of the unique features and pay-offs of this approach to learning since I design them to cover the full range from personal to theoretical. In the more advanced group classes in which I include the elements of leadership training, consultation, and program design, innovative student proposals have been developed, and sometimes carried out, which integrate running with more traditional verbal approaches in a variety of mental health settings. To date, feedback on the courses has been very favorable. The consensus from papers, interviews, and formal research seems to be that running has considerable value as an adjunct to this kind of learning experience.

The Running and Personal Growth workshop and the Running and Therapy Groups that I lead or co-lead are based upon a model similar to the educational one already described. Once the general design and procedure is established, it is not difficult to vary it somewhat according to the specific goals and client needs for a particular situation. Thus, for a group geared to serve people who are struggling with the discomforts of stress or depression, extra attention would be directed to the dynamics of these issues. For example, the facilitation in the running phase could be structured to bring awareness to the experience of physical and/or emotional stress while the post-run discussions could provide space for a more thorough exploration of the dynamics of depression. In fact, what usually works most effectively is not to provide a structure that is tightly defined; the issues and central themes seem to come to the fore on their own accord.

The subjective reports of the clients indicate that positive personal and interpersonal changes do result from active participation in these groups. My findings seem to be consistent with work such as that by Greist (1978) who reported the

beneficial effects that running has on depression and with Diensbier (1978) who noted personality changes to be correlated with regular running activity, e.g., more energy, less anxiety and depression, and improved body image and sense of well-being. In spite of the pioneering work of such individuals and the increasing number of therapeutic applications being made of running (e.g., Higdon, 1978; Gratch, 1979), the field of running and psychology, and more specifically running and group therapy, is still relatively unexplored territory. Applications like the ones I have described would benefit from some evaluative and comparative research. The field is ripe for positive development, creative application, and controlled study. It's exciting to be a part of its evolution.

Practical Implications and Potential

1. Running is a cheap, readily available medium which can stimulate awareness at the sensory, emotional, and mental levels. As such, it is an ideal vehicle to include in applied learning or personal growth settings.
2. The community mental health field, e.g., day treatment centers and mental health facilities, could gain immensely from the skilled inclusion of running-based activities in their program.
3. Research is gathering which indicates that running, even when carried out without therapeutic support, is a positive therapeutic vehicle.
4. Running may be a representative of other such powerful, available, do-able techniques which serve to better bridge the body-mind chasm when it comes to therapy and personal learning.

REFERENCES

Diensbier, R.A.: Running and Personality Change. *Today's Jogger.* Jan., 1978, Vol. 2. #1, 3-33, 48-49.

Glasser, W.: *Positive Addiction.* New York; Harper & Row, 1976.

Gratch, S.E.: Run For Your Life. *The Running Psychologist.* Fall, 1979.

Greist, J.H., Klein, M.H., Eischens, R.R., & Faris, J.T.: Running Out of Depression. *Phys. Sportsmedicine,* Dec., 1978.

Higdon, H.: Can Running Cure Mental Illness? *Runners World,* Jan. & Feb., 1978.

Jorgenson, C.B. & Jorgenson, D.E.: Effect of Running on Perception of Self and Others. *Perceptual and Motor Skills,* 1979, *48,* 242.

Kostrubala, T.: *The Joy of Running.* Philadelphia; Lippincott, 1976.

Sacks, M.H. and Sachs, M.L. (Eds.) *The Psychology of Running.* Champaign, Illinois: Human Kinetics Publishers (in press).

Sheehan, G.: *Running and Being.* New York; Warner Books, 1978.

POSITIVE AND NEGATIVE ADDICTION TO RUNNING

Michael L. Sachs (Canada)
Université du Québec à Trois-Rivières

Running addiction may be defined as addiction, of a psychological and/or physiological nature, upon a regular regimen of running, characterized by withdrawal symptoms after 24-36 hours if participation is interrupted. These withdrawal symptoms appear to be critical in the determination of the degree of addiction to running. Reported withdrawal symptoms include feelings of anxiety, tension, irritability, restlessness, guilt, bloatedness, muscle twitching, and discomfort. The development of running addiction may take

place within a period of a few weeks or months, or may require as long as 20 years.

Running is generally viewed as a positive addiction. The concept of positive addiction, first popularized by Glasser (1976), views certain addictions as supportive of the individual's psychology and physiology. Positive addictions, such as running and meditation, are seen as providing psychological strength and increasing the satisfaction derived from life. Glasser's thesis is that: "Many people, weak or strong, can help themselves to be stronger, and an important new path to strength may be positive addiction". (Glasser, 1976, p. 11)

Most runners do indeed view running as a positive addiction because running is seen as providing numerous physiological and psychological benefits. The positive physiological benefits may include improved cardiovascular system functioning, reduced body weight and percent body fat, improved muscle tone, and "more energy". Numerous positive psychological benefits have been cited as well, including reduced levels of anxiety and depression, the "feel better" phenomenon, and improvements in self-confidence, feelings of control, imaginativeness, and self-sufficiency. These reported benefits help make running an important but considered aspect of the runner's life.

In negative addiction, on the other hand, running moves from this important, but considered aspect of the individual's existence, to a controlling factor, eliminating other choices in life. Symptoms of negative addiction may take form in decreased ability to concentrate, listlessness, fatigue, constant thought about running, and other subtle signs. More obvious symptoms include skipping appointments because of the need to run. The negatively addicted runner "continues to exercise even when it is medically, vocationally and socially unadvisable; he ignores pain or takes strong pain relievers, and disregards job responsibilities and family commitments".

Runners tend to be, on the whole, well educated, and many negatively addicted participants will be able to acknowledge the existence of withdrawal symptoms and the effects of running on their lives. A first step is to provide general information on the phenomenon of addiction to running, and the effects of negative addiction in particular, on the individual, and on this person's family, friends, and work. Group meetings and distribution of written information could be effectively used as part of this educational process.

Programs of therapy for those who wish to go beyond this step should be made available. The key in treating the negatively addicted runner is getting this individual to decrease the level of involvement, and learn to cope with the initial withdrawal symptoms associated with this reduction. Running would then remain an integral part of the individual's lifestyle, but one that would blend well with responsibilities of work, home, family, and other aspects of human existence.

The running therapist in these cases should be a professional who is also a runner, and who can therefore understand more "intimately" the nature of the problems encountered by the client. One particularly important task that awaits the running therapist is the development of coping strategies for the withdrawal symptoms for both positively addicted and negatively addicted runners. The use of coping strategies to help the runner with symptoms brought on during times of injury or encompassing familial or work

responsibilities that preclude participation is essential in maintaining a stable, positive relationship between the individual and running.

There are some runners, to be sure, who will make a considered decision that running is the most important thing in their lives, and therefore will take precedence over family, friends, and work responsibilities. Given that these runners are aware of the factors underlying their decision, and the control exerted by the activity, their decision is a "final" one. However, it is likely that many negatively addicted runners have not made such a conscious decision, but have crossed that fine line between positive and negative addiction without realizing that this transition was taking place. It is to these runners that help should be directed if they wish to be helped once they discover the nature of their relationship to running.

There is much still to be learned about the process by which addiction to running develops, and the specific effects of addiction on participation in running. The precise nature of the withdrawal symptoms, and strategies for coping with these must be determined. Further clarification of the fine line between positive and negative addiction must be made, and delineation of particular strategies for dealing with the negatively addicted runner may be envisioned in the future.

Practical Applications

1. Addiction to running is an important area in the psychology of running, with implications in both running therapy and adherence to participation.

2. Strategies for coping with withdrawal symptoms experienced by the addicted runner must be developed.

3. Particular strategies for working with negatively addicted runners are suggested. These strategies include education and counseling.

REFERENCES

Glasser, W.: *Positive addiction*. New York: Harper and Row, 1976.

Jacobs, L.W.: *Running as an addiction process*. Unpublished doctoral dissertation, University of Alberta, 1980.

Morgan, W.P.: Negative addicition in runners. *The Physician and Sportsmedicine*, February 1979, *7*(2), 56-63; 67-70.

Peele, S.: Addiction: The analgestic experience. *Human Nature*, September 1978, *1*(9), 61-67.

Sachs, M.L.: Running addiction. In M.H. Sacks & M.L. Sachs (Eds.), *The psychology of running*. Champaign, Illinois: Human Kinetics Publishers, 1981.

Waters, B.: Defining the runner's personality. *Runner's World*, June 1981, *16*(6), 48-51.

AGEISM: ANOTHER -ISM AFFECTING SPORT PARTICIPATION

Andrew C. Ostrow and David D. Spiker (USA)

The physiological and psychological benefits of participation in physical activity across the life cycle are well documented (Clarke, 1977; Ostrow, 1980; Shephard, 1978). Yet, there is also evidence to suggest a gradual reduction in participation in physical activity and sport with advanced age (McPherson & Kozlik, 1979; Robinson, 1967). Data from the National Adult Fitness Survey (Clarke, 1973) indicated that only 39% of Americans aged 60 or older (N=979) participated in any systematic exercise (primarily walking), and that there was a sharp decline in *vigorous* physical activity participation

with increasing age. While the better educated and more affluent members of society are more inclined to participate in physical activity, a general pattern of disengagement from physical activity and sport emerges. Apparently, the joy, beauty, and personal meaning of sport have not been universally accepted and adopted across the life course of each individual.

This paper summarizes a series of research investigations by the authors Ostrow & Spiker, 1981 (Ostrow, Jones, &

Spiker, in press; Ostrow & Spiker, in progress) that suggest that this gradual disengagement from sport and physical activity may be due, in part, to a blatant system of *age grading* of physical activity and sport. Several authors (e.g., McPherson & Kozlik, 1979; Snyder, 1980) have alluded to the potential restrictive function of age as a socially constructed category defining appropriate role behaviors, including involvement in physical activity, at specific points in the life cycle. For example, in West Virginia, the Monongalia County Consolidated Recreation Commission sponsors an "Over the Hump" Basketball League for individuals over 30 years of age. Until two years ago, one of the modified basketball rules in this league was that no "fast-breaks" were allowed. Participation in sport tournaments is primarily stratified by age. The United States Handball Association sponsors the "Golden" Master Tournament for individuals over 50 years of age. Vintage defensive linemen and linebackers formed the famous Washington Redskin professional football team "Over the Hill" gang during the 1970's.

These examples serve to illustrate that age, like race or sex, is an attribute that clearly regulates many of the normative expectations affecting participation in sport and physical activity. Age-related norms tell us that kids go to school, adults get married, and the elderly should not be interested in sex, or singles in tennis.

In two recent investigations by the authors Ostrow & Spiker,(1981), (Ostrow, Jones & Spiker, in press), college students (N=93; N=444) at West Virginia University were asked to rate how appropriate they felt it was for 8 referent persons, who varied in assigned chronological age (20, 40, 60, or 80 years old) and assigned gender, to participate in 12 designated physical activities including bowling, tennis, ballet, basketball, swimming, marathon race, bicycling, etc. For example, these subjects were asked to rate how appropriate they felt it was for an 80 year old healthy female, a 60 year old healthy male, etc., to participate in swimming (and 11 other physical activities).

Results of the 4-way univariate ANOVA across physical activity indicated that the age of the referent person (rather than the gender of the referent person) was the more potent factor influencing subjects' responses. These college students felt that participation in these physical activities was less appropriate as the age of the referent person increased from 20 to 40 to 60 to 80 years old. Generally, these subjects appeared to have clear, age-regulated social prescriptions regarding the extent to which people should be involved in physical activity as they grow older.

These preliminary investigations warn us of the self-fulfilling prophesy — i.e., if these college students view physical activity participation as less appropriate with advancing age, they may, in turn, gradually disengage from sport and physical activity as they grow older. It is apparent that through socialization, individuals acquire specific roles based on age. Older adults are typically portrayed as decrepit and toothless consumers of laxatives, denture adhesives, or sleeping pills. Aging is seen, generally, as a period of decline. We have failed to recognize that older adults can and should have fun and be physically active. After all, older adults drink Pepsi too!

Clearly, socializing agents responsible for protraying the older segment of our population as in a period of decline need to be re-defined. Older role models need to be portrayed on television as being physically active and not decrepit.

Textbooks for young children need to emphasize the relevance of physical activity across all ages. Participation in tournaments should be based on developmental experience rather than chronological age. Most important, the parents and grandparents of young people can be effective role models by maintaining and being advocates for a physically active lifestyle.

Without these changes, we run the risk of promoting ageism in sport and physical activity. Ageism -- views about aging that are discriminatory and prejudicial in nature, may parallel racism and sexism as an important social issue impacting on our profession during the coming decades. Research in progress by the authors (Ostrow & Spiker, in progress) suggest that college students may view physical activity participation as inappropriate with advancing age because of the stereotype that older adults cannot learn new skills. Clearly, research examining the motor learning capacities of older adults needs to be conducted.

If we are to promote programs of physical fitness and activity for older adults, we must be more aware of the social barriers that have precluded older adults from maintaining physically active life styles. Socialization into physical activity must occur during youth and must be continually encultured and reinforced throughout the life course of each individual. Age-related social sanctions must be eliminated if the joy, beauty, and personal meaning of sport are to be universally accepted and adopted across the life cycle.

REFERENCES

1. Clarke, H.H. (Ed.). National Adult Physical Fitness Survey. *President's Council on Physical Fitness and Sports Newsletter*, 1973, 1—27.

2. Clarke, H.H. (Ed.). Exercise and Aging. *Physical Fitness Research Digest*, 1977, 7, 1—27.

3. McPherson, B.D., & Kozlik, C.A. Canadian leisure patterns by age: Disengagement, continuity, or ageism? In V.W. Marshall (Ed.), *Aging in Canada: Social perspectives.* Pickering, Ontario: Fitzhenry & Whiteside, 1979.

4. Ostrow, A.C. Physical activity as it relates to the health of the aged. In N. Datan & N. Lohman (Eds.), *Transitions of aging.* New York: Academic Press, 1980.

5. Ostrow, A.C., Jones, D.C. & Spiker, D.D. Age role expectations and sex role expectations for selected sport activities. *Research Quarterly,* in press.

6. Ostrow, A.C., & Spiker, D.D. *The stereotyping of sport participation based on age role and sex role appropriateness.* Paper presented at the North American Society for the Psychology of Sport and Physical Activity annual convention, Monterey, Ca., 1981.

7. Ostrow, A.C. & Spiker, D.D. *Validation of a conceptual model characterizing the age role stereotyping of physical activity.* Research i progress, 1981.

8. Robinson, J. Time expenditure on sports across ten countries. *International Review of Sport Sociology,* 1967, 2, 67—87.

9. Shephard, R.J. *Physical activity and aging.* Chicago: Year Book Medical Publishers, 1978.

10. Snyder, E.E. *A reflection on commitment and patterns of disengagement from recreational physical activity.* Paper presented at the North American Society for the Sociology of Sport convention, Denver, 1980.

SPORTS MOTIVATION AND PHYSICAL ACTIVITY

Martti Silvennoinen (Finland)

INTRODUCTION

This report presents a survey of the properties of motives that are connected with Finnish schoolchildren's sports and other physical activity, and the relationship of these motives to so-called manifested physical activity. The present research was carried out in 1977—80 and financed by the Ministry of Education. The earlier results have been presented at the World Congress of Psychology of Sports held in Prague in 1977. The data have been collected by interviews of school-children of 7—9 years (N=346) and by questionnaires sent to 11—19 year-olds (N=3106).

The theoretical starting-point of the study lies in the establishing of the normativity vs. intrinsic value of motives related to sports and physical activity. To achieve this, the structures of the motives have been compared with variables describing manifested physical activity. The study does not aim at a mechanical classification of the motives into extrinsic and intrinsic ones. Rather, it is assumed that as physical activity becomes more internalised, processes which are intrinsic by form also become more controlled by consciousness.

Problem-areas of the present study

The aims of the present study are the following.

1. To find out which motives are the least goal-oriented, i.e., of the shortest duration, among school-children, and which of them retain their significance longest.[1]

2. To show the connections between the basic motive factors and the manifested activities with its internalised traits.

3. On the basis of the above mentioned study tasks, to prepare ground for the evaluation of motives especially in schools and in voluntary sport club activity.

Results of the present study

1. The motives which lost their importance most rapidly were performance-oriented motives as well as motives related to normative health and sociability. Correspondingly, the motives which remained most stable were those related to the experience of recreation and relaxation as well as the motives of outdoor activities and functional health.

1.2. A comparison of answers to open-ended vs. multiple-choice questions showed that, among the former, there was much less variation and a great number of vague or disorganised answers. In the lowest age-groups the answers to open-ended questions emphasised the intrinsic value of the activities, which indicates identification of activities and motives instead of goals and motives (for instance, "one has a chance to play", "a chance to run" or the like).

Answers which spontaneously mentioned motives expressing aesthetical experiences could only be found in answers given by girls.

2. A/D analysis [1] was used to examine the relation between the eight motive factors previously subjected to factor analysis and variables describing manifested physical activity and its internalisation. A summary of the results is given in Table 1.

[1] Observations on the differences are based on comparison of the importance significance of the motives as indicated by the different age-groups (interindividual differences). As an investigation of general motivation (so-called habitual motivation), the present study is not concerned with analysis of different situational motives and/or the intraindividual development of motives.

Motive factors		Manifested physical activity
I	Motor ability	Reasoning about interests, Participation in sports club training
II	Recreation-Relaxation	Reasoning about interests, Age (+)
III	Sociability	Frequency of physical activity, Participation in sports club... Age (—)
IV	Outdoor activities	Frequency of physical activity, Sex (girls), Participation in sports club training (—)
V	Normative health [2]	Reasoning about interests, Age (—)
VI	Performance orientation	
VII	Physical appearance	Age (—)
VIII	Functional health [3]	Reasoning about interests Intensity of physical activity Sex (boys) Participation in sports club... Frequency of physical activity

TABLE 1. Summary of the A/D analysis results

[1] Automatic Interaction Detector

[2] Eg. "Fitness exercise is everybody's duty", "healthy habits of life".

[3] Eg. "Maintaining one's health", "improving endurance".

(+) a positive relationship between factor and variable

(—) a negative relationship between factor and variable

3. Conclusions

1. In the data of the present study there appear both *normative* (see normative health) and *more intrinsic* features (see functional health) of sports and exercise motivation.

2. The significance of normative motives decreases with age.

3. For the internalisation of the motivation of physical activity as well as of manifested activity, *personal experience* plays a more decisive role than external "propaganda" or information. There is an obvious connection between motive factors and voluntary sports club physical activity.

4. *Cathartic experiences* of sport and physical activity/exercise (recreation, joy, etc.) have an obvious connection with *regular manifested* activity. In this sense they can be called conscious goals of physical exercise/activity.

5. In the present data, *social motives of the young are connected with performance orientation* and *achievement of social status*. Their importance decreases with age. However, social motives gain a new importance in adulthood.

6. The motive factor of *outdoor activities* has a specific independent character. It even stands *in opposition* to

157

physically *active* and *effective* sports club training (see table 1). Motives related to outdoor activities are in the clearest opposition to "the phenomenal world of sport" (eg. the motives of performance orientation, sociability, motor ability and functional health).

7. *Conscious* consideration (internalisation) of physical activities is most clearly related to motives expressing *regular* and *effective* exercise such as recreation-relaxation, functional health and motor ability.

8. The need of motor ability is most clear-cut with 11—13 year-olds. At this age, education or educational institutes should offer the possibility to develop many-sided physical skills.

9. The structure of the motive factor of performance orientation is most clear-cut with 17—19 year olds, which indicates *consciousness* of the competitive purpose of

physical activities. In younger age groups motives of sociability and motor ability are related to the motives of performance orientation. With age, performance orientation clearly decreases.

REFERENCES

Silvennoinen, M. (1979) 11—19 - vuotioaiden koululaisten liikuntamotiivien rakenne ja kehitys sekä yhteydet harrastuskäyttäytymiseen. (Structure and development of the physical activity motivation of 11—19 year-old pupils and its relations with pupils' interests.) P.E. Lic. thesis. Jyväskylä. University of Jyväskylä, Department of Physical Education.

Telema, R. & Silvennoinen, M. (1979) Structure and development of 11 to 19 year-olds' motivation for physical activity. Scandinavian Journal of Sports Sciences, Helsinki 1(1), 23—31.

INTERESTS IN SPORT EXPRESSED BY CHILDREN AND ADOLESCENTS

Paolo Bonaiuto and Gabriella Bartoli Bonaiuto (Italy)

For a long time, our research group has been carrying out polycentric investigations on *interests* about motor activities-especially sporting activities but also school and other recreative activities-expressed by *children, pre-adolescents* and *adolescents* of various urban centres of different cultural trends (1,2,3). We gathered a second series of data, on which we will report.

This second research was carried out in five Italian cities, from North to South (Bolzano, Milan, Bologna, Rome and Salermo). We examined 1,200 subjects in each city; in other words, 100 subjects (50 males and 50 females) for each age level from seven to eighteen years of age inclusive. The subjects constituted a representative sample of different city school students; on the whole 6,000 subjects were randomly selected. Each student completed two inventories, part verbal, part pictorial, assigned in subsequent days according to systematically assigned order.

The inventories investigated how subjects would like different kinds of activities to be organized in the school and extra-school environment.

Respondents willingly expressed their views, giving direct and indirect information on their trends, wishes, motivations, emotional valences; how they live their own experiences and make their decisions.

The results point out some practical implications of this kind of research.

1) One result pertains to the importance of interests in sport and the exact acknowledgement of the *range of preferences*. For all the motor activities, the greater part is represented by sporting ones; the subjects at every age level expressly indicated the kind of activities they preferred (number intensity and time). They also requested the opportunity to practice motor activities such as cultural and recreative sedentary activities. This kind of request could be realized in sport centres and playgrounds, with qualified teachers, according to the perspectives of development and personality.

2) A second finding pertains to the *relations* between the interests in sport and the psychological *period of development,* the *actual opportunities* and the *cultural type of values.*

It was noted that there is a characteristic way of articulating these kinds of interests. The subjects, examined in

various conditions, show their deep self-affirmative needs, in accordance to a progressive development of critical skills, also conditioned by the values of the culture where they live. This has to be considered for applicative purposes. Some cities (Salerno and Rome) are urban areas, more traditional, low industrialization levels with an economy based upon bureaucratic and artisan — agricultural activities and tourism.

In this social situation the range of interests expressed by subjects is not very ample; their choices indicate a dichotomy between free time (extra-school) activities and school activities. Most of the subjects, for example, don't plan activities common to school and playground. In urban areas, well developed, with industrial and business economy (Bolzano, Milan, and Bologna), the range of interests is more ample; the subjects show a tendency to integrate the two environments of activity; this is especially true for pre-adolescent subjects.

There is a common characteristic of adolescent personality to gather and specialize their interests. This is more clearly evident where people have poor opportunities.

So the interests in sporting activities reflect the various human motivations (movement, comfort, self-affirmation, emotional tension etc.) and also the social motives and cognitive skills; which lead people to adapt themselves to environmental norms and social rules. That's why the development of interests in sport is conditioned by actual structures and cultural trends of the environment in which subjects live.

REFERENCES

1) Bonaiuto, P. and Bartoli Bonaiuto, G.; Proceedings 1st Internat. Conf. Phys. Education, Bologna, 1967.

2) Bonaiuto, P. and Bartoli Bonaiuto, G.; Proceedings 1st Med. Cong., Cattolica, 1969; publ. also in: Minerva Pediatr., 1970, 22, 44, 2156-2163.

3) Bonaiuto, P., Naldi, R., and Bartoli Bonaiuto, G.; An Intercultural Comparison (Italy-U.S.A.) Regarding Interest for Motor Activities in Children, Pre-adolescent and Adolescents; Laboratorio di Psicologia, Università degli Studi, Bologna, 1977.

ATTITUDE TOWARD PHYSICAL ACTIVITY OF FEMALE STUDENTS

Faiza Mustafa Salman (Iraq)

The purpose of this study was to evaluate the attitude of Ottawa University female students toward physical activity as a means of recreation, to determine whether they were participating in the amount of physical activity they desire, and if not, to determine what they felt to be the underlying reasons for this lack of participation.

The sample was made up of 100 female students attending Ottawa University, in the winter semester of 1981. A 12 item questionnaire was administered to measure attitude towards physical activity. Personal interviews were conducted with 20 of the students (i.e., 20% of the sample).

The data tabulation was done to find frequency and percentage for each item answered.

The results of this study show that a favorable general attitude toward physical activity was held by Ottawa University female students.

In contrast to this finding is the fact that the average amount of time spent in participation in this type of activity is low. Approximately 60 percent of female students participate less than four hours a week. The number of female students spending no time at all is 10 percent.

Eighty-five percent stated a desire to spend more time than they are currently spending in activity but find it impossible primarily due to a lack of time.

This study shows, that the interest and participation of Ottawa University female students are definitely more strongly related to individual sport activities (tennis, swimming, ice skating etc.) and social activities (dancing, social games etc.) than to organized team sports (basketball, volleyball etc.)

Forty-three percent of the subjects do not participate in the five programs which are organized by the sport services of Ottawa University. These programs are as follows: a. free play program; b. sport clubs program; c. Intramural program; d. Instructional and Initiation program; e. Intercollegiate program.

Thirty-one percent participate in the free play program.

These female students participated more in physical activity in the secondary school than in University of Ottawa.

Ninety-five percent of Ottawa University female students do not think that participation in physical activities and sport make women more masculine, the other 5 percent think this participation makes women somewhat more masculine.

REFERENCES

Allport, Gordon W., "Attitudes", *Handbook of Social Psychology,* ed. Carl Murchison, Worcester, Mass.: Clark University Press, 1935, p. 810.

Bullock, M. and Florence D. Alden, "Some of the factors Determining the Attitudes of Freshman women at the University of Oregon Toward Required Physical Education", *Research Quarterly,* 4:63, December 1933.

Eastgate, Carole Ann, *Attitudinal Differences Between Female Participants and Non-Participants in a Middle School Extramural Meet,* Master thesis in PE, University of Wisconsin — Madison, 1975.

Horner, Rhonda, *The Effect of Interscholastic Athletics in Junior High School on Girls Attitudes Toward Athletics,* Master thesis in PE, University of Kansas, 1967.

Kenyon, G.J., "Six Scales for Assessing Attitude Toward Physical Activity", *Research Quarterly,* Vol. 39, 1968, pp. 566-574.

Kenyon, G.J., "A Conceptual Model for Characterizing Physical Activity", *Research Quarterly,* Vol. 39, 1968, pp. 96-105.

SENS CULTUREL DU JEU SPORTIF

François Bregiroux (France)

Le sport actuel, d'avenement récent passe en dépit de sa popularité, pour une activité d'expression primaire plutôt utile mais sous-culturelle.

Les définitions courantes, médicales (développement, exutoire d'agressivité) ou philosophiques (défoulement fetiaire, discipline morale ou pédagogique) retiennent quelques caractères étroits de son exercice, oubliant tout acquis culturel singulier qu'une expérience sportive soutenue puisse permettre à l'athlète de faire reconnaître socialement.

Aucune théorie ne semble explicitement rendre compte des ressorts contribuant à soutenir la démesure dans l'application et l'effort tendus pour des exploits peu ordinaires, apparement gratuits dans leur mise en oeuvre et leur objectif.

Ne produisant rien matériellement en dépit d'une immense et intense consommation de temps et d'énergie, le sens de sport ressortit des catégories de la psychologie qui se doit de poser la question: Quelle réalité psychologique profonde hausse-t-elle les exercices élémentaires d'une fiction ludique au rang de fonction sociale passionnée jusqu'à la dimension internationale?

Le sport est d'abord jeu et représentation

La tâche ludique est fictive. Ce sont des règles qui la délimitent comme un espace dans lequel convergent toutes les tensions, tous les efforts. Les règles existent spontanées ou non dès les jeux enfantins. Règles qui ouvrent entre "ce" qu'elles délimitent, un espace de libre échange social: le jeu.

Psychologiquement (par delà le pragmatique) ces règles ouvrent (sans l'écraser) le conflit relationnel-concurrentiel principe dynamique du jeu sportif. (ou social = lois créatrices d'espace positivement viable). Mais à l'opposé du conflit "primitif", en expansion aveugle, le jeu sportif offre entre ses repères (d'espace-temps-règles) l'issue positivement sanctionnée d'une démarche à la fois totalement engagée et totalement maîtrisée. (plaisir sportif = jouissance redoublée, "retrouvée" du pulsionnel et du social)

Car le public voit — grâce à l'intelligibilité des régles — il "rejoue" synchroniquement en miroir, et sanctionne l'enjeu: régulation du conflit par adresse et puissance, mais surtout dans les règles: l'acte le plus fondamentalement puissant dans le corps à corps, aux limites de la loi culturelle relationnelle admise.

Pousser sans cesse l'action aux confins des limites socialement admises (engagement/risque — puissance/violence), proposer en compromis entre pulsion (légitime) et cadre social (légal) une attitude dynamique moyenne ("loyale"), telles sont les fascinations du sport dans des sociétés qui n'ont de cohérence que la loi. Et sans loi point de culture.

Trop ouverte l'action est floue: corrompue par toutes les agressions sociales et pulsionnelles non confiées. Il n'y a pas "jeu": la brutalité domine. Trop serrée l'initiative dynamique d'action disparait écrasée (de l'extérieur) par la règle: défilés, démonstrations grégaires synchroniques anonymes où il n'y a plus jeu. En mécanique trop de jeu et l'énergie se perd, inutile. Pas assez et la machine se bloque.

Le jeu enfantin, comme le jeu présportif (au sens actuel du terme) ne sont ouverture que de relations privées, partielles entre individus, groupes, classes corporatives ou sociales, castes . . .

L'instutition sportive en transforme le sens en ouvrant égalitairement la participation dans une représentation publique. Jeux de représentations dramatiques et jeu sportif ont des points communs . . .

• récemment laïcisés par émancipations de leurs formes religieuses puis festaires

• se côtoient à leurs limites respectives (cirque, music-hall)

• spectacles où les "acteurs" s'éprouvent dans les fugires d'un jeu.

Mais ils différent profondément: ils "jouent" autre chose

• "Pièce" de théatre: représentation fermée et répétitive d'une même relation entre les figures.

• "Partie" sportive: représentation limitée arbitrairement dans le temps. "Partie" d'un mouvement de confrontation continu (calendrier cyclique naturel — générations successives).

• Rôle théatral: prêter son corps "diguisé" — figures et mouvements définis — Sens idéologique.

• Rôle sportif: s'impliquer entièrement (nudité) dans des figures à créer ("fonction héroïque" du sport) — anonymat idéologique.

• Production théatrale: acte fictif, artifices et discours imaginaires autout d'un "drame réel".

• Production sportive: acte réel, tangible et muet autour d'un "drame fictif".

L'expression dramatique passablement réductible au discours et considérée comme un sommet du culturel se démode cependant jusqu'à l'incongruité parfois d'une civilisation, d'une société, d'une époque, voir d'un moment à un autre.

L'expression sportive dans son institution idéale libre et ouverte se maintient dans l'espace temps qu'elle intègre étroitement selon un modèle qui confine toujours aujourd'hui au rite et au culturel. Ce modèle qui se passe des approximations et contradictions du discours (et dont l'audience souligne l'importance) sous tend toute culture égalitaire entre générations et individus en appelant à la diversité affrontée de l'expression des talents, à l'affirmation concurrentielle pour la reconnaissance de mérites avérés.

Le jeu sportif est ouverture symbolique. Préjeu (athlète) rejeu (public) d'un modèle social entre la violence anarchique aveugle et la paralysie de la loi "totale". Il constitue le modèle d'une voie subjective d'intégration personnelle dans une ouverture sociale de tensions extrêmes contenues qui s'éprouvent corporellement et affectivement (et se réfléchissent en spectacle) dans leur véracité vitale actuelle et active d'expression toujours renouvelée.

Le sens du jeu sportif est la "modelisation sociale" de l'espace étroit d'initiative entre la violence informelle et l'assujestissement formel. Un équilibre dynamique d'ouverture distributrice entre l'individu et le groupe.

L'expression sportive "joue" la réinstitution sociale des tensions vitales fondamentales. Elle est ainsi ouverture culturelle.

Le mythe sportif

Le sport fonctionne comme un mythe, et se fonde comme tel sur un exploit primordial ("prophétique") qui en reconstitue le principe au tréfond de l'affectivité socio-individuelle ("circularité"). Le principe curieusement retrouvé par le XXème siècle se fonde à Olympie où Zeus à l'origine affronte et triomphe loyalement (sans mutilation ni meurtre) de la souveraineté tyrannique de son père Kronos pour fonder son règne. Cet avènement de Zeus (Dewos, Dieu) fonde la civilisation préco-latine (Jupiter) et par conséquent la notre.

La ritualisation en fut consacrée sur le lieu même (Stade d'Olympie) en compétition sportive.

Geste prophétique primordial, métaphorisant un principe social, geste "oedipien" mais sans dimension névrotique. L'affrontement du fils au père se propose comme:

• légitime: défense de son existence sans vengeance sanglante

• légalisante: puisque le règne acquis inaugure un système nouveau de dynamique sociale où chacun (père frère fils) trouve existence et honneur selon ses mérites et différences (Olympie).

Schéma d'avènement (archaïque) de la loi distributrice moderne sur la domination violente de la force que le sport renouvelle aujourd'hui en modèle d'avènement filial dont le schéma oedipien ne serait que l'avatar pathologique (Oedipe n'étant qu'un mythe. secondaire).

SPORT	MYTHE	PSYCHOLOGIE DU SPORT
Engagement (ou maintien) du défi au niveau ancien de performances locales	défi à l'ordre paternal frustrant	Défi d'affirmation personnelle à la génération établie. Schéma maturant
Stades: espaces d'obstacles naturels normalisés	Olympie: lieu de l'acte prophétique où Zeus affronte Kronos — Stade consacré Ritualisation en compétitions sportives	Territoire symbolique revendiqué
Temps: parties arbitrairement limitées d'un continuum cyclique Affrontement au chronomètre	• Affrontement à Kronos (temps: Chronos) • Temps originaire (Sujetion filiole) • Temps indéfini du règne avenement personnel)	Temps génératif • crise adolescent • de projets autonomes • de réalisations personnelles
Règles: • maîtrise dynamique d'aggressivité • intelligibilité sociale • loi du sport: distinction sur seuls mérites réellement avérés — hors les a priori et a postériori rationnalisateurs du discours	Acte prophétique signifiant • mesuré — légitime non mutilant • légalisateur d'un mode de régulation social dynamique	Apprentissage de maîtrise spatio-temporelle dans des conditions collectives de conflits concurentiels socialement régulés.
Perspective sportive: espece temps rercréatif Jouissance créatrice des plus hautes capacités d'implication dans l'intelligence de la puissance. Selon un cadre socialement significatif	Perspective espace/temps symbolique (Olympe) de régulation dynamique des civilisations gréco-latine (racines des civilisations occidentales)	Perspective surmoïque d'espace temps Projection implicative (athlète) speculaire (public) de régulation idéale. • Egalitarisme des chances et des moyens • dynamique concurentielle mobilisatrice non-violente • distinction socio-affective pour capacités éprouvées • réinstitutionnalisation constante dans l'universalité fraternelle.

SPORT ET VIF DE L'ETRE

Georges Rioux (France)

La domination rationnelle et technique de la pensée moderne implique la deshumanisation de la subjectivité au profit des représentations de type mécanique, censées représenter au plus près la réalité.

Pourtant, tandis que le dedans de la chose s'avère aussi extérieur que l'extériorité des dehors, chez l'homme tout n'est pas objectable. Une force intérieure, une puissance, un mouvement expressif animent le vivant.

L'élan de la nature procure la qualité à l'être, mais cette qualité, jamais plénitude, n'appraît que virtualité et absence: les innovations réussies en matières sportives proviennent d'athlètes qui peuvent et qui savent de déterminer librement; l'expérience subjective vécue doit demeurer une expérience privée.

Tandis que chez l'animal le monde extérieur apparaît comme un lieu de signaux et de simples valences organiques, la présence du monde s'impose à l'homme; tandis que chez l'animal le cerveau se trouve au service exclusif de l'organisme, chez l'homme, l'organisme devient un simple exécutant au service du cerveau. L'homme refuse fondamentalement et obstinément d'accepter l'aliénation sous toutes ses formes.

L'intériorité humaine marque l'absence de distance de soi à soi et souligne l'identité de la réalisation de soi et de l'unité de l'être: l'homme s'affirme être au monde dans l'être en soi. Le sport se révèle ainsi lieu privilégié du face à face; mais l'athlète doit se montrer capable de vouloir et surtout se révéler capable de bien accomplir.

L'homme apparaît de l'extérieur "unitas multiplex"; en réalité, il adhère de l'intérieur à sa substantifique diversité. Le corps appartient à la subjectivité; l'activité est l'être même, tout entier actualisation. Comme la plante qui s'épanouit retourne en même temps dans ses racines, l'homme effectue aussi un retour vers soi qui ne cesse d'être un épanouissement: dans le geste sportif qui émane d'une source dont il ne se détache pas, l'unité en profondeur se vit intensément.

L'homme échappe à l'actualité strictement définie; l'acte ne peut en effet subsister que dans la relance permanente de la pulsation. L'unité de l'être et du phénomène réalise la synthèse humaine. Les activités sensori-motrices sont des activités d'un sujet responsable; l'erreur grave consiste à les reduire à un simple processus neuro-musculaire entraînant mécaniquement le déplacement des organes periphériaux de réception. Aussi longtemps que dure l'application de techniques auxquelles il n'adhère pas, l'athlète se sent réduit à des réflexes composés et à des gestes vides de sens. Le sport doit, tout au contraire, se révéler intimement comme vérité profonde et unifiante; le moi doit éconcer cette qualité que la liberté se donne à elle-même à travers les changements.

Affirmer, comme le fait Piaget (1961) que les activités sensori-motrices constituent des schèmes en se généralisant et en s'intériorisant, c'est verser dans la pétition de principe; on ne peut pas expliquer aussi simplement l'intériorisation d'activités assimilées à des mouvements mécaniques; il n'est pas possible de saisir de l'extérieur la manière dont le mouvement se tient en continuité étroite à l'intérieur de soi, au cours de son effection animée par la visée. L'athlète vit le geste d'une seule coulée; l'unité de l'expérience motrice se prolonge constamment dans la diversité des mouvements et souligne par là le décalage entre la connaissance anatomo-physiologique des processus et des segments du corps mis en jeu et l'accomplissement du vécu. Les liaisons mécaniques restent incapables de rendre compt e des liens unitaires entre diverses centrations; l'unité vécue ne peut pas provenir de processus extérieurs les uns aux autres et caractérisés par l'absence d'unité intérieure.

Dés le départ, le mouvement porte en lui l'unité liante de l'effection. Il ne s'accomplit que par unité fondatrice. Le bon contrôle et le bonne exécution échappent au jugement. Dans les profondeurs vitales tout demeure inséré en symbiose auto-adhérente avec stricte identité du spontané et du pathique. Etre conscient dehors, c'est être inconscient de soi. La prise de conscience, par contre, sépare et compte d'une manière unilinéaire, liée au coup par coup des fixations attentionnelles; l'excès d'attention joue parfois un rôle perturbateur!

Le passage du sentir au percevoir transforme en relations tracées du dehors, les liens d'un seul tenant qui unissaient les réalités agissantes, en les assemblant de l'intérieur; le JE de l'initiative se disjoint de la vitalité qui le porte et sépare les choses emportées par le temps des choses épurées par la pensée.

Cependant, percevoir c'est aussi dégager le senti; les deux modes de connaissance s'entrelacent: la conscience séparatrice et symbolisante implique la connaissance sourde du devenir des symbioses vitales. C'est au sommet du vivant que l'athlète affirme sa liberté et accroît son efficacité.

Dans l'expérience intérieure s'insère l'acte de choisir qui appartient à la seule nature humaine. Choisir les principes de son devenir suppose la liberté d'expression au delà de soi. Tout fait humain prend signification dans l'espérance permise. Le véritable fondement de la réussite se trouve parmi les choix portées dans la manière d'être, car la liberté reste totale comme les responsabilités. On ne peut être véritablement sportif que si l'on choisit sa sportivité. Dans l'acte de "vouloir être", la liberté s'exerce et obtient le maximum d'efficacité; elle devient risque, pari, décision; elle s'éprouve et se

prouve. Vouloir est la seule chose qu'un homme puisse sans réserve.

Le langage humain suppose l'expérience d'unités significatives où l'absent vient tremper dans l'actualité par le vocable qui l'éprouve. Mais, une culture ne consiste pas seulement dans l'extension d'un champ de domination lucide, elle procède aussi de réactions vitales inconscientes qui lui donnent une impulsion première. Toute domination technique privée de la direction interne des forces vives conduit au déclin. Le sport doit être, avant tout, l'occasion d'une élévation intérieure qui donne un sens aux épreuves, en développant la passion de vivre.

A l'origine de l'action se trouve l'unité dynamique avec spatialisation de la subjectivité, champ unitaire d'action. On n'explique pas, non plus, l'existence de l'expérience consciente unitaire et de la subjectivité directement attestée, par le simple jeu de fonctionnements mécaniques!

La constitution de l'homme s'avère essentiellement pathique. L'affectivité demeure le ciment de l'être, la base essentielle de toute existence subjective. L'homme saisit le monde du dedans; le vécu manifeste subjectivement ce qui se trouve éprouvé dans un certain rapport au monde. L'affectivité réside dans le non perçu du perçu qui en forme le soubassement. Les hommes restent sensibilisés prioritairement à ce qui présente pour eux un intérêt affectif; rien ne les touche autant que ce qui parle à leurs besoins, à leurs désirs et à leurs craintes.

Le premier relief est toujours celui de la motivation. L'athlète doit s'y affirmer dans son unité et dans son identité; la passion contrôlée entraîne et rectifie. Lorsque retentit sur le sujet le résultat espéré, l'unité affective se réalise pleinement. Seule créature refusant ce qu'elle est, l'homme ne vise qu'à se conquérir constamment sur lui-même; aussi, l'athlète ne doit-il jamais se réduire au simple objet d'un savoir qui lui demeure extérieur; son initiative doit pouvoir assurer l'orientation de son propre devenir.

"Toute pédagogie sportive préparant véritablement à l'accueil de la vie, doit nécessairement se construire sur une constante mise au point de l'équilibre existentiel, étroitement relié à l'activité fonctionnelle naturellement unitaire; toute pédagogie sportive doit aussi nécessairement s'exercer selon un bon ajustement de la liberté au niveau de 'l'être vif' qui exprime l'être au sens le plus profond". (Rioux et Chappuis, 1981)

REFERENCES

1) Piaget, J. *Les mécanismes perceptifs"*. Paris: PUF, 1961.
2) Rioux, G., et Chappuis, R.: *Développement unitaire et succès sportif*. Paris, Vrin, 1981.

MEANING IN SPORT THROUGHOUT LIFE: CONCLUSION

Leonard M. Wankel

How can we ensure meaningful sport experiences throughout the life span? A valuable contribution towards this end was realized by drawing attention to certain key issues and posing a number of significant questions. Still, many questions remain. The difficulty of dealing with the topic "meaning" was amply illustrated by the divergent meanings ascribed by different authors to the theme. Any summary comment on the theme, therefore, must not be a unitary statement but rather must reflect the different dimensions emerging from the theme sessions. In this closing section attention will be drawn to the major issues addressed and some observations will be offered as to possible future directions for research and practice in the area.

Psychological Effects of Sport and Physical Activity

Although considerable research pertaining to the psychological effects of sport and physical activity was reported or referred to during the Congress sessions, it is obvious that much remains to be investigated in this area. As Morgan clearly points out authors often go beyond the evidence in interpreting the psychological consequences of sport or physical activity engagement. Morgan indicates that biochemical and neurophysiological research may be required to establish that it is physical activity itself which causes certain psychological effects. Equally important at the program level is the need to identify the significant dimensions of the overall program (physical activity-type, intensity, and duration; leadership; social relationships; support services, etc.) related to positive outcomes. For the practitioner a number of papers indicate considerations for implementing activity programs to have desirable psychological effects. These guidelines can serve as a useful purpose although it should clearly be understood they reflect only tentative knowledge which is subject to change with further research. This emphasizes the need for the practitioner to keep abreast of the relevant rersearch affecting his/her field of practice.

Going beyond the more circumscribed view of psychological outcomes in terms of reduced anxiety and depression, Csikszentmihalyi outlines a model for assessing outcomes from sport. Such a view which adds a social or cultural outcome component to the individual outcome perspective warrants further examination. Although there might be disagreement with the particular dimensions which Csikszentmihalyi identifies as criteria for desirable sport outcomes, this basic approach is instructive as clearly if any evaluation is to be made of the contribution of sport some criteria must be established. The continuing emotional rhetoric of the supporters and detractors of sport indicates the futility of reaching any general agreement on the merits of sport without first setting some criteria for making such an evaluation. Having once established such standards it would then be possible to go ahead and investigate more systematically what organizational and leadership practices are particularly conducive or anathema to realizing these desired outcomes. While such research will be both complex and time consuming, a beginning in this direction can be seen in the work of Csikszentmihalyi (this volume) and Smith, Smoll and Curtis (1978).

The Sport Delivery System

The opportunities made available for sport involvement throughout the life cycle will have a significant effect upon involvement at different age levels. Kunath's description of how different agencies play a role in making sport available for all in the German Democratic Republic provides one model for encouraging widespread sport participation. Although such a highly centralized organizational system would not be acceptable to most western countries, it does provide one example of how widespread sport involvement for all ages can be provided. Elements of this system (e.g., sport club concept) might be introduced to good advantage into the sport delivery system of other countries where current systems based on elitism and excellence of the few appear to be effective methods for eliminating participants from sport (Orlick, 1974, 1978).

Target Groups Requiring Special Attention

Certain groups require special attention if the goal of meaningful sport involvement throughout life for all is to be more fully attained. As indicated by Kirjonen, sociological research indicates that age, sex, education, and socio-economic status are factors influencing sport involvement (see also McPherson, 1980; Statistics Canada, 1978). More specifically it is found that females participate less than males, and lower socio-economic groups participate less than higher socio-economic groups. Further, participation rate is positively related to level of education but negatively associated with age. It becomes important to understand why these groups are underrepresented and to identify strategies for encouraging their participation. A number of factors including available opportunities, social norms, perceived importance and attitudes toward sport involvement may be involved.

As Ostrow and Spiker indicate, social stereotypes in the case of "ageism" may be one of the most important factors inhibiting greater involvement of older citizens in physyical activity. Similar social stereotypes and limited opportunity sets have been identified as major factors limiting the involvement of females in sport and physical activity.

Further research is needed to more clearly delineate what factors operate to inhibit the involvement of certain population groups. At the same time, sport organizers and administrators should make immediate changes in their programs to remove those barriers which have been shown to preclude or limit the involvement of certain groups.

Motivation for Sport for All

Probably the topic which surfaced most regularly throughout the "Meaning in Sport Throughout Life" theme session was "how can greater widespread involvement in sport and physical activity be realized?" This question was addressed from several different perspectives.

Dishman advocated a psychobiologic model as one means of working with individuals in an attempt to increase adherence to a regular exercise program. Wankel, together with his colleagues (Wankel, 1980; Wankel and Thompson, 1977; Thompson and Wankel, 1980; Wankel and Graham, Note One) has utilized a program intervention approach to promoting more regular attendance of activity programs. A decision balance-sheet technique and perceived choice of activities have been shown to positively influence attendance. An attempt has been made in the more recent research to categorize participants on the basis of self-motivation level as indicated by the Self Motivation Inventory and then to introduce motivational treatments in order to determine if such treatments are differentially effective for different individuals (Wankel and Graham, Note One). Preliminary evidence indicates that individuals who have low levels of self-motivation may benefit more from external interventions than will individuals who have high levels of self-motivation. More research, however, is needed to substantiate and extend these results before such findings can be useful in a program context.

Such studies addressing physical activity as a form of preventive health are extremely relevant as large numbers of individuals currently join activity programs in the search for health benefits but after joining they find it difficult to persist in regular attendance of such programs. Thus any systematic intervention which increases the probability of more regular attendance warrants further investigation.

Such attempts to promote physical activity as a health product, however, would appear to have a basic limitation. As Dishman notes, for continued involvement greater attention must be given to self-motivation which is not dependent on the support from a formal program. Increasingly, evidence points to the necessity for an active program to become enjoyable in its own right if a participant is to continue in it (cf. Department of Youth, Sport and Recreation, Melbourne Australia, 1975; Fitness Ontario, 1981; Wankel, 1981), Sheehan makes this point in his lead-off paper when he distinguishes between the concepts "play", "sport" and "exercise" and indicates the essential aspect of each for promoting widespread involvement in sport and physical activity. Sheehan notes fitness has been essentially viewed as a physiological domain with the result that it has not received the attention from psychological researchers that it should. He argues that for lifelong commitment to sport it must be enjoyed in its own right, not just viewed as something that is good for one. Arnold similarly supports the importance of the playful attitude for continued sport involvement. Kirjonen and Silvennoinen, in their papers, present evidence in support of this perspective. They report research with Finnish populations which indicates that intrinsic motives (aspects related to enjoyment of the activity) are more closely related to participation than are instrumental health related motives. Similarly, considerable evidence exists to indicate that although individuals join physical activity programs initially for health related reasons, continued involvement is more closely associated with factors related to enjoyment of the activity and other program factors (cf. Wankel, 1980, 1981).

In emphasizing the role of enjoyment in promoting physical activity, attention necessarily shifts from emphasis on a medical compliance model to a leisure or recreation perspective. In this context physical activity and sport are viewed as a means to attaining the positive affective state termed the leisure state or recreational experience (cf. Driver and Tocher, 1970; Mannell, 1980; Murphy and Howard, 1977). Some progress has been made in identifying different dimensions related to enjoyment of an engagement (Csikszentmihalyi, 1975; Iso-Ahola, 1980; Wankel, 1980, 1981); however, much further research is required. In the meantime it must be emphasized that attention should be focussed beyond the mere involvement of an individual in an activity to consider the quality of the experience. That is, is the individual truly enjoying the involvement, what is his/her psychological reaction to the engagement? This becomes the most important factor influencing whether the individual will continue to be involved or not.

To date most research on enjoyment has been of a short-term or cross-sectional nature. Although some progress has been made in identifying factors related to sport enjoyment which may be related to long-term involvement (cf. Csikszentmihalyi, 1975; Gould, 1982; Robertson, 1982; and Wankel and Pabich, 1982), further research should address developmental changes in enjoyment factors. Are enjoyment factors relatively stable over time or do they change over the period of involvement? Longitudinal research utilizing a more in-depth, qualitative emphasis should be conducted to gain insight into this area.

While acknowledging that research into factors related to sport enjoyment and intrinsic interest is still in its infancy and much needs to be done, still some general guidelines may be offered for sport organizers and coaches. At the organizational level, increased attention should be given to alternative programs which cater to different psychological meanings. The almost exclusive emphasis on sport as an achievement oriented activity with outcome factors emphasized accounts for much of the attrition from sport (Orlick, 1974, 1978). Sport and/or physical activity programs emphasizing affiliation, cooperation, skill development, meeting realistic personal challenges, just engaging in stimulating activity, etc., would provide opportunities for those who are not primarily motivated by a desire to outperform someone else.

At the level of coaching, greater emphasis should be placed upon treating each athlete as an individual in an attempt to make sport an enjoyable exercise for him/her. The quality of the sport experience is unique to each individual and only has meaning in terms of his/her psychological needs and interests. Meaningful lifelong sport involvement will only become a reality if the individual's needs are met through his/her sport involvement. Although this places a tremendous leadership responsibility on the coach and requires far more sophisticated skills than are required for a unitary emphasis upon maximizing team performance and "winning", it is the only approach which can lead to the optimum development of each individual while at the same time fostering peak performance. It is encouraging to note that such a perspective has been made an integral part of some large scale coaching development programs (cf. National Coaching Certification Program, Coaching Association of Canada, Coaching Theory Level One, Level Two, and Level Three Manuals).

REFERENCES

Bannister, R. The Meaning of Athletic Performance. In E. Jokl and E. Simon (Eds.) *International Research In Sport and Physical Education.* Springfield, Ill.: Charles C. Thomas, 1964.

Csikszentmihalyi, M. *Beyond Boredom and Anxiety: The Experience of Play in Work and Games.* San Francisco: Jossey-Bass, 1977.

Department of Youth, Sport and Recreation. *May 1975 Attitudinal Study: Fitness and Recreation in Victoria.* Melbourne, Victoria, Australia: Department of Youth, Sport and Recreation, 1975.

Driver, B.L. and Tocher, S.R. Toward a Behavioural Interpretation of Recreational Engagements with Implications for Planning. In B.L. Driver (Ed.) *Elements of Outdoor Recreation Planning.* Ann Arbour, Mich.: University Microfilms, 1970, pp. 9-29.

Fitness Ontario, *Those Who Know But Don't Do.* Toronto, Ontario: Ministry of Culture and Recreation, 1981.

Frankl, V. *Man's Search For Meaning: An Introduction to Logotherapy.* Boston: Beacon Press, 1962.

Frankl, V. Sports — The Asceticism of Today. In *The Unheard Cry for Meaning: Psychotherapy and Humanism.* New York: Simon and Schuster, 1978.

Gould, D. Fostering Psychological Development in Young Athletes, Proceedings of the 5th World Sport Psychology Congress, Coaching Association of Canada, Ottawa, Canada, 1982.

Iso-Ahola, S. *The Social Psychology of Leisure and Recreation.* Dubuque, Iowa: Wm. C. Brown Co., 1980.

Mannell, R. Social Psychological Techniques and Strategies for Studying Leisure Experiences. In S.E. Iso-Ahola (Ed.) *Social Psychological Perspectives on Leisure and Recreation.* Springfield, Ill.: C.C. Thomas, 1980.

McPherson, B.D. Social Factors to Consider in Fitness Programming and Motivation: Different Strokes for Different Groups. In R.R. Danielson and K.F. Danielson (Eds.) *Fitness Motivation: Proceedings of the Geneva Park Workshop: March 26 to 28, 1980.* Toronto: Orcol Publications, 1980.

Murphy, J.F. and Howard, D.R. The Nature of the Recreation Experience. In *Delivery of Community Services: An Holistic Approach.* Philadelphia: Le a and Fabiger, 1977.

National Coaching Association, *Coaching Theory: Level One.* Ottawa: Coaching Association of Canada, 1979.

National Coaching Association. *Coaching Theory: Level Two.* Ottawa: Coaching Association of Canada, 1979.

National Coaching Association, *Coaching Theory: Level Three.* Ottawa: Coaching Association of Canada, 1981.

Orlick, T.D. and Botterill, C. *Every Kid Can Win,* Chicago: Nelson Hall Publishers, 1975.

Orlick, T.D. The Athletic Drop Out A High Price for Inefficiency. *C.A.H.P.E.R. Journal.* (November-December), 1974.

Orlick, T.D. *Winning Through Cooperation: Competitive Insanity — Cooperative Alternatives.* Washington, D.C.: A. Hawkins & Associates, Ltd., 1978.

Robertson, I. Sport in the Lives of South Australian Children. Proceedings of the 5th World Sport Psychology Congress, Coaching Association of Canada, Ottawa Canada, 1982.

Smith, R., Smoll, F.L. and Curtis, L. Coaching Behaviours in Little League Baseball, In F.L. Smoll and R.E. Smith (Eds.) *Psychological Perspectives in Youth Sports.* Washington, D.C.: Hemisphere, Pub. Corp., 1978.

Smoll, F.L. and Smith, R.E. *Psychological Perspectives in Youth Sports.* Washington, D.C.: Hemisphere, Pub. Corp., 1978.

Statistics Canada. *Culture Statistics — Recreational Activities, 1976.* Ottawa: Statistics Canada, 1978.

Thompson, C. and Wankel, L.M. The effects of perceived activity choice upon frequency of exercise behaviour. *Journal of Applied Social Psychology,* 1980, 10(5): 436-443.

Wankel, L.M. Involvement in Vigorous Physical Activity: Considerations for Enhancing Self-Motivation. In R.R. Danielson and K.F. Danielson (Eds) *Fitness Motivation: Proceedings of the Geneva Park Workshop, March 26 to 28, 1980.* Toronto: Orcol Publications, 1980.

Wankel, L.M. Social Psychological Dimensions of Physical Activity Involvement. *Proceedings of the Third Canadian Congress on Leisure Research* (in press).

Wankel, L.M. and Thompson, C. Motivating people to be physically active: self-persuasion vs. balanced decision-making. *Journal of Applied Social Psychology,* 1977, 7(4), 332-340.

Wankel, L.M. and Pabich, P. The Minor Sport Experience: Factors Contributing To or Detracting From Enjoyment. Proceedings of the 5th World Sport Psychology Congress, Coaching Association of Canada, Ottawa Canada, 1982.

MODULE III
Cooperation in Sport and Life

FOREWORD

COOPERATION IN SPORT AND LIFE

Terry Orlick (Canada)

"The destiny of the world is shaped by those who can get
their ideas across, for better or worse. — John F. Kennedy

The purpose of this module is to share with you some ideas which relate to cooperation and the development of healthy values in sport and life. The ultimate aim of our efforts is to stimulate individuals, teams and societies to greater harmony, happiness and self-fulfillment through cooperation and healthy competition. Our overall focus here is more upon cooperation as a playstyle and lifestyle than upon cooperation as a specific strategy for improving competitive performance.

In the first section of this module, four invited contributors with extremely diverse backgrounds present some of their perspectives on cooperation in sport and life. This is followed by an invited reaction to some of their thoughts. In the second section, a selection of shorter papers which relate to this theme is presented. These will hopefully stimulate more work, study and most of all action, which reflects positively on the whole realm of harmony in sport and life.

The first section begins with two papers by Ashley Montagu, a native of England and long time resident of the United States. One paper is on the decay of sport and the nurturing of sport in perspective and in the other he reflects upon the related values of education, love and children.

Montagu, a well known anthropologist, proclaims that if we do not change our current path, we may live up to the prediction to be the only species that ever completely destroyed itself. This should cause us to seriously reflect upon how we play and how we live. One of his major concerns is that many industrialized people accept moral sickness in sport and life as normal and inevitable and often do not recognize the need for change. Another of his concerns is that competition, particularly as it is practiced in industrialized power-hungry societies, works contrary to the biological nature of humankind.

Wang Min Qi, a native of Beijing, who grew up under Mao's influence in the People's Republic of China, presents a blueprint for developing cooperation and sportsmanship which was utilized successfully in the People's Republic of China. Drawing upon his background as a former athlete and coach at the Beijing Institute of Physical Culture, he presents some very practical means for nurturing sportsmanship, fair play, and cooperation, within the context of competitive excellence. Some of the strategies utilized in China might well be adapted for use in other cultures as well.

Naomi Tulaha Martin, the daughter of a tribal chief who was raised in a small village in the North Solomon Islands, shares with us some of the traditional play and games of her people, a people whose traditional language does not include a word for "winning". In her paper, Martin, currently a professor in education at the University of Papua New Guinea, discusses how the most cherished values of her village people (i.e., cooperation, respect, generosity, and responsibility) were taught through traditional play and how these values have been seriously threatened with the introduction of foreign "knowledge". Her paper forces us to reflect upon the right of one culture to invade another with conflicting values; and upon whether this intrusion can ever be turned around.

My own work in Canada has focused on the humanistic education of children, primarily through play and games, as well as on the healthy pursuit of personal excellence. In my paper I discuss how cooperatively designed games can help us learn to live together in greater harmony. I also outline some obstacles to constructive change and present specific suggestions for improving the quality of our games and lives.

Leonard DeVries, a native of Malaysia, whose heritage and perspectives make him a truly international citizen, agreed to serve as our reactor for this theme. He is a professor in sport and education at the Universiti Sains in Penang, Malaysia, and has a special interest in sport psychology, particularly as it relates to people in developing nations. DeVries points out the desirability of consistency if one wants to truly implement a system which cherishes humanistic values. He cautions us about the need for careful consideration and appropriate adaptation when using approaches developed for one culture in another and finally warns of a danger in going to extremes with respect to enforcing either conformity or rampant individualism.

The backgrounds of Montagu, Wang, Martin, Orlick and DeVries are literally worlds apart; yet they have arrived at some common beliefs which have implications for all of us.

- it is desirable and possible for people to play and live in harmony, whether they grow within populations which are large or small;
- there are vitally important human values quite apart from science, technology, material possessions, and power which need to be understood, valued and cultivated;
- when certain values are consistently promoted by various arms of one's culture, these values will be acted out in the day to day lives of the people (regardless of whether the values being promoted are desirable or undesirable);
- because human values are initially acted out, learned and promoted through children's play and games, play is a realm of great social and cultural significance.

Most of us now playing and living on the global arena — earth — have not witnessed an abundance of human cooperation and compassion. There are a great many injustices, as well as ruthless disregard for human life and the quality of life, especially for those who dare to think differently from those in power. This occurs both within societies and between them.

It is time to seek more constructive options which will ultimately benefit all of us. Those of us who are interested in the human arena of play, games and sport have a significant contribution to make in this regard. Perhaps through revised values within play and games we can provide children with a more positive beginning; perhaps by promoting sport in perspective we can provide a model of harmony and healthy interaction from which other branches of this planet can learn.

Of course this will be a very difficult task. If the Chinese are correct when they proclaim that "failure is the mother of success", then we have a very bright future. But only if we are able to learn from our past and willing to commit ourselves to a better future.

The second section of this module begins with a paper by Czula who clarifies the inherent problems within contemporary competitive sport structures. He suggests a direction for sport which focuses on allowing people to compete for improvement without turning others into "the enemy". The subsequent paper by Pauwels demonstrates that players with relatively low skill levels are often left out of the action in contemporary team games. His work reinforces the necessity to seek out alternative approaches for youth games which allow for more inclusion and related social benefits. Sohi's observational study of soccer in Nigeria supports the proposition that introducing competitive sport structures and placing importance on outcomes increases player susceptibility to exhibit aggression on the field. Heil then points out that the effects of participation in sport are largely a consequence of the attitude taken into it. He maintains that by focusing on the Eastern (oriental) concept of "do" (a way to live), we can begin to limit inappropriate aggressive behavior in sport and further enhance personal growth.

Gillot presents his experiences with "les fêtes de la vigne", a festival of traditional songs, dances and sporting activities which are approached with a feeling of fraternity and joy. The atmosphere described is much like that generated by our original Inuit (Eskimo people) during their traditional northern game festivals. The participants control the competition rather than the competition controlling them. He suggests the expansion of this approach to include divided peoples from many places in the world with the aim of improving international harmony and peace.

Antonelli and Gatti report data which supports the position that sport can result in greater cohesion and rapport between man and wife. They conclude that doing sports together is a good way to strengthen the rapport between couples. This, of course, would necessitate taking either a positive attitude or recreational approach to the activity.

Provost presents an overview of a study which assessed the effects of videotaped cooperative game exposures on 2 and 4 year old children. He found that these exposures had beneficial prosocial effects on the children. This study points to the positive prosocial potential of cooperatively oriented television programming. Kerr's study supports the general proposition that well designed activity programs can positively influence human interaction. He found that learning-disabled children aged 6-10 increased their cooperative behavior by 50% after being exposed to a physical activity program which stressed cooperative games and a variety of other modified activities.

All authors in this section would agree that games and sports have the potential to be benefitial to personal and interpersonal growth. However, this kind of growth does not occur automatically. Team games, for example, have the potential to increase cooperation, sensitivity and harmony among participants but often do not, particularly when opposing team members or members of one's own team are viewed as the obstacle or "enemy".

In order for contemporary games and sport to fulfill humanistic and personal growth objectives, something in the real world has to support this growth: the structure of the activity itself, the environment and reinforcements surrounding the activity, the attitude towards the activity, the orientation towards players or feelings about oneself. Our challenge is to change environments and people so that together they nourish meaningful and positive human qualities.

TABLE OF CONTENTS

THE DECAY OF SPORT VALUES AND THE NURTURING OF SPORT IN PERSPECTIVE

Ashley Montagu (USA)

It was Dr. Arnold of Rugby who, in the 1840s, introduced sports into an English public school as a continuing and intrinsic part of education. Its principal role was to serve as a training in character. It was the way you played the game, with style, skill, and elegance, the grace of doing your best under stress, that mattered, not whether you won or lost, but how you played the game: "To love the game beyond the prize." This view of sport so appealed to the English that it quickly spread to all other schools, to the universities, and to the secondary and elementary schools, when the latter were finally instituted for the children of the working classes, in the 1870s.

Having spent virtually the whole of the first 23 years of the twentieth century in England, I am able to speak from personal experience as a boy scout, and as an athlete who eventually rose to the exalted position of captain of my college boxing team, about the manner in which one played the game. There were definite rules: the first of these was gentlemanliness, *noblesse oblige,* which meant not only fairness, but never, under any circumstances, to take advantage of the weakness of any member of the opposite side. If during a game of tennis, for example, your opposite number (one avoided words such as "opponent") happened to slip, and the ball was in your court to return, you deliberately hit it into the net. If, during a boxing match, the other man slipped, you retired to your corner, to allow him time to re-erect himself. In boxing it was considered bad taste to knock a man out — any slugger could do that. The idea was to use your skills, just as you would in fencing, and to accumulate your points by skill and elegance. What was most admired in an athlete was style, to be unobtrusively stylish, which is what most people understood by "sportsmanship," a humanity of elegance which detested violence in any form or taking an unearned or foul advantage of another. This was the rule of rules, and it was not for nothing that it gave rise to the universally adopted phrase, "It isn't cricket," to indicate that it was a matter of honor to play by the rules.

To play by the rules wasn't at any time considered a constraint of any sort, but a privilege. One played the game for fun which, if at the same time it also turned out to be a discipline of character, then so much the better. Winning or losing was not the point, doing one's best within the rules *was*. One took pleasure in the skill of the game, perhaps even more in the skill of the other than in one's own. And so one constantly strove to play with players who were better than oneself, for in this way one would constantly be challenged to improve. One played *with* the other, rather than competed against him.

And whoever won, one rejoiced in the performance of the other and congratulated him. The same held true for group games. Certainly the element of competition was present, but one competed *with* the other side, not *against* them. They were not our adversaries, but our challengers. And what each challenged in the other was to bring out the best in each other. The competition was *cooperative*, not *competitive.*

Today cooperative competition is a dead letter, and has given way entirely to competitive competition of the worst kinds. Professional sports have corrupted and degraded every form of sport, and have demeaned the ways in which almost everyone "plays" the game. In fact, the corruption is so generally recognized, that when one businessman inquires of another what his business is, he is as likely as not to ask "What game are you in?" What is implicit in that question is that one is playing the game according to the rules of the business world, a world in which business is pursued as a way of life, instead of a way of making a living. Business principles have, in large part, been responsible for the breakdown, corruption, and degradation of sports. It was a President of the United States, Mr. Calvin Coolidge, who informed the world that the business of a democracy was business.

Up to 1914 games were generally played on gentlemanly principles. With the breakdown in values during and following the First World War, and during the period between that and the Second World War, we witnessed the completion of that breakdown, and the concomitant rise of violence and ruthless competition in sports. When it gradually became clear that huge profits were to be made from the commercialization of sports, both for the businessman and for the players, the full corruption and debasement of sports was finally achieved.

The corruption and debasement of sports reflects the corruption and debasement of the fans who support such spectacles, for without their encouragement professional sports would be impossible. The word "fan" is short for "fanatic," and *the fanatical ferocity of the fans who support the more popular sports such as football, soccer, ice-hockey, and basketball, represents an emotional involvement of such powerful charge, that were it directed toward more creative ends it might succeed in changing the world.* In a violent world it is not surprising that it is the violence of the sport that most appeals to the fans. Toward this end the players are taught to be brutes, and the brutes in the arena are surpassed only by the brutes in the stands. Football (the North American version) is no longer a contact sport, but a collision sport, and while the helmet may protect the head, its principal function is to serve as a battering-ram. The resulting injuries are staggering.

It would be a vast oversimplification to attribute the corruption of sports entirely to big business, for big business is itself as much a victim of the breakdown in values as is virtually everyone else. If we take the United States as the example which stands out in high relief among the nations of the world for the addiction of its citizens to sports, and inquire into the value system at the altar of which Americans are taught to worship, all students of the American scene are agreed that it is SUCCESS. As William James, in 1906, wrote to H.G. Wells, "The moral flabbiness born of the excessive worship of the bitch-goddess SUCCESS. That — with the squalid cash interpretation put on the word SUCCESS — is our national disease." (James, 1920:260). From the earliest possible age, the American child, and particularly the boy, learns that the great American opportunity is not education but success. He must be competitive, he must be better than others, he must excel in sports, and as that much venerated American culture hero, the football coach Vince Lombardi put it, "Winning is not everything. It is the only thing." No one ever tells him what an infinite loss it is to win in such ways, or shows him what the people who have "made it" have in fact made, or explains to him how it comes about that the human propensity for spiritual creation and the struggle for value are matched, or even surpassed, by a mindless and devilish ferocity. All that he is told is that he must do well in all things possible, all toward the end of success. One must learn to be aggressive, for in the struggle for life, he is informed, the weakest go to the wall, and fall by the way, and are never heard of again. In Junior High School, sports, especially football, are up there with what is significantly called "academics," and if "academics" fall by the way, so much the worse for them. The very term has a sort of derisory effluvium about it that suggests that it is not to be taken seriously. Junior High School boys are frequently held back in their class so that they can play an additional year, in the hope that they may some day become professionals. In January 1981, on the TV program "60 Minutes," Morley Safer reported on football in Junior High in a small town in Texas. In that town football is Number One. The Principal of the school was formerly its football coach. At this school, as in many others throughout America, parents not only approve but ask for their boys to be held back another year in class, especially if they are not physically mature enough at 83 pounds. Football is considered much more important than "academics," because, as one of the boys' influential father put it, "The sooner and better they're able to compete, the better they'll do in life — knock 'em on their butts." Or as a commercial put it (this time relating to trains), "Winning is more than a goal; it's an attitude which helps you know where you're going." But to that it may be replied, that knowing where you're going doesn't mean that you are necessarily going to get the right train, and if you do that, that you're going to get off at the right station.

In another "60 Minutes" program (9 March 1980), during an interview with Bobby Knight, the University of Indiana basketball coach, he said that he placed the emnpohasis on toughness. He yells at the players, screams at the referees, and berates the home crowds for not yelling loudly enough. He humiliates, intimidates, and motivates his players by fear. It is the team, not the individual who counts. "I have to take away individuality," he said. On occasions he has threatened journalists with violence. The thing is to win at all costs, and his job is to prepare his players to win. He sees coaching as being very similar to hunting, and the game as more suited to a battleground than a playground. Basketball income in 1980 was more than a million dollars, and in that year the alumni gave the university over two million dollars. Of his players, Mr. Knight said, "Basketball is the greatest education they received at Indiana University." And that, alas, was probably only too true, for with such attitudes towards sports in America players have been enrolled in college and universities who couldn't read or write.

It is generally agreed that to be able to read and write is desirable, but as every schoolboy knows by now, it is not absolutely indispensable, for the easiest route to success, many of them are taught to believe, especially blacks, is through sports. Coaches seek out high school boys who have excelled in some sport and offer them contracts with enticingly large sums of money to play either on college teams or commercially. The very word "play" in such a context grates on the ear, for that boy is being seduced to go into big-time business, and perhaps to become one of America's culture heroes, as well as a multimillionaire, before he has reached 25. What he will be engaged in is not in playing a game but in making money. In a sport like basketball, if a player happens to be exceptionally tall and can simply drop the ball into the net, it makes it that much easier. The absurdity of having players of excessive height matched against shorter players doesn't appear to have struck anyone as being unfair — it is as if one were to pit a heavyweight against a lightweight in a boxing or wrestling match, when it is clearly no match at all. No one seems to perceive anything incongruous in such extreme disparities in basketball players, and in any event, it would appear that the fans in the stands couldn't care less.

Many of these athletes, from major universities and colleges, have maintained their eligibility through extension courses at smaller colleges. Scores of them have received credit for courses they never even took. When the Los Angeles District Attorney's office began studying athlete's cheating, investigators found that the problem spread beyond sports. "Teachers," the Deputy District Attorney said, "appear to be abusing the system at least as much as athletes." He might have added that many colleges were not less guilty of providing teachers with credits for taking a one-evening five hour workshop (including dinner) on collective bargaining, worth two hours of academic credit. That could be worth an increase in salary of $50 for every year taught. Teachers in America are not, in any event, valued anywhere nearly as highly as athletes, and are therefore generally paid no more and frequently less, than the janitor who cleans their classrooms. Hence they are only too often forced to supplement their low salaries by the readiest means available to them. In keeping with the prevailing debased and destructive values, it need hardly be said that the football coach should receive a higher salary than any of the teachers.

As John Underwood has written, "The educational system is itself in chaos, its spirit preoccupied, its standards blunted to a point where almost anything that passes for curriculum is permissible, and almost anyone who can walk and talk admissible. Not just underprivileged young men who need a chance, but unqualified young men who have no chance in the classroom. High schools — many of them — have such meager requirements that they are fertile ground for coaches who must cheat to keep players eligible. The sins of the high school and junior college are visited on the major colleges, where the buck stops" (Underwood, 1980).

What has become clear is that intercollegiate sports, instead of building character are, in fact, deforming it, "by making the athletes willing victims," as Dr. George H. Hanford, current head of the college board put it, "of today's highly structured industrial complex . . . through exposure to the unethical practices in which the athletic establishment indulges."

The willing victims are exploited in the name of success with fabulous salaries at the end of the rainbow. No one ever tells them, in the fast shuffle to which they are exposed, that the chances of making it are less than 1 in 20,000. It is a myth which many colleges and universities serve to perpetuate because the ends that they have in view are the alumni who take a special pride in their alma mater's prowess in sports. They are, in fact, the primary cheerleaders. For the alumni, as well as for the members of these institutions, the annual games constitute ritual celebrations at which they can renew something of the happy days of their youths, a Dionysian occasion which they can share with their families and old friends. The "game" is not simply a game, it is an event, a metaphor for life, a kind of theology. One cheers, exults, drinks, and sings "Back to Good Old XYU," which seems rather redundant, since many of the vocalists seem never to have left it.

As commentary on this state of affairs it is told that at one university an illiterate athlete who was considered quite indispensable had, by some means, to be kept on the team. A special tutor was therefore assigned to him and told to do what he could. On the day of the examination a small crowd gathered outside the building, and when finally the athlete and the tutor emerged, an impatient fan rushed forward and asked the tutor how the athlete had done. "Oh," said the tutor, "I asked him who wrote Aristotle's *Politics,* and he said Plato. That was

wrong, so I asked him who wrote Plato's *Republic,* and he said he didn't know. That was right. So I gave him 50 percent, and so he passed."

With the C-average rule for admitting student athletes to college, that is what only too often happens. The rule should, of course, be abolished, and admission standards elevated to their proper levels, with no special favors for anyone.

Ultimately, as John Underwood has said, "the solution to the problem is caring. Caring about young people, caring about their being educated, caring about the contribution they will be able to make to society."

In our time, alas, sports have only too often become a means of evading education, and caring about society.

In the matter of games, of sports, I would bring about a complete revolution in the understanding of what games are for, and therefore, how they should be played. By this means I believe one may significantly help to change the value-structure of society. That would appear to some to be a difficult task. Perhaps it is; but, then, difficulties are made to be overcome.

It is true that the degradation of sports has, in the Western world at least, affected so many nations that the task seems insuperable. Professional sports have become gladiatorial shows. Ice hockey, which has been described as "war on ice," is supported by the media, movies, magazines, newspapers and the public. Major sections of newspapers and magazines are wholly devoted to the report of sports, and among the most popular of these is ice hockey. The appeal of that form of mayhem is much the same as that of auto racing. The Indianapolis 500 is the success it is largely because there is always the promise of the relief from the tedium of watching racing cars go round and round, by a really serious accident, which then makes the whole boring spectacle worth while. Ice hockey without violence is unthinkable. As one owner put it, "The crowd has an instinct for violence and blood, and we give them what they want." From the behavior of the crowds at such events it is clear that the real beast in the arena are the fans, the players are merely doing what the crowd wants them to do, and what they are paid to do.

Ice hockey is a so-called contact sport, which in reality is understood by everyone to mean physical assault. It is calculated violence routinely practiced and implicitly condoned by the National Hockey League. As one N.H.L. general manager admitted in private, club owners hate to tamper with a lucrative formula. (Editorial, 1980:22).

Professional hockey has been courting violence since the early 70s, when the Philadelphia Flyers discovered the commercial value of paying extras from "A Clockwork Orange," to slug it out nightly. A not inappropriate employment for extras from a movie based on Anthony Burgess's chillingly violent novel celebrating rape, violence, sexual sadism, brutality, and "the eternal savagery of man."

However, do not let us blame the players, the coaches, or even the businessmen who exploit the players. They are all victims of the same corrupt value system. For as Christopher Lasch has said, "What corrupts an athletic performance, as it does every other performance, is not professionalism or competition, but the presence of an unappreciative, ignorant audience and the need to divert it with sensations extrinsic to the performance. It is at this point that the ritual, drama, and sports degenerate into spectacle (Lasch, 1977).

The national media seem to be engaged in a compulsive drive to create heroes for their voracious audiences. The amount of printed space devoted to sports has already been mentioned. Television and radio also devote a disproportionate amount of time to sports. The sportscasters often become celebrities. What sells newspapers and magazines also sells TV and radio programs, so the networks pay huge sums for the rights to broadcast every variety of sports event, thus further enriching the owners as well as the players. The artificially created heroes of these sports, ranging from Olympic gold medal winners to skiing champions and everything in between, are assured of considerable financial rewards from the advertising world for the loan of their endorsements. And so the corruption is spread like an epidemic disease which knows no boundaries. The result has been to turn virtually every form of play into a contest. At an early age small children are trained for highly competitive sports, by methods which are shocking in their psychological crudity. Errors committed by Little Leaguers, in the presence of their Gung-Ho parents, elicit from coaches the most brutal criticism, coached in barroom language, or even more searing terms. The psychological damage done to many boys in this way is probably appreciable, and may be permanently disabling to those who do not "measure-up". It is certainly often enough handicapping to those who do, for it gives them a distorted view of life in what they have been told is the broad competitive arena of the world, a world in which the glittering prizes go to the strongest and most cunning: "the survival of the fittest". No one ever tells them that they have their biology wrong, that it is not the survival of the fittest, but the survival of the fit; that the fit remain flexible, malleable, and adaptable, whereas the fittest, being too specialized, become too rigid to be able to adapt to rapidly changing conditions.

The oft repeated statement that sports are a training in character, in the sense in which that word used to be understood, is a myth. It is a training in dehumanization, in violence. It is not surprising that the country with the sixth highest crime rate in the world, should have violent athletes, violent fans, and violent coaches, coaches who boast, as Woody Hayes, the famed coach of Ohio State University, did, "We teach our boys to spear and gore....We want them to plant that helmet right under the guy's chin....I want them to stick that mask right into the opponent's neck". (Sharnik and Creamer 1962:16).

After a long career of attacks on newsmen, photographers, and others, Woody Hayes outdid himself by punching an opposite number at the 1979 Gator Bowl, for which he was finally dismissed because of the widespread publicity, and was subsequently presented by his admirers with an award "for character building". No one said what kind of character building. But I will say it: the worst kind of character building, a training in dehumanization and violence, self-aggrandizement, disrespect for culture and education, in the debasement of humane values, in cheating, and the addiction to money-oriented commercialization.

It is this kind of training that contributes the 2 million members to the Americal Rifle Association, to one of the highest murder and violent assault rates in the world, to killers of defenseless animals, killers who, with peculiar irony, are called "sportsmen", and it contributes to far too many people who are ever ready to resort to violence to solve personal, interpersonal, and international problems. Paul Hoch, writing in 1972, commented, "More than twenty-five million Americans fostered their own dehumanization each weekend last fall as fans of big-time football....Collegiate and especially professional football reveal the fascist streak in our society....Football's totalitarian authority structure....reflects the militarism prevalent in our culture" (Bianchi, 1972:31). In similar vein, in the same year Paul Hoch argued that football surpassed baseball in popularity in the late 1960s because of the basic militarism in American life which found violent expression in games as well as on the battlefields of Vietnam (Hoch, 1972:7).

The truth is that in the United States we live in a culture of violence. It is therefore not surprising that sports, far from acting as a counterbalance to that violence, should be an expression of it, that football which is euphemistically called a contact sport, should have become a head-on collision sport. In the 1979 National Football League season over 20 percent of the players were out of the game because of serious injuries. Dr. John L. Marshall, Director of the Sports Medical Clinic at New York Hospital for Special Surgery, estimates that some 12 million Americans under age eighteen suffer from permanent, sports induced injuries. Thirty young people die each year from playing American football, and well over three hundred thousand are treated annually in hospital emergency rooms for football injuries. Battering ram helmets are responsible for more than 80 percent of highschool football fatalities. The number of injuries sustained in American amateur and professional sports is simply staggering, not a few of which incapacitate the victims for the rest of their lives. It has even been claimed that injuries dignify the game and give it zest, and that violence in football is "its special glory" (Stade, 1966:173). Coming from George Stade, Professor of English Literature at Columbia, who is a great admirer of Konrad Lorenz's On Aggression, the remark should be no surprise. As Allen Guttman (1978) has pointed out in his admirable book *From Ritual to Record* , there does seem to be a readiness to accept if not to seek injury as a way of dignifying the game. As one player put it, "You have to show that you don't care about your body" (Bloutut, 1974:117). And as Guttman remarks, "Injury for the contemporary football player is comparable to the duelling scars proudly borne by the nineteenth-century Prussian aristocrat. Injury becomes, therefore, a certificate of virility, a badge of courage" (Guttman, 1978:121). It is the kind of courage that led to the greatest collective murderousness, the holocaust, in the history of this planet. It is the kind of courage and virility that led to the conduct of American troops in Vietnam.

It would be tedious, were it even possible, to list the injuries which Americans inflict upon one another in the name of sport, a destructiveness which is exceeded only when the fans decide to play an active role in the game, in the form of what Peter Marsh (1978) has called "aggro". In May 1964 the worst stadium riot in history resulted when Peruvian fans protested what they considered to be an unfair nullification of a home-team goal in a pre-Olympic soccer game against Argentina. Nearly 50,000 Peruvian fanatics surged out of the bleachers, breaking up everything in sight, the intervention of the police only adding to the mayhem. At the final count there were 318 dead and over 500 injured. A final irony was a march by angry fans on the presidential palace demanding official intervention in declaring the game a tie. On another occasion during a soccer match between El Salvador and Honduras in 1969 each side claimed the other had used unfair tactics. This led not only to a riot, but to a three-day war between the two countries during which a thousand people were killed and rioting Honduran crowds attacked Salvadorans living in their country, sending a stream of more than 10,000 fleeing refugees into El Salvador and Nicaragua (Martz, 1979; Yeager, 1979).

The pervasive pathological brutalization of contemporary sports, and their dehumanizing effect upon the individual and society, has produced a widespread acceptance of them as perfectly normal--which indicates once again that pathogenic ideas and values can be quite as destructive, if not more so, than viral and bacterial pathogens. Pathogenic values can lead to the downfall of a society. It is, therefore, urgently necessary for us to identify those pathogenic ideas and values, if we are to succeed in returning games and sports to a state of health.

In order to do this with any promise of success we must first dispose of a number of myths. The first of these is the notion that violence or aggression, that is, the desire to inflict injury upon another, is instinctive in humans. In support of this view what is known to behavioral scientists as "the hydraulic theory" is often cited. This is the common belief that motives or tensions behave like a fluid under pressure, ready to break out through a weak spot when the pressure becomes too great. "Letting off steam" is the common phrase for this idea. Freud, McDougall, Lorenz, Tinbergen, and "the man on the street" have been the leading proponents of the hydraulic model. But the fact is that it is a complete myth, as Robert Hinde (1980) and others have shown.

It is quite unsound to believe that what is released in violent behavior is accumulated aggressive energy from a reservoir fed by a constant source. There is no evidence whatever, with the exception of rare pathological cases where a tumor of the brain is usually involved, that violent or aggressive behavior can occur spontaneously. On the contrary, the evidence indicates that such behavior is *reactive*. That is to say, the motivation to violent behavior is not always present, ready to be drawn upon, but is produced by external stimulation. Aggressive behavior is an *emergency* action, not a *maintenance* action. The presence of "a constant aggressive driving force would be counterproductive since there is no homeostatic equilibrium to be maintained, as in the case of hunger. Instead there is only adequate coping with environmental emergencies" (Klaus et al 1975:56).

A second popular myth, related to the hydraulic energy myth, is that the violence exhibited by sports crowds produces a cathartic effect, that it is, as Peter Marsh has claimed in his book *Aggro: The Illusion of Violence,* very similar to animal ritualization. By "ritualization" ethologists mean the modification, during evolution, of a behavior pattern, so that it becomes a social signal, (Burnett, 1981:616) a specialized behavior for communicating a specific message (Smith 1977:10). There is nothing whatever even remotely resembling the genetically evolved modification of behavior to serve communication involved in violent, so-called "aggro" behavior. The behavior of crowds, "aggro" behavior at sports events, is learned behavior and may be called "conventionalized" (Smith 1977:327). It has become the conventional way to behave at soccer and similar events, in exuberant and often violent ways. Ritualized aggression in animals rarely results in injury to others, being for the most part limited to feigned rather than actual aggression; it is threatening, but not injurious. It is, then, quite unsound to speak of the hunting factor in humans as posing a special threat, as Marsh does, and to argue that combined with the human ability to dehumanize our fellow humans, the hunting factor provides the basis for massacre, genocide, riots, and violent behavior at sports events. The total weight of the evidence indicates that far from having a cathartic effect sports and the violence displayed at them, on the contrary, breeds further violence and reinforces it.

The claim that aggressive sports redirect aggressive behavior away from violent activities of every sort, and are therefore to be encouraged as catharses, is also quite unsound. Anthropologists tested the hypotheses, and found that cultures that indulge in violent sports are the most violent and warlike, while those that engage in non-violent sports are the most unviolent and unwarlike (Sipes, 1973).

Americans play games violently and have one of the most violent crime rates in the world. Manhattan, with a population of 1.4 million had about 2,000 murders in 1980. Tokyo, with a population of 13 million had 50 murders. Americans, for the most part, seem to be blithely unaware of the violence of their culture, and take the terrible daily crime rates for granted. I have even heard one psychiatrist remark that perhaps it is the price we have to pay for American virility. The solutions offered by politicians and others like them are typically obtuse: restore capital punishment, institute stiffer sentences, build more jails, recruit more police, and Mr. George Wallace of Alabama said that if he were elected President he would put soldiers with fixed bayonets on every street corner. Such solutions are themselves an evidence of the violence of the culture: punish the criminals. What we hear too little of is discussion of the causes that produce criminals.

The problem is not crime, nor violence, nor sports, nor human nature. The problem lies with the values by which we live. In the land of Rugged American Individualism, in which competition and success are the principal values, ruthlessness becomes a virtue. For the many who fail in "the rat race", the frustrations are devastating. The individual in the lonely crowd feels rejected, disengaged, unrelated, and the response to the dried-up inner life which follows, to the frustration, to the need to fill the vacuum where there is no relatedness, is violence. As Rollo May has said, "When feeling decreases and apathy increases, when one cannot affect or even genuinely *touch* another person, violence flares up as a daimonic necessity for contact, a mad drive forcing touch in the most direct way possible" (May, 1969:31).

If the affectless individual cannot affect or touch anyone, he can at least shock them into some feeling, force them into some passion through wounds or pain. In this way he at least makes certain that both feel something, and thus force the other to take notice of him and know that he is there.

In almost any form, what is violence, if not love frustrated? If it takes violent behavior to be noticed, and even condemned, then it is better to be noticed and felt than ignored and untouched.

> I am one, my liege, whom the vile blows and buffets of the world have so incensed that I am reckless what I do to spite the world.
>
> *Macbeth*, III.1.

These are the men who lead lives of unquiet desperation. These are the men who have been failed in the opportunity to fulfill the promise they once gave, in common with all other human beings, of growing into healthy creative creatures. By health I mean the ability to love, the ability to work, the ability to play, and the ability to use one's mind as a fine instrument of precision. At this moment I think of the ringing words of John Stuart Mill in his 1859 essay *On Liberty* , "It still remains unrecognized, that to bring a child into existence without a fair prospect of being able, not only to provide food for the body, but instruction and training for its mind, is a moral crime, both against the unfortunate offspring and against society"(Mill, 1959:189). In a society which offers less than a fair prospect of fulfillment for so many who should never have been born because they have been deprived of their birthright, to grow and develop as healthy fulfilled human beings, there are going to be many victims who are thoroughly frustrated and deformed, sick with bitterness, and understandable hostility ready to visit itself upon the nearest target.

We are not going to eliminate violence from our sports until we reduce, at least, the sanctification of violence in our society in all the varied forms it takes, from the singing of our violent national anthems, with "bombs bursting in air", through our military-industrial establishments, our ritual incantations, uncritical patriotisms, and worship of success, winning, and competition. Nor will we get far until we reform our instructional systems and turn them into genuine educational systems, in which the most important of all the arts and sciences are taught: the art and science of love, of compassion and committment, of relatedness, of cooperation. The three "R"'s are important, but mainly as secondary skills which enable each of us more effectively to live as if to live and love were one.

At present our children are schooled in brainwashing institutions that meet corporate/nationalistic ends, not human needs. We give our children answers, but do not teach them to ask questions. To deny children the tools to solve problems, to make inquiry, to create a reality, an environment which is fulfilling and sustaining to them, is a denial of basic human rights.

Unless we undertake a fundamental revision of the values and convictions by which most people live in our shrinking world, we are doomed to realize the prediction that we were the only species that destroyed itself. Remembering, however, that the only philosophically tenable position for a pessimist in a time of crisis is optimism, there is a great deal of work for us to do. We must work as if by our labors we can bring about the changes which cumulatively may turn man around from the disastrous course he has lately been pursuing at an exponential rate.

One of the wonderful things about our species is that we are the most educable creatures on this earth. That is why to be human is to be in danger, because we are not only capable of learning more sound things but also more *unsound* things than any other creature. And when you combine the two you don't get intelligence, you get confusion. And truth, as Lord Bacon remarked more than 400 years ago, grows more readily out of error than it does out of confusion.

It will not be easy to rectify the confusion which has been produced in so many millions of victims. It is nevertheless a challenge to which we must all rise, for our very survival depends upon whether we do so or not.

Where, then, do we begin? We begin where charity (which I remind you is but another word for love, "caritas") begins: at home, with ourselves. To the extent that we have been failed as warm loving human beings, it is never too late to mend. All that is required is that we begin behaving as if we were loving people. For what we are, is not what we believe or what we say, but what we do. The meaning of a word is the action it produces. And love is demonstrative, it means to communicate to the others by demonstrative acts your profound involvement in their welfare, your deep interest in their fulfillment as the unique beings they are, that they may depend upon you standing by ministering to their needs for growth and development, giving them all the supports, stimulations, and succor they require for the realization of those marvelous capacities with which they are endowed, for sensitivity, for joy, for curiosity, creativity, learning, play, inventiveness, song and dance, and many others, and above all for love. (Montagu 1966; 1970; 1974; 1975; 1978; 1981; Orlick, 1978; Walsh, 1981).

It is only through such means that the human community can be brought back into being, and it is by this means, through love, that most, if not all human problems will be solved — including the restoration of sports to their true role: a major contribution toward the humanization of humankind. Teaching that sports can be a beautiful expression of the humanity of man and woman, an expression of art, science, skill and love — of love of the game and love of one's fellow players, that above all one plays for joy, always doing one's best, hoping that one's opposite number will bring out the best in oneself, as one does in him, and rejoicing in the play of the other, as well as one's own, whoever wins. Winning, contrary to Vince Lombardi, is not the only thing or everything; the only thing and everything is being a good sport, and that means playing the game for love, as a metaphor for life. Though it has been many times cited and perhaps has become hackneyed in the process, nevertheless I fully subscribe to Grantland Rice's view:

> For when the One Great Scorer Comes
> To write against your name,
> He marks — not that you won or lost —
> But how you played the game.

We can begin teaching the children the difference between competitive and cooperative competition, as a model for the nobility and dignity of humankind, that losing well is as much to be honored as winning well, and that with a logic that few understand, the true winner in a race is often the one who comes in last.

In the world toward which we should work there would be no professional sports, not competitors but cooperators, lovers who play for the love of the game. Neither to win nor to lose, but to do one's best and have fun.

REFERENCES

S.A. Barnett, *Modern Ethology*. New York: Oxford University Press, 1981.

Blount, R. Jr., *About Three Bricks Shy of a Load*. Boston: Little, Brown, 1974.

Bianchi, E. "Pigskin Piety", *Christianity and Crisis*, 21 February 1972, pp. 31-32.

Guttmann, A. *From Ritual to Record: The Nature of Modern Sports*. New York: Columbia University Press, 1978.

Editorial, "Blow the Whistle on Ice Hockey Violence", *The New York Times*, 2 January 1980, p. A.22.

Hinde, R.A. "Energy Models of Motivation", *Symposia of the Society for Experimental Biology*, Vol. 14, 1960, pp. 199-213.

Hoch, P. *Rip Off the Big Game*. New York: Doubleday-Anchor Books, 1972.

James, A. (editor), *The Letters of William James*. Two volumes, Boston: The Atlantic Monthly Press, 1920, Vol. 2, p. 260.

Lasch, C. "The Corruption of Sports", *The New York Review of Books*, 28 April 1977.

May R. *Love and Will*. New York: W.W. Norton, 1969.

Martz, M.J. *The Central American Soccer War*. Athens, Ohio: Ohio University Press, 1979.

Marsh, P. *Aggro: The Illusion of Violence*. London: Dent, 1978.

Mill, J.S. *On Liberty*. London: John P. Parker & Son, 1859, p. 189.

Montagu, A. *On Being Human*. Revised edition. New York: Hawthorn Books, 1966.

Montagu, A. *The Direction of Human Development: The Biological Bases of Love*. Revised edition, New York: Hawthorn Books, 1970.

Montagu, A. (editor), *Culture and Human Development*. Englewood Cliffs, N.J.: Prentice-Hall, 1974.

Montagu, A. (editor). *The Practice of Love*. Englewood Cliffs, N.J.: Prentice-Hall, 1975.

Montagu, A. *Touching*. Second edition. New York: Harper & Row. 1978.

Montagu, A., and Matson, F. *The Human Connection*. New York: McGraw-Hill, 1979.

Montagu, A. *Growing Young*. New York: McGraw-Hill, 1981.

Orlick, T. *Winning through cooperation — Competitive insanity: Cooperative alternatives*. Washington, D.C.: Acropolis Press, 1978.

Scherer, K.R., ASbeles, R.P., and C.S. Fischer, *Human Aggression and Conflict*. Englewood Cliffs, N.J.: Prentice-Hall, 1975.

Sharnik, M. and Creamer, R. "A Rough Day for the Bear", *SI* 26 November 1962.

Sipes, R. "War and Aggression: an Empirical Test of Two Rival Theorioes", *American Anthropologist*, Vol. 75, 1973, pp. 64-86.

Smith, J.W. *The Behavior of Communicating*. Cambridge: Harvard University Press, 1977.

Stade, G. "Game Theory", *Columbia Forum*, Fall 1966.

Underwood, J. "Foul Play in College Sports", *Sports Illustrated*, 19 May 1980.

Underwood, J. *The Death of An American Game: The Crisis in Football*. Boston, Little, Brown, 1980.

Walsh, A. *Human Nature and Love: Biological, Intrapsychic and Social Behavioral Perspectives*. Washington: University Press of America, 1981.

Yeager, R.C. *Seasons of Shame: The New Violence in Sports*. New York: McGraw-Hill, 1979.

REFLECTIONS ON EDUCATION, LOVE AND CHILDREN[1]

Ashley Montagu (USA)

EDUCATION

If you want one word that distinguishes human beings from all other creatures on the face of this earth it is educability. We are creatures that are capable of learning anything, not only under the sun but over the sun, anything not only that you can think of but anything that you can't think of. And therein lies the rub — because if you are such a creature it means that you can learn more rubbish as well as more sound things than any other creature on this earth and it means that if you put the rubbish and the sound together you don't get intelligence, you get confusion and this is the state that human beings are in and have been for some time now — not homo sapiens, the wise guy, but homo sap.

But the sapiens — the wisdom is there — as a potentiality. We are capable of being the most wonderful creatures on this earth. At the moment we have become the most destructive creatures on this earth. Not only destructive of the whole rest of animate and even inanimate nature but destructive of ourselves. Not the lion or the tiger or the elephant are the most endangered species — it is the homo sap that is the most endangered species — *self-endangered* — who stands at the very end of a very short time on this earth if he continues to go on in the direction in which he is at present doing.

Can education change this direction? What is school today? It's not an educational institution — it's an instructional institution. We don't have any education. Instruction is mistaken for education. Education in brief is the art and science of being a warm, loving human being.

LOVE

What is love? Love is something that has been the most important factor in the evolution of the human species. It's a word that we use very frequently but that very few of us have any real understanding of.

Yet we can now show you its effects in X-rays, in test tubes. Biochemically there are differences between a person who has been loved and one who hasn't been loved and this begins from the moment you are born. We can show you because if the mother hasn't been loved, the baby suffers. If the mother is emotionally disturbed during the pregnancy you can pick this up in the baby. Often the baby will behave like a neurotic. If you know what to look for you can look at X-rays of his bones and pick it up in the bones. If you haven't been loved during the growth of your bones — (i.e. in the womb and after birth while the bone is growing) then the deposition of the bone will be such that there will be condensation of bone — lines of varied thickness. This deposition will occur because not being loved is a very serious biochemical deficiency of a very complex nature. If this kind of change occurs in the body of the unloved fetus, the unloved child, the unloved adolescent who is still growing, then you can imagine what may be happening in the brain — in the mind.

We can define love as the process of demonstrative acts by means of which there are conferred upon the other survival *benefits*. You confer survival benefits upon the other in a creatively enlarging manner. If you want the basic pattern and pattern model for love it is what the loving mother does with her dependent baby. That's love. And with it being the most important factor in the evolution of our species, *the role of human beings is to live as if to live and love were one*. Why? — not because I said so or because God said so or anyone else said so, but because the marvellous creative process we call evolution shows us that this is the way which human beings managed to survive through their long and difficult history over the last 3-4 or more million years.

Total populations of human beings up to the very recent years (i.e. the period when agriculture was first discovered) lived in small populations. Agriculture enabled one for the first time to stay put in one place instead of hunting by food gathering and wandering all over the earth. This enabled one to enlarge one's population and is where our miseries really began. This is a fascinating story itself—how we departed from these marvellous people — the food gathering/hunting peoples — because this is how we lived up to 12 thousand years ago. Populations were comprised of between 30 and 50 people — that was the total size of human populations up to 15 thousand years ago. The average age of death was 33 years and increased by a third only up to 1865. But longevity is not important — the duration of the number of years that you live is not important — what is important is the quality of the years you live — not the quantity. If you can put a larger quantity of years into that quality — so much the better. Always remember that it is the quality of love, not the quantity of love, that is important. It is the one thing of which you cannot give anyone too much because it has its own discipline, its own "yes" and its own "no" which is understood perfectly by those who have been truly loved; some of you know from your former experience, of those who have consistently loved you, that everything they have done has been from love for your benefit.

CHILDREN

Children are the most honest creatures in the world; they are also enormously imaginative; their curiosity, their explorativeness, experimentalism, their open mindedness, their need for love — not only to be loved but to love others, to think, to learn, to wonder and sensitivity are all enormously important. You see we are deformed babies, deformed children, brought up by people who haven't the least idea of what babies or children are for, what they need. Adults have imposed their own deformed ideas upon the child — in other words, the child has become like themselves. The poor child often questions whether adults ever were children and then decides out of charity they probably never were but were all created adults. So he keeps his own true self to himself and suffers alone until he becomes completely dehumanized as do most people who have to go through life acting out roles according to their betters, their educators. Mother, father know best and the culture does this by imposing its ideas upon the schools, school boards, teachers and so forth. So we are all victims and *what we all end up as being is no more or less than deteriorated children*. What we are designed to grow and develop as, were those qualities that I have named. As children we're designed to grow as children, not as adults — not to be arrested at the level of the child but to grow in all those wonderful traits of the child. To grow and develop — to grow means to increase in amplitude — to develop means to increase in complexity. And that is what we are designed to do. And those of us who grow this way sometimes do say of another person we particularly like — he or she has childlike qualities. Isaac Newton was described as childlike. Albert Einstein was a neighbour of mine and friend. The first time I ever met him, I rang the door bell, it was opened by a

---

[1] The material in this article on education, love and children was extracted from Ashley Montagu's oral presentation at the Fifth World Sport Psychology Congress.

secretary and he danced down the long corridor like a child. And he laughed like a child, fought like a child but a highly developed child. This has been said of many great and distinguished and wonderful human beings — several of whom I have been privileged to know.

What we need are men who have become more like women — all those qualities we call feminine but which are not feminine at all but are human qualities which men have denegrated because they are the possessions of women. We need gentleness — just imagine gentleness — that he is a gentle creature being said of a man, and yet that is the only true strength. Brawn is not strength, it is weakness. That's what is wrong with the U.S. foreign political policy at the present time. We use our weakness, the American weakness, which we call strength, against the weakness of the Russians who also believe in arms and brawn. It is not brawn which we need to fall back upon but brain — humanity.

In so far as sports are concerned, what this means is that sports should be a loving interchange in which one brings out the best in each other.

THE DEVELOPMENT OF COOPERATIVE COMPETITION AND SPORTSMANSHIP IN CHINA

Wang Min Qi (The People's Republic of China)

Tradition

China is known for its long history, distinct culture, rich philosophy, literature and art. Chinese people, since ancient times, understood the importance of cooperation which among other things was considered to be the guarantee of victory over the enemy as well as natural disasters. We have been told many classical stories on cooperation. In first year primary school we learned the following story from the textbook. Although it is simple, it does tell us a truth: unity and cooperation is strength.

"Once upon a time, there was an old man who had ten sons. When he was dying, he called his ten sons over, and took out ten chopsticks. He gave each son a chopstick and asked them to try to break it. Each son broke one chopstick without any difficulty. Then the old man took out another ten chopsticks and this time he bundled them up and asked each son to try again to break them. None of them could break the ten chopsticks tied together no matter how hard they tried. They looked at each other in blank dismay. Then the old man said: See, each of you is just like one chopstick, one chopstick is easy to break. If you unite and cooperate, your strength is so great that no one can easily destroy you".

The more important aspect of studies on cooperation in the modern world today are undertaken with a view to deliberately modifying the cooperative conditions in which children and younger generations are living and will live. The effective and ideal way to create a cooperative environment and educate the young is interesting to psychologists and educators of different countries regardless of its culture, tradition, or political system. No one would deny that cooperative behavior is a learned behavior which, in all kinds of fields including sports is dependent upon education. Because cooperation is strongly influenced and shaped by the social environment, I would like to share with you how this social environment of cooperation functions in China.

The Policy

In China, the government policy on education is "to enable everyone to develop morally, intellectually and physically". The guiding principle in sport is — "to promote physical culture and sports and build up our people's health". Since 1949, educators in schools and other institutions generally have followed this policy and principle. *The government and educators have paid great attention to inculcating within students and athletes an understanding of the importance of cooperation, unity, fairplay and sportsmanship when taking part in physical activities, sports and competitions.*

Unfortunately, the development of cooperative behavior is not as simple as that of planting a seed. A seed can naturally grow to be useful once it is planted, but the development of children and their concepts can follow in a desirable or undesirable way depending on how they are educated and are influenced. When a child is born, his character is a blank paper. It is the societal opinion and education that make him either cooperative or competitive, or whatever.

Collective Beginnings

Perhaps the first time many Chinese children experience collective life is in kindergarten, where life is comprised mainly of play, games, handwork, dancing, singing, story-telling, sight-seeing and other group activities. Kindergarten is an extension of the primary school which most children attend from age 4-6.

It has been demonstrated that children prefer play and games which correspond with the intellectual, psychological and interest development, to other activities. Most play and games not only improve health, develop basic motor ability and physical fitness, but are fun. Through subtle ways play and games (along with other activities) develop the children's ideas of unity, cooperation and discipline. They become active and helpful to each other. Take the role-play-game "Locomotive Engine" for example. When the game starts, the child station-master gives the signal for several "passengers" waiting in the line board the "train". The "driver" pulls the whistle and starts the train. At the same time, passengers begin to sing: "Hong long long long hong hong, hong long long long hong hong ...", imitating the sound of moving train, rhythmically. All participants have their own roles for which they must be responsible and all participants must cooperate with others and observe the discipline; otherwise the game is ruined.

Another role-play-game example is called "On Duty". A child "on duty" plays the role of a teacher who is in charge of "students" doing extracurricular activities and thorough cleaning. The "teacher" gathers the "students", assigns the tasks and the whole game occurs in an orderly fashion. A parent once shared his impressions with me. While he watched his child in the game, he had "the feeling that his child became, in the twinkling of an eye, much more capable and mature". The child performed a role which the parent could not imagine the child doing at home. In the game, the child who plays the role of teacher must understand his or her duty and must be concerned with the reaction of the "students". He or she must encourage everyone, who has his or her own "student role" to cooperate with the "teacher" and others. Here every role is experiencing cooperative and disciplined interaction and this concept can be accepted easier through the game.

When I was young, every time when I joined the role-play game, I could not help becoming more honest and attentive. In the role-play-game, you realize that you are not alone. You are in a collective, so your actions are not only responsible for yourself, but also for the others and collective.

In the game, "Big Fish Net", a group of children hand-in-hand serve as a net catching some children serving as fish in a given space. Every child can find truth apparently from their own actions: if all the children serving as the net move cooperatively and coordinately, like one child, the fish is caught; if not, the net may be "broken" and no fish caught.

I was once deeply touched by the dance-game "Planting Trees For The Community". You could not believe without seeing with your own eyes that such young children's performances could be of such high quality, demonstrating unity and cooperation, joint effort and high spirit.

I believe that this kind of play and games have a substantial influence on Chinese children. *In many countries teachers in kindergarten and curriculum design are more concerned with activities to develop the children's physical skills and fitness, rather than developing cooperative ideas at the same time.*

It is not without meaning to probe into the educational role of different play and games and design

better and better ones.

An eyewitness account by an American visiting a nursery school in China reports:

"Outside, one section of the school was in recess, and almost a hundred children were engaged in a game of tug-of-war. Some of our American women started choosing sides and shouting encouragement. As if to answer us, the children stopped in the middle of the pulling and chanted to each other, "Friendship first! Competition second! Friendship first! Competition second! We learn from you. You learn from us. We learn from each other!"

Suddenly an American leaped into the fray, she chose a side, picked up the end of the rope, and pulled with all her might until all the children fell down. The other American women laughed and applauded, but I noticed that the children were very confused and the teacher looked mystified.

The children got up, and the teacher started shifting the players, so that some of the stronger children would balance out the sides. She blew a whistle and they started again. This time, another American jumped in. She added her strength to one end of the rope, and managed to topple as many children as another American had.

The children were looking at us as if we were violent and aggressive strangers who had come to play games to which we did not know the rules. We had disturbed their game, and we had even applauded the disturbance. If the lesson of the game really was to make competition secondary to friendship, we had made a mess of the lesson" (MacLaine, 1975).

School, Physical Education, and Interest Group

Two 50-minute PE class per week for high school and two 45-minute for primary school are obligatory. In addition to this, one-hour of physical exercise or group activities every afternoon is recommended. The teachers and instructors are challenged to discover the students' different interests and to provide the proper environment and opportunity, which can be best used for cooperative behavior and cooperative ideas. Without such environment and opportunity for students to develop their interests and to participate in cooperative activities, school life would be rather dry and uninteresting. The students could not stay in the classroom all day long.

I may forget some of the lessons I have learned in the classroom, but I will not forget the things I experienced in the "interest group". I may forget some classmates, but I will not forget the playmates in the "interest group". The "interest group" was offered to students in the primary school and high school which I attended as an extracurricular activity. As the term suggests, it is a group for interested students. Most schools in China offer the same sort of group. The "interest group" may consist of a variety of activities, such as drawing, singing, musical instrument playing, poetry, drama, hi-fi, chess, but above all, sports, which are able to attract the students' interest. A sports group can consist of different events, such as track and field, ball games, soccer, basketball, volleyball, table tennis, badminton, swimming, gymnastics, Chinese traditional boxing and general physical exercises.

Most students choose their own interest group and join group activities at a regular time, usually in the afternoon. The instructors who are good in these fields, guide the members of the group. They practice techniques collectively, give performances and take part in games and competitions. Through these team activities, group awareness and mutual aid are cultivated. Discipline, cooperation and organization can be instilled through collective activities.

Cooperative education is better undergone in the process of activities in sports and physical training. The students must inevitably show different behavior in the collective. The instructors should be good at observing students behavior in activities from their language and actions, in which their attitudes are exposed. The instructors should take full advantage of the educational opportunity and give the timely feedback.

The experienced instructors may arrange some special or unusual conditions for the members of the group. For example:

• Offer better and worse, new and used equipment at the same time to the students to see if they take better or new ones for themselves and let the playmates have worse and used ones, or just the contrary;

• assign a skilled and unskilled student to practice together to see if the skilled will help the unskilled warmly or show impatience;

• ask a successful student to introduce and demonstrate his experience and technique to the group to see if he is willing and eager to do that or if he is not willing and does so with reserve;

• offer a less sufficient amount of equipment or apparatus to the group to see if everyone will "grab" the opportunity for practice himself or let the playmates have the practice opportunity first;

• set the contest with strong team and weak team to see how students react during the match and after the match, in other words, how they look at winning and losing;

• whenever a game or even just a practice session is finished, organize a short meeting, ask the students to sum up what (and how) they have learned and done, and what has been desirable or undesirable;

• whenever and wherever a problem occurs (either personal or group) let students voice their own opinions, let them judge which is a proper way to deal with the problem and which is not, then adopt the reasonable suggestions of the group.

• Let every student become aware that some problems one alone cannot solve, but the cooperative group can.

From the reality, the students become clear and accept the truth:

"More people mean a greater ferment of ideas, more enthusiasm and more energy".

"If we are all of one heart and one mind, we can change clay into gold".

"Three cobblers with their wits combined equal Zhuge Liang the master mind."

(Zhuge Liang was an historical character in Three Kingdom Period. He is said to have been exceptionally wise and full of strategies).

Positive and Negative Behavior

You might be interested to know what our basic standard is in judging and evaluating positive and negative behaviors in a group. *Simply speaking: "Be devoted to others and cooperate with others" reflects the positive. "Go one's own way, benefit oneself first and care not about others" reflects the negative.*

For positive behaviors, the instructors should lose no chance to encourage and praise and set up a fine example for the others. For negative behaviors, the instructors should not hesitate to redirect them enthusiastically, rather than letting things drift. It is better to adopt methods of reasoning, talking to them patiently, assisting them to analyze the disadvantages and advantages, fostering their ability to tell right behavior from wrong ones. It is important that the students know the significance of cooperative behavior; in other words, what is right and what is wrong, furthermore, why it is right, why it is wrong, and that they can display the cooperative actions conscientiously. Once the students have established positive ideas and behaviors in early group activities, sports and competitions, *these ideas and behaviors may remain with them to higher level sports and competitions, as well as in other endeavors.*

The spirit of cooperation and comradeship are seen in many aspects of "interest group" activities where students gradually understand and accept contribution as a part of a group, *and move from that demarcation line of when self is paramount, to when the group takes on the greater importance.*

The Young Pioneers

In China it is believed that under the guidance of an instructor and under the leadership of organizations, a collection of individuals comprising a group realizes that they can solve problems better through joint action than by taking individual action.

The "Young Pioneers Brigade" is found in every primary school. Education aims at the all-round development of the young students, in the sense, that it aims to develop a young student's body, mind and morals. The motto of the young pioneer is to be a "Five-good" and "Five Loves" student, that is, good in study, good in work, good in body, good in thinking, and good in labour; love of the fatherland, love of the people, love of labour, love of science, and love with respect of public property.

The Brigade brings the young students together, organizes the meeting discussing the tasks the members should do, and evaluates the students' positive and negative behavior in order for them to make better progress.

The members in the Brigade are encouraged to do good things for others, to do public good and to help each other. In the Brigade, the members are formed as a group and this group is characterized by cooperative behavior.

The moment I was admitted as a member of the Brigade, I felt different from what I used to be. I was a member of collective. I must exert to do better for the collective where every member is required to be coactive and cooperative.

"The Youth league" admits young people 15 above. It is a continuum of "Young Pioneer Brigade". Since the members in Youth League are older than young pioneers, they are subject to higher demands. The general goals are the same.

Media Support

There are several newspapers and journals for the members of the Youth League as well as for other people. Chong Nien Pao (China Children News) educate the members and other people by publishing many articles reporting exemplary real life people and deeds from which the members can constantly absorb new ideas and learn from those examples.

They also publish articles and caricatures criticizing and mocking poor and ill behavior. Typical cases would be those who benefit oneself at the expense of others or seek private gain at public expense. Every time I read and saw those articles and caricatures I would look at those poor behaviors, then warn myself: "Oh, I will never follow that!" They made quite an impression on me as a youngster.

In the 1960's, China raised the campaign to learn from Lei Feng, who was an ordinary soldier and is distinguished by finding it a pleasure to help others. His selfless deeds and excellent diary, when published, found a tremendous echo in the hearts of thousands upon thousands of Chinese people, old and young. Lei Feng helped an old lady find her relative when she lost her way in the rain; gave money to a passenger who lost his train ticket; sent his deposit to the community suffering a flood; served as a voluntary instructor of a school Pioneer Brigade, to name just a few. In one word, he did help others wherever and whenever possible at the expense of his own interest and his own leisure time. He wrote in his diary: "The purpose of my life is to make others live finer and more glorious".

Lei Feng is considered to be a "fool" by some people, but the majority of Chinese think Lei Feng's unselfish spirit and deeds have been the example of the most lofty ideals and noble-minded behavior of human beings.

It is my belief that this campaign greatly and deeply influenced the Chinese people's moral ideals and behaviors, especially the students. It has been one of the biggest and most significant campaigns on moral education, thus far. Many students did their best to follow Lei Feng's good example of doing others good, which became the order of the day at many schools. Actually, this campaign still exists and is advocated.

Coaching Values

In China, teachers are held in high esteem by students, perhaps more so for PE instructors and coaches. They are teaching an attractive subject, passing on interesting techniques and worthwhile activities. They have an essential and indispensable role. They work with students at daily tasks, physical training and competitions. They have frequent opportunities to see student's behavior, his ways of doing things, his responses to others and theirs to him or her. In this case, the viewpoint of PE instructors and coaches themselves is very important, for they are supposed to teach the right concept of value, and teach students how to live up to it. They teach what they think is right to the students. The students learn what is right in terms of them, according to them, from them. So Chinese say: "An educator should be a paragon of virtue and learning".

At school, I frequently took part in games and competition. I was never told or made to feel: "You must win!", "If you win, you will be awarded . . .". When the contest came, the coach told us simply: "Try your best!" That is all. On my teams, no one was reproached when losing, but instead was encouraged. *One was supposed to be blamed only if he displayed poor sportsmanship.* After each game or contest, the coach would organize a summary meeting and he never just said how so and so won, so and so lost. He would say how so and so displayed fine sportsmanship and asked us to learn from him or them. Then he would ask the players who did not display fair-play, to undergo self-criticism (or self-reflection) which also served as a warning to others.

Who could be sure, from the very start that you could display only positive behavior and no negative behavior? In games and competition, we had quarrels and occasionally even fought with other teams and among ourselves. But whenever it occurred, the coach would come to stop the game; the fighter and quarreller were ordered to quit. Then the coach would have a person-to-person talk with you, tell you and explain why you were wrong, until you understood and admitted the mistakes and promised not to do it again. Otherwise you were not supposed to re-enter the game or competition.

Every other week our coach would take all the members of the team to watch the local sports games. The coach commented on the athletes' performances — technique, skill, discipline, cooperation, fairplay etc. At that time, we worshiped some outstanding athletes and followed their good examples. Once in a while, the coach invited some athletes to school to give performances and lectures, telling us how they were brought up to maturity and excellence.

The coach did his best not only in teaching us skills, but more important, in establishing a cooperative relationship within the team and with others. He made us recognize and do our share for others' needs and our concepts of discipline and cooperation were rooted in our mind at that time.

As I grew up, I participated in more games, visited more places, talked with more people, read sport reports and also coached my young teams and college teams. I realized my coach did like many other coaches in China.

Cooperative Competition

This seemingly conflicting topic has been widely discussed from different fields by many people interested and concerned with both theory and practice.

Competition is defined as rivalry between opposing forces in which the interests of both are not mutually obtainable. From this definition, it seems competition and cooperation are regarded as antithetical. But in China, we do not look at competition and cooperation as conflict in sport contests.

When we have finished a reading and writing course, we are given an exam. Through the exam, we can become aware how much we have learned and how much we have failed to learn. The results provide us the information which serves as a guide for future effort and progress. By the same token, when athletes have learned and practiced sports skills, competitions and contests — (some sort of exam) — are held to test how many skills they have obtained and mastered and how (in what areas) they have lagged behind. Without any exam or contest, without comparison by certain standards, how could you know that? But contests have much more meaning than paper exams.

On the sports fields, the athletes and players can directly observe each other's performances and compare each other's techniques. Is it not the very opportunity to learn from each other, gain from watching each other's strength and make up one's own weak point? Is it not the opportunity for athletes and players to gather together to know each other, exchange sports experiences, benefit from each other, spread the values of sports and get more people involved? A brilliant performance is also an "art" through which spectators can gain enjoyment, get aesthetic feelings and make cultural life more colorful.

In China, friendship is indeed placed above winning. In all sports games, either at the school level, or national level, the importance of the athletes doing their best rather than winning against others is stressed.

A lot of people have heard about the slogan "friendship first, competition second" which serves as our sporting philosophy. The "Friendship first, competition second" concept was widely publicized both inside and outside China in the 1970s, whenever sporting competitions took place among the Chinese themselves or with other countries. This motto greatly influenced and continues to influence sports contests. The younger athletes and players are brought up by the belief that friendship, which can be established through sports competition, is eternal, while winning and losing are temporary. The slogans "good health is more important than material rewards" and "missing a shot instead of hurting the other" represent the desirable attitude of Chinese athletes toward contest.

Easier said than done. In real contests, every athlete is challenged to face different situations where individual interest, the interest of the collective, the interest of opponents, and the attractive outcome, reward, fame, social status, prize, tour...are all involved. The contest is really a trial of the athlete's behavior.

Imagine this situation: A scoring chance occurs, but an opponent happens to slip down in front of you. Your score may be at the expense of injuring him. You have one of the two choices, which do you choose? In China, giving up the scoring chance instead of causing the other's injury is encouraged and is considered sportsmanship. Choosing to score and injuring the other is not acceptable. No one will cheer and applaud for your score.

Play rules are the most rudimentary principle in sports and competitions. But the moral excellence of human beings should be more than just obeying the rules. Play rules do not necessarily include sportsmanship. Does any rule say athletes should help each other? But athletes do. In China, skilled athletes pass their successful and unique techniques to younger athletes during contests and do not care about gain or loss. Those things happen often and are praised. Also, sports clinics are everywhere, between teams, districts and between countries.

In order to enhance unity and cooperation among team members and between various teams, sports teams often start some sort of "drive". "One help one" drive is a within-team activity. Every team has better and "so-so" athletes in skills and concepts. One-Help-One means each better athlete matches up and cooperates with a "so-so" one and gives him constant person-to-person help. In this way, the whole team can make better and quicker improvement.

Another drive is called "emulate, learn from, catch up with, help and in turn surpass each other". As the words suggest this drive calls for every one on the team and among various teams to do better.

Before beginning any contest, whether school, local or national, the teams acknowledge each other with the greeting "we learn from you" and then shake hands before the contest starts. Whoever makes a foul, or offends the opponent, shows his hand immediately to the referee, or shakes hands with the opponent on his own initiative, meaning "sorry". The athletes on both sides are encouraged to demonstrate their best technique and give a good account of themselves and display fine sportsmanship.

As a result of the education in the schools, the early experiences in sports and competitions, the influence of public opinion and the societal context, most Chinese athletes look at the competition and contest as the demonstration of a combination of sportsmanship and performance.

In our country, negative behaviors still happen sometimes in competitions and contests. For example rough play, lack of respect for the referee, impoliteness to the opponents. But these negative behaviors are under constant criticism and redirection, under the pressure of public opinion, so these negative behaviors do not become so serious and do not become too pervasive.

In 1958, the first National Boxing Match was held in Tianjing -- one of China's biggest cities. In the first round, one boxer was injured by an opponent and died on the spot. A lot of athletes and citizens were rather disturbed and the government adopted the decision of prohibiting the boxing event. Of course that was not the only or necessarily the most ideal way to solve the problem. However the Chinese had and still have this view in looking at sports and competitions: If it can seriously cause injuries and deaths, it is no good. What can violent behavior give our younger generation?

If all athletes understood that contests are for athletes to show two qualities - sportsmanship and performance - the whole game would be more beautiful and glorious than ever.

In China, there are usually two kinds of prizes for all levels of competitions. One is of course for individual performance, and the other is for teams and individuals who display fine sportsmanship, cooperation, fairplay, etc.

The excellent players and fine performances should be, without fail, praised and acknowledged, but every player should know that individual achievement could not have been achieved without the help of the teammates, coaches and others. Could a volleyball player succeed in a good spike without the cooperation of the setter and other teammates?

In my country, the winners are, time and again, exhorted that success and achievement are the results of the collective team, the result of cooperation, but not a person alone. Once success is made, the players are warned not to let the success go to their heads but try to find out where they fall short. *Can it be that they leave nothing to be desired?* "Modesty makes people progress, conceit makes people lag behind".

Losing

An inevitable outcome of competitive sports is that there are always losers as well as winners. Winning and losing describe a temporary difference by certain standards which exists not only in sports contests but in many other fields as well. Sports contests are considered an opportunity to "learn from others' strong points to offset one's own weakness" and this Chinese idiom is often told to athletes.

Players and athletes are impressed upon from the beginning that losing a game, well and seriously and honestly played, is part of the natural uncertainties of life and is an experience which should not lead to shame. When losing, the younger athletes are often reminded of the fact that even national and international outstanding athletes have to start from obscurity. But through repeated practice and competitions, learned strength from others, and new experiences from each competition, their technique improves from each loss. They finally, became excellent. When you see national or international competitions and the high jumper clears the bar with ease, have you ever thought that he might have failed to clear the bar thousands of times before? Winning is based on countless losses. The Chinese people have summed up, from long experience, a motto: "Failure is the mother of success".

Spectators

I want to say something about my impression of watching American football. Once in Dallas, the Dallas Cowboys played against the Philadelphia Eagles. The moment the Eagles appeared on the field, the spectators began shouting "boo". My neighbor told me to shout "boo! boo!" all the time, even if the Eagles made a score or successful play. He shouted with all his might. But whenever the Dallas cowboys made a score or something, my neighbor would stand and shout a cheer.

This occurred again in Tallahhassee, Florida when the Florida State University football team played Pittsburgh University. The spectators cheered for only the home team and sneered at the visitors. When the home team made a score, the electronic scoreboard would display: "What a score! What a kick! Go team go!..." Then on the electronic scoreboard a picture showed a ball flying fantastically over the bar. But when the visiting team made a score, I looked at the scoreboard instinctively, but what would happen? Nothing!

I was very much surprised and confused. Because in my country, the spectators applaud and encourage the good performances of both sides, regardless of whether the visiting teams come from other schools, cities or provinces. The same is true when teams from other countries visit our country and play a match there.

I watched American basketball teams play in Peking several times. I, among thousands of spectators, applauded and cheered for the excellent performances of the American team and our home team, perhaps more for the visiting team. No one ever told us to do so: it is not mandatory, it is voluntary. In my country "boo" is only used when the spectators find the athletes engaging in poor sportsmanship and rough behavior, which seldom happens.

Would it not be better if the spectators expect and enjoy good performances from both sides -- home teams and visiting teams -- instead of just expecting the home team to win? Would it be conducive to cooperation or violence if the spectators applauded and encouraged players on both teams?

Mass Media

Mass media is the strongest voice of public

opinion. China has a centralized leadership governing all sports and physical education programs, including mass media propaganda, such as movies, radio, television and press. The mass media had done a big job educating the players, students and children. I will give some examples:

The popular movie "The Diving Girl" depicts a young diving girl who won the championship. Then, she became arrogant, looked down upon her teammates, did not listen to their criticisms and estranged herself from the teammates. Although she still practiced hard, no progress was made in her technique. Finally, she realized that personal success was not entirely a personal effort, but must be under proper guidance and instruction, with the help and cooperation of the others. Educated by these facts, she saw her mistakes and became modest, cooperative and honest. She made rapid improvement, and conquered a new and difficult feat.

Another vivid movie is the "Young Soccer Players" which describes some undisciplined school students who organized a soccer team without correct ideas about leadership and cooperation. When playing against a team from a middle school, which was well-disciplined and cooperative, they neglected the rules and attempted tricks. They quarrelled with players from the other team and quarrelled even among themselves. Although their individual skill could match, or was even superior to the players from the other team, they suffered a great defeat. After some reflection, they realized that they took a wrong way, amended their undesirable behavior and became a cooperative and well organized young soccer team.

The educational role of movies is very extensive and the spectators are so numerous...millions and millions of youngsters. The sports theme movie is more suitable for children and young players' interest, because these movies draw their source material from actual life and reflect it critically and instructively.

Many movies I saw I have forgotten, but the ones with sport themes still remain fresh in my memory. They help us experience collective strength and collective wisdom. They help us understand and accept that individual strength and effort should cooperate with others, then collective success and accomplishment can be expected.

More new movies with a sports theme have been made and are being made. In order to encourage more students to watch those movies, "student specials" are offered in theaters, where students may pay about 10¢ to watch.

The press plays an enormous part in fashioning the way in which sport and competition are conducted. In China, the main newspapers and journals on sports are the monthly "New Physical Culture" (Xin Tiyi) and the third weekly "Physical Culture News" (Tiyi Bao). They take a clear-cut stand in reporting positive and negative behaviors in sports and competitions. I will give some examples.

In a national track meet, the champion and the runner-up in the 1500—meter race stood on the platform shaking hands warmly. You may not know, this runner-up was the champion at the last track meet and this new champion was the third. They were on the same team. Since the last meet, they began to train together. The former champion told all his successful experiences to his teammate without reserve and tried his best to help him. In this recent meet, they both made improvements but the former third place finisher became the champion and the former champion placed second. The report praised both of their achievements but gave more attention to the cooperative and unselfish behavior of the former champion.

In 1975, our national mountaineering team conquered Mount Everest. When the team was only several dozen meters from the top, a serious problem occurred, the oxygen was not enough for every mountaineer to get to the top. At that moment, one mountaineer looked at the top, where every one was now capable of climbing, then, did not hesitate to offer his oxygen to the others. All others succeeded in getting to the top. But he stayed behind. Unfortunately he was blown down by a gale of wind. He died, but his heroic behavior will never die. Many Chinese athletes were deeply moved by his heroic behavior when it was published and praised highly by the newspapers.

The newspapers also publish and criticize those undesirable behaviors in sports and competitions, such as rough play, unsportsmanlike conduct, which every reader, athlete or citizen, can compare with other behaviors such as those mentioned in the above two news stories. Which should be the real model of a human being?

In my opinion, the newspapers have not only the responsibility to report but also have an educational purpose. Why not make full use of this propaganda means and opportunity to let more cooperative behavior appear and let sport and competition advance in a healthier atmosphere?

Concluding Remark

You can draw your own conclusions. I simply want to raise a question, *"For What"*. What should be the main and best purpose for people and athletes and children who participate in sport and physical activities?

In China, ideology governs the goals, purposes and reality of sport. We believe sports have a personal meaning conducive to improving health and fitness, and above all, have social meaning conducive to understanding and cooperation, to friendship and peace.

REFERENCES

Butt, Dorcas Susan. *Psychology of Sport*. 1976, Litton Educational Publishing, Inc.

Galliher, J.F. Sports Competition and International Capitalism. *Journal of Sport and Social Issues,*

Spring/Summer 1979. 13.

MacLaine, Shirley. *You Can Get There From Here.* New York: Bantam Book, Inc., 1975.

McIntosh, P.C. *Values and Competitive Sport.* Development of Human Values Through Sports.

Proceedings of National Conference Held at Springfield College, Springfield, Massachusetts, October 12—14, 1973.

Orlick, T.D. *Winning Through Cooperation.* Washington, D.C.: Acropolis Press, 1978.

SOCIALISATION THROUGH TRADITIONAL PLAY AND GAMES IN THE HANAHAN SOCIETY OF BUKA

Naomi Tulaha Martin

(Papua New Guinea)

At present, very little is known about the many forms of *traditional* play and games of the Hanahan society and of Papua New Guinea (PNG) as a whole.[1] As part of a way of life, these forms of play and games are a very neglected aspect of PNG culture in our present education system. Very few schools have a physical education programme having anything to do with the traditional play and games of their particular areas and locality. This is partly because strong emphasis and support is being given to the promotion of introduced (Western) games and sports throughout the country and also, because of a lack of understanding and appreciation of the cultural and social significance of our forms of play and games in contemporary PNG society. This attitude has its roots in the colonial regime (1800's-1975) during which Western knowledge was projected to be superior to those of so-called primitive societies. Both the early missionaries and the colonial government prohibited the practice of many PNG forms of culture as a condition for entering their "new schools". To them, encouraging the perpetuation of "primitive" forms of knowledge was another way of refusing to do God's will in doing away with paganism, and it was anti-development: they wanted a shift from a "primitive" stage to a higher stage which is considered rational and scientific, hence better than the first stage. Many PNG societies have since become conditioned to the misconception that in order for Papua New Guinea to develop, she must necessarily accumulate Western culture to the total exclusion of her own ways of life.

Literature on PNG play and games has so far been limited to nothing more than a few collections of games from selected areas of the country. The most recent of these being that of Pensa Roleasmalik (1979), who acknowledges the importance of traditional games in the education and socialisation of PNG children, but unfortunately does not treat the subject beyond his game descriptions.

In anthropological studies (see e.g. Sorenson,

1976; Burridge, 1960) reference to the subject has taken a pattern confined to sex roles, with boys said to be more explorative than girls. Children's play experiences according to these accounts usually take place within the confines of garden and house chores for girls, and hunting, gardening and other "more boisterous" physical activities for boys.

In her 1930 *Growing Up in New Guinea,* Mead saw no logical connection in the play activities of the Manus children and thus came to the conclusion that play has no positive influence on the lives of these children. Mead's views may be said to have been influenced by some early accounts on play in certain African societies (see e.g. Spencer 1899; Monroe 1906; Davidson 1909), where so-called primitive children's play was said to be sporadic, aimless as well as lacking in ingenuity and creativity. Working from this premise, Whitting and Child (1953), while acknowledging imitative play as an element of socialisation, portray the role of adults as the primary agent for socialisation. This in turn is re-created by children through imitative role playing. However, the essence of this view is the interaction between adult and child (or vice versa); if this interaction is absent, then it follows that imitation of adult roles by children is also absent; the result of which is an incomplete, asocial and acculturated being (Schwartzman 1974). This is particularly evident in Margaret Mead's belief that the lack of "proper family life" in the Manus society of PNG is responsible for the cultural poverty and lack of discipline amongst children in that society. The cultural significance of such accounts, if not their authenticity in the context of PNG life styles, awaits new evidence.

Rosentstiel's (1953) unpublished ethnography is so far the only known detailed account on play and socialisation amongst the Motuans of southern Papua New Guinea. Rosenstiel stresses games of physical skill, strategy and chance as necessary elements of socialisation in that they elicit certain behaviour patterns which are important not only for the development of the child but also its survival against the "harsh" environment of the Motu people.

My own interest in traditional play and games in

---

[1] The term "traditional" is used in this paper to refer to the form and play activities of Papua New Guineans in the period preceding extensive colonial influence in 1945.

the socialisation process stemmed largely from the results of the *North Solomons Education Research Project* (NSERP) in which I participated.[1] Significant amongst the results of this study was the parents' complaint that their children no longer respect them, other adults or the laws of the land in general, despite the education they are being given in schools. Parents felt that the present formal system of education is educating their children out of their own village society, in that it encourages individualism and elitism amongst the young people rather than the co-operative lifestyle characteristic of PNG societies.

There was great unanimity on the need to combine new knowledge with traditional knowledge, with greater emphasis given to the development of social conduct and behavioural norms acceptable in the Hanahan society.

When parents were asked how this might be done, many different suggestions were offered, but the one which seemed to interest me most was their description of how certain values were learned through traditional play and games. It was felt necessary therefore to examine closely the significance of traditional play and games in the socialisation of Hanahan children, in the hope of exposing new avenues for making the present education system more relevant to the peoples' way of life.

The People and Their Cultural Patterns

In order to set clarity and proper perspective to the discussion, it is necessary at the outset to briefly say something about the people and their basic cultural patterns as they existed prior to extensive colonial influence in 1945. This should provide a preliminary sketch of the social horizons of Hanahan children and how such horizons affected or were affected by traditional play and games.

The Hanahan number approximately 1,000 out of an estimated 2,400 people living in the Hanahan district as a whole. The people see themselves as the most skilled and fearless seamen on Buka; they were the only islanders to have had long expeditions to the Cateret Islands to the east of Buka. They eventually colonised these groups of islands and established trading and kinship ties with them, as well as with the Nissan islanders to the north. They were also the only groups of people in Buka whose domain extended the width of the island, to the small west coast settlement of Banis.

Cultivation and fishing were of equal importance in the lives of the Hanahan people. It was from these

activities that relatives observed and marked prospective wives or husbands for their kin. For marriage was seen as both the beginning and the end of the social network: a child is born and is socialised into Hanahan society, so that he or she in turn may ensure the continuity of the society through the installation and development of a well-respected family. It was therefore a great honour to parents to have their daughters "marked" or promised in marriage to a man at an early age. This was a sign that the community admired her conduct and respected her family for bringing her up in a respectable way.

Every male child was expected to learn how to fish, hunt, make a garden or construct a house at an early age, so that by the time they reached *marriageable age,* they would be proficient in these skills.[1] Likewise, girls had to learn everything their mothers did, to prepare them for adulthood.

At first, the child's learning took place within the limits of its household and the people he or she came in contact with at a young age. As the child became older, the whole community began to take on the responsibility of guiding and correcting the child in its daily activities and behaviour. This sense of responsibility and co-operation in the upbringing of the child was seen as an extension of the inter-dependent relationship between and amongst the web of kinship ties which permeated almost the entire population of Buka. Until very recently, the Hanahan did not distinguish between how close or distant their relationship with their kin was, as in the Western notion of first, second and third cousin relationships. Rather, kinship relationships are explained through matrilineal or patrilineal blood lines, so that everyone within that line has the same social obligation and responsibility towards each other, or their possessions. For example, if a member of family A owns a radio, and if he or she is from the same blood line (e.g. matrimonial lineage) as the boy in family B, then that boy has family lineage right to use the radio or even keep it without too many questions being asked.

In the case of non-relatives, a number of social mechanisms operated to maintain the co-operative relationships inherent within Hanahan life. Firstly, an individual's need for recognition and acceptance in the society often led to those individuals going out of their way to please other members of the Hanahan community. For example, if person C happened to be passing by while person D was eating, the proper thing to do was to offer food to C, even if it meant D going without it. Or if a tsunono (an important man who plays a prominent role in rituals and feasts) quite innocently admired something in front of the owner, he would not be too suprised if he found whatever he had admired on his doorstep when he returned home. For it was common practice to offer gifts to the tsunono as a sign of respect and courtesy

[1]This study was conducted by the Education Research Unit (ERU) of the University of Papua New Guinea (UPNG) in response to an invitation to ERU by the North Solomons Provincial Government to carry out research into several areas of education that were of concern to them. This was the beginning of the Province's attempt to try and make its education system more appropriate to its peoples' way of life. The research began in July 1979 with the assistance of university students from the North Solomons Province.

[1]Marriageable age was measured according to the maturity of the breasts and in the case of the boys, "shaving" was an indication that a boy was old enough to marry.

for their seniority and social status in the community.

Any person found to be operating outside the norms of Hanahan society (a very rare case) was sneered at and gossiped about. In the children's case, they were often by-passed as undesirable when prospective wives or husbands were being sought.

The whole society therefore, as a unit sharing the same social goals, endeavoured to inculcate in the minds of their children those social values based on the accepted behavioural codes of Hanahan life.

Behaviour goals

The Hanahan goals for the development of good behaviour and conduct was summed up in one word: *Matsingolo* (v) or *Nimatsingolo* (n); a concept which is difficult to translate adequately into any single English word or phrase. The closest single translation is "respect" which again defies the actual meaning of the term in context.

The concept of nimatsingolo bears reference first and foremost to respect and honour others and of the land in general. It also refers to politeness and courtesy, or even shyness — which is often associated with gentleness or being "ladylike". Any young or adult female who displayed too much openness especially in the presence of the opposite sex for example, was seen to be a promiscuous type of person — hence tabuna matsingolo or having no shame or respect for herself.

All children were demanded to express nimatsingolo in all their actions at all times and in all places. Expressing nimatsingolo necessarily meant being helpful or co-operative, obedient, kind, responsible, respectful and all other virtues upheld in Hanahan society. According to Hanahan tradition, nimatsingolo as a virtue is a pre-requisite to all other teachings in the life of the child. In other words, if a child has learned to express nimatsingolo from the beginning, then he or she will be in a better position to learn from and practise the teachings of others.

When a child was summoned before its father, uncle or any other adult including older brothers and sisters to answer for any mischief or bad behaviour, that child had to listen without saying a word while being scolded.

Children were constantly called upon to help with domestic chores and attend to other adult requests. However, parents were always careful not to overwork their children for a number of reasons:

1. the Hanahan, and generally the whole Buka society, believe that children who are over-burdened with work from an early age onwards will always look unhealthy and unattractive — even before they reach adulthood;

2. too much work at an early age is thought to slow down the growth of the child. As one old woman explained:

   "A healthy child's body should glitter in the sunlight; the child should grow to a certain height each month. This is possible only if the child is kept away from heavy and untidy work as much as possible."[1]

Much of the children's time was therefore devoted to play, for play as a concept was also seen as children's work — apart from the enjoyment it afforded its participants.

Since the Hanahan concept of play is very much interwoven with the way they rationalise their culture, it is necessary to first explain the Hanahan view of culture in order to establish the meaning of play in the Hanahan context.

The Hanahan View of Culture

Elsewhere I have found it useful to explain culture as a concept by using the analogy of a tree with its branches, leaves, fruit —, all of which constitute the tree as such. The branch, for example, may represent a form of culture (e.g. spiritual beliefs), a dying branch may represent a disappearing form of culture (e.g. traditional play and games) and so forth. These physical manifestations of the thing called tree are not the tree itself, but parts which make up the tree.

Similarly, culture in the Hanahan view manifests itself in various forms, whether physical, mental, spiritual or otherwise. It is abstract and undefinable except through the various forms in which it is anatomised. This view suggests that culture is universal, but latent until it is exposed through its various forms which can be visualised as part of that culture.

In discussing traditional play and games therefore, we are specifically concerned with a particular aspect of Hanahan culture which, although it may emerge separately from its component parts, plays a role which is an integral part of the whole culture. In other words, there is an element of play present in all forms of culture in the same way as culture permeates and transcends all these forms. To attempt to separate play from what is not play therefore, is to search for problems where such problems do not exist.

From what has been discussed so far, it appears we have established an adequate framework upon which we can build a discussion on how the Hanahan explain play and its role in the socialisation process, as well as its relationship to the whole Hanahan culture:

A Classification of Play

The Hanahan classify play into three types:

(i) HIHIKUMA — a part competitive and part co-operative type play. Although hihikuma games

---

[1] Extract from recordings of interviews held with village people in Hanahan in July 1979.

187

may be competitively structured, their end results are usually co-operative;

(ii) HAKOKOPEITS — a non-competitive simulation type play in which the daily, seasonal and annual cycles of adult life are re-enacted. It is often referred to by adults as children's work;

(iii) RORO — the closest English translation of the term "roro" is "to relax", though this translation defies its real meaning in context. Roro activities may include telling stories, playing with younger brothers or sisters, or any activity which is more exploratory in nature rather than competitive.

To the extent that both (i) and (ii) are also a means of refraining from strenuous physical work, both can also be regarded as "roro" activities. However, unlike roro, hihikuma and hakokopeits follow a permissive pattern in Hanahan, whereas roro becomes permissible only after the more serious and specific tasks (helping with adult chores) have been completed.

Given their permissive nature, therefore, it seems necessary to examine both hihikuma and hakokopeits as concepts, so as to establish their significance in socialisation.

Hihikuma

Two types of hihikuma games are distinguished —

- those played by children; and
- those in which both adults and adolescents take part.

In the first type there is often, though not necessarily, an adult who assumes a supervisory role in the game (as in the game "Mothers and Fathers"). In the absence of an adult, the whole team automatically becomes responsible for everything that goes on in the game; single referees are uncommon in such cases.

The second type is usually played during the day and only in certain seasons such as the *galip nut* season.[1] One of the main attractions of such games is the large crowds, amongst which there are chiefs and other important elders from different areas.

Everyone brings food (e.g. taro, kaukau, fish, betel nut and very often a pig) to the host village.[2] The food is shared amongst everyone and eaten to celebrate firstly the coming of the galip nut season and secondly the end of hihikuma; *not* the victory of the winning team as is the case in modern sports.

With the assistance of the elders, the tsunono and especially the Monihil (the paramount chief whose status and authority out-ranks all others) reserve the

right to formally judge how best each individual or team is able to master the skills of the game. Although a particular team or individual may demonstrate an outstanding level of excellence in hihikuma and eventually become the winner, winning in the Hanahan concept is not necessarily the end result of the game. For winning is nearly always manipulated by the monihil and other tsunono, to maintain or strengthen ties with other groups. For example, if a team from tsunono A's village proved outstanding in hihikuma, he may either accept the public praise (usually in the form of a pig) on behalf of his team, or he may decide to improve his peoples' relations with tsunono B's people by offering him the pig instead. Tsunono B in turn may want to show his nimatsingolo (respect and honour) to the most important tsunono — the monihil, by giving him and his people the pig.

Similarly, children's hihikuma games are mainly structured along a co-operative basis. Within this structure there is ample allowance for flexibility, an element which is necessary in preventing conflicts amongst participants, especially in cases where the rules of the game become too rigid. For example, in the "Hohopu-tula" game (see appendix) it would be easy for the participants to ridicule anyone who is too frightened to fulfil the requirements of the game. In which case, therefore, allowances are often made (quite outside of the rules of the game) to have another child accompany another to the cemetery over a specified period of time, or at least until that particular child is no longer afraid to take part in the game on his or her own. It becomes clear here, that competing against another child to see who is best at that particular game is secondary to socialising children into achieving those values taught in the game.

Hihikuma games therefore, were mainly seen as occasions during which social ties with other groups were improved or reaffirmed and secondly, as mechanisms through which individuals were able to show to the adults their different levels of mastering the skills or values involved in hihikuma. In other words, it may be said that although hihikuma was partly for finding out individual levels of performance in the physical, intellectual or social skills and values involved, the underlying social values relating to the maintenance of group solidarity and harmony was regarded as more important than anything else.

Hakokopeits

As a concept, hakokopeits designates the aggregate of adult life in microcosm; it is a children's world within its own. An adequate description of hakokopeits would thus be impossible within the limited scope of this paper. However, a few examples of the type of activities involved will suffice to describe hakokopeits as a social process.

Since Hanahan life centered around fishing and civilization, we shall examine how these activities were reproduced in hakokopeits and what type of learning went on in the process.

---

[1] Galip is a small nut with a hard brown shell and white fruit. It grows mainly in the tropics and is used in puddings or eaten on its own. The galip nut season (that is when the nuts are ready to be collected) comes every six months of the year.

[2] A pig is a status symbol in Papua New Guinea. It also symbolises the importance of the ceremony itself; to give it to someone else is to show them the highest respect and honour.

(a) Cultivation

From dawn till dusk, children from as young as 3 years to *"near-marriage adolescents"* became engrossed in *taro* gardening.[1] Before the gardens were started, everyone would get together to decide on the site and the time the gardens were to be started, and how best the whole group should be organised for maximum results. Very often, the group would be organised into temporary "husband and wife" pairs. Anyone without a partner or considered too young would simply join in as a relative or friend.

When the time finally came to start the gardens, everyone ensured that they were all up before sunrise. Whoever was up first would wake the others up. Usually, the "wives" would be up at the crack of dawn to prepare food not only for themselves, but also for the rest of the household. For it was considered good training for girls to give their parents or relatives a treat now and then by doing the housework or the cooking on their own. The "wives" would only get enough for themselves and their friends and leave the rest of the food for their families, who upon waking up, would be so relieved to find hot food waiting. By this time, all the children would be up in their new gardens working. The "husbands" would be chopping trees and cleaning the bush while the wives did the planting. All the time they would be simulating adult forms of speaking. For example, a wife may complain to another in a "woman-like" voice, that her husband was too slow in cutting trees. Or she may pretend that a tsunono was approaching and so all had to speak in low voices as a sign of respect while the tsunono was passing by.

At mid-day, everyone would come together to eat and monitor what they had done so far. Comparisons would be made on the amount of area cleared in each garden. Often, everyone would agree to help any particular couple whose garden was thought to be lagging behind so that everyone's garden would be exactly the same on the first day of clearing and planting. The period after that would be left to each couple to see to their own gardens, though from time to time the whole group would take turns to work on each other's gardens. At other times, all the matrilineal relatives would come together to help. Patrilineal kin were only allowed to help out of respect, especially if they themselves offered help. Otherwise it was improper to expect them to help, granted that their relationship was only through marriage links and that it is only in matrilineal blood lines that family members are allowed to take each other for granted. Such practices of course were reproduced only in as far as the children understood them and therefore never to the same degree as in the real adult world.

At dusk, the wives would bring home little knapsacks of firewood or vegetables to their homes. On other occasions, everyone would agree to bring food to the village elders, whether they were relatives or not.

The next stage in gardening was weeding, which often required co-operative effort; so too did harvesting — the most exciting and final stage, which in itself became an epitome of adult social life.

At first the neighbouring hakokopeits groups from a different moiety[1] would be *notified*[1] about the harvesting day. For example, if the Naboin children were harvesting their gardens, they had to invite the Nakaripa children or vice versa.

When harvesting day finally came, the whole place was filled with excitement as the girls prepared their knapsacks to go to the garden while the boys were busy organising themselves into different groups for the different tasks to be done. Shelves for the food display needed to be put up, while coconuts, betel-nuts and other necessities had to be prepared.

By mid-morning the girls would return home with the harvest, singing and with their hair festooned with pretty flowers. The biggest taro would be placed on the shelves for display and distribution later to the other moiety while the rest were cooked. Many parents often used the occasion as an opportunity to evaluate their children's garden produce by comparing their size, quality and number. It goes without saying here that another major attraction to children's harvesting day was the food distributed to any onlookers. For harvesting not only meant gathering in the food crops; it also meant learning how to share the crops as well as prepare them for consumption or distribution, all without which harvesting would not have been considered complete.

When food was cooked, it was placed on the shelf and later distributed to everyone by the oldest members of the hakokopeits group. The important thing was to make sure that each child had a different basket of food and not her own, the reason being that everyone was expected to taste and comment on someone else's food. The uncooked taro would then be distributed to the guests. Most important of all, the best and biggest taro had to be given to the tsunono of the village as a sign of respect to him. Since the tsunono represented the community as a collectivity, the gesture of respect given him necessarily meant a gesture to the whole

---

[1] Once adolescents got married, they no longer participated in Hakokopeits, since they were now regarded as adults.
Taro is a starchy root plant found mostly in the Pacific region. It is one of the main foods in Hanahan.

---

[1] The Hanahan are divided into two great moieties. Although in theory these moieties form separate groups, members of both groups often live together on each other's territorial boundaries as a result of ceremonial ties and inter-marriage links.

[2] The term *notified* is used here in the sense that the Hanahan do not invite people individually or selectively. One is simply notified through appointed messengers that a particular village is about to have an important gathering. Usually, the message is given to the tsunono's messenger in each village, who in turn will pass it quietly to his tsunono, and eventually to everyone else in the village, who are expected to appear with their tsunono in the host village.

community.

(b) Fishing and Other Activities

Fishing became the next big activity when the children were not gardening. Girls would spend hours collecting shellfish or fishing in shallow waters, while the boys concentrated on reef fishing. In between shellfish collecting, the girls would often come together to play such games as "Kikimits Kari" and "Naha Naha". When the boys returned home with their catch, everyone would then share the fish, after which they would all decide on the next activity. Some of the favourite beach games include "Pupu Soli" and "Ha Rak Raku" (see appendix).

Although children of different age groups often come together to play hakokopeits, there were also occasions when children played in their own age groups. For example, 3 to 4 year old children often spent the whole day at the beach playing "Mothers and Fathers" under the watchful eye of their grandparents. Make believe babies were bathed, dried and sung to sleep in grandmother's favourite lullaby song while father went out hunting in the nearby beach-shrub. Mother would then prepare food out of sand or stones, feed the baby and then play with it a while and when father returned, they would all tell stories and then go to sleep.

The Hanahan believe that whenever children played "Mothers and Fathers" near a newly-married woman's house, this meant that the woman was in her early stages of pregnancy. Similarly, when children pretended to hold a funeral, adults believed that this was a warning that someone was about to die.

Toddlers and young infants were also encouraged to engage in what I shall call "infant play" for convenience of presentation. Infant play is classified under "roro" and is observed when babies and toddlers become engrossed with whatever objects they come across. This form of play is seen as important for two main reasons:

1. It is said to distract infants from crying and demanding adult attention unnecessarily. The people believe that a child who is constantly picked up becomes conditioned to remain in the hands of adults and will therefore refuse to play on its own. According to the Hanahan, over-indulging in the physical handling of a child leads to a weak and mentally less receptive child. Children should therefore be allowed to play freely and learn how to manipulate their environment at a young age.
2. Infant play is also believed to toughen up the child's body and speed up its growth.

Young mothers were therefore advised to let their children play freely and to pick them up and cuddle them only when they cried or became tired.

It is clear from the preceeding discussion that play cannot be discussed in isolation from the Hanahan culture; for play, as Johan Huizinga (1949) once put it, arises in and as part of (that) culture. Through play, the social values surrounding the concept of nimatsingolo in Hanahan society are learned and reinforced, thereby socialising children into adult life which, in essence, is the highest point towards which all learning is geared.

Infant play (roro) focusses on the physical and social adaptation of the child into its environment. From childhood to adolescence, play centres on hakokopeits (role play) and takes on a more specialised role in hihikuma.

As a concept, play is an integral part of the social mechanism which binds Hanahan society together. When part of that social mechanism is upset by external forces, certain imbalances necessarily take place, thus disturbing the social system in its totality. This is evident from the current conflict between the Hanahan values and those resulting from the pursuits of modernisation.

The view that the creation of a modern and materially advanced PNG society is dependent upon the accumulation of Western knowledge not only presupposes certain deficiences in the PNG culture, it has also led to the failure of the existing education system to socialise young Papua New Guineans into the social values acceptable in their own communities, hence the persistence of current conflicts in value systems. Since the modern school removes children from their village societies at an early age (7 years), and granted that most of the children's time is spent inside the school, the community at large expect the school to develop acceptable codes of conduct and behaviour appropriate to their way of life. This is not to suggest, however, that modern values should be completely rejected in favour of reaffirming traditional values. For the current situation in PNG is such that Papua New Guinea would resist a complete shift from traditional to modern ways or vice versa. The implication of this statement suggests that the ideology which influences our attempts to make education more relevant to the needs of PNG is neither essentially modern nor essentially traditional. In other words, the ideology which informs the development of culture education vascillates between these two polar positions. There is therefore obvious need to synthesise modern knowledge with traditional knowledge.

Synthesising the Old and the New

Having briefly presented some of the weaknesses of the present formal education system and having established the relationship between traditional play and games and the Hanahan socialisation process, we are now faced with many questions, one of which is how our traditional play and games can be made an integral part of the present physical education programme in our schools.

At the present time there is not one Papua New Guinean game included in the physical education activities for each grade. Although there are a few body control activities which give children the opportunity to play with each other co-operatively, nearly all the games played from grade three onwards are competitive. One team always ends up the winner while the other, the loser, the result of which is nearly always seen as a devaluation of one's character and sense of worth. Amongst most males for example, winning is often seen as a means of reaffirming one's strength and masculinity, while the loser is reduced to nothing more than a weakling, especially amongst young children.

Another important consideration is the type of environment (i.e. school) in which learning takes place and the transaction involved between the teacher and pupils. The school atmosphere is usually characterised by formality and time regimentation, which in themselves can pose problems in teaching children to be responsible, in that it encourages a high degree of dependency upon a higher authority. For example, most schools have rules which regulate children's behaviour in the school grounds. A child, for example, may not remove a ball from the storeroom unless prior permission is sought from the teacher. While such rules may be necessary in the school situation, they are basically for administrative convenience, and not necessarily for the good of the child. For once that child steps out of the school grounds into his own village, he knows that he does not have to ask permission from his parents to use anything in the house. He knows too that whatever he may own is as much his as it is the entire family's possession. The important thing he is expected to remember is never to inconvenience anyone else; that being part of the family means sharing or sacrificing one's wants for someone else's, a principle which governs all children's behaviour in their village community.

The fact that physical exercise is stressed in school games is a mere truism according to Hanahan belief. For any physical activity (whether it be working in the garden, doing daily chores or playing) necessarily provides the body with the exercise it requires. What the Hanahan consider important in play is to prepare the child for life, the fundamentals of which are the social values which hold society together as one whole unit. This implies that play must be one with the highest human values of the society and not a separate learning experience devoid from this as our modern games appear to be in the eyes of the Hanahan people.

Suggested Directions

It might be useful to offer some questions relating to social development which may contribute at least some serious thinking into present attempts for a more relevant physical education programme.

• What does the community expect and want children to learn from their play and games?

• What social values are actually learned or elicited by (a) introduced games and (b) traditional games?

• Are these values in line with the aspirations of the village community, the provincial community, the nation or meaningful survival as a whole?

• By what criteria should selection of games and values be made?

• Where, when and how are these games (and values) to be taught to the young children and by whom?

• How can conflicts in value systems be ameliorated and by whom can this be done?

• How can possible conflicts between the teaching approach of the school (formal) and that of the village or community (informal) be overcome?

• Should (and for what reason) games from other ethnic groups be included in the physical education programme? (The pursuit of a united country [or world] is an important consideration here)

• How is the programme to be evaluated, how often, by whom and by what criteria?

This list can be continued to include many other possibilities. Axiomatic to all possibilities considered however, must be the necessity of making life-enhancing traditional play (along with other forms of humanistically oriented games and values) a part of all children's learning experiences.

Reflections (Post Congress)

I feel so grateful to have been given the opportunity to take part in the congress. To say the least, I met and learned much from different people who came to share their views. As for my contribution, I came back with the idea that perhaps developing countries like PNG have far to go in really making highly powered nations (e.g., America) appreciate the simple values of co-operating and putting one's fellow-man first, before oneself, in the field of sport and play and in life generally. I felt that most delegates accepted that sport without competition would be self-defeating and were therefore not willing to appreciate or even see the value of co-operative sport and play. In any case, I am happy that I was able to at least listen to the views of the different speakers; it taught me to appreciate the difficulties of having to justify one's views on certain important issues.

REFERENCES

BURRIDGE, K.O.L. *Mambu: A Mellanesian Milleneum.* London: Methuen, 1960.

Community School Syllabus — Grade Six Physical Education; Konedobu, Papua New Guinea: Standards Division, Ministry of Education, Science and Culture, 1978.

DAVIDSON, T. *A History of Education,* London 1909.

HUIZINGA, Johan. *Homo Ludens: A Study of the Play Elemewnt in Culture.* London: Routledge & Kegan Paul, 1949.

LANCY, D.F. & TINDALL, B.A. (ed.) *The Anthropological Study of Play: Problems and Prospects;* Cornwall, New-York: Leisure Press, 1976.

MEAD, Margaret. *Growing Up in New Guinea.* New York, N.Y.: 1930.

ORLICK, T. *Tumbuna Pilai: Games from the Great Ancestors.* North Solomons Education Research Report #5; Arawa, Papua New Guinea: North Solomons Provincial Government, August, 1980.

ORLICK, T. *The Second Cooperative Sports and Games Book.* New York: Pantheon Publishers, 1982.

ORLICK, T.D., McNALLY, J., & T. O'HARA. Cooperative games: Systematic analysis and cooperative impact. In F. Smoll & R. Smith (Eds.), *Psychological perspectives in youth sports*, pp. 203-225. Washington, D.C.: Hemisphere Publishers, 1978.

RIMALDI, M. The Hahalis Welfare Society: A.N.U., 1971.

ROLEASMALIK, P.M. *Traditional Games of Papua New Guinea*. PNG Ministry of Education, Science and Culture (Cultural Activities, Box 2051, Konedobu, Papua New Guinea(, 1979.

SORENSON, E.R. *The Edge of the Forest Land: Childhood and Change in a New Guinea Protoagricultural Society*. Washinton, D.C.: Smithsonian Institute Press, 1976.

Summary of Statistics (PNG) Port Moresby, Papua New Guinea National Statistical Office, 1978.

Appendix A*
Sample Games
POPU SOLI

This game is the children's interpretation of an initiation ceremony into adulthood.

Two groups of both boys and girls stand about 6-8 metres apart facing each other. One child lays face down in the middle of the two groups which then begin to sing the Pupu Soli song, clapping hands and moving slowly in unison towards the child lying down. When both groups are close enough to the child, they continue to sing, clap hands and dance and at the end of the song they jump over the body (in opposite directions) and immediately commence singing, clapping and dancing, but this time moving away from the body, until they reach their starting positions. Then they all turn around and once more move slowly towards the child lying down and jump over him as they did before. At the end of the third jump, both groups pick the child up and dance around with him over their heads, until a child gives a signal to put the child down. At the end of the song, the child is put down with loud cheers from everyone.

The game may continue with another child lying down until the group decides it is time to stop the game.

HA RAK - RAKU

Raku is a method of cooking with hot stones. The food is wrapped in leaves and placed over hot stones. Additional hot stones are then placed on top of the wrapped food, after which several large leaves (e.g., banana leaves) are added to keep the hot steam inside. Most people will add sand on top of leaves to ensure that no steam escapes.

Ha Rak - Raku is a child's version of the method described above. The usual practice was for children to make "casava pudding" by wrapping sand in leaves and then pretending to "raku" them. When they are "cooked" they are distributed amongst friends and relatives.

At other times, however, especially amongst older children, real food (e.g., banana, taro etc.) was cooked — very often overnight, using the raku methods. Children could bring their own food home from the garden and prepare them at the beach for the raku. Usually this was done in pairs or groups of children. By sunset, the whole beach would be ablaze with stones being heated. When most of the wood has burnt out, the stones would be just hot enough for the food to be placed on them. After every detail of the raku is covered, the children would light fires on top of their raku and then very often would

camp on the beach until morning. Then the food would be shared, making sure that some of it is given to the parents and other adult relatives.

HOHOPU TULA

This game which is designed to develop courage is played only in the darkest of nights. Any number of players can participate either within their own age groups or in mixed age or sex groups.

Children gather together at a certain point in the village. An adult or a child who is not afraid of the dark is instructed by the whole group to take a piece of lit wood to an isolated area, usually a cemetery some distance away from the village. When that person arrives at the chosen spot, he/she must stand the lit piece of wood firmly onto the ground so that the lit end faces upwards. This is so that the next player(s) can easily locate it. It is also to ensure that children follow instructions and do not throw the piece of fire anywhere they like.

Once the piece of fire has been placed in the right place, the player(s) return(s) to join the group. The next person is then instructed to collect the fire from where it had been left and to take it to an area or cemetery even further away from the first spot. If a player does not follow the instructions of the game — as say, for example, in cases where the fire is just thrown near the cemetery, he or she will always be found out by the next player, who then has to take the fire back to the group and report that the player concerned has not followed instructions. This same player may either be instructed once again to repeat the requirements he/she has failed to carry out previously, or if he/she is too frightened, another player may be asked to accompany him or her, making sure that he encourages that child all the way.

The game would continue for sometimes 2 to 3 nights until all children or interested adults in the village have a turn to take the fire to a cemetery. As the game continued, the distance between selected areas and cemeteries for the fire would be increased into somewhere within the range of 3-5 miles.

This game, and others like it, helped in teaching children to get rid of their fears and to obey their parents. When children who had played this game many times were asked to fetch something or someone in the next village, they would always go alone because they no longer feared the dark, no matter how far the village or how dark the night was.

---

* For descriptions of additional traditional gameplays in the North Solomon Islands, write to the author at P.O. Box 4850, University of Papua New Guinea, Port Moresby, PNG and see Orlick, 1982 and 1980 in references.

ENHANCING LOVE AND LIFE
MOSTLY THROUGH PLAY AND GAMES

Terry Orlick (Canada)

When village people in the North Solomon Islands were asked what were the most important lessons that schools could teach their children, they responded with such things as: Cooperation, kindness, generosity, responsibility, respect for others, respect for nature, and a sense of justice. Their concern is that children gain human skills which enhance the experience of life.

But their contemporary schools (which follow the format of industrialized countries such as ours) do not teach important life skills. They do not draw upon traditional wisdom; they do not promote responsibility within the community; they are not based upon interdependence and mutual help, nor do they rely on observational learning, on learning through doing, through play, games, stories, songs, dances, movement and activity which was always the case with the transmission of knowledge in the past. The applicability of what is learned in school is not readily apparent to the villagers. As one parent put it, "everything children learn in school belongs to the school alone, it has no place in our village" (Kemelfield, 1979, Orlick, 1980a).

For the past decade I have grown from my experiences in many aboriginal cultures. These exposures have inspired me to seek out ways to improve relationships and human values in more industrialized societies.

I have attempted to operationalize and act upon some global concerns reflecting the need for more love and compassion. I have sought out practical possibilities for implementing real world change, primarily in and through the medium of play and games.

The contemporary work being done in the area of cooperative games is a new beginning which draws from and expands upon long standing wisdom. It was largely through play and games that the most humanistic people on this earth gained their sensitivity advantage. Their play was neither competitive nor cut throat in nature. It had been carefully developed to nurture some of the most important educational lessons of life (Orlick, 1978b, 1980a; 1982). In cultures where people are considerate and respectful of one another and the land, these values are initially acted out and assimilated through children's play and games.

Play is a realm of great social significance. As a medium for positive social learning, it is ideal because it is natural, active, and highly motivating for most children. Players are continuously in the process of acting, reacting, feeling, and experiencing. Play, when approached in a sensitive and thoughtful way, is a beautiful medium for bringing people together. However, if you distort children's play by rewarding excessive competition, physical aggression against others, cheating and unfair play, then you risk distorting children's lives.

The distinctive feature of cooperative games that separates them from all other games, old and new, is their structural makeup. For example, in the game "King of the Mountain", the rules dictate that one person be King while all others are shoved down the mountain. The game has a competitive structure in that it demands that players act against one another and excludes all but one from attaining the object of the game. In the cooperative version, "People of the Mountain", the structural demands of the game are completely reversed. The objective is to get as many people as possible to the top of the mountain, and children play together to accomplish this. This frees the players from the pressure to compete against others, eliminates the need for destructive behavior, and by its very design encourages helpful and fun-filled interaction.

When you place children in competitive "King of the Mountain" structures and you make them feel as if their personal acceptability or self-worth is dependent on being on top, you create problems. These problems surface in the form of high levels of anxiety, dropping out, insensitivity towards others, destructive aggression, and sometimes depression. If the outcome is made to seem important enough, people will deceive, cheat, hurt, and even kill to get to the top. And the rules they learn as children may affect them all their lives. By accepting the competitive goal as all-important, people not only become more willing to destroy others but may also destroy themselves and their families in the climbing process (Orlick, 1982).

When designing a game or counseling a player, consider trying to integrate some of the qualities which help with the growth of meaningful working and loving relationships. Structure the activity as well as time-outs within, between or after activities so that participants can practice and subsequently perfect some of the following life and love enhancing skills.

Empathetic Responses — Try to develop the skills necessary to climb inside another person's feelings, to know how she feels and to act on the basis of this knowledge.

Appreciative Responses — Try to develop the skills necessary for one person to recognize, appreciate and express appreciation for another person's

193

perceptions, contributions and personal growth needs.

Cooperative Responses — Try to develop the skills necessary to share the daily workload whether in the game or home, to share experiences, good times, bad times, and promote the idea of solving problems or seeking solutions together with others.

Communicative Responses — Try to develop the skills necessary for individuals to express their own feelings, as well as to encourage others to express their feelings, knowledge, appreciation, problems, concerns and perspectives.

Balanced Responses — Try to develop the skills necessary for participants to respect the various phases of their lives so that one area (e.g. sport or work) does not result in the exclusion of important others (e.g. family, relationships, relaxation).

One of the major goals of cooperative learning experiences is to enable children of the future to become more receptive to *sharing* both human and material resources, (e.g., ideas, talents, concerns, feelings, respect, possessions, equipment, turns, time, space, responsibility, and the betterment of each other's lives). With this in mind, we created a series of games and conducted several studies to assess the social impact of well-designed cooperative games programs. The results have consistently shown an increase in cooperative behavior in games, in free play, and in the classroom setting for children involved in these programs. The cooperative change does not occur overnight, but over a period of several months, most children seem to become more considerate and caring human beings (Orlick, 1981a; 1981b; Orlick and Foley, 1979; Orlick, McNally, & O'Hara, 1978; Jensen, 1979; Slack, 1978; Witt, 1980; Provost, 1981; Fritsch, 1981).

Based upon our work and observation to date, the following conclusions can be drawn:

• cooperatively designed play and games are an effective medium for introducing children to the concepts and skills involved in cooperation and sharing (Orlick, 1978b);

• very young children of both sexes (even 1 and 2 years olds) are fully capable of cooperation and sharing and will do so with some regularity if their natural gestures of giving are encouraged and re-inforced (Orlick, 1982; Pines, 1979).

• team harmony and mutual helping among players on competitive teams can be developed and enhanced through the use of group awareness sessions and on-site reminders for positive action (e.g., cue cards), (Orlick, 1980b);

• television can be an effective medium for introducing young children to cooperative games and cooperative values (Provost, 1981).

Perhaps the most significant finding emerging from our work is that we can design games and intervention techniques, with pro-social objectives in mind, and actually influence participants behavior in a positive direction as a result. Through thoughtfully designed play and sport experiences we can provide valuable opportunities for children to act out, and acquire important life skills. Learning to cooperate and share is only one area of potential impact. Others include the learning of stress control strategies, the improvement of non-verbal communication skills, the enhancement of self-acceptance, increased enjoyment and so on (Orlick, 1980b; Orlick and Botterill, 1975).

Our most recent studies have shown that after an exposure to a cooperative games program of several months duration, pre-school children cooperate more during recess activities (Orlick, 1981a), and share more with their peers when given the option to keep goodies (candy) for themselves or share with others (Orlick, 1981b). Overall prosocial effects appear to be speeded up with the use of television (Provost, 1981).

Though our cooperative game studies have shown significant positive effects and suggest that physically active learning has great potential for humanistic development, there are several pervasive problems which may negate potential long term impact.

• the number of children currently exposed to active cooperative learning opportunities is relatively low, their relative time involvement is minimal and programs are usually not continued from one age group to the next (e.g., year to year);

• those children who do experience cooperative learning opportunities live in a system (or world) which often supports contrary models of behavior (e.g., violent heroes in television programming, in pro-sport, and in films; highly competitive structures in school and sports programming). These mediums (T.V., school and sport), as well as peers in the street, provide a very powerful yet largely insensitive model to overcome, particularly for boys.

There is a certain sense of futility one experiences when swimming against the current, but to go with it, in this case, almost ensures disaster. . . "The winners will win themselves the same grave as the losers. Everywhere you look, insanity rages, all over the world. Because the whole world is infected with this way of thinking, believing in winning and losing, never thinking about just what it is you win or lose" (French, 1980:269).

We need to work together to develop a special kind of balance between cooperation and individualism which frees people to help and enjoy each other, to play and love joyfully, to live and work in harmony and to compete in a psychologically healthy way. In our society it is important to allow for individual initiative and creativity but also to nurture the ability to work well as a team in a responsive and caring way.

Too much self-interest is a losing proposition in terms of harmony within relationships, societal peace and balanced growth. But too little concern for individual needs also curtails both personal and societal development. By demanding too much conformity we risk removing not only much needed creativity but the smile from many people's daily lives.

To help with the development of more healthy and balanced lifestyles for future generations, at least three points of intervention could be considered: Parental education, Pro-social television programming, and Screening of teachers and coaches.

We currently do not have an effective process for educating young parents in a way which will help them to help their children grow into empathetic and responsible people. We have no significant pro-social impact on North America's window to the world — television. Nor do we have any guarantee that the people working with our children (i.e. teachers and coaches) behave in a way which reflects a humanistic concern for children's overall development. With respect to real-world impact these media would appear to be primary targets for constructive change.

Parental Education — The roots for caring and sharing are established surprisingly early in life (Pines, 1979). My work with 3, 4 and 5 year-olds made clear the vast differences in young children's willingness to cooperate with their peers. My more recent experiences with one and two year-olds leads me to believe that parents' responsiveness can effect differences which are quite dramatic even within the first couple of years of life (Orlick, 1982). To help children's warm and loving qualities grow during the early years, parents or parent substitutes can:

- freely demonstrate their affection towards their children (and other children) so children experience people as kind and loving,
- through example, play, games, role playing and discussion, repeatedly teach cooperation and empathy, and conversely that children must not hurt others,
- repeatedly acknowledge and encourage children's responsiveness and sharing gestures towards others (whether "others" are real or imaginary),
- play with their children for the sheer joy of play,
- clearly demonstrate their concern for the distresses faced by their own children as well as by others (even strangers),
- empathically demonstrate dissatisfaction with their child's behavior (or other children's behavior) if he hits or hurts another person (Pines, 1979),
- explain why he should not hurt others either physically or psychologically and have him practice a more appropriate response,
- promote children's natural tendencies towards sharing and empathy (catch them being good!),
- have children practice sharing behaviors after disruptive acts (Barton and Osborne, 1978), and before anticipated problems,

- learn to utilize play experiences to promote altruistic behavior (Orlick, 1982).

Parents and parent substitutes (including other children) can be especially influential because infants get their first exposures from these people. Other important lines of intervention come from professionals who work and play with pre-school children, from those who design children's toys, games, play equipment, school curricula and T.V. programs, and from those who are in a position to influence the parents and teachers of young children. Programs designed with a social conscience in mind and people who support this type of programming will lead to the kind of essential social development which is most needed today.

It is particularly important for boys to be exposed to experiences which allow them to grow into sensitive and empathetic people. Mothers (as well as supportive fathers) are in a position to help boys gain the sensitivity advantage that girls now experience. If, with boys, parents simply begin to encourage responsiveness to others, (both in and out of games) as they now do with girls, we would take a giant step forward. I am speaking about freeing boys and men to become more fully human, and in so doing, freeing girls and women to live more fully.

When it comes to one's capacity to achieve in a way which respects life, women have a distinct advantage. It is woman in our society, who has the greatest understanding and sensitivity. It is unidirectional self-centered man who has the least to offer humanity; yet he continues to wield the greatest power. This is largely the reason for the sickness which permeates all modern societies.

Men are emotionally (and humanely) handicapped largely due to socialization towards competition, aggression, power, winning over others and the denial of feelings. Many are so insensitive to real feelings and needs (their own as well as others) that they do not recognize their own insensitivity. A confrontation on the issue will likely lead to either a "not me" response or an attack on the person who raises the issue; rather than to serious reflection and an attempt to understand. Competitive conditioning has helped put men in this state; cooperative learning will help free them.

Mothers (and other females) might consider making a special effort to help their sons (and other males) grow into warm and considerate human beings with the kind of qualities that they themselves would have appreciated in a marriage partner. To allow a child of either sex to grow into a selfish, non-empathetic, or morally void adult is to ensure interpersonal problems, unequal relationships and inner hollowness in the end. A child's best chance for a future of lasting meaningful relationships, which is the essence of human life, is to focus on nurturing the feeling and loving dimensions of life.

Many North American "parents to-be" attend prenatal classes designed to help mothers and fathers work together during the active birth process. These classes could be extended to include post natal classes which provide parents with strategies for promoting helpfulness and self-confidence among their children, for helping them with their own inter-personal relations and for coping with the new stresses they themselves are about to face.

Television Programming — Television has a significant impact on the behaviour of children. Those who watch are directly influenced. Those who do not watch, observe their peers who do. Thus to the dismay of some concerned parents, their lovely little pre-schooler comes home saying "pow-pow" or "smack", while acting out these behaviors. To remedy the negative influence of television the following actions could be considered:

- provide children's TV programs which help children learn how to play in creative, constructive and cooperative ways (e.g., by showing other kids doing it),
- use television to promote the use of cooperative games and competitive games played in a coope-rative fashion,
- replace children's cartoon and puppet shows which depict violence and insensitivity to others (which includes almost all of them) with those which depict pro-social behavior,
- provide television programming which depicts boys and men in a variety of settings interacting with others in sensitive and caring ways,
- provide positive male models in television pro-gramming (and TV by advertising) who respect the personal growth needs of women, treat wo-men as equals, do their fair share in the home, and become tenderly implicated in child rearing,
- provide alternative models on TV which show games and sport being played in a fun way with-out concern for score and with coaches acting in the best interest of players (e.g., encouraging per-sonal involvement, fair play, etc.),
- request the Players Associations to generate guidelines for their own behavior which reflect a responsible stand with respect to how they influ-ence the millions of children and youth who watch them.
- have respected sport figures (heroes) relate the ways in which sport can get out of perspective (turned into work or war) and have them provide constructive suggestions to help youngsters to continue to enjoy and benefit from sport,
- educate sports reporters and sport casters so that they understand the effects of their medium on children, and encourage or require them to reflect a more socially responsible perspective (e.g., they are in a position to help promote sportsmanship and eliminate the glorification of violence),
- use television to help with the pro-social educa-tion process for parents and coaches.

Teachers and coaches — The screening and humanistic education of teachers and coaches needs to be further developed and expanded. We need some guarantee that those people working with our children and youth are in fact the kind of people who should be working with them. Some considerations which may ensure that educators sti-mulate and model more balanced and sensitive life-styles includes the following:

Personnel considerations

- begin to select teachers and coaches based on human values, compassion, their ability to com-municate and the model they project,
- do not allow adults to teach or coach until such time that they can *demonstrate* that they operate solely in the best interest of the child's or athlete's overall development (e.g., by following humanis-tic guidelines),
- put some of the assessment of who is allowed to teach or coach in the hands of the students and players,
- expand teaching and coaching certification so that the *demonstration* of constructive and posi-tive responding to students and players is neces-sary to be allowed *to continue* in this line of work (e.g., do on-site behavioral assessments).

Program considerations

- provide more opportunities in communities and schools for self-paced activities, cooperative game experiences, and non-competitive games (e.g., activities with no score, games with collec-tive scores, games aimed at tie scores, outdoors experiences) (Orlick, 1978a; 1979; 1982),
- leave lots of time and facilities open for free play in the community with qualified humanistic in-struction available for those who want it,
- provide experiences for children in school (from pre-school on) which promote playing for enjoy-ment, trying many different activities and con-tinuing healthy activities throughout life,
- provide a variety of active group learning situa-tions in school (and in outside projects) which in-volve cooperative interdependence and which also eliminate the need to compete (Aronson et al., 1978; DeCharms, 1982; Johnson and Johnson, 1975; Sharan, 1980; Sharan et al., 1980; Slavin, 1980; Kohn, 1980),
- make full use of a child-to-child approach in school and sport (i.e., where empathetic older children teach younger children skills and posi-tive lessons) (Aarons and Hawes, 1979),
- provide interdependent play equipment, play ac-tivities and play materials which are designed to facilitate social development in a variety of set-tings (e.g., in community playgrounds, play areas, parks, nurseries, classrooms, family living rooms, playrooms, back yards, etc.) (Doyle, 1976; Orlick, 1982),
- replace children's toys which encourage the act-ing out of the destruction of others (e.g., war toys) with toys which encourage more construc-tive interaction,
- replace hitting sports for children with non-con-tact sports, or with non-contact version of "hit-

ting" sports, (Orlick, 1978b),

- teach stress control strategies, coping strategies for loss, and skills for enhancing team and family harmony to children and adults engaged in competition at all levels (Orlick, 1980b),
- consider postponing competition in organized sport until children have undergone training in stress control,
- integrate children (and coaches) from different teams together in interdependent ways (e.g., shifting team members, sharing locker, shower, coping strategies, ride to and from the game, etc.),
- use interdependent sharing rituals at the conclusion of games . . . where athletes engage in mutually beneficial activities together (Orlick, 1980a; 1982).

Moving On

We have a great deal of knowledge but have suffered from an inability to get our good ideas across. We have lacked the collective motivation to seek out and implement positive change in media thinking, government thinking, and corporate thinking, as well as in the education of people in the home, school and community. Until this begins to change our dreams will remain distant from our reality.

Some among us talk a wonderful game, but fail to act upon our proclaimed humanistic beliefs in our day-to-day living and interaction with others. The most important consideration is *not* how we write, produce or even preach. But rather how we live. Each of us must look at ourselves and our priorities in this light.

REFERENCES

Aarons, A. and H. Hawes. *Child-to-child.* London, England: The MacMillan Press, 1979.

Aronson, E., Blaney, N., Stephan, C., Sikes, J., & Snapp, M. *The jigsaw classroom.* Beverly Hills, CA: Sage Publications, 1978.

Barton, E., Osborne, J. "The development of classroom sharing by a teacher using positive practice". *Behavior Modification,* 1978, 2, 231-250.

De Charms, R. "Intrinsic motivation, peer tutoring and co-operative learning". In J.M. Levine & M.C. Wang (Eds.), *Teacher and student perception; Implications for learning.* Hillsdale, N.J.: Lawrence Erlbaum, 1982.

Doyle, P.H. "The differential effects of multiple and single niche play activities on interpersonal relations among pre-schoolers", In D.E. Lancy & B.A. Tindall (Eds.), *The anthropological study of play.* Cornwall, New York: Leisure Press, 1976.

French, M. *The bleeding heart.* New York: Ballantine Books, 1980.

Fritsch, H. "It's gotta be we — towards a humanistic physical education". Unpublished master's thesis, Dept. of Humanistic and Clinical Psychology, The Merrill-Palmer Institute, Detroit, Michigan, 1981.

Jensen, P.K. Effect of cooperative games programme on subsequent free play of kindergarten children. Unpublished doctoral dissertation, Faculty of Physical Education, University of Alberta, Edmonton, Alberta, 1979.

Johnson, D. and R. Johnson. *Learning together and alone.* Englewood Cliffs, N.J.: Prentice Hall, 1975.

Kemelfield, G. "UPE": The getting of wisdom in the North Solomons". Paper presented to the Extraordinary Meeting of the Faculty of Education, University of Papua New Guinea, Port Moresby, PNG, Sept. 18, 1979.

Kohn, A. "Why competition?". *The Humanist,* 1980, 49, 14-15.

Orlick, T. *The cooperative sports and games book.* New York: Pantheon Publishers, 1978a.

Orlick, T. *Winning through cooperation — Competitive insanity: Cooperative alternatives.* Washington, D.C.: Acropolis Press, 1978b.

Orlick, T. *The second cooperative sports and games book.* New York: Pantheon Publishers, 1982.

Orlick, T. Children's games: Following the path that has heart. *The Elementary School Guidance and Counseling Journal,* 1979, 14(2): 156-161.

Orlick, T. and C. Botterill. *Every kid can win.* Chicago, Illinois: Nelson Hall Publishers, 1975.

Orlick, T.D.; McNally, J.; & O'Hara, T. Cooperative games: Systematic analysis and cooperative impact. In F. Smoll & R. Smith (Eds.), *Psychological perspectives in youth sports,* Washington, D.C.: Hemisphere, 1978.

Orlick, T. and C. Foley. "Pre-school cooperative games — A preliminary perspective". In M.J. Melnick (Ed.), *Sport sociology: Contemporary themes* (2nd ed.), Dubuque, Iowa: Kendall/Hunt, 1979.

Orlick, T. "Tumbana pilai — games from the great ancestors". North Solomons Education Research Report #5, North Solomons Provincial Government. Arawa, Papua New Guinea, 1980a.

Orlick, T. *In pursuit of excellence.* Ottawa. Ontario: Coaching Association of Canada, 1980b.

Orlick, T.D. "Cooperative play socialization among pre-school children". *Journal of Individual Psychology,* 1981, 37(1), 54-64.

Orlick, T.D. "Positive socialization via cooperative games". *Developmental Psychology,* 1981, 17(4), 426-429.

Pines, M. "Good samaritans at age two". *Psychology Today,* 1979, 13(1), 66-77.

Provost, P. Immediate effects of film-mediated cooperative games on children's pro-social behavior. Unpublished Master's thesis, Dept. of Kinanthropology, University of Ottawa, Ottawa, Canada, 1981.

Sharan, S. "Cooperative learning in small groups: Recent methods and effects on achievement, attitudes and ethnic relations". *Review of Educational Research,* 1980, 50(1), 241-271.

Sharan, S.; Hare, A.; Webb, C.; and Hertz-Lazarowitz, R. (Eds.), *Cooperation in education,* Provo, Utah: Bringham Young University Press, 1980.

Slavin, R.E. "Cooperative learning".*Review of Educational Research,* 1980, 50(2), 315-342.

Slack, J. The effects of a cooperative perceptual-motor program in the learning disabled child. Unpublished Master's thesis, Dept. of Kinanthropology, University of Ottawa, Ottawa, Canada, 1978.

Westland, C. and Knight, J. (Eds.) *Playing, living, learning: A worldwide perspective on children's opportunities to play.* Ottawa, Canada: Canadian Parks/Recreation Association, 1982.

Witt, W.M. "Comparison of a traditional program of physical education and a cooperative games program on the co-operative classroom behavior of kindergarten children". Unpublished Master's thesis, Dept. of Education, Temple University, Philadelphia, PA., 1980.

REACTION TO WANG, MARTIN AND ORLICK

Leonard A. de Vries (Malaysia)

Let me begin by pulling out a few points which I thought were interesting. There is much that we can learn from Mr. Wang's paper. China has implemented specific strategies for the learning of cooperative behaviors from kindergarten to high school involving teachers, coaches and the mass media. I was particularly impressed with the methods used for structuring the learning environment. For example, they provide different quality soccer balls, observe the choices made by students, then provide feedback on cooperative behavior including the value of placing others before self. I also found the standards used for judging positive and negative behavior with emphasis given to cooperative behavior useful. The feedback provided by teachers and coaches focuses not only on skill performance but also on co-operation and other desirable behaviors. There are other examples which could be used by those interested in teaching cooperative behaviors to children and youth.

We also hear that China has been successful in implementing cooperative behaviors not only in the school system but in society as well. Perhaps Mr. Wang could share with us some of the evaluative measures used to assess the success of their efforts. We get the over-all impression that a very humanistic Chinese society is emerging through the implementation of the concept "Friendship first, competition second" and through the promotion of other human behaviors such as concern for others and cooperation. However, mandatory military training in society and in the educational system is in existence. Since this aspect was not considered, Mr. Wang might share his views on the two systems emphasizing very different values, namely, human (concern and care for people) and destructive (death). As someone from the Third World, I am also curious about China's policy towards international competition. I believe China will be making her first appearance at the next Olympic Games. Will China attempt to dominate, as all superpowers do, with strategies to win as many medals as possible, a task she has the capacity to do, or will "friendship first, competition second" be applied? Will she use her influence to reform the Olympic movement and by so doing align with the Third World?

Naomi Martin from Papua New Guinea shares with us her research on indigenous cultural activities and her proposal for their inclusion in the school curriculum. Her paper has great relevance for all third world countries, which have the same intentions, but not the plans for implementation. The concept of cooperation as practiced in her country, extends further and across matrilineal blood lines. In other words, relatives in her society have the same responsibility and social obligations as those within the immediate family. For example, my mother-in-law would have the same rights to my car!!

I was also interested in her people's concepts of work and play, both being totally interrelated. It would be enlightening if she could expand upon these important concepts. I agree with her concern, that the implementation of indigenous sports and games is much more difficult for secondary than primary school, due to the influence of international sport.

Dr. Terry Orlick, the "guru" of the cooperative movement in North America has sometimes been criticized for idealistic preaching and not being specific or realistic about his ideas. Not in this case. He has given very simple and practical suggestions based on his research, for integrating coopera-tive behaviors in school, at home, for the mass media and in particular television. His paper should greatly facilitate our efforts in the area.

I would like to make a few general remarks. All speakers have emphasized the use of sports and games for the learning of cooperative behaviors. They have emphasized the connection between cooperation in sport and cooperation in life. They are determined to use sport for non-physical ends, and are hoping that cooperative behaviors will transfer to non-sport-situations, that is, life. I suggest we review some of the teaching and learning requirements necessary for effective transfer of these behaviors.

1) the learner must be totally absorbed in the activity;
2) teachers and coaches must be extremely competent and concerned people, if they are to fully influence coopera-tive behaviors;
3) there must be specific instruction on the behavior;
4) provisions must be made for the learner to practice the behavior;
5) the outside social forces must reinforce the behavior.

Not only the potential but also the constraints of the sport environment should be considered.

Cooperation in sport and life, as a concept, has relevance to all nations. However, because many of the world's popula-tion live under highly structured, authoritarian policies, where collective societal needs and goals are given priority over individual goals and freedoms, positive behaviors traditionally associated with competition, that is, committment to excel-lence, individual goals & decision making, should be given similar importance. I suggest that we also consider competition in the context of these countries.

And finally, we have come to Ottawa, Canada, from all corners of the first, second and third world. Irrespective of the stage of development of our sport system, there is much from which we can benefit, if we have the openness, sincerity and humility to share and learn from each other. Terry Orlick, it seems to me, exemplifies these qualities. Although from a developed country and sport system, his experiences with the cultures and people of China, Papua New Guinea, Australia, Malaysia and others, have provided him with knowledge and insights for the improvement of self, his research and the general human conditions. I hope the papers in the coopera-tion theme and your subsequent deliberations will be of similar benefit to you.

A NEW DIRECTION FOR OLYMPIC SPORTS

Roman Czula (USA)

The aim of this paper is to suggest a new format for the Olympic Games based on a re-interpretation of Muzafer Sherif's (1958) "theory of contact under conditions of super-ordinate goals." Increasing understanding and improving relations between culturally diverse sports participants has long been a cherished hope among sport leaders despite the fact that there is little empirical data to support the hope. The research that does exist is outside of the Olympic Games and is generally based on Sherif's contact theory. Essentially, the theory states that "coordination between groups necessitated by a series of situations embodying superordinate goals will have a cumulative effect in the direction of reducing existing conflict between the groups." (Sherif, 1958, p. 355) Super-ordinate goals are defined as "goals which are compelling and highly appealing to members of two or more groups in conflict, but which cannot be attained by the energies and resources of the groups separately." (Sherif, 1958, p. 349) While Sherif's pioneering research project, The Robbers Cave Experiment," did not deal directly with the effects of sport participation or with different ethnic groups, it is often cited as being the strongest empirical evidence supporting the efficacy of the contact hypothesis in reducing intergroup prejudice and stereotyping.

It is easy to see how researchers who are interested in sport could relate Sherif's conclusions about intergroup dynamics to sports teams. That is, on a team the prime objective is to get everyone working together to obtain the mutually appealing superordinate goal of victory; and, generally, that victory is only possible if the individual team members subordinate themselves and their differences for the good of the team. Working together to achieve a common goal should lead to improved relationships between the participants and, ultimately, group success. This interpretation is consistent with the views of most social scientists who have studied race relations in sport, despite the paucity of data to support the theory. The general acceptance of the theory is exemplified by the fact that Gordon Allport and Thomas Pettigrew, two acknowledged leaders in the field of race relations, have each singled out the athletic team as an example of the validity of the contact theory. Consider the following:

> The principle is clearly illustrated in the multi-ethnic athletic team. Here the goal is all important; the ethnic composition of the team is irrelevent. (Allport, 1954, p. 264)

> Athletic teams furnish a pertinent example . . . the black and white members cannot achieve their common goal of winning without the assistance of each other. (Pettigrew, 1971, p. 276)

Sport researchers (e.g., Ibrahim (1968), McClendon (1972) and McIntyre (1970)) have also worked under the assumption that athletic teams provide validation of the contact theory. They have adopted Sherif's theory of superordinate goals and tested athletes and teams to see if they were less prejudiced. The result of this line of research will, in my view, continue to be ambiguous or negative because a basic component of Sherif's original study has not been adequately considered.

A careful review of the design of the second stage of Sherif's project makes it clear why attempts to improve human relationships in traditional athletic programs typically end in frustration. The Robbers Cave Experiment consisted of three carefully planned stages:

1. Two matched groups were independently formed at isolated and separate camp sites. The subjects were not known to each other before the project began.

2. HOSTILITY AND FRICTION WAS NATURALLY CREATED BETWEEN THE TWO GROUPS. (my emphasis)

3. A series of superordinate goals, goals that could not be attained by the efforts of one group alone, were introduced to reduce the intergroup hostilities.

Despite the fact that the second stage of the experiment is the only portion that deals directly with sport, it has been historically neglected by researchers. Ironically, sport at this point in the study is used to destroy interpersonal relationships. All Sherif did to create hostility between the two totally independent and homogenous groups was to form each into teams, give them a team name, and have them compete against each other for desirable prizes that were only awarded to the winning team. As Sherif, with grand understatement, wrote: "Specified conditions conductive to friction or conflict between groups were introduced." (Sherif, 1958, p. 353) He set up competing teams!! For sports researchers this bit of information is as valuable as his conclusions about superordinate goals. Apparently, all that is necessary to create intergroup hostility is to form two teams and have them compete for one prize. (Sherif also discovered that the competition negatively affected intra-team relationships because, as the going got tough, players used teammates as well as opponents as scapegoats.)

The research literature is clear on this subject — in situations characterized by competition for a prized goal, interpersonal relationships will be sacrificed and suffer. Thus, also by definition, traditional sports programs in this country cannot be expected to consistently have a positive effect on intergroup relations. Actually, it is likely that interracial and interpersonal relationships will be negatively affected. And, in the traditional sports program as successful teams move up the competitive ladder, they represent and oppose larger and greater entities. They compete in the local league, then the regional championship, the nationals, and then they play other countries. The ultimate example of this competitive process pits countries or political systems against each other in the often not-too-friendly strife of the Olympic arena. For instance, the victory by our Olympic Hockey team in 1980 was hailed as a great unifying event for the country. Indeed it was, but it brought us together by creating a "common enemy" of the Soviet Union, her people and the Soviet way of life. This is hardly the basis for bringing people together through sport. For every unification in our traditional sports program, there is a division. And there are many more losers than winners. We have been on a perpetual treadmill to nowhere when it comes to unifying mankind through sport.

Traditional team and combative sports programs do have positive attributes that justify their existence and support. However, consistently improving interracial and interpersonal relationships is not one of them. That is not to say that they should be abolished as many radical sports activists have suggested; it simply states that these programs do not have any magical powers when it comes to unifying mankind or even a team of 10 players (recall that Sherif's subjects represented a homogeneous sample and sport participation had a devastating affect on team relationships).

In my view, however, the cause is not lost. If we analyze the third stage of Sherif's study — the introduction of superordinate goals — we can find the basis for a sports program that helps build positive interpersonal relationships without sacrificing competition or maximal performance. Sherif, in the third stage of his experiment, introduced a series of natural events that could only be overcome by both groups working together: (1) A water shortage in the camps was created by rolling two large boulders over the main water valve and clogging the pipes. (2) A truck going for food for the two camps was "accidentally" driven into a ditch. (3) Equipment for the tents was mislaid.

In each situation, the groups, realizing that they had a common stake in cooperating to defeat their "natural" opponent, set aside their hostilities and solved their problems. With each success the groups erased more of their previously held animosities until they eventually became united. Implicit here is the fact that if sport is to effectively serve as a unifying agent, we must find "natural" opponents to defeat. My suggestion is to create Olympic Games which are truly unique;* Olympic Games which are more than another prestigious collection of world championships that happen to pay lip service to a tired series of idealistic homilies about brotherhood and unity. Let us begin the era of the "superordinate Olympic Games" by eliminating from the Olympic agenda team sports and all sports whose ends are the physical or symbolic vanquishing of a human opponent. Let us no longer, not even psychologically or symbolically, strive to defeat a human opponent in the athletic arena. Let us make the universe our common enemy. Let us strive to defeat time or distance or gravity or weight or a standard of excellence as in gymnastics or diving. Let us unite all the athletes of the world in the struggle to defeat those natural barriers that limit human potential and mark human boundaries. Let nature be

---

* The basic concept for these Olympic Games was originally outlined by me in a response to a presentation by Harry Edwards at the Olympic Symposium at Skidmore College, February 9, 1980.

every athlete's opponent. When a barrier like the 4-minute mile or the 8 foot high jump is defeated, all of mankind is victorious. It is a moment when every human being's limits and potentials are expanded and it is just cause for universal rejoicing.

The possibilities for this "superordinate" approach to sport are exemplified in any marathon race. The cheers for the last finishers are as loud and as genuine as for the first. And the sense of accomplishment is as strong for both. All marathoners (and spectators) are united in the common struggle to cover the distance and defeat time. The comraderie and love extant in a marathon field represents the attainable ideal in sport. It is possible in dozens of other events. Think back. Try to recall those rare instances in sport which have momentarily erased national boundaries and unified humanity. They have occurred as a result of victories against nature: Bob Beamon. Alekseyev Nadia. Roger Bannister . . .

This superordinate sports perspective, radical though it may appear to some, is not far in philosophy from that which was espoused by the founders of the Olympic Games. Faster. Higher. Stronger. Unity through sport. And, the salvation of the Games may lie in changing the current format to more accurately reflect this philosophy. All events removed from the "superordinate Olympic" agenda would still have their yearly championships and they would continue with as much importance as ever. But, the inclusion of only those sports strictly adhering to the concept of the "natural" opponent would be a long overdue substantive change that would place the Olympic Games into a realistic position to achieve its lofty

goal of unifying humanity through sport. Once the Olympic program is humanized, national and local programs would have to follow. The potential is there. We can get off the treadmill . . .

REFERENCES

1. Allport, G., *The Nature of Prejudice*. Cambridge, Mass.: Addison-Wesley, 1954.

2. Ibrahim, H., "Prejudice among college athletes." *Research Quarterly*, 39: 556-559, 1968.

3. McClendon, M., "Interracial contact on collegiate basketball teams." Doctoral dissertation, University of Kansas, 1972.

4. McIntyre, T., "A field experimental study of cohesiveness, status, and attitude change in four bi-racial small sport groups." Doctoral dissertation, Penn State University, 1970.

5. Pettigrew, T., *Racially separate or Together?* New York: McGraw Hill Co., 1971.

6. Sherif, M., "Superordinate goals in the reduction of intergroup conflict." *American Journal of Sociology*, 63: 349-356, 1958.

7. Sherif, M., O. Harvey, B. White, W. Hood, and C. Sherif, *Intergroup Conflict and Cooperation: The Robbers Cave Experiment*. Norman, Oklahoma: University of Oklahoma Book Exchange, 1961.

HOW COOPERATIVE ARE TEAM SPORT GAMES?

J.M. Pauwels (Belgium)

Situating the problem

In Western Europe there is now a continuing effort to devote more time in the lessons in physical education to team sport games. Formerly in physical education medical and physical aspects were central concerns. Today games have a broader educational purpose.

A movement towards developing the *socio-motor* aspects of participants began in the 1970's in Western Europe. According to those who are so directed, sports games are a social event where one, as a participant, can speak, understand, believe, and feel and where there is no closed system in which each player serves as a cog in a machine. Not competition but cooperation is important. The emphasis is placed primarily on interaction and much less on motor skills.

The purpose of this contribution is to investigate to what degree the unchanged team sport games in school offer a chance for interaction and cooperation. The project includes three areas of research.

Overview of the study

Within a group of 79 pupils (15-18 years old) the relationship was studied among sociometric status, motor status ("How proficient do you find your classmates for each of the 3 sports, Basketball, European Handball and Soccer?"), participative status (the number of times someone holds the ball during a game), and a proficiency score given by the teacher. The results show a close relation between participative status and the proficiency estimated by the pupils (r = .80) and the actual proficiency measured by the teacher (r = .85). The correlation between participation and social status, on the other hand is low (r = .40).

A group of 22 pupils (age = 16 years old) was tested two by two. Twenty slides of European handball were shown with 2 offensive players, one in possession of the ball and one without the ball. The subjects had to observe the situation and press one of two keys (1 = action: shoot at the goal; 2 = interaction: pass the ball). Several hypotheses were tested, and most of the time, the player without the ball tended more toward interaction than the player with the ball.

Video recordings were made of 20 pupils (age = 17 years old) while playing basketball. Each player, was scored on the number of passes, shots, dribbles, and the total time he was in possession of the ball. There are very serious differences in participation in favour of the skillful pupils. The relationship between the total time a player is in possession of the ball and a proficiency score for basketball given by the pupils and the teacher is very high (r = .82 & .81). The weaker players have the ball much less often.

Discussion

The results of this investigation demonstrate that not all pupils are equally brought into interaction through playing team sport games, nor do they participate to the same degree. Cooperation, where it exists in such games is largely selective in favour of the most skilled players.

When we want to strive for the benefitial social aspects of games, placing the accent on cooperation and interaction for all, then we have to adapt the games to allow weaker pupils to be drawn into the games more quickly and as equal partners. We have to change the games so that they require less technical competence, or indtroduce simpler or different approaches.

COMPETITION AND AGGRESSION: OBSERVATIONS

A.S. Sohi (Nigeria)

Soccer in Nigeria is the most popular game with respect to being played and spectated. The popularity of the game gives prestigious colour to victory, and hence a fierce competition and higher level of anxiety are the outcomes. In view of this the organizers have attempted to take various organizational precautions in order to avoid unwanted aggressive behaviour during the competition. In spite of this, aggressive behaviour continues to be observed.

This study was an attempt to give us a better understanding of the conditions under which sport aggression occurs. Aggressive behaviour expected during soccer competitions, was categorized operationally as: 1) ritualized and permissive and hence not punishable aggression, 2) aggression punishable under normal rules and 3) aggression explosions outside cultural expectations. These categories are in ordinal hierarchy of degree of magnitude.

The data was collected during the inter hall varsity soccer competition in an institution of higher learning. For each match three observers were assigned to score for aggression independently. The rounded averages for each type of aggression were taken for analysis. In all there were eight teams representing each hall of residence and were pooled into two pools. The teams played first on a league basis and the two top teams on the tables from each pool played on knock-out basis, thus altogether totalling fifteen matches. The aggression categories have been added together for analysis purpose.

In this study we considered progress of competition, number of matches played, match outcome in each case with goals scored and incidence of aggression under three operationally defined categories during first and second halves. It is obvious that aggression took place during all the matches. The permissive aggressive behaviour occurred very frequently both during first and second halves. This is followed by incidence of aggression which is punishable under rules, especially Law 12 of the game. The incidence of socially disapproved behaviour in terms of aggression was also observed but its incidence was far less than those found in the other two categories.

In soccer there are two halves separated by an interval for rest and change of sides. There is a possibility that as the teams compete, tempers heat up or teams start the competition with high aggressive tendencies. Both situations can result in hard fought attempts to frustrate the opponent. In such a rallying milieu an outburst of aggression in any form cannot be ruled out. Similarly such a behaviour may occur interruptedly and in chain like fashion. To see whether there is any patterning of occurrence of aggressive behaviour, the same has been seen with a comparative view in relation to its prevalence during first half and second half. It was observed that aggression, all categories combined, occurred more frequently during the first half than it did in the second half. The differences were found significant (t = 2.445; df = 14 and P < .05). This type of patterning perhaps can be attributed to a general psychological adjustment of the participants in the course of play.

During the competitions, there is a movement of teams on a broad-based pyramid fashion and this movement brings the ultimate objective closer to realization. This upward movement has been broken into four stages of the competition. As the teams approach the final victory, the competition gets fierce. The average incidence of aggressive behaviours, all categories combined together, increased from stage one onwards to the last stage. The differences were found significant (x^2 = 11.828; df = 3 and P < .05).

In a competition, victory can be very hard fought or won with ease and a margin of superior performance. In the present case the outcomes of matches have been categorized as hard fought matches and easily won matches. Draw (tie) matches and those decided with a margin of one goal were categorized as hard fought and the remaining were put under second category. In all there were seven hard fought and eight were easily won matches. The observations showed that during the hard fought matches, the incidence of aggressive behaviour was more but the differences, however were not found to be significant.

To finish at the top is a well earned prestige and most of the teams, if not all, try to achieve this merit. It is assumed that such a team has to fight out the competition with great vigour and spirit. It is possible that while struggling hard to be on the top, such teams may be more aggressive than those who rest satisfied with lower achievement. In this context it is interesting to know whether there is any relationship between the finishing rank and rank on the committing of aggression. The final results tabulated for the competitions furnished the rank each team got on the hierarchy of finishing order. The rank for each team from the highest to the lowest with respect to committing aggression was worked out. To get a true rank for a team, averages of aggression committed were taken since all the teams did not play the same number of matches. It was found that aggressiveness was more on the part of those teams getting higher positions on the final ranking. In other words, the positions on final placings and aggressiveness were found correlated to each other. (Rank difference correlation = 0.738, df = 6 and P < .05).

The soccer matches at the university attracts a good number of spectators and supporters. Some of the halls of residence organize the supporters very well in order to boost the morale of their teams. The number of the spectators cannot be estimated exactly since there is no seating arrangement. But on the other hand a fairly good estimate of them can be affected when considering the space they occupy around the field while standing. With the help of space occupation estimates the number of spectators was categorized. It was observed that the larger the number of spectators, the higher was the incidence of aggressive behaviour. These differences were found out to be significant (x= 4.406; df = 1 and P < .05).

This university is fairly old when seen with respect to the development of formal higher education in Nigeria. The intramural programmes in soccer were started as far back as thirty years ago. Every year's engagements and encounters have developed certain rivalries among a few halls of residence and these rivalries are jealously nurtured, sustained and exhibited during the soccer competitions. During these competitions, the halls having rivalries met each other during 6 matches and glancing at magnitude of aggressive behaviour during the mentioned matches, it is obvious that there was a higher degree of aggression. (For a complete breakdown of aggression statistics recorded write to the author).

Conclusions: The following conclusions can be drawn from the study:

- Inspite of a strong supervisory structure, aggression of different natures did occur.
- there was a temporal patterning of aggression since it was more during the first halves of the matches.
- there was a tendency towards an increase in aggression as the teams moved up in the stages of the competitions.
- the nature of victory (small or large margin) was not seen associated with the degree of aggressive behaviour.

- the rank of team on the degree of aggressing and position on the final standings of teams were seen as correlated.
- the greater the number of spectators the higher was the incidence of occurrence of aggressive behaviour.
- old rivalries among some of the teams were associated with a higher degree of aggression when teams engaged in an encounter.

Implications:

Some implications emerging from the study are given below.

Today it is "normal" to see aggressive behaviour in soccer but at times it becomes explosive in nature which should be of concern to everyone.

It should be remembered that aggression occurs in activating socio-psychological environments. The coach (and organizers) have to understand them.

Competitive sport is a double edged sword inculcating higher values on one hand and nurturing ruthless drives on the other. As human beings let us teach and learn positive values in competitive sport.

The effectiveness of checking a ruthless drive to aggress in competitive soccer is a dependent upon changing value orientations of the participants. Winning through fairplay is the ideal to be cherished, while facing the fact that competi-

tion strengthens the susceptibility of aggressive behaviour. To curtail explosive aggression in competition, the competitors must be taught to be aggressive only within the cultural limits provided by rules of the game.

REFERENCES

Ardrey, Robert, *The Territorial Imperative.* New York: Atheneum, 1966.

Cratty, B.J., *Psychology in Contemporary Sport.* New Jersey: Prentice Hall, 1973.

Loranz, Konrad, *On Aggression.* New York: Harcourt, Brace and World, 1966.

Morris, Desmond, *The Naked Ape.* New York: McGraw-Hill, 1968.

Montagu, Ashley (ed.), *Man and Aggression.* New York: Oxford University Press, 1973.

Scott, J.P., "Sport Aggression," in William F. Straub (ed.), *Sport Psychology — Analysis of Athletic Behaviour.* Mouvement Publishers, 1978.

Starr, Anthony, *Human Aggression,* New York: Athenemum, 1968.

Volkamer, M., "Zur Aggressivitat in Konkurrenz — Orientierten Sozialen Systemen" *Sportweissenschaft,* I, 1971.

PERSONAL GROWTH AND AGGRESSION CONTROL IN SPORT

John Heil (USA)

To assess the contribution of a social institution to the society it serves, it is necessary to examine both the positive and negative consequences of the influence of that institution. Traditionally sport had been recognized to offer a host of positive benefits including: physical fitness, aesthetic appreciation, and socialization (Kenyon, 1968), as well as political and social mobility (Figler, 1981). More recently claims have been made supporting the role of sport in the enhancement of psychological health and well-being: in regard to personal growth, where Maslow's (1977) concepts of self-actualization and peak experience have been demonstrated to be both conceptually interesting and empirically useful (Ravizza, 1977); as well as in the areas of stress management (Cogan, 1976) and therapy (Kaplan et al., 1980). Among the negative consequences of sport participation (direct or vicarious) the greatest concern is directed toward its aggression enhancing potential. The more salient manifestations of this influence include: spectator violence (Gaskell and Pearton, 1979); the high frequency of injuries occurring legally within the participatory context of the collision sports, notably professional football (Underwood, 1978); and, the public spectacle of fighting that commonly occurs in the sport of ice hockey (Reed, 1976). The psychological literature offers ample theoretical bases for the concern that the formerly cited examples represent only the "tip of the iceberg." Alderman (1974) suggests that all competitive sports are by design frustrating (in that they involve each contestant or team attempting to block the goal-directed behavior of the opposition) thereby serving as an instigation to aggression.[1] Perhaps the gravest concern is that the widespread exposure to aggressive models provided by sport (especially in the television medium) may subtly raise the aggression baseline of all who participate, directly or vicariously, in sport.[2] In contrast, Lorenz (1971) has characecrized sport as "war without weapons," which offers a safe arena for

the ritualized catharsis of aggression. This author suggests that enhanced aggression is not an inevitable consequence of sport participation, but that it is an effect subject to modification.

The purpose of this paper is to explore a strategy of sport education which at once seeks to limit inappropriate aggressive behavior and to enhance the growth potential of sport participation. It is assumed that the aforementioned concerns are not distinct but represent different aspects of the same problem; and, that the net, positive or negative, effect of participation is largely a consequence of the attitude or mental set that each person brings to the sport context. An additional assumption is that it is through the training of sports educators (who will in turn train athletes) that a constructive attitude toward sport participation may be most widely and most effectively nurtured.

At this juncture, a critical question appears to be, "Can the adoption of a particular attitude or mental set toward sport participation limit inappropriate aggression within a context as potentially frustrating and violent as that of the collision sports; and at the same time, enhance the growth element?" Harris (1973) suggests that even the highly competitive sports context may be managed so that it may serve as a paradigm for training in frustration coping skills. Bandura's (1973) work with hyper-aggressive boys offers empirical support for this contention. Shifting to an historical focus it is notable that the military skills of the past, in particular, fencing in the West (Bower, 1976) and the martial arts in the East (Huard and Wang, 1977), have made the transition from highly volatile activities to workable, reasonably safe, modern sports. The code of Chivalry (later Honor) which guided knightly (later gentlemanly) behavior in Western society (Baldick, 1965; A. Traveller, 1836); and, the code of Bushido which guided the behavior of a comparably elite group in

Japan, the Samurai (Huard and Wang, 1977) both are designed to limit violence within a violent context. In each of these traditions, training in the use of weapons and indoctrination into the code of behavior (which prescribed conditions for the appropriate use of the weapons) took place simultaneously (Baldick, 1965; A. Traveller, 1836; Huard and Wang, 1977). Both codes are based on the fundamental assumption that the superordinate goals of personal honor and collective justice, when embraced by their adherents, would limit the indiscrete use of violence. While the abuses of the custom of formal dueling are well documented in Western society, it appears that this practice failed to the extent that its adherents deviated from the spirit of the code (Baldick, 1965; Kane, 1951).

Most salient among the criticisms of modern Western sport is that the spirit of "good sportsmanship" is being supplanted by a "win at all costs" attitude. It seems reasonable to assume that the reestablishment of sportsmanship as a superordinate goal may best serve as a fundamental conceptual focus to guide sports educators in their efforts to simultaneously limit violence and enhance the growth element in sport. Having once identified the essence of a constructive attitude toward sport participation, it then becomes necessary to develop a systematic strategy for the implementation of the educational program designed to instill this attitude. However, the role of sportsmanship in Western athletics, though prominent in lore, has not been systematically articulated. Traditionally, it has existed as an implicitly held assumption highlighted by anecdotal accounts. In Eastern societies, where physical culture and athleticism play a prominent role in the traditional philosophies; and are viewed as integral to the process of personal development, a strategy has been articulated. The difference between the Western and Eastern views is well conveyed in the contrast between the Japanese concepts of "do" and "jutsu." The term "jutsu" refers to technique, the "how to do" of exercise. In contrast, the term "do" means "way," in particular, a way to live. In the West, the "jutsu" concept traditionally prevails with sport treated as a physical discipline; while, in the East the "do" concept holds implying that the sport experience may be treated as a vehicle for the pursuit of personal growth.

Fortunately, the "do" concept is not without precedent in the West. In the *Loneliness of the Long Distance Runner*, Stillitoe (1959) portrays the sport experience as a microcosm of the larger microcosmic world of everyday life; and, shows how this may serve as a context for reflective self-examination. More recently, this concept has been explored in relation to the world of sport by the humanistic psychologists Murphy and Leonard. In *Gold in the Kingdom*, Murphy (1972) creates a "fantasy" rich microcosm for the game of golf. George Leonard (1975) develops the concept of the "ultimate athlete" as one who plays at sport in such a way as to enrich and enliven one's experience in the "larger game" of life. The focus on the process rather than on the consequences (i.e., victory or defeat) of participation, which is a critical element in the microcosmic concept, is reflected also in the "Inner Game" (Gallwey, 1974), "New Games" (Fluegelman, 1976) and "Cooperative Games" (Orlick, 1978) approaches. Gallwey relies on an intuitively based training program and directs students away from an overriding concern with objective evaluation of performance. Fluegelman and Orlick provide an "anti-frustration" alternative offering participants the opportunity to choose from a selection of activities that to a varying degree emphasize cooperation over competition. The spirit of "playfulness and spontaneity" which characerize these latter approaches has begun successfully to make inroads into collegiate intramural programs (Gilbert, 1975; Orlick, 1978).

In conclusion, it is suggested that through the inclusion of a psychologically sensitive training component in the curricula of sports educators, the growth potential of sport participation may most effectively be enhanced. The practical implications in regard to the implementation of this program are twofold, one theoretical and the other applied:

A. Development of a personal systematic strategy for sports education based on:
   1. The Oriental concept of "do."[3]
   2. The related concept of the microcosm as articulated in Western literature on psychology and sport.
   3. Relevant mainstream psychological literature, in particular, that dealing with the concepts of self-actualization and peak experience.
B. Continued exploration and application of existing alternative models of sport education including:
   1. The "Inner Game" approach.
   2. The "New Game" approach.
   3. The "Cooperative Game" approach.

Footnotes

[1] This statement is supported by the frustration-aggression hypothesis of Dollard, Dobb, Miller, Mowrer and Sears (1939) and by Bewrkowitz' (1974) "angry" aggression theory as well as by contemporary empirical literature (Baron, 1977).

[2] This assumption finds theoretical as well as conditional empirical support in the work of Bandura (1973).

[3] A brief list of appropriate readings follows:

Herrigel, E. *Zen in the art of archery* (Hull, R.F.C., trans.). New York: Random House, 1971.

Hyams, J. *Zen in the martial arts.* Los Angeles: J.P. Tarcher, 1979.

Kauz, H. *The martial spirit.* Woodstock, N.Y.: The Overlook Press, 1978.

Musashi, M. *A book of five rings.* (Harris V., trans.). Woodstock, N.Y.: Overlook Press, 1974.

Suzuki, D.T. *Zen and Japanese culture.* Princeton, N.J.: Princeton University Press, 1970.

REFERENCES

A Traveller. *The art of duelling.* London: R. Willoughby, 1836. Reprinted in Haven, C.T. (Ed.), *Shooting muzzle loading handguns.* Falmouth, Mass.: Guns Incorporated, 1947.

Baldick, R. *The duel.* New York: Clarkson N. Potter, Inc., 1965.

Bandura, A. *Aggression: A social learning analysis.* Englewood Cliffs, N.J.: Prentice-Hall, Inc., 1973.

Baron, R.A. *Human aggression.* N.Y.: Plenum Press, 1977.

Berkowitz, L. Some determinants of impulsive aggression: The role of mediated associations with reinforcement for aggression. *Psychological Review,* 1974, 81, 165-176.

Bower, M. *Fencing.* Dubuque, Iowa: William C. Brown Company Publishers, 1976.

Cogan, M. The possible role of physical activity in adaptation to psychological stress. *Proceedings of the American Association for the Advancement of Tension Control.* Louisville, Ky.: AAATC, 1976.

Dollard, J.; Doob, L.W.; Miller, N.E.; Mowrer, O.H. and Sears, R.R. *Frustration and aggression.* New Haven, Conn.: Yale University Press, 1939.

Figler, S.K. *Sport and play in American life.* New York: Saunders, 1981.

Fluegelman, A. (Ed.) *The new games book.* Garden City, N.Y.: Doubleday and Company, Inc., 1976.

Gallwey, W.T. *The inner game of tennis.* New York: Random House, 1974.

Gaskell, G. and Pearton, R. Aggression and sport. In Goldstein, J.H. (Ed.), *Sports, games and play: Social and psychological viewpoints.* Hillsdale, N.J.: Lawrence Erlbaum Assoc., 1979.

Gilbert, B. Imagine going to school and learning to play: Program at Emporia State College. *Sports Illustrated,* 1975, 6, 84-87.

Harris, D.V. *Involvement in sport: A somatopsychic rationale for physical activity.* Philadelphia: Lea and Febiger, 1973.

Herrigel, E. *Zen in the art of archery* (Hull, R.F.C., trans.) New YorkZ: Random House, 1971.

Huard, P. and Wong, M. *Oriental methods of mental and physical fitness* (Smith, D.N., trans.). New York: Funk and Wagnalls Publishing Company, Inc., 1977.

Hyams, J. *Zen in the martial arts.* Los Angeles: J.P. Tarcher, 1979.

Kane, H.T. *Gentlemen, swords and pisols.* New York: William Morrow and Company, 1951.

Kaplan, H.I., Freedman, A.M. and Sadock, B.J. *Comprehensive textbook of psychiatry.* Baltimore: Williams and Wilkins, 1980.

Kauz, H. *The martial spirit.* Woodstock, N.Y.: The Overlook Press, 1978.

Kenyon, G.S. A conceptual model for characerizing physical activity. *Research Quarterly*, 1968, 39, 96-105.

Leonard, G. *The ultimate athlete.* New York: The Viking Press, 1975.

Lorenz, K. *On Aggression.* (Wilson, M.K., trans.). N.Y.: Bantam Books, 1971.

Maslow, A. *The farther reachers of human nature.* New York: Viking Press, 1971.

Murphy, M. *Golf in the Kingdom.* New York: Viking, 1972.

Musashi, M. *A book of five rings.* (Harris, V., trans.). Woodstock, N.Y.: Overlook Press, 1974.

Orlick, T. *The cooperative sports and games book.* New York: Pantheon Books, 1978.

Ravizza, K. Peak experiences in sport. *Journal of Humanistic Psychology*, 1977, 17(4), 35-40.

Reed, J.D. Week of disgrace on ice. *Sports Illustrated*, 1976, 44 (17), 22-25.

Sillitoe, A. *The loneliness of the long-distance runner.* New York: The New American Library, Inc., 1959.

Suzuki, D.T. *Zen and Japanese culture.* Princeton, N.J.: Princeton University Press, 1970.

Underwood, J. Brutality: The crisis in football. *Sports Illustrated*, 1978, 49(7), 69-82; 49(8), 32-56; 49(9), 30-41.

COMPETITIONS DE DANSES FOLKLORIQUES ET CONVIVIALITE INTERNATIONALE

M. Gérard Gillot (France)

I. Présentation générale

Depuis plus de 30 années, un groupe de bénévoles de la ville de Dijon organise des rencontres internationales d'ensembles amateurs de musiques et de danses folkloriques, qui rassemblent chaque année au cours de grandes fêtes populaires plus de mille athlètes et artistes et les mêlent à la vie bourguignonne.

L'auteur a pris des responsabilités actives dans ces festivités, comme organisateur, présentateur et metteur en scène de spectacles, folkloriste ou photographe. La présentation et les réflexions suivantes sont le fruit de 20 années d'expérience.

La devise des Associations qui se sont relayées pour cette action, devise explicite ou implicite, est: "Pour la Bourgogne, ses hommes, ses arts et ses traditions". Terre de la vigne, du vin et des vignerons, la Bourgogne est aussi une terre historique, riche de traditions humanistes: terre d'accueil, terre de gastronomie, terre d'oecuménisme. Les compétitions qui *affrontent* chaque automne ce millier d'hommes et de femmes pour la conquête du "Collier d'Or" ou du "Tonneau d'Or" sont donc une véritable compétition sportive, très connue dans le monde de la danse et du folklore; mais c'est aussi et surtout une occasion de fraternité entre des peuples, qui parfois se haïssent, ou plus souvent, qui ne se connaissent pas.

A Dijon et dans toutes les bourgades de Bourgogne sont organisés des défilés et des spectacles folkloriques, à la fin desquels les spectateurs apprennent les chants et les danses de leurs invités. Une grande opération "Amitié" permet à des familles, des associations, des entreprises, des hospices d'accueillir pour un repas, une journée, soit un couple, soit un groupe entier de danseurs: ainsi ne vit-on pas seulement au rythme des spectacles, mais enracine-t-on profondément les amitiés.

C'est donc chaque année, au moment des vendanges dans le vignoble des grands crus entre Dijon et Beaune, — vers le 15 septembre, que ce rassemblement traditionnel a lieu. Chaque année, un hommage solennel est rendu aux vignerons d'une commune rurale: Gevrey-Chambertin, Beaune, Mercurey, Nuits-Saint-Georges, Vougeot, etc. . . On déguste ensemble le vin nouveau, on offre le raisin aux enfants et aux vieux, on offre son travail au Bon Dieu au cours d'une grande messe à laquelle les groupes de compétiteurs s'associent par des chants et des musiques. Ainsi le sport et le spectacle artistique sont-ils enracinés dans les traditions rurales et dans les rythmes de la vie actuelle.

La centaine d'animateurs qui organisent bénévolement cette grande occasion de rencontres internationales se réunit souvent, en grand groupe ou en petites commissions techniques, pour réfléchir aux résultats obtenus et pour imaginer ce qu'il convient de faire pour se rapprocher toujours davantage de ses objectifs: ainsi a-t-on intensifié l'effort de mêler les visiteurs étrangers à la population; ainsi a-t-on très vite réinséré le spectacle sportif dans une Fête en hommage aux Vignerons, car la Fête réduite au spectacle avait perdu son charme et son âme. . . Ainsi réunit-on chaque jour tous les ensembles au "Cellier de Clairvaux" pour les repas qu'ils prennent en commun, tous réunis sous les voûtes de l'ancienne cave des moines bénédictins, tous mêlés au fur et à mesure que s'avancent les Fêtes. . .

Ces Fêtes de la Vigne ont enfin un effet non négligeable au sein même du groupe des nombreux bénévoles qui les organisent: l'association qui les réunit regroupe des personnes de tous les horizons politiques et confessionnels, séduits par cette grande occasion de fraternité et de paix par le sport. Car c'est bien de sport qu'il s'agit: et le Maire de Dijon l'a si bien compris qu'il contribue fortement à l'organisation des compétitions, par des subventions, mais surtout en confiant aux soins de toute cette jeunesse le grand Palais des Sports de la Ville.

II. Elargissements et opinions personnelles.

Il y a de nombreux spectacles, organisés dans les théatres et salles des fêtes de toute la Bourgogne. Mais le vrai spectacle est ailleurs. Il est dans la rue, à Dijon, lors du grand défilé, où la foule se mêle aux danseurs et musiciens pour une grande fête populaire. Il est encore dans la rue, devant le Cellier de Clairvaux, où les groupes déjà arrivés donnent l'aubade aux arrivants, font l'assaut de prouesses dans des spectacles improvisés que les ménagères savent apprécier, elles qui en sortant du marché aux légumes s'arrêtent là pour un grand moment de joie collective. Le spectacle enfin est dans le Cellier, où, après une semaine de compétitions acharnées, chacun reprend en choeur les refrains des autres.

Il reste bien sûr des problèmes à résoudre, car ces Fêtes sont d'abord une compétition, avec ce que ceci comporte d'agressivité, d'âpreté, voire de violence. Dans leur désir d'amitiés internationales, les organisateurs d'hier avaient multiplié les catégories et les récompenses; l'actuel Festival a restreint les catégories et réduit les prix. Cette exigence de qualité sportive n'est pas sans poser des problèmes "diplomatiques", car chacun a à coeur de rapporter dans sa patrie le fruit de ses efforts. Pourtant, il en est ainsi en sport: il n'y a qu'un vainqueur. Un grand effort est donc à faire pour préciser nettement les règles du concours, afin que le vainqueur soit indiscutable, et que tous les concurrents puissent le féliciter.

Pour ce qui est de l'amitié, il semble que l'on soit sur la bonne voie. Mais l'expérience d'une année sans hommage aux vignerons a suffisamment montré que la fête, pour être réussie, doit avoir des racines populaires, et que cette convivialité ne peut se confondre avec un simple spectacle, — fût-il de qualité. Il importe que les Bourguignons dans leur ensemble aient l'occasion de participer à la Fête, et parmi eux, d'abord les artisans de la vigne et du vin. Qu'on les honnore, qu'on les fête en appréciant, au milieu des rires et des chants, leur vin.

Mais il reste un dernier projet pour rapprocher plus encore ces hommes et ces femmes venus des 4 coins du monde: des EU, du Canada, d'URSS, de Hongrie, Tchécoslovaquie, Bulgarie, Pologne, Albanie, Turquie, Allemagne, Suède, Norvège, Phillipines et j'en passe. . . Il reste à leur donner d'autres occasions de se mieux connaître. C'est pourquoi nous formons le projet d'un Centre d'Etude du Folklore International, — qui a déjà fonctionné par le passé, et qui ne permettrait pas seulement à des folkloristes français de mieux connaître ce folklore qui leur rend visite à domicile, mais qui en outre, permettrait aux groupes de s'étudier mutuellement, de s'influencer, de s'apprécier. Comme athlètes et artistes, mais aussi comme Hommes. Et il y a pour ce faire des solutions simples à mettre en oeuvre.

III. Conclusions.

1. Les Fêtes de la Vigne de Dijon sont une grande compétition de danses et musiques folkloriques.
2. Le but de cette manifestation est triple:
   * rendre hommage aux arts et traditions populaires locales, et en particulier aux arts et traditions de la vigne,
   * faire vivre le folklore international,
   * renforcer la convivialité internationale,
   * accessoirement, renforcer la compréhension locale.
3. Les Fêtes de la Vigne s'inscrivent donc dans la grande perspective des JEUX OLYMPIQUES rénovés par Pierre de Coubertin: elles sont apparemment une simple occasion de compétitions sportives. Mais elles sont au fond une fête à la gloire de l'Homme, une contribution à la Paix.

SPORT PAR COUPLES

Ferruccio Antonelly et M. Gatti (Italie)

Cette recherche, menée à l'aide d'un questionnaire, démontre les effets positifs que la pratique sportive exerce en ce qui concerne le rapport du couple. Tous les hommes et femmes ont répondu (100%) d'être satisfaits si le partenaire pratique des sports. Parmi les raisons fournies, on peut constater: "Cela fait du bien à la santé". "Le partenaire rentre à la maison plus détendu". "Il y a un autre intérêt à part de travail". Les taux de réponse de ces alternatives sont chez les hommes 78%, 48%, 56% et chez les femmes 69%, 61%, 62% respectivement. L'activité sportive s'est avérée également salutaire en vue d'améliorer la cohésion du rapport du couple.

En fait 68% des hommes et 75% des femmes ont déclaré d'avoir remarqué des améliorations dans leur ménage après avoir commencé à pratiquer ensemble le sport. Parmi les raisons de cette amélioration, il faut signaler: "Nous avons un intérêt en commun" (hommes 61% — femmes 68%). "Nous déchargeons notre aggressivité" (hommes 41% — femmes 65%). "Nous pouvons connaître d'autres amis" (hommes 42% — femmes 32%). "Nous avons un meilleur rapport avec les enfants" (hommes 36% — femmes 57%).

Avant le mariage, 76% des hommes par rapport à 49% des femmes pratiquaient l'activité sportive. Cette différence est confirmée du fait que 39% des femmes ont été initiées au sport par leur mari, alors que 9.1% seulement des hommes pratiquent le tennis sur stimulation de leur femme. A la question s'il est important de pratiquer ensemble le même sport, 70% des hommes et 81% des femmes ont répondu d'une manière affirmative. Les raisons les plus fréquentes pour cette réponse sont les suivantes:

"Le partenaire me stimule à pratiquer ce sport" (hommes 24% — femmes 43%). "Nous pouvons rester ensemble plus souvent" (hommes 65% — femmes 60%). En général, sur la base des résultats obtenus on peut affirmer que le sport pratiqué en couple, représente un moyen efficace pour renforcer la rapport du couple, tant en améliorant sa cohésion et harmonie qu'en sauvegardant la santé mentale.

EFFECTS OF VIEWING VIDEOTAPED COOPERATIVE GAMES

Pierre Provost (Canada)

Recently cooperative games and sports programs have been implemented in a variety of schools, pre-school centers, community centers and homes (Orlick, 1978, 1982; Provost & Villeneuve, 1980). In this report, the researcher summarizes a study that investigated the use of television (Provost, 1981) for teaching cooperative games and values. Possible implications are outlined and suggestions are made to facilitate teaching cooperative games and sports.

Method

Subjects. Subjects were drawn from 700 pre-school children between the ages of 2 and 4. Six groups were randomly chosen to balance sex and socio-economic status. At the end of the experimentation, a total of 77 children had not missed a single period of experimental treatment; the data from these 77 children was used in the statistical analysis.

Procedure. Each group of children was randomly assigned to one of three treatments: 1) The presentation of five cooperative games with video reels (VTR), 2) the presentation of the same five cooperative games with slides and 3) the viewing of non-related animated films. Each treatment was replicated for a morning and an afternoon group.

With the help of a videotape recorder the children were observed and measured on cooperation, competition and individual behavior by two blind observers for five weeks of experimental treatment. In each case observations were made immediately after the experimental treatment. In addition after the five weeks of experimental treatment, the children were measured on a donation behavior to their friends. The cooperation and donation measures were analyzed together with multivariate analysis of variance to compare the three different treatments (i.e., VTR, Slides and Films).

Results

Behavior observation. A comparison of the total number of cooperative, competitive and individual behaviors recorded by two blind observers in each group shows that in the non-related film treatment, the subjects exhibited 25 cooperative behaviors, 75 individual behaviors and 0 competitive behaviors; in the co-op slide treatment, the subjects demonstrated 64 cooperative behaviors, 54 individual behaviors and 1 competitive behavior; finally in the co-op VTR treatment, the subjects initiated 75 cooperative behaviors, 61 individual behaviors and 2 competitive behaviors.

Multivariate analysis. A multivariate analysis of variance (MANOVA) using the cooperative and donation scores allowed a more in-depth look at the immediate effects of modeling cooperative games on children's prosocial behavior. The results show a significant difference in the means of the treatments under study ($V = 0.638$, $p < .05$). See Table 1 for means and standard deviations.

A post hoc Bonferroni confidence interval analysis on contrasts for each dependent variable shows that the non-related Film and co-op VTR means are significantly different from each other for both variables.

Table 1
Means and Standard Deviations in Three Viewing Conditions

	Donation Means S.D.		Cooperation Means S.D.	
Non-related Films	3.33	2.16	0.24	0.10
Co-op Slides	6.42	2.36	0.49	0.29
Co-op VTR	6.77	2.10	0.49	0.27

Discussion

Videotape recordings of cooperative games were effective in teaching cooperation and donation to groups of 2 and 4 year olds in comparison to non-related animated films. Videotaped cooperative games can serve the educational process. Teachers, parents and students could rapidly learn cooperative games from viewing videotapes (Singer, Singer, & Zuckerman, 1981), and widespread implementation could have far reaching implications on the development of prosocial behavior.

It would thus be advantageous to:

- make and use viodeotapes of cooperative sports and games for widespread applications;
- make and use slide and TV packages of cooperative sports and games;
- make and use posters and pictures of cooperative sports and games.

REFERENCES

Aronson, E., Blaney, N., Stephan, C., Sikes, J., & Snapp, M. *The jigsaw classroom.* Beverly Hills: Sage, 1978.

Orlick, T. *The second Cooperative Sports and Games Book.* New York, N.Y.: Pantheon Books, 1982.

Orlick, T. *Winning through cooperation.* Washington, D.C.: Acropolis, 1978.

Provost, P. & Villeneuve, M.J. *Jouons ensemble: Jeux et sports coopératifs.* Montréal: Editions de l'Homme, 1980.

Provost, P. Immeadiate effects of film-mediated cooperative games on children's prosocial behavior. Unpublished master's thesis, University of Ottawa, Ottawa, 1981.

Singer, D.G., Singer, J.L., & Zuckerman, D.M. *Teaching television: How to use TV to your child's advantage.* New York: Dial Press, 1981.

IMPACT OF A SPECIAL PHYSICAL ACTIVITY PROGRAM ON LEARNING DISABLED CHILDREN

Robert Kerr (Canada)

The most basic operational definition of a learning disabled child, would be a child of normal or above average intelligence who is one grade or more behind at school. This group, therefore, does not include the retarded or the physically handicapped but does include those who have perceptual problems, e.g., letter reversals. Conservative estimates of the number of learning disabled children in North America place the figure at 12% of the school population. Because some children were expected to fail at school it is only with the growing interest in special education that this disability group have been identified. By 8 or 9 years of age these children already see themselves as failures because they cannot keep up with their peers and are bright enough to comprehend the consequences.

While the major characteristic of this group is their academic problems, a properly structured physical activity program may provide a means of helping them to deal with their problems. The rationale for this is based on the premise that there is little difference between learning to swim and learning to read, at least in terms of the basic classroom survival skills of *attending* to instructions, *communication* — which involves both comprehending instructions and being able to express ones own ideas — and *cooperating* with at least one other person — the teacher. Learning disabled children, in addition to their academic difficulties, lack social skills and demonstrate emotional and behavioral problems. In general, the learning disabled child has difficulty in forming productive inter-personal relationships.

By taking the learning disabled child out of the problem environment — the classroom — where they expect failure and placing them in the non-stressful and fun atmosphere of a recreational-type physical activity program, it may be possible to foster those basic survival skills which they require in the classroom and elsewhere. The purpose of this study, therefore, was to assess the impact of a special physical activity program on the basic survival skills of learning disabled children.

The subjects in this study were all participants in the Lone Star Program at the University of Ottawa. This program emphasizes physical activity and is structured specifically for learning disabled children. The program ran for 5 days a week from 8:30 am - 3:30 pm for a six-week period during the summer. A random sample of 20 children, from a total of 65 participants, were selected for this study. The ages ranged from 6 to 10 years and all children were referred from special education classes.

The children were involved in a wide range of activities each week including cooperative games, modified versions of soccer, basketball, volleyball, track and field, gymnastics, combatives, dance and daily aquatics period involving swimming, diving, and other water games. These activities, and others, were presented at 6 activity stations with the children changing stations approximately every hour. All games were, however, adapted to the level of the child. Thus, at times, an observer might have difficulty in recognising the adapted activity as a version of one of these traditional games.

Each activity would be led by one instructor. For example, in a group of 20 children and 5 instructors, the instructors would interpret the activities in terms of their own children. Initially the children could work within their small groups of 3 or 4, but over time they were encouraged to work within the group as a whole. Whenever possible the children were encouraged to make their own suggestions for games within the context of the particular activity station they were using.

The children's behavior was assessed twice, once in the first week and again in the final week of the program. The assessment involved observing each child for 5 two-minute periods in at least 2 different activity sessions, and recording their behavior every 5 seconds. The major categories of the observation scan focussed on the amount of work (task) related activity and an assessment of cooperative and aggressive behavior. The observations were conducted by a trained observer not associated with the program.

From a descriptive point of view, the data indicated that the children spent nearly 60% of their time on work related activity (i.e., including cooperative acts). This figure increased slightly in the final week, overall, a surprising result for a group characterised by their distractability and inability to demonstrate normal work habits *in the classroom*. The most notable change over the 6 week period, however, was a 50% increase in cooperative behavior. Again for a group of children who traditionally fail in group of class situations this is a highly positive step. Of interest also is the fact that while aggressive behavior was minimal, perhaps a reflection of a less stressful or physically active environment, physically aggressive behavior in the first week was replaced by verbal aggression in the final week.

Although the observation scan identified 28 sub-categories, these could be reduced to 4 major types of behavior. The average frequency of occurrence of each of these major categories is indicated in Table 1. The increase in cooperative behavior was significant, $F(1, 19) = 4.64$, $p < .05$.

Table 1

Mean Frequency of Behavior (major categories only)[1]

Behavior	Pre	Post
Task: related (work)	67.8	67.4
unrelated (play)	21.2	17.4
Cooperative:	9.5	15.8
Aggressive: physical	1.0	0.2
verbal	1.0	1.6
Unclassified	19.5	17.6

[1]based on 120 observations per child

Implications of study

1. Physical activity may provide a means of helping learning disabled children deal with their problem by helping them to improve their basic work habits, particularly in the areas of attention, communication skills and cooperation.

2. While physical activity may not directly improve either intelligence or reading ability, by allowing the children to perform closer to their abilities in a more active setting, their academic performance may improve. However, this study represents only the first step in demonstrating this possibility.

REFERENCES

Hendry, J. & Kerr, R. Communication through physical activity for the learning disabled child. Paper in preparation.

Kerr, R. Adapted physical activity: a ray of hope. Paper presented to Canadian Associations for Health, Physical Education and Recreation, June, 1980.

Kerr, R. & Booth, B. Principles, practices and sports programs. *Recreation Research Review*, 1980, *8*, 2:16-21.

Kerr, R. Madness out of method. *Education Canada*, 1977, *17*, 22-25.

Mender, J., Kerr, R. & Orlick, T. A cooperative games program for learning disabled children. Paper in preparation.

Names and Addresses of Principal
Authors

Ferruccio Antonelli
ISSP Editor via Della Camilluccia,
Roma, Italy.

Peter J. Arnold
Dunfermline College,
Cramond Road North,
Edinburgh, Scotland
EH4 6JD

David Beaver
Western Illinois University
Macomb, Illinois
U.S.A. 61455

Bonnie G. Berger
10 Waterside Plaza, Apt. 2A
New York, N.Y. 10010

Stephen Bindman
School of Journalism
Carleton University
Ottawa, Canada

Paolo and Gabriella Bartoli Bonaiuto
Prof. of General Psychology
Universita Degli Studi
Via dei Sardi 70
Roma 00185 Italy

François Bregiroux
X Allée Traversière
Fresnes, 94260
France

Toller Cranston
c/o Tom Hess
International Management Group
767—5th Ave., Suite 601
New York, N.Y. 10022

Mihaly Csikszentmihalyi
5730 South Woodlawn Ave.,
Chicago, Illinois
U.S.A. 60637

Roman Czula
P.E. Dept.
Vassar College
Poughkeepsie, N.Y. 12601
U.S.A.

Hélène Dallaire
107 Sweetland Ave.,
Ottawa, Ont.
Canada

Leonard de Vries
School of Educational Studies
University Sains Malaysia
Penang, Malaysia

Rod. K. Dishman
Route 1, Box 360
Strafford MO. U.S.A. 65757

Jack Donahue
1 Lismer Cr.
Kanata, Ont. Canada
K2K 1A1

Catherine Garnier
384 Isabelle Moyen
Ile Bizard, Que. Canada
H9C 1T2

M. Gérard Gillot
14 rue General Joubert
Dijon, France, 21000

N.A. Gomez, F. Peronnet, D. Massicotte
and M. Gagnon
Education Physique,
Université du Montréal
H3C 3J7

Wayne L. Halliwell
Education Physique,
Université de Montréal
Montréal, Qué.
H3C 3J7

John Heil
Psychology Dept.
"Roanoke College"
Salem, Virginia, U.S.A.
24153

Leo Hendry
University of Aberdeen
Aberdeen, Scotland
AB9 2UB

Abby Hoffman
Sport Canada
Kent & Laurier
Ottawa, Ont.

Vaclav Hosek
Sadova 5 161 00
Prague 1
Czechoslovakia

Leif Isberg
Kyrkyardsgatan 6
5-78155 Borlange
Sweden

A.H. Ismail
Dept. of Physical Educ.
Purdue University
Lafayette, Indiana, 47907

Robert Kerr
Human Kinetics
University of Ottawa
Ottawa, Ont. Canada
K1N 6N6

Juhani Kirjonen
University of Tempere
SF 33101
Tempere 10
Finland

Paul Kunath
DHFK
Leipzig
German Democratic Republic

Larry M. Leith
Physical Education
Latichend University
Thunder Bay, Ontario

Carol Anne Letheren
129 Davenport Rd.,
Toronto, Ont.
Canada

Mary Jo Weaver MacCracken
H&PE. 110C Nem Hall
University of Akron
Akron, OH 44235
U.S.A.

Naomi Tulaha Martin
University of Papua New Guinea
Box 4820 University PO
Port Moresby
Papua, New Guinea

Y. Matsuda
The Leisure Research Center
Toronomen Bldg.
Tokyo
Kasumgasek I, Chiyoda-Ku,
Japan

H. Keith McConnell
197 John St.
Oakland, California
U.S.A. 94611

John McKay
Canadian Amateur Swimming Assoc.
160 Vanderhoof Ave.,
Toronto, Ont. Canada
M4G 4B8

Ashley Montagu
321 Cherry Hill Road
Princeton, New Jersey
U.S.A. 08540

Bernard Morelle
Groupement d'Etude en Psychologie du Sport
4, avenue du Maréchal Ney
91800 Brunoy   France

William P. Morgan
Dept. of Physical Educ.
2000 Observatory Drive
Univ. of Wisconsin Madison
Madison, Wisconsin
U.S.A. 53706

Sue Moxley
School of Physical Education
Dalhousie University
Halifax, N.S., Canada
B3H 3J5

Robert M. Nideffer
12468 Bodega Way
San Diego, CA. U.S.A. 92128

Terry Orlick
Human Kinetics
University of Ottawa,
Ottawa, Ont. Canada K1N 6N5

Andrew C. Ostrow
268 Coliseum
Virginia University
Morgantown, West Virginia 5   U.S.A. 265

John T. Partington
Psychology Dept.
Carleton University
Ottawa, Ontario, Canada   K1S 5B6

J.M. Pauwels
Tervuurse vest 101
23030 Heverlee
Belgium

Pierre Provost
180 Murray #10
Ottawa, Ont. Canada
K0N 5M8

Wang Min Qi
Beijing Institute of Physical Education
Beijing 100084
People's Republic of China

George Rioux
Société Française de Psychologie des
Sports
22 rue Sibuet
Paris 25012
France

David A. Rose
35 754½ Keystone Ave.,
Los Angeles, California
U.S.A. 90034

Michael L. Sachs
Education Physique
Univ. Trois Rivières
Trois Rivières, Qué.

Faiza Mastafa Salman
Physical Education
University of Alberta
Edmonton, Alta.

Gurbakhsh Singh Sandhu
Dept. of Physical Education
Punjab University
Chandi-Garh,
India

Guido Schilling
ETS
Magglingen
Switzerland

George Sheehan
Red Bank
New Jersey, U.S.A.

Thomas J. Sheeran
4661 Apple Drive
Lewiston
New York 14092

Martti Silvennoinen
The Institute of Physical Culture & Health
40700 Jyvaskyla 70
Finland

A.S. Sohi
Dept. of Physical Education
University of Ibadan
Ibadan,
Nigeria

Hans J. Stollenwerk
Shulpsychologisher Dienst Koln
Gronewaldstrabe 2
5000 Koln 41
German Federal Republic

Katherine Switzer
Avon International Running Circuit
9 West 57th St.
New York, N.Y.
U.S.A. 10019

Raymond Thomas
12 rue du Soleil
94380 Bonneuil
France

J. Tiainer
Viertajant 208 13, 40320
Jyvaskyla 32
Finland

Pepa Pueyo Uson
Independencia 25
Spain

Robert T. Vallerand
University of Montreal
Montréal, Qué. Canada
H3C 3J7

Hans van der Burg
Amsterdam
The Netherlands

Miroslav Vanek
FTVS UK Ujezd
450 Mala Strana
11807 Prague
CSSR

Leonard M. Wankel
Recreation Administration
University of Alberta
Edmonton, Alberta
T6G 2E1

Ma-Qi Wei
Beijing Institute of Physical Education
Beijing 100084
Republic of China

Thomas Wilke
Behavioral Science Division
University of Wisconsin-Parkside
Kenosha
Wisconsin, U.S.A. 53141

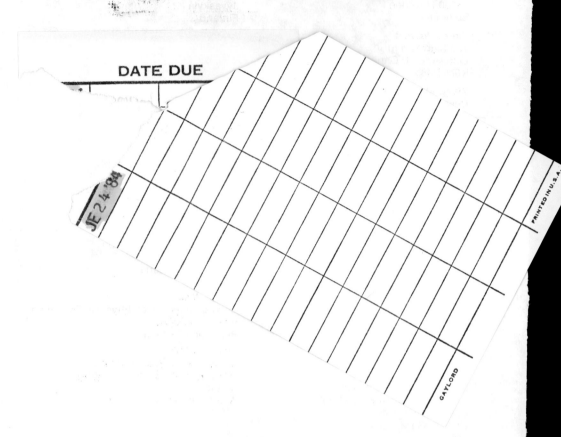